BOLLINGEN SERIES L

*

The Notebooks of Samuel Taylor Coleridge

VOLUME 4

TEXT

Anonymous: *Samuel Taylor Coleridge*
"painted from the Life at the house of James Gillman in the Grove, Highgate"

THE NOTEBOOKS

OF

Samuel Taylor Coleridge

Edited by Kathleen Coburn
and Merton Christensen

VOLUME 4

1819 – 1826

TEXT

BOLLINGEN SERIES L

PRINCETON UNIVERSITY PRESS

THIS IS THE FOURTH VOLUME OF
A COMPLETE EDITION OF THE NOTEBOOKS OF
COLERIDGE WHICH CONSTITUTES THE FIFTIETH
WORK IN BOLLINGEN SERIES SPONSORED BY
BOLLINGEN FOUNDATION.
THE VOLUME IS IN TWO PARTS: TEXT AND NOTES
LIBRARY OF CONGRESS CATALOG CARD NUMBER 56-13196
ISBN 0-691-09906-5
COMPOSED AND PRINTED BY
PRINCETON UNIVERSITY PRESS
PRINCETON, NEW JERSEY
BASED ON A DESIGN BY ANDOR BRAUN

IN THE PREPARATION OF THIS VOLUME THE EDITORS ARE
INDEBTED FOR SPECIAL KNOWLEDGE AND CO-OPERATION

TO

Lorna Arnold

Joyce Crick

Trevor Levere

George Whalley

CONTENTS

LIST OF PLATES

THIS fourth volume of *The Notebooks of Samuel Taylor Coleridge* is comprised of entries made between March 1819 and December 1826, in many notebooks already drawn upon in Volumes I, II and III, and in addition it taps five new ones, one of which is complete in this volume. The notebooks here present wide contrasts in size, from the small pocketbooks N 27 and N 28 to the largest of all, made up of folio-size pages. But Coleridge's habits of note-making do not vary greatly with the size of his pages, or the passing of the years. The range of reading, the endless questioning, the recondite sources, continue to baffle and stimulate. There are some changes in emphasis and interests, but almost any generalisation one makes can be almost immediately called in question. One may say, for example, that the most pronounced movement of mind is towards theology and the relation of church and state, and yet perhaps the most startling development in this volume is Coleridge's greatly expanded interest in chemistry, the chemistry of the laboratory that was discovering the elements in the Royal Institution of Great Britain, and the theoretical chemistry of the German transcendentalists such as Oken, Steffens, and Oersted.

It has been just as necessary in this volume as in the three earlier ones to call on specialists to help in meeting the editorial demands of Coleridge's range and depth of knowledge. It is a pleasure to record that the three main consultants who helped steer the course of Volume III have also contributed very considerably to this volume, Lorna Arnold, Joyce Crick, and George Whalley. Lorna Arnold as classical consultant to the Bollingen edition of the *Collected Works* of Coleridge has brought her classical scholarship and her experience of Coleridge untiringly to bear on our problems. To these names must be added that of Trevor Levere of the Institute of the History and Philosophy of Science in the University of

Toronto. It is impossible to measure quantitatively or qualitatively the extent of his elucidation of some two hundred and more entries in the general area of eighteenth- and early nineteenth-century science, in particular the chemistry, the very language of which defeats all but a handful of scientists today. His generosity and patience in clarifying and re-clarifying notes for which he had provided the substance, only to be confronted by unforeseen complications pulled by us out of the maze of the tangled materials in this volume, made the editing of these baffling entries possible. He also laboured to answer our questions about the progressive changes in Coleridge's views stemming from his scientific reading, and was ready (with appropriate diffidence) to discuss its relation to the broader reaches of Coleridge's thought. Where the notes have achieved this kind of elucidation, it is owing largely to him.

Editors of the Collected Coleridge team have, as always, been very helpful, especially in this volume Heather and Robin Jackson. Having read it carefully in manuscript, they provided us with many useful addenda from their work on the *Logic* and *Shorter Works and Fragments*. R. A. Foakes and John Beer also made their materials usefully available.

As usual, the list of persons who have contributed richly to the volume by bringing their learning to bear on single problems, or sometimes on several, is a long one. It is a pleasure to remember and record most gratefully their assistance.

Professor G. E. Bentley, Jr, University of Toronto, answered some questions about Flaxman; Sir Isaiah Berlin, about Vico; Professor J. H. Burns, University of London, about a Bentham problem. Professor Douglas Bush, Harvard University, interrupted his own work to trace in detail the sources of an entry on early Greek history. The late Professor Otto H. Christensen was helpful with some theological entries. Professor Maurice Cope assisted a search in the history of Renaissance art. Mrs W. T. Cutt, University of Victoria, B.C., gave painstaking references to Mrs Barbauld. Valerie Eliot, London, provided an elusive Plato reference. Dr Dorothy Forward, University of Toronto, gave informed botanical guidance in a search for an early reference to hydroponics. Professor Ryotaro Kato, Nagoya University, Japan, generously put at our disposal an annotated copy of Kant's *Anthropologie* he had procured for the library there. Professor Gordon Keyes, Principal of Victoria College, Toronto, clarified some obscure Latin. Professor J. A. Leo Lemay, University of Delaware, answered questions about Colonial American literature. Professor Stephen Lukashevich, University of Delaware, gave assistance on entries dealing with Italian history. Mr Arthur W. J. G. Ord-Hume, President of the Musical Box Society of Great Britain, answered a question about musical boxes. Professor John Grant, Emmanuel College, Toronto, dealt with a problem in Scottish church history. Professor F. B. Newman of the English Department, University of Delaware, assisted with an Italian passage. Professor Mary Priestley, Elon College, North Carolina, was helpful through her knowledge of the Southey collection in the Keswick Museum. Chaim Raphael and George Spater illuminated an entry involving an English constitutional problem, and William Rees-Moggs one involving the Bullion Controversy of Coleridge's day. Professor Jack Robson of the Toronto J. S. Mill edition has always been good about throwing tidbits our way. Dame Teresa Rodrigues O.S.B., of Stanbrook Abbey, identified a baffling early Pope. Professor John W. Scott, M.D., gave useful information on medical electricity and mesmerism. Miss J. Stainton responded with ornithological as well as bird-watcher's zest to a question about the migrations of nightingales. Dr Ann Tracy, Plattsburgh University, gave part of a London holiday to a dogged search in the British Museum. Mrs Eunice Turner of Kent found a Ramsgate street cry. The late Professor Gershom Scholem of the Hebrew University, Jerusalem, gave attention, such as he alone could give, to questions about the Cabbala. Dr Tuzo Wilson, Director of the Ontario Science Centre, provided some lucid geological answers.

To certain libraries and institutions on both sides of the Atlantic we are indebted for much help and many kindnesses, which it is not always possible to acknowledge personally.

In Britain by far the largest debt is owing, over many years, to the British Library in the British Museum and its knowledgeable staff, of which in this volume particular mention must be made of Mr Geoffrey Arnold, helpful at many points but especially for zealously using a holiday and his knowledge of Dutch to find the source of 5363. Thanks are due also to the Bodleian Library,

Oxford, and to Cambridge University Library. Smaller or more specialized libraries have also contributed from their archives. The Central Library, Manchester, and the Manchester Local History Librarian, Mr D. Taylor, and the Central Library of Bradford, provided local material on the manufacture of cork legs in the days of Waterloo. The librarians of Christ's Hospital School, Mrs O. Peto and Mr N. M. Plumley, found some answers for us in the school records. Miss S. M. Hare, Librarian to the Worshipful Company of Goldsmiths, was able to produce useful information about their awards to Derwent Coleridge. The Hertford County Archivist clarified a problem of place-names. Mrs Gosling of the Highgate Literary and Scientific Institution clarified at various points references to the Highgate of Coleridge's time, and to the Institution we are also indebted for permission to use as an illustration a little-known unpublished portrait of Coleridge (frontispiece). Of the National Library of Scotland we wish to thank Alan S. Bell; of the Queen's Archives, Windsor, the Registrar Miss Jane Langton; of the Royal Institution, London, the Archivist Mr James Friday; and of Sion College Library, Miss J. M. Owen, Librarian. University libraries in Britain, always generously open to overseas scholars in Cambridge, Edinburgh, and Oxford, as well as in London, have our gratitude for otherwise unavailable materials.

In Canada and the United States we are also indebted to many institutions for freely given help. In Toronto the William Boyd library in the Academy of Medicine, a useful resource, was particularly helpful through Mrs Sheila Swanson. From the Pontifical Institute of Mediaeval Studies in Toronto we had the invaluable assistance of the Reverend Walter Principe with some difficult theological and Coleridgian Latin, and of Dr Roger Reynolds, who put us on to other specialists in the early history of the church, Dr John O'Malley of the Western School of Theology, Cambridge, Mass., and Dr John Tedeschi of the Newberry Library in Chicago. The University Library (Robarts) in Toronto has become increasingly useful throughout the four volumes. The Victoria College Library, housing as it does a significant Coleridge Collection, and by the unfailing interest of the library staff, has supported the work in innumerable ways. The University of Toronto Press gave skilled attention and help with Coleridge's little drawings.

We are grateful to many institutions in the United States: in California to the Huntington Library, San Marino; in Chicago to the Newberry Library and the Federated Theological Schools of The University of Chicago; in New York to the Public Library and especially to the Berg Collection and Dr L. L. Szladits, to the Pierpont Morgan Library and especially Mr Herbert Cahoon, and to the library of the Union Theological Seminary; in Pennsylvania to the Library Company, the Lutheran Theological Seminary, the University of Pennsylvania Library, the American Institute of the Natural Sciences, and to the library of Dropsie College.

Various research assistants from time to time have by their diligence lightened certain tasks: Miss Patti Hanigan, Mr Scott Baker, Miss Carla Mulford, Miss Michiyo Ishi, and Mrs Ruth Jackson, all of Delaware; Mrs Ann Bonnycastle, Kingston, Ontario; Gregory Hollingshead, University of Alberta; and the late Heather Bremer, Tunbridge Wells, Kent, over considerable periods in the British Museum.

In the wisdom of Bollingen Foundation we have had the incalculable advantage of the services of an indexer throughout all the work on the volumes. In this volume Mrs Gertrude Stein has by her steady thoroughness contributed her own objectivity and accuracy.

The work done by Mrs Freda Gough as the Toronto clearinghouse for the *Collected Works* and as a secretary of twenty years of invaluable service far beyond the call of duty in crisis after crisis cannot be adequately recognized here. She has made herself the crucial hub of the work on the Coleridge *Notebooks*.

Victoria College   KATHLEEN COBURN
in the
University of Toronto

INTRODUCTION

THIS fourth volume of Coleridge's *Notebooks* begins with entries made in 1819 just after the conclusion of the last of the
Philosophical Lectures which ended the two successful courses of
public lectures, literary and philosophical, given from December
1818 to the end of March 1819. The volume ends, somewhat
arbitrarily, partly from considerations of bulk, at the end of 1826.
It comprises entries made during Coleridge's struggles to formu-
late and to dictate to amanuenses, his Logic*, what he called his
"Opus Maximum"†, probably parts of what came to be known as
his *Theory of Life* (some of which was evidently begun earlier, in
1816–17), and during the long drawn-out writing of the "Beauties
of Leighton", which became *Aids to Reflection* published in 1825.
By the end of 1826 he enjoyed increasing fame from the publication of *Aids to Reflection*; although the first American edition was
yet to come, in 1829, the work was already well-known in New
England. As a Royal Fellow of the Royal Society of Literature he
had delivered a lecture on the symbolism of the *Prometheus* of
Aeschylus, and only Lord Liverpool's sudden death prevented him
from being put on the Civil List. The year 1827 saw the beginning of a marked decline in Coleridge's health, and a prolonged
illness. In 1827 he began a more systematic reading of the Bible.
His interest in the Church as an institution, though by no means
new, was given fresh affirmation in *On the Constitution of the
Church and State* (1829). On Christmas Day of 1827 he took the
sacrament for the first time since his first year at Jesus College,
Cambridge. His next seven years of remaining life were domi-

* Vol 13 of the *Collected Works* in the Bollingen edition, ed R. J. de J. Jackson.
† To appear as Vol 15 in the *Collected Works* in the Bollingen edition, ed Thomas
McFarland.

nated by biblical, theological, and cultural interests, which drew many pilgrims up Highgate Hill to pay homage to an *eminence grise*, mellow and charming, but sometimes evidently frail.

To the end he was still the passionate inquirer. In April 1819, with obvious relief, he had abandoned lecturing to turn student again, seizing upon the latest textbooks in chemistry. On the publication in May 1819 of Brande's *Manual of Chemistry* he read it from cover to cover. By this time he was suspicious of the pseudo-science of the German *Naturphilosophen* and wanted to investigate for himself by juxtaposing to their largely theoretical conclusions those of the British chemists working experimentally in the Royal Institution. Hence in this volume, Oken, Steffens, Schelling, Oersted, Eschenmayer, are often present in the intellectual debates, but Thomas Brande, Thomas Thomson, Davy, and Hatchett are there too, in specific detail, consulted in corroboration or contradiction, with many others both German and English brought into the fray. The approach was no longer that of 1801/2—when Coleridge said he went to Davy's first chemistry lectures in the Royal Institution to improve his metaphors. He now felt that transcendental metaphysics had to be tested by empirical deductions, and vice versa, the results of laboratory experiments must be subjected to logic and philosophy.

Similarly, in the period of the 1820's, social theories and practices received his fresh examination stimulated by the painful disclosures of corruption in privileged places and the outbursts of mob violence. These were aroused partly by demagogues, but demagogues who appealed to physical miseries, social disparities, and witless attempts to govern by suppression, as by Sidmouth and "all the King's men". The popular uprisings from Peterloo onwards bore out Coleridge's fears in his *Lay Sermons*. His social discussions now were not so theoretical as some times in the days of Pantisocracy, but they were not utterly dissimilar in that they now raised in new forms the old questions of the relation of government and authority to the quality of human life and its needs. In this period the gap widened between Coleridge's kind of conservatism and Wordsworth's and Southey's. Never a thoroughgoing partisan, Coleridge was more *against* George IV than *for* Queen Caroline, and like most English people was deeply shocked by the whole royal debacle. It led him to further probing of the moral roots of English society, as well as quite practical interests in the economy, education, civil liberties, and constitutional law. All these topics appear in the notebook entries. There is also in the moral dilemmas a turning towards the Bible, a taking of his own advice to regard the Bible as the "Statesman's Manual".

One misses in this volume much of the exquisite observation of nature, there are fewer attempts at poems, and less of the critical literary reflections of earlier days, although all of these appear here occasionally, sometimes all the more touching for being imbedded in darker matters. The psychological insights still astonish, and should not be underestimated in this volume because they some-times are directed to new courses less congenial to the psychoana-lytically orientated than some of the earlier prescient observations in *CN* I, II and III.

The notebooks drawn upon for the first time here are N 26, N 28, N 30 in the British Museum, N 60 in the Victoria College Library, Toronto, and the Folio Notebook, to which no number was ever assigned, now in the Henry E. Huntington Library in California, from the library of the late Anthony D. Coleridge. It was prematurely hazarded in the Introduction to *CN* III that except for known gaps in the numbered series (31, 32, 57, and 58) "the question of lost notebooks hardly arises after Highgate." At least one more loss is now known, that of a small, red, leather-bound book like N 27 and N 28, and "like them bought at Mr Bage's but elder and thinner"—as described in N 28 Gen N. and in 4645.

A few minor changes in manner of presentation have become necessary in this volume. As in *CN* III, quotation from Coleridge's own works is reduced to a minimum because of the publication of the *Collected Works*. Likewise in the interests of saving space and expense, Biblical citations are in the main reduced to references only. For the same reason, quotations from foreign authors are given in the notes in English translations only, not in both lan-guages, unlike the practice in earlier volumes. Exceptions have been made where Coleridge's direct quotations or discussion of diction or style make the original language essential to his argu-ment. The loss of the German, e.g., in the long Creuzer entries, and of the Italian original in which Coleridge read Vico, is regrettable but unavoidable. As the volumes have proceeded it has become more and more necessary to conserve space; for instance, the reader should bear in mind that a reference to a note is intentionally also to any cross-references in that note.

The progress of the *Collected Works* has dictated some minor changes also in abbreviations and in the style of reference, e.g. to *Marginalia*. It is hoped that these, and similarly some changes in the manner of indexing works formerly in manuscript but now published, will cause no inconvenience. Another change we have rightly or wrongly resisted. When our Volumes I, II, and III were being edited the Coleridge notebooks were in the "BM." We have left them there, without moving them to the British Library, *"BL"* having been pre-empted as an abbreviation for *Biographia Literaria*.

It was always the intention, from 1952 onwards when Bollingen Foundation undertook to support the editing of the Coleridge *Notebooks*, to bring into the editing at some point someone equipped by training in theology to deal with this aspect of Coleridge's notes. In Volume III and still more at the beginning of Volume IV it was clearly imperative to do so. Merton Christensen, who had studied the impact of German biblical criticism on English literature in the early nineteenth century and was working on Coleridge's marginalia on the German theologians of his day, happily took on this aspect of the annotation. The preparation of *CN* IV until June 1985 was a joint undertaking. Unfortunately Merton Christensen died after a severe stroke. In the emergency thus created, it was fortunate that Anthony John Harding, whose work had many close connexions with Coleridge's thought and reading, was able to commit himself to editing the fifth volume. Certain tidying-up matters like Addenda and Corrigenda for the first four volumes, and the supervision of a concordance-type subject index for all five volumes, will be my responsibility in bringing the publication of the *Notebooks* to completion.

KATHLEEN COBURN

EXPLANATION OF EDITORIAL
SYMBOLS

⟨word⟩   A later insertion by Coleridge.

[?word]   An uncertain reading.

[?word/wood]   Possible alternative readings.

[word]   A reading editorially supplied.

⌜word⌝   A tentative reading, through crossings-out all but obliterative
                  and usually post-Coleridge.

[. . .]   An illegible word. Each additional dot beyond three, up to a
                  maximum of ten, indicates another word. Longer omissions
                  are referred to in the notes.

⌜ . . . ⌝   An obliterated as distinct from an illegible word or passage,
                  whether obliterated by ink, acid, or excision of page or
                  pages. A maximum of ten dots is used to suggest the longer
                  obliterations.

Other brackets, strokes, dashes, and devices are Coleridge's unless described
otherwise.

THE NOTEBOOKS

1819 – 1826

Entries 4505–5471

4505 27.25   Christies Vases—in Mr Westmacott

4506 27.26   Holding weights in the arm affected—since the
swelling & occasional cramps in the hand & all down the side.—
[?He/JG] has been electrified—daily for a quarter of an hour.—

4507 27.27   Olen, Hymnist, inventor of Hexameter verse,
a Lycian—Lycia, Pamphylia, evidently congenous with the
Greeks.—Lydia even in Herodotus's time very nearly resembled
them in Laws & Manners—Trojans spoke the same language—
Olympus, the father of Grecian Music, a Phrygian—Thamyris,
Orpheus, Musæus, Eumolpus, Thracians—(all Ioaones—Descendants of Javan.)—
    So too the Pelasgi, I doubt not—an earlier migration, barba-
rized by the pioneering which made it successively more easy for
the following tribes of the same Family.
    Hesiod in a poem *on* husbandry makes no mention of *manuring*
the ground—The Odyssey l. 17. v. 299, does.—Now it is only
within little more than a century, that the Dung was thrown away
in the N. of Scotland—a farm advertised with the recommendation
of a fine Beck (= Brook) thro' the Farm Yard to carry off the
Dung—. It argues a more populous state as well as a more cultivated—in as far as it supposes tillage and pasturage carried on on
the same Farm.—Q.ʸ How far is this one addition to the various
presumptions of the juniority of the Odyssey to Hesiod & the elder
or contemporary Iliadist? In the Odyssey Nestor produces Wine
eleven years old—and the manufacture of Wines as well as the ~~the~~
Culture of the Vineyard were practised with great skill & delicacy.—Is there any thing equivalent to this in the Iliad—especially, if we consider the Shield of Achilles as a later addition—a

point conceded by many scholars who utterly reject and anathe-
matize the theory of Wolfius.—

f34ᵛ   4508 27.28   What was my own case has so often come within
my observation in others that I am almost disposed to generalize
it into a rule—that the more vigorous the Volition, (as in sanguine
lively young men of quick abilities) the less the indisposition to
the denial of the Free will and the doctrine of Necessity or absolute
preformation of every possible act in the one Causa causarum—
Nay, that from the same law of mind that at the æra in which we
are most rich in any thing, that thing we least *stickle* for. The
young *think* more highly of chastity than the Man of 50–60.—

4509 27.29   5ᵗʰ—12 + the Good Friday Boon if possible
1. Boosey
2. Blackwood
3 Colburn
4 Holland
5 [?Hart/Visit] [?Der/Dev]. Mʳˢ C.

8,10ᵈ

f35   4510 27.30   Now for the re-possession of this golden Age
we must, I fear, wait as long as Rabbi Barchana for his Hat—
which (he having in his travels arrived at the place where Heaven
& Earth meet) he had incautiously put in a window of the former—and on going immediately after to get it again, the heavens
had carried it off—and he is condemned to stay there till the revolution of the annus Magnus, 36000 years, shall bring it back—
all the interim he is employed in peeping into every window as it
passes by him—it being the *Fortunatus Cap* which alone had enabled him to transport himself thither./

f3   4511 29.14   ⟨16 April, 1819.⟩ "Oppressive and irritative
combination of restless Curiosity and contriving Suspicion: the result being, that one can scarcely take a pen in hand, or even obey
a command of Nature by a walk into the garden, without having
the sense of free agency put to the question—a true inquisitorial

Torture of one's Individuality by a succession of Pin Stabs. I have already detected the impression made on more than one of my friends, that I am made over, in absolute right of Property—that whatever time I give to them is a robbery from my Owners, and they ~~are~~ regarded with an evil eye as Receivers of Stolen Goods. Whatever can be required from a Brother living in the same House, my affections would of themselves prompt me to anticipate: provided only, it does not exceed what a Woman may properly expect from a Man who must both *be* and *appear* a Free Agent.—More than this is equally degrading to both parties: for if it can be justified, it proclaims the one a dangerous Lunatic, and the other his hired Keepers." Henry Somerville, a Novel in a series of Letters, Vol. I. P. 163.

4512 29.15   If additional proof respecting the facts or real   *f3ᵛ*
phænomena of Animal Magnetism were necessary, it might be found in the contrast between the Reports of the German Magnetisers and those of the French. Suppose the facts real and grounded *quovis modo* in some general Law, but not yet brought into clear connection with our former experience, and the Attesters would feel, act and express themselves, just as the German Naturalists & Physicians do and have done.

Suppose them ~~tricks~~ *subjective* accidents, ~~or~~ & illusions, or intentional tricks, observed without caution and recorded without accuracy, and you have the natural Product in the Bibliothéque magnetisme animale, or Magazine by the Société du Magnetisme at Paris—first published 1 July 1814.—Yet the German Credulity and its honorable derivation from their own scrupulous Veracity (to which, however, we must add their rage for Theory and Prepossession in favor of whatever strange phænomena they think, that they have found out how to account for) are amusingly exemplified in Kieser's reflections on this Contrast. An English Physiologist with the same facts before him (ex. gr. that the most powerful Magnetizers in Germany out of a hundred sick Patients all females do not produce or expect more than one or two Somnambulists ⟨often after a month's manipulation,⟩ while according to the French Account a First Beginner makes 5 out of 6 healthy Persons of both sexes Somnambulists in the first attempt!!) would ex-

claim—What a nation of LIARS the French are! Only where immediate Detection is foreseen (as in Mathematics & Chemistry)
can you rely on a word, they say!—Not so honest Kieser's "*most*
f4 *believing mind.*" He takes both statements for granted: & gravely
sets about a solution of the difference.—See the third Heft of Es-
chenmeyer's, Kieser's, & Nasses' Archiv fur [für] den Th.
Magn.—p. 127.—If there were any ground for Kieser's speculation on the dependence of the *sorts and comparative excitability* of
⟨the⟩ magnetic State on national character, so that France being =
10, Germany is but = 1, I fear that old England will be − 1 =
+ 0 : i.e. not mere absence of sufficing evidence with its consequent Unbelief, but positive *Dis*belief.—

    As to my own creed, I am more and more inclined to revert to
my first notion, that the French Report under Dr Franklin was a
glimpse of the truth, but such as might be expected from French
Eyes filmed and gummy with French Sensualism/. Relying on the
German Statements exclusively, and the special circumstance that
it is always *der* Magnetiseur, and *die* Magnetesirte, I infer that the
sexual relation excited by and thro' the Skin ex contains the *main*
solution, if we do not forget to take in the properties of the Skin
(among which I for the last 20 years have reckoned *Voli*tion) and
the re-actions of the Nerves, as well as the re-actions of the whole
& of all the parts, some parts more remarkably & with a sort of
specific Sympathy, as must needs be the case when so very important an organ as the Skin is aff- and inf-ected (contagiïum quasi
in*generatio*)—but then I hold that the very contrary of the French
Reporter's Theory is the Fact—namely, that the Act of Magnetism
is to *transmute* the infra-abdominal Appetite into pectoral Sentimental Fruition or Sensation. Opium ⟨will⟩, in a less degree, will
produce the same effect on men of feminine Constitution—Hence
its temporary effect cures in women's hysterics—it dissolves the
uterifaction or rather the tumultuous struggle of the whole nervous
f4^v system to resist the despoinism of the Uterus—and diffusing calms
it as by an equation./S.T.C. 16 April, 1819

    Whether he Mesmer were the Discoverer of a New Power,
standing in a similar ratio to Galvanism as Galvanism to common
Electricity, or only of the surprizing both psychological and medical effects of cutaneous excitement or sedation, in either case the

phænomena remain the same, and the cures unquestionable. Our Memory suffers no revolution: tho' our Hopes of the Future may be narrowed. On either supposition, therefore, Mesmer deserves that we should proceed to the examination both of his claims as a Physiologist and of his character and conduct, as a Man, without *prejudice*—nay, I do not hesitate to add, with a prepossession in his favor.

4513 29.16   The ancient Mathematicians conceived a line to   *f*5
have been engendered by a point *producing* itself in one dimension: or supposing the point to produce itself in all directions, then the *theorem* (i.e. Actus contemplantis sic et non aliter, se ipsum ut rem contemplatam contemplans)—then, I say, the theorem of the Line is obtained by fixing the attention exclusively on the production in any one direction. If this production is to be contemplated as finite, there must be two positions taken as its extremes—each both equally and neither with any inherent claim to priority, positions or theses (θεσεις) but as each has the relation of opposite to the other, whichever from whatever cause is assumed first preoccupies the *name*, Thesis, and gives to the other that of Antithesis. In the pure Di Theorems Diagrams of Geometry this is determined by the inner margin of the page, in dependence on the custom of writing from left to right or from right to leaf. In real subjects the stronger or more desirable is chosen as the Thesis, and is marked + or & called Positive or Plus, and the Antithesis, marked − , is entitled the Negative or Minus. Thus if a Man's Capital were 7000£ & his Debts 6000, it would be the same in calculation whether I stated it + D. and − C. or + C and − D—; but no one would hesitate in adopting the latter.—

Now to manifest itself is to *produce itself*, & to produce is to manifest, as is implied in the very terms. Absolute oneness in the manifestation may be known, indeed, or *inferred*, as Oneness; but cannot *appear* except in and by *the many*, or not-one, as the condition of the Distinct—an angle requires two lines to manifest it— &c—It follows, therefore first that Since then the One Monad or Indistinction can be made manifest only by *the Many* (*the Dyad* we will suppose;) and as each is distinct in relation to that from which it is distinguished; it follows, that all manifestation is by Opposites, each opposed to the other as Thesis and Antithesis, and both (*as* both) opposed to the Prothesis or that which is thus manifested, as ~~the~~ distinct Multeity to absolute Identity. *Both* I say as both: for neither *as* either is opponible to Identity, inasmuch as they *exist*, ~~each~~ severally, in ⟨and by⟩ contradisting~~uishable~~ction to each other.

f5ᵛ   Thus then: Unity is manifested by Opposites. But it is equally true, that all true Opposites tend to Unity. For the further Fleeing each from the other is here precluded by the assumption of the Line as finite, i.e. the assumption of a punctum indifferentiæ midway between the extreme points, and the distance of each from the mid point is the exponent or measure of the equal *attractive* power of the mid point over each extreme in controlling *their* centrifugal, ~~power of the latter,~~ or the measure of ~~the finite degree of the~~ its own projective power: ~~of the former,~~ according as the mind imagines the forces to be placed, the result being the same, and the difference ~~i~~ only in the imagination of the sort and the subject of the agency

f6 **4514** 29.17   The same excessive irritability, the same exquisite susceptibility of impression in the Skin which forms ~~a~~ the leading character, in Hydrophobia, is found to result from the poison of the false Angustura Bark from the East Indies—Angustura ferruginea virosa. See Lond. Med. Repos. Vol. VI p. 92. 1816. Professor Emmert on *Sp. Ang.* anxious and frightened Look—diminished control over the ~~organs~~ voluntary muscles of ~~convul Volition~~, spasms, convulsions, tetanus—irritable, startled, frightened—every impression, however light, as the Touch of a Fly, electrifies & often convulses or brings on a tetanic state—. *The imperfect conversion of the venous into arterial blood*/Qʸ (how far may this contribute to the septic inflammation of the Stomach &c of the rabid Dog ?—O!—Emmert notices the resemblance to Hydrophobia, in the absence of Mania—the undistorted Consciousness—the increased Sensitiveness, in sight, hearing (odors?).—Few and doubtful organic changes discoverable after Death!—(Much to be regretted that Berzelius, Davy, or Woolaston, have not procured quantities of Sp. Ang. sufficient to yield an ample sufficiency of the Rubigo virosa, for analysis.—? *Fluate* of Iron—. Excess of Astringent + Contractive.—

This poison, like the Saliva rabipea, acts thro' the medium of the circulation.

N.B. Respecting the occasional re-origenation or in all but the first case—*tradition* of Rabies, ~~note~~ note the 2 senses of the term, Probability—1st that which has the a priori conditions of being proved—the *absence* of all that precludes its future confirmation by facts: ⟨this⟩ being the minimum reale waxing according to the presence of analogies. 2. The *feeling*, of ex. gr. A having fixed at haphazard on a Lottery Ticket by diving (we will suppose with his hand into a revolving wheel, which contains the whole number of Tickets, has taken one that afterwards corresponds to the 20,000£ *f6ᵛ* Prize. The next year, in a lottery and under circumstances in all respects the same A does the same. Now according to Sense the 1st, it is equally *probable* that it should prove a 20,000£ prize, in the year 1802, as in the year 1801. But according to Sense 2— few indeed are there, who would not *feel* an increased improbability. Here probability is = familiarity, improb. = strangeness—. —⟨*Mem.* Something repulsive in an απαξ φαινομενον to the scientific sense as in an απαξ λεγομενον to an Historian—& this aggravated because if ~~in~~ in the Rabies, then in Plague, Small Pox, in short all contagions & infections—. The theory of the Solifidianists, or *mon*⟨*mi*⟩archists (μονη η μια της λυσσας αρχη) either innate (as malignant fever) or extrinsic—as the bite or sting of an Insect, eating of a poisoned plant or the like—⟩

4515 29.21   Leibnitz brought forth two imposing Ideas: *f8* one, that all the varieties of existing Things consisted in the More or the Less, i.e. in different degrees or quantities of the same X: the other, that the vis representativa (Vorstellungskraft) was this X or one prime fundamental Power (Grundkraft).

The latter is obviously either false, if it exclude the Will, and vis essendi: or nugatory and an illogical generalization if it subsume them: just as if the ~~term~~ Cherry-tree were made the universal, including all Plants.

To the former it has been objected, that such an Analysis would require an infinite Mind, Yes! (Leibnitz might justly reply) to *compleat* it. But it is proposed as an Idea, for regulation and guidance—as the ultimate Insight, at which we are to aim; the unattainable Ideal, by which we are to measure our approximations. There is, however, another Objection which has not, I believe, been advanced, and less easily to be removed—viz. that Leibnitz's Idea contains a probable Truth turned topsy-turvy—proposing Quantity as the ground of Quality, ⟨⟨Qualitas *primaria*⟩⟩ i.e., the Phænomenal and merely Relative for the Real or Actual, Quality being in fact pre-demanded in order to determine the amount of Quantity. Thus the magnet acts in *length*. Length being the product & exponent of the magnetic Quality or Power—the Electric Fluid in surface, the Galvanic in Depth or Body, Surface and Depth being severally the Products of these. It is to be suspected, I fear, that Leibnitz's Ground-Power subsisting in an infinite scale of More or Less in Quantity, amounted to little more than the *f8"* abstract Universal, Power. But substitute Quality as the *Vis* Qualitativa, and it is susceptible of a positive sense in the Idea, Will, as that which is essentially and originatively causative of reality.

S.T.C.—

4516 29.22   We all consider Sight as the most perfect Sense: and the Improvers of Locke's psychology, Hume, Hartley, Condillac, and our Materialists generally, who reduces ⟨all⟩ Perceptions to mere modes of *Sensation*, have drawn from the Eye, as the sense of Sight, not only their most plausible arguments but the very Ground, Principle and Criterion of the Omne Scibile: the whole Philosophy of the modern Epicurists resting on the term, *videre*, et videri, as the fundamental Axiom or universal Antecedent, in contra-distinction from the Agere et Pati of the Platonists. (I have called the Eye *the sense of sight*: for with the Materialists an organ of sight would convey a false meaning, inasmuch as it presupposes the Sight or visive Power, in order to be its Organ. At least, the term could be used per catachresin only, as = the machine that organizes Sensation into the Species, Sight, for itself.). Turn over to p. 28.

f12 *continued from p. 20*—And yet let us examine any single instance of Sight, and observe to what it owes its superiority over the inferior senses of Smell and Taste. Almost wholly to conceptions of Relation, Acts of Comparison, *&c.* Taking for instance a Tree as seen and we shall find the so called Idea thus impressed almost composed of Relations and Judgements—so that we find it difficult to abstract the actual Impress, so dim, confused and evanescent is it, in its sensuous nature exclusively.

4517 27.70   The common sense of mankind attributes Being   *f98ᵛ*
where it does not attribute Life, nay where it does not attribute Christallization or any form of arrangement, beyond that of simple Cohesion: and even in this it supposes as prior in order of nature a being or beings that *have* the active and passive qualities of co-hering. But it never attributes Life without Being. So again Life without sensation (in Plants) Sensation without Consciousness (as in the Zoophytes) Consciousness without Self-consciousness; but not vice versâ. Nature leaves nothing ~~being~~hind but still takes up the lower into the higher, still refining and ennobling what it elevates.

The most convenient Formula therefore would be, X − Y for the Object of the merely physical Sciences: X + Y for the Object of the Zoological Sciences. The latter might stand as the representative of X + y z, of X + y z w, &c: as the same reasoning would be repeated in each: i.e. what was said of Life or *living* Beings would apply to Sensation, Reflection, and Selfness or *Personity*.

Now the position of the argument is, that Philosophy originates in the feeling of a desideratum not supplied by any one Science, nor by all the Sciences, quoad *Sciences*, taken collectively, in the seeking after this supplement; and in the finding of the same: and these three, as beginning, middle, and end, comprizes the total meaning of Philosophy, which therefore falls into three subdivisions, or stages of growth: viz. incipient, progressive, and conclusive or final. In proof of the first, namely the existence of a desideratum supplied by no Science, a residuum of Darkness common to all, we sho~~uld~~w, first, that for the purpose of the present argument all the Sciences may be represented in one or other of three classes—namely, those which have for their Object X − y, in   *f97ᵛ*
which X is *pre*sumed; those that have X + y, in which both X and y are *pre*sumed, as well as the efficient connection between X and y in X + y, and ~~of~~ between X + y with X − y; and the Science, which has for its professed Object the common ground and copula of both. In other words, Physics, Zoology, and Theology. If then the third, or Theology, should be found to have

failed in its professed Object, i.e. if the solution of the Problems left unsolved by the two former should appear to rest on a mere *pre*sumption, including the darkness, ~~of~~ or residua, of both the former, and even when granted yet inefficient to its purpose the inevitable conclusion is, that in *no* science is the supplement of the Desideratum to be found—Q.E.D.—. Philosophy therefore is not

f9 a *Science*; but a Supplement of Science. Consequently Philosophy is not the same as Science; and yet cannot be wholly heterogeneous. Furthermore, its Existence depends on the proof of the insufficiency of the *Science* of Theology: in as much as that which contains the ground of all, its own Existence included, is by universal admission = God, or the Supreme which has in itself the ground of its own existence, and in this, its necessary or self-existence, is the sufficient cause of all other existence. Thus, the failure of Theology, as the Science of Sciences, gives rise to incipient Philosophy, and Philosophy completed passes into the Object of its pursuit and becomes Theosophy.

f96ᵛ 4518 27.71   Atoms.—If understood and employed as xyz in Algebra, and for the purpose of scientific Calculus, as in elemental Chemistry, I see no objection to the ~~assumption~~ Fiction not overweighed by its technical utility. But if they are asserted as real and existent, the Suffiction (for it would be too complimentary to call it a Supposition) is such and so fruitful an absurdity that I can only compare it to a Surinam Toad crawling on with a *wartery* of Toadlets on its back, at every fresh step a fresh Tadpole. The contradictions, which it involves, were exposed by Parmenides, 460 years A.C., so fully as to leave nothing to be added. An atom is a body which contradicts the constituent character of a Body, namely, that which fills a space, ~~for~~ and consequently must have

f96 the relations of Space, viz. two Poles and the point of bisection. But if it be answered, that they are physically indivisible, in consequence of an invincible Hardness given to them by the Creator—what are we to think of a Theory which commences with a Miracle, that could be known only by inspiration, which inspiration could be accredited only by another Miracle—? It is evidently a mere picture-word for the joint properties of Cohesion and Divisibility, and besides rests on the gratuitous position that what is divisible must be dividuous. Again, when the Theorist has got his

Atoms, he must then make a new set of Atoms still less in order to compose his subtlest Fluid, by which they are to be dilated, attracted, repelled, and generally put in motion.

The Subtle Fluid. To this likewise I have no other objection, if used as a mere sign, than that it indulges that slavery to the Eye from which the Philosopher should take every means to emancipate   *f95ᵛ*
his mind. When it is argued, that all properties ~~presume~~ must have a substratum to inhere in, the position, that is *meant* by this ~~pictur~~ metaphor from a pincushion, is a truth; but would be much better expressed in plain words, that Properties presume an objective reality. Pythagoras is believed to have first taught the existence of a Subtle all-permeating Ether, which entering from without into bodies are diversely organized into their Souls and active Powers.—But this must have been intended hieroglyphically/for what could it be but an exciting cause which supposes an excitability from within? But if it be the identity of excitement and excitability, i.e. an Object that is its own Subject, and vice versâ, what is this but another word for Mind? We say to children, what did Thought do? Lie a bed, and p—— itself!—But tho' I have heard of a fluid-making Thought, a thought-making Fluid would be like gun-pow-   *f95*
der exploding into a Syllogism, which in the form of a Congreve Rocket dried up the subtle Fluids of a dozen Troopers.—If however I found it a convenient metaphor, I should still object to calling it Electricity—for if it be a fault in nomenclature to designate a genus by the name of one its Species (ex. gr. to say, Greyhounds when we mean Dogs generally) it is still more objectionable to christen a Power by the name of one of its Forces.—A very convenient, perhaps, a necessary Form of Thought in the physical Sciences it assuredly is: and for this Reason. Physics ~~should~~ must be confined to Phænomena, and yet must not be grounded on a mere fiction. How can these two equal claims be reconciled?— Only by taking some result of metaphysical Dynamics, as the prior Science, ~~for~~ of the truth and objective reality of which it refers to   *f94ᵛ*
that Science for the proof—and then representing this by ~~an imag-~~
~~inary~~ some natural phænomenon, sufficiently flexible to the Imagination by its power of more and less by comparison, to become the fancy-language of the truth so embodied. Now this is the case with *Air*—& therefore I greatly prefer (as we know from History than Mankind have in all ages preferred metaphors so drawn, as

f94

animal, spiritus, &c, aura ignea, &c) the old word, Ether, to *Fluid*—(for Air and Water are in my belief generically ⟨*better omit*⟩ diverse, the one presenting the predominance of Repulsion over ~~Attraction~~ Cohesion, both being present, while Water is the Indifference or Equilibrium of Contraction and Dilation, in chemical phrase, the neutralization of Hydrogen by Oxygen, or more accurately of Positive by Negative Electricity.) ⟨Omit the lines within the ( ), as *peculiar* opinions.⟩

f93ᵛ

There ~~was~~ escaped one position from Mʳ Abernethie which I flatter myself he will be disposed to retract on reconsideration. Having shewn the diversity of Life from Corpuscular Substance, and the separateness of Feeling (which he identified with Consciousness) and having superinduced both *from without*, he declared that all the rest, the superiority of animals, ~~to~~ one to the other, and of men to animals, resulted wholly from their organization. Now not to mention, that the moral and religious Consequences of such a Doctrine are the very same with those of the crudest materialism, he seems to have forgotten, that according to John Hunter and himself Organization is itself an effect of the vis vitæ/therefore, his position would not essentially differ from that of Steam fabricating the Engine which it worked, and yet deriving the quantum and quale of the Power from the Engine.—If the vital fluid that formed the Brain and nervous system of a Man be the very same with that which formed the organism of a Fish, for what purpose did it degrade itself in the latter instance? By what caprice did it choose to play on a Jews harp when a Pan harmonicon was at its service? This is assuredly a ὕστερον πρότερον which involves all the mystery of ~~the~~ Spiritualism with the *pre*posterousness of ~~the~~ Materialism—in the latter ("Mind is the result of Structure," *says Mʳ Lawrence*) the House begets the Mason: in the former the Mason makes the House ~~and~~ in order that the House may make the Mason.

f93   4519 27.72   ~~On~~
                    The Philosopher's preference
                    Matters of Belief.

It is true, that my own inward faith being taken as the standard of orthodoxy (and that of course every ~~man~~ Believer must do: ~~and~~ or where would be his *Faith* in his Faith?) the Romanists and Protestants (Arians & Unitarians excluded, and likewise Mahometans) appear to me equidistant from the Truth / And yet I would on any trying occasion suffer martyrdom for the cause of Luther—at least I hope that I should & pray that I might.—Here lies the difference or rather the contrariety. Both are equidistant as, ex. gr.

Let C. = the true Faith, R. = Romanism, L = Lutheranism—the former is equally or more near to C. as or than the latter—and paradoxical as it may sound, it is nearer because it is farther out of the way. But every step on the line R. increases the distance, while every step on the line L. is an approximation. /   *f92ᵛ*

4520 27.73   *f89ᵛ*
 f90

4521 27.74   *f92ᵛ*

Yet One word more on
Subtle Fluids.

I would wish it to be understood, that I do not attribute Individuality, or an ἐγωειδες τὶ (egöitas, Ichheit, Selfness) to Life as Life: and that therefore I have no more and no other objection to a vital than to a magnetic, or electrical, or Galvanic, Fluid. But the subject is altogether new, with exception of a few ~~wandering flashes~~

uncertain rash Hints in Jacob Behmen that are = flashes & flame-fits (flammulæ errantes) that seem to have lost their way in the smoke or like a swallow that has fallen down the chimney into a

f92   chamber and dashes itself about from cornice to window-blind/The subject, I repeat, is altogether new: tho' the theme is, as old as the days of Job, and the notion of its *materiality* (N.b. not its *corporëity*) apparently authorized by Moses.—It is indeed not only a very subtle, but a very complex, Problem, and the satisfactory insight thereinto belongs exclusively to the Epoptæ of the intercirculation (περιχωρῆσις) of the Genneēsis, the Genesis, and the Procession, and to the Historians of the Apostacy and the Anastasis. (*How luminous! As plain to be seen, as an Eel in an old Fish-pond, from which the water has been just let off, or the Sun glittering on the mud and sparkling on the Duck-weed!*) But *physically* I should perhaps affirm this *Matter of Life* to be the *Product* (tertium aliquid e Syn-thesi) of the Energy of the total Organism (vis systematis solaris,

f91ᵛ   and proximately of our own Planet) and the Principium Indivi-duationis, or the nisus of each part to manifest, no i.e. réalize, ~~or~~ (were not the phrase too ludicrous) to thingify, in itself the im-manence of the whole—fieri microcosmus. But as it is itself con-tained in the total organism, and tho' an individual for itself is Nature (or a part of nature, as we say) for all other individuals, it must needs be, that Life only can assimilate Life.—Again: it does not seem probable (and so far from having proved by chemical experiments that the presumptions from chemical induction are against it) that even Plants assimilate the material Elements, or elementary *Stuffs*†, which latter, eodem modo quo fluidum se-

f91   minale auram seminalem irretire et vehere habetur, is rather than the involucrum of *the materials of Life*. ~~Yet~~ For there are two Principles (= *Grundsätze*) or opposite Poles, which must both be retained & satisfied, and therefore, of course, ⟨are⟩ to be recon-ciled. The first, ~~that~~ SIMILE SIMILI GAUDET, or NULLA DATUR ACTIO, NISI SIMILIUM IN SIMILIA: and QUICQUID SIMILE EST, NON EST IDEM, or NULLA DATUR ACTIO, NISI INTER DIFFERENTIA—

f91ᵛ   † *Stoffen* of the German Chemists: and much is it to be regretted that in this as in so many other instances, we have made ⟨the term unuseable by deturpation—⟩

both positions being combined in the formula, NEQUE IN CON-TRARIUM, ⟨(heterogeneum)⟩ NEQUE IN OMNINO NON DIFFERENS, AGITUR. The requisite difference is given in the present case by the affinities between the vectum and the vehiculum, Δυναμιν τήν οχουμενην, και το οχημα: and the form of action is an extrication. But this affinity and consequently a difference (∵ for quod ad fines, non intra fines est) must likewise be explained—which can be effected only by the suspensive interpenetration of two forces, as the + and − ℇ in Water, which therefore is the great menstruum and Vehicle of Nature. Take Water saturated with Oxygen (= Hydrogen ⚌ Oxygen, + Oxygen), and you have an instance in illustration of my position: and doubtless, the observation of this truth, *ap*prehended perhaps rather than *com*prehended, ~~is~~ lies at the bottom of the Thalesian Πρωτον μεν Ὕδωρ, and παντα εκ του υδατος, as well as the Heraclitic and Parmenidean πυρ υδατι ενοχουμενον, πῦρ ὑγρον, ὑδατοειδες, &c.—The vital Principle, or vis vitæ ~~supero~~ præter organica, of John Hunter can in no wise therefore be identified with the Pythagorico-abernethian *Vital Fluid*, the latter : the former : : agens : patiens, or as the Combustible to the Comburent; or the +ℇ = Hydr. to −ℇ = Oxygen. It is therefore no mere Play on Words, but on the contrary a most important distinction, when I say, while the man *lives*, his body *is alive*, being the mid term between the Vis vivax (or Vis vivendi) and the vital fluid, (or materiam vitæ.) The last neither lives nor is alive: ~~the second~~ for it exists in a fixed tho' loose combination with a compleated interpenetration, or neutral = death, dormant Life, or natura naturata. The second is = the last, but existing in a fluxional as well as loose combination with the first, or the Uncombined Power, and therefore is *alive*, tho' it does not live. Thus we have, 1. ab intra. 2. ab extra. 3. inter ambo = 1. Vis vitæ. 2. Materia vitæ. 3. Organismus vitalis, at once the party-wall and the conductor of both, connecting and dividing, binding and bounding, a true Natura gemina quæ fit et facit, recreat et re-creatur./

This appears to me the only sciential or scientific Form, in which the ~~electro~~ ηλεκτρικο-πυροειδες Fluid or Ether ab extra advocated by Mr Abernethie is representable. Under any other form, and endued with any higher properties, it would enforce results

f90ᵛ

f90

f89ᵛ

f89ᵛ

f89

the most inimical to those truths, both moral and physical, the ~~im~~ warm Interest in the support and defence of which does so much honor to his heart, and ~~enables him~~ establishes his claim to the title of Restorer of Common Sense, in the theoretical, as his Writings and Lectures had done before in the practical, department of Medicine and Anatomy.

f88ᵛ   **4522** 27.75   Zeno's demonstrations of the non-existence of Motion—I ~~was~~ am astonished to find them held valid or even ingenious by Tenneman & others—the whole Sophism lies, 1. in making a false assertion, that Space is divisible into infinite portions, each infinitely divisible—Now Space has no parts, & so far from being infinitely partible is *not* partible at all—2. in assuming the ~~pa~~ actuality of an Impossibility under the cover of an If.—3. In supposing separate & comparative magnitudes, where they do not exist, and abstracting them where they do—So in the Achilles or Tortoise—Achilles stride has here no appropriate magnitude. 4. That if Things in Space are real, Space must be so; but Sp. is

f88   not, ergo, Things are not.—i.e. If the Table, I see, be a Thing out of me, my *Seeing of* it must be out of me—Space is a mode of Seeing. N.B. There are visualities of negation—positions of Negation. A man in a Balloon (supposing him not to look at his Balloon) with his eyes open has a visuality tho' he see no thing, no image, very distinct from the same man in pitch-darkness or with his eyes shut—this requires to be explained—it is like the appendages of Images, as A taller than B—&c, which is neither in A or B—but rises out of both, like Tartini's third-sound/

When I express my wonder at the reverence shewn to the conundrums of Zeno, and their elevation into Antinomies of Reason!! I do so the more, because the Object to be attained (= the non-existence of ~~an~~ corporeal *Object*, as an Object only, and separate

f87ᵛ   from the Subject, cui objicitur seu Objectum est,) might be & often has been, so easily proved by analysis of What is meant by it—namely, Color, and the sensation of being repelled—&c &c.

4523 27.76

f87   I am = Verb active sui generis, causative but not transitive.

That I am = ~~the~~ a sentence, as the Noun substantive in the Objective case governed by the preceding Verb active, I am.

The second I am = Verb substantive, or the act of Being.

Fieri facio me ipsum. Facio me esse quod sum. And *I* am *all* that truly is, and yet *"Thou art*—how?—*my* Son: in the eternal *This* DAY have I ever begotten thee."

νοῦς ποιων active, transitive

— πραττων active, intransitive

— πασχων passive

from Aristotle. Hence τί ποιεῖς; what are you doing?—τί πράτ-τεις; how do you do? τί πασχεις; what ails you?

4524 27.77 Truth = the system or kosmos of Ideas, which conceived as self-possessed is Reason—. N.B. Like all ~~perfect~~ absolute definitions, applicable absolutely to the Supreme alone.— Thus God is the Truth, and the Supreme Reason.

Truth = Idea Idearum. Reason = Principium Principiorum.

Idea = that which successively we may be evermore realizing but totally can never have realized.

Human Science, Erkenntniss = an asymptot in successive approximation to the Idea, and Philosophy the Geometry of Asymptots.—

4525 27.78

Καὶ Ζήνωνα φάσι λέγειν, ἐι τὶς ἀυτῷ <u>τὸ ἕν</u> ἀποδοιῇ τί ποτε εστι, *f86ᵛ* λέξειν τὰ ὄντα.

Simplicius in Physica Aristot: p. 30

4526 27.79

As to Forgery

What? would you deprive the Throne of its Mercy? Make it a mere instrument of the penal Law? Proud like School-boys when first at their Greek exercises to turn a king into αναξ?—an ax.

4527 27.80

ως και εγων οφελον πυκινου νοου αντιβοληℴσαι *f85ᵛ*
αμφοτεροβλεπτος, δολιη δ' οδω εξαπατηθην,
πρεσβυγενης ετ' εων και απενθηριστος απασης
σκεπτοσυνης· ὅππη γαρ εμον νοον ειρυσαιμι,
εις Εν Ταυτο τε παν ανελυετο· παν δε ον αιει
παντη ανελκομενον μιαν εις φυσιν ισταθ' ομοιαν.

Xenomanes apud Sext. Empiricum.

f85   4528 27.81   "TOMORROW WILL NOT TAKE PLACE."

Second Advertisement, second Column, first page of the Morning Advertiser, Friday, April 23, 1819.—

Substitute "may" for "will": and it is a Lesson for all men. But even as it stands, to how many! and in how many instances! "I'll part ⟨with⟩ the Wench tomorrow."—Tomorrow will not take place.—

f84ᵛ   4529 27.82   Augustus IInd K. of Poland, intimate *Friend* of Friedrich Wilhelm I^st K. of Prussia (this is the *strangest* part of the Story! Two Kings, *Friends*!!) warned against wine on account of an inflammation einer Zähe—and Field-marshall Grumbkow who attended him to the Borders, and in the last Prussian Royal Palace as Frederich's Proxy-Host, cautioned / Too fond himself of Champagne to stand Augustus's entreaty—got drunk & broke his ribs, and was carried in a sled next morning to receive Augustus's last commissions—Augustus ausser einem vorn geöfneten Hembde [Hemd], nur mit einem kurzen Polnischen Pelz bekleidet.—In this very dress, only with closed eyes, Augustus appeared on the first of February, 1733, about 3 ºclock in the morning to the Field-marshal—& said,

Mon cher Grumbkow! Je viens de mourir ce moment a Varsovie—.—The rest of the story I omit, the essence being in the my dear *Grum Cow*! ※

f85   ※ Pity the F.M. had been the ghost himself—it is such a happy Ghost's Name.

f84   4530 27.83   If I understand the terms aright, a radius is the *exponent* of a Circle, as 6 is the Exponent of ³⁰⁄₅; and a Circle ⟨with infinite radii⟩ is an *Exponential* of Space—, ~~being to Space as its own center to itself~~ i.e. a center the radii from which in all directions are equal ⟨—so far it is an Exponent—⟩—but the circumference being no where & the radii, of course, infinite, this is transcendental—. But an Exponent of the Transcendental is an Exponential—.

An Ideal = the Exponential of an Idea. The *poetic* Imagination the Exponential of the Reason/. A statue an exponent of an Ideal?—

4531 27.66
    Revd Mr Hornbuckle,   *f99^v*
            St John's
                Cambridge

4532 27.68
    3. 10. 17. 24. 31. 7. 14.

4533 27.69   Throughout these Memoranda the symbolic   *f100*
marks are and mean as follows.
    =   equal to, one with.   )(opposed to, in antithesis.
    ⊝   the same as.   ⋕   contrary to.
    —   without, less by.   +   added to.   ⋕   combined
with.
    ×   multiplied into.   ÷   divided by.
The Letters from A to W mean known Quantities or degrees.
X, Y, Z   mean each any not yet determined Quantities or Degrees.—

4534 .322   One *source* of Calumny (I say *source*: because   *f163^v*
~~Alph~~ Allophoby from hëautepithymy is the only proper *cause*) may
be found in this:—every man's life exhibits two sorts of Selfishness—those which are, and those which are not, objects of his own
Consciousness. A. is thinking, perhaps, of some plan in which he
may benefit another.—and during this absorption consults his own
⟨little bodily⟩ comforts *blindly*, occupies the best place at the Fire
side, or asks at once *"Where am I to sit?"* instead of first enquiring
after the health of another.—Now the error lies here—that B in
complaining of A. first takes for granted ~~that~~ either that these are
acts of conscious Selfishness in A. or if he allows the truth yet
considers them just as bad (& so perhaps they may be, in a certain
sense) *but forgets*, that his own Life presents the same/Judges of his
own life ⟨exclusively⟩ by his consciousness, that of another, by
conscious & unconscious in a lump. A monkey's anthropo*morph*
attitudes we take for *anthropic*: & so &c.

4535 18.323   As Paülo became Pagolo by change of u into   *f164*
v, and of v into g (Grazzini, alias, Lasca writes *Pagolo* IV)—so in

the German orthography of the 17th Century & still later Krays for kreis—Hence our Craw fish, and our *Crab*—which the Egyptians made the symbol of the cyclical motion of the Planets round the sun—i.e. at every point the strait line falls back on itself, whence of course a circle.

4536 18.324

f163^v I adopt the following Symbols—

Z = Carbon. Y = Oxygen.

$X^{(1}$ = Hydrogen. $X^{(2}$ = Nitrogen or Azote

+A = Light. −A. Gravity or Ether.

⟨Ω = universal, O = partic., Organism.⟩

f164 It is often observed and in fact it is curious, that no mention is made of the Minerals and Metals in the Mosaic Cosmogony. But our present chemistry enables us to solve this difficulty, greatly to the credit of the inspired Historian. For he distinctly enumerates, first Light and Darkness, i.e. Gravity; second, Water, or Hydrogen; thirdly, Air or Azote, both having the common term, Oxygen; fourthly, Earth, as the astringent or rather subject of homogeneous Attracter = Carbon in combination with the former. But Carbon + Azote, supporting Hydrogen and Oxygen = Metals and their Oxyds. But all the Earths are metallic Bases. Therefore the apparent Defect in the Mosaic Account resolves itself into full Insight and freedom from idle and erroneous Supernumeraries.

f164^v Q.E.D.—Still more evident will this appear when (as I confidently anticipate) Azote and Hydrogen shall be shewn to be the same Element or *Stuff* diversely modified, and interchangeable—varying, in short, as Dilation and Repulsion.—Call this Element X.† The Mosaic Chemistry would be expressed in the following brief formula—

Chaos or Indistinction = Gravity ÷ Light.—From GL in di-verse interpenetrated in pre-established proportions/the Arithmi of the Pythagoreans & Material Numerationes of the Cabbalists arise—

† and call the Attraction of Cohesion or Carbon Z: Contraction call Y.

Y (Oxygen)   + $X^{(1}$ = Water
Y (Oxygen)   + $X^{(2}$ = Air
Z (Carbon)   + $X^{(2}$ = Metals
Metal   +   Water = Chrystals ⎰
Metal   +   Oxygen = Oxyds   ⎱ Earth

The same process repeated in infinitely smaller spheres, = cycles of Individuation. Symbol o

The material World is one Individuum. Symbol Ω.

O counteracting (contr'actio) or contracting, at the same moment that it is both contained and potenziated by Ω = semina, organismi, $\omega\alpha$.

O Ω under the predominance of $ZX^{(1}$ = Vegetable Life; of $YX^{(2}$ = Animal Life—

$A\lambda\eta$ $\Theta\varepsilon\iota\alpha$ + Ω $OYX^{(2}$ = Man.—

4537 18.325   Thursday Morning, probably between 4 and   *f165*
5, May 6th, 1819—at Highgate. I have this morning had a fearful Dream in which I saw Mrs Morgan, threatening to publish all my letters to them, shewing how grateful I felt myself—and to abuse these over flying feelings of Gratitude to give confirmation to their scandalous Lies—Then poor J. J. Morgan himself, frightfully distorted with Palsy, attempting with shaking and tottering limbs to assassinate me, first with ⟨a⟩ pen knife and then with a Razor.

The night before, Wordsworth & SH, $\mu\alpha\mu\mu\alpha$ $\pi\upsilon\lambda\chi\varepsilon\rho\rho\iota\mu\alpha$ $\alpha\pi\varepsilon\rho\tau\alpha$.

4538 18.326   ⟨)(is my mark for "distinguished from".⟩   *f165^v*
                    Abstraction)(Generalization
Abstraction is to Generalization as the Numeration below the Unit is to the Numeration above it, the Unit being the Fountain of both.

$$4$$
$$3$$
$$2$$
$$\overline{1}$$
$$''2$$
$$''3$$
$$''4$$

In other words, in abstracting we give the Character of an Integer to a component fraction of the Integral. We super-individualize in order by means of an intenser *individuity* or *propriety* to find the Genus or *common* Form. And this we ⟨do⟩ in the feeling (almost I might say by a sort of *instinctive* Reason that leads us to expect) that in the Generic or Common we shall find, as in its natural word or symbol, the true forma formans ab intra: i.e. as far as it is *proper* to the Subject in question, and as distinguished from the

f166   operation of the *circumstantia*. Hence Abstraction is a preliminary step or necessary Antecedent to Generalization. And hence too Abstraction ~~or the~~ affords a Test of the ~~genuiness~~ *genuineness*, the *real* and philosophic truth, of a Generalization—which test is given, when *both* acts, that of Abst. and that of Gen. are found united in the common Base of another and higher Individual, and an IDEAL is born. Whether this Individual occurs in the World of Experience, or is a Birth of the Mind embodied in a statue, is nonessential. Thus certain Forms and Exponents have been abstracted, from the person, countenance &c of Pericles we will say—then generalized—and lastly, re-individualized—& we have an Ideal, a God.—Where this union does not take place, the Generalization is at best but a technical Mnemonic—for the aid of the Memory and as a mode of Arrangement. Nature herself sets the example— Thus from the Plant she abstracts the irritability of the anthers &

f166ᵛ   stamina of the flower, as the acme of vegetable Life, and the perfection of the Planet in its most perfect state—and generalizing this and again re-individualizing (i.e. embodying) it, she produces the Insect Race—

Receptivity, or Excitability, at one pole, and Agency or Excitancy ⌐. . .⌐ at the other, are the opposite states in which the **one** Activity, ~~of Nature~~, which is the Substance of both, and their identity, reveals itself. There can be no *Product* without an Antecedent Power, that produced it, and is known to *be*, and to be that particular Power, by that ⟨particular⟩ Product. In relation to Existence, the Power determines the Product; in relation to ~~the~~ our *knowlege* of its Existence, the Product determines the Power.—But again no Power can produce but under the condition of passing out of its Oneness or Identity, nor manifest itself except by Opposites, ~~that~~ each of which *suppose* the existence of the other in

order to the possibility of its own existence. ~~Each~~ These twin Opposites I call the Poles; and the process itself, in which THE ONE   *f167*
reveals its Being in two opposite yet correlative Modes of Existence, I designate by the term, Polarity, or Polarizing. The ~~on~~
Poles themselves are entitled, either plus (+) & minus (−); or
positive and negative; or Thesis and Antithesis (in English, Position and Counterposition) and the Antecedent One, which is the
sole *reality* of Both, and in both is *pre*supposed, I call the **Prothesis** (in English, the Pre- or Ante-position) or the **Identity**; or
the **Radical**.—I will illustrate this by the simplest instance. You
must in the first place think of ~~Life~~ a vital, or generative Power,
& carefully exclude from your mind all mere mechanical composition—i.e. you must not think of a Line as *made up* of an indefinite multitude of points, which is the mechanical notion; but of a
Point producing itself into a Line (you may say, *generating* a Line):
and if by the Point you will understand a something that, like a
Mother, remained after and together with the Offspring, you
would then say that the Point *produced* the Line.   *f167ᵛ*

Now the Point taken as producing itself into the Line, and of
course existing no longer as a Point, but transformed into the Line
and as it were lost in the Product, ~~is~~ would be the proper representative of all purely *Chemical* processes; and the Point taking as
producing the Line of all *vital* production; but that the Prothesis
in both cases is no true Identity, but itself a Composition (as in
chemistry) or a Combination or Union, as in animal and sexual
Production—in both instances we *commence* with a Dyad, or Dual
Number. Still whenever it is assumed as antecedent to the Product
and thus standing in the place of the Identity, we apply the same
reasoning—with this difference that in lifeless substances the Point
re-appears ~~as~~ in the Line as the imaginary midpoint or punctum
Indifferentiæ—. Thus the Male & Female considered in Union
as one Being would be represented by the Point, A, and the bipolar
Product by the Line B. C.

but an ~~chemical~~ inanimate productive Power by the Point A in the
Line B. C.

A
B———/—— . ———C

But in both instances, (that is, when real ~~and integral~~ Things are spoken of) as we *begin* with a *synthesis*, the Production can only be, in the first instance, a reproduction of itself, as 2 = 1, in a third, ex. gr. the Union of the Stamen and Germen of the Flower in a Seed; or in a third expressing at once the Union of the Productive Powers & their separation. Thus the Male & Female produce a

f168ᵛ Child as the compound or quotient of both Parents, but the Child is ~~now~~ either a Male ~~& now~~ or a Female, ~~or~~ either in succession or both at the same time.—But a chemical Synthesis, or 2 = 1, produces only by decomposition into the original 2—Thus Oxyde of Mercury produces (i.e. produces itself into) Oxygen as one Pole and Mercury as the other.

4539 27.90

f73ᵛ   Who first invented work, & bound the free
           And holyday-rejoicing spirit down
           To the ever-haunting importunity
           Of Business, in the green fields, & the town—
           To spade, loom, anvil, plough—& oh most sad,
           To this dry drudgery of the desk's dead wood?
           Who but the Being ~~tw~~ unblest, alien from good,
           Sabbathless Satan! he who his ~~unblest~~ unglad
           Task ever plies 'mid rotatory burnings,
           That round & round incalculably reel—
           For wrath divine hath made him like a wheel—
           In that red realm from whence are ~~not~~ no returnings

f72ᵛ   Where, toiling & ~~returning~~ turmoiling, ever & aye,
           He & his thoughts keep pensive workyday.

                                                    C L

f35ᵛ 4540 27.31   A position, which occurred to me 20 years ago as an objection to Idealism (as Berkley's &c) recurs with additional weight to me as often as I think on the subject.—Idealism & Materialism are both grounded in the impossibility of inter-mutual action between things altogether heterogeneous—and here again it is assumed by both parties that *Perception* is but a sort of, or at least an immediate derivative from, *Sensation*—so that the changes or modifications of the Percipient's own Being are exclusively the objects of his perception. But is not this gratuitous? Is not sensibility just as mysterious, equally *datum*, haud intellectum, as Percipiency?—If I assume, as I have a far better right to do because all men do so naturally, that Percipiency ⟨in⟩ *genere* is an attribute   *f36* of the Soul, and that sensation is nothing more than ~~or~~ a species of Perception modified by the Object—(Just as Colors, and Sounds difference it, while they realize it) which in this instance is the Percipient's own existence/and all is clear.—The Soul $\neq$ Existence + Percipiency = 1.—~~Then~~ there arise two Sorts—α. Percipiency as Perception. Percipere is like scire a verb active—qui percipit, percipit *aliquid*—i.e. a verb active must have an objective case belonging to it—. Now this is in its most general expression, Existence—. And Perception of E − E = Perception simply: Perception of E + E = Sensation.—

Or perhaps still plainer. Percipience confined to one Object ⟨α⟩   *f36ᵛ* = Sensation. Perception of β, γ, δ relatively to α, or to each other, = Sense. The *one* Object α is *most* often the Self or proximate existence—but sometimes it is not so, as in sublimity and intensity, ex.gr.—a sweet strain of music. "*I lost myself*"—and the perception becomes a sensation—even in an aweful mountain Form, Color, &c. do not act at that moment as form—.

$$\text{Existents—} \begin{cases} \text{non-perceptive} \\ \text{perceptive} \end{cases} \begin{cases} \text{~~of its own existence~~ } \gamma \\ \text{without comparison } \alpha \\ \text{with comparison } \beta\gamma \end{cases}$$

α = Sensation
βγ = Perception

incomparative absolute, *no ~~re~~ Memory*. Ergo, the *act* of Being not   *f37* *memorable*†: its *Product continuous* = condition of the dim commencement of self-consciousness?

† neither continuous nor discontinuous; for it is transcendent to Time, Space, and Motion. *Product* of the act of Being = Act of Perception? And in this double nature, Product + Act, the ground of Consciousness, and Memory?—

4541 27.32

f37ᵛ Geometrical Elements: Fibre, Leaf, Cell.
Chemical —— — Fibrine, Albumen, Lymph
~~Modes~~ Forms of existence—Solid, Fluid, Aeriform, Impondera-
ble.
Modes, Soft, Hard-Solid.— (N.B. Solid a bad term, as
                                      properly ⋇ Hollow. Firm?
                                      firmamental?—*Fest.*)
Hard-solid.

———

  Bone
  Nail
  Hair.

———

Soft-solid
  Skin
  Flesh
  Marrow.

———

Combine the Solid with the Fluid, and we have Systems.—1.
~~Lymphatic~~ Glandular. 2. Blood-vessels. 3. Nervous.
~~Lymphatic~~ Glandular = 1. Absorbent. 2. Exhalant.
Absorbent = 1. Lymphatic, properly. 2. Lacteal.

f38 Exhalant = 1. Vapor, collects in all the cavities & exhaled from
the vessels of the Hair. 2. Gas, separated by the Lungs. 3. XY
(= Ether?)—from the Brain. (perhaps.)
N.B. Lacteals those that in the intestinal Canal suck out the Chyle
from the Food and carry it to the Blood. Lymphatic suck out the
Lymph from all parts of the Body and likewise convey it to the
Blood.
2. Sangui-vascular System.
As the Glandular hath its duplicity in Absorbent & Exhalant, so
the sangui-vascular hath its in
        1 Veins—that carry the Blood from all parts of the Body back
        to the Heart.
        2 Arteries, that propel the Blood from the Heart to the Pe-
        riphery.

3. Nervous System.   *f38*ᵛ
    1. Adductive, nerves of sensation
    2. Abductive, nerves of motion.

Compound Systems
    divided into three according to the great Cavities.
1. ABDOMINAL, formed by the LIVER, Spleen, Pancreas, Stomach, Gut.—
Functions = Digestion, Assimilation, Secretion, Excretion.—Preponderance of the Venous
Common Object = Reproduction.
2. PECTORAL, formed by the Heart and Lungs.—Functions, Circulation, and Respiration.   *f39*
Common Object. Vitality Irritability—The Systole and Diastole of
the Heart, the In- & Ex-spiration of the Lungs—indefatigable—
Preponderance of the Arterial.
3. Cerebral—formed by Brain, Cerebellum, Spinal Marrow.
    Functions. Sensation, Loco-motion, & perhaps conditions of
Memory.—
Common Object. Sensibility.

In the Brain   Organization at its Maximum—and as Extremes
meet, so here Form sinks under Form, and self-conquered approaches to Formlessness—or that which has no outward Dimension, but Depth.—without fluidity it has the character of Fluid—
These are the three interior Systems, to which correspond three   *f39*ᵛ
exterior Systems, viz.
    1. the Osseous System.
    2. the System of the voluntary Muscles
    3. the Sensuous System.
    In the first, coresp. to the Abdominal, Reproduction
    In the 2ⁿᵈ, ——— — — Pectoral, Irritability.
    In the 3 ——— — — Cerebral, Sensibility.
In the muscularles Contraction, Expansion—as in the Heart Systole, Diastole. In the M. voluntary, in the H. involuntary. Oscillation—& so in the Pulmonary In- and Ex-halations.
    In the voluntary Muscle the Longitudinal Fibre predominant,   *f40*
that oscillates, as the perpendic. Pendulum, in shortning and

lengthning—in the involuntary (arterial & vascular) the circular
fibre, as in the circle-shaped Pendular, in narrowing and opening
out—In the Heart both are found—hence its self-dependence—.
As the exterior Muscular System to the Will, +, so the interior
Pectoral to the Passions, Affections, Emotions—
The Senses are outward Brains.— = Brain-colonies—. Hence a
sort of Life of its own in Eye, Ear &c.—
As the Blossom of all these, the Speech = Sensibility over Irritability—? Intellectuality? Generative = Irritability over Reproduction

f40ᵛ The Analogies, = Higher, to Interior. Lower, to Exterior.
Wind-pipe, close by Gullet. Urethra, passage of Ourin and
Sperm, close by ανυς—Glans, Lips.—

But of these my conceptions are but chaotic at present—. Yet
the testicles & brain-convolutes have a striking analogy.

Does the supinduction of Intellectuality call upward the Sensit.
and Irritab. into an Identity, or Indifferency of both, so that instead of Sens. submerged in Irritab. and Irrit. no longer Irrit.
from the evanescence of its antithesis, Sensib.—and both therefore
lost by the internecinisme susception, into the forms of Reproduction—or swallowed up *into* it—instead of this, I say, we have N
= the unity of Irritability taken up into Sensibility, (or N =
~~irritable sensibility~~ sensible Irritability) as the negative and Intellectuality as the positive, with *Intellectual* ~~Re~~Production as the
f41 Product, which is here become a Genesis, or Gennēma?

Whatever I may or may not make out of this, still the Relation
of Higher and Lower, as attributes of the Dimensionless *rising out
of* the perfected Tri-dimensional, the Dimensionless Superra-di-
mensional, therefore attributes of *Spirit* in ~~opposition~~ contradiction
to infra-dimensional *Matter*, and Opposition to dimensional
Body—is important and fruitful.
Thus we have,
    1. Length, Breadth, Depth.
    2. Inward, Outward
    3. Higher, Lower
All the Organs are themselves modes, or rather ascending forms,
f41ᵛ of Perception—and as in the higher Mathesis shorter and yet shorter
Exponents are found, that, all below existing, contain in themselves

the power of all below, and are entire in themselves—but only under the condition that all below or anterior still existed in other forms—9 is no less real and individual than 1, if only 1, 2, 3, 4, 5, 6, 7, and 8, exist each in its own place & function—. 9 in nature is not a mere mark of one added nine times, but a true × of 8 into a one, capacious of the 8. Thus the embodied Soul is individuated from all external & below it; but yet could not be, were these not. And thus, the Soul may be disembodied, and no longer need Senses for its Brain, nor the Brain for its Organs—& yet could not be so, had not these been & were they not still—·
—i.e.—in the scheme of Ascent, or Anastasis.—N.B. the advan- *f42* tage of this system is that it *realizes* Mathematical Truths, by making Mathesis or Perception a co-efficient of Being—a principium *essendi*. We live when we live as we ought to do by a successive carrying over of the Balance to a new Leaf—. The Balance at the 50th leaf being as true a unit, as the first *one* of difference in the first leaf—.and thus farthings may disappear in pence, pence in shillings, shillings in pounds, and the Mint of God is more copious in its Money Table/and yet it too has its highest which then is never lost, but increases in itself—namely, *act of Will*, resolving itself into the Will of God.—In the lower Life-world Habit is the exponential of this increaseing Unit.

But before it is possible for me to proceed, I must first and foremost be clear concerning Repulsion & the Magnet/

4542 27.33   In a long-brief Dream-life of regretted Regrets *f42ᵛ* I still find a noticeable Space marked out by the Regret of having neglected the Mathematical Sciences. No *week*, few *days*, pass unhaunted by a fresh conviction of the truth ⟨involved in⟩ of the Platonic Superscription over the Portal of Philosophy, Μήδεις ἀγεωμέτρητος εισίτω.—But surely Philosophy hath scarcely sustained less more detriment by its alienation from Mathematics

4543 27.34   Mile End, Bow. Stratford, Ilford. Chadwell, *f43* ⟨Heath opposite⟩ Rumford 12 Road velocipedous throughout— dry, hard, level and dustless. Sat. June 8, 1819/Brookstreet (to the Left Weald Church on a Hill, woody) Brentwood, 18 Miles, in 2 Hours & 5 Minutes—from the Town/Ingatestone—Whit-

ford. Chelmsford, 29, in 3 H. 35.—Great Baddow—Danbury
Place/Runsell

4544 27.35

f43 Attraction = Attraction Appropriative
Astringency = Attraction Conservative
Q? Whether Repulsion can be conceived under the latter form—
how far astr. is diverse from Contraction and Rep. from Dilation,
whether attraction baffled, i.e. at its maximum, must not re-act on
the attrahent body?

4545 27.36

f43ᵛ Objective Perception × Objective Memory
Subjective Perception × Subjective Memory
Thus to
Ob. (or perceptional) Perception,
belongs
Sub. (or Sensational) Memory.
while to
Sub. or Sensational Perception
belongs
Ob. or perceptional Memory.
But in this latter I have sacrificed the true force of Ob. and Sub.
f44 in order to attain a rememberable and seemingly more comprehensible order of opposition/For that Memory which in our natural
and waking state is ever on tiptoe to rush out on & flow into the
exciting Perception, must in all consistency be deemed *Objective/*
1. it is all, or all but all compulsion, or necessity as opposed to
choice—2. in the Subject but not for the Subject, but Nature as
contrary to Consciousness.—3. It is elementary, ~~an~~ atomic, as it
were, and linked by Laws ~~systems~~ of primary construction as opposed to secondary, integral, and combined by laws of association.—Even the word Sensational is false.—
f44ᵛ   Far better therefore adhere to the strict nomenclature—.⟨To⟩
Objective Perception (= βγ) belongs Objective Memory: to Subjective Perception (= α) Subjective Memory.—The objective
characters of Obj. Mem. (= βγμ) we have given over leaf—and
the subjective characters of Subj. Memory (= αμ) at the same

time per antithesin—viz. first, choice ⌇ Necessity. 2. Consciousness ⌇ Nature. 3. Secondary, integra~~lers~~ or rather wholes, associative ⌇ elementary, fractional, constructive.—

We proceed then.—The Objective Perception is integrated by $f45$
the Objective Memory—βγ ~~supplies or implies~~ implies comparison, and supplies it to βγM—βγM supplies an objective *Unity* to
βγ—And thus Comparison + Unity = full integral objective
Perception.—But here specially observe, what is meant by *Objective Unity!*—no other than the very opposite of true (i.e. Subjective) Unity, namely, indistinguishable Multeity, elementary Nature—And this is the unitas phænomenὴ, & reconciles Leibnitz
with Kant. In like manner must the Subjective Perception (= α) $f45^v$
be integrated by the Subjective Memory (= αM.) And here per
antithesin requisitam α supplies the Unity, and αM—the plurality
or stuff of Comparison—and here again we have the *same* factors,
~~which~~ and as far as we can at present see in no differencing difference of position in reference to the *Product*, which therefore as
before must be objective Perception ~~relativ~~ in the Subject relative
to the Objects in the Subject—in other Words, the Sensation (or $f46$
Perception non-perceptive) ~~was~~ is elevated into Perception (commonly so called) relative to the organs &c = Objects, that had
been previously objects of Sensation exclusively.—Internal Vision
in Clair Voyance—magnetique.—

4546 27.84   Religion defended against its Defenders, intro- $f84$
ductory to a Demonstration of Christianity, the moral conditions,
essentially indemonstrable, being present & conceded.

4547 27.86   June 10, 1819. St Lawrence, Essex. $f83$
    Mrs J. Green presented me with the first Cherries, I had seen—
& on the 9th made my silk Breast plate/—on which Days M^r
J. Green & myself were evolving the state, constituted by A ⌇
B, as the *Adjectives*, Centrifugal ⌇ Centripetal, and C ⌇ D. =
the Substantives, Fluid and Firmamental.

    Ditto, while making this memorandum Mrs J. Green brought
in to her Husband and me, each the first Strawberry of the year, $f82^v$
relatively to us the Eaters.—Moats Farm (alias, in old title deeds,
Motts) in the parish of St Lawrence, scarce a mile from the arm

of the Sea, called the Black Water, six miles from the *Station*, where it becomes open sea.

f82   4548 27.87   Generosus = in full possession of the qualities & of the degree, ~~or~~ intensive or extensive, of the qualities by which the Genus was originally formed and characterized.

Degener = the contrary of Generosus, and yet contra-distin-guished from Bastard, Hybrid, crossed—in short, from the Off-spring of Parents, of different Origin, whether of greater, lesser, or equal dignity.—~~An~~ Apples *degenerate* where *Grafting* is not in use.

Thus Semitæ Generosi, or the cultivated Descendant of Shem, signified by ○; Semitæ degeneres, by ⊖.

f81ᵛ Iapetidæ generosi, ♀ Descendants of Japhet.
Iapetidæ degeneres, ♀̵ Ditto degenerate.
Chamitæ generosi, ♈ Descendants of Ham
D? degeneres ♈̸ D? degenerate.

N. S. E. W. all relatively to ~~Asia Minor, or~~ the Countries of Palestine, Syria, as far as Mesopotamia as the extreme ~~South~~ North and East Boundary: ~~Eastwards~~ and Arabia the South B—/~~rather Westwards~~ But Mesopotamia I extend Southward, as far as the plain of Babylon—/

Palestine, Syria, Arabia and Mesopotamia I consider as = the Tents of Shem.

♅ = the Teutonic Branch of the Iapetidæ: ♀ = the Greek Branch—or the N.W. and the S.W.

f81   The Semitic Race forbidden to intermarry with the Descendants of Ham and Canaan—but disobeyed the command so that the whole Race is lost by dilution of Intermarriage, except only the ⊖ Jews and the ⊖ Arabs.

The ♅, my N.W, includes Sarmatia, Dacia, Germany, Sweden, Norway, Denmark—

The ♀, my S.W. Macedon, Greece, the Archipelago, and Italy as high up as Rome.—and some of the Spanish Coast.

My *West*, the intermediate Parts of Europe, namely, France, N. of Italy, the Northern Half of Spain, the Island of Britain and Ireland—all the Celts, in short.

f80ᵛ   My East comprehends the Breadth thro' Tartary to China, and China.

My South = Africa including Egypt.

My N.W by N.—the Sclavonic Nations, as Poland and Russia. S.E. Persia. SE by South, India.

America by itself; but linked on to the Noachic World by the S and SW of the SE by S, Polynesia to wit, and the Isles of the Malay Races; and by the N. of NW by N—/

General Rule. The Generosi of the Mixt Races *emigrate* first and farthest—thus ○ ♈ to China and ♀○ + ○♈♀ to Japan.—The prior marks the predominant Blood.

Emigration not to be confounded with Conquest, and Coloni-   *f80*
zation by the conquering Race. Thus of N. G⟨aul⟩ by the Franks and Normans, Britain by the Saxons.—

These things understood and admitted I cherish a hope border-ing on a belief, that I can explain the origination and geographical position of Blumenbach's five Races, the Caucasian with the ~~Tartar and~~ American and Tartar on one side, and the Malay and Negro on the other, on the Mosaic Triad, Shem, Ham and Japhet—nay, what is yet more difficult, reconcile the Kantean diagnostic of *Race* with the Mosaic Documents respecting the *Deluge*. For Kant's,   *f79ᵛ*
which was the germinal and Substantiating Idea of Blumenbach's, as it first enabled us to distinguish diversity from variety, or dif-ference in *Kind* from difference in Degree, and to appropriate the term, Race, to the former,—seems at first sight to agree with the Sons of Adam, ⟨in⟩ whom we might easily ~~be~~ conceived the germ of a fivefold modifiability to have evolved, by the time of the Deluge; but not with the Sons of Noah, in all of whom ⟨some⟩ one, and ⟨that⟩ the same, Mode must, it should seem, have already been developed irrevocably. For it is a bold assumption, that the Caucasian had no evolution—and rendered improbable by the characteristic peculiarity of the Jews and Arabs;—still more by the   *f79*
absence of ~~all~~ any greater tendency to modification in the Caucasian than in the American.—

The possible cases are: I. That Adam was Φ, containing v. w. x. y. z; but a some one different from them all. Or II. that he was V = v, and modifiable alike into w, x, y or z.—If we take the former, the Caucasian v will be a fixed evolute of Φ, and precluded from further or other evolution by the hypothesis of Race as herein contra-distinguished from Variety. If we take the latter, then it must be affirmed either that the ~~human~~ children of *f78ᵛ* Men from Adam to Noah had not peopled the earth so far ~~or~~ for so long a time as to have passed into any race exciting diversity of Climate, Soil &c, or that the Earth had no such diversity before the Deluge, which again is astronomically supposable only under the supposition that but a small portion of habitable Land had as yet emerged from the ante-diluvial Ocean.—Or that the Ancestors of Noah had continued under the same circumstances as Adam, and that Noah himself was in all respects a second Adam.—And this is certainly the most probable hypothesis in all respects—for so Shem, Ham, and Japhet will all be V = v, and no more difficulty will be found in deriving 5 races from 3 than from 5—and 5 will have no advantage over two or three—nay, the very con-

f78 trary. For my Scheme comprizes all the influences which Blumenbach supposes, and adds to them the effects of intermarriages, and the mighty contribution of Causes from the Moral World.

1 Φ in the Tents of ○.

2 Φ + ○ = Φ͡○ in the Tents of Shem.

3 Φ + Φ ○ pass into Persia.

4 ○ Ψ͡Φ Eastward, pressing on to China

5 ΦΨ + ○ΨΦ, at the same time, & separating from the first Horde evince the predominance of the Iapetic Blood by finally passing into the Isles of Japan.

f77ᵛ 6. These followed by ♄ ⊖, ⊖ Ψ, and other bastard tribes from the intermarriage of the degenerate Semitæ with the Chamitæ, & probably mixt again with a mixture of Ψ♃, = degenerate Iapetidæ and Chamitæ or ♃ alone, forming the various tribes of Tartars.

7. Φ͡○͡Φ pass out of Persia into India, and pressing on, till they probably blend with Detachments from Nᵒˢ 4 and 5, descending Southward—and intermixing form the nobler Races of India, as the ancestors of the present Burman Race, and of the Japanese in part—

8. In after times a ~~more~~ degenerate race of Semito-Iapetidæ from

f77 Persia, ⊖♃, pass into India and blend with S. detachments of Nᵒ 6—And enriched at ~~a~~ later periods by refugee Semites, and Chamo-Semites from the ~~plain~~ Plains of Tigris and Euphrates, and by both Ψ and ♄ from Egypt and the Countries towards the Heads of Nile & the Sea Coast, form the Ancestors of the Hindostanese.

N.B. As the Celts differ from the Tartar or *Eastingners* by ○ predominating over ♈ in ○ ♈, and by being ○ ♈ while the Tartars are for the most part ↑ ⊖, i.e. the predominance of Ham over Shem, and of both in degeneracy, so do they differ among themselves, first by the degree of cultivation of the ♈ from whom they originated, and the ♈ (Phœnicians, Carthaginians, for instance) by whom they might afterwards be colonized; and secondly, especially towards the North Line of the vast Isthmus, which they formed between the Φ and ♋, by their greater admixture of Blood thro' Intermarriages with the Φ.

f76ᵛ

So the Scythians or Φ ♈, and the Sclavonic People, all either ♃ ♈, or Φ + ♃ ♈—and ameliorated by ○ or ○ Φ—as the Russians by the asiatic Greeks ♃ .—

4549 27.85 The weather-bound Travellers: or the Histories, Lays, Legends, Incidents, Anecdotes, and Remarks contributed during a detention in one of the Hebrides—

f83ᵛ

by ~~Lory McHaroldson~~ ⟨their Secretary,⟩

Lory McHaroldson,

Senachy in the Isle of ——.

"Tho' not all fact, must it needs be false?" These things have a truth of their own, if we but knew how to look for it. Every period of Life has its own way of representing the humanity common to all periods, that I mean which constitutes ~~man~~ ⟨us human beings⟩ in contra-distinction from all other creatures. Thus in whatever ~~most deeply~~ layed firm hold of us in early life there lurks an interest and a charm for our maturest years: which he ~~to~~ will never draw forth who merely mimicking ~~the~~ the ~~style~~ forms and unessential tho' natural defects of Thought and Expression ~~cannot~~ has not the skill to remove the childish yet leave the childlike untouched. Let each then relate that which ~~m~~ has left the deepest impression on his mind, at whatever period of life ~~it~~ he may have seen, heard or read it—but let him tell it ~~as he shapes it to his own~~ in accordance with the present state of his Intellect & Feelings, as he has perhaps, Alnaschar-like, acted it over ⟨again by the parlor fireside of a rustic Inn, with the fire for his only companion—⟩

f82ᵛ

4550 27.89

f74   Nitrogen = 13, Hydrogen being = 1
Oxygen = 15 in specific gravity; but as ~~occupying only half~~ in a
volume of equal size—But as the equivalent number of Oxygen
taken from water is 7.5, if this be called *its* volume, then Nitric
Acid in its dry ⟨state⟩ is composed of one Vol. of Nitrogen = 13,
and 5 volumes of Oxygen = 37.5 = 50.5.

But liquid Nitric Acid is 50.5 + 17 of Water, i.e. two pro-
portionals, at †8.5 each—therefore L N A = 67.5

But Muriatic Acid = one V. of H. = 1 and the same Vol. of
Chlorine = 33.5 = 34.5—But as no equivalent number has been
given for the liquid Muriatic Acid, and we only know that W.
takes up 480 times its own bulk, it will be fairest perhaps to take

f73   the Nitric Acid–water = 50.5—in order to set about solving the
problem of the Aqua Regia. Neither 50.5, nor 34.5 by itself will
dissolve gold, but mixed they *become yellow* & readily dissolve
Gold—

That Nitrogen is as Steffens first asserted (Anglicè, conjectured)
one Component of Metal, I am strongly inclined to believe—that
Chlorine, Iodine, and Oxygen are significant of Fixture (North,
Carbon, − Magnetism) differently contracted—I likewise suspect.—And again that philosophical Carbon never exists but as in
some state of Contraction, and that probably Ox. Chl. and Iod.
are but 3 of many primary, and therefore in the present ratio of
the Numbers, constituting the Solar System, indissoluble Products
of attraction + or × contraction, various Proportions not of the
Stoffs (as Steffens mistakenly supposes) but of the constructive

f72ᵛ Powers—And so in like manner that Nitrogen never *exists* but as
Dilation + Contraction—i.e. that it a modification of that of
which Hydrogen *at present* is the only known representative—that
others will be discovered, is probable—and that others have been
discovered, or rather have presented themselves, but have been
confounded with Hydrogen or supposed to be *chemical* compounds
(just as Chlorine was) is not improbable—.

I have therefore here, as every where, not 4 primary *powers*, as
the Natur-philosophen, but a Triad with a Prothesis. My tetra-

†one vol. of Hyd. = 1, and half *that* vol. of oxygen = 7.5—

grammation is not ⟨⊕⟩ but thus ⟨⊙⟩ where the Circle represents the Prothesis, or Princi a(• •)c pium simpliciter essendi
—·A = Dilation and ·C = contraction are the only opposites,
while ·B = Astringency, Cohesion, is ~~an~~ equi-distant from both—

In short, all depends on the proper application of + and − . In $f72$
my present view, which is not however in *this* point (viz. the denial
of a primary potence to Volatility, as a co-equal and opposite of ~~the~~
Fixity) essential to my system, I ~~regard~~ name Volatility Incoher-
ency or Incohesion and regard it as O (= materia, principium
essendi passivum) − B (= Astringency, Cohesion). Thus O +
A − B. could appear only as a Power or Quality, Heat for instance. O + B − A as Cold.—But O + A + B, would produce
the Dilate, Hydrogen, and O + A − B ⨯ (i.e. + the Counter
agent) C would be volatility—/*Consequence*: that Air supposes an
Ether in which it exists.—But I feel at every step, how much all
this requires reconsideration—. The Test will be whether I can $f71^v$
clearly explain Nitrogen ⟨*Gas*⟩ and Oxygen ⟨*Gas*⟩ in this view.

4551 27.88   The gathering together of the Land and for- $f76$
mation of the Sea close the actuation which was necessary to all
alike, as the condition of that self-actuity which henceforward consists in the degrees of conversion & opening out toward the Love
in the Distinction, the recipiency of the Distinction in the Love,
~~by~~ on which depends the capability of ascent, as the Balloon must
be filled with air in order to *keep* in the common air (in organized
Body = *flat* bladders), and with a warmer and more dilative air
(universality) in order to *rise* in the common air. The process of
vegetation ~~in~~ of masses, yet not the loss in and on masses—
~~Unity with Multeity Indistinction implies~~
Indistinction with Unity cannot be actuated but that at the same $f75^v$
time there is actuated Multeity with Distinction—these acts *form*,
give both existence and locality to, the first Water, the second
Earth.—i.e. Metal. Analogies of Water & Metal, relatively first
to Figure, and secondly to Light, Rejection of Light by Metal,
imperfect Passage to Light in Water; but neither take it up into
itself, as its centre—This first effected in Vegetation/the first Trial,
or *Tentation* of the Apostacy/
Mem. the predominance of Light over Heat, which latter did

not then exist but in nascence, because Gravitation was not yet perfected, marks the date of vegetable creation—yea, even now.— Already one cause of the Intervening of the 4th day.—

f75   In the separation of "the Dry Land from the Waters" we would not even be suspected of favoring the absurdities of the Precipitation-Scheme, a scheme the most extravagant in its assumptions yet the most barren in its consequences of all the many phantoms, with which the whole continuity both of Nature and Thought is crumbled down in modern Analysis—Neither Earth nor Water are *Data* with us, but like all Product of a living Powers mutually call ~~forth~~ each forth, and never can exist in a shew of separation but by the intervention of the series, in which they have modified each other—

(N.B. Essential difference between E = Metal becoming the Bearer-Supporter of Light as in W—i.e. of + Light as Oxygen or of − Light as Hydrogen (observe that I use + and minus in

f74^v   the opposite application to Schelling & Steffens, − with me always meaning the *Base*, or *Ible*—Thus + Light = the Comburent or Combustive, − Light = the Combustible) and E × W taking up the Light into itself as its Center and Punctum saliens/Hence tho' I regard the kernel of the Earth as Metallic, and Metallity as the unchangeable Supporter of the Directions, O and H.—I do not affirm it to be *Metal*—On the contrary I with Steffens regard all the metals in the Mountains as reductions, and likely a priori to be more common as the actions organic of the Masses are more complex.—Schubert's objection from the paucity of metals in the oldest Granite is at once answered by the fact, that the organic action of Granite is the simplest, & thence least favorable to Reduction.—

f46^v   4552 27.37   Bell's Weekly Messenger, June 14, 1819 Monday's Edition—
p. 1901, col. first, last §.

SUICIDE. "A student of Vienna, (✻but) a native of Prussia, lately blew out his brains in a tavern at Leopoldstadt." He and an auf ewig dein went to Vienna, and both Friends fell desperately in love with the same young Lady—challenged each other—but neither could bring himself to level a pistol at the head of the other.

Not Love alone but eternal Friendship too had its inviolable rights, its claims, that must be heard.—They threw down the Pis- _f47_ tols, rushed into each other's arms, kissed and wept, wept and kissed. "It was therefore agreed to decide the affair by a Party (*a game?*) at Piquet, in an undertaking (*agreement?*) that the party who lost (*the Loser?*) should blow out his own Brains. The Game was accordingly played: and the Loser, a youth of 19, instantly payed the forfeit by shooting himself thro' the Head."—N.b. The words between " and " are those of *the Newspaper*—those with ( ) mine.—I wish, that this were as common in England/viz. let our youths keep the skulls on instead of blowing the Brains out—

✻"but" added by the Transcriber. S.T.C.

4553 27.38
1 Abdominal = Attraction. appropriative potenziate[d] into ap- _f47ᵛ_ propriation selective—⟨ponderific. potenziated into⟩ organific.
2 Pectoral = Oscillation, projective, modificatory, circulative— calorific pot. into vitific
3 Cerebral = Convergence divergent, radiative, ~~focusal~~—lucific poten: into sensific.
1. Ponderific, chrystallific(2, organific(3.
Rectilineal potenziating per nisum ascensivum into the Curve / = cylindrical, rhomboidal / Linea recta a directione eluctans.
2. Calorific, caloric(2, zöic(3.
Curve potenziating into the transcendent, or finitely infinite— Cone, Hyperbolon
3. Lucific, lucid(2, sensific(3.
Transcendent, formæ in τὸ super formam adluctantes/Oval, fo- _f48_ cal, vertical, potenziated co-adunation of the Straight and the Curve, of the projectile, and recurrent—radius and arc—. Subject of the Objective, Object of the Subjective.

4554 27.39   Still the Multeity actualized must eâ ipsâ actu- _f48ᵛ_ alitate, which in this case is that of the *Word's* influence in the Multeity, become active, and a power—And if the Influence of the Spirit in the Indistinction appear as cohesion, and that ⟨too⟩ be ~~astringency~~ a power—from attraction appropriative, then the for- mer must be not mere Volatility but Repulsion/& I am wrong.—

f49   4555 27.40   Glossary of Characters, employed by me in my
Dialogues de finibus et methodo Philosophiæ.—

/ Carbon = Attraction. − Magnetism. North ideally. N by N.E.
really. Fixity.

/ C = chem. carbon.

∴. Nitrogen = Repulsion, as the *power* of separative ✳ Projection. + Magn.

South ideally. South by SW really. Volatility. n∴. = chem. n
gas.

.... Oxygen. Contraction. − Elect. East. Particularization. N.b.
        ⠂⠂⠂ when disting. from chlor. or Iodine.

∽ Hydrogen. Dilation. + Elect. West. Universalization. ♄
        chem. hydr. gas.

⊙ Centrality.   Involution of each in each, or 4 = 1, and then
N.B. As Quality,   1 + 4 = 5. Pan, the 5ᵗʰ Numen, and 3ʳᵈ
ad intra.   Deity, the offspring of the two Deities / and
                         ∴. with their numina .... and ∽.

f49ᵛ ⊕ Gravitation. | + ⊙ = the Centripetal
N.B. As *Property*, | − ⊙ = the Centrifugal
or Power ad extra.
⊘ Weight. Specific Gravity.
□ Ether. Actualized Space.
> Light
≡ Caloric
∪ Sulphur   ∪ ate ∪ ite.
∩ Phosphorus   ∩ ate = phosphate. ∩ ite.
[...] Chlorine   .⚥. ⠂⠂⠂ or .ϫ.

f48ᵛ ✳ when coerced and restrained from actual separation and projection by the preventive Predominance of Appropriative Attraction
in the form of Cohesion. Thus Cohesion supposes ∴. under the
predominance of /, and / again *resisted* by ∴., as the conquered
Steed presses forward against the Curb which holds him in—and
in this way Attraction & Repulsion become *powers* as well as Contraction and Dilation; but the former Powers *of*, the latter powers
acting *on*.

Glossary of characters, employed by me in m[?] /49

Dialogues de finibus et methodo Philosophiæ.

1 Carbon = Attraction. — Magnetism. North ideally.
N by N.E. really. Fixity. /z = chem. carbn/

∴ Nitrogen = Repulsion, as the power of separative
×. Projection. + Magn. South ideally. South
by S W really. Volatility. ♄ n̄ ᵌ = chem. nitgn.

.... Oxygen. Contraction. — Elect. East. Parti-
- cularization. N.b. ⊥. when disting. from
chlor. or Iodine.

~ Hydrogen. Dilation. + Elect. West. Univers-
- alization. ♄ chem. hydr. gas.

⊙ Centrality. Involution of each in each, or
N.B. As Quality, 4 = 1, and then 1 + 4 = 5. Pan
ad intra. the 5ᵗʰ Numen, and 3ʳᵈ Deity,
the offspring of the two Deities
1 and ∴ with their numina .... and
‿

⊕ Gravitation. + ⊙ = the Centripetal
N.B. As Property, or Power — ⊙ = the Centrifugal
ad extra.

⟁. Weight. Specific Gravity.

□ . Ether. Actualized Space.

⟩ Light

≡ Caloric

∪ Sulphur ∪ate ∪ite.

⌢ Phosphorus ⌢ate = phosphate. ⌢ite.

⊛ . Chlorine ⊛ .... chl. or ⋅×⋅ᴰ....

⌐⫶⌐ Iodine *f50*

Alkalies   Triangles with the Apex upward, and the initial†
~~inclosed~~ ⟁ following

Earths   Triangles with the Apex downward, &c

Metals   Circles, with the Initials following—

> N.B. Seldom used, the name (or the Initial where it is the
> only Metal beginning with that letter) being as brief or
> briefer.

Metal, metallëity. ○. Metals collectively or indefinitely

    ○ ○, or ~~ou~~ ○s

▽, △ and ○s = the Earths, Alkalies, and Metals.

╼⊢ Oxyds ∨ Chlorides ⌐...⌐ ⫶∨Iodides ⌐...⌐ ⫶∨ ⫶∨ or ⟩ ∨.   *f50ᵛ*

⌐...⌐ Acids ⌐...⌐ ◇. Chloric Acids χ◇. Iodic Acids ⬦ or ⟩ ◇

∿ Water. ∵∵ Fire. ˙⫶˙ Air.

M (from Μορφη) ~~Fund~~irmamental, − μ = Fluid, αμορφον

λ Logos. πν. Spirit. X̷. Matter. ζ life. Σ Body. σζ organization.

    σζ ∼ Vegetation. σζ .... Animality, animalization. 3 =
counteracting.

    Ɛ = auxiliar to.

III. 3 Mechanism. 8 Chemical Compound or Product. ⚌8
Neutralization, Balance, ⊢8 Predominance. ⊖8 ⌐...⌐ Thus
Water is ⊻8. Coal ⊖8 —. The latter always supposing a third   *f51*
something, or common Base, of the two opposite numina—, independent of the *primary* co-existence of the four in each, under
the predominance of the one placed first, or rather singly. Thus /
is / ˙∵. .... ∼ under the predominance of /—& so with the
rest.—

    Observe. .... used simply means the Power generally, and
includes Chlorine, and Iodine, as well as Oxygen: ⟨and so ∨ means
Oxyds generally, without special reference to Oxygen.⟩ But Oxygen as a *Stuff* or Element of the Laboratory is signified by ˙⫶˙.

P.S. For marks of Relation see the Insides of the Covers of this
Pocket Book.— These 22 + 12 = 34 Characters will suffice for
all my purposes—For I do not call the ⫶∨ ⫶∨ and ⫶∨ and χ◇, χ◇ and
i◇ for Oxyds from Oxygen, Chlorides and Iodides, & for the   *f51ᵛ*

~~† I.e. in MSS. In Printing I would have the Initial inclosed as in~~   *f50*
~~Nicholson's Ch. Dict.~~

Acids in like manner, separate Marks. These are easily recollected.
A very little practice either in reading or writing them will make
them as familiar as 1, 2, 3, 4, 5 &c.—To add more would be
burthening and perplexing the memory, and wasting the readers'
time ~~by~~ in references to the Glossary, in order to save an infinitesimal of Ink, Paper, and digital motion.—

4556 27.41   The difference between Attract. + Repul. and
Contraction + Dilation is—that the former are acts of the
προπλασμα that results from the first descent of the πν.—The Chaos
= Indistinction + Multeity becomes an Etwas, Ether/. These acts
f52   *constitute* Cohesion, and then re-appear as polar powers of Cohe-
sion/in ludicrous language, are reborn as their own Grand Sons.—
We must therefor distinguish the primary and constituent Att. +
Rep. from the secondary and proceeding, the acts from the powers.—

Prothesis

  1. Thesis   1. Antithesis
          1. Synthesis = Cohesion (nascent) as *Continuity*.
          1 Synthesis = Continuity
  2 Thesis   2 Antithesis
          2 Synthesis./~~Conditions of amassment~~. ⟨cohesion⟩

and these ~~are~~ belong to the *Eve* of Creation
~~But~~ Contr. and Dil. are Generations of the first *Morning*—off-
springs of a distinct Act, that of the Logos—an Act *on* that Etwas,
which the πνευμα had prepared—

f52ᵛ 4557 27.42   The less the ⋰. is modified by ...., and the

⋰/ by ⌣, the more distant must they be from each other, so that
/ to ⋰. shall be as the Earth to the Air, for .... counteracting
⋰. tends to *assimilate* it *to* (not *identify* it *with*) /. This dispa-
rateness without opposition, αλλο μεν, ου δε τ' εναντιον γενος, of
*Con*traction and *At*traction, is the subtlest Idea of the whole Anastasis, or rather the most slippery and difficult of *detention*.

4558 27.43 It is very striking, that as ☉ is 4 = 1, the Pan *f52ᵛ*
begotten by the ‾1̅ ‾+̅ ‾1̅ × 1 + 1. or 2 Divi with the two numina)
and consequently ☉ is a 5ᵗʰ, generated by the co-involution of the
4—so in the Mosaic Scheme the Birth of ⊕ and with that of central *f53*
> is on the 5ᵗʰ day—and as the first separates the Light from the
Darkness, & so gives birth to the former, so the 5 *unites* them
distinctively, and gives birth to the latter in the form of Gravitation—and the second great Birth-day to the former—even as we
celebrate the Birth-day with especial Splendor, when the Heir
passes out of his Minority and becoming *of age* enters on his
⟨proper⟩ realm and dominion.—And even as the Ves⟨pertine⟩ Act
preparatory to the Birth of Light was the *Spirit* of Life, so here
the *incorporation* of Life (in the vegetable creation) to the glorious
Birth-day and Enthronization of Light. And again as the *Spirit* of
Life was but preparatory, so here it is Life general preparatory to *f53ᵛ*
Lives individualy, or *living* Life.—There all was enlivened, but
no each alive ⟨and all is formless⟩—next *each* is alive, but no *one*
lives, and the *forms* are diffused, the *distinctions* outward—last,
each *lives*, the essential forms become *central*, the distinctions *inward*—and the outward still simplifying is the reflex, not of the
Life, but of the distinctions of the Life. (*Qʸ Comets : Veget. : :
Planets : Animal?* If so, whether it furnishes a presumption in
favor of the Parabola versus the Ellipse?)
—A mistake in the *Day!* 4ᵗʰ instead of 5ᵗʰ—Still the main points
remain—& I have but to take the *Eve* of Creation = 1./But in
my last conversation, for *all* (now Fluid, now Firmamental) I
ought at least to have added all *successively*—which almost subverts
the all not before used—and opens out a wholly different & vast *f54*
field of causation.—Item/I have not sufficiently adverted to the
atmosphere—. In short, I must commence next time with the *Powers*, as evolved out of the *matter* of *Light*—and ~~to~~ inquire concerning *Cohesion* whether I have not antedated it as firmamental cohesion—giving too much to the *N. & S.*

4559 27.44 The generation of water and fluids most near *f54ᵛ*
pure water a feature of *nervous* action—Qʸ Is it an act of life anterior to or at least at the minimum of *organic* function/Life in its

simplest state and nearest to the life of the Elements/are hydrogen-
ation of azote (I mean, not a superinduction of $\sim$ on $\cdots$. but a

f55   transmutation of $\cdots$. into $\underline{\text{H}}$) similar to the formation of Rain
in the atmosphere, in cases where nothing but a theory would make
us suppose the presence of aqueous vapor in quant. suff.—

N.b. I do not suppose ~~that~~ such an absurdity as that the *Power*
$\cdots$. should be ˌcome the *Power* $\sim$, but Hydrogen is not the
Power $\sim$, but $\cdots$ under the predominance of $\sim$.—
                    /

4560 27.45   Phosphuret of Mercury, = formed by heating
Phosphorus $\cap$ with an $\vee$ of M., gives a sectile Solid of bluish-

f55ᵛ   black color.—osmium = insolub. in $\Diamond$s, ready Sol. in $\triangle$, ease
with which it is oxydized, its great volatility, peculiar smell, and
purple color (purple blue) produced in its solution by tincture of
galls.

4561 27.46   I had taken a right tho' not a precisely accurate
view of Breadth, as the mid product of the figureless and lineal,
~~or~~ which is the essential of figure—and so of the fluid and firmamental.—Illustration in Mercury as compared with $\sim$, and in the
sulphuret and bisulphuret of Mercury. You can give no breadth to
Mercury but by the containing Vessel—still splits and splits into
globules—. For the $\sim$ is globulous by negation of the power
of Length, and finely poised but easily disturbed balance of the 4
powers, superficially. Centrality[1]. Mercury = Centrality[3] or potenziated from $\odot$ into $\oslash$.—W. continuous—M. Attract. with Rep.
curbed in.—Hence allied with Dilation it soon *volatilizes*.

f56   Granite. Quarz, pure Silica—proper Firmamental (= M.) ×
freedom by the Figureless (− ~~mμ~~, or $\alpha\mu o\rho\phi o\nu$) chrystallization.—
Mica, lamellar breadth. Feldspar, Density as the tertium aliquid
of Linear and Globular—under the power of $\oslash$ and commencing
$\oplus$. Potenziated $\odot$

A most important point, I mean the essential character of $\Diamond$s
generally, as differenced from $\vee$s, I have yet to discover. I have
not even examined whether the class itself is philosophically justi-
fiable—i.e. whether the properties common to all the substances
classed as Acids are essential or merely belong to them as included

in a genus generalius.—Especially whether Acids in the fluid form
are not different from the gaseous and so far diverse from the **M**
$\Diamond$ as that the latter are but $\forall$ or bi-oxides?—   *f56ᵛ*

4562 27.47   I was perfectly right in considering the genesis
of the Solar System as the 5ᵗʰ day—tho' mistaken in supposing that
Moses had so *named* it—and this pleases me, for it is a proof, as
far as it goes, of the independence of my System on any preconceptions of mine derived from Moses—. From *legislative* motives
Moses had made the first Evening & Morning commence with
the Logos.—This according to his own account is the second *distinct* operation—and instead of the day of rest, I consider *the rest*,
i.e. present organismus cosmicus to be the continuance of the 7ᵗʰ
Day—We are now in the 7ᵗʰ day, but count it as the first, to mark
the *new creation*—Mem. the ~~present~~ B.C. *World* the spiritual chaos,
the Aft. Chr. World as the second, nominal first day??—Nay!—
Christ has still sent his *Spirit*—the Spirit of Comfort & Prophecy—the Preparative for his Coming in his own celestial name.—
     But tho' right in the main, yet the mistake of dividing the **M**   *f57*
+ (− μ) from the genesis of the Expansion □, $\cdot\cancel{}$. &c (v. 6.
7. 8.) has led me out of my way and into a jungle./

4563 27.48   Malleable as differenced from ductile is an ill-
chosen smithie sort of a word. Surely, expansible, or dilative are
better.—

4564 27.49   Gold in a state of high ductility per- or rather
sur-meated by an electrical discharge gives a purple powder—is
this rightly called an oxide? The answer must depend on the result
of my investigation into the nature of $\Diamond$ s.—It seems clearly to be /
counteracted by ...., simply—but this must be determined by
the comparative weight.—To remember to ask Mʳ Hatchett,
whether the purple powder so produced is more heavy than the
same in its metallic state, or less heavy than the Muriate of Gold—   *f57ᵛ*
i.e. if the quantity electrically procurable allow it to be weighed—.
Item whether there be any absurdity in suspecting, that the modern
Chemists have sometimes confounded in their speculation, the
Power or ideal Agent, with the particular Stuff in which it pre-

dominates—? that there may be hereafter discovered some *Stuff*, having a similar relation to Hydrogen that Iodine has to Oxygen?— nay, that there may even now be among the different supposed compounds of Hydrogen + x y z some analogon to Chlorine, as the ci devant oxymuriatic Acid? Lastly, whether the Nitrogen may not be an hydrate of the ideal Azote, as the *Suppositum* philoso- phium vel scientificum of nitrogen, tho' requiring the vis vitæ cosmicæ to decompose ~~or~~ ⟨it?⟩—and most *audaciously*, whether such decompositions (cosmozöic) may not in *phænomenology* be equiva-

f58 lent to transmutation—so that the ∵. shall appear in its effects, as ⟨subsumed into⟩ potenziating the Oxygen, and facilitating the dispersive needle points of aqueous vapor with their minute elec- trical atmospheres?—It is at least a beautiful conception/in the me- tastasis of the Terraqueous into the Atmospheric there must be a given Point, common to it with the anametastasis of the Atmos- phere to the Terraqueous—.so that a high cloud would differ from the Atmosphere by substitution of ∴ as the puncta centralia for ∵. curbed in by ...., with ⌣ for the inter et circum jacencies.—But the action of .... on ∵. is among the most difficult if not *the* most difficult of the whole *Method*. Probably, the contractive energy reveals itself in the ponderability of Air—.

f58ᵛ —P.S. There would be great convenience in appropriating the words, Diamond, Nitrogen, Oxygen, and Hydrogen to the ele- mentary Stoffs, and then designating the *elements* or supposita scientifica by Carbon, Azote, Zöote or Zote, and Röote (from ρεω, fluo.) or Fixity, Volatility, Contraction and Dilation—or P~~oten~~sote = Azote, Antipot~~ens~~ = Carbon; Eurrhöe = Hydrogen, and Antirrhöe = Oxygen—or Pezon = Carb., and Peteinon, or Po- tēnon, = Azote.

4565 27.50   Mem.—the *Fluorine*, or Phthore,—the hydro- fluorine—. *Why* classed with Oxygen, Chlorine, Iodine, rather than with Hydrogen/Methinks, ⌣ West by South, would make analogous to Chlorine as probably E by S.—Thus it would be ⌣

f59 in alliance with ∵. and hostility to ╱—.and hence its character- istic attack on Silica.—P.S. I am convinced that Quarz or still better *Chrystal* simply is preferable to Diamond & still more so to Carbon as the name of ╱.—The *hardness* of the Diamond makes it

plainly N.E. of Quarz—so that Silica being NE by N. or the
nearest to the Carbon scientificum, the Diamond would be N.E.
and Charcoal perhaps NE by E. and Fixed Air E. by N.

Rock Chrystal 6 sided Prisms, ended by 6 sided pyramids. Alumina as Corundum, in six sided Prisms—sp. gr. 4.—The sp. gr.
of Rock *Chrystal*, 2, 6—of Alumina not chrystallized 2.—its intense tenacity of water—thus 2 = water + water.—The different
colors of corundum, blue sapphire, red ruby, yellow Topaz—gems
found principally in *alluvial* deposits—.

Wavellite or Hydrargillite = alumina + water, found in small
radiated nodules on clay slate/(very striking)—The clay slate +
alumina perfects the dense breadth into centrality-nodules and then
the Line is born anew.

The gelatinous solutions formed by acids on Silica (ex. gr. 50,   *f59ᵛ*
24) + Alumina 29,30 + Lime, 9,46 + water 10,00.—Again
what are Acids—rather what is an Acid?

The existence of *potassa* and *soda* in some minerals otherwise
similarly composed—as Apophyllite and Chabasite.—Connected
with the beautiful circumstances of Carbonate of Lime in shells ⚹
Phosphate of Lime in human Bones.—

Silica = Silicium 50 + Oxygen 50—or 15 + 15 = 30. A
confirmation of the *alliance* of *Con* with *At*-traction.

Of the complex composition of many minerals that occur only
in small quantities—as the Greenland Sodalite or Natrolite. ~~Alum~~
Silica 38,42/Alum. 27,48/Soda, 23,50/Lime, 2,70. Muriatic
acid, 3,00. Oxide of Iron 1,00. Volatile matter 2,10.—Pity that
its ordinary matrix is not mentioned.

45 per cent of Silica and 33 of Alumina with 18 of Potassa *and*
Soda = Elaolite or Fatstone—with ditto of Lime = Scapolite—
while Lime 12,7 with Soda, 10,7 *and* Potassa 8,5, and ⁷/₁₀ of
Oxides of Iron & Manganese, with 7,4 water and loss, make the   *f60*
Jade or axe stone—hard & tough.

Lepidolite, massive and lamellar Silica 54,5 + Alumina 38,25.
Potassa 4. Ox. of I. + Man. ⁷⁵/₁₀₀—purplish: white the nearly
white, *fibrous* and semi-transparent Tremolite Sil. 62, Lime 14,
Magnesia 13, Ox. of Iron 6—While Asbestos, soft, *fibrous*, flexible, Silica 60, Magnesia 30, Lime 6, Alumina 4.

Suppose the Bases divided into two classes, N. and S. (each

subdivided into 2, N.E. N.W. S.E. S.W.—) to examine whether any generic character can be discovered by Induction, distinguishing from the noble Metals.

f60ᵛ   Query. Whether in some of the rarer Oxides as Glucine, Ittria, Zirconia, Thorina, it may not be supposed that the Base itself may be modified by its combinations—so that the slight difference in the properties of the Earths may be owing to the different proportions of Oxygen and the complicated attractions of the matrix at the moment of formation of the particular Earth, affecting perhaps the inward texture of the Whole? The exceedingly small quantities & rare occurrence of these Earths plead strongly for such a supposition. As far as we dare use the word "accident" as applied to Nature, they seem to be accidental results of complicated Action/ —the nascence or dying away of the Energies—or feeble re-awaking of the Antagonism in the minima, or small remainder not

f61   interpenetrated, and thus acting for themselves. How striking this in the ores of Platinum—Gold, Iron, Lead (as representative of the upswallowed Links of Silver and Quicksilver, Rhodium, Osmium, Titanium, Palladium).

4566 27.51
Vegetables
Brand, p. 345.—"tho' the disappearance of the enormous quantities of carbonic acid gas continually pouring into our atmosphere can, I think, scarcely be referred to the purifying action of Vegetables alone."

If measured by pints & quarts, certainly not—not by *contribution* of the *Plants*—but tho' not this, nor yet in a higher sense of the words, than the Author had in mind, by the action of vegetables alone—yet by *vegetable* action and its analogy in the minerals & waters on the surface of the Earth the restoration may be as readily effected in the living atmosphere as in a living Man.—

f61ᵛ   Remember the singular statement in Gilbert's Annals from the younger Saussure (which Gay de Lussac doubts only because it seemed so surprizing to him, without detecting the least inconsistent or suspicious circumstance in the Experiments in the report: or the deductions—) of the great variation in quantity of the Carbonic Acid of the atmosphere in Winter and Summer—

"The cause of the motion has never been satisfactorily accounted for: tho' perhaps principally referable to the contraction & expansion produced by changes of temperature." Brand, 345.

Will these changes with the consequent cont. and exp. account for the qualities acquired by the Sap, diff. in each diff. veg.? If not, if Life must be taken into the Company of causative agents, why not ascribe the particular motion with the particular mode and degree of Ex. and Con. to Life & the specific Life of each Sort of Plants?—But Zoophobia and Misothelēsia are the epidemic *distemper*, the Influenza, of our Naturalists of the Anglo-Gallican or School regnant.— *f62*

Again, p. 346. § 705. "It is thus (i.e. *from the soil*) that the alkaline, earthy and saline Ingredients of Plants are furnished"—Query? whether the *same* in sort and in quantity, particle for particle? or only as excitements of reproduction, as a quart of water poured down a dry pump will sometimes bring it into play again, gallon after gallon? *N.b. illustration by simile, not instance or analogy.* If an Equisetum could be raised ⟨*from seed*⟩ in flannel moistened by distilled water—or Grass or a Rattan in a pot of Soil carefully desilicated—. Why should particular plants take up Sulphur, others Nitrogen, others Sulphate of Lime (as clover)—⌈. . .⌉ many but not all marine plants common Salt—the barley nitrate of soda, the Sap of the Sun flower nitrate of Potassa, Oat seeds phosphate of Lime, the Grasses & Canes Silica—while *all* *f62ᵛ* have Carbon, Hydrogen and Oxygen, ~~in~~ live in them and reproduce, at least re-exhibit them, if it were not that *their* formative functions have an analogy with the vires formatrices of Nature, in the primary production of these *Stoffs?*—

(It would be especially desirable and expedient for Viridis and Carbojuge to devote a whole day to a careful Reading of all the dictations hitherto—marking the differences and oscitations.)

4567 27.52   Ox ⸫ as 48,31 with /c 45,39, ♄ 5,90 and an 0,40 of n⸫. does *not* work as an *Acid*. The ? is, whether it be not chemical pedantry to consider the Starch even as an Oxide?—I propose it as a hint to myself, whether Oxide should *f63* not be confined to a plain *superinduction*, not amounting to an

Acid—and another term found, when it is a component of the *Base-composite?*

100 parts of Starch sugar (made by boiling starch with very dilute Sulphuric Acid) /c 37,29 ..ˣ.. 55,87 ⌐ʰ 6,84. n'··. 0,00.—No part of the acid decomposed (= Saussure), the contact of the air unnecessary, no gas evolved—and the Starch Sugar : the Starch : : 10 : 9.—*Solidification of Water inferred.* If Saussure's analysis be accurate, a great deal more and more important may be suggested—the increase of the ..ˣ.. by 7½ & a trifle more, of the ⌐ʰ by 1 − ⁶⁄₉₀; the decrease of /c by 8¹⁄₁₀, not to mention the disappearance of n'··.—and thus when the sulphuric acid has been *taken up by chalk*, and must therefore have acted as *a power*, not as a *thing*—altogether most confirmative of my system. For

f63ᵛ here seems a transmutation of Carbon into ..ˣ.. , by − El. the primary ⌐ʰ ation adding itself to the ⌐ʰ, making 5,90 be 6,84.— Neither can I agree with Brand & Gay Lussac that the small portion of n'··. is accidental & "no essential component."—

4568 27.53   Gluten, Vegetable Albumen, in Wheat—that affords ammonia in destructive distillation—contained likewise in the sap of the House leek, Cabbage and most of the Cruciform plants.—*Animality in vegetation.*

4569 27.54   Tanning ⚹ Rusting a good illustration of N ⚹ E, Att. ⚹ Cont.—

4570 27.55   N.b. The *blue* compound (characteristic of Starch) produce by *Iodine* on Starch—a peep into the nature of Iodine as − Light + Shade. or Darkness
                                                              ——————
                                                               Light.

f64 Extractive matter. Ulmin. Polychroite (suffrote) Hematin. *Bitter Principle.* THE YELLOW BITTER PRINCIPLE. PICROTOXIN. *Nicotin.* Asparagin. *Fungin.* Inulin. Ematin. Woody Fibre. Cork. *Cotton.*—.p. 368. Particular notice the action of *Nitrous Acid*, and the *Volatility* of Nicotin in Alcohol.—Then, the insolubility of Fungin in water & alcohol. = *metallic, electro-conductive, principle of Fungi?* Ditto, *Cotton*, as combining with several metallic Oxides. Qʸ termed Gossipium as being the Dress in which women go about Gossiping??

The use of *Alumina* as base mordant to the *colouring matters*.

Alcoholic solution of Soap a test for the fitness of water for washing. If it becomes very turbid, it is unfit.—Opium = Morphia $\triangle$ + $\lozenge$ called *meconic*. Q: the *peculia* of the latter? A $\sigma\zeta\smile$ $\lozenge$: $\sigma\zeta$.... $\lozenge$: : $\sigma\zeta\smile$ Albumen (= Gluten) : $\sigma\zeta\cdots$. Albumen? By exciting resistance or facilitating, to the narcoma?   *f64ᵛ*

The great importance of .... to / and the effective alliance of the former to $\odot$ and $\oslash$ is exemplified in Naphtha as 87.21 /c + 12.79 $\underline{h}$ = 100.—Lighter much than water, highly inflammable, *volatile*. The $\smile$ here allies with $\cdots$. in the $\angle$, and tends to *unbit* the $\cdots$., or relax the curb rein, ~~on~~ ⟨by⟩ which it had been *held in* by this astringent Dynast /.

In Maltha it becomes heavier than water—inspissated—by ..ˣ..? Q: Whether − > without x or i ever acts as ....?   *f65*

Pit coal = 1. Brown Coal. 2. Black Coal. 3. Glance Coal. Coke from black Coal *sonorous*.

Solubility diminished by $\lozenge$ s.—

"By distilling oxalate of Lime Dr Thomson resolved the Oxalic Acid into 1. Water. 2. Carbonic Acid. 3. Carbonic Oxide. 4. Carburetted Hydrogen. 5. Charcoal — And by a very elaborate analysis (of *these gases?*) he determined the composition of the acid as follows.—Oxygen 64; Carbon 32. Hydrogen 4."—Q: How could the water be formed? Ans.—The Q: was *silly of me*—had only so minute a portion of the Acid been applied, as supposed in the 100, it could not—but suppose ~~21~~ x y portions, and the Ox. to draw [. . . . .] the Hyd. from in each portion till it = ~~87~~ 15 when then combining ~~with 13~~ 65 Ox. ~~out of the 64, would~~ might form Water, and ~~51 remain for the Carb. $\lozenge$ and $\curlyvee$.~~

4571 27.56   Gluten both in wheat and the juice of the Grape/$\sigma\zeta$ $\smile$ + $\sigma\zeta$ .... /Σ + $\pi\nu$., but Σ itself Υ + $\pi\nu$. ⟨The Bread & Wine unite = hyper$\pi\nu$. $\dot{\upsilon}\lambda\eta$.⟩

⟨—The Romanists therefore disturb the *symbol* & pervert its *significance* by pretending to *unite* what ought to be connected indeed, but yet successive.⟩

4572 27.57   Finely bruised Galls, 3 Oz. Green Vitriol (= Sulphate of Iron) Logwood Shavings, and Gum Arabic; each 1 oz. Vinegar, 1 Quart.—If about an ounce of Indian Ink be dissolved   *f65ᵛ* in this quantity, the Ink greatly improved—by keeping a few cloves in the ink bottle prevented from become mouldery, or by adding to the Quart of Ink 6 grains of corrosive sublimate.—Wash faded writing first with vinegar, then with infusion of Galls.—

4573 27.58   To collate all the veget. Acids, as to their different proportions of /c, ..ˣ.. and ᴸ, and the results—thus by increasing the pr. of /c at the expence of the ..ˣ.. , the ᴸ remaining 5.16.—the Benzoic Acid sublimes in *soft feathery* chrystals. But what throws a doubt on the depend. of acidity at all, much more of the properties of particular Acids, in the comparative Quantities of the simple Compon. is that pure alcohol consists of H. C. and O. as $13,70/51,98/34,32/ = 100$. But if we substitute Olefiant Gas, 61,63. Water 38,37. the problem is shifted. Qᵞ
◇ s = *proper* combination of 3 Elements. Alcohol = proper combination of 2—and maximum of *Solution* in a third, itself a Dyad in equilibrium ✳ predominance?—I have before expressed a doubt of Brande's confusion of intimate commixture with positive intussusception—a legitimate consequence, I grant, of the mechanical Daltonian Theory, or the Corpuscular Scheme forced upon Chemical Phænomena—.—But the fact of alcohol & many others of the same kind not only subvert the coarse idolatry of the sic est or sic Deo placitum Atomists but tends to prove that 2 from 1. × into 1 (I purposely put × for +) is as truly a third Unit, as either of the antecedent *Ones*: just as the Son is as truly an Individual as his Father or his Mother. So Water = 1. Olefiant Gas = 1.—and still it remains possible that ◇ s may demand 3 antecedents and Alcohol 2. But how is Saussure's Analysis of Alc. to be reconciled with the other—whence did the one obtain the Oxygen, the other the Chlorine—Olefiant Gas being chloric Ether, or chlorine + carburetted Hydrogen? Could any thing like Alcohol be formed by any more of *blending* Olef. gas with water? Or by combining the supposed Elements of Water *separately?* or successively? or together, but still as H. 87. and Ox. 13?/Yes!—"By abstracting the water wholly from Alc. we obtain Olefiant Gas; if but half, we convert the Alc. into *Ether*." Not (adds Br.) that we ever *do* obtain either perfectly in any of our processes. This, however, sufficiently favors my notion, & gives a *sense* to my queries & suggestions, written before I had come to this passage.

f66

f66ᵛ

f67

The quid pro quo (..ˣ.. for ..ˣ.. in Saussure & its tacit acceptance by Brand is still more prominent on p. 416.—

Pity that the exact quantities of Carbon in the combustion of Oleum Ethereum (= a portion of the result of ether distilled with its bulk of sulphuric acid) should not have been determined—and compared with the total proportion of Carbon in the whole of the Ether and Sulphuric Acid employed, as known by calculation: and the remainder of the Result from the Distillation carefully analysed.—It *might* substantiate a − magn. conversion of ..ˣ.. into /c, correspondent to the before-hinted-electric Conv. of ~~carbon~~ /c into ..ˣ.. — *f67ᵛ*

(n.b. an objection to χ for chl. from its resemblance to x.— better ..ᶜʰ.. or c, suffic. dist. from carbon by the .... subscription/

4574 27.59   Since I have read the latest and best compendia of chemistry with courage enough to cross-examine its details, I see a world of desiderata, and matter for new experiments—proving my assertion, that the more initiative Ideas, the greater the impulse to experiment. Among others, the action of *Water* as *Water* in the processes of composition demands looking into. — And so of muriatic Acid, whose power to act as a unit may have occasioned ⟨some of⟩ the semblances that have indisposed chemists to the reception of Chlorine.—. *f68*

4575 27.60   The precipitation of ⌈. . .⌉ G. S. Pl. Mʸ and Cpʳ from their solutions in a metallic state by the Lampic Acid, the constitution of the acid itself, an acid so powerful, by carbon (5,7) ⌣ (1) water or ⌢⌢ (8,5) one proportional each; and the pure or concentrated lampic acid, obtained on distilling the lampate of Mʸ, in the form of a *very dense* Liquid with an intensely suffocating odor—are fruitful facts.—But I am not *sufficed* by the theory of proportion, as founded on weight *only*—. No! I can think of no substitute—yet in many cases I should dwell on the volume, or comparative space occupied under equal pressure and temperature. For spec. gr. seems ⚹ to energy.—So in water the 15 grains of ⌣ must fully ..ˣ.. /counter-energize 85 of ..ˣ.. /tho' not counterpoise. *f68ᵛ*

4576 27.61   When Acetate of Lead is submitted to dest.
dist., a consid. quant. of a peculiar fluid is obtained, smelling and
burning like Alcohol./

f69   4577 27.62   Albumen, which in actu is fibrine, and the firmamental principle of the animal, as Carbon + $\cdot\overset{x}{\cdot}\cdot$ of the vegetable, is still / in predominance. /c 52,883. $\cdot\overset{x}{\cdot}\cdot$ 23,872. $\underline{\overset{h}{ }}$
7,540 n$\cdot\cdot\cdot$. 15,705. And whatever be the verdict of the Labo-
ratories respecting the difference between Berzelius and Brande
respecting the Coloring matter and crassamentum—the philosopher sees the truth oscillating in an arc that includes both their
accounts. He sees the *nascent* metallization, tho' the chemical ides
and ates he refers to the chem. process. Thus with Br. he deems
it a "proximate principle" of animality, and with Berz. (tho' in a
very different point of view) he refers it to oxide of Iron &c.—
"The coloring matter *incinerated* affords a residue consisting of $\vee$ I
50. Subphosphate of I. 7,5. Phosphate of Lime with magnesia 6.
Lime 20. Carb. acid & loss 16,5.—
        The magnetic action in the albuminous films on boiling milk.
f69ᵛ Bile / in the *liver* from *venous* blood. Ergo, especial product of the
/ $\cdot\cdot\cdot$. or reproductivity + $\odot$. Its intense Bitter $\odot$—rapid putrefaction and heavy nauseous odor in that state $\cdot\cdot\cdot$. + $\odot$. N.B.
The urgent importance of *auseinander*ing the twofold possible relations of each of the 5 elementary Powers to each one of the remaining. Thus $\odot$ by *counteracting* / would ally itself to and virtually strengthen $\cdot\cdot\cdot$., and vice versâ. Which of these it shall be,
antagonist or auxiliary, must depend on the third then co-present.
Item, the expediency of appropriating 4 characters to counteraction
and alliance. Thus 3 = counteraction. $\mathcal{E}$ = alliance, ⟨aided or
aiding⟩

4578 27.63   Qʸ Solution = $\oslash 3$/, where / = appropriative
attraction, $\mathcal{E}$ by the equation of $\smile$ and $\cdots$? The lineal or primal
firmamental act $3 \odot$, while $\smile 3 \oslash$. For $\odot \mathcal{E} \cdots = \oslash$.—
f70 Solution therefore is the intermediate term between III and $\uparrow$:
and this answers all the phænomena.

4579 27.64   Mʳ Brande has more than once expressed a
doubt whether a substance (Thenard's *Picromel* for instance, as

$^{69}/_{100}$✳ of Bile, water $= {}^{900}/_{1000}$ being removed) be a *product*, or
a mere *educt*, ipso processu analytico artefactum. It is matter of
regret, that he had not devoted a chapter to the nature of this
important Distinction, and the rules for its application. The Dy-
namists, much more the Zöodynamists, would regard most of his
own Products, as Educts.

✳The remainder $=$ Soda, hydrochlorate of Soda and Potassia; ∪,
⌒ates of Soda; yellow matter: as 4; 3,5; 0,8; 2; 4; ⌒ate of Lime
& Magnesia, 1.2; and a trace of ∨ Iron.

4580 27.65   Lymph, seemingly a very weak solution of Al-   *f70ᵛ*
bumen, but like all things that have passed the laboratory of σζ,
peculiarized.—Mucus, "a peculiar *albuminous* combination, not
coagulable by the usual means"—i.e. Lymph ⟨as Saliva⟩ inspissated
by xyz.—
      Urine : Water; Carb. Phosp. and Uric ◇s; ⌒·ates of Lime,
Ammonia, Soda and Magnesia; ∪ate of Soda, Common Salt; Albumen; Urea.—The solid πς of Serpents and some Lizards, pure
Uric Acid.—complex as might be anticipated of that which is to
rinse and carry off the scourings of so many Chambers—furnishes
per antithesin a confirmation of the valuable hint $=$ the resolution
aqueous of the *ante-organic* agency of the nerves, in nervous diseases &c from mouth-watering, and tears of grief to Hysteria,
cholera Morbus of India (Dʳ Anderson's account) and Hydroen-
cephalus/Now here e contra in injuries of the spine, diminishing
the action of the nerves that supply the kidneys the Urine is always
turbid, often alcaline, and disposed to form calculi—✶ urina
ebria.—The ζωη προυργανικος must ipsis terminis be a simpler, less   *f71*
modified ζ—of course nearer to the κοσμοζωη—or ♄ ζ. *ογρ̲γανικη*
of the ~~Earth~~ Planet.

      Cuticle $=$ Albumen. Skin, cutis vera, rete mucosum $=$ Gela-
tine. Gelatine $=$ potenziated Albumen? or Alb. $+$ dilute nitric
Acid? ‡—Not precipitated in solution by corrosive sublimate, or
bichloride of Mʸ.

‡ more animalized by ˙··.n, and inspissated by ..ˣ.. ?—*Ta-
nnin*.—Thenard's *Osmazome* (Have I not somewhere a memorandum on this substance as .... $=$ pungent (✶ insipid) $+$ ˙··.
$=$ putro-volatile, with ⌐ʰ as the Base?—

Fat—instance of the dualism in firmamental & fluid, the former by *Stearine*, the latter by Elaine—See Sir E. Home's Paper—. This too an antecedant in the lowest forms of Life (Tad-Poles) and the relapse in the higher—& therefore nearer the κοσμοζωη—(Sea water)

f71ᵛ   Cerebral Substance—Water ⁸⁰⁄₁₀₀. Albumen 7. Fatty Matter (white 4,53, red 0,70 =) 5,23. Osmazome 1,12. Phosphorus 1,50—Acids, salts, and Sulphur (the two first probably *Educts*) 5,15.—How strikingly composed of the σζ nearest to the κοσμοσζ!

Shell and Bone.—Hatchett admirable as every where—certainly superior to Davy.

Shells. 1. porcellaneous. Carbonate of Lime—& very little animal matter; but that (n.b.) gelatine (maxima evoke m.) 2. Mother-of-Pearl. 26 animal matter to 66 carb. of l.; but all Albumen.—

Higher up—Hen's egg shell. *Phosphate* of lime 5,7; animal matter, 4,7. C. of L. 89,6—yet higher Lobster-Claws &c Phosp. of Lime—14. Cartilage 26. C L 60

f99   ⟨*Turn to the last Leaf, onward to the Right.*⟩ ⟨Shells and Bones— *continued from 27 Leaves back.*⟩

Still higher, Zoophytes repeat the process, in 4 classes.—White coral (madrepora virginea) an example of the first—resembles the porcellaneous—the second, madrep. ramea, and m. fascicularis, the mother of pearl shell. The third (red coral, Gorgonea nobilis) to the cartilaginous matter of the second adds *phosphate* of Lime, while the 4ᵗʰ class (Sponges) consist almost entirely of *albuminous* matter.

At the summit, Bone in its dyad of soft and hard combines the animal matter (fat, gelatine, albumen) ~~with~~ in a minute overbalance of σζ.... (51) with Carb. of L. 10. *Phosp.* of Lime, 37,7, and Phosp. of Magnesia 1,3.—A beautiful Harmony—and all ascending.—Scarcely less pleasing is the nascent disanimation or ζ in its mid transit to − ζ in the *Enamel* of Teeth ⌒ ate of L. 78. /ate of L. 6. Gelatine 16. — or in the true order, 16; 78; 6. and here too the − ζ evokes the gelat.

f99ᵛ   The Carbon (as the σπασμα, Spannung of − ζ) evoking (or losing itself in) the albumen, the albumen rises into Gelatine—and the S. pole or ⌒ assumes the dynasty over the − ζ or Lime.

4581 27.67   Resurrection = Parturition Divæ Mortis!—   *f99^v*
Mem. A strange but striking instance of the facility in the person-
ifying of General Terms produced by the habits of *Idols* under the
ancient polytheism is St Chrysostom's gloss on the text "having
loosed the pangs of Death."—He at once make a Diva Mors, that
suffered the pangs of a Woman in labor till she had been *delivered*
of Christ.

4582 28.1   W. P. Esq.   *f2*
                     Broxbourne
                   Waltham Cross

4583 28.2   ▽ Silica ▽ alumina ▽ Lime ▽ Magn   *f1^v*
S. appropriates ☉, or takes it up into itself. L. (primitive) is taken
down into ☉.
⚸ chemically combined with = ×
   Al. balances ☉. Magn. ~~is~~ counteracte~~ds~~ ~~by~~ ☉.
   ÷ means a division which is yet not an absolute chasm. It ~~plows~~
dips underground and then filtrates for ascension, and reappears as
a spring in a diverse *Kind.*

4584 28.3   16 July 1819. Highgate   *f2*
   Continued from the red pocket-book marked Χημικο-φιλοσοφικον
on the outside cover.
   That book like most of its Predecessors begins at beginning,
middle, and end—and to prevent the Jumble of Heterogene subjects resulting from this ταραξια κ'αταξια, I have paged the last
† 28 sides ⟨separately,⟩ the side next the Cover being p. 28: and
devote these exclusively to Miscellanea.

† recommencing p. 1 after p. 160   *f1^v*

4585 28.86   *f78*
                     Miscellanea
vel cogitationum vel otiorum vel negotiorum.

f92   4586 28.100   Thor Somerled
                         —— Haroldson

f90ᵛ 4587 28.99   The Oxyglucius, a small red fruit in the Ashan-
tee Country which gives acids (De Marchais adds, Bitters) the
flavor of Sweets, making Limes taste as Honey. *T. Edward Bow-
dich, Esqʳᵉ* strongly confirms my ⟨Hemispheric⟩ scheme of *Tastes*,
in which the Pungent and the smooth (fluent) Insipid (examp.
Gum Arabic) are the proper opposites—Sweet and Sour compounds differenced by the proportions, and declinations, namely
Acid E. toward N. Sweet, W. toward S.—but A. *within* the E.
and Sw. *within* the W. so as to be relatively W. to the extreme E.
(Acid) relatively E. to the extreme West (Sweet)—.

f91   A globe would give the scheme with clearness beyond words—
either by single characters (either marks or Letters) with a glossary, appropriating them to the intended Colors, Sounds, Tastes,
~~and~~ Smells and Touches—or with the whole words, Sharp, Acid,
Scarlet &c. the middle word marking the place of all, when it is
common to all—. The only difficulty would be in the expression
of comparative centrality.

   Dʳ Joseph Reade (of Cork) his Essay in proof that the inverted
Image on the Retina is the mere joining of two Images sent hem-
ispherically from the Cornea, and the true Overt Image by which
the mind perceives and judges is that on the transparent Cornea
(Tilloch's P.M. July 1819)

   N.b. so confusedly worded and the sentences arranged with such
genuine Hibernian perplexity, in addition to the *Pother* of Passion,
Scorn, and Positiveness, that it is difficult to appreciate its claims.

f91ᵛ   Fox, of Falmouth, = the intense chemical action of Tin heated
in contact with Platinum—~~thus~~ Have a new confirmation of the
Genetic Philosophy as ⠂⠂⠒⠂ × ≡s as at once superinduction and
alloy, so ≡T × ≡ Pl as at once alloy and superinduction.—

The French Chronometer!! (Qʸ Z)—Impossible

Allizeau (of Paris) His *Metamorphoses* (14 Franks, or 0″ 11″ 8.—
To procure as a present for James.

At 73.5 of Far. and the Bar. 27-44 Inches Sounds moves 1,227
Eng. Feet in a second.

Sawdust of the *less harder* woods mixed with gunpowder in equal
parts triples the force of gunpowder in blowing of rocks, Capt.
Warnaghen† (of Brazil) Q.ʸ Excess of Dilation beyond Power in
the Gunp. for that purpose? The Dust instanteously charred, and
✳ ⌣?

Thenard's new Liquid = oxygenated Water. Evolution of Light
when dropt on Metal. ◯ 1.453—sinks like a syrup in water; but   *f92*
very soluble. Thickens the saliva. Taste peculiar & emetic-like.

Monge's Pyroligneous Acid—and MacSweeny's boiled Water,
covered with oil, with bright Iron or Ir. Filings in the Water, to
be kept in a dark place—prevent putrif. sine die.

† An apt name for a Rock Blaster.   *f91ᵛ*

4588 28.101   The proper unmodified Dochmius, i.e. anti-   *f92*
spastus hypercatalecticus—

    Bĕnīgn shōotīng Stārs/ĕcstātīcst dĕlīght
or   The Lord thron'd in heav'n, ămīd āngĕl troops
"   Amid troops of angels God thron'd on high.

4589 28.37   Vi divinâ compositum; ⟨idem vero hic⟩ *vidi*   *f46*
vini vi non compos situm.

    I was not trained in academic bowers,
    And to those learned streams I nothing owe
    Which copious from those twin fair founts do flow;
    Mine have been ~~very~~ any thing but studious hours.
    Yet can I fancy, wandering mid thy towers
    Myself a nursling, Granta, of thy lap;
    My brow seems tightening with the Doctor's cap,
    And I walk gowned, feel unusual powers;
    Strange forms of logic clothe my admiring speech,
    Old Ramus' ghost is busy at my brain,
    And my scull teems with notions infinite;
    Be still, ye reeds of Camus, while I teach
    Truths, which transcend the searching schoolmen's vein,
    And half had stagger'd theat stout Stagirite

4590 24.8   2 Sept. 1819. Ramsgate. I *begin* to understand *f6*
the above poem: after an interval from 1805, during which no

year passed in which I did not reperuse, I might say construe, *parse*, and spell it, 12 times at least, such a fascination had it, spite of its obscurity! A good instance, by the bye, of that soul of *universal* ~~meaning~~(significance) in a true poet's compositions in addition to the specific meaning. S.T.C.

P.S. After the 4 first lines the Hand writing is that of my old, dear, and honored Friend, Mr Wade of Bristol.

f35 4591 24.69   The aversion to the doctrine of the theletic Life of Nature is worth investigating. 5 Sep^t/. 1819. Cream, tending to sour, in the Tea—I turn it round in a vortex by a tea-spoon—this *is* an act of Will—and no one starts from it.—But that there is *any continuation* of Will, any series of Wills—that the unseen Producents of the Cream particles &c act likewise by any the remoter analogy to a Will—from this we all recoil.—And why?—Answer. Free Will in an Individual, or rather Will at all in a Finite Existent is so utterly incomprehensible that nothing but the fact itself can prove the fact—as soon therefore as the *self-known*

f35ᵛ *Doing* & *Being* it remits, the proof, the only possible sufficient proof, ceases, the conviction ceases—and we deny it of all but the *first* link, i.e. our *own* act. It is God. But God (as ~~opposed to~~ working *in/not* as working *with*) the Finite, is the same as Mechanic Causation—Thus in Religion must even Irreligion be grounded!!—

I must not forget to add, that there is a mistaken latent in the mind of most men.—They think that nature being thelematöid is the miracle, because they *feel* that their own will—i.e. an *individual* Will in a *finite* Being, a Will tota et omnis et nullo modo *pars* in non toto, is indeed miraculous/But such a Will containing its source in itself is by no maneans attributed to Nature—far less to the parts, particles & partial phænomena—but still the power of producing them is thelematoid, i.e. of the nature of Will, just as much as the muscular movements of the Musician's hand & arm are—& instead of being a miracle, twould be a miracle were it otherwise.

f1 4592 24.3   Lackington's Cat: 1819.
p. 666. N.º 20571—Bruining. Schediàsma de Mesmerismo ante Mesmerum—

4593 29.13

Comparative *f2ᵛ*

1. Accommodations, including the compar. chances of Rooms in the College.

2. Expences necessary, & *style* of respectability.

3. Society.

4. Chances of Exhibitions and the like from the College, or *for* the College.—

5. Value of the Tutors' Lectures. ~~esp~~

7. Influence, if there be any, in the distribution of Honors, Univ. Scholarship, for instance—

8. *Degree* likely to secure a man a fellow-ship,—higher or lower at Sᵗ John's than at Trinity?

9. Comparative Time before a man can hope to be elected?

10. Value of Fellow-ships, Chance of private pupils, family Tutorships, College Livings—Schools &c—

11. Competition among the men—

4594 21½.72   The Devil (saith Luther) now dallieth and *f36* playeth no more with People as heretofore he hath done with and by rumbling spirits and strange knockings and noises: for he well seeth that the condition of the time is far otherwise now than it was twenty years past. Truly he now beginneth at the right end and useth great diligence. The rumbling and clattering Spirits of old times and old houses are now mute among us; but the grumbling and chattering Spirits of Sedition above measure do increase and get the upper hand, God resist them.

N.B. Sᵗ Austin writeth of one that knew the thoughts of men, as when one thought of a Verse in Virgil—but (said/Luther) the Devil had before possessed him with that verse.—*Schelling's Correspondent.* MAGN.

The hint of Undina in Luther's Table Talk p. 386.—of the Noble family, born of a Succuba—or Nixy—i.e. Water-woman.—

Cogitations of the Understanding do produce no melancholy: it is the cogitations of the will that produce sadness. p. 388.

?~~Ker~~ Cerberus (Κερφερός) from the Hebrew, Scorphur.   *f36ᵛ*

In proof how Superstition can hurry the noblest and most compassionate natures to injustice and inhuman Cruelty take this passage from a 100 others in Luther's writings equally striking.

"The Magistrate should *make haste* with Witches to punishment. The Lawyers in such cases will have too many witnesses and proofs. I had lately a matrimonial Cause on hand. A wicked woman by poison intended to make away her Husband, insomuch that he vomited and cast out little vipers. When she was put to the Torture, she refused to confess any thing: for such Witches are altogether dumb and contemn the rack. The Devil will not suffer them to speak. But such actions are sufficient proofs for them to receive condign punishment to the example of others!!!

Table Talk 390

The natural good sense of Luther bursting thro' even this dense mist of Superstition evident in this—that all his advice against Possessions, Tribulations, & other Familiarities of "my Gentle-

f37   man, the Devil" precisely the very same that a sensible Physician of the present day would prescribe/Society, employment either in company or purely intellectual and even that chiefly of the outward arts, and Sciences, a merry Cup, Confidence in God's Redemption, Scripture and other Proofs that the best men have commonly been most plagued in this way, and "That the Devil may be driven away by ridiculous contemning and jeering" (p. 381) of which he giveth sundry *savory* instances in his own case and self-experience. "When I could not be rid of the Devil ~~with willing~~ by shouting Texts at him and pelting him with sentences out of the holy Scriptures—but that he still would be vexing my faith & abringing me to the Question—Hast thou not a befowled Conscience &c—I often times said unto him, Devil! I have bewraied my breeches— Can'st thou smell that?—Or when he threatened me—Aye, aye— Master Luther! I have recorded thy sins in my register—I have answered/much obliged to you, kind Gentleman! make you a present of them for your trouble—~~they will~~ Put them in your fine Chaff-granary with the rest of the chaff from Christ's Corn. You will find them burn very well, I doubt not—. and still as he

f37ᵛ   bawled into my Conscience, Sin O! Sin O! I have bawled in return—Winnow! Winnow!—And at other times, If Christs blood, that was shed for my sins, if the intercession of the crucified Lord, be not sufficient, will you, as ~~now~~ you seem to take such an interest in my affairs, be so good as to pray for me yourself?—We know from your scholars, the Shavelings, and your idolatrous Masses and Invocations of dead Monks and Mummers—how skilled you are in praying! ⟨Sancte Satan! ora pro me!⟩—Whereat he would leave me—Quia est superbus Spiritus et non potest ferre contemptum sui.

Luther often disquieted by the Devil's objecting to him the confusion, and divisions that had been occasioned by his Reform, says heroically—But better it were that the Temple brake in pieces than that Christ should remain therein obscure and hid.—

Is not Christ the foundation and the Corner Stone?—Then tho' the Earthquake should split the temple from
   [*] yet if it but gave us a glimpse of the Foundation Christ, that had been hidden from us, we ought to rejoice—

"We should have no dealing with such poisoned Back-biters and Slanderers, that appear not openly on the plain   neither do they come right in our sight, but out of a frantic hate they scandalize and scorn with promiscuous bitterness."—Applied to Jeffrey & Hazlitt—

Nullus et Nemo mordent se in sacco. Quarrel between Hunt & Dr Watson.

Swill and Quaff, the names of the two Devils—German in Luther's Times—

A Friar super latrinam reading Horas Canonicas—to whom the Devil saying, Monachus super latrinam non debet legere Primam, the Friar answered
                    Purgo meum ventrem
                    Et colo Deum omnipotentem:
                       Tibi quæ infra
                    Deo Omn. quod supra.—

4595 21½.73   The Theologian, who in the present age, should appeal to Luther's particular expressions or dogmata against

[* Coleridge's blank.]

the *Spirit* of Luther, would resemble the Physician who should servilely copy Sydenham's Prescriptions in opposition to the clearest deductions from Sydenham's *Principia*. Who does not know that no great man who is at the same time a wise & practical man, can or will make the application of his Principles commensurate *f38ᵛ* with the same—*at once*. If he be indeed born to act on his contemporaries, he will not even see, nay, he will be zealous, against many an application which a later age will perceive to be an inevitable consequence—Now such a Principle was that of Luther's that the Bible was to be withheld from no man, under any pretence—and that no man had a right to control the spirit of his Brother but by the Spirit—

4596 21½.74   Of those who object to a rich and empassioned style (as formerly the Answerers of Burke) Juno's who conceive Mars at the very smell of a Flower—and who would fain attribute the Cuts they receive, not to the sharpness but the brightness and polish of the Sword—

4597 21½.75   There are in every Country times when the few, who knew the truth, cloathed it for the Vulgar and addressed the Vulgar, in the vulgar language and modes of conception, in order to convey any part of the Truth. This, however, could not be done with safety even to the Illuminati themselves, in the first instance—but to their successors—habit gradually turned Lie into Belief, *partial* & ~~imperfect~~ starveling truth into Ignorance, and the Teachers of the Vulgar (like the Franciscan Friars in the S. of Europe) became a part of the Vulgar—nay, because the Lay, men *f39* were open to various Impulses & Influences ~~from~~ which their Instructors had smelt out, (compare a brook in open air, liable to rain streams & rills from new opened fountains to the same running thro' a mill guarded by sluice-gates and back-waters) they became the Vulgarest of the Vulgar—till finally, resolute not to detach themselves from the Mob, the Mob at length detaches itself from them, and leaves the Mill race dry, the moveless rotten Wheels ~~for Owls~~ as Day-dormitories for Owls and Bats, and the old grindstones for Wags and Scoffers ~~and~~ of the Tap room ~~Witlings~~ to whet their Wits on—

4598 21½.76   The curiosity of an honorable mind willingly   *f39*
rests there where the Love of Truth does not urge ~~him~~ it farther
onward and the Love of his Neighbor bids it stand still.—
(stop—)
     or willingly halts ⟨stops⟩ at the point where the Interests of
Truth do not beckon him onward and Charity (bids him stops)—
cries, Halt!

4599 21½.77   Of Antony, the Monk, and his Compeers—
"Put in case, they led a private and a *grizlie* kind of life, yet it
was far from a holy life. I believe (said Luther) that they are in a
far lower degree in heaven, than an honest god-fearing married
man and house-father." P. 351.—"falleth from the matter, and
goeth the wrong way to the wood" 352.
     When it falleth out (saith Luther) that two Goats meet the one   *f39ᵛ*
the other upon a narrow plank or style that is laid over a deep
water, how do they behave themselves? Neither of them can turn
back again, neither can they pass the one by the other—and if they
should thrust each other, both would probably fall into the water
and be drowned. Nature hath taught them that the one layeth himself do~~ne~~wn and permitteth the other to go over him—Even so we
should submit in points where the Interests of Faith are not concerned, to be trod on rather than fall at debate & discord.

                                                      469.
     After this Luther's Excuse of Cursing—the same as Lessing's.
The Christian curses not the Heretic; but *Faith* curses the Heresy.
     If we may trust the Table Talk, Luther himself taught at last
the true christian doctrine of the Sacrament—Christus est *spiritu-
aliter* in Sacramento—quo modo, non nobis est perscrutari. Rem
credimus: modum nescimus.
     Quote the passage respecting Copernicus, collate with Sir
T. Brown's—

4600 21½.78   "We are better prepared for, and more inclined to, Despair than Hope: for Hope proceedeth from the Holy
Spirit and is his Work; but Despair cometh of our Spirit, and is
our Strength, our work and act. Therefore God hath forbidden it
under highest penalty." p. 223.—*Profound.*

f40   4601 21½.79   Scriptural, nay, evangelical ⟨authority⟩ sanctions the use of such names as Tommy, Jacky, (n.b. not, however,
the misappropriation of Jacky to Johannes instead of Jac-obus/the
true name is divided in halves of which we have the first in John
and the Germans the other in their *Hans*. James is either from
some Spanish provincial dialect: or a compensatory quid pro quo
from I'annes) Billy and the like. For as Alexas for Alexander,
Antipas for Antipater, Artemas for Artemidorus, and Kleopas for
Kleopatros, so is Demas for Demetrius (Demmy) and Lucas for
Lucius or Lucillius: as we say Lucy for Lucinda.—

4602 21½.80   Of the sentimental *Can*tilena respecting the
benignity and loveliness of NATURE—how does it not sink before
the contemplation of a pravity of nature, on whose reluctance and
inaptness a form is forced (the mere reflex of that form which is
itself absolute Substance!) and which it struggles against, bears but
for a while and then sinks with alacrity of self-seeking into dust or
sanies, falls abroad into endless nothings or creeps and cowers in
poison or explodes in havock—What is the beginning? What the
end?—And how evident an alien is the supernatant in the brief
interval?—

f40ᵛ   4603 21½.81   I have written (in pencil) a serviceable Note
ending p. 600, Vol. I. Eichhorn: Einl. in das Neue Test.—If
instead of the absolute inspiration and infallible res ipsissimëity of
every sentence, yea, vocable of the O. and N. Test.—a tenet contradicted by so many facts, irreconcileable with all analogous experience, nay, a tenet, of the possibility of which is inconceivable,
and without the assumption of an unbroken series of Miracles, no
one of which has ever been even † suspected, even deniable—and
lastly, a tenet, of which the assertors themselves have no intelligible notion—and define the terms, by which they would convey
their opinion, in a circle—if instead of this we are contented to
adopt the plain doctrine that the Canonical Books contain as faithful an History of the Doings and Sayings of Men impelled by the

† Unless the Aristean Fable of the 70 Translators be admitted as
an exception

Spirit of Truth and Holiness, as written History *can* be—a History not only adequate but admirably adapted to all the purposes,
for which it was intended, and for all really desirable ends—and
then instead of unrecorded miracles would dwell on the heart-rais-
ing co-incidence of *providential* circumstances in the first writing,
the diffusion, and the preservation of the Scriptures, a ~~mo~~ proof
would result most fitted to human Nature, and in minds not unfit-   *f41*
ted ⟨to⟩ & by scripture ~~to~~ itself declared ~~incapable~~susceptible, of
Christian Faith, capable of inspiring the same tranquil confidence,
~~as~~ in the moral world, that the coincidence of the different organs
in a plant or an animal does in the physical world—. Among these
may be placed the very defects charged by Worldlings & classical
infidels—namely, that so large a portion of the New Testament
was *occasional*—that even Luke, the most polished writer & schol-
arly of the Evangelists, was yet a Jew, & adhered scrupulously to
the Jewish conception of ~~what~~ History—the *word for word* tran-
scription from his documents, except where other and securer information intervened—but more especially with respect to
Speeches, of their Rabbis—this being characteristic of the Jews in
the time of our Lord, to *take notes* &c—The amazing Collection
of their Gnom~~onai~~, the result of this practice, proves the great
antiquity of this—bearing no comparison with the few gnomonic
Poems of the Greeks & Romans before Christ—/The most glorious
instance of this, however, and for which we cannot be enough
grateful to Providence, is the large Memorabilia peculiar to Luke
and inserted by him in his Gospel, from C. 9, v. 51 to C. 18, v.
14.

4604 21½.82   Experience, raised indeed by speculative philosophy above mere observation, but unaided by instruments and
not yet experimentative, was necessarily imperfect & often illusive.
In the countries and ages, in which Observation ⟨Experience⟩ un-   *f41ᵛ*
aided by ~~scientific~~ Instruments and ⟨not yet experimentative⟩ Experimental Inquiry was necessarily superficial, it was a common
belief that the smaller animals were produced by an abnormous
generation—for instance that Frogs were sometimes rained from
the clouds, and that at other times the warm prolific rains after
long drouth had impregnated the brute earth and ~~ma~~ gave it the

self-alchemy of transmuting itself into multitudinous organic
Lives—The Egyptian Naturalists in particular having their attention roused by the swarming mud deposited during the Overflow
of the Nile believed themselves to have ~~saw~~een Frogs, whose extremities (fore and hind legs) were complete, while the head and
trunk were still a lump of mud, ⟨rudis indigestaque moles⟩ yet
waiting for the vis plastica—A chaos on which the Spirit of Life
was but brooding, and preparing the dark confused semi-fluid for
the reception of the Lucific ~~Word~~ *Fiat*, the distinctive Light, the
solving Word of the plusquam-Sampsonian Riddles—~~Tho' this is
exploded as a physical fact~~, That this was an error and for us a
vulgar error I need not add yet like the greater number of the
ancient Fancies and Traditions, ~~it still remains supplies an emblem~~
that exploded as facts still remain to supply apt emblems and happy
illustrations, so this seems to me a most ~~logical~~ appropriative type
of the process of our intellectual and moral Life—for a ⟨natural⟩
Death, which is but the Life of a lower order of Natural Power,
f42   (the chemical, for instance) begins at the extremities and so dies
upward till it reaches the Heart and finishes its course in the Brain,
so the true life (the Individual's own Life or the *Life of the Person*)
begins in the extremities, the *subservient* and *instrumental members*.

And the ~~Objection~~ Difficulty too is the same in both/For the
Circulation in the Legs of the Frog supposes the co- if not the pre-
existence of the Heart & nobler Vitals—& this is indeed an unanswerable objection to the story taken as a *fact*—but not so to that
Life of which it is here made an emblem—for the Life, we speak
of, is but the Life of God made *our* Life by Acceptance & grateful
love—by a clear *consciousness* of its *eternal* Being and that it alone
truly lives, we realize it *in time* and uniting it with ~~the~~ Time conquer the Temporal and lead away *Captivity Captive*/even as Fire
uniti~~nges~~ with the opposite thereby to *manifest* itself by the conversion of the op. into itself. i.e. the self-preserving, social and civil
duties, those which the Penalties of Human and of Nature's Laws
ordinarily suffice to enforce, by the influences of Fear, and Shame,
and Disease—the Prison or the Hospital, the Sword of the Exe-
cutioner or the Knives and Saws of the Chirurgeon (The Punitive
~~Law~~ Code of Human Law is but a poor and meagre extract lamely
copied from the vast *Common Law* of Nature ~~contra~~ in reos læsæ

Majestatis suæ, rebelles, veneficos, hæreticos, insolentes—and the
Carnifices of the Inquisition can neither hang strangle, drown,
rack, ram saw, burn, distort, stretch, mutilate with half the vigor,
and inventiveness of Disease—)

N.b.—I am not at all satisfied with the preceding, It does not f_{42}^v
solve the difficulty if the assumption were true (viz. that the true
Life begins in the extremities) and I doubt the fact that it does
begin there.—Perhaps, the emblem would better apply *ad contra*—
a *galvanism* vita non vita, data a⟨b⟩ arbitrio alieno—or the true fact
in nature—the Tadpole in its Metamorphosis—When the Higher
Life is really beginning in the heart, but *manifests* itself by the
production of its instruments—to *others*—but the Calf butts before
it has *horns*, and the tadpole *seeks* the mud before it has legs to
crawl or hop, quits the world for which alone its actually present
members fit it, and lies passive in the other in order to *become* co-
organized therewith—and then returns to its first element, when it
has been enrolled as a Citizen of the second, a Free Man of both
Worlds—but thenceforward it merely *uses* the first state & element,
lives and draws life only in the second—and dies *wholly* if it attempts to *live again* in the first or if it re even remains too long a
space, without intervals, s immerged in the same—. *This* is a beautiful and commensurate series of Emblems.—And the mud-body
and antecedent fore and hind legs of the vulgar Zoology is as
proper an exposure of the Hartleyan &c Doctrine of Self-love
perfecting itself into the Love of God—in opposition to the doctrine of *Conversion* as taught by the soundest of the Moravians/and
meant by both Calvin and Luther/—
⟨The Egyptian Frog a good emblem of the Priestleyan Education
from Selfishness to Virtue.⟩

4605 21½83   There are many, alas! too many, either born
& who have become Deaf and Dumb—So there are too many who
have lost perverted the *religion* of the *Spirit* for into the Superstition of Spirits, that peep, and mutter, and mock and moe, like f_{43}
Deaf & Dumb Ideots—. Plans of teaching the Deaf & Dumb
have been invented—for these the D. and D. owe thanks & we
for *their* sakes—Homines sumus & nihil humani a nobis alienum/
But does it follow therefore, that in all schools these plans of teach-

ing should be followed—?—Yet in the other case this is insisted
on—and the Holy Ghost must not be our *guide* because *Mysticism*
& *Ghosts* may come in under this name—Why?—Because the Deaf
and Dumb have been promoted to *Superintendents* of Education at
large & for *all*!!—

⟨n.b. *begin* at "Save only—⟩

Save only in that, which I have a right to demand of every *man*
that he should be able to understand me, the experience or inward
witnessing of the Conscience, and which every man in *real life* &
(even the very disputant who affects doubt or denial in the moment
of metaphysical Arguing) would ~~for~~ hold himself insulted by the
supposition that he did not understand it—Save this only and that
what if ⟨it be⟩ *at all* must be *unique* and therefore cannot be supported by an Analogon, and what if it be at all, must be *first*, and
therefore cannot have an antecedent, therefore may be *monstrated*
but cannot be *de*monstrated—I am no Ghost-seer—I am no believer in Apparitions—I do not contend for ~~un~~indescribable Sensations nor refer to, much less *ground*, my conviction on *blind
feelings* or incommunicable Experiences,—but far rather contend
against these superstitions in the Mechanic Sect & impeach you as

f43ᵛ   guilty of the same habitually and systematically, which at worst are
but exceptions and *fits* in the poor self-misapprehending Pietists
with whom under the name Mystics, you would fain confound and
discredit *all* who receive and worship God in spirit and in truth,
and in the former as the only possible mode of the latter. According to your own account of your own scheme *you* know nothing
but your own *sensations*/~~which the very definition of which implies
that they~~ indescribable in as much as they are *sensations*—for the
appropriate *èxpression* even of which we must fly ~~after the parts of
speech~~ not merely to the indeclinables, in the lowest parts of
Speech, but to ⟨human⟩ articulations that only ⟨like musical notes⟩
stand for ~~the~~ *inarticulate sounds*—Οι, Οι, παπαι, &c of the Greek
Tragedy—or rather tragic Oratorios—. You see nothing but only
by a sensation that conjures up an image in your own brain, or
optic nerve (as in a night mair) have an apparition, in consequence
of which, as again in the night mair, you are *forced* to ~~infer~~ believe,
for the moment, and are *inclined* to infer the existence of a corresponding reality out of your brain—how, by what intermediation,
you cannot even form an intelligible conjecture—. During the

years of ill health from disturbed digestion I saw a host of Apparitions, & heard them too—but I attributed them to an act in my
brain/You according to your own see and hear nothing but appa-   *f44*
ritions in your brain, and strangely attribute them to things that
are out ~~of~~ side of your skull/—which of the two notions is most
like the philosopher, which th~~ate~~ ~~of~~ Superstitionist—. Mine who
make my apparitions nothing but apparitions, a brain-image nothing more than a brain-image, and affirm, nihil super stare—or yours
who schemically contend that it is but a brain image, and yet cry—
ast *super*stitit aliquid—. Est *superstitio* alicujus quod *in externo*, id
est, in *apparenti* non *apparet*—[?(ss/55/§)]—What is *outness, external*, and the like but ⟨either⟩ the *generalization* of Apparence, or
⟨the result⟩ of ~~an~~ given degree, a comparative intensity, of the same—
"I see it in my mind's eye"—exclaims Hamlet while his thoughts
were in his own power—the same phantom, in a higher intensity,
became his Father's Ghost & marched along the Platform—I quote
your own expositions—and dare you with these opinions charge
others with *superstition*—You, who deny aught permanent in our
being, you with whom the Soul, yea, the Soul of the Soul, our
Conscience & morality are but the *Tune* from a fragile ⟨Barrel-⟩
Organ, played by Air and Water—and whose whole Life therefore must of course be ~~but descent~~ but a pointing to, like as of
Marcellus or Hamlet—Tis here!—Tis here! Tis gone!—Were it
possible that I could actually believe such a system, I should not
be scared from striking it—from its being so *majestical*.

4606 21½.84   Oct. 20, 1819. Wednesday—49 (My Mother   *f44ᵛ*
told my Wife, that I was a year younger & that there was a blunder made ~~in~~ either in the Baptismal Register itself or in the Tran-
script sent for my admission into Christ Hospital‡—& Mʳˢ C,
who is older than myself, believes me only 48. Be this as it may,
in *Life* if not in years I am, alas! nearer to 68)—beautiful Flowers
as a Birthday Present from Miss Bullock—~~seat~~ up till past 2ᵒclock,
writing (in vain, I fear) to *Williams*, to dissuade him or rather to
prepare for my attempt (this afternoon, 2ᵒclock) to dissuade him
from acting as an ungrateful Serpent to Mʳ Gillman.

‡ I forget which—but I believe, the latter.

4607 21½.85   Oct. 21,—Snow and Sleet for the first time,
this 11°clock. Morning.

4608 21½.86   N.B. A Sonnet on the Child collecting shells
and pebbles on the Sea shore or Lake side—and carrying each with
a fresh shout of Delight and Admiration to the Mother's Apron,
who smiles and assents to ~~the~~ each—There's pretty! Is it not that a
nice one?—and then when the Prattler is tired of its *conchozetes̶y̶tic*
labors, lifts up her apron and throws them out on the Sand—Such
are our first discoveries both in Science and Philosophy—/

4609 21½.87   Truth is a good dog; but must not bark too
near the heels of an Error or it will get its brains knocked out.

4610 21½.88   Milton versus Salmasius—hic latrat, ille
rugit.

4611 21½.89   Ille veritatis defensor esse debet qui quum
recte sentit, loqui non metuit nec erubescit.
                                        Gregor: Homil.
     The old Law of England punishes those who dig up the bones
of the Dead, for superstitious⟨or⟩magical, purposes—i.e. ~~to~~ in order to injure the living. What then are they guilty of who uncover
the Dormitories of the Departed to throwe their Souls into the Pit
f45 of Hell—in order to cast odium on a living truth?/
     An excellent Sermon might be written on ~~the~~ Luke, 6.26. Woe
unto you when all men shall speak well of you for so did their
Fathers to the false prophets.—The sum is this—you will then
have merged *all* duties into those of worldly social duties.—The
Quakers are so neat, so sober and quiet, and foremost in public
Charities. They may equivocate and take advantages, but never lie,
swear, or ~~unlaw~~ illegally defraud—and so tolerant in all points of
religion, that they neither trouble others nor themselves therewith—Compare this their present favor with all men, with the
time when by their more than heroic passive resistance before the
Bull inn, Aldsgate S! they purchased Toleration for the whole
Kingdom/. This is admitted, nay, asserted and declared by Baxter;
and yet in that very § Fanatics and poor deluded Souls are the best

words that he can afford them. Elsewhere they are *possessed by Devils*—Dæmoniacs who have delivered themselves up to Satan, &c.—And Baxter was of all Anti-tolerationists the least intolerant—say rather, that he used and understood the word "Toleration" in a different sense from the present—for he pleaded for subscription only to the Belief, Lord's Prayer, and Ten Commandments, in order to the higher Magistracies, and for Presbyters added no more than, I believe all articles of faith necessary for salvation are contained in the canonical Scriptures, and promise that I will use all the means in my power to discover the true sense of the words, and that I will interpret accordingly.—

"If we consider the generality of mankind, either in respect of their inclinations and dispositions, or of their breeding, education, state and circumstances, we shall not find one of an hundred either by nature inclined or by education fitted and qualified to search forth and understand the Truth.—And even of that comparatively small number, who have been trained up in Learning, how much larger portion move wholly in the trammels of their Teachers, and merely receive the other men's opinions unsifted and unwinnowed; or perhaps only repeat their phrases, with as little thought of their *f45ᵛ* meaning as Parrots or Echoes have. If then there be an hundred to one drowned in ignorance, and of the remainder so few fitted to understand or disposed to investigate the truth of things either divine or natural, it must needs follow that it is not safe to embrace, or adhere to, an opinion because of the great number of those that hold or maintain it, but rather to stick to the smaller number: tho' neither simply ought to be regarded, but Truth itself."

Webster "Disp. of Supposed Witchcraft," p. 13.

In addition to Tertullian & others cited by Lessing, this of Augustine (de Libero Arbitrio) Si de veritate Scandalum sumitur, utilius permittitur nasci scandalum quam veritas relinquatur.

Naturæ ignari, libris solis ⟨de Naturâ⟩ eruditi, ut qui de Imperatore Sinensi vel Duce quolibet Tatarico historiolas quasdam legebant, secretarios tamen Naturæ se præsumunt: quicquid autem ipsos latet, vel ⟨a⟩ lectionibus suis alienum sonat, vel αδυνατον, vel falsum, vel præstigiosum atque diabolicum esto! Helmontius *de Inject. Mater.* p. 597.

Nam et omni miraculo quod fit per hominem majus miraculum est Homo. Quamvis igitur miracula visibilium naturarum, viribus autem præter visum effecta, videndi assiduitate vilescunt, tamen ea quum sapienter intuemur, inusitatissimis rarisque majora sunt.

Augustin. de Civit. Dei. lib. 10.—

MEMENTO. An admirable Passage in Webster (p. 19. 20:—the whole §. 1. of Chap. II.—on the equal claims of Experim. Research and of Logic. It is congruous with but more clearly & nobly expressed than Bacon's, who scarcely holds the Scales evenly: and it *shames* Lock—who affirms that Geometry supersedes the necessity of logic, and Experimental Research metaphysics.—

f46   John 9. 6.7.—The Miracle of the Blind Man, whose Eyes our Lord anointed with Clay, is one of the most exact and significant allegories, I ever remember to have read—& thus confirmative of the (*at the time*) secondary but now & in their prospective intentions primary Purpose of the Miracles in general—symbols namely of the everlasting *Good Tidings*.—The Mouth of Christ was symbolically (not merely metaphorically) = Divine Philosophy, in S͟t͟ ͟J͟o͟h͟n͟ our Lord's own words—*The Way* and *the Truth*, the means, the method and the End itself—it is the way to the Truth but being the true way it is itself a portion of the Truth— or even the form, in which the Truth itself is partaken of by finite spirits. The Spittle = the lower, and instrumental Excretion of Philosophy, by which it assists in first dividing (masticating, ruminating) then a͟s͟consimilating, and lastly assimilating the earthly food (facts of the senses) to its own higher Life—namely, *Logic*, which like Geometry, and common Arithmetic, had its source in the highest Philosophy, and could never have been derived from the empirical life.—This Logic applied by a Master's Hand to the commonest, most incoherent, sand-like facts of the senses whose lapse merely fills up and measures the t͟h͟e͟ vacuous flux of mortal Time, will communicate a coherency to the same, & give it virtues capable of opening the eyes of the Blind, provided there be a passive Resignation of the Will—and provided, the Blind Person proceeds & washes himself in the waters of *the Sent*, Siloam = the Messiah—the purifying moral discipline, το προπαιδευτικον, of Faith.—By a truly scientific Logic applied to and combining the commonest Facts and Phænomena the Philosopher can prove to the

most Ignorant, if only merely ignorant & not repugnant, ~~to~~ that
the knowlege of the Truth can be no otherwise obtained—that
done, the next step is—*Try therefore*—~~you are~~ it has been demonstrated that a, b, c, d, are not and cannot be the *road* to the   *f46ᵛ*
Temple or the Oracle—that e is the only remaining Road—try it
therefore, travel along it, trust in it and ~~let your steps~~ obey in all
respecting the various guide-posts both at its entrance & those
which you will find along it—and this is the method, nay, this is
from the nature of the thing the only possible method of converting your negative knowlege into direct and positive Insight; and
Possession. Believe (says Augustine) and to understand will be the
result and reward of thy Belief.—In all things worth knowing our
knowlege is in exact proportion to our *faith*: and all faith begins
in a predisposition, analogous to instinct, inasmuch as the particular Will could not be awaked and realized into an actual Volition
but by an impulse and communication from the universal Will.
This latter is the vital air, which the particular Will breathes, but
which must have entered & excited the faculty ~~in order to~~ as the
previous and enabling Condition of the first disposition to breathe,
as well as of the power of drawing the Breath. It must be "in us
both to will and to do." And not only at the beginning but thro'
the whole Life do we need this *prevenient Grace*—Note too—that
it is the †*Pool* of Siloam—an inclosed Collection of Water—a
Church, or positive Religion—from the predisposing Grace &
application of natural reason divinely potenziated to the Church—
the appointed reservoir of the waters from above—καὶ ηλθε
βλεπων—i.e. where ever he had occasion to go—in all departments
of Life—he walked in light./

The first act of the Infant—feels ⟨exerts⟩ its Individuality in
⟨announcing⟩ its helplessness ⟨and its wants⟩ & the sensation of
being acted upon—is *placed* at the Mother's breast—is rendered a
cupping machine—and *then* is entrusted with it, and from *being* it
rises into *having* and using it. N.B. The dust becomes *clay*—not
only a *salve*—but capable of being moulded into vessels wherewith
to draw up and apply to individual and domestic use the waters
from the reservoir of *the Sent*—

† τὴν κολυμβηθραν—απῆλθε   *f46ᵛ*

f47   **4612** 21½.90   It is probable that Christ implied his divinity
in the active ~~voice~~ Substantive of the Messiah, viz. *Unctor* as subsisting and incarnated in the humanity or passive *participles* Messiah, viz. Unctus—and that in the *Siloam* he alluded especially to
the Paraclete, the Spirit of the Lord *sent* by him, sic ut patris, ita
suo ipsius jure et nomine demissus.—The incarnate Logos was at
once Anointed and Sent; and the Anointer and Sender.

4613 21½.91   There is a ~~praise, a hope, a sympathy~~ species
of applause a scarcely less ~~necessary~~ genial to a ~~man of genius~~ Poet,
whether Bard, Musician or artist, than the vernal warmth to the
feathered Songsters during their Nest building or Incubation—a
sympathy, an expressed Hope, that is the ~~May~~ open air in which
the Poet breathes, and without which the sense of Power sinks back
⟨on itself⟩ like a ~~Sickness~~ sigh heaved up from the tightened chest
of a sick man.

4614 21½.92   Anonymity is now an artifice to increase ⟨ac-
quire⟩ celebrity, as a black Veil is worn to make a pair of bright
eyes more conspicuous—

4615 21½.93   There is a curious fact which fully solves, and
without which it would be impossible to solve, the absurd impro-
prieties of the ordinary schemes of the defences of Xtnty—it is
this—that the majority of readers as well as the Writers, are Christians, & not Christians—the first in their wishes and in profession,
the latter in the want of all living *faith*.—Hence the stickling for
Daniel, & the acrimony with which the opinions of Dodwell &
Bentley are treated. Hence the palpable circle in which the arguments move—D. is true because C. is said (by them) to have
confirmed his prophecy—& C. is true because D. prophecied of
him—

f16   **4616** 29.26   Abstine a fabis. For (says or is said to have said
Pythagoras) they resemble the Gate of Hell which is kneeless,
αγονατον—inflexible, yields no homage, & heeds no supplication.
Numa too forbad the eating of Beans: and the Priest who sacrificed
to Jove dared neither touch or even name them, because there was

connected with the Bean an idea of Death incompatible with offerings to Jupiter, Zeus or Ζῆς, ζωῆς πατηρ, the Father of *Life*—.
Seek the obscure cause in the word—
κυω, originally, to contain passively, as a vacuum. Thence
κυανος, the *dark-blue* of the Hollow of the Sky. 2. To contain a
child, to be the womb of, to be pregnant. κυαμιζειν, to be mann-
able, fit for marriage—& κυαμος, the first milk in a virgin's breast
after puberty, making the nipple rigid.—Thus both senses in κυαμος, our Horse-bean. κυαμοι μελανοχροες, black-skinn'd Beans,
Homer—hence symbolical of the blind appetences, cravings, like
the Gate of Hell, αγονατον; out of which we *rise* into distinct
Existence & the realm of Light, but to which and thro' which the
retrograde and sense-subdued carnalized Soul returns & passes into
the dark chaotic fire—the Infera—

4617 29.27   Picus asserts the scientific certainty of three   *f16ᵛ*
Worlds—corporeal, celestial, and divine = intellectual. So Swedenborg. The Mystique has fair claims to the rank of a *Subjective
Science*, all men in all ages and countries who have cultivated it,
having proceeded from the same grounds to the same conclusions
by the same deductions. Picus Mirandula had little speculative
power, but enormous & restless speculative curiosity—overlaid his
genius or constructive power by his pantoïomathy.
    Superiority of the oldest trichotomy, phytozoic, zoic, and no-
erozoic to Bichat's dichotomy, zoic and zoophyte—. Abdominal,
pectoral, cerebral = sensation, sentiment, sense—the intermediate
term being the synthesis, semi conductor, or Drawbridge of the
first & third.
    The true norma loquendi philosophicè can only be detected in
common life by placing the words in *antithesis*—Thus, Reason &
Understanding, Vernunft und Verstand—you may employ in a 100
instances indifferently—but put them in antithesis—~~God~~ That
God is all in each, totus ubique, ist ganz unverständlich; nicht
aber unvernünfting [*unvernünftig*]—quite incomprehensible, and
yet apodictically rational. Vernunft, veritatum consociatio, Zunft
der Wahren—Verstand, fixatio, et—substantiatio der Wahrneh-
mungen, perceptionum pro veris sumptarum.
    In the 7ᵗʰ B. of ~~thi~~ P. Mirandula's Heptaplus, would the Uni-

tarians if they were wise seek his interpretation of John & Paul, not in the repulsive effrontery of making the Apostles *mean* the direct contrary of what they say—but then they must either give up their Jesus, or their Lock and Hartley; but then in the latter instance they would lose at the same all their motives for disbelief in the Christ of the Christians, namely, God made manifest in the flesh by the incarnation of the co-eternal Son.

Dicæarchus, contemp. with Arist. denied all soothsaying, even the most venerable, but was compelled by the notoriety of the fact to except the predictions of *morbid sleep* and a certain species of derangement tho' of so narrow a sphere as to be of little or no use except as sometimes guiding the Physician in the cure of the unhappy Prophets themselves.—*Second Sight.*

f17   4618 29.28   Axiom.—Where ever the Choice lies between the Incomprehensible (praeter intellectum, sive intelligentiam *definientem*) the Absurd (rationi contrarium) and a palpable Shuffle (nihilismus turpis), to choose the former.—Again. 1. incomp. 2. absurd. 3. evasive—3. denial in toto. But then look for the positive ⟨of the negative lest greater evils than the one removed.⟩

2. Φρονημα σαρκος, intelligentia carnis—I call upon the Socinians to explain this phrase—so that St Paul shall not be made guilty of a puerile identical proposition—That wicked thoughts are wicked thoughts—την σοφιαν των σοφων, την συνεσιν των συνετων, σοφιαν του κοσμου τουτου.—Scorn and abuse will not be accepted in lieu of Answers.—The Commentators of all the Xtn Churches (for the Socinian I will not call a Christian Church) explain these words of Isaiah and Paul as signifying all the ~~wisdom~~ philosophy (for that is the manifest import of σοφια in this place) and Understanding natural and acquired, which is merely intellective, and not *grounded* on moral Postulates, or Faith—ex. gr. on the assumption of Will, God, and responsible Agency.—I render φρονημα σαρκος—the Understanding referring to the Objects of the senses as its substantiating ground or πληρωμα, which being therefore a passive faculty, or mere repository, must needs be a result of the ⟨bodily⟩ Senses, & literally therefore the Understanding of the *Flesh*—the flesh being the Scriptural term for an organized living Body & its necessary accompaniments—φρονημα σαρκος is thus distinguished from σοφια των σοφων or Philosophÿic Intellect

self-grounded = Spinosism, Dogmatism, and perhaps from συνεσιν των συνετων, or skilful adaptation of actions to worldly
ends, moral prudence as the substitute instead of the subordinate
of Moral Goodness—but all contradistinguished from the wisdom
of the spirit, Faith and Love. Now I have this advantage over the
Unitarians—Every interpretation, they can offer & which can appear supported by any passages in Paul or John, must be included
in mine—& yet excluding th mine as far as it is not theirs, becomes a mere sophisma pigrum—

I asked myself—what is the import of *Religion*—in what sense
must it be taken, in order to distinguish it from & yet to be
capable of combining it with Revelation as *Revealed* Religion? and
vice versâ. As to *Revealed*!

Item—What is the Pauline sense of *Mystery* as applied to Christian Faith.

That this φρονημα, συνεσις, σοφια = the Mosaic Οφις, accord-   *f17*
ing to Paul, can, I think, be supported by proofs sufficient and
satisfactory for any Reader of his works collectively: and conversely, that the Serpent—sensu Mosaico—meant this φρον. &c
has not only in its favor the presumption of unanimity in the inspired Writers, but likewise the test of transferred interpretation
to the Scriptures throughout—that I mean, that if you assume this,
there are numerous passages which gain a significance & local ap-
positeness, that it would be difficult to establish by any other
means, and there is not one, with which it is not consistent.—
Serpens from creeping into the interior mind, say Webster &
others—. They might have quoted Virgil Æn. L. 3. 89

Da, Pater, augurium, *animisque illabere nostris.*

Q. Is the plate in Tooke's Pantheon of the Trunk-like Club, with
the Serpent twined round it, the little woman on one side, and the
God-Man, Esculapius of any classic authority, antique gem, bas
relief, or extant or described?—If so, I should guess it to have
been originally borrowed by the Greeks from some Egyptian
Hieroglyphic or Emblem—or perhaps Phœnician—Of the Eve,
(Homo inferior, Humanitas passiva) the Tree, the Serpent, and
the *Jah*, Son of the Monas (α πολλων) sent to Hades for raising
Men from Death, but re-ascending from Hades into Deity, &
thence the God of Healing—Θεος σωτὴρ, φιλανθρωπος, θεάνθρωπος.

Syllogyzari non est ex particulari, sive εξ απαξ λεγομενου. Suppose the Serpent to be the discursive Understanding, discursus intellectualis, then the arguments & words put in the mouth of the Serpent are most apposite—but if bonâ fide a serpent, absurd.

f18   4619   29.29   Mat⟨erialism⟩ versus *Im*mat.—a mere Skiomachy of the Schools—among the Fathers, Tertullian, Augustin, Nazianzen, to which add the venerable Bede, were Materialists, the Schoolmen on the other side—but the dispute is of mere disputative interest, a play or trial of definitions/not however without use nor without scientific Interest, as determining the *senses* of terms, historically & as what would be most conducive to a harmony of language—in short, ⟨would⟩ finds an honorable rank in the Prolegomena to a philos. Lexicon—provided only, it be not supposed to alter or add to, existing sum of knowledge de *rebus*—Zanchius, one of the learned *iss*- & er[r]-imuses of the [*]   Century, concludes, Mihi videtur ex iis quæ Scripturæ tradunt de Angelis, probabaliorem esse Patrum sententiam quam Scholasticorum—utram tamen sequaris, non multum peccaveris, nec propterea inter Hereticos haberi poteris.

4620   29.30   Compare the atchievements of the Church of E.—during its call it Calvinistic or what would be better & truer, Melancthonian, Oicolampadian, but best of all & alone correct, Scriptural & apostolic Period from Elizabeth & *parliamentary* Religion, when in *heart* the People in general were Papistical, i.e. attached to all the pomp, & superstitions they & their fathers had been accustomed to, & in head—nothingists—to the full triumph of Arminianism (that brood-hen wch Socinianism, Unitarianism, Deistic † Atheism for her Egg—egg within egg, like Aphides or Spallanzani's animalcules)—compare, I say, what was done for Religion by these *Calvinists* with the works of the Period since!—in which I confess I see but one thing to boast of—the clearing up of the genuine Doctrine of the Trinity by Bull & Waterland—

† Bolingbroke's God without *moral* attributes.—

[* Coleridge's blank.]

4621 29.31   Quicquid agit, agit vel mediatione suppositi vel   *f18ᵛ*
mediatione virtutis, ※"by immediate or virtual contact"—i.e. with
or without contact! a *profound* truism!

Mem. Tertullian makes *Spirits* a sort of *Lumbrici*—Δαιμονες
hæc sua corpora dilatant et contrahunt ut volunt, sicut Lumbrici
et alia quædam insecta.—

To Zanchius add S. Bernard—Videntur Patres de hujusmodi
diversa sensisse nec mihi perspicuum est unde alterutrum doceam:
et nescire me fateor. *Super* Cantic. p. 504—

Stillingfleet observes that God only can really alter the course of
nature—ergo, the miracles of the Xtn Religion are alone *true* miracles. ~~Mir prove~~ i.e. M + C = T: because T + M = C.—
Who dares deny it?—But teach us, dear Divine, what is a proof
of course of N. *altered*! 500 years hence the raising of ~~animals~~ men
from what *we* now call death may cease to be a miracle just as the
raising of men from what the *ancients* called Death has ceased to
be a miracle now except in the metaphors & compliments of the
Humane Society. No true miracles except those worked for the
establishment of Gospel Evidence in the apostolic age! says the
Grotian low Church Protestant. None since the 3ʳᵈ Century, says   *f19*
the High Church Protestant. No where but in the bosom of the
holy Catholic Church, but there now & in all times, says the Romanist. Thick as Hops in all religions, says the Brahman: and
where applied to confirm a man in his own religion, in all alike to
be received with pious acquiescence—but when worked to evince

※this is Webster's phrase—more accurate would be, immediate,
intermediate, or virtual—the word "contact" is evidently idle † in
either case, being involved in *agit/*. It can have no other than a
visual sense.—Ergo, the true maxim is as before—Whatever acts,
acts either with or without the sensuous phænomena of Contact—
or Quicquid agit, agit vel mechanicè vel magicè—for such (as I
have a 1000 times observed) is the true and original as well as the
only philosophical import of the word *magic.*—

† Perhaps, I should say that the word has but two possible
senses—either phænomenal, or potential = repulsion—in the latter sense, it would say whatever acts, acts solely by its repulsive
power—which is a frequent but unproved & I doubt not false,
Assertion—*Vide Kant.*

the falsehood ~~of another~~ or inferiority of another, then we are to take them only as a proof that the Gods have a difference among themselves, and it in no wise becomes us to take sides & aggravate matters, like officious Servants when their Masters and Mistress happen to quarrel—.

4622 29.32   Axioms. I An Argument applying equally for or against B and A, is valid for both or neither.

COROLLARY. 1. An argument which if valid would disprove a certain truth is ex absurdo invalid.

COROLLARY 2. An argument which equally applies to an admitted position cannot without gross inconsistency by adduced by the Admittent against a position disputed by him. He cannot grant A + C, and assign C as his ground for the denial of B + C, A and B being ejusdem generis. SCHOLIUM. Let C be = Error, ⟨the same or equivalent:⟩ A = *Newton*, B. Des Cartes ~~I cannot assert~~ and D = Philosophy; I cannot ~~admit~~ssert A D + C, and B + C − D. I must prove a specific difference in the Errors, before I can assign the circumstance of having occasionally erred as a proof that Des Cartes was no philosopher, having admitted errors in the Philosopher Newton. For here the terms are ejusdem generis. But let C = Reason, ~~and my~~ A a man and B an Ox, my belief in A + C is no objection to my disbelief of B + C.—

II. The point in dispute cannot be brought as an argument primo loco for or against. Thus in order to discredit the evidence for animal magnetism, I must not bring the belief in the physical powers of the Will & Imagination as proofs of disqualifying Credulity in Bacon, Boyle, Helmont, Wienholt &c.

f19ᵛ ~~Nay what~~ Nay, a theory in accordance with the general belief of the age, even of the learned, is no sufficing proof of a man's ⟨*comparative*⟩ *credulity*† in point of Fact, however absurd it may now appear, provided it be adduced only as a Theory.—That Van Helmont was disposed to explain the substances occasionally vomited or found after death in the body of epileptics by a transplantation by evil spirits is no fair proof that he did not see what he declares himself to have seen—but I must suspect every fact of Corn. de Gemma that rests wholly on *his* authority after his assurance of having seen a girl void a three pound Cannon Ball with an eel in its secundine—or an Ox ⟨that⟩ having taken 3 herbs did vomit a Dragon with a tail like an Eel, a leathern Body, a Serpent's Head, and not less than a Partridge.

† but yet admit that in such an age such a theory would unduly dispose a man to receive facts with less investigation—& vice versā, that the theory of the age, and up to a given point of time that of the Individual is toto cœlo against the probability of a fact, is an argument for its reality, as far as it goes. So Wienholt, and Blumenbach.

4623 29.33

> And there was young Philosophy,
> Unconscious of her self, pardie,
> And now she hight—Poesy—
> And like a child, in life-ful glee,
> Had newly left ~~of~~ her Mother's knee,
> Prattles and plays with flower and Stone,
> As if with faery play-fellows
> Revealed to Innocence alone—

Exerts the power excited in her as ~~the~~ passive or negative subject by the Mother & becoming in her turn positive acts upon her Toys, like Light, that meeting eyeless things falls back & so reflects the image of her inward self.

> Yet what she now attributes in her play,   *f*20
> She shall here after, armed
> With stedfast stronger will, *awake* and *find*—
> ~~And~~ For Metaphor and Simile
> Are notes of lisping prophecy—

New Creation—"fell not out in man & by man must arise—St Paul—

> Then Poesy shall rise into Philosophy
> When Philosophy hath known herself as Poesy (ποιησις)

4624 29.34   The Rhabdomancy, the Ring or Sword suspended over Metals, or Water—. The Baquet of Zoo-magnetism—the potenziation of Galvanism in inanimate Substances by
organic correspondents—these & countless others, the Redemption
of the *Life-in-death* by Man.—Θέος φιλάνθρωπος—θεάνθρωπος—
Ανθρωπος ~~εν~~ προς θεανθρωπον φιλοκοσμος.—

Is not Οπιυμ και ολον το ναρκοτικον γενος βοτανων, example and
proof of the βακυετ μαγνητικου? Why, should we deny the possibility of similar effects by combination of water, metals, wool,
glass scientifically arranged?—The Surgeon ⟨(Stott)⟩ near Blooms-
bury Square, I forget his name, can vomit, freeze, blister, nay
send to sleep by local and quantitative application of common Electricity.

ὑπνος = ὑπο νοοϩοῦν—I incline to think the latin, animus,
nothing more than a pronunciation of the ~ by an m, a sort of
spelling mode of pronouncing νοος or νοῦς—rather than from ανε-
μος—and somnus to be *sub animus*, or sub nous—the m for b as
in summitto.

4625 29.35   First Chapter of Genesis. 1 V.—Is the created,
schuf, the same Hebrew word as that in the 7ᵗʰ verse?

2. Pott (D. J.) ⟨David Julius in letters to Herrn Bergrath von
Crell: Berlin und Stetin, bey Fr. Nicolai, 1799⟩ renders our
"void" by *ordnungslos*, & "without form" by schmucklos.

5. Are we quite sure, that is mere *senseless-popular*? If not, what
is the latent sense of God's *naming* the Light Day, and the Darkness
Night? Evidently, Light and Darkness are here used as the *Powers*
of Light & of Darkness—distinguished from the *Phænomena*, positive or negative, and truly therefore did call make Day the manifestation, id a quo noscitur, of *Light*—its natural *Name*.—Origin
of the Cabalistic Philosophy, and the Key of the Cypher of the
Cabala. Christ as the Logos is the *Verbum* Dei; as the fixed Word,
the verb in the form of the Substantive, he is *Nomen* Dei.

Hence the Evening in its process to the Morning makes the first
Day—the Evening (Light struggling with Darkness) not Night—
and hence the M. of the first day is the Evening of the 2ⁿᵈ/as still
preserved in the diurnal motion of the Planet.

6. 7. Pott translates "firmament" by Wolbung [Wölbung],

cope, vault. Q͟ꭚ—Here again the vaulted Sky is most evidently, even in our ordinary unphilosophic Physiology, the *Name*, diagnostic, of the *power*. And of what power?—Of that whatever it be which converts hydrogen + oxygen into ~~Azote~~ Nitrogen + Oxygen—that, which acting, Hydrogen becomes Nitrogen—and consequently keeps the water suspended above and divided from, in the only sense of division that can *really* obtain. Visible interspace is mere not-seeing—the negation of a faculty, not the position of a thing.

Horne's Comment. on the Psalms, Vol. I. p. 76. "Now the Hebrew word Chebel = 2 things a cord ~~&~~ or a band & a pang. Hence the 70 meeting with the word, Ps. 18. where it *certainly* signifies χινια, cords or bands, have yet rendered it ωδινας, pangs: & from their example here Sᵗ Luke hath used τας ωδινας θανατου, the πangs of Death, when both the addition of the word, λυσας *loosings* and κρατεισθαι *being holden fast* do shew, the sense is *bands* or *cords*". In the opinion therefore of this super orthodox divine, *f21* Inspiration did not preclude mistakes in the sense of texts & words—/

14. God said, let there be lights in vault of Heaven, to form the boundaries of Day & Night, and to point out the seasons, days & years—. The Sun well accounts for the Year, the Moon for the Months; but exclude the Mosaic Cosmogony, and that too in this sense in which I interpret it, and whence arise the week—the first order of the Egyptian Gods—whose name (the n. of the week) was Mendes—& Mendes, i.e. *Pan*, says Herodotus, excluded—they were seven.—Now without denying this, in a certain secondary sense, I hold the Παν = the Spirit of God on the face of the waters—which I make a *first day* or pre-annexed Vesper of creation—& so have *8*. These were the Cabiri—των οκτω των πρωτων λεγομενων θεων.—

In the 2ⁿᵈ Class (says C. F. Dornedden, Eich. Bibl. X. p. 360) there were, Hercules included (*mit Einschluss des H.*) Twelve Gods Ηρακλης ⟨Theuth⟩ των δευτερων, των δυωδεκα λεγομενων ειναι.— And in the third class were (mit Ausschluss allen übrigen) *all the others excluded*, Dionusos (Osiris). ~~Di~~ Διονυσος τε των τριτων. Now why this change from in- to ex-cluded?—Dornedden replies—because Osiris is the name of the Year. Still it is odd to say that of the gods of the third order or of the third Gods Bacchus is the only one./I should therefore translate the words—Διοννσος τε των τριτων, οι εκ των δυωδεκα θεων εγενοντο—as = But Dionysus is the common Name (Nomen, Νουμενον, Copula) of the tertiary Gods who arose out of the Twelve—. And after all it is quaint arithmetic to make 8 Gods out of 7 and their Sirname. There were 8 Brothers of the Coleridge Family. J~~oh~~nack, Jam~~e~~sim, ~~Harry~~, Bob, Bill, Tom, Ned and Dick—That's but 7—Aye—but Jack, Jim, Bob, Bill, Tom, Ned and Dick Coleridge—now there's *8*!!

f21ᵛ 4626 29.36   That Sᵗ John by αιμα και υδωρ meant no more or other than true real human Blood, globules + lymph, in contradiction to those fancies of an ειδωλον εμπνουν, σωμα πνευματικον, &c which in the next generation rose into Name and Sect as Gnosticism, is evident to me, both from the context, from Sᵗ Paul, Corinth.—on the Resurr.—& because all the early commentators so understood it—(the distinction between apparent & real death not thought of by any, friend or foe)—Marcion supported a fancy of this kind—Irenæus adver. Hær. IV. 57. p. 357. Ed. Grabe. Quomodo cum Caro non esset, sed cum pareret quasi homo, (homo putativus, hominis umbra) crucifixus est et e latere ejus puncto *sanguis exiit et aqua?* (not a word of coagulum or the water after death in pericardio!—Exactly so Tertullian, de Carne Christi. p. 358—Christi carnem quæstionibus distrahunt tanquam aut nullam omnino aut quoquo modo aliam præter humanam. Crucifixus, &c—resurrexit—sed hæc quomodo—si non vere habuit in se quod figeretur—Carnem scilicet sanguine suffusam, ossibus structam, nervis intextam, *venis implexam*—thus p. 366. Ipsum certe corpus nostrum—utriusque originem elementi confitetur—*carne, terram; sanguine, aquam*.—Still stronger perhaps, the apposite passages in Origen contra Celsum—Lib. II. ~~p.~~ T. I. p. 416 *ed. de la Rue*—
Φησιν ο κελσος· ~~p.~~ τι και ανασκολοπιζομενου του σωματος ποιος ιχωρ
    οιος περ τε ρεει μακαρεσσι θεοισιν;
εκεινος μεν ουν παιζει· ημεις δε απο των σπουδαιων ευαγγελιων, κ᾽ αν μη Κελσος βουληται, παραστησομεν οτι ιχωρ μεν ο μυθικος και Ομηρικος ουκ ερρευσεν αυτου απο του σωματος.—

4627 29.37   26 Decr. 1819.—To collate all the passages   *f22*
(vide Concordance) of the O. and N. T. in which Αγγελοι are
introduced?—Q^y *the Hebrew Word?*

4628 29.38   Q^y—How far the revival of Metals may be attributed to decomposition vegetable? Whether at all ~~ex~~ at all modified by the infinitesima of animal—medusae &c?—Iron by grav-
itating Chemistry in cold Peat Climates? The ductile, in hot
climates, by sublimation? See Bracconnot's experiments on the substances formed from Wood by sulphuric Acid—i.e. the elements
of Water & Sulphur, and Oxygen—.

4629 21½.94   We live in a busy Commonwealth, with the   *f47ᵛ*
forms, and by means of our various elective and municipal magistracies, our juries and our periodical Press with as large a portion
of the *Substance* of Freedom as hath ever been possessed by any
Country ⟨of⟩ equal population and with the same inequality of rank
and means of living. ~~It~~ As the ways of obtaining Wealth are more
in number & more various, than elsewhere, and these open to all
classes, except as far as they are blocked up or rendered difficult
by the success of prior Competitors acting as Capitalists; and as
Wealth, when obtained, ~~secures in a~~ raises & benefits the mere
possessor immediately, & in a far higher degree & ⟨in a far⟩ more
desirable kind than in Countries less free, and where ⟨Rank &
Influence and⟩ the privileges of Birth or of ~~Office~~ Court Favor; so
it is nature, that the desire of Wealth should be stronger and more
general. Another Consequence of such a state of things, is, that the
different ranks tread close on each other, and far more in dress,
manners, & other appearances than in their comparative Fortunes.
For many men ~~intellectual~~ popular Talents and Acquirements, especially from the frequency of public Meetings, and Associations
of all names and purposes, arising out of the confederative & vol-   *f48*
unteer Spirit characteristic of a State, the Citizens of which have
learnt & ~~been perm~~ are priveleged to exert, the powers of social
co-operation, fluency of Speech, are necessary, as means of acquiring a fortune; & Wealth is now so common, that of itself it does
not suffice for a distinction, and the wealthy are anxious to ~~display~~

acquire the same accomplishments in order to ~~obtain~~ display ~~the character of~~ Talent, as the former to display Talent in order to the acquirement of Wealth. Now tho' it is possible, that I dare not affirm, that ~~two or three men may please each the other by avowing & exulting in the principles of conscious and deliberate Selfishness common to all; and~~ that the feelings & sentiments ~~so admirably~~ represented ~~by Macklin in~~ by Sir Pertinax McSycophant ⟨in the incomparable⟩ Sketche~~s~~ of his past Life, given by him for the instruction and incitement of his Son, are ~~at least as~~ less common ~~as~~ now than in any former age/yet ~~it is not possible to~~ man cannot so far abjure his ~~better~~ nature, ~~but that~~ as not to be pleased by the ~~shew~~ of a noble principle, or at least of more generous impulses. It is, I own, to be feared, that Sir Pertinax McSycophant, Macklin's *Man of the World*, in the incomparable Portrait ~~of himself~~ which he draws of himself for the edification of his Son, is less singular in his maxims of conduct than in the ~~courage with which he~~ hardihood of ~~his~~ Conscience with which he reflects on

f48ᵛ   4630 21½.95   Excellent instance of the Abstraction, that results from attention converging to any one Object, is furnished by the oily Rags, broken Saucers, greasy Phials, dabs, crusts and smears of Paints in the Laboratory of a Rafael or a Claude Lorrain or a Van Huyssen—or any other great Master of the Beautiful and Becoming. In like manner the mud and clay in the modelling hand of a Cha~~u~~ntry, whose total Soul is awake, in his eye as a Subject, and before his eye as ~~the~~ some Ideal of Beauty *Objectively*. The various Objects of the Senses are as little the Objects of *his* Senses as the Ink, with which the Lear was written, existed in the Consciousness of ~~a~~ Shakspear.

4631 21½.96   The Humming Moth with its glimmer-mist of rapid unceasing Motion before, the Humble Bee within the flowery Bells, and Cups, and the Eagle *even* ⟨level⟩ with the clouds, himself a cloudy speck, surveys the Vale from Mount to Mount. From the Cataract flung on down in the Gale the broadest Fleeces of the Snowy Foam Light on the Bank. Flowers or the Water-lilies in the stiller Bay, below—

4632 21½.98   ~~In~~ Youth ~~we~~ beholds Happiness gleaming   *f50*
~~ever~~ in the ~~distant~~ prospect—~~in~~ Age ~~we~~ in the retrospect. It is the
happiness of Age to look back on the Happiness of Youth; and
instead of Hopes ⟨we⟩ seek our enjoyment in the recollections of
Hope.

In Youth, our Happiness is Hope: in Age, The Recollection of
the Hopes of Youth. What else can there be? for the substantial
Mind, for the I, what else can there be? Pleasure? Fruition? Filter
Hope and Memory from ~~it~~ ⟨Pleasure: & the more entire the Fruition, the more⟩ and it is the *Death* of the I—a neutral Product
results that ⟨may⟩ ~~exists~~ for another, ⟨but⟩ no longer for itself—a
Coke or a Slag. To make the Object one with us, we must become
one with the Object—ergo, *an* Object.—Ergo: the Object must be
itself a Subject—partially, a favorite dog—principally, a friend;
wholly, *God*—the *Friend*—God is Love—i.e. an Object that is
absolutely Subject—(God is a Spirit) but a Subject that for ever
condescends to become the *Object* for those that meet him subjectively—Eucharist—verily & truly present to the *Faithful*, Neither
Trans- nor Con- but Substantiation.

4633 21½.97   Increase of Number is increase of Value only   *f48ᵛ*
in relation to the Focus, and not to the ~~singular~~ Rays, singly. It is
Increase, or rather intensive Augment, of Worth, that alone raises   *f49*
the value alike for both, for the Convergents no less than for th~~ane~~
Concentrant.—The ~~usual~~ lofty Exposition of the Newtonian System, ~~provided us taught us the introduction to Guthrie's Grammar, and to~~ in all our popular Introductions to Astronomy, and
which usually forms the contents of the first Chapter in Books of
Geography, ⌈ . . . . . ⌉ failed to impress me with any correspondent feeling even when I was a Boy, and first read it in my Guthrie's
Grammar—But in later life the contemplation has ~~produced~~ rather
⟨had⟩ a depressing, ~~effect,~~ I might almost say, a revolting effect—
The very Nature of the process ⟨(and endless series of ~~ascending~~
comparisons⟩ ⟨a Ladder with ever increasing Interspaces between
the Rounds, & the least of these so great, that the Second Round
is already out of Sight⟩ seen obliterates the first *sensation* of the
positive Magnitude, of the Heavenly Bodies—for so we may call

the preliminary Comparison with our ordinary measures and their own *apparent* size.—and as the indefinite measure of more numbers The Earth we are taught to know think a mere Mote speck in Comparison with some other enormous body which actually is a mere Speck for our senses—a bellum internecinum commences between the Understanding & the Imagination, which soon terminates in the utter expulsion of the latter—& we proceed with

f49ᵛ ever increasing *Numbers*, [. . .] and never-altering Images, like Children repeating the storyies of a Giants—He was a mile high, says the first—O interrupts the other, but the Giant, that little Jack killed, was a hundred miles high—and in afterwards, when the Understanding has obtained its under unshared supremacy, what is the Abstract; but so many Circles Balls of lighter or heavier Metal spinning in round a Ball of Fire—which Ball with all its Tributaries spins round some larger—and so on ad infinitum—I said, that the effect, was I repeat, is not only depressive from its monotony but revolting from its want of analogy to what all our other experiences of the Nature, so simple in her ends but so infinitely various in the means by which she accomplishes them. It reminds me of the Homœomery of one of the elder Greek Physiologists, in which the Heart is made up of infinitely of little Hearts/—I have derived more pleasure by imagining that the Ellipse might be the Law only of the planetary Systems—that the Solar Movements may be parabolic—and the Nebulæa or System of Suns, might be in the Hyperbola—and into which the Great Fountain-World might pour itself forth on each side—& when I

f50ᵛ had proceeded so far, I found ⟨the next page but one⟩ that I was no longer contemplating a created Mass but a Creative Energy—& that all else is less than the Wish and Wax of the human Soul—which soon detects & turns away from the trick of putting passing off Bigness for Greatness—. Hence I find no satisfactory employment for our Eternity a post, in oute astral circumnavigation, or the Grand Tour of the Material Universe—Nor in truth in any supposed Ladder of Beings—Why, should the Earth contain a More worthless Chaos than Jupiter—or one Sun Sirius be a whole more Seraphic than our own Apollo. There The Inhabitants must be either Men or Beasts—. For we might as well attempt to conceive more than three Dimensions of Space as to imagine more than three kinds of living Existence, God, Man, and Beast—& even of these the last is obscure, & scarce endures a fixt contemplation without passing into an unripe or a degenerated species of Humanity.

4634 17.209   Brandes' Journ. of Science and the Arts.   *f128*

N.º XII. p. 223.—To Mirbel's disallowance of the possibility of equivocal generations—first, I suggest primitive or initial gener: as the juster epithet—then I remark, that to be or to have been ⟨vitally⟩ organized may be, and probably is, the same as to be or become generative, whether by projection (= egg, seminula &c) or by production (= propagula, ramenta &c)—but to be generative is not the same, necessarily, as to have been generated. Adam became a Father, without having been a Son.—The latter position may be true *in fact*; but there are strong, at least very plausible Objections to its reception into the same universality as the first, and objections drawn from apparent experiments, ~~whi~~ the error of which no more accurate Experience has hitherto detected. The locality of Plants and the Insects thereon, the groups or rather series of undeveloped germs in the Uredo (Veg.) and the Volvox (anim) strike me as favoring rather some deviation from the pantogamic hypothesis—i.e. the belief, that the last mentioned class of facts are so many proofs against primitive (= equivocal) Gen., rests in part on the ~~confusion~~ equivalence of the ~~former~~ latter position— (Adam was a ~~Father~~ Son) to the Former (Adam was a Father.)— Apply analogically what Brande himself has said of the Meteric Metals (as possibly *children* of the *Air*, &c, last §. p. 294. N.º X.) and Mirbel's own remarks on Linnæus's assertions/No Mushroom   *f128ᵛ* of an herbaceous green—nor gives out Oxygen under the Water— Some transpire Hydrogen Gas, others acid carbonic gas—Azotize products, obtained from them, Albumine, Oxmazone, Adipocire, a fatty matter, and Braconnot's Fungine.

Their forms resemblances & rude prophecies of human Artefacta—Globes, mitres, clubs, hats, bowls, powder puffs, ~~manes~~, carding instruments, Strips of Parchment—some *manes* (?) coral branches, scum on standing water, &c &c &c

Now the tuberous root of the Truffle that gives liberty to its seminules only by its own total dissolution—by what right are *these* called *seminules?*

So see p. 225. No. XII.—In whatever way we explain (the intestinal ~~plants~~ fungi, Genera Uredo, Oecidium, Puccinia, that grow no where but within the cellular texture of (other) plants,) *always keeping clear* of *fortuitous re-productions*—Now what is this but Theory tyrannizing over Theory—who contends for *fortuitous re-productions*—? ~~and~~ Not those at least who assert that the *possibility* of primitive Productions has not yet been disproved—that new races may spring up, and old races de novo, for aught that *f129* has been logically *proved* to the contrary! without denying the greater probability of the other hypothesis. Sæpissime is not = semper: nor *fere* ubique = ubique.

f164   4635 17.220   The progress of human Intellect from Earth to Heaven not a Jacob's Ladder but a Geometrical Stair-case with 5 or more Landing-Places—that on which we stand, enables us to see clearly & count all below us, while that or those above us are so transparent for our eyes, that they appear the Canopy of Heaven— we do not see them, & believe ourselves on the highest—

4636 17.221   I by itself + He, by meditation of the subject on itself *as Object*—therefore in the 3rd person/this done often by *f164^v* Pain, Sorrow &c—& enables ~~us~~ *man* to love his neighbour as himself—thus I + He = Ye, the Aspirate of the latter *me*lted away by the former—the former *tenuis, Iotism,* Ιψιλον—enriched by the latter—~~then~~ the H is Eeta. I + H = Ye—& *I* rises into *f165* *Eye*, in which the Sense is lost in the Sentita, or Sensa—*I + He* = *Ye*—all men become *Ye* to me, I composing part of them & they part of me—/. This is the moral *Eye.*—The He or Er of the German, as the ος & ως, ωτος, of the Greeks, = the Ear—Thou from the Mouth or moving Lips—/thouth— ➤—the first Θ changed into M.—

f148^v   4637 29.184   With Solon (rifattore di Omero) & Thales began the intellect of Greece as a nation, the War of Greeks against the combined might of Persia strengthened & invigorated the nation intellectually as well as politically the 7 and 20 years Peloponnesian war of Greeks against Greeks wore out both—and with Demosthenes who survived the conqueror in the arch-contest for Liberty, died the last Writer who acted as an elementary *power* on his Countrymen & thro' these the world. A polished, intelligent, tasteful people the Greeks continued to be to the very last—and under the Ptolemies in Egypt a were a more learned and scientific race than perhaps in the fairest days of their freedom—but as a *nation* they ceased to act—and it is only in a nation, a state, that poetry, the fine arts, true eloquence, genuine History, ~~& even general~~ can arise. (Science a hardy Pine-tree—vide Steff./They left in their stead a Greek-Asiatic Philosophy important in its influence on the Jews at one pole and on the Romans at the other—

The Greeks before Solon differed no otherwise from their Brethren of the North than in the early formation of their sweet language, which is attributive to three causes—all arising out of their situation—1. The modification & enriching of the same by the Phœnicians, and the attainment of an Alphabet—~~their~~ nearness of ~~var~~ states ~~always~~ to each other, & War under [?their] earlier king's republican whence oratory (= Chili)—and of the effects of genial climate on the organs of Speech—the chi, & the theta Gothic—the digamma found in all rude nations, the unpronouncable gnang of the Hebrews—the rude Traditions, Songs of War, Love, and Devotion—Homer before Solon = Nibelungen—

4638 29.3   J. Gooden, Esqre   *f1^v*
                46.Wooburn Place
          (between Russel Square & Tavistock S^t)

4639 29.39   Warmth midway upward to its appearance as   *f22*
Light)(W. m. downward from L. towards Grav.—The difference qualitative: & this one of many instances of the actual and not only realizable but real distinct existence of the Dimension Zenith and Nadir, as well as Arctic and Antarctic; ~~and~~ the hemispherical surface-dimension. Orient and Occident interchanging at their maxima, center & circumference, in the horizontal Circle; and Nucleus and Rind in the Globe. Nay, even these would be defective, unless we add a nobler and a meaner, = higher and lower

in Dignity where Extension becomes evanescent & the Power & Product being identical can be contemplated only as Intensity. This *diversely* higher is always a double Copula, the Unity reflected in the Totality of the meaner Order, and the mediative evanescent or subinfime Link of the nobler—. Thus Animal Life (Life proper: for the term is misapplied i.e. misappropriated to Vegetables, a misnomer for self-*growth*. I doubt even the legitimacy of the Life of Nature, or Life universal,—as confounding Life with the essential Will in its awakening, = Tendency, Trieb.—

W. anterior to L. = Vegetable—. W. post. L = Animal—. Relative Indifference (as Water) ≠ Absolute Indifference, as Latent Heat. the identification of + and − Elect. as Temperature— is the relative Indiff. Q? Is ⟨not⟩ abs. ind. a superfluous Term? Would not the Subject at all times sufficiently determine whether the Identity spoken of was specific, or absolute & supreme.— Surely it would: for we need only know whether we are speaking of God or ⟨of⟩ the Creation. N.B. *Is there any discoverable Relation of Latent Heat & Capacity of Heat to Specific Gravity?* Self-organization, veg. = Diurnal motion—the variety of the former in contrast with the simplicity of the Latter the result of the variety of relations which an ~~fra~~ infinitesimal fraction of ① has compared with the simplicity of the relations of ① itself.—Co-organization = disturbance & balance by cycles of time in the Planets = not in Veg. *Tendency to be in a Higher Orbit.* Subordination of organs.—Animal life a step higher than Solarity—this in Life as linking Sentiency &c.—Ergo, the Worlds *not* animantia as Giord. Bruno holds them.—Q? Zamboni's columns proofs or not of Galvanism from two heterogene surfaces—and therefore of its reducibility to mere Electricity?—Or does Galvanism at present include two powers that will hereafter be known by proper names?—If all that is now called G. can be reduced to two surfaces then we may confidently look out for some higher power, in which 3 Heterogenes are of necessity in act.—Of great interest is the double Heart, or the two chambers, in the warm-blooded animals; & the one Ch. in the cold-blooded—compare too the many vegetable analogies in the latter. Experiments on the comparative Temperatures of Veget. and cold-blooded animals very desirable.

f22ᵛ

4640 29.40   ? Multeity—planetary plurality—diurnal Revolution—Tell us, O Earth!—Mars, Jove, Saturn, must there not
have been, nay is there not implied in the existing equilibrium a
prior oscillation, a varying of distances, sufficient at least to account for such an influence of the several masses on each other (the
material ⟨Lux⟩ *lucifutura*, as Caloric [1]) as to make each, our Earth
perhaps chiefly, from its apparent middle rank a focus of the *proper
radiant* heat. May not the *radiant* Heat of the present Epoch as
distinguished from the dilative *conductible*, have light thrown on it
from this view?—. Would not such an hypothesis correspond happily with the facts of or huge strata of vegetable Origin, with equal
strata of mere mineral strata action intervening, to explain which
enormous *Years* & Seasons (Age-long Winters & Age-long Sum-
mers) have been imagined by Steffens—which still accounts not
for the want of regularity—Now on my plan this regularity was
not to be expected—. Then at the maturity of the vegetal act,
establishing a relation between each Planet, as Lifeght germinal &
central, & the Soil, Air &c as Universal, the distances of the
Planets might be fixed, & while the Vegetal Life arose by the
introsusception of Light [1] (= Calor lucifuturus), by the rejection
of the same & consequent projection by the remaining Mass
(which *because* it had not taken with it the antagonist of the Self-
principle, or Centripetalism, must of necessity appear a vastly
greater *Mass*—i.e. incomparably more *Time* in the same space) a
focus must take place (the Ellipse having been previously shown
to be necessary) & that Focus the Sun—. Instead of deriving the   *f23*
Planets & their distances &c from the Sun with all former Theorists I take the contrary—Eschenmayer's fanciful derivation of the
Sun from an accidental focus of the Ether ⟨from the Natur-cen-
trum⟩ refracted into Solar Light by the nebulous systems would
(besides its fantastic wanton arbitrariness) not account for the *Body*
of the Sun—or rather precludes it. Mine has yet *possibilities* for
this—which may serve as guides for further *discovery*—Maxima
interchanges—the extreme of Light (relatively) must find a pole in
itself—& it must have an attractive power—how many small bodies may have been, must have been, attracted to the ⟨Positive⟩
Focus of the Ellipse—nay, the *Matter* of Light is not unigrade—

the lower grades—tho' light relatively to the Mass projecting it, must become Mass when all the contributions were aggregated— Even now the Solar Beams are not homogenous—. If there be aught of import in the anticipations of Titius & Schubart, they would follow as naturally from my view, which regards the Sun as posterior to the Planets, as from their's who suppose the Sun planetific.

The geological facts correspond with this theory—the vegetable remains, chiefly found in the Regions toward the pole, & in the northern extremity of the temperate Zone, are 1. few in *kind*— palm-tribe & fern, that are now the indigenæ of tropical and juxta-tropical Climates—2. La place having determined that the obli-quity of the Poles is cyclical & can never exceed a degree & a half, it remains only that either these Vegetables were anterior to the Solar System in its present adjustment, or that there was a warmth not so immediately dependent on ~~the~~ the position of the soil relatively to the Polar light—Schubart ingeniously proposes an atmosphere more banded with vapor—. Neither is the "or" here of necessity disjunctive—Both, & even Schubart's supposition, are included or inclusible in mine,—For a vaporous atmosphere would be the natural form of the presence of a Warmth ascending toward the nature of Light—not to mention the obvious predominance of a dilative ad extra Power in vegetable growth, and that Warmth is to Light as Hydrogen to Oxygen—.—but in this chemical qual-itative Warmth we should have $\frac{\text{Dilative}}{\text{Contractive,}}$ in the Solar Heat & in Animal growth $\frac{\text{Contractive}}{\text{Dilative}}$.— ⟨Qy Whether the air itself anter. to Sol. Light and not more Hydr. than Azote.⟩

f23ᵛ   At this point likewise the Earth's specific Magnetism, as well as the universal, must be taken into consideration; and here too it is all so far a thing of promise, that the Vegetable Creation is clearly the passage from Magnetism to Electricity—~~as the Animal is the~~. Of course, a potenziated Magnetism as Reproduction—even as Animals are a potenziated Galvanism (M + El.) while the Insect World with their Spiracula are Electr.—substantiation of surface power.—Now as both Extremes must exist before the reconciling Mean—ergo, Moses places the insect world as the last of the mere animal—Man's penultimate. (Is it wholly fanciful that this detects

a ⟨particular⟩ relation of the Insect world to Man, the link &
commencement of a higher Order—& that even this must not [be]
overlooked in the contemplation of the marvellous arts & sciences
of Insects, which in so very many instances are anticipations &
Alphabetic Elements, of Human Inventions?—Or shall we dare
suggest, that it was not by mere accident that Moses in one verse
interposes and in the next *post*poses, the Insect Creation: as if the
certain tribes were created first, others last, & others in all the
different Lines of Interval.—

In Magnetism not to overlook the law of Tripolarity discovered
and confirmed by Brugmann, Hamberger, and Van Schwinden—

$$+m \; \frac{o \qquad -m \qquad y}{\mathrm{I} \qquad\qquad \mathrm{I}} \; +m$$

As in Electricity the One is in two, so here the two are in one,—.
It is a sort of magnetized Electricity.—The operation of this potenziated Potence, which we may regard either as Electricity recalled into Magnetism, or Magnetism impregnated by Electricity,
as the lower by the higher—a shadow too of Consciousness, as
contrasted with unconscious Causality—namely, what A has produced by projection, it strives to produce *in* itself & by retention—
this operation, I say, we may expect to find in the *Planets* versus
the *Planets*, distinct from Plan. vers. Sol.—

4641 29.41   Jahrb. d. Med. (ed. by A. F. Marcus and   *f24*
F.W.J. Schelling) Vol. I. p. 51.—Marcus asserts that the (so
called) external Nature produces in Animal Life only the disease,
under which itself at that time is laboring: or rather that the same
cause produces both, both considered as one Organismus; tho' with
the action and re-action, found in all causation realized—the body
sometimes diseasing the Atmosphere, the Atm. sometimes the
body—. The atmosphere has *contagious* Fevers &c—

Were this true, thus nakedly taken, all organized individua in
the same district would have be diseased at the same time—nay,
no part of the Atmosphere could be disturbed without more or less
disease of the whole—. Yet (with great modifications indeed) the
Notion might be adopted—Let the Atmosphere be taken, as an
organism indefinitely lower & more centerless ⟨than,⟩ yet analo-

gous to, that of the Jelly-fish, Polyps', and the class of divisible zoophytes generally—and let every organized body be a room sui generis, excluding all but what it has modified in the act of admitting, & is capable of modifying when admitted. Thus we know, that an atmosphere may be so loaded with vapor or miasma, as to baffle the greatest precautions—. The most anxious attention to windows, doors, stoves, &c could not wholly prevent our late dear old King, who became immortal on Saturday night last, from suffering from the northern exposure of his apartments during the late severe & changeful weather. So with *Bodies*—the rooms & work-shops in which our Souls live.

Q?—It is evident that in the temperate Zone Spring & Autumn have more Fever, & inflammatory (so called) or typhus, than Summer or Winter—especially when the Summer is regular Heat & the Winter regular Frost.—But do not the diseases of Spring differ from those of Autumn, tho' of the same Order, correspondently to the differences between Cold followed by Heat, & Heat by Cold?—

f24ᵛ   4642 29.42   Michael Scott, the Person: Homo Agonistes, the Ens personans (seu personificatum) and the Title.

Homo Agonistes.—The advantage over Dʳ Faustus, 1. that the Scene may be laid in Cumberland, 2. Time that of Wickliff.—

Prelude—Interpretation of the Bible—The language of the Senses, first, the only possible vehicle of early instruction, and the facts that must be assumed in order to the language of Science which arises only out of the explanation of the order & series of these facts, relatively & comparatively so as that one should not contradict the other: secondly, as the proper language for that which is superscientific, namely, Morality (for only to the ~~Objects~~ Things without us as Objects of our senses does our practical duty extend). The Sun as rising or setting may determine my conduct, for my own Good & that of my neighbours; but as the center of the System it is a pure Object of my *speculations*. Likewise, of Religion no less. For religion contemplates the heavenly Bodies as God's Ministers to us as men—consequently, that which ~~acts on us~~ properly exists & acts *in* us as well as *on* us, viz. the Phænomena, are in this view our proper Sun, Moon, & heavenly Bodies— Rightly, therefore does Moses place the Moon, as next or rather as equal in dignity with the Sun, while the Stars are spoken of collectively as minor forms. For so to & for us they are.—Then the Parable of *the Garden*—to be fenced, from wild-beasts, &c & weeded, & the grain given—would you have Loaves ready made come down from Heaven?—Tend the *Corn* & the Vines—the Elm, their future Support, will grow of outself if only the *ass, the goat, the Hog* are kept out—

4643 29.43   Good Friday, March 1820.—Can not it be that so celebrated a passage as Peter's more sure word of Prophecy should have been hitherto universally mistranslated?—Yet so it appears to me—The words seem plainly to be—Therefore *we* have an additional confirmation of the prophetic Word—

4644 29.44
1.

Grammar and Logic mutually support each other. Grammar   *f*25
must have been learnt in order to the teaching of Logic; and Logic must have been taught in order that Grammar may be understood. The result from both, or the perfect knowlege of ~~the~~ Words and the positions and relations of Words as representing and corresponding to, the sensible Objects & the bodily, imaginative, moral and intellectual processes of Man whether active or passive, is Metaphysics, or Philosophy as far as it is Science.

2.

The first great Truth which all men hold implicitè and the knowlege of which it is the highest business of education to make *explicit*, ut sciamus nos scire—in other words, to lead the mind to reflect on its knowlege and by reflection to bring it forward into distinct consciousness—the first great Truth is—GOD. This unfolded (—or rendered *explicite*) amounts to—God is: and is self-existent and a pure Spirit.

3.

But a Spirit is, 1. a substance impassive, i.e. a substance having the nature and perfection of an Act, and, 2. an Act substantial, i.e. An Act having a ground in itself, and in itself a principle of permanence. It is therefore one and the same meaning, when we say in the words of Scripture, God is a Spirit, and when we say

f25ᵛ   with the School Divines, Deus est actus purissimus = God is a
most pure *Act*.

4.

Place these two ideas together, viz. Self-existent and Spirit or
the preclusion of all that is not Act, and there arises that unique
Idea, which can belong but to one Subject and can therefore be
elucidated by no ⌈ . . . ⌉ analogy, but which the Fathers, School-
divines, and both Greek and Hebrew Theologians have struggled
to express by the terms, αυτοπατηρ, αυτονιος, causa sui, &c; but
which the great Ineffable and Incomprehensible has himself as
most sublimely so most adequately, conveyed in the words—*I am,*
that I am, or to give the literal sense of the Hebrew words—I
shall be that which I will be—the Future here involving a fortiori
⟨both⟩ the Past and the Present, being used as the fittest symbol of
an Eternal Act, to God an all-comprehending Present, to every
finite Being a Future; in which nothing that is Past is wanting or
left behind. The whole Host of Heaven and Earth from the mote
in the Sun beam to the Archangel before the Throne of Glory owe
their existence to a Will not their own; but my own Will is the
Ground and the sufficient cause of my own existence—What I will
to be, I eternally am.—

5.

f26   Eternity is the ground and necessary Condition of Time, even
as the Space ⟨in the Hour-glass⟩ is presupposed in the succession
of the sands that fall thro' it—And no less is the Idea of Time
necessary in order to that of a series of Causes and Effects.

6.

Again: as this series is impossible without supposing some First
(and such as is First, Midst, and Last) in which Cause and Effect,
Antecedent and Consequent are co-inherent, some *One* who *is* in
that he affirmeth to be, and who affirmeth to be in that he is (which
is the predicate and definition of an *Absolute Will* or of God contemplated abstractly as the Absolute eternal *Source*): so Time must
in the first instance be brought into some relation to Eternity, in
order to render Time itself the subject of distinct Conception, and,
as such, of legitimate Reasoning.—

7.

Now whenever we apply the accidents of Time to an Eternal,
there necessarily arises—the semblance ~~either~~ of a contradiction,

or of an argumentum in circulo. In Nature this is perpetuated &
recognized as the Law of reciprocal Action, so that in every act of
bodies that which is taken as Cause in the first instance is by the
necessity of re-action declared to be in the same indivisible moment
Effect & vice versâ. But in the human mind, the succession of
whose thoughts constitutes *Time* for us, and of course therefore in
Grammar and in Logic we assume one circle, ⟨like the staple of a
Chain,⟩ as the only means of letting all other Links follow each
other in one Line of Dependency, so that A B having been assumed   *f26ᵛ*
= B A, thenceforward D shall be the effect of C but the cause of
E, E the effect of D but the cause of F; and so on. In other words,
we must ~~assume~~ yield to one argument in a circle as the only way
of precluding it ever afterward and in every other case.

8.

In Grammar the Nomen, or Substantive, corresponds to the
Subject, Object, or Thing in Logic; and the Verb to the *Act* of the
Logicians. (N.B. This comprehends not only the Act of Acting
(= Verb Active) but the act implied in † suffering (= Verb Passive.)—The *Identity* of the Noun and Verb, viz. that which is both
in one not by *synthesis*, whether it be mere juxta-position or mechanical union; or uniform solution of A in B. as salt in water; or
a tertium aliquid engendered by the introsusception of A in B, i.e.
proper chemical combination, as Carbonate of Lime, from Lime
+ Carbonic acid—neither of these forms of Synthesis are = Identity, which means One containing the power of *two* as their radical
antecedent, or as ~~the~~ a point *producing* itself into a bi-polar Line but
contemplated as anterior to this production, and *containing* the two
Poles or Opposites in unevolved cöinherence.—I have adopted the
term, *Identity*; but the term *Prothesis*, would not be amiss—in the
distinction of the first four Parts of Language it would be perhaps
preferable;

	1 Prothesis	
2 Thesis		3 Antithesis
	4 Synthesis	

†This may be illustrated to you by contrasting a blow received by   *f26ᵛ*
a man or animal with the *same* force falling on a body insentient
and (*per hypothesin imaginariam argumenti causâ*) perfectly inelastic.
In the former the suffering implies an act by which it chooses
&c—

*f*27　　but Identity contrasts better with INDIFFERENCE.—Be the thing,
however, called Identity or Prothesis, this Co-inherence of Act and
Being is the I AM IN THAT I WILL TO BE, of Moses, the Absolute
I AM, and its grammatical correspondent is the VERB SUBSTAN-
TIVE.

9.

Hence in all Languages there are Five essential Forms of Speech,
1. Verb Substantive, 2. Substantive (= Noun) 3. Verb. 4. Participle. 5. Infinitive Mood—and the two Modifications, viz. of the
Noun by the Verb, & vice versâ of the Verb by the Noun. In all
then we may count them as *Seven*. More really distinct parts of
Speech no language can have—and perhaps we might voyage to
the savages of New Holland before we could find one that had
less.—These seven are tabled overleaf.

　　P.S. Interjections are mere explosions of *voice*—express sensations rather than thoughts—& are common to man & beast. Articles ~~in Conjunction~~ are Adjectives (*Adnomen*): while Conjunctions
and Prepositions are one or other of the 7—and become such
whenever a word has lost its *particular* meaning in the general
position, which it is used to express—even as we use a *yard* as a
measure, indifferent whether it be *mahogany* or *oak*.—Observe I
confine myself to parts of Speech existing as distinct words. Otherwise I should have added as an 8th, *syllables* of *position* ⟨in Space
& Time⟩ latent in Cases, Tenses, Augments &c.

*f*27*ᵛ*
　　　　　　　　　⟨N.B. For the explanation of the
　　　　　　　　　Terms, Prothesis, Thesis, &c,
　　　　　　　　　turn back to p. 5. at this end of
　　　　　　　　　the Book.—⟩
　　　　　　　　　　　　Identity
　　　　　　　　1.　　　or
　　　　　　　　　　　　Prothesis
　　　　　　　　1.　Verb Substantive

2. Thesis	3. Antithesis
2. Noun	3. Verb
4. Modification of Thesis	5. Modif. of Antithesis
by Antithesis	by Thesis
4. Adnoun or Adjective	5 Adverb

6. Synthesis

6. Participle

7. Indifference or that which may be ~~both~~ either, namely, Noun or Verb; but not both in the same relation.

7. Infinitive Mood

"For not *to dip* the Hero in the Lake   *f28*
Could save the Son of Thetis from *to die*"—

Here "to dip" is both a Noun, the Nominative Case to the verb "could save", and a verb governing "the Hero" as its Accusative; but it is Noun in one relation & verb in another. Tho' this form is ~~not~~ less frequent in our Language, in the Greek and Italian the *Indifferency* of the Infinitive Mood is of constant recurrence.—

10.

The most orderly way of arranging them would perhaps be— 1 Verb Substantive. 2. Noun. 3 Verb. 4. Participle. 5. Infinitive Mood. 6. Adnoun. 7 Adverb.—(Conjunctions & Prepositions being some one or other of these, in while ⟨*which?⟩ the expression of some relation in time or space is attended to, ~~so as to~~ abstracted from the original or concrete meaning of the particular word. "I saw Lælius striving to enter the House & Caius *withstanding* him. Here we have a participle.—Caius stood in the way; ~~but~~ I got in, not*with*standing. ~~Here~~ Or *yet* I got in. Here it answers to a conjunction.—Yet I passed, notwithstanding his resistance. Here it is a preposition.—

4645 28.4   Coleridgii Fides et Doctrina de Deo, Mundo, et   *f2ᵛ*
Homine. Theosophy, Cosmogony, Zöonomy and Anthropology.   *f3*
⟨Fides Coleridgiana: or the⟩ System of Philosophy and philosophic   *f2ᵛ*
Science taught in a series of Conversations during the years 1817-1820.

In the two red books elder than this and both like this bought at Mʳ Bage's, but more particularly in the Junior and thinner of the two, I have flitted on, transcribing, criticizing, suggesting, side by side with Chemistry and her present Hierophants, Sir H. Davy, Dʳ Thomson and Mʳ Brande, ⟨above all, with Hatchett,⟩ thro' the Life of Nature in the organismus of our Planet to her potenziation by the ~~thre~~ co-presence of *insulated* Life, both σζ

f3   ⁀ and σζ. . . . / and concluded with the Teeth and Bones. Now
I recommence with Life (a. and o.) queening it in her own right,
and *using* Chemistry, as one of her Hand maids, but Chemistry
penetrated by her influence, transfigured and become vital. As I
confine myself, however, to the actions and products, that have
been watched, imitated, analysed by the Chemists and Galvanists
of the existing Scottish and Anglo-gallican or Gallo-anglican
School, the Subject will occupy but a small number of pages—and
then turning round vault back again to the Life and Exploits of
Nature, geologically considered—wholly in order to collect the
facts that have been observed and recorded by our Geologists and
Mineralogists of best repute.

f3ᵛ   4646 28.5   CHYME. Saliva—chemical analysis of in the preceding P. B. (which I shall henceforward mark in any refer-ence,
I may have occasion to make, Π_2 and the other Π_1.) The food
comminuted and mixed with Saliva in and by the act of mastica-
tion, and propelled thro' the gula into the stomach and undergoing
the solvent and other unknown actions of the various secretions,
that form the gastric juice, becomes after a few hours *Chyme*, an
apparently homogeneous ⟨pulpy⟩ mass which passing onward into
the ~~bow~~ small intestines blends with bile, and separating into two
portions, the one passing down-ward to the larger intestines (see
Sir E. Home's Lectures, in ~~how~~ what various ways and have
adapted to the abundance or scarcity of local productions of food
the ~~latter~~ food is changed and in the latter case (as in the ostrich
f4   of the Desart as ✕ to that of Java, becomes literally alter'd—as
⟨observed to me by⟩ a philosophic friend, who is characteristically
quick and delicate in perception of tho⟨se⟩ accidental (but which
he will by no means allow to be ~~more~~ wholly accidental) coincidences of the sound, and the sense in words which furnish the
materièl and occasion for the paronomastic art—yea, and so that
he addeth to the Orphic epithetical Polyonomy of the Natura Naturans the title of ~~Punstress diapanta~~ the Diva Diapanta Punifica,
or the divine All-punstress, and deemeth the Natura Naturata one
great complex *Pun*, ⟨or⟩ Pun of Puns! ~~vere rebus in rebus~~ the
other, white as milk, is the CHYLE.

        CHYLE—absorbed by the Lacteals, and by them conveyed to

their common Trunk, the Thoracic Duct—therese mixed with var-
iable proportions of Lymph (v $\underset{2}{\text{II}}$) is poured into the veins.—Chyle
is an *opaque white Fluid* of a *sweetish saline* taste (Q.ʸ the double   *f4ᵛ*
taste mixed not united a character of incompletion and a preparatory state) ⊘ less than Blood—exhibits slight traces of alkaline
power when tested with infusion of violets—soon after removal
from the thoracic duct, ⟨spontaneously⟩ gelatinizes and ⟨then like
the Blood⟩ coagulates spontaneously, gradually separating into a
firm *yellowish* white curd and a transparent colourless Serum—the
coagulum closely resembling the caseous portion of milk, therefore
= a variety of albumen: of which the Serum when heated gives a
few flakes and by evaporation a small portion of an = sugar of
milk. (See Hatchett's admirable communication in Sir E. Home's
Paper in Phil. Trans.) Small portions likewise of ∩ ate of Lime,
/ ate of Soda and common salt may be detected in the chyle—but
whether from gramini- or carni-vorous animals no distinctive difference—the n˙∵. an abundant ultimate principle in both alike.—   *f5*
    Remarks. This is the sum of Brande's statement but it is defec-
tive, ~~in not~~ at least deficient (which of the two I must examine
Bichat & Blumenbach to discover) in not marking the properties
common to Chyle with Chyme/ex. gr. whether the nitrogen ⟨al-
ready⟩ abounds in the latter, or if found at all is found in the
Chyme in a determinably less quantity—& whether in the chyme
of graminiv. animals?) and of course those which it has acquired
by its change into Chyle. 2. It is asserted that to become chyle it
must be blended with the *Bile*, which (it is *supposed*) contributes
its aqueous and perhaps alkaline parts, reserving its albumino-re-
sinous matter for the future excrement or the excrementitious portion—But as these former are not peculiar to Bile—the water certainly not, and the alkali is proposed with a *perhaps*—no *proof* is   *f5ᵛ*
afforded—and the emaciation consequent on the absence or deficiency of Bile may be more naturally and analogically be attributed
to the sympathy of the different parts and functions implied in a
living and interorganized Systema, as the condition of its Unity:
while the disorder of the Bowels from the morbid secretion of Bile
supplies a presumption against its commixture with the chyme.
Indeed, the very stuff, it is alone supposed to contribute, aqueous
and a minute portion of its alkali *perhaps*, are almost = 0, and

might be supplied nearer at hand even if they were not already existing in the food, or supplied first by the Saliva & then by the Gastric juices. These juices are, I doubt not, different in different animals according to the kind of their food, and perhaps different *f6* at different times in omnivorous animals such as man; but that in birds of prey (and presumptively therefore in other carnivori proportionally to the resemblance of their appointed *game*) ⌈ . . . ⌉ the gastric juice is of the nature of an Alcali may be conjectured from the indistinguishable Likeness of the Mice which had fallen into a bason of caustic Alkali at the Royal Institution with the Nostoc or tremulous transparent Jelly vomited by Hawks, Kites and Owls, ~~one~~ ⟨in⟩ one Mass of which that fell swop on my Hat at the foot of Bowscale, behind Skiddaw—& which seen falling by the Light of a crescent moon, immediately after a f shooting Star had been noticed, ~~wou~~ might naturally be referred to the latter (vide the exquisitely ludicrous explanation of the word, Nostoc, in old Bailey's Dictionary—and in another large mass which fell, *f6ᵛ* during another walk, behind Saddleback on Blenkarthur I found the ear of a Mouse, and frequently have found parts of the Legs of Frogs.

The n⁻⁻. in the chyle of the graminiv. has extorted a question from Mʳ B. which joined with his poetic admission, ~~in~~ that
                    "those meteoric Bodies
Brande,   That thus salute the Earth with stony Showers,
p. 293   May be the children of the Air, created
               By union of the simpler forms of matter"
(printed as and meant for *Prose!*) promises or threatens a presensation of the dynamic View of Nature, substantially the same with ⟨"hypotheses of so chimerical a cast,⟩ ~~short~~ (i.e. Steffens, Schelling's, Oken's and the Natur-philosophic generally) ~~which man~~ "as rather to resemble "Eastern Allegor~~y~~⟨ies⟩["] than European Philosophy, and therefore defy all criticism"—Brande, p. 480. Recoil, and retreat in good time Man of Fashion—. O Endive and Cellery of *European* and R. I. Philosophy—a single inlet of Light would disblanch your snowy Beauty and unfit you for the palates *f7* of Lords and learned Ladies—. Right about to the Left and advance backward!—

But it is unfortunate for the sober *Philosophers* (~~i.e.~~ n. bene. to philosophize in the modern sense is "to cook what cannot be eaten"—but like a cucumber, must be divided, combined, looked at, smelt to, weighed, recorded—& then thrown out of window!— Assuredly as much intellect and as various knowledge is requisite for a first rate French Cook as for a Chemist on the plan of *Facts and nothing but Facts!*) it is unlucky, I say, that they have lately excluded all absorption of Air (even of $.\overset{x}{.}.$, much more of $n\overset{\cdot\cdot\cdot}{}$. ~~by~~ in the Lungs—. So that while Mr Ellis bars up one door (the pulmonary) and derives all the constituents of the plant from the Soil, Messrs. Brande and Brodie ~~double lock~~ stultify the other inlet of conjecture. For here no $n\overset{\cdot\cdot\cdot}{}$. exists—ergo, none ~~could~~an enter—and yet there the mysterious Element *is*—and as   *f7^v* substantially as where the Gula was regularly and cordially opened for his reception, viz. in the *carnivori*.—But a third suspicious symptom of a reluctant approximation to the "Eastern Allegory" or Dynamic Scheme, occurs in the next article on

Respiration, and threatens two *Things* in this *Rebus* of the *thing-ical* (= corpuscular) Psilosophy! The ~~mu~~ veins are ramified in the Lungs into vessels of such thinness as to permit the *action* of the Air on the blood, exciting it to excrete its carbon, while the vessels in their turn, we must suppose, excite the air to decompose itself, and then excite the Oxygen, so separated from the Nitrogen, to combine with the excreted carbon in the formation of carbonic acid   *f8* Gas, at a temperature below a 100 F.— The *thinness!* what is that to the purpose? Are or are not the Coats of these minute vessels air-tight *both* ways? or so valved in their pores or otherwise con-structed as to let in what it cannot let out, i.e. to *keep in* what yet it lets in?—or lastly, if these are too improbable & too unsupported by induction or analogy to be asserted, must we say that the Air communicates a chemical power by vibration, as in Sound, or by electric tremor? Something like this seems to lurk in the dynamic phrase "*action* of the air." And if so, what becomes of the whole system of Pores, and of ~~thaeir~~t marvellous Progression, at once the supporting and the stumbling Block, ~~the muffler and the mystery~~ of the atomic Newtonian Theory, the *Muffler* of its Miracles, itself the greatest of all, staring down Objection "in the Lion's skin of mathematical calculation! Why, our eyes and microscopes may   *f8^v* have told the truth, and plate Glass transmit the *tone* of Light without pores?—/It would not be utterly impossible, even that the few drops on the Florentine Globe of Gold might be accounted for, without ⟨porous⟩ pertrusion, by an act of the metal in the air?—

And again the ubiquitarian *Thing*, that *fills up* all the *Pores* and thus determines the expansion of all Bodies and their specific gravities, doubtless with an infinity of Porelets itself which ~~is~~ *sometimes* are strait & thus Thoroughfares for the yet smaller particles of Light, &c &c—for an atom is a Pig with a buttered Tail, the instant you catch it, you lose it/even the Caloric is in Jeopardy. For while an artificial respiration can be kept up (and in some

f9 animals this may be effected for hours after their decapitation) the venous blood undergoes its due changes, and decarbonates, but ~~the~~ no Caloric is supplied—the body gradually and rapidly sinks down to the surrounding temperature. Ergo, the Caloric is given by the *action* of the nerves! But what we have not, we cannot give. If it be a *thing*, where did the nerves get it? All outlets are closed! But if to *excite* be to give, then again we fall back to an *action*, as before, in the nerves—and a *mode* of existing, or correspondent action in the blood and Muscles!—and we have the specific *Tone* of Heat instead of the *Somebody*, Caloric by name—and so with the matter of Gravitation, that other Somebody, hight Newtonian Ether—and so good bye to the only sane, ⟨sound,⟩ sensible, ~~and~~

f9ᵛ solid *European* Philosophy, which, as suits an Age of *Amusement* and accords with the genius of its Birth place (*Abdera*, a *European* City in *Crim. Tartary* or thereabouts) is *au désespoir* and good for nothing *sine Rebus in Rebus*—⟨i.e. a succession of Rebuses! and Riddles—⟩ What would the Lady Chem'stresses, the fair auditory of the Royal Institution, do without *Things* in *Things*? Why, nothing could come of it. ~~A~~ Much better, disguise Defeat in Devotion, and admit that these *things* "remain among the mysteries of Nature, which, doubtless for the wisest purposes, are hidden from our view." Sham, Flam, and Saintship, Humbug and holy-cant, rather than plead guilty of the horrid Heresy of Zoodynamism, and the *Life* of Nature.

f10   4647 28.6   Davy, Brande, &c. cannot die "that vital Powers exist, not less manifest than physical". Nay, whenever the ex-

planation of the former by the latter is in question, they favor the
attempt and cordially announce every semblance of success as a new
triumph of Science. Where then is even the discordance with their
own position in supposing that the latter may be not so completely
heterogeneous from the former, as the vulgar System assumes?
"Aye! But tho' we would make the vital physical, we do not want
to make the physical vital." But does not this amount to the denial
of any *Life*? Or is it a quarrel about a name, a word? Call them
physical, if you will—all we require is, that they act in a lower
power analogously to those hitherto called vital in a higher state.
Now this is the mere converse of your own position. A. The pow-   *f10ᵛ*
ers, called vital, are but higher states of the ~~same~~ powers called
physical. The kind is the same, the degree alone different. B. The
Powers, called physical, are but lower states of the Powers, called
vital. The kind &c.

Besides, where would be the extravagance, wherein do they detect anything lawless, if we had of two possible hypotheses chosen
one when they had preferred the other? Here in both cases the
ground of the Foundation is likewise the quarry from whence both
the materials and the cement of the Superstructure must be sup-
plyied. Let us then see which will build the ~~building~~ mo~~s~~tre consistent ~~in itself~~ ⟨edifice the more durable in itself⟩ and on the more   *f11*
abiding foundation. To the result we appeal. What and who else
shall judge us? It may be long before the final sentence can be
pronounced. What then! Employ yourself with hand and heart in
~~the~~ realizing the Plan of your own election—and Industry ~~will~~ may
shorten the period, whi~~eh~~le Quarreling, and Scoffing will only
interrupt the Laborers on ~~the~~ both sides.—Remember,

~~Intr~~ Iliacos intra muros peccatur et extra.
Can even the "Eastern Allegorists" afford a more palpable extravagance than Mʳ Brande's assertion, that since the confirmation of
Hutton's Theory by Davy's discovery of the Nature of the Earths
(which by the bye belongs jure philosophico to that Heresiarch
~~among~~ and Eastern Allegorist, H. Steffens) no other Agents are
required to explain the whole surface of the Earth with all the   *f11ᵛ*
various [?suites] of their formation, but Fire and Water—senseless
as a Truism, mad if it be meant for more.—

Qʸ The huge Boulder Stones ⟨of Granite⟩ descrᵈ by Saussure,

one resting on a pillar of Lime Stone, another in a glen surrounded by Lime Stone mountains—might we not suppose a ⌈ . . . ⌉ reduction to Granite ⟨and *then* &c.⟩ just as if a metallic Mass ⟨⟨(which had been reduced ages before perhaps)⟩⟩ had been left bare by the wearing away of the more perishable circum et superincumbents. The ? is not—is it probable? But is it less or not more probable *f12* than the Deluge, and Debacle System, to which the *small* number, relatively to the asserted origin, and the want of granite rubble ~~near~~ scattered about the Boulder is a most serious objection—were there no other.

4648 28.7   The proper objects of knowlege and which may be regarded as the Poles of true Learning, are Nature and History—or Necessity and Freedom. And these attain their highest ~~form~~ perfection, when each reveals the essential character of the other in itself and without loss of its own distinctive form. Thus *f12ᵛ* Nature attains its highest significancy when she appears to us as an inner power (= vis ab intra) that coerces and subordinates to itself the outward—the conquest of Essence over Form—when by Life + ⟨superinduced⟩ Finality she reveals herself as a plastic Will, acting in time and of course ‡ finitely. . Here there is Process and Succession, in each Plant and Animal as an Individual, and in the whole Planet as at once a System and a Unit—and the Knowlege of Nature becomes Natural History. History e contra has ~~its~~ her consummation, when she reveals herself to us in the form of a necessity of Nature—when ⟨she appears⟩ as a power ab extra ~~she~~ that coerces and takes up into ~~her~~ itself the inner power—the conquest of ~~ordinant~~ Form over ~~the acting~~ Essence, when the Essence *f13* is rendered instrumental, = *materia*, and the Form ordinant.— But here is *Law*, and the *Ever-present* in the moving Past, the Eternal as the Power of the Temporal—and the Historic Science becomes a higher Physiology, a transcendent Nature—appearing in the first ascension of History above the Horizon of Chronicle, as Destiny—in the Zenith, as Providence, and anterior to Chronicle itself, and in the rich purple of her Dawning, as Mythology, the interference of Gods and Goddesses.—

‡ This maintains the necessary distinctⁿ of N[ature]. from Deity, and consequently the reality of both. ~~Life~~ The Finality (or

establishment of one End) as *superinduced*—not inherent; and Life
— Finality is = a Wen ⚹ a man With a most mistaken zeal, et
impiâ pietate, has it been fashionable to speak of Nature as a mere $f13^v$
Paganism for God, at best a Synonime & useful as preventing a
too familiar use of th an aweful Name. But these good folks forget,
that in making Nature God they make God Nature, and fall into
all the chaos of Eastern Pantheism. If they include Man in Nature,
they annul all morality: if they exclude him, all science—and how
is the latter possible, if Nature be God? Nowo! God is neither but
the ineffable Presupponens (and in logical usage, the Presuppositum) of Both: the A and Ω, the Base and the Apex of the Isosceles
Triangle, Man and Nature being the sides. Take your stand at the
foot of the Throne of God—contemplate Nature from thence, as $f14$
she exsubists only in the being known—contemplate Knowlege,
and it exists only in Nature—in the one, as Idea, in the other, as
Law. Therefore these must be the two forms of the same Essence,
the the two opposites of the same Unity, essentially one, *form*ally
two: and Nature is known as knowing—self-knowning, self-
known. Nature seen as subsisting in ⌈ . . . ⌉ Knowlege is Idea:
Knowlege contemplated in Nature is Law.—But this applies *in
verity* only to Nature considered as an ⟨divine⟩ Ideal Integral and
Total—as Life compleatly subordinated to Finality—⟨Nature in
Apotheon⟩—the Beatification of a Nature that *has* been redeemed—
and the momentous Error of the best Schellingians consists in their
applying this to the process of Redempt[ion] nay, worse still, to $f14^v$
the *necessity* for the Redeeming Act, to the *Materia*—to the very
resistance to the redemptive Power, and with a so as to supersede
and nullify all Redemption when they ought rather to have en-
quired whether all the materia is redemptible.—The true Philosophy, therefore, treating of Nature historically and in fact contemplates it as subsisting *in Will*—an evil will and *potentially* only—
existing by a power not its own, and so far only existing in *mind*,
by communication of the πν Λ in the Πν—Law has here its proper
sense—i.e. not = God, but to the Power of God in Nature, with
which all Nature must comply, whether by obedience or by diso-
bedience. Hence *for us* and for Nature in its present state relatively $f15$
to *us*, it is not true that Nature has its *esse in percipi*—as I have
demonstrated in Π. This *is* not true where (wo) but *will* be true

when (wann) die Natur keinen Schatten ins Erkennen wirft, das Erkennen keine Gewalt über die Natur ausübt, wo beide völlig unzertrennbar *geworden sind.*

4649 28.8   Anticipation : Idea :: Theory : Law.
Genius : Anticipation :: Cleverness : Theory.
or *Antic.* : *The.* :: *G.* : *Cl.*—or As A to T, so G to C: ⟨or in a yet richer metre,
                    As A to THe, so G. to CL:
                    Pay the Post and go to Hell.⟩
PRACTICAL Anticip. + Theoresis = Idea. (the most likely way of begetting it, I mean.—Then, as by a sort of *Cohobation* in intellectual pharmacy, Theoresis + Idea = Law.

f15ᵛ **4650** 28.9   Qʸ The compleat detachment of σζ.... from the mass, may not this require a balancing Attraction, in order to constitute a *neutral* ground? The Bird shoots or soars itself upward: to the filmy Fly the Air is terra firma: the Height of the Camelo-pardalis follows the ~~upward~~ root-continuing Growth of the arbo-rescent Shrub: Man alone seems *drawn upward*, his Base narrower than his shoulders. He ~~too~~ *stoops* to *procure* (labor improbus)—but he *enjoys* with his face and eyes fronting his fellow man ~~(naturâ~~ ~~suâ~~ (*consociat* se dapibus)—haud minus, amplexus et oscula, vel stanti vel sedenti dare fas est, cum virgini desponsæ tum matri et
f16 sororibus, ita ut pietas ejus non sine amore sit; amores casti esse possint—.—In specie suâ conservandâ, fateor equidem, ⟨servus videtur;⟩ Naturæ et Telluris *Minister* fit; ~~tam~~ mancipium vero, suâ nisi ipsius injuriâ, non fit. Prosternit se ad naturam, facie humanâ humanam faciem occulente. Oculi desuper in terram defixi, at in Terram vultu futuræ Matris ⌐ . . . ⌐ interceptam, et præventam vultu ⟨isto⟩ amanter pudico ⟨versus⟩ cælum cælo vultûs maritalis propiore et domestico reflexum potius quam occlusum obtuente.—Homo in fine vere ANIMAL SOLARE EST.
                    With feet adhesive to the earth, we shun,
                    Headward we gravitate toward the Sun.

f16ᵛ **4651** 28.10   Conceive an inundation or *Overspread*. Still there is a stronger force, a current in the mid stream; with this it wears ~~en~~downward and makes itself a channel, with this it finally removes the opposing rock—when this is effected and the River moves in its own broad & deep Curve to the Ocean, who would ask, why does not the River make inundation and remove the rocks now?—Yet such is the question put to the Lucretians by the Miraculists, who unwisely attack those ships of the hostile fleet which are manned by their own sailors, factiously discharged. Why does not the Sun make animals now? Ans. Because they & with them the Sun itself, in your meaning of the word, are already made.

4652 28.11   "The Bound *poned* as Boundless (the Line as itself space) is the Square of itself or A^2.—But as in opposition to the Boundless, $A - B = B - A$." But there is no Square of 1.   *f17* Ergo, we must take the Infinite in the Finite = 2: and vice versâ, the Finite in the Infinite = 2. But how can this be on the Identität-lehre? We might as well multiply the Head into the Tail, and then call the Halfpenny the Square of itself.—This, however, is *their* concern. It may be illegitimately deduced from their system, and yet be Truth and a rightful consequence in ours.—To work, therefore, to work! and first to state the 3 Laws of Kepler for this is the number assigned by Steffens—

1. The *Squares* of the periodic *Times* are as the *Cubes* of their (the Planets') mean distances from the Sun. (This alone given by Long as a Law.)

2. (If I understand St. aright.) The *relative* Difference of the Planets is made known by the Ellipses of their orbits, so that no orb for itself, but yet all taken collectively, describe the compleat *circle*—not indeed for the immediate Beholding (Anschauung) but   *f17ᵛ* yet for the intellectual. Hence (adds Steffens) the necessity of the second Keplerian Law; which he no where however gives.—Is it the same as the Newtonian Law, that the Gravity universally increases in the inverse ratio of the Squares of the Differences (i.e. Distance)

3. The Planets moving in Ellipses, which have one of their Foci in the center of the Sun, their motions are all unequal, and *vary* so that a Ray, supposed to be always drawn from the Planet to the Sun, describes equal areas in equal times.

In the first law, the Identity of the Planet with itself; in the second, the relative Difference; in the third, the Synthesis of the Identity and the Difference; are expressed.

f18　　Now for the life of me, be the cause in my unusedness to Algebraic Symbols or my dullness or in the § itself, I cannot make out why A taken as relative and therefore supposing a Ground in another as its antithesis or correlative, and so far = B, should when taken as absolute and one with its ground, be A = A, or A², or the *Square* of itself. Yet I remember that Kant in the commencement of his Einz. Mog. Dem. speaks of the Square as demonstrably equal to the Infinite, and of the wonder with which the Demonstration affected the Math. Student. Is it that A multiplied into itself is its own bound exclusively, which is equivalent to unbounded, inasmuch as it is *irrelative*, and so relatively absolute? But that "Das Endliche" is *absolute* in the highest sense of the term

f18ᵛ　is a mere assumption of the Natur-philosopher. In the Planets all opposition of Forms is resolved into one Form and this = to and one with the Essence—in the particulars of a Planet the several Forms are in counter position to each other, so that the Idee-Einzelne holds itself to the Whole as to its ground—In the first, T. and Sp., Motion therefore & Rest, must be affirmed identical.

4653 28.12　　No need of Fire to account for the Basaltic Columns—. Porphyrooid ⌣/③ ($\frac{\text{Alumina}}{\text{silica}}$ + Iron) ℉ .⋰. Magn.

"The four Basaltes in the British Dominions, 1. Bris-m hawk, in Sky. 2. Humble, 20 leagues south. 3. Staffa. 4. The Giants'

f19　Causeways, run in one line f̶r̶o̶ ⟨due⟩ North to South, / Pennant /

—i.e. in the Magnetic Axis ⊙

⊘Silica ⊖ Alumina ☉Lime (·⊙, Magnesia Qʸ)

ⱳcounteractive of + ⱳdirectly − ⱳindir.

+ or − ♒ di- or indi-rectly auxiliar to.

　　　　　　　　　　　　　Magn.　　　　　Lime

Thus ....　+ ⱳ ☉ diversifies ·⊙· from ☉ and vice versâ ∠ − ♒ ☉ div. L. from M.

But remember, the "good Excellion" (bono auxilio) a fine old word! is itself auxiliar by counteraction.—N.B. ∇ instead of ○

f18ᵛ　**4654** 28.13　　ʟime relatively to Space = Motion. Ergo, M = T.—Therefore M. to realized Space = Time actual; but Time actual is contraction—the phænomenon of contraction in Ether can *f19* be nothing but Light i.e. luminous Ether.—But what *gives* the motion in the Ether?—

4655 28.14
Ad Lectorem. *f19ᵛ*
~~One~~ The Author's one Request.
~~Read the work Thro', before you.~~
Do not hold yourself authorized to ~~revile or~~ scoff at this work, ~~the labor of 5 and 20 years of a fellow creature's life~~, till you have read it. What? throughout? Yes.—But will that be possible? For him who puts this question without having read any part of it, probably not. But there is another thing not only possible but easy,—⟨and honest to boot⟩ ~~Be silent and knowing nothing, say nothing.~~ Say nothing about it. ~~This at least you can do and this by every tie of Justice and Veracity you ought to do.~~

This work is the Labor of five and twenty the best and ripest *f20* years of my Life. I brought to it the advantages and preparatory aids of a learned education—and I have woven into it the flower of constant study, Travel, Conversations and Correspondence with a very large proportion of the greatest Geniuses in Arts, Science, and Literature, at home and abroad, among ~~my~~ our contemporaries, and ~~above all~~ much and ~~various~~ multiform experience in more and more various relations & circumstances of life than have fallen to the Lot of ~~men~~ literary men in general, and above all, habitual commune with the moods and movements of my own moral and intellectual Being. I seek not money or reputation; and *f20ᵛ* it would indeed betray a pitiable ~~ignorance of the world, a reall~~ simplicity, and specially an ignorance of the ~~present~~ existing state of Society and the present Fashion of Literature, in this Country, if I expected either. Yet I have one request to make, Christian Reader! and only one. &c.

But I have it to review!—O!—You are a Reviewer? I beg your pardon. Farewell.

4656 28.15   A system of Science ~~much more~~ *presupposes,*— a system of Philosophy and philosophic Science must *begin in,* ⟨—⟩ an Verity (ἀληθὲς τὶ) a ~~Verity~~ so far negatively definable that it shall be neither particular, general nor abstract—neither a par-

ticular Fact, nor a generalization—, nor an abstraction (i.e. an
f21   heuristic Mark for the purposes of calculation, imparting in the
first instance a subjective form, or Handlungsweise of the Mind
intuitive or conceptive—thus the Infinite, Space, Time, Matter
and Spirit (*add Identity?*) are abstractions]—

And this Verity ~~reduced to~~ in its terminal expression ~~shall be~~ will
appear as an *Assumption* but yet an *unquestionable* assumption—for
it is the Bond between the Teacher and the Hearer, and if refused,
no connection has taken place, consequently no opposition can
arise, since inter res heterogene~~ou~~as nullus datur antagonismus.
The examinant like the Ox in the field, must smell to it and leave
it.)—This then being understood, we will commence anew with
f21ᵛ   the necessary conditions of a *System* in mundo intellectuali.

A system of Science *presupposes*—a system of Philosophy and
philosophic Science must *begin with*—a Verity (ἀληθὲς τὶ) *negatively* definable as being neither a particular fact, nor A a generalization, nor an abstraction; and which reduced to a verbal proposition shall be an *unquestionable assumption*—an *assumption* by force
of its negative definition (A) and *unquestionable*, because, if it be
not conceded either from conviction or argumenti causâ, all argument is precluded (as when you go up to a man with an intention
f22   of conversing with him and at the first look discover him to be a
stranger, and as from his first words that he speaks a language,
you do not understand.) In this assumption an Idea must arise, and
in this again the Principles of its Construction into distinct Conceptions—whence begins a series of Constructions, each productive
or procreative of the succeeding—and as soon as the nature of the
subject renders it possible, a parallel series of Correspondences in
~~the world of~~/ facts of Experience, as learnt from Observation or
Ascertained by Experiment—but not as proving the truth of the
Principles or the legitimacy of the Constructions which must stand
f22ᵛ   on its own ground and be established independently in the ever-
accompanying Light of the Idea, out of which they all arise, even
as Wave begets wave yet all collectively obey the attraction of the
Moon; but yet as not only confirmative and illustrative, but likewise and principally as demonstrating the *universality* of the Truth,
~~as both~~ namely, that it is at once real and ideal, ~~in~~ not only *objective*
in the Subject, but ~~as~~ subjective in the Object—and by this coin-

cidence realizing the Idea and Ideal Constructions into *Laws* ~~and~~
~~Laws,~~ of Nature and their genesis out of each other into powers
and forces.—In the Light of Law arises Theory, and the principles   *f23*
of Classification—and from these again scientific Hypothesis, ~~arise~~
the ~~Determination~~ (~~or~~ Proschema) of Observation, and the ~~Ration-~~
~~ale and Direction~~ Determination of Experiment—and generally,
the Architectonique and Organonlogy of Discovery and Invention—lastly, as an accessary advantage from the whole process, a
compleat System of Logic both transcendental and applied, both
demonstrative and detective.

4657 28.16   Q? The precise relation of Abstraction to Outline, under which name there are some excellent remarks in Rees:
Cyclopaedia, Vol. XXV, P. II. May we say, that all outline is
Abstraction; but not all Abstractions Outlines? or that Outline =
Abstraction + Association reproductive, or Pars sui completivus   *f23ᵛ*
in Totum suum? So that $\genfrac{}{}{0pt}{}{\text{Space}}{\text{Time}}\Big\{$ a Line, and the Figures in Flaxman's Homer, Eschylus & Dante may be regarded as gradual
potenziations of Abstraction by the plastic Imagination?

4658 28.17   That chlorine is, sensu philosophico .... +
⁚.. its incombinability with Charcoal, and its eager alloys with
the metals suggests—as well as its poisonous effects on breathing.

4659 28.18   It is more and evident to me that little can be
done to any purpose in philosophic Chemistry, till the nature of
Heat and Fire in their various manifestations be satisfactorily enu-
cleated—and the proportions of $\smile$ and .... established/ex. gr.
the action of the *red heat* on some sorts of the Black Oxyd of
Manganese in the emancipation of ..ˣ.. gas, and that of the Sulphuric Acid on other sorts. At present, I should say conjecturally,
that ignition implied the maximum of *antagonism*, the wrestling   *f24*
war-embrace of the Contractive and Dilative—and that melting =
the superiority of the latter, and Gas that of the former, the struggle still continuing, tho' with greater energy & endurance in the
Gas than in the Flux—in this latter therefore becoming a *property*.

4660 28.19   The Osteocolla, or Hammosteus of the Germans, and its ground of connection with the rotten wood substance (probably, submerged small Trees) round which this marly spar concretes—why always in sand? never in clay nor any solid soil, not even in gravel?—That it is never found in the same ground but around this rotten substance, suggests a query or two respecting the true genesis of the Fluorine or Phthoric Principle.—There is one part, however, of the account in the Phil. Trans. N? 39 which I do not understand—viz—its growing again in a year or *f24ᵛ* two in the same pit after it has been all cleared out—/ Did a new quantum of the woody basis appear with it?

4661 28.20   Among the most momentous Constructions of my Systema ενκυκλοπαιδευμενον is this: that in consequence of ⌣ and ...., / and ⋰. are capable of acting as Powers, and vice versâ in consequence of / and ⋰., ⌣ and .... are capable of subsisting as Bodies. Thus Cold is not a mere comparative − Heat, ~~but~~ which is true only by an equivoque of our sensation which we *f25* call Cold, & which has no no effect in Nature, but with the diminution of ⌣ as ≡ the power of / increases, as the Chrystalline power: and subordinates to itself the contractive, as its auxiliary. The contraction of frozen Iron ist nur scheinbar, being in part only increased Cohesion—which takes place in water with *lineal* enlargement, as M ⚹ − M.

4662 28.21   Each and every chemical process (says Steffens, Handbuch p. 61) forms ~~apropern~~ individual life of its own—ein eigenthumliches individuelles Leben (eine momentane Identitat *f25ᵛ* der Schwere und des Lichts)— Identity of Gravity and Light!! What this *means*, lies beyond *my* comprehension. It does *not* mean Indifference or the Neutralization—for Caloric, he has told us, is the Indifference or Common Mean of ⊕ and >, as Water is the Neutralization, ⟨ 8̄ ⟩, or Corpus mortuum of ♄ and ⋰. / Neither can it be an 8, or tertium aliquid from the superinduction of ⊕ and > or a common Base, either in equipollence, or predominance of this or that: for > = the whole E and West, ⊕ the whole magnetic axis, i.e. N.S. and ☉. Consequently, nothing is left to *f26* supply a Base. However, we may help ourselves out of this difficulty by the Rule of Converse. ~~If by Z, ⟨⟨Life⟩⟩ = the > Identity~~ ~~(understood) of > and ⊕, both, (Life) the Identity of > and ⊕~~ ~~must be Z.~~ If Z = Identity of > and ⊕, the Ident. of > and ⊕ = Z. But as the Identity of α and β, as distinguished from the combination of the same α and β, whether as Synthesis or Indifference, can be no other way conceivable than as the Prothesis to the Thesis and Antithesis, in which it manifests itself under the form of correlative and interdependent Opposites—it follows, that the Life must be anterior to the chemical Process which is to form this Life. Now the whole scheme of Evolution, according to the Iden- *f26ᵛ* tität-system, is grounded in the impossibility of a retrocession to Identity—the constant tendency being constantly counteracted by the equal tendency to Manifestation, and ⟨either⟩ Neutrality or Synthesis, ~~being~~ the Product of the composite Force.

But if it be said, that the Life = Prothesis be Life Absolute and universal, and the Life = the ~~Product~~ Synthesis, be Life relative, ergo finite, and particular, I again demand, by what right and in what sense the term, *Identity*, is applied to the latter? An Identity subject to More and Less, to this sort and that sort? a *f27* modified Identity? An Identity of > and ⊕ under the *preponderance* of ⊕? And what after all does the whole amount to but ~~the~~ ⟨a chain of⟩ bald Truisms?—that when the identity of α and β appears in Division as $\alpha \times \beta$, it appears the opposite to Identity, or is disidentified and Iden. of $\alpha\beta$ being + Life, the Disidentification must appear as − Life or Death—and when in this Disidentity it reidentifies itself *it comes to life again*—and inasmuch as ~~it is~~ this identity re-identifies itself *here* and not *there*, in *this* and not in *that*, it is not universally re-identified—therefore particularly—and *f27ᵛ* therefore as *particular* Life! They give two or three several names to the same thing, and you may exhibit a finer display of irrefragable Logic by mere shuffling of the Synonimes!—But the worst of it is, that it is all nothing but appearance after all! Now an appearance without a correspondent reality is an Illusion; and (which is the case here) and Appearance contrary to the reality is a Delusion. Finally, *to* which and *for* whom is it to appear?—Can the universal Life cheat itself, and by force of habit come to believe its own Lies? A appears to B is = B perceives A. Now to *appear* to have an appearance, or it appears to me to appear, is downright *f28* nonsense.—In like manner, the *momentaneousness* of chemical Life, &c, are at best mere fantastic phrases ~~for the~~ ⟨and⟩ nicknames for the simple fact, that the flame of Phosphorus combining with Oxygen is not so long-lived as an oyster.—at *best*, I say: for in fact it falsifies the fact, and makes the latter differ from the former by a mere comparative *quantity* of Time. For if *momentaneous* be the positive opposite to *permanent*, they must differ *diversely*, as *no time* to *sometime*—so that in the one sense the assertion is notoriously false—in the other sense it is the same as the chemical agents are

f28ᵛ at no time living agents, and chemical Life = no Life. Nay, were the Logic less absurd, still this momentaneity and this permanence are the PROBLEM to be solved—If they are essential and not accidents, what is *that*, ⟨that⟩ gives permanence to xy and withholds it from yx? Nothing in xy or yx: for that the same y + x ~~is~~ are differenced into xy and yx, is the very thing, the cause of which we are seeking after.—

It is the chief merit of the anastatic System to have got rid of this Identity—except in that state in which it is at its proper Home,

f29 namely, in the Chaos as the realm of contradictions—In our Absolute (i.e. the ineffable Godhead) there is no Dualism, no antithesis, consequently *no* "Identity" in the sense ~~of~~ affixed to the term by the New *Decorators* of Spinosism. We have the eternal Prothesis and the co-eternal Thesis, εν δε πληρωματι τω τῆς ἀυτῆς τιθεται τα παντα οσα μεν οντως εισι. In the apostasis indeed the word has been used, but with the fixed signification of an inherent suicidal *amphoterism*, or the agony of contradictory Potentials—and here the term ceases—. Instead of making the recurrence or the nisus redeundi in Identitatem the mask of progression in melius, it is

f29ᵛ with us the symptom of relapse into the Evil One, the Identity of Multëity and Indistinction—.—In the proper creation we have ~~communion an~~ no αμφοτερον—ουδετερον of Light and Darkness—They are Contraries, with whom no communion is or can be—The Darkness may by Light be converted to Light; and the *effect*, in the Darkness, of the *Influence* of Light may by the Darkness be converted to Darkness—but no Identity.—In short, Schelling's System and mine stand thus:—In the Latter there are God

f30 and Chaos: in the former an Absolute Somewhat, which is *alternately* both, the rapid leger de main shifting of which constitutes

the delusive appearance of *Poles*—just as if a Ball rapidly changing
from Black to White and from White to Black should be moved
from right to left ~~with say~~ so momentaneously as to leave the
impression White at the right end still remaining on the eyes at
the time that it receives the impression of Black at the left end—
no wonder that all ~~is~~ ⟨the changes are⟩ explained into *nur scheinbar*—and that the problem, ~~is~~ repeated in another formula ⟨of ⟨f30ᵛ⟩
words is *passed off*⟩ for the *solution*—How should it, how *can* it,
be otherwise, where the cause and the effect are the same ⟨absolute,
unchanging, & unchangeable⟩ thing?—If only that unmanageable
"We", the spectator, the Eye, das Auschauende," could be disposed
of, the Schellingian Philosophy might pass as an ingenious scheme
of Psychology or Subjective Logic. But ⟨then⟩ if ~~these~~ Births and
Successions of Mental Forms are real, there is no reason for denying real correspondents to them.—and if these are themselves
appearances that are not real appearances, then the whole may be
summed up into—a something which ~~being at the same moment~~ ⟨f31⟩
is everything, and being ~~both~~ neither cause ~~and~~ ⟨nor⟩ effect ~~and~~
appears to be each severally and both at once to a something which
~~is~~ not being every thing is therefore nothing, which being ⟨in itself
and in the same moment⟩ all things and the ⟨one⟩ only thing is
neither cause *nor* effect; ~~yet~~ ⟨but⟩ appears ⟨to be⟩ each severally and
both at once, to a Something which *not* being all things is really
nothing—on an apparent Focus, ⟨to wit,⟩ where Nothings, itself
⟨being⟩ one of them, converge to Appearances!!! It (the Natur-
philosophie) cannot tell us *why* it *is* so: for *so* it IS not—nor even
why it *appears* so—but merely, *how* it happens that it must so
appear to us.

　　Hence throughout Steffens's Manual, spite of the many excel- ⟨f31ᵛ⟩
lent Anticipations which wanted only ⟨the vis mascula of⟩ a πρωτον
Αληθες to have been pregnant Ideas, there is a manifest præposition
of the empirical Fact in the author's mind and then such an arrangement of relations ⟨— of punctual productions⟩ and oppositions ⟨and re-unions⟩ and re-unions relatively opposite, as will
solve the mode of its appearance ~~by~~ from the possibilities afforded
by the laws of *Perspective*! There is no necessity ab et in precedenti,
that X or Y is so—but being *found* to be such, it ⟨may or⟩ must
be explained—not *by*, but—*into* such and such relations. Conse-

f32 quently, the whole Process is improgressive Analysis in the shews and forms of productive Synthesis: and the *Sum* of Steffens's ~~Philosophy~~ Organology is reduced to the following identical position grafted on an implied Postulate.—That which ~~it~~ attempting to compleat what is wanting to its ⟨relatively⟩ independent ~~Totality~~ Integrity ~~and~~ (or self-subsistence) by taking up its Opposite into itself, ⟨wholly⟩ fails ⟨and perishes⟩ in the attempt, and only forms another Gegensatz, is Chemical Power—and that which ⟨partially⟩ succeeds in the same attempt, ⟨and partially survives it,⟩ is organic Life. Who does not see here a verbal, at least a merely *formal*, Definition palmed on us for a real definitive Construction?—To be convinced of the hollowness we need only substitute another defi-

f32ᵛ nition of the same kind and of at least equal merit—ex. gr. That ~~which~~ Product, which demands and supposes a product specifically the same as itself for its ⟨own⟩ productive Antecedent is = individual Life ⚸ chemical Action. In this definition we find the *rationale* of the fact contained in Steffens's; but only to affix a new question to the same unsatisfied "*Why?*"—But that St. had been dazzle-dimmed by the interpolat~~ioned of the~~ empirical generalization, Polarity,—this point alone would have detected for him the fundamental equivoque and duplicity of his *Nature*, ~~of~~ his ⟨irrelative⟩ *Identitaty*, and his *Absolute*. ~~but~~ In contra-distinction

f33 from, and additively to, the sense in which his "irrelative Identity" = chaos, every Germ would have Disclosed to him the other sense, in which it and its Synonimes are ill-chosen Terms for

THE WILL, THE WORD, THE BREATH—THE LIVING GOD Giver of Life, and Lord of Life in Death!

So again individual Ident. of > and ⊕ = the Soul!!

4663 28.22   The Tabasher in the nodes of the female bamboo, curious opt. phænom. from minus of refract. comp. with water.—Some all silic.—other specimens 70, Sil.—30 per cent potash, Lime and water!—~~t~~ between water and the Gasses. Immersed in water, from semi-tr. it becomes wholly tr., but—small portion of water dropt on it converts it to opake and chalky-white—How this dep. on Refr. I must learn.

4664 28.23   What Luther (Table Talk) says of Dyonisian Mystic Theology holds of Schelling—"Omnia sunt non ens, et omnia sunt ens, & so leaving all *hanging* in frivolous & idle sort. *Schwebend.*—And so of the School Divines who "talk most of the   *f33ᵛ* Union of the Will with the Understanding."—Both are capable of a sound meaning; but then the *meaning* must have preceded, or they will lead to the most dangerous perversions not only of Faith but of common sense.—Thus in God : Will = Reason—ergo, the human will being one by obedience with the divine Will, is in union with Reason. But all this is but a Periphrasis of "Seek after Godliness." And where are we to seek, but in God's Word? But if the Understanding mean the human Understanding, in like manner as the Will mean the human Will (and this is the natural and grammatical sense of the words) a fouler error cannot be conceived: for the Understanding is but the secondary Reflex of the Will, the senses being the first Image, as the underst. the Reflexion of that Reflex.

4665 28.24   I intended many times (said Luther) well and   *f34* thoroughly to search and find out the ten commandments, but at the first sentence I stuck fast—the very first word (I) put me to a non-plus. Table Talk, p. 5.—

I have grounded my preaching on the literal word: whoso pleaseth may follow me, he that will not may chuse. Dᵒ

The most perfect human Mind is to God or divine Truth as a Globe on a Table—the G. toucheth the T. but at one point at a time, ~~but~~ while the T. at each point supporteth the whole globe.— (N. b. a good Emblematic Vignette.

The opposite errors of the Neologists and the ψευδο-evangelicals—These demand the same process of Faith for ~~the~~ Bibliology as for the mysteries of Religion—those submit the latter to the same aweless criticism as the former.

Memento. To read thro' the Ταφελταλχ, hoc modo, as soon as possible.

4666 28.25   No Sophister was ever able to understand these   *f34ᵛ* words: The Just liveth by Faith

4667 28.26   Among other apparent differences almost =
contradiction, at least to diversity, in the I, and ⟨v⟩ 1. 2. 3. of IInd
C. of G. ⚹ II from 4 inclusive, v. 11, 12 C. I. and v. 5 of C II
not the least striking—In the latter namely the *Jehovah* Adonaim
"made every plant of the Field *before* it was in the earth, and every
herb of the Field *before* it grew": in the former Adonai bade the
Earth bring forth &c./~~the second~~ To reconcile the two we must
say, that the second, probably the elder and ruder document speaks
of the *Germs* as in the air.

4668 28.27   The speedy ennobling ~~of~~ *and* re- or disde-gen-
erating of the human Form, in the Instance of the nobler Ranks
of the Turks, of the Persians, but especially of the Georgians &

f35   Circassians, from the ~~F~~ Tatar Race ~~of Ham & Shem~~ = Shem +
Ham, mixed with the Grecian = the Descendants of Ja~~van~~phet in
the noblest line, that of Javan (Iaphetidae Iao~~n~~anes), probably with
a primary oxidation (Iapetidizing) of the (Sh + H). The Bassiani,
a confluence of the Bulgarians, ~~the~~ of Nogay and Tatar Tribes and
of Greeks in the vicinity of the Elbrus, the highest Point of Mount
Caucasus, at the source of the four streams, Kuban, ⌐ . . . ⌐
Tscherek, Backsan, and T'schegem.—If the Bulgarians be a relict
of the N. W. Iapetidæ/, the Reduction of the ore or alloy to the
original Regulus, Metals-könig becomes still more conceivable:—
viz. Ham zurück gedrängt durch die stärkere affinitat [*Affinität*]
oder vielmehr der übergewalt der Sch. + Japhet.—

4669 28.29   Sonnet to a Bird that haunted the waters of

f36   Lacken, in the winter, by Lord Thurlow.

> O melancholy bird, a winter's day
> Thou standest by the margin of the pool,
> And, taught by God, dost thy whole being school
> To Patience, which all evil can allay.
> God has appointed thee the fish thy prey,
> And giv'n thyself a lesson to the Fool
> Unthrifty, to submit to moral rule,
> And his unthinking course by thee to weigh.
> There need not schools, nor the Professor's chair,

Though these be good, true wisdom to impart;
He who has not enough, for these, to spare
Of time, or gold, may yet amend his heart,
And teach his soul, by brooks, and rivers fair:
Nature is always wise in every part.

4670 28.28   The exudation of the Gum Arabic from the   *f35ᵛ*
Acacia vera ⟨or Mimosa Nilotica⟩ *after Rain*—while from the Acacia *Senegal*, the still finer, Tor or Siung, quite colorless & transparent—these spontaneous, the latter wholly so, the former somewhat reddish-yellow & turbid is forced by *somewhat* by ⟨arts of⟩
cultivation, but by making cuts in the Bark in March, they procure from the *Siung*-tree a still redder sort, and n. b. *bitter*. (In
the spontaneous the *West* (Insipid, colourless) loosed from the ☉:—
in the forced still under its dominion.—
    The Acacia Arabica, which forms the link between the Nilotic
& the Senegalensis, and the durable Timber of which is when old
almost black as Ebony, is the Shittim Wood of Moses.

4671 28.30   Spinosism in all its forms, εποπτικοις (as in the   *f36ᵛ*
Hindú Polytheism) η νοητικοις (as in Spinoza's own works), or in
both conjointly (as in Schelling and his followers) is principally
and eminently forbidden in the 2ⁿᵈ Commandment, and the same
Veto is implied in the first. Thou shalt not worship God *under* any
image—thou shalt not hold God to be the substrate of ⟨Nature⟩ or
immediate invisible Cause of the phænomenal World or of any
single Phænomenon. for it is an "*I*" that is alone the Lord God—
and *him* thou shalt personally worship. Now W. without Pers.
is = 0.
    But again as the fontal God can only be known in the Logos, so   *f37*
neither can the Logos be sought aright but in the divine Humanity—this is the doctrine of Luther, p. 17—as well as that of the
Moravians & not less expressly tho' less fantastically than that of
Em. Swedenborg.

4672 28.31   [I] can truly affirm, that of averaging one with
another there is not a Chapter, which has does not contain the a
full year's labor of Thought and Study, and but few, the devel-

opement, application and detail of which, a as far only as the Author himself has carried them, do not fill a Mss equal in volume
to the whole work. Nor is there any subject here treated, which I
have not studied from its first elements and and for the acquire-
f37ᵛ   ment of all existing information concerning which I have not, as
it were, gone to school, as far as it was requisite or expedient for
the proposed end. And here let me state one fact that may perhaps
not be without a beneficial influence on some among the undergraduates at Cambridge—viz. that year after year not a month
passes, in which I did not receive fresh proof of the ⌈ . . . ⌉
superscription over the Platonic School — Μηδεις αγεωμετρητος
εισιτω, not one in which I did not look back with a regret not
unmixed with remorse on my own neglect of my Mathematical
Studies both at School, and at Jesus College—in both of which I
enjoyed the greatest possible opportunities, and in the latter not
only every help and facility, but likewise every motive, & inducement that the most kindest assurances and the most friendly solic-
itations could supply—till at length the trouble of my own mind
f38   drove me to take it up at a late period, when with less active
memory and less bodily strength to endure a long continued pass
effort of passive intellection I had no helps but those of Books &
no counsellor even in the choice of these—. One ⟨rather⟩ ludicrous
instance of my ignorance and of the loss of time and labor thereby
incurred often awakes a⟨n⟩ rather almost sardonic smile at myself—dissatisfied by the usurpation use of the names, Th × and
÷ in common arithmetic, which I regarded as usurped by antici-
patively from rightful claimants, after long and eager thought,
dishearted by repeated failures, I stumbled on the system of natural
Logarithms a scheme which I entitled the organ of amalgamation
negat aggregative position and negative Catena of [*] and shewing
it to a Schoolmaster found that I had invented the *natural Logarithms*, essentially the same with those of Napier.

4673   28.32
f38ᵛ   The Logosophic System and Method
by S. T. Coleridge
Subject. On Philosophy as supplying the real ground and comple-

[* Coleridge's blank.]

~~ment of Science, the regeneration of Science in Philosophy, and~~
the Pursuit of Wisdom, in relation to theoretical and speculative
Truth: comprizing the grounds ⌐ . . . . ⌐ and outlines of the several sciences ~~in the order of their~~ ⌐ . . . . ⌐ ⌐ . . . . ⌐ ~~reproduc-
tion~~ as integral parts ~~of philosophic Science~~ and ~~organs~~ products
of sciential Philosophy with an organon criticum et heuristicum
applied to investigations, experimental or observatii̶v̶eonal, proposing scientific e Truth as their direct end. A ~~system~~ ⟨series of
Disquisitions de D.M. et H.⟩ which commenceing with a postulate, ~~of~~ morally coercive, ~~and not inconsistent with logic~~, first demonstrating the inherent imperfection of all exclusively intellectual   *f39*
~~and~~ or theoretical Systems, ~~then exhibits the completion of Science
by Philosophy and the realization of Philosophy in the Christian
Religion~~ proceeds to establish the ~~true~~ proper ~~nature~~, character and
function of Philosophy as the supplement of Science, and the realization of both in Religion or the Life of Faith, as ~~at once and
alone~~ the process and only possible mean of the one only wise and
desirable End.—Sᵗ John, C. I. v. Θεον ουδεις πώποτε εωρακεν ·
ο υιος, ο εν τῳ κολπῳ του πατρος &c—

Organum verè organum: seu Logicè instrumentalis, tum critica,
tum heuristica, in Physicis vel observatione vel experimento indagandis utillima—i.e. ~~Logic as the organ of Judgement and~~ the
Method of scientific anticipation, ~~and~~ or the Pioneer of Invention
& Discovery

The L. S. and M. by S.T.C.   *f39ᵛ*

On the inherent imperfection of all systems exclusively intellectual—i.e. professing to be *grounded* in Reason or in the Understanding. On the true definition and proper office of Philosophy,
as the Supplement of Science; and on the realization of both in
⌐ . . . ⌐ Religion or the Life of Faith, as the only possible mean
of the only wise End, and the appointed process thereto.—and
comprizing first, the grounds, and outlines of the several Sciences,
as integral ~~parts~~ and co-organized Parts of sciential Philosophy,
each in the order of its primary developement—secondly, a scheme
of instrumental Logic, or the Method of scientific anticipation, as
the Pioneer of Observation and Experiment, and entitled, Organum verè organum, tum criticum, tum heuristicum, in physicis
sive per observationem sive per [. . .] experimenta indagandis
utillimum—the whole forming a series of Discourses and Dia-

f40   logues held with a fellow-enquirer during a succession of Tours at
       home and abroad during the years 18167–1820.

4674 28.33
~~Matter~~ Physica, singly as in the Vocabulary of abstractions
_____

Matter = verb impersonal, videtur
Materiale
     or $\left\{\vphantom{\begin{array}{c}a\\b\\c\end{array}}\right.$ = existit
mater. Substance
Body = subsistit.
_____

Ditto, in the phraseology of Nature
Matter = existit alterius vice
M. S = existit suo jure et suas habens proprietates, at nons nisi
in altero
Body = ⌈ . . . ⌉ ~~existit~~ subsisit et sibi et ut Basis alterius, viz.
MS superinductæ

4675 28.34   *ff 40ᵛ–43* [Notes toward a Greek Grammar: in
SWF.]

4676 28.35
f43ᵛ   Criterion of Obscurity
       Suppose yourself to have read a passage repeatedly and at length
(~~say at~~ but not, we will say, till the 3rd or 4th perusal) to have fully
mastered the import. *Then*
       1. If you exclaim O, it means so and so—~~using other~~ substitut-
ing words ~~than those of the author and which convey the same~~
~~sense — & it might advantageously be substituted for those of the~~
~~author~~ which if the author had used, you would have understood
him at once, you are entitled to condemn the passage as obscure—
& if many such occur, to ~~nominate~~ charge the Author with Obscurity.
       2. But if having mastered the sense at length you say—Yes! I
see it now—it is &c. using the author's words—then you may
f44   think it an obscure (more properly, a difficult) subject, but have

no right to call the Author an *obscure writer* or the Book an obscure Book.—Lycophron is an obscure writer; but Euclid's 37th Pr. is a *hard passage*. Tacitus is a difficult author &c—

4677 28.36   Of Life *in genere* we see clearly so far, that it consists in an Entelechie or inward Act, as the proper Causa exis- tendi determinatè/herein differing from the inanimate (= soulless) or Life of Nature, that the latter is indeed likewise an entelechie or Act ab intra (for no mechanical motion, i.e. motion continued thro' the medium of *Impact*, can be original—) but it is simply as entelechie, a causa communis existentiæ indeterminatæ—~~as~~ this   *f44^v* *phænomenal* ‡ individuality being given to each thing by the posi- tion—while it is indispensable to the Idea of proper Life, that its position ~~in on and what is~~ is predetermined, and ⟨at least⟩ de- manded⟨ed⟩ ~~one's~~ if not produced, *by* the Entelechie.

‡ That is, even in those things which do bear a semblance of Individuality, this Individuality is purely & merely phænomenal; Either *Schein* as in dendritic Stones & the like—or Erscheinung as in Chrystallization. It is never an *Individual* properly, ~~but~~ tho' possibly ~~an~~ Unique; but always a species—i.e. it has nothing but its simple Existence that is not determined ab extra, according to   *f45* some general Laws.—

All this is clear—clear therefore that however endless the grades of descent may be in living things, there must ~~be~~ still be a chasm between the lowest, & the inanimate— Anticipation: God, the Word, even here as *Pre-substitute—imputed* Righteousness even before *they* were (St Paul, IX Rom.)—Light in its *identity* or *Prothesis*; but what is this? Evidently an *act of Will*—or rather *a Will*—but how is this to be conceived?—Music in the un*self*conscious Muscles of the Musician's Fingers?—A fuller scheme of Mineralogy than ~~my~~ the limits allotted to it in my Totality would have better prepared the Mind for this great moment. For already we ~~face~~ should have seen the prophetic em-   *f45^v* blem in the paths, in which the Self-seeking or apostatic was de- termine[d] by the influence of the L + Pr to diverge—namely, in the Salts and the Metals—these taking up Light, and those following ☉—those again so far assuming Light as to subsume

their entelechie in the Light—they *shoot* and mimic vegetation—
these (Os) combine indeed with an embodied Light (∿, oxygen)
but use it for *multeity* and increase of the Spec. Grav.—in the
aggregate—tho' the Mass a should be destroyed).)—

But *in Life* Light must be the Entelechie, the central Point, that
takes up, & not is taken up—The Word is *Light*—in it is *Life*—
and this Life is the Light of man—The divine Cycle cannot be
more adequately expressed, from Light to Light thro' Life—.—
Inoculation—

4678 28.38

f46ᵛ   ⌜ .... ⌝
         ⌜ .... ⌝
         ⌜ .... ⌝
         ⌜ .... ⌝
         ⌜ .... ⌝
         ⌜ .... ⌝
         ⌜ .... ⌝
         ⌜ .... ⌝
         ⌜" .... ⌝
⌜with us" Thursday April 6, 1820⌝
         ⌜ .... ⌝
         ⌜ .... ⌝
         ⌜ .... ⌝
⌜Again moods mentioned of another⌝
⌐nota bene Monday April 10, 1820⌝

f47   **4679** 28.39   Without the potential moulds, ανευ μορφαις
μορφογενεσι of the Understanding the notices supplied by the
Senses would have no *substans*, no substance—could not be *formed*
into Experience. Without the materials contributed by the Senses,
the forms of the Understanding would have no *reality*, no content—or as the popular Language, always more philosophical than
the Individuals that slight it, truly says—There is no *sense* in it.—
Being thus interdependent, both are necessarily confined to such
subjects as have the predicates of Time and Space—strange are the
Bulls that are engendered, where the Logic of the mere Under-

standing is allowed to bring the entia of the supersensual World to its Procrustes Bed.—See Note MSS, in Behmen, vol. 3, p. 33.

4680 28.41

Quid vult iste equitans? et quid velit ista virorum   *f48ᵛ*
Palmifera ingens turba, et vox fremebunda, Hosanna!
Hosanna Christo, semper semperque canamus.

Palma fuit senior pictor celeberrimus olim.
Sed palmam cedat, modo si foret ille superstes;
Palma, Hadone, tibi: tu palmas omnibus offers.

Palma negata macrum, donatque reddit opimum,
Si simul incipiat, cum famâ increscere corpus,
Tu citó pinguesces! fies et, amicule, obesus.

Affectant lauros pictores atque poetæ—   *f49*
Sin laurum invidea⟨n⟩t (sed quis tibi?) laurigerentes,
Pro lauro palmâ viridanti tempora cinge.

4681 28.42   The Rustic apprehensive of a *delirium in his* feet was recommended by the Physician, to whom he applied, to take the *Juice of Cotton*—*Qʸ to apply a Corn-plaister to his Temples?*— bathe his head with Tender-Juice from baked Corn-plaisters.—

4682 28.43   My Master never sees *any*body before one   *f49ᵛ* o'clock; & then he goes out. *Mʳ Kenyon*—

                        5 May *1820*

4683 28.44   Sir Christopher Heydon, Knight. His—A Defence of Judiciall Astrologie in answer to a Treatise lately published by Mʳ John Chamber—

                     Legat, Cambridge, 1603.

P. 10—a droll distinction between Mathematics a mathesis and Matematics from ματαιος,—*vain*—

4684 28.45   Churches, but no church; and churches only   *f50* enough to preserve the establishment as the head *sect*, for the sake

of the Lay Tithe-holders—this is the Creed and scheme of our
great Agriculturalists in and out of Parliament. A most short-
sighted, selfish & blundering Body of Statesmen never existed,
than the present Country Party, with M̶r̶ Messrs. Western, Bennet,
Sir John Sinclair, and other He Mer- or Terre- maids for their
Leaders.—The overbalance of the Landed Interest in the H. of
C. is the true Evil of the Borough System. Admirable is the *Idea*
of the English Constitution—1. a whole Branch of Legislature,
the self-representing Major Barons. 2. A powerful minority in the
other House of the representatives of the Minor Barons. 3. A
majority of the representatives of the Inhabitants & the Interests
f50^v of the Ports, Towns, and Cities/sure to join with the minority
(County Members) in all cases, when the interest of the smaller
Land occupiers is opposed to or threatened by the Magnates or
Major Barons, while the County Members are sure of being supported by the Upper House & enabled to baffle any attempt of the
Majority in the lower, to encroach on the interests of the Landed
Body collectively.—The reply to this from the Power of the Purse
in the H. of C. is a mere sophism—no such power exists except
as the power which every man has of murdering his child or cutting his own throat—& this predomination of the H. of C. is the
result of the Lords' own grasping ambition, by which in attempting to extend they *transferred* their power into the lower House,
and thus compelled the Crown to follow their example. All our
Const^n. wants is, a circulating movement of the Elective
f51 Franc⟨h⟩ise whenever a Borough falls below a certain degree of
independent Manufactural, Commercial, and Trade (i.e. distrib-
utive, wholesale or Retail) Welfare (Wohlstand:) & the obligation
on each Borough to chuse *one* of its two representatives from its
own bonâ fide Burghers, and the other from its own number or
from the bonâ fide Citizen of some other Port, Town, City, or
Manufacturing District, ad libitum.

I am inclined likewise to hold that in good policy not to say
common Justice, the Clergy, as a Property sui generis, ought
either to have their Convocation restored or to elect a ⟨parliamen-
tary⟩ Representative in each diocese, or one from two or three
Dioceses, according to number &c.

Um nicht *Kirchen* allein, sondern auch *eine Kirche*, zu haben oder zu werden, fehlt uns ein *Centralbehörde*, ein *aüsserer* Mittel-punct unserer Vereinigung: ein Mangel, der uns der katholischen Kirche gegenüber, die durch ihre Verfassung in der engsten Ver-bindung steht und sich mit der grösster Leichtigkeit in Masse bewegen kann, aüsserst nachtheilig werden muss, indem dadurch so leicht der Fall eintreten kann, dass in Collisionsfällen jede ein- *f51ᵛ* zelne unserer Kirchen mit der ganzen katholischen oder Method-istischen oder auch (wie neulich im Falle des Lord Sidmouth's Bill) mit der ganzen mannichfaltigen *Dissenter*, Parthey [*Dissenter-Parthey*] zu thun hat—die Landes-herrn und ihre Clienten nicht zu nennen.—S.T.C.

4685 28.46   A Piony how long (3 weeks some) they remain in the Flower-Waterpot, fresh as in the garden, yea, as long may-hap as if they had been let die on the Root./But when ~~they~~ it once begins to drop a leaf, or two, tomorrow they drop l~~eaf after leaf~~ves in companies, no breath stirring, no vibration given,—this batch now—an hour hence, or half an hour, or two hours, another—and so may it be, that it will be a Summer's day, dropping at causeless fits (why say, it drops the leaves—the Leaves like tired friends, drop from it!) & you shall see its loss only beneath it, this red Heap on Table or Mantle-piece./But the next day, in early morn- *f52* ing, then indeed the poor Flower looks storm-pillaged—a fine-feathered Bird picked & plucked, here a piece of naked stubby white Skin, and there a smaller or a large—and those, that remain, they have no thanks, no thanks to them, the Flower looks only the more miserable—he feels, he does not grasp *them*—& he feels too that they are loose at their roots in his heart. Why do they stay?— Habit, perhaps. Why don't they go now? This Hour!—Procras-tination! Because it may be done the next day.

4686 28.47   A courtezan or Venus Plebeia, with a wreath of Syringa and Dutch Myrtle around her carrotty wig—made from the Cæsaries of a Scotch Corporal who died of the ποξ.

4687 23.18   I think Sᵗ Peter's assertion that "in every nation *f17* he that feared God & worked righteousness, was accepted by him"

has been dangerous⟨ly⟩ misinterpreted by the naturalists & Socinians—for in the first place, it would clearly supersede the *necessity*
of a faith in Christ, & secondly, it would be irreconcileable with
all those many & more explicit Scriptures which assert this neces-
f17ᵛ sity. I rather take it as a confirmation of my opinion, that Christianity was intended as a perfecter of ~~the~~ human Nature—& pre-
supposed Natural Religion & a good Conscience, as previously
necessary to the capacity for a firm Faith in Christ—Hence the
Elias went before to preach Repentance, to sweep the Temple clean
before the Lord of Glory entered—& therefore Peter's meaning
was, that Fear of God & answerable Conduct were the only conditions of being accepted by God—i.e. brought to a Faith in
Christ—not the descent from a nation, nor the observation of the
Jewish Law.—

4688 23.19   In the English Translation (published 1584) of
Calvin's comment on the Harmony of the Evangelists (dedicated,
from Geneva, 1 August 1555) the word "merry" is still used for
joyful—"they may very well & fitly be called Evangelists: that is,
bringers of merry news"—(The Argument)

f18 4689 23.20   June 30ᵗʰ, 1820—Night, & 1 July, Morning/
strange & fearful Dreams, so distinct & conscience-like/after the
σαδ νευσε φρομ Οριελ—The effort, I believing myself to have departed this life. O let me still pray to God!—God must still be
here! & the prayer, soon after which I awoke.—How like the Hell
of Swedenborg it appeared, how completely conceivable (some malignant, but all perfectly unbenignant, Spirits) did the different
human Beings appear.—But the terror which I write this to preserve is—Life *without breathing*—not always a positive torture of
deprivation of Breathing, but often a *mere negative—not to
breathe*—fearfully symbolical of a spiritual Life, but why say I
Spiritual only?—of Life without continued successive feeling of
dependence on God, of food of Life asked each moment &
granted—O recollect in waking thought, that every free Breath is
= God has not yet rejected me.

f18ᵛ 4690 23.21   Magic—Michael Scott (Edward I time) Zoroaster Disc.—Medes, Apuscŏrus and Zarātus, with Marmarides

of Babylon. And Hippocus from Araby/The Assyrian, Zarmoceni-
das/

Histaspes and Astrampsyches
And Dardan of Phœnicia
Whose works in chest sepulchral found
Democritus becommented/

⟨Gnostics,⟩ *Ephesian Letters*. Besama Camosi Bue Anoora Mysta-
dia, Rhuda, Custaba, Phagor Calathi—i.e. O qui es supra omnem
virtutem Patris, te invocamus, qui lumen et spiritus bonus nomi-
naris, quoniam in corpore regnasti—(Swedenborgianism.)

4691 23.22   Perhaps, from confluence of calamities, my
Son's *persecuted* imprudence at Oxford, & my own wretchedness
of mind, body and estate I may look at other objects & see the
general state of affirms thro' a film or haze of melancholy.—May
it be so!—For if neither my Sight nor the medium be in fault   *f19*
there is a most ominous resemblance between the present times of
George IV, and those of Charles II. and the differences are ὡς
ἐμοιγε δοκεῖ by no means to our advantage. The hatred of the Sectarians and of the Scrupulists, with the dread of the Commonwealth men with whom the Royalists confounded the friends of a
limited Monarchy could not be stronger then than the horror of
Jacobinism & popular Riots is at present/

4692 23.23   Metaphys. is Speculation : Phys. :: Observation. All metaphysic (as is proved by the Hist. of Philos.) is in its
origin poetic:& in Poetrysy, that highest in which Phil. & Poetry
interpenetrate, & mutually co-inhere it must end. Hence all the
so called Analysts, peripat. or epicurean, from Aristot. to Locke,
Hartley & Condillac, attack all Speculation: for they leave off
where Speculation begins, viz. at the precinct of IDEAS. And yet
without these *their* Philosophy is either negative & like Tartar
Skirmishers, annoyant only—or a sensual dream—or a branch
from stolen from their Antagonist, & vainly grafted on a dead
Tree. (Such is Locke's Religion.)
    But only as Man is capable of Ideas, is he a Philosopher by   *f19ᵛ*
birth-right—and as far only as he is capable of an Ideal (practical
product having its cause & impulse in *Ideas*, & its End, Aim, and
Object in the approximative realization of the same) is Man a

Religious Being.—But neither the one nor the other is possible except thro' the Imagination (*not* Fancy which is but the aoristus primus (or Indefinitum ad *omne* tempus) † of Memory, in the service of *Choice*: & which in the absence of Choice or conscious Volition becoming the slave of Association, while present bodily *Sensation*, abdominal or pectoral, is the Usurper or Vice-gerent of *Choice*, loses the name of Fancy, & is called *Delirium* or *Dreaming*)—neither, I say, are possible but ~~except~~ by means of the IMAGination, by force of which the Man,

1. creates for himself, and for the use & ~~orderin~~ furtherance of his *Thinking*, Representations or rather *Presences*, where *Experience* can supply no more, but had already stopt payment;

f2o   2. feels Wants (πoθov, desideria) and proposes to himself Aims & Ends (*Zwecke*) that can be gratified and attained by nothing which Experience can offer or suggest, and to think of which is at the same time and by necessary involution to think and to form the notion of a higher purer Existence & a limitless Futurity. The Alogist or Metapothecary who from this absence of facts of Experience, & because these Presentments, Desideria, and Aims flow from out the Imagination, would degrade them into mere Dreams, and delusive phantoms, does but betray his own ~~crass~~ sensual *matterish*, crass & yet substanceless, notions of the Agency of the mind of man & ~~his~~ the powers that constitute his proper humanity, & knows not or forgets, that in every manifestation and to every product of his mind, *all* ~~the~~ its powers must co-operate.—Whether a given result proceeds or appears to proceed in a greater degree ~~of~~ out of one or the other, & is attributed to *this* RATHER than (more correctly, MORE than) to *that*, is ~~of~~ comparatively of small concern——~~The one important point is~~ Enough if truly and actually such Result be in accordance with our *whole Nature*, homogeneous ~~&~~ with & conducive ~~to~~, perhaps indispensable to, its collective *developement*——: if ~~in~~ under the condition of this developement of *f2oᵛ*   the moral and intellectual faculties collectively to a certain extent, & with the more clearness & confidence in proportion to their fuller developement, such Result ~~belongs to~~ as is received & recognized by the whole rational World, belongs to Man as *Man*, not

† The aorist. secundus, is the Indefinitum ad tempus *præteritum*.

as the peculiarity of one or of several Individuals, but if subjective
is yet universally subjective—nay, farther yet—if in addition to
this which for this high dignity is possessed by the truths of pure
Mathematics, & most awful on this account those truths are—if
the Result be impregned ⟨& actualized⟩ by the *Will*, which (as
concentric with the absolute Will that is one with the universal
Reason) is the source or index of all reality, and thus the *Objective*
rise up, as a celestial Birth, in and from the universal Subject—O
let it still be a ⟨mere⟩ Dream—for to Dreamers, an empty sound
to the Blind, an Apparition in the Limbo of modern Psilosophy,
an alien Substance.

The one sole Substance
And guest unwelcome to their shadowy den
That frightens Ghosts as Ghosts here frighten men!—And O!
    that

if only the souls of better mould, made to live in the courts of the
Sun, could be drawn called into the Valley of Vision—if only I   *f21*
could raise *them* by magnetic power from their present twilight of
Somnambulism to Clairvoyance—what a new Heaven & a new
Earth, would begin to reveal itself. Ah! mighty Phantom, whose
of which all their sensual reality is but the perverted Refraction!
Ah faithful Delusion, in which alone Nature speaks the Truth! Ah
lovely Dream without the faith in which maen must for ever have
been have walked in their sleep, the somnambulists of Savage
Life—or rather, rushing against an other, or falling from preci-
pice, or into gulph, would (as the history of savage tribes unanswerably demonstrates) have ages back ceased to exist. The faith
then in these Ideas, as the condition, & ground, and cause of a
positive Religion, is necessary even to the continued existence of
Man. Now a yearning & presentiment necessary to the existence
of a creature is an Instinct—but every Instinct is correspondent to
the kind and destination of the creature, to which it is connatural—
the instinct of a rational creature must therefore be a rational Instinct—and the Ideas or Faith as defined by Sᵗ Paul, is the Instinct
of Man—

It is given by Nature? If so, can Nature lie? And is it in her   *f21ᵛ*
last & noblest work, her Master-piece, that she utters her first and
only *lie*? (Here the various instincts of animals, in all of which she

keeps her promises, to be adduced)—But if from another than
Nature, then from a Power above Nature—and can *that* deceive?
But if the Instinct be a gift above the power of Nature, neither
can we expect from Nature alone the fulfilment—& Nature's fulfilments ~~are~~ to ~~the whole~~ Plant & Animal are Pledges & Prophecies to Man from the God & Lord of Nature—& with this *sealing*
evidence, that the incapability of Nature to fulfil this human Instinct is a necessary condition, an essential part, of the instinct
itself.—

f22 **4693** 23.24   Priesthood, as the conservatory of sacred tradition.—In the Zend Aptè or Haptè, in the Pehlvich Aft or Haft,
is a Hand—the 𝔚 or sch, the mark of 3—B or, soften'd, P = 2,
then by epenthesis Ha*p*te, the hand + 2 = 7, Asc*h*tè the Hand
+ 3 = 8.—Deschtè, both Hands, the Dual of Apte, in Greek
Δεκα—Haptè, ἑπτα/Aschtà (Sanscrit;) ⟨Greek⟩ οκτω; Tamul. asta,
eptu; Malabar epta, etta; Nepaul, ax; Bengalese, acht; the posterior, or hindward Hindost., awtoa, afto, awt; the anterior Hindost. at, aute; Gypsey, okhto; Zend, aschtè; Pehlv. hascht; Persian,
hest; Kurd. achst, chaschtu; Armenian, aut, utu; Russian, osm, w
ossim; Albanese, actini; Irish, ocht; Gaelic, ochd; Cymri, öis;
Welsh, wyth (pronounced *ooit*); Anglo-saxon, euhta; English,
eight; old belgic, afft; Dutch, acht; old Friesl. achta; old Gothic
achto; old Franconian, acht, achtoe; Frank, Bavar. and Austr.
achtè, achti; Runic & Islandic, aatta. Swed. åtta; Danish, otte; Ital.
Otto; French, huit./Lapland or Finland, kautze.—And curious at
least it is to observe the resemblance of the Zend, Aste or Aschti;
Sanscrit, Asti; Pehlv. Ast; Pers. Hash; Sclav. and Latin, Est;
Greek, εστι; for the Verb Subst. in the 3ʳᵈ· Person/or rather *objective* form.

The first P. Person   3 object
              Thesi[s]   Antithesis
f22ᵛ while the second is the punctum medium or punctum indifferentiæ—partaking of both, and capable of being contemplated as
either.—E contrario, however, there is much plausibility in my
original counting; man or I, one; δυ tu, two; τε ερ; ~~three~~, and *he* =
3; τε ετερον, *que* ater, quatuor, and another; πε = τε, εν, τε, πεντε,
and one yet; εξ,? out of that hand, to the other thumb; επειτα,

επτα, *then*; ο εκειτα; & what follows or is next; nᵣ . . . ᵀovem, νεον, a fresh one; δεκα, Digiti, all the Fingers.

4694 23.25   Tu verò crassis auribus et obstinato corde respuis quæ forsitan verè perhibeantur. Minus hercule calles, pravissimis opinionibus ea putari mendacia, quæ vel auditu nova vel visu rudia vel certe supra captum cogitationis ardua videantur, quæ si paulo accuratius explorâris, non modo compertu evidentia sed etiam factu facilia, senties.

APUL. Met. L. I.

Zoomagnetism.—The following sentence records the feats of our late Indian Conjuror as seen by Apul. himself—His Conjuror swallowed equestrem sphatam præ-acutam mucrone infesto (Qᵞ a spear?)—et venatoriam lanceam, quâ parte minatur exitium in ima viscera condidit.

4695 23.31   I propose the following Terms for Classifica-   *f26ᵛ*
tion.

1. Class. 2. Order. 3. Kind. 4. Race. 5. Tribe. 6. Family.
7. Branch. 8. House or Household.—

P.S. Where seven only are required, I omit Branch, & make House the 7ᵗʰ Example—

~~Order~~ Class.	ANIMAL
Order.	MAMMALIA.
Kind.	Man.
Race.	European.
Tribe.	Gothic.
Family.	Teutonic.
House.	English.

4696 23.32   Phthoric (Fluoric) Gas?—Let us suppose it   *f27*
n⸪ i.e. Nitrogen + Oxygen or Chlorine—or in the language of Dynamics a Power from the union of the *Contractive* Force with the *Separative-projective*, or Repulsive Force. These then are its Parents, ..., and ⸫. From the *former* it derives the power of acting on. /. *Carbon* (the power of Astringency or Appropriative Attraction, the energy of Cohesion)—for two extreme Opposites, or in other words two simple Forces in extreme

opposition cannot combine (decomponibly at least) but by mediation of a third, or collateral Power. The proof a priori is easy. If
not without mediation, then by numerical proportions; but these
are essential, primary, *reific*—ergo, by nothing could they be attracted, so as for the one proportion to leave the other. It is ~~highly~~
probable that the Metals are a series of Products of different primary Proportions of Carbon & Nitrogen (*Ideal* C. and N.) from
~~Quartz~~ Silicum to Potassium—and the metals are all simple *Bodies*.—But .... is the weaker, the subordinate Force: and ∴.
the predominant. The Product therefore, __∴__ , *discerps* only
the Silex.

f31 **4697** 29.45   Etymolog~~y~~ies sought in a different language,
tho' they should be true, are matter of curious information & instruction, but are not necessary for ~~the~~ a philosophical insight into
the purpose of the word~~s~~ or its inflections.—I am much delighted
to find my theory of the 3 Sons of Noah, & especially of the N.W.
N.E.~~&~~ Emigration of the Japetidæ (Descendants of Japhet) with
exception of the S.E. Passage thro' Persia into Hindostan, in the
latter only as a superior *race*, confirmed by the undeniable Identity
of Groundwork in the Teutonic, Greek, and Sanscrit—. But my
conviction that the inflections of persons in the verbs are expressed
by the verb of existence, as εω, ειμι, εομαι, ειμαι & its tenses is
not added to by finding σεβομαι, σεβεσαι, σεβεται. σεβομεθα,
σεβεσθε, σεβονται, in the Sanscrit, Sebāmi, Sebasi, sebati, sebāmas,
sebatha, sebanti (active voice)—and Sebe, sebase, sebate; seba-
mahe, sebadhava, sebante (Middle voice.—for asti and ~~est~~ εστι;
and bhavati = is; *ast* and ~~bh~~ubud, ⌈. . .⌉ is and be, in Persian—
bhu is the deficient root, in latin *fu*—Greek φυω.—So τετρεφα,
Sanscr. Tetārpa.—bharan, Acc. bharantam. φερων, φεροντα. Fer-
ens, ferentem. See Franz Bopp über die Conjugations System der
Sanscrit sprace in vergl. mit ~~den~~ jenen der Gr. Lat. Pers. &
Germ—Frankfurt am Mayn.

4698 29.46   Derwent, I believe it was, expressed his surprize, that Οδυσσευς should become Ulysses. Answer. Οδε is Ille,
οδ'εις ullus, ουδεις nullus— . —The wh = F preserves the f
sound in broad Aberdeen Scotch. Fat o deed he? What did he die
of?

4699 29.47 πίθι ἢ ἄπιθι = sauf oder lauf. The Bacchic used by Plautus, for Wives' Gossip & broad Soliloquy or Self-contemplation of the low Humour.

4700 29.48 Monday Night, July 9, 1820. The Alien Bill *f31ᵛ*
passed the H. of C. without a division, & without any reply to
the unanswerable arguments of Grant, McIntosh, Scarlett, &cc on
the strange ground, that the powers are so enormous that it would
be insulting to suppose that the Ministers should abuse them!!—
Nay, Mʳ Canning declared the omission of a Statute against Par-
ricide in the Roman Republic a fair analogy & a precedent in
point!!—as if it ~~were~~ had not been already provided for in the
statute against Murder.—O! how many thousands will this & the
former Sessions of Parliament have converted into Advocates of
Parliamentary Reforms, and of these how many too men who had
~~for 20 years~~ like me stood proof against all the arguments & facts
adduced by the Reformers ⟨themselves⟩ from Lord Russell to
Brougham and from Br. to Burdett, & from Burdett to Cart-
wright, Cobbett, Hunt and Co! Woe! woe! woe! to the Country,
once free, ~~of~~ in which a sober-minded Patriot can whisper to himself—✳ ✳ ✳ ✳ ✳ ✳ ✳! *If* the attempt could be made without
occasioning a civil war—*if* the success were morally certain—it
would be expedient: and IF it were *expedient*, it would be JUST.
Woe, woe, I say: for where the opinion of its *Justice* has once
struck root in the general mind of a Nation, what chance is there
of a calm judgement respecting its *expediency*, in the intense glow
of Feeling which such an opinion must either suppose or engender?
Lord! grant us Peace in *our* times.! And even this prayer for the
deferring & transferring a calamity, the entire prevention of which
we cannot pray for *in faith*, selfish, unconstitutional, unenglish as
it is, but nevertheless permitted, as the least evil, to a true Patriot—even this Aspiration is a deadly symptom!—

4701 29.49 On the state of mind ~~deman~~ requisite previ- *f32*
ously and in order to a fair examination of ~~the Old and New
Testament in relation to~~ the divine Origin of the articles of Faith
held in common by the ~~Greek~~ Eastern and Western Churches before the Council of Trent, & since then by the Greek, Roman,

Evangelic (or Lutheran) Reformed and English Churches—.—
Or rather thus—

There is a Religion, consisting of Doctrines, Commandments,
Precepts, and Histories held in common, ~~by~~ or with exceptions
too few and ~~of~~ too recent to ~~offset the truth invalidate the~~ invalidate
the assertion, by the members of the Greek, Roman, Scotch, An-
glican, Evangelical or Lutheran, and Reformed Churches. Of
this, the common Faith of Christendom, it is one Article, that
whatever ~~is the~~ Doctrines & Commands are evidently contained ~~in~~
~~or may~~ or implied in certain Books entitled collectively the Bible,
or the Old and New Testaments, are to be received as of divine
authority. All the Churches above named agree that nothing confessedly contradictory to these Scriptures can be a *true* part, while
the Protestants assert further that nothing not contained in or immediately deducible from these Scriptures, can be a *necessary*, part
of the Christian Religion. The sum of the Religion thus derived
is: that there is only one God, the Father, the Son, and the Holy
Ghost, the Creator and Governor of the Universe; that Man has
become corrupt in nature yet so as to remain justly responsible for
his deviations from original rectitude; that to remedy this corruption, and for the redemption and restoration of this fallen creature
the eternal Son, very God of very God, became incarnate, uniting
the human with his divine Nature, and submitting to the Death of
the Cross ~~ascended~~ rose from the Grave ~~and~~ & ascended unto his
Father's Glory, ~~and is now~~ to be our Mediator and Judge; lastly
that the plan of Redemption commenced ~~or prepared~~ with preparatory dispensations ~~to that of the Gospel~~ before the incarnation of
the Word in Christ Jesus, namely, with the Patriarchal, the Mosaic, and the Prophetic; and that it is still ~~condu~~ carried on ~~for as~~
~~many as can receive the Gospel in repentance and faith~~ by reading
& hearing of the Scriptures, by the aids of the Holy Spirit, and
by the ⟨continued⟩ intercession of the Redeemer, ~~obtaining~~ thro'
whom there is forgiveness of sins and a blessed immortality for as
many as ~~repent~~ receive ~~the Christ crucified as their Lord and Sa-~~
~~viour~~ the Gospel, loving the Lord ⟨Jesus⟩ in faith and manifesting
their love by obedience to his Commandments.

f32ᵛ

4702 29.50   In Hebrew all *aorist* Truths (generals) are expressed in the Future. Thus in Gen. 2. v. 24. our Transl. *There-*

fore shall a man (where the Future Hebrew led our Translators to attribute the verse to *Adam*, as part of his Speech, is truly to be rendered "*Hence does a man* or This is the cause, origin, & occasion of mans' doing so & so.

the "Therefore" in Hebrew is strictly *before this* or *On so*—

עָיָר	the term for dust
	⌜. . .⌝
אֵפֶר	ashes
אָבָק	dust as the dust raised by a crowd
דָם	**dam** = blood
אָדוֹם	**adom** = red
אָדָם	**adam** Adam
אֲדָמָה	**adamah** ground
דם	to imagine
מַיִם	water סָ **ya** sea = יום **ma** מַ **ma** from מַיִם water
ד	principle of fixity as what? from water †
נד	a wall
עד	eternity
אוֹד	substance very
מאד	very, ad.

f33

†how natural this is to the imagination, our modern phrase of the *Mother*-waters—i.e. before Chrystalization, proves—a quâ? ὕδωρ originally, *humor? udus?*

4703 29.51   The first use of the word, *Shem* or *Name*—co-existent with Language—when the Beasts were called before Adam, ~~to see what he names he~~ that he might see what he ought to call *it* (= each;) and whatever Adam called every living creature, IS its NAME. Ὄυνομα.

f33ᵛ

Necdo which our T. render Helpmate is strictly *Counterpart*— just as the Image in a Looking Glass—

4704 29.52   The evils of confounding or not determining the precise limits of the several Sciences are elucidated by the ill consequences of a similar confusion in the several Professions of the Learned, of the Theologian with the Jurist, of the Physician ~~of~~ and the Jurist with the Theologian, of the Chemist with the Physician, of the Naturalist ~~with~~ (= *Physicien*) with the Moralist and *Meta-*

physician, of all with the Philosopher, and the Philosophist or
*Psi*losopher with all!—and lastly, as at once Accompaniment and
Consequent, the Confusion of the Learned Class in genere ~~with~~
(the docta respublica: the res Literatorum communis: universitas
doctrinas supremâ potestate sancitas vel sanciendas explorantium
custodiantium, docentium et competentium privilegiata)—

4705 29.53   Known strong minds with imposing undoubt-
ing Cobbett-like manners; but have never met with a *great* Mind
of this sort—and of the former, like Cobbett, and Rickman, they
were at least as often wrong as right. The truth is, a great mind
must be *androgyne.*

Great minds (Swedenborg's for instance) never wrong but in
consequence of being in the right—tho' imperfectly. Such was the
case with his adherence to the mechanic philosophy, even to the
last—as in his notion of the human Will being placed in the punct.
indifferentiæ between the Heavens & the Hells—

f37   4706 29.56   Mournful yet of deep and concerning Interest
to reflect on the two ~~opposite~~ extremes, into which the Christian
World is divided respecting the nature and character of the canonical books of the Old and New Testaments, tho' in⟨to⟩ very
disproportionate Halves. With the immense Majority the Authors
of the Books are mere Automaton-Amanuenses, every word having been dictated to them by the Holy Ghost, in person—With
the other party the⟨se⟩ Books, & especially those of the New Testament, are mere *occasional* Writings, addressed to and ⟨exclu-
sively⟩ intended for the first Converts, but especially for Jewish
Converts, full therefore of accomodations to Jewish Prejudices,
and interesting or binding to Christians of the succeeding ages only
by accident!—~~and~~ But still stranger is the union, rather I should
say the juxta-position, of the two Contraries by the Clerg~~y~~ical Reverend Professors of the Orthodoxy, now in Fashion with the *liberal*
Divines of the Established Church. The former ⟨opinion⟩ in all its
blazonry of epithet & paraphrase: ex.gr. "the *very words* of Omniscient Deity", "the immediate Dictates of the Holy Ghost to the
inspired Penmen", "the infallible Amanuenses of the Spirit~~s~~" &c
&c they predicate of *the* BIBLE at large; and *the latter* they adopt

and avail themselves of, with regard to each several ~~word~~ part &
passage, as often as they happen to be discontented with the literal
sense, and no Socinian fancy is at hand to make a different Construing of the words plausible or possible.—O then it was for the
Jews only and in that particular time—The World, which was to
be avoided by Christians, the World which could not but hate
them, the promises, Blessed are ye when all men speak ill of you—
meant only the wicked Jews & idolatrous Heathens—& not at all
applicable to the present Communities professing Christianity—
For them there has ceased to be any World & of course any Christian Warfare with that World—Do not all good religious men &
the Public at large, extol and honor Mr Wilb.—Lords Sidmouth,
Eldon, &c. &c.—

4707 29.57   The attempts of some of the sentimental Uni-   ƒ37^v
tarians, ex.gr. Mrs Barbauld, to give a religious Splendor to the
Man, Jesus as p. 93 of her Hymns for Children—Who is he that
cometh to burst open the Prison Doors of the Tomb; to bid the
Dead awake, and to gather his Redeemed from the 4 winds of
Heaven? He descendeth on a fiery Cloud—the sound of a Trumpet
goeth before him—1000s of angels are on his Right Hand! It is
Jesus, the Son of God!—Now all this is, part, insincere falsehood,
meaning one thing, & conveying another—and part, the Lord
Mayor's Show—only not so well contrived.—

4708 29.58   The Object of the Mosaic Legislation *a Nation*/
In this one consideration lies the complete answer to & confutation
of Warburton's Fancies in his "Divine Legation of Moses". Compare the 1 and 2nd Chapters of the Wisdom of Solomon, 200 ante
Christum, with the plainest enunciations of a future State in the
Schools of Greek Philosophy of the same date—& if this was the
result of the Constitution established by Moses, notwithstanding
the almost continual corruptions of & rebellions against it—what
must it not have been calculated to have produced, had it been
retained in its perfection?—The non-destruction of the conscious
principle was undeniably held by the Jews—*Sleep* with their forefathers.—Jacob's Pilgrimages & *Promises*—go to Abraham's
Bosom—the Story of the W. of Endor—&c on/—/. The unity &

monotheism of God & all his attributes were everywhere *taught*, and kept present and prominent before their eyes—. How is it conceivable that these attributes should not be brought to bear on the nature of the Future State? That they *were* so, we know—. P.S. The Tendency of the vivid & *super* alia omnia eminent— Belief of a future State in the earliest & semi-barous states, 1. to Idolatry, Magic, Nec⟨r⟩omancy &c—& 2. to *denationalize*—i.e. to counteract the peculiar final cause of the *chosen people*.—Moses answered *all* purposes, without injury to any purpose—Made the Jews fit for that state by the same steps as led each Individual to

f38   the belief of it as a necessary *Inference* from the Attributes of God, aliquâ futuritate presuppositâ—but this *after* & out of the habits of Nationality—i.e. the *We*, ergo *I*. But this and this alone is the Christian *Soul*—it is ever a Class, comprizing all souls under given & established characters—the Christian as a Christian cannot think of ⟨"my"or⟩ "*I*" but as a conditional & humble deduction from *It* or *They*.—Under any others, alas! the far more common notion or rather fancy, the Soul becomes a selfish *Superstition*—an imagined Survivance of the earthly & perishable Slough.

f132ᵛ   4709 29.195   Misnah collected by Judah the Holy, under Marcus Aurelius, Severus, and Caracalla: tho' many additions were made in after times, as appears from both Judah himself & his Sons being cited in the work.—~~Other~~ Under the above mentioned Emperors the Jews enjoyed great privileges & prosperity: & the Academy of Tiberias became famous.—Jochanane, † the Beautiful, Chief of the Amoraiim, whose portrait was hung up in the ⟨Women's⟩ Baths callopædiæ causâ per vires imaginatrices, wrote a commentary on the Work of his Master, Judah, intended as a supplement.—⟨This the Thalmud of Jerusalem.⟩

The Targums were Chaldaic Paraphrases of the Law & the Prophets—~~and~~ some of them long before the Birth of Christ.— ⟨while one by R. Scessiath at the close of the 3ʳᵈ Century, who likewise wrote a Cabalistic composition of the Sephiroth, once in the Heidelberg Library.—⟩

Hillel II. Grandson of Judah was converted to Christianity in

† Called likewise, John the Son of Eliezer.

the beginning of the reign of Constantine—Judah himself born
about 135, died at a good old age 210, or 215.—This at least
seems the only tolerably consistent Chronology! as Basnage proves
against Bartalocci Mem.—Bartal. compared with Georgius Vene-
tus!—How is it that Basnage never refers to the latter! Not later
than Basn. ?—I fancied at least, that our Donne had attended to
Georg. Ven. in his whimsical Catalogue of Books.—

R. Nathan Collection of the Sentences of the Fathers layed the
foundation of the Thalmud of Babylon—230.

About the times of Heliogabalus, Alexander Severus—down to
Zenobia, and Odonatus, the number of the Syncretists or those
who would fain reconcile a neo-platonized Polytheism with Judaism & Christianity, some with a larger portion of the one, others
of the other, must have been considerable—.

4710 29.196   A grave Problem. Whether and in what de-   *f13ᵛ*
gree the advantage obtained by the transmutation of the numberless
minims of animal and vegetable matter into ~~living~~ vitalized Fly-
stuff, and the consequent prevention of noxious effluvia & miasma
by the anti-septic property of Life, are diminished, or counter-
poised, or outweighed by the dung and other excretions and extru-
sions of the same Flies ?—Aye or No, in an inhabited House ?
Ditto, in the air at large ?—

A practical Problem, suggested by the Grave Problem—
Whether it be practicable by ~~to~~ breed or education to rear a race
of House flies having the ⟨cancrine⟩felisity of going backwards and
performing burial-service.

> Sit alba, sit fusca
> (Ni res est absurda)
> Quod fuit Merda in Muscâ
> Jacet Merda *in Merdâ.*

4711 29.194   Distinguish as finely and subtly as you can, but   *f133*
not *drily* ⟨*dryly* or drily ?⟩ not *hostilely*. ~~Your~~ Light ceases to be
Light, when it oxydates & pulverizes, acts divisively instead of
distinctively. Nature sometimes melts into difference by a continuous diminution of intensity as in the petals of the Cabbage Rose;
sometimes as in the Rainbow, the Peacock's Tail and the many-

colored Butterfly defines without interspace by common boundaries; and where she makes segments, as in the Vine, Oak, or Fig-
leaf, unites them in a common expanse, from a common pedicle.
So ~~must~~ will you do, if you think, speak, and compose in the Spirit
of Nature—Your light must arise out of her *life*—φυσεῖ γαρ ενεστι
ζωη, και η Ζωη εστι φῶς ανθρωπων. Distinguish in order that you may
understand, remember, and communicate, but still silently sub-
suming the Unity that you may have wherewithal to distinguish.
For in all things capable of acting on each other, A, the Antithesis
of B, is itself = a ⨉ b: or A ⨉ B = α)(β ⨉ β ⨉ α.
()(for opposite to, the antithesis of ⨉ contrary to—Sweet)(Sour
: Sweet ⨉ Bitter.⟩ However small the extreme point, which you
call North relatively to a distant opposite spot, which you make
the South, can never be so small but that it must contain in itself
a South of its own relation to its own North.—Let us apply this
to your objection, that I do not sufficiently distinguish the historical from the doctrinal in my defence of the Pentateuch. In a certain sense every fact, worthy the name of a fact, is an Allegory—
it is equally unsafe to *heterogorize* and *not* to *alle*gorize. We cry,
Halt! to the streamy march of associate Thoughts & fix our attention on some one appearance only as far as we anticipate a representative value therein—and all such appearance have, besides their
common and individual import, a higher significance, and only in
the apprehension of this do we live a higher Life. And this is emi-
f131ᵛ   ⟨(turn over one Leaf)⟩-nently true of ourselves as individuals:—
"unless above himself He can"
"Erect himself, how mean a thing is Man!"
I do not however deny ~~that~~ nay the contrary I have myself enforced
(see Statesman's Manual) the propriety and strong expediency of
expressing the representative plusquam = individual function of
Particulars by the term, *Symbolic*; of heedfully distinguishing Symbol from Allegory; and of confine~~d~~ing the latter to a Total composed of connected Metaphors, such as the Tablet of Cebes or the
Vision of Mirza; a Metaphor being a Simile, where the subject
intended by the Likeness together with the conjunctions or particles
of Similitude or equation (*as*, *like as*, *so* &c) is understood, but
not expressed. A Symbol on the other hand I define as "representing the Whole of that, of which it is itself an essential Part". Ex.

gr. the Eye is a Symbol of Vision. Instead of being *alle*gorical, it is therefore so far necessarily *taute*gorical.

4712 29.193   Αυστραλ. βεσλειου βιος. My friend, Surgeon   *f133*
Γρῆν observed—I can't tell, whether he is in jest or in earnest, or where one, where the other.—But it's worse with me: for I see that he is neither in jest nor in earnest—ἑρμαφροδ.

4713 29.197   18 Sept.ʳ 1820.—Mʳ Gillman's just observa-   *f132*
tion of the Senses, not enumerated with those so called, Sight, Hearing, Smelling, Tasting, & Touch—He instanced *Handiness*—but many others might be stated, tho' this is very striking, permeative, & contra-distinguishing. In some of these indeed that recipiency, capacity, active-passivity, which seems essential to our notion of *Senses*, as far as we appropriate the term, a sense, to the 5 so called, is wanting—as in Handiness, which might therefore seem to require the name of Faculty (innate facility) rather than that of a Sense—but this is not the case with all, as ex. gr. the sense of Time, the sense of Relation, either in Place or Time (Mem. a word wanting that should be to Time what Place is to Space) but even with regard to the former, as the Faculty of Han-   *f131ᵛ*
diness, there must assuredly be co-inherent some feminine or receptive power, some ~~org~~ peculiar organ of assurance, some assurability of an outward correspondent, waiting, as it were, to be raised from Being into Existence by the formative Handiness.—

4714 29.198   Friday Evening, 18 Septʳ 1820—A̶n̶ half an   *f131*
hour later—. Found Mʳ G. with Hartley in the Garden attempting to explain to himself & co Hartly a feeling of a something not-present in Milton's Works, i.e. the Par. Lost—Par Reg. & Samson Agon.—which he *did* feel so delightedly in the Lycidas—& (as I added afterwards, in the Italian Sonnets compared with the English)—& this appeared to me, the *Poet* appearing & wishing to appear *as* the *Poet*—a man likewise? For is not *the Poet* a man?
As much ⟨as⟩ tho' more rare than, the Father, the Brother, the Preacher, the Patriot?—Compare with Milton Chaucer's Fall of the Leaf &c &c, & Spenser throughout—& you can not but *feel* what Gillman meant to convey—. What is the solution? This, ⟨I⟩

believe—but I must premise, that there is a *synthesis* of intellectual Insight, including the *mental* object so *anschaut*—the organ & the Correspondent being indivisible & this (O deep truth!) because the Objectivity consists in the universality of the Subjectiveness— as when A sees, & Millions *see*, even so—& the Seeing of the Millions is what constitutes to A & to each of the Million the *Objectivity* of the Sight, the *equivalent* to a Common Object—/A Synthesis of this, I say, and of proper external Object which we call *Fact*—Now this it is, which we find in Religion, & the Contents of Religion—it is more than philosophical Truth, it is other & more than Historical Fact; it is not made up by the addition of the one to the other—but it is *the Identity* of both—the Co-inherence.—

Now, this being understood, I proceed to say—using the term, *Objectivity*, (arbitrarily I grant) for this identity of Truth & Fact—that Milton hid the Poetry in or trans*formed* (not transubstantiated) the Poetry into this objectivity—while Shakespeare, in all things the divine Opposite or antithetic correspondent of the divine Milton, transformed the *Objectivity* into *Poetry*.—Mr G. observed as peculiar to the Hamlet—that it alone of all Shakespeare's Plays presented to him a moving along *before* him—while in others it was a *moving indeed*, but with which he himself moved equally in all & with all, & without any external Something by which the Motion was manifested—even as a Man would move in a Balloon, out of the sight of all objects, but himself and his Balloon—a sensation of Motion but not a sight of moving & having been moved—and why is this? Because of all the char. of Shakespeare's Plays Hamlet is the only character, with which by contradistinction from the rest of the Dram. Pers.—the *fit* & capable Reader identifies himself, as the representative of his own contemplative, & strictly *proper* & *very own* being—(action &c &c belongs to others, the moment we call it our own)—hence the events of the Play with all the characters *move* because *you* stand still—in the other plays, your identity is equably *diffused over* all—Of no part can you say, as in Hamlet, *they* are moving—but ever it is *we*, or that period & portion of human action which is *unified* into a Dream, even as in a Dream the personal unity is diffused & severalized (divided to the sight tho' united in the dim feeling)

f130ᵛ

into a sort of Reality.—Even so the styles of M & Sh.—with the same *weight* of effect from the exceeding felicity (subjectivity) of Sh.—& the exceeding *propriety* (extra arbitrium) of Milton/.

4715 29.199   Discourse = Ratiocination, but ⚹ Reason. Or   *f130* if not opposed directly (which I mean by the mark ⚹, even as by ⚹ I mean "contrary to"—thus Sweet ⚹ Sour, but ⚹ Bitter) yet □ disparate from Reason.—It is but a mean compliment to the Age that I ~~now~~ find it expedient to shelter my use of these terms by Authority—. Inopem me copia fecit—I take the three, that first occur to me, each from a different School, Peter of Mastricht, from the Aristotelean, Gassendi, from the Epicurean, and ~~Limborch from the Platonic~~ Limborch from the Christianized Stoic.
1. Petrus de Mastricht, Theolog. lib. II. Cap. 13. § VI. In Dei intellectu duo etiam requiruntur, conceptu nostro diversa: *idearum* præsentia et earumdem *speculatio*, in quo intellectus Dei haud aliter definiri possit accuratius, quam perfectissima *sui*, seu *idearum, intuitio*. Sed absque ullâ earumdem *receptione* seu *intellectu patiente*, absque ullâ etiam compositione ac divisione, absque ullo *discursu*— quód illa imperfectionem involvant, quæ a perfectissimo religiosissime est secludenda.
2. Gassendi in Lib. X Diog. Laert. de moral. phil. Epicur. Animad. de perfect. Dei—p. 56.—Nos multa, gradatim unum post aliud, ac deducendo varia per varias consequutiones cognoscimus; ipse (*Deus*) intuitu simplici, et nihil *ratiocinatione* per *discursum* indigens, intelligit omnia.
3. Limborch Theol. Christ. L. II, Capt. IX, 25.—simplici *intuitu* omnia cognoscit per nudam et simplicem intelligentiam. Non enim Deus, hominum instar, *discursu* utitur: omnis namque *Discursus* imperfectionem sapit. To which add Leibnitz from the Platonic School, Nouv. Ess. sur l' Ent. humain. Liv. IV. Chap. XVII— & Milton cum tercentum aliis.—

4716 29.200   Thursd. Sept. 21, 1820. It would be a useful   *f129ᵛ* exercise for youths liberally educated to *compress* Papers of Business, such as Reports of Committees, &c, & prizes attached to those who deliver the *same import* in the fewest words without sacrifice of 1. ~~transparency~~ perspicuity: 2. logical connection. 3.

energy & total impression. Then might follow compressions of Narrations—then of Orations, on principles of manly demosthenic *Taste*— & lastly, of argumentative Disquisitions.

It is greatly to be regretted, that the inveterate usage of borrowing from the French & Latin only (and in excepting a few technical names in the Sciences from the Greek) renders hopeless all attempt to enrich our Language from its own source primitive main stream the Saxon, and from the sister tho' ampler Flood, the Teutonic. For instance, having the noun, adjective & verb, content, in *sensu morali*, from the Latin, why not instead of the barbarous and equivocal *Contents* adopt the Teutonic Inhalt, or Inhold—thus complying with the general Rule, that where there exist two synonomous words, as swerve & deviate, from one Saxon, the other Latin, the Saxon word should be 1. the nomen generale; & 2. express the physical act, fact or phænomenon: while the Latin should be appropriated to the moral & figurative application of the word.—It is not so much the pedantry displayed, as the feeling of this Rule having been transgressed, that displeases us in Milton's Elephants indorsed with towers.

4717 29.201   Mem. To give a more *plain* as well as a more satisfactory Demonstration than I have hitherto met with, that alles Bewüsstein durch das Bewüsstein meiner Selbst bedingt ist sey, or (generally) that *all* Consciousness is necessarily conditioned by Self-consciousness—. Might not an animal scire truncum arboris *cum* ramis, as well as *se* cum arbore, or arborem cum *se*? If it be answered, that it must have *begun* in Self-consciousness, as the first Link, we must either allow Self-consciousness to animals, or find another term either for "Self" as objective Self, distinguished from the Subjective by abstraction, or for Consciousness, as Self-Consciousness.—The latter will perhaps be more advisable;—as Self-sentience, Self-percipience, as we might then say, that all *consciousness* is conditioned by Self-consciousness, tho' it may not be demonstrable, that all Consentiency supposes Self-consentience, or all Conpercipiency Self-conpercipience.—

f129

4718 29.202   I hold it scarcely possible to be ⟨too⟩ jealous of the purity of Language, even in technical terms, or the terminol-

ogy of Art and Science.—Yet when a great convenience & of one
of very frequent recurrence, is obtained, and a source of probable
confusion avoided, it would seem hard to refuse to Metaphysics &
Psychology alone a permission readily granted to all the other Sciences, and systematic Researches—hard that the Philosopher alone,
and that, too, even in those higher parts of Philosophy which even
more than Mathematics itself must ever be addressed to a Learned
Class, should be confined to the language of the Market and the
House-hold.—For instance, the term extension requires intension
as its antithete: to imply the *act* of making or becoming intense.—
& this cannot be ~~accurately~~ precisely expressed by intensity or in-
tenseness, which have another & appropriate sense & are wanted
for themselves. ~~The~~ Its homophony or sameness of sound with
Intention is an inconvenience but ~~one in which Philosophy shares
with~~ one which may be easily supersed by a more accurate pronunciation of the two words, assigning the s sibilant to Intension,
Inten-si-on, thus making it a quadrisyllable, and the *sh* to Intention, Intensh-on as a trisyllable.—But in the participle, the spelling will be same, as well as the sound—& tho' even this would be
an evil which ~~Philosophy~~ the Mathematician is allowed in more
than one instance, yet in so very common a word, as intended for
purposed, I consider the inconvenience sufficient to justify the
~~forma~~ introduction of a new word, even tho' it be irregularly
formed, & have preferred the somewhat barbarous intensed)(
extended to *intended*, and intensify to intend—on the principle that
it is more perplexing to have to attach a new & strange sense to
an old & very common word, than to have to learn a new word
~~for~~ with its appropriate sense.

f128ᵛ

4719 28.48   It strikes me (Octob. 9, 1820) that it would be
well, as a Ζητητικον π⟨ε⟩ρι 'Υδροφοβιας, to trace the Vorregungen
& first appearance of Saliva in the animal creation—then its potenziation as poisonous in the Toad's back-warts, in the Saliva direct
of the Egyptian Gecko (—3 persons died in Cairo from having
eat a cheese which the Gecko had beslimed with its saliva, of vis-
ceral inflammation)—& so on to the Serpents. It appears *characteristic* of the proper Amphibia; consequently, in the mammalia to
be a retrogressive Metamorphosis. Item, to seek (tho' this indeed

f52ᵛ

f53

is expressed in Vorregungen) the prophetic Avant Courier, in the vegetable world—here it is, surely, the milk that dries into gum, resins, opium—& in a lower state the corrosive milk of the Euphorbias—or both mixed apparently in certain Thistles./The Lettuce Opium to the poison of the Lactuca viridis—/—. In animal Life therefore we are to look for its resurrection in the reproductive processes, but the reproductive in the service of that which characterizes animal life, viz. *sensibility*—but yet in an early stage, & probably from a certain affinity to Azote obtained by its animalization, even as Opium seems to be the last power of Carb. + Hyd., in those that breathe in the atmosphere—& here indeed it does appear in the amphibia—& finally ripens (like an animal Anti-Opium) into a gummöid—as Opium to Carb. + Hyd.—So the Adder, Cobra di Capello [*Cappello*], &c. Poison may be to Azote + Pthoric Gas (Fluoric)—In the process of digestion in mammalia, Saliva an Expression of Hunger—the mouth fills, &

f53ᵛ its tendency is to the Stomach, intractive, reproductive—but in anger (how many the analogies of anger & Hunger, which in animals are almost always united) it is explosive, therefore collected—Cats, ~~wom~~ children, women *spit*—the application to *Wolves, Dogs—Thirst!* Hunger's tendency to bite wood, stones &c.—In short, whatever harmless on the nerves is α + A, becoming connected with some dilative power attacks B (= Irritab. Syst. Blood, Muscles) producing therein an awakening of the power A (Sensib. Sys. Nerves) would tend to *Hydroph.* But here, observe, that in my Scheme I combine two principles of Classif. First & highest, the Powers—

Magn. Elect. Galv.

Repr. Irrit. Sens.

and then each according to the ~~three~~ Circumstances of the Planet (for I have nothing to do with Elements, but follow Moses) viz. ~~Water—Dry Land, Water + Dry Land, Water + Air~~ Water— or Subaqueous Air, Dry Land or Superterrene Air. And these again with the Links, 1. Water + superaqueous Air (Whales &c.)

f54 Water + Dry-land (Amphibia) Dry Land + Water i.e. those that live most on dry land, and yet haunt the water, as Swans—&c.— This *Combination* is most important ~~from~~ in reference to the former, or Principle of the Powers—thus Fish pass from a lower form of Reprod. (Water plants) into Sensibility—Insects from the highest forms of Veg. Repr. into Irritability, & present Irritability tending to Sensibility—while the Bird in which the sensibility of the Fish exists as promoted, pauses, as it were, to combine itself with the irritability of the Insects & their Art-instincts and then commences the harmonizing & equilibrizing of the three powers in the Udder of the Mammalia—/

In short, my plan comprizes Oken's & Steffens's without the fictions of the one or the deficiencies of both—& this, not by any mixture of the one with the other but as a necessary deduction from the difference in my first principle.

4720 28.49   Effects & Cons. of Despotism in high states of $f54^v$
Civiliz. far more pernicious than in Barbarism. The Prudential Proverbs that truly regulate the conduct of Italians, whenever their passions are not masters (as in Marietti versus Brown)—the facility of obtaining esteem by negative virtues flattering to the self-interest of others, spite of the most shameful public Depravity. & in this in two classes—*Honor*—Castlereagh Goodness, Piety = Sidmouth the Feelings of the higher Classes, of the Females above all, from the moment the Prince's Dislike of his wife was known— & their excessive hard-heartedness—This has never been effectually displayed—& yet never was there such a moral necessity of displaying it. Fodder the man, beasts well—be a knowing Grazier &c! it is a paternal Government. What results? Austria!—Italy!—

State comp. of England, Ch. I and II & the present times.—
How full of Confidence the Cavaliers, at the outburst of the $f55$
War—& with what a shew of reason! In each *County*, what a splendid decisive majority, what a tantum non omneity, of Gentry & Nobility on the part of the King!—& with these the majority of the populace in the cities, London itself forming scarcely an exception. So now *perhaps*, as to the higher class! but, not so now with regard to the populace. And O! compare the number & information of the latter, & the means of making that number & information be *power* by influence of the ubiquitarian Press! Compare the influence of the Landowners, & the Prelates then—of an Earl of Newcaster who could himself bring into the field a force of 50,000 men, with the influence of our absentee Gentry, who

for the most part belong by accident to their Places of Residence, & whose Farms are let by auction or equivalent

f55ᵛ   4721 28.50   What seems to me wanting in our fashionable vocal Music is *Eloquence*. As Oratory is Passion in the service of Reason, so should vocal Music be Passion connective in the ~~source~~ service of Passion.—Præcipitandus est liber Spiritus. If there were as much Spirit, and Liberty as *Feeling* & *Sweetness* in her singing, Mrs. Gillman would excel, to my Judgement, all the Singers I ever heard—

Oratory = Passion ~~enlivening~~ in the service of Reasoning, fusing the links of connection, so as to soften away ~~its~~ the angles & fill up the interspaces without destroying the distinctness—

Vocal Music = [?C.] Connection in the service of Passion, giving it at once order and progression.

f56   4722 28.51   Man the fiercest beast of Prey ⚹ the most servile Beast of the Stall—the handsomest Monkey & the ugliest Baboon—the haughtiest War-steed, the most sluggish & insensate *Sloth*—the faithfullest Dog, the most treacherous Cat—the most magnanimous (vs innocence) Elephant, the most cowardly-ravening Hyæna, at once the lordliest Lion & the most venal Jackall—the pious (frommste) meekest Doe, & the most untameable (ausgelassenste) Rat. In parts, Man is like to (find an equation) every ~~part~~ Class of the Creation; as an Integral total, equal only to himself, Nature, & God.—

Men are black, olive-brown, copper-red, and white/Qʸ—Why no green & blue men? The reason may be—that the perfection of animal life consists in the continued antagonism of powers; but blue is the negative Pole of Life, & marks deficiency—Green, the Synthesis, & where Synthesis should not be, *Confusion*, or Indifference—Bruise. Putridity

f56ᵛ   4723 28.52   Stercore fucatus Crocodili. Horace. The dung of the Warane, a species of Lizard skin to the Crocodile, only something smaller, yet commonly confounded with it, is still collected by the Coptic Peasantry & sold to the Turks, who still use it as a *fucus*. The ψευδο-άγιοι—Sidemouthry ⚹ Yare or Yardmouthry—

The Plumage of the polished brilliant Colibri & Bird of Paradise used as a FAN, with the Arm-bone of an assassinated Enemy for the Fan handle, by the Malay Tribes, viz. the Friendly Isles in the South Sea. An Ax he met her os! + Castellum re age.

The retrenchments & reforms done with the consent of a rapacious canting Government = the little Bird that the sleeping Crocodile suffers to creep down its throat, & pick off the small Slugs and Leaches ⟨& Efts⟩ that annoy the monstrous King-Eft himself. ⟨The Bird, Trochilus by Herodotus, the Charadrius Ægyptius of Mod. Ornithol.⟩   *f57*

4724 28.53   Nature-history on a new scheme of Classification—first, of Powers, each Power subdividedstinct into its Force & all each Force again according to the *proportion* of its predominance in the Species of animals subsumed; & then according ⟨to⟩ the kind (E. or W.) and degree of its modification, as the Substantive or ens substratum modificabile by the adjectives = επιθε-τον modifaciens—⟨These the Distinctions of the first order—then the Divis. & Subdivis. of the⟩
Second; according to the circumstances or habitats. First Non Atmospheric)(Atmospheric
  − A. a. Terrene subaqueous *Grubs*, ex. gr.
        b. subaqueous   Fish
  + A. +a aqueous   whales
        +b superaqueous
        +c subterrene
        +d terrene
        +e superterrene
              Entozoa & Parasites   *f69*
1. Those on the surface of the internal organs
2. Those in the parenchyma
3.   —   in the Fluids and Humor—
4   —   in the Solids

4725 28.54   The greatness of the kingly power ought to be   *f57ᵛ*
as guarded a state-mystery, potestas celata, in a free country, as the power of the People under an unlimited Monarchy. What a desertion or ignorance, then, of the true *craft* of a British Statesman to have bared this secret to all eyes, by making the H. of Lord's his

Majesty's Breech, cocked out of a Window. His organ of elimi-
nation & explosion!—

4726 28.55   I purpose to collect from Oken all the words
f58 which he gives as the sounds of the different Birds. The number
of consonants, I confess, startles me, & makes me suspect that the
pre ~~forming~~ existing forms or Moulds of a German Ear were
fellow-artists with the Birds' Larynxes in the ori- and auri-facture
of these vocables Dadigöi, Dasida, Girrahia, Gack-Gop,
Schwoine, (Hizärizäri Zsuss-döng döng, Histhisthehi, gip gip gip
gip dihöija dihoija—Gäga ga. these 2 lines = the song of ~~the~~ one
Bird, the Loxia curvirostra, or Fir finch!) I remember my friend,
Von Einem; & my vain attempts to persuade, he me that the
Cuckoo said, Gück, gück, & I him that that the Guckguck said,
Coo! coo! I am inclined to think, that the clacking sound, the
guttural flung sharp thro' the hollow under the palate is the nearest
sound to a consonant—but not one—for it has no vowel to sound
WITH it—& that what the German hears as consonants are gut-
f58ᵛ tural, aspirated vowels.—Birds make divisions of sound, and likewise distinguish ⟨by⟩ high & lower in continuous sound—but they
do ⟨not⟩ articulate, distinguish the ~~same~~ sounds without references
to high or low, & yet link one to the other without absolute dividing.—Yet we know, that physically speaking, they *can* speak as
well as whistle. i.e. they can repeat but cannot *make* words./? ?
Because they do not reflect, express *sensations* only, while man,
infants at least, attempt to imitate sights & modes of *Touch* by
sound, using the organs of speech as embryo hands, moulding the
voice or sound./

4727 28.56   Striking instance of the bad effect of Wit in
Swift's Sermon Upon Sleeping in Church the text Acts xx. 9.—
"But because the Preachers now in the world, however they may
exceed St. Paul in the art of setting men to sleep do extremely fall
f59 short of him in the working of miracles; therefore men are become
so cautious as to ~~take~~ chuse more safe & convenient postures for
taking their Repose, without hazard to their persons; and upon the
whole, chuse rather to trust their destructions to a miracle, than
their safety." In what state of mind are the Auditors thrown, to
hear a grave sermon on the subject?—

4728 60.1   final a Cause. Adjungit *voluptatem*—atque   *f1*
utinam Virtutibus semper vel Innocen[tiæ] saltem; at nec non et
vitiis, eheu!—

What is the definition, not verbal but real, of PERSONAL-
ITY? What constitutes a PERSON?

The union of a Self-subsistence with a Basis independent of it,
so that both, ~~are~~ mutually interpenetrated, ~~and~~re but one Being.—

The *Ground* of God's existence independent of the Ideal Principle, or his Self-subsistence—God therefore in whom the Basis &
the Self-subsistent necessarily unite to form one absolute Existence,
is in the highest sense a Person, a⌈nd⌉ the very Principle of all
⌈Per⌉sonality. If this be Manicheism, i.e. a doctrine of two Prin-   *f1v*
ciples — or if it be Pantheism too, as making the *ground* or *Basis*
of human Existence the same with the *Ground* or Basis of God's
Existence—both which in any offensive or irreligious sense I utterly deny — yet still I affirm that without *such* Manicheism &
Pantheism neither can the Personality or Free Will of God be
maintained without gross contradictions—not ~~from transce~~ incomprehensible from Transcendence, but [?yet/not] comprehensibly
ABSURD. Hence in the 3 different Systems, the Vulgar, that of   *f2*
perfected Idealism, ~~an~~ such as Fichte's, and that of perfected Realism, such as Spinoza's, God is no *living* God, but either an infinite
Power without personality or Consciousness,—of which all other
things are modifications—infinita cogitatio sine centro—Spinoza,
or a mere *Law* of the Universe, Lex generalissima—ordo ordi-
nans—moralitas infinita sine centro—Fichte/or an anthropomorphic Deity, a *part* of the Universe—& therefore itself requiring a cause beyond itself—the Jehovah of the unthinking Crowd—
whose Creed is a mere Theriacum multi-compositum, like the Pre-   *f2v*
scriptions of the Empirics in the old Books of Pharmacy—. It is
Pantheism counteracted by a positive denial & anathema of Pantheism—it is Manicheism with a declared abhorrence of Manicheism—& Idolatry which the juxta-position of the first & second
Commandments is to disidolize & renders innocuous.—

Our Being is in the Being of God—and yet God created our
Being out of *Nothing*—The Devil is the Principle of Evil—but   *f3*
yet God created—i.e. is the Principle of the Devil—/Aye, but God
made him an Angel of Light, all Light & Holiness; & he made
himself a Devil.—What *Light* make Darkness?—If Light &

Darkness are co-present in a Being, it is conceivable how that Being may choose Darkness instead of Light, or subordinate at least the Light to the Darkness—but the Darkness must have been—or we make a creature a Creator—& what do we gain by it? The supreme Creator is still the Causa Causæ. If he made the Angel of Light including in him the power of transcreation to

f3ᵛ Darkness—(for it is either creation or annihilation, accordingly as the Dogmatist predicates of Evil that it is a Positive or a mere negation of the Positive/as Augustin, the Schoolmen, Leibnitz, Spinoza, teach)—then he created the Darkness.—If we are forced to assume a Devil in order to conceive the Fall of Man, how much more must we assume a Devil's Devil to explain his own Fall—& so on ad infinitum, in diabolos Diabolorum per secula seculorum!—

f₄ 4729 60.2   There is a deficiency in all the languages, I am acquainted with, of a fourth gender or genus commune in the pronouns relative, ⟨& demonstrative.⟩ We have masculine αυτος, ος, *he*, er, egli, &c—feminine, she &c—neuter, *it*; but we want a fourth, which instead of being neuter, i.e. neither Masculine or Feminine, is common to both—or rather abstracting the sex (withdrawing it from the Attention) not denying it. Thus the Greek

f4 Ανθρωπος, the Latin, Homo, the German, Mensch, & in English the word, Person—

I wish for instance to conceal the sex, & say "a Person, whom I shall not name, called on me and made a request—I however asked—*him?*—or *her?* whichever I used, I baffle ~~my~~ the very purpose, ~~of~~ I had in choosing the word, a Person, instead of "a man" or "a woman"—& yet our Language will not permit ⟨us⟩ to say, *It*—/nor the Greek, or Latin, ὅ or quod as the pron. rel. to Αν-

f5 θρωπος or Homo—and the same inconvenience is felt when I mean both sexes, or either indifferently—as for instance I wish at present to describe Love as it exists in common both in the Man & in the Woman—& unless I use *it*, I destroy my own thought in the very second ~~&~~ or third sentence. *It* therefore I will use.

4730 60.3   PROBLEM.—Is *true genuine* LOVE of necessity

f5ᵛ RECIPROCAL? that is, can I really be *in Love* with a woman, ~~whom~~,

I *know*, does not love me?—If I were asked merely for my own
~~ex~~ self-experience, ~~for~~ as an *instance* in favor of the Neg: or the
Affirm-ative, I should not hesitate to answer—"No! *I* at least could
not." But if Reasons & Grounds are required, and the question be
that generally, I should support the Negative *thus:*—We are talk-   *f6*
ing of Love/but under that term many & diverse meanings may
be, and have been conveyed. What do we precisely mean in the
present case?—I for myself wish to be understood as meaning by
LOVE (in the present question)

Exclusive sexual Attachment, such as may exist in the best &
noblest conditions of human nature—*that attachment* of a refined
& honorably honest Man, which is *exclusively* felt to some *one*   *f6ᵛ*
Woman; & vice versâ, that of a Woman to some one Man.—

Well!—and where-in does this Love consist? What is its universal cause, its *indispensable Condition?* (i.e. that, without which it
could not be.)

Here are two questions: and I will answer the last first.—The
cause of this Love taken generally, that without which it would   *f7*
not be, is

The Necessity ~~in all Noble Dispositions~~ in all men of human
Sympathy, ⟨&⟩ ~~whence~~ ~~the~~ a in nobler Dispositions, the yearning
after that full and perfect Sympathy with the *whole* of our Being
which can be found only in a Person of the answering Sex to our
own.—In this statement is implied a two-fold Truth: 1ˢᵗ that no
human ~~B~~ Individual is self-sufficing (ἀυταρκὴς): 2ⁿᵈˡʸ, that the con-   *f7ᵛ*
sciousness and impulsive Feeling of this Self-insufficiency ~~increases~~
is more awakened, is stronger & more active in proportion ~~as the~~
to the *natural* Sensibility & *fineness* (which, when preserved &
aided by the moral choice, is called *Refinement*) of the Individual,
and to the cultivation & more or less compleat developement of all
his ~~moral~~ bodily, mental & moral, Powers & Impulses. This in-   *f8*
stinctive Sense of Self-insufficingness is indeed common to all men.
But in vulgar Natures it breaks forth in the turbulen~~e~~et Inquietude
of mere *Appetite*, with little other determination as to its *Object*
than the same Instinct in Beasts—namely, to any one indifferently
of its own kind & the opposite Sex/or if they think at all, yet their
whole attention is swallowed up in the effect, (i.e. the Desire itself)   *f8ᵛ*
and in the fitness of the *Object* to gratify it—the visual form being

to them the *word*, as it were, which signifies their Lust. Thus as low & ignorant Persons ~~never~~ always ~~confound~~use the *Word* ~~with~~ and the *Thing* so as to be incapable of separating them ("damnd

f9 fools! to call a Hat 'Chapeau'! How can a *Hat* be chapeau? a Hat is a Hat.") *to love* ~~means~~ signifies no more than an appetite represented to the eye or Imagination under the form, ~~of~~ which accidentally excites it.—To do them Justice, they seldom take the name (of Love) in vain/they have a *Liking* for such or such a Woman.

In the Steps above these which yet differ in *degree* only from them, but are of the same kind, the Instinctive Sense of Deficiency

f9ᵛ manifested in Appetite may be appropriated to some one Object with a perception of good or agreeable Qualities in it; but still so, that their ~~Love   i.e.   their Liking~~ bodily Desire is the true Origin, Cause & occasion, of their Love (i.e. especial Liking) not their exclusive Preference the occasional Cause of their Attachment. Enough of these!—In ⟨a⟩ pure & ~~harmonious Being~~ noble mind,

f10 the sense of ~~his~~ its Self-insufficingness, the sense that it is of itself *homo dimidiatus*, but *half* of a compleat Being, exists *consciously*, ~~becomes~~ & with *reflection*—and this is extended to the *whole* of his complex Nature, to the Understanding, to the Affections, as well as to its animal organization—& by this very extension, united

f10ᵛ with the habit of associating all fairest thoughts & images all mental & corporeal Perfection with the Desire to be both in mind & body perfected, we—without effort ~~subordinate~~ harmonize the cravings of each part of our Nature with the whole by subordinating them according to the rank of the Faculty which is their Birth-

f11 place/making that which ~~is~~ originates in our moral nature not only the Master & Lord, but likewise the cause & occasion of those feelings which have their birth-place in what we possess in common with Animals. "I *love* ⟨her⟩ & *therefore* I occasionally *desire* her—I *occasionally* desire but I *always* love her"—For him, who can truly before God & his own inmost Heart affirm this, his very

f11ᵛ Desire is transmuted and glorified into Love—and ~~on~~ with the contrary this Love itself, however recommended by moral or tasteful associations, as it is the mere Effect so ~~it~~ is it only a mere mode of Desire.—

Observe the Question was, what Love ~~is~~ must be? not in what

manner it takes possession of the mind—no, nor what it *is* in its   *f12*
inmost Essence. We say only, Love is *a* Passion, that effects this
or that—but what *the* Passion is that effecting this & that is Love,
& its Causes of existence in ~~the~~ a given *Individual*, & the *mode* of
its origin, all this is beyond our present Discussion. For our purpose it is enough that ~~rational~~ Living Beings have no other means
of Union but Sympathy & Inter-communication/~~that once, at one~~   *f12ᵛ*
~~& the same time, in the same kind & the same degree~~, in the same
moment, same Kind, same Degree, ⟨and⟩ by one and the same
Act, to receive & to give, to give what I receive, to receive what
I give.——~~Defin~~ Understand Union in this sense—& then I say—
that Love is the Desire of ~~my whole~~ all my Being to be united to
some other Individual ~~as the~~ (conceived as alone capable of per-   *f13*
fecting my Being) ~~in its our present finite state~~, by ~~the~~ all the
means which Nature, ~~dictates~~ Reason, & Duty, permit or dictate—
the means observing the same harmonious relation to each other,
as the Body, the Soul, and the Spirit do—and with a similar Co-
adunation & due Subordination—. Thus Soul & Body are united,   *f13ᵛ*
yet it is the Soul especially that I call "I"—so ~~Love~~ exclusive Preference & Desire may be united in one Feeling, but still the former
only ~~is~~ may be taken by itself & be still called Love.

We shall now then find little difficulty in justifying our first
Negative/For how can we conceive the ~~origin~~ appropriation of   *f14*
Love, as a co-alescence of all our Powers & Receptivities, to one
particular Object except as the result of a secret Intuition of a
Sympathy in ~~the~~ its Being with our own?—Unless ~~both~~ the Head,
⟨the⟩ Heart, & ⟨the⟩ Body concentrate their separate desires of
perfecting them selves by union ~~with~~ the Head, ~~with the Head~~,
the Heart with the Heart, the Person with the Person, ~~of~~ to one   *f14ᵛ*
Individual, it is not *Love*,—for Love is a Passion of the whole
Being in harmony.—And how is this possible or conceivable, unless the Lover *imagines* at least an essential, tho' perhaps not fully
developed or realized Sympathy, ~~with~~ in the inmost Being of the   *f15*
Beloved?—In short, dismissing the notion tho' obliged to retain
the metaphor of Time (as when I speak of the Sun & his Rays, or
of a co-eternal Filiation)—with my first Definition as of Love in
its ~~first~~ moving *Elements* & *before* it has an Object (in order of

Thought merely)—& then see whether any cause of its appropriation to one out of 1000,000 can be conceived, but the conviction
that this is the Object?—

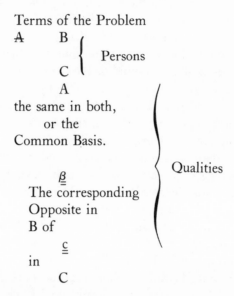

Terms of the Problem
A   B
{ Persons
      C
      A
the same in both,
    or the
Common Basis.

        β̲
The corresponding
Opposite in
B of

        c̲
in
      C

Qualities

so that the qualities β and c from the corresponding Poles meeting
in the Equator = A.

‾B + A + β‾ + ‾C + A + c‾ = B.C. = A.A.—But B being =
A, and C being = A, B = C—they are one Flesh—i.e. living
Soul.

Persona duplex, dupliciter una, per intus-susceptionem mu-
tuam.

4731 60.4 German Words, for which I am still to seek for an exact Correspondent in English.
Anmuth.

4732 60.5 ⟨Identif ⟨Sir John Seabright⟩ of H. of C. with administ.⟩ N.B.—To appropriate a Blank Book for such notitiae et annotationes as the perusal of the M Papers, especially of the Debates & other Proceedings in Parliament may daily suggest.— Ex. gr. Wed. 18 Oct. 1820.—a motion in H. of C. on Sir R. Baker asking Governm. to commit an act of Suicide!

4733 60.6 Few Sophisms more frequent than that which ⟨where two things fall under some common property as weight, measure, motion &c.,⟩ shifts changes the contingent subject in order to *shift* or give the a impress the belief of having shifted, the Predicate/—tho' in truth it is at all times an equal tho' not at all in all cases an equally palpable absurdity as if I should object to the measurement of a room by a given yard, tho' I had agreed to the same measurement before, under the protest—aye! but that was a garden & earth—this is a room & of wood.— *f17*

4734 60.7 *f17ᵛ*
Elements of Music
1. There is a *pleasurable sensation* from sweet sound, dal corpo del' suono, in & of itself, & independent of congruity of successive notes, ex. gr.—the first note struck on an Harmonica or Steel Organ (Claggett's Aeieuton).
2. There is the like from succession of sounds in accordance with the original and inherent Congruity of A with B rather than A with F.—This I call pleasure from Melody, calling into act (actus receptivus, analogous to—Elect. in Physicks) the intensityon of the Sense.
3. There is a pleasurable effect from congruity of co-existing, & co-existence of congruous, sounds = the picturesque in Music, *f18* in which Time avails itself of the an attribute of Space, calling into act the *capacity* of or *extension* of the Sense. This I call *Pleasure* from Harmony.

f18   4. There is a *delight* † (S̶t̶a̶t̶u̶s̶ ̶V̶i̶r̶i̶u̶m̶ ̶(̶s̶i̶v̶e̶ ̶F̶a̶c̶u̶l̶t̶a̶t̶i̶s̶ alicujus
b̶e̶n̶e̶ ̶s̶e̶) from the seeking, expecting, and finding according to a
Law.—G̶e̶n̶u̶s̶. ordo.—

5.α and a *specific* delight from the perception of Proportion,
f18ᵛ common to all the Fine Arts. S̶p̶e̶c̶i̶e̶s̶ ̶c̶o̶m̶m̶ Genus speciale.

β These in union & applied to Sound, I call Delight from from
the *Act* of following, perfected by the *Fact* of finding, order and
calculable Proportion.

Species Musica.

5. There are certain appropriate effects or movements produced
on the nerves as far as the̶y̶ nerves are the instruments, or the
conditional cause, or at least the admitted Exponents of our Sensibility as distinguished from mere sensation—and probably pro-
f19   duced on & seated in the *pectoral* Nerves especially, the *Plexus
Solaris* &c.

Now these specific movements in the nervous system m̶a̶y̶ = A,
B &c may be excited in their nascent quantities, = a, b, &c, &
in any of the *degrees* from a, or b, up to A or B—: so that, tho' A
or B. should be painful, and incompatible with Order and calculable Proportion, yet a, or b, or some one of the higher quantities
short of A or B. may be pleasurable, and reducible to Law, Order,
and Proportion. But whether thus or by any other means, it is a
known fact, that different Agents may produces similar movements
on the nervous system, so that

f18   † = Status Virium sive Facultatis alicujus bene se habendi, &
have the same ratio to the *intellectual*, that *Pleasure* has to the *animal*, Life.

4735 60.8
f20   Mʳ J. Bishop
Mʳ Eggleton's
Church Lane
Chelsea

4736 60.9
                        Music

Sweet discontent

Of a Contentment overflowing,
Jet of a Pleasure striving with its fullness

a joy that strives with its own fullness—

or Sweet Overswell and mimic Discontent
Of a too full Contentment.

4737 60.10   In Sir W. Jones's vi[th] Diss., that on the Per-   *f*2o[v]
sian's (Vol. I. p. 203 of Dissertation &c relating to the Arts, and
Literature of Asia) we have the most pleasing account of the Pantheistic Scheme of Theomonism of the Persian and Indian Philosophers. But here, as in Europe, the System is either the same as
religious Idealism, = the Berkleian Scheme: or subject to all the
odious consequences of Spinosism, such as the indistinction of good
and evil, of moral and physical, of God and blind Fate—and after
all, leaving the main problem unsolved & unsolvible, viz. the
ground of the existence of Multeity, or the passage from the Infinite to the Finite. The re-union of the Soul after Death with God   *f*21
is a mere Bubble of words and contradictions in a Scheme which
makes God all, and all God. If the Body be God, how i̶t̶ can it
disjoin from God? If the Body be Maia, i.e. a subjective Illusion,
a mad perception or cycle of Imaginations without any correlatives
in Being—whence came they? from Finiteness?—But whence came
that?—From moral evil? But that supposes a *will*, and that a finite
will, & this again supposes a plurality of wills, as the bounds, each
of other/—for a boundary *from* nothing is as absurd as a boundary
of Nothing.—

4738 60.11   Twixt thro'—twixt in—Zwischen Branches—   *f*21[v]
swelling Branches.

4739 22.79   Sherlock's "Vindication of the Doctrine of the   *f*57[v]
Holy & Ever blessed Trinity &c—1690. Sm. Q[rto].—p. 69.—
Exquisite instance of the state of metaphysical Lore at the æra of
our Revolution in 1688, and after it—of the famous fruits of
Mr Locke's Confusion of ιδεα with ειδωλον, of νουμενον with
phænomenon!

"We can form no *idea* of Substance (*i.e. ejus quod stat subter*) but what we have from Matter—(i.e. *ab eo quod super faciem jacet, seu, rectus, a facie quæ supra videtur*)—that it is *some thing* extended in a triple dimension, in length and breadth and depth, which is the SUBject of those Qualities, ["] which inhere and *sub*sist in it!—

N.b. The words in parenthesis are mine, not Sherlock's.—The next sentence is—

And therefore as Matter is the subject of all sensible Qualities, &c—*therefore/* —Now either Matter means objectivitas = quod *f58* videtur mere/ or the opposite = quod est et videri nequit—take your choice—In the former case, it is a contradiction in terms, in the latter a pigra iteratio = the subject is the subject.

f59   4740 22.81
                              Lancelot Wade, Nov. 1820—
Hints of Mr Gillman's conversation with Lancelot concerning the nature and management of his Case.

1. Irritable Stomach with highly irritable Lungs, acting and re-acting on each other, in a patient constitutionally of ~~too great~~ extreme nervous ~~activity~~ mobility.

2. The complaint partakes of an asthmatic Character without being directly asthma. ⟨So too the Lungs are subject to disordered actions & even organic injuries which are not necessarily that specific malady, called De⌐cline⌐.⟩

3. Whether pulmonary *Disease* has already commenced, & is among the causes, ~~of~~ that keep up the irritation, ~~tho' the Disease be not what is called Decline~~, there are no means of *deciding*; & therefore we are entitled to hope that there is not.

4. But even if ~~there were~~ Disease ~~in addition had~~ in its slighter forms ⟨should already exist,⟩ be~~en superinduced on the disorder'd actions of the pulmonary & digestive Organs~~, still there is every encouragement to believe that it might be suspended & finally worn out by a strict & regular adherence to a judicious alterative & curative process.

f59^v   5. And on the other hand tho' there should be no Disease at present, yet ⟨if the Patient neglect or long defer the proper means, or adopt a wrong means⟩ it is to be more than suspected that ~~it~~ Disease will ~~sooner or later, and that later~~, take place and probably under more unfavorable symptoms.

6. The remedial & preventive Process consists of (**A.**) cautious and persevering systematic attention to Diet, to the *quality* of the Food doubtless, but still *more* sternly and steadily to the *Quantity*: in respect to both of which not the Appetite, but the experienced Digestion must be the Test and the Guide.—In this rule attention to the after-processes of digestion, the feelings after eating and the state of the Bowels is included, under this one maxim, that where relief can be obtained by reforms in the quality and *quantity* of the Food & the Liquids taken, recourse should not too often or rashly be had to Drugs, Emetic or purgative. ⟨The question, not whether you *want* more, but whether you *need* more & can digest *so much?*⟩

(**B.**) Choice of Temperature, or an Atmosphere neither chilling nor hot nor damp but dry and warm, and as little as possible subject to great & sudden charges.—South of Sicily, with Malta in the 3 winter months. **C.** exhilartive Circumstances of occupation, Country and Society. **D.** Quietness in motions, Spirits, Talking &c—& re estab. of Health the one sole Business—

4741 22.80   —the Word of God does not work as a natural *f58ᵛ* agent but as a divine instrument: it does not prevail by the force of deduction and artificial discoursings only but *chiefly by way of Blessing in the Ordinance, and in the ministry of an appointed person.* Bishop Jeremy Taylor's Holy Living, p. 215.—/Sect. IV. Ch. 4.—

Now this is the Point. Is this assertion of the superloyal suborthodox Bishop (God bless him!) *truth.* If so, the present Church of England ~~is~~ with all other Protestant Churches are fools and suicides—

4742 22.82

                    000001   and   *f59ᵛ*
        then behold   100000——

4743 28.40   Quæ enim facilior res quam linguæ rabies et vilitas morum: alter ex aliorum contemptu, alter ex sui? Nam viliter semet ipsum colere, sui contemptus est: barbaré alios insectari, audientium contumelia est. An non summam contumeliam vobis imponit, qui vos arbitratur maledictis optimi cujusque gaudere? qui vos existimat mala et vitiosa verba non intelligere: aut si intel-

ligatis, boni consulere? Quis ex rupiconibus bajulis, tabernariis
tam infans est, ut si pallium accipere velit (i. e. choose to turn
reviewer) disertius maledicat?
    Apul. Lib. Floridorum I. *ad finem.*—Hazlitt, Jefferey & Co.—
f48   By the bye, these two Books of Florida seem to be transcripts from
Apuleius's common-place Book of *Good things,* happy Hits &c.,
which he had not had an opportunity of *bringing in* in his writings—& so put them together much as Ovid's Metamorpheses—
    Walking ~~in Newgate Street~~ with W. out near ~~by~~ Newgate—a
fine piece of architecture—Phidias—Mr Knight on Taste—Lord's
Mayor's Dinner—Ministers—Spanish Revolution/
    hoc quoque genus invenitur, qui meliores obtrectare malint
quam imitari: et quorum *similitudinem* desperent, eorundem affec-
tent simultatem: scilicet uti qui suo nomine obscuri sunt, meo in-
notescant. Si quis *igitur* ex illis Libitinis splendidissimo huic au-
ditorio velut quædam macula sese immiscuit &c,—*Do.*

f38   **4744** 29.59   22 Novr. 1820.—Proclus in Plat. Theol. given
me by my dear Friend & Fellow Inquirer, ⌐ . . . ⌐ Joseph Henry
Green, Surgeon of St Thomas's &c &c—
    Surely never did any Writer, before or since, perpetrate such
verbose and *littery* periods as Proclus—and this in his introductory
Chapter. I can compare them only to what the Germans call a Rat-
king, that is, *a Huddle* of Torpid Rats whose Tails have inter-
twisted, stuck and *grown* into each other. It is the more strange:
for Marinus, his Disciple & Biographer, writes an elegant, & tho'
too *exquisite,* yet a perspicuous, style.—I felt repeated pricks of the
conscience as if my own periods in the FRIEND were too many &
too often, of the Proclian† kind.—Nothing can be more elegant
than Marinus's Character of Proclus, from the passage—Μαρτυρες
δε μοι του λογου οι εν πεπονθοτες—to υπο συμπαθειας εφερετο—on
the first & second page of the last leaf but one of the Life.—
    A motto for my Work, Assert. of Religion.
    Οὐ⟨τε⟩ γὰρ νοῆσαι τὸ θεῖον ἄλλως δυνατον, ἤ τῳ παρ᾽ ἀυτῶν φωτὶ

†Mem. likewise the *splendid* sentences intermingled—making it
still more difficult to take up and knit on the ravelled skein of the
Construction.—

τελεσθέντας, οὔτε εἰς ἄλλους ἐξενεγκεῖν ἢ παρ᾽ αὐτῶν κυβερνωμέ-
νους καὶ τῶν πολῃειδῶν (υ?) δοξασμάτων καὶ τῆς εν Λόγοις φερομένης
ποικιλίας ἐξηρωμένους. Οὗ δὴ γινομενοι, σύμπασαν τὴν περὶ αὐτῶν   *f38ᵛ*
ἀλήθειαν ὑποδεξόμεθα, καὶ τέλος τὸ αριστον ἕξομεν τῆς ἐν ἡμῖν
ὠδῖνος, ἥν ἔχομεν περὶ τὰ θεῖα, γνῶναι τὶ περὶ τούτων ποθοῦντες
καὶ παρ᾽ ἄλλων πυνθανόμενοι. καὶ ἑαυτοὺς εἰς δύναμιν βασανίζον-
τες.—

And what follows, i.e. the first § of Cap. II : tho' indeed this latter
would better suit the Logical Prolegomena—down to οι περι
ταῦτα δεινοί.

4745 29.60   Sincerum est nisi Vas, quodcumque infundis
acescit.

HOR. EP.

4746 29.61   Εν ἄπασι δὲ τὸ Σαφὲς καὶ Διηρθρώμενον καὶ
'Απλοῦν προθήσομεν τῶν εναντίων—τὰ μὲν διὰ <u>συμβόλων</u> παραδε-
δόμενα, μεταβιβαζοντες εἰς τὴν ἐναργῆ περὶ αὐτῶν διδασκαλίαν·
τὰ δὲ δι᾽ <u>εἰκόνων</u> επι αναπέμποντες ἐπὶ τὰ σφέτερα παραδειγματα.
Καὶ τὰ μὲν <u>ἀποφαντικώτερον</u> ἀναγεγράμμενα τοῖς τῆς Αἰτίας βα-
σανίζοντες λογισμοῖς· τὰ δὲ δι᾽ <u>ἀποδείξεων</u> συντέθεντα διερε-
υνώμενοι καὶ τὸν τρόπον τῆς ἐν αὐτοῖς ἀληθείας ἐπεκδιηγούμενοι
καὶ γνώριμον τοῖς ἀκούουσι ποιοῦντες. Καὶ τῶν μὲν ἐν <u>αἰνιγματι</u> κει-
μένων, ἀλλακόθεν τὴν σαφήνειαν εξευρίσκοντες οὐκ εξ ἀλλοτρίων
ὑποθέσεων ἀλλ᾽ ἐκ τῶν γνησιωτάτων συγραγραμμάτων.—

The above, annecting the first extract (Ουτε γαρ νοησαι) as the
motto to the Religion Asserted—and the part of the §, p. 3, and
4, from Ο μεν αυ των προκειμενων δογματων ακροατης to—
Σωκρατης.—last line but 9, p. 4.—for the Logical Prolegomena.
This last extract, in which Proclus details the successive steps necessary in the ascent to Theology, as the philosophic Apex, beginning with purity as the absence of evil, & thence thro' the various
Learnings as so many courses of discipline, viz. Grammar, common Logic, Physics (i.e. Εμπειρια istorum omnium quotquot *ab*   *f39*
extra dantur) Dialectics and Metaphysics, and ending with the entire Love of *Truth*. (Truth as the being the immediate Form and
proper *Person* of the Good) as the presence of Good, Truth being
the immediate Form of the Good and its proper Person—is one

instance among many of the superiority of the philosophic Mystics, even of those whose peculiar doctrines are most transcendent, nay, fantastic and grotesque, in subjects within ordinary comprehension. Barren and clouded as the mountain summits may be, to which they have clomb, the point in their descent at which they emerge from the cloud, into the common day-light on the mountain's breast, commands the vale below, and gives them ⟨not only⟩ a more comprehensive but likewise a more distinct and orderly view of the fertile fields in relation to each other as well as to the Uplands by which they are all in common surmounted than is possessed by those whose exclusive domain & abiding place they are. Interpret what I have called the fertile fields as representing the practical arts and empirical attainments, and the Uplands as corresponding to the Ideas, *Forms*, pre-existing the plastic *Moulds*, as it were ⟨pre-existing⟩ in the Mind itself, and all the *formal* as so many conditions a priori of all Experience, themselves therefore in the order of Thought to all or particular experiences, and lastly to the *Ideas*, that transcending both experience & how its mental forms Correlatives furnish the grounds of both speculatively, and the the Exemplar practically: & you have the *sense* of the Allegory.

f59   **4747** 24.104   Books for Mr Stuart
                              Orme's History of Indostan/

4748 24.103

A Simple Question   ⟨opposite page⟩
Does it follow, I say, that because Bacon was Very Lamb, Pork must therefore be Mutton? By no means! Even tho' I should waive, out of courtesy and to avoid the suspicion of over captiousness, a possible Objection that in some & these ancient & authentic Documents VERY LAMB is written VERULAM? The difference, I admit, is small, as Verulam, that is, Lamb super Veru, or Lamb on the Spit, must have been Lamb verily—For local accidents *f59^v* cannot affect *essentials*—thus a King on a Close Stool is still a King, and a Close Stool tho' lidded by a King's Breech,

ε ω; θ.c; η :

natheless remains a close stool.

Modern Oratory.   *f58ᵛ*
—Suppose then, that out of Courtesy and to preclude all suspicion
of Captiousness, suppose then, I say, Mʳ Speaker! that I should
waive the important Objection, that in the best and most ancient
~~mod~~ Documents and these of most authentic orthography the word
is written, nay, I will even add, *spelt*, with a variation that of itself
would give the Death-blow to the learned and eloquent member's
argument, a variation essential, not accidental, Mʳ Speaker, a
variation which ~~informs~~volves two ~~out of~~ in three of the three main
Forms of Variation, variation by false substitution, and variation
by fraudulent ~~Omission~~ addition—a variation, Sir, ~~too~~ likewise in
two out of the three places of all possible ⟨variations⟩ in the middle
and in the End—and perhaps therefore, Mʳ Speaker, ⟨when⟩ the
learned and Eloquent Member's argument ~~having alr~~ shall have
been proved deficient ~~with~~ both in the middle and the end, it may
appear to some persons desirable, that it should have wanted a
Beginning too. (*a* Laugh). But suppose, that we submit to waive
this, yet does it therefore follow, I say, Mʳ Speaker—does it, I
say, follow that because Bacon was very Lamb, Pork must therefore be Mutton?

⟨Modern oratory *continued*, from over leaf—(this being the sec-   *f58*
ond page)—
But, Sir! I will not consent to waive the Objection, I will not
thro' ⟨a⟩ false & idle Facility submit to throw behind me a Javelin
which will pierce, Mʳ Speaker! thro' the sevenfold Shield of the
learned Member's Logic into the very heart of his Cause—I assert
then, Mʳ Speaker, that the word so far from being Very Lamb, is
not Lamb at all—neither Lamb in its innocent & sportive state of
voluntary Motion in the fields, nor Lamb in its compelled state of
rotatory Motion having for its axis the culinary Spear, the trivial
name of which will, I doubt not, occur to the Recollection of the
⟨hon.⟩ House without aidance on my Part—. Sir, the word is of
topographical Origin, derived ~~either~~ from a *Town* ~~or Village~~ in
his Majesty's imperial Realms. Here then, Sir, is a town inhabited
doubtless by men, women, & children, all rational & featherless
Bipeds! [?confounded/compounded]with ~~an~~ one irrational & fleecy
Quadruped—The animate substituted for the ⟨in⟩animate, one lit-   *f57ᵛ*

tle Lamb, ~~for~~ or perhaps one joint or limb of one little Lamb, for many Houses—(House-Lamb indeed!) A LAUGH. On the other hand the irrational for the rational. Many Men sacrificed in order to introduce in their stead one Sheep, and that, Mr Speaker, a Sheep in its Minority. (*Here* the learned member took occasion to advert to, and particularly animadvert on, the recent depopulation of the Highlands, by the new system of Sheep-farms/We regret &c.

But this is not all—Here is a Y forced upon us instead of U, Mr Speaker! (a *loud Laugh*)—a why, which ⟨if⟩ the learned and el. member had put to his own mind he would have spared ⟨me⟩ the painful but necessary Duty of asserting, that it is a why, to which no answer can be given! And here too, is a Bee, which ~~ought not to Be to us as our great Dramatic~~ to use, Sir, the emphatic Language of the greatest of Dramatic Poets, ought *"not to be"*. O Verulam! Verulam! quàm maluisses subire Ferulam, than to have this over-bold, busy-body Bee buzzing at thy Bottom, O beautiful Borough! But Mr Speaker! I more than suspect & shall conclude by anticipating the same opinion on the part of this honorable House, that those who have planned and attempted to execute this forgery will find ~~the Sting of this Bee in their consciences~~ this their culditatious Bee, honeyless, but not stingless—the Honey, ~~I trust~~, they will find no where, but the sting, I trust, they will feel in their own consciences.—(Great applause)—

M^r —— rose in answer.—Mr Speaker, after so long, so severe, & let me say, so unmerited an attack ~~both~~ alike, on my cause, my argument, & my motives, I claim the indulgence of the House merely for one observation. But that will suffice. For I ~~will~~ shall not ⟨attempt to⟩ follow the eloquent Member thro' his long ⟨logical, philological,⟩ orthographical, topographical & chorographical Gallop, but content myself with ~~returning at once~~ one arrow out of a Quiver-full, but that (to return to my assailant at once his menace & his metaphor) aimed successfully at the very Vitals of his Vituperation, at the very Heart of his Harangue.—Sir, I assert that there is no such Borough in his Majesty's whole imperial Realms as Verulam. If there ~~are~~ is, let the honorable Representatives of that Borough stand up & confute me.—I pause for a reply. None—Then there being no Members, there can be no such Bor-

f57

f56^v

ough—This was the main foundation of the Antagonist's reasons/ & this you find, swallowed up at once by no Giant ⟨argument of Monster Length no⟩ or a logical Polypheme, but by a dwarf syllogism, a short yet irresistible and Jacko-giganticidal Enthymeme, ⟨who atones for for his want of monophthalmic Defect of Color clear Sight by width & length & height.⟩ *f56*

Having thus by a single Gust, as it were, of articulated Air dried up the wet sand which formed the Pediment (it might perhaps not have impaired the eloquent Member's reputation, had it been the Impediment) of his high vaulted Column of Invective, and by the same momentary desiceative Gust scattered it on the vacant Air, I shall need no blast stronger than the mere Blast of a Kitchen Bellows to blow away the superstructure, the Rope of Invective, with which the eloquent assailant hoped to have strangled my Cause, ⟨or kept it at least in opprobrious patibular suspense.⟩ I shall need no Blast stronger than the mere Blast of a common Kitchen Bellows to blow away whatever remains of this his Logical ⟨philo-log⟩ Sand-whip-cord (a Laugh)

As to the addition of the final B. so heavily charged upon us, is it not notorious to all legal Scholars the frequency of the omission *f55ᵛ* of final Letters in ⟨all⟩ e older Documents! And shall the removal of obscurity supply removal of a Defect by the Supply & Cure of a Contraction be deemed a Fraud!—Forbid it, Candor! forbid it, Correctness! ⟨Ortho-Typography⟩ As well might the renowned Lancashire Maker of mechanized wooden Cork Legs be indicted as a Counterfeiter of Heaven's Coin, or exposed to public rendered odious in the eyes of the Public, as a Corker-up of the understandings of his fellow-men. ⟨The Bee with which the document ends, proves a humble Bee—buzzing in every Mouth, as if it had been a whole Apiary—Lilyies Convolvuluses-garden of Eloquence/nectarium large, but stamina wanting, the sting is barbless, the honey- *f56* bag empty.⟩ As to the medial u, Mʳ Speaker, had it been *you* *f55ᵛ* yourself, that had been vi et armis dragged into the middle of this astonished House, instead of a poor one meagre little Vowel, the poor Penultimate of Vowels, which the wise Grecians degraded by the perpetual annexment of the Epithet, slender, therein so probably instructed perhaps by the perhaps wisdom of that Phœnix of Letters, the famous Phœnician Cadmus.—But Sir! I will indulge *f55* my Antagonist. I will recall my Y, tho' I see no wherefore, & restore this repair the daring, and Parisian Rape, the direful Source of the ⟨long⟩ fierce Siege, with which the Ilium of your Patience has been sustained, I will restore this Helen of Vowels to her former rank and station—and for very ⟨Lamb⟩ behold once once more the ancient Veru lam. But what will my Antagonist gain by this—Veru lam, it even must be evident to all etymologists, is Lamb super Veru— or in an unmixed with that mixture of two Languages rendered venerable by its frequency, nay, constant recurrence in our ancient Law-books—in the unmixed English of the present Style Lamb on the spit—. But spitted Lamb cannot ceased to be Lamb because it has been transpierced with the Spit— nor tender young Lamb ceased to be contradistinguished from that transitional state analogous to the Hobbidihoy Period in the human Animal, in which it is neither Lamb or Mutton, by the appropri-

f54ᵛ ate Epithet of Very Lamb—so that here we have at once Very Lamb of Veru Lam'—& the assailant has only occasioned me to return pace a circle in triumph back again to my first position. Local accidents, and accidental Conjunctions, as that of the kitchen & the spit in the present Instance, cannot affect Essentials. The King on a Close Stool still remains a the King: & the Close Stool tho' honored with a living & temporary Lid by one of the fundamental Parts of our constitution still continues a close stool & it would be as much an high absurdity to question the latter, as it would be high Treason to deny the former.

Here the honourable member sate down—& a loud cry of Question! Question!—Indeed after two such speeches from such speakers who & what could be after listened to—The comparative merit of the two Orations divided the opinions of Judges as much as those of Eschines & Demost. de Coronâ.

f54 We have only to regret that in consequence of our temporary exclusion from the Galleries which the Member for —— had ordered to be cleared, but afterwards was induced to permit our readmission, the whole introductory Portion of the former Speech is irretrievably lost—It is, alas! a fragment; but a large & precious Fragment—a Mercury compleat, all but the Head.—

f59 4749 24.105   os = mouth and os = bone—meaning that the Os should be quasi ossified, whenever it is in Nominative Case.

4750 24.101   Launcelot Wade and myself are agreed as as to *f49ᵛ*
the following:

1. That we are opposed equally to all attempts to explain any
thing *into* Scripture, and to all attempts to explain any thing *out* of
Scripture/—i.e. to explain *away* the positive assertions of Scripture
under pretence that the literal sense is not agreeable to *reason*, i.e.
their notions drawn from *Their* school of phi- or psilosophizing.
Thus a Platonist would ~~anticipate~~ believe as ideally true certain
doctrines independent of Scripture and therefore anticipate their
Scriptural realization which an Epicurean will not receive on the
most positive declarations of the divine Word.—   *f50*

We both agree likewise, that as the Unitarians (and a large part
of the Arminians who will not allow themselves to be Unitarians
in the ⌐ . . . ⌐ fashionable plusquam-socinian sense) err grievously
in the latter point, so tho' less grossly the Pædo-baptists err in the
former. We both appear to ourselves to see, that there is no end
or determinable Limit ⌐ . . . ⌐ to these inferences and probable
deductions; but that the final decision in each particular dispute,
pro tempore isto et quo ad disputantes ipsos will depend on the
accident of ⟨superior⟩ logical skill and rhetorical address and
fluency in the victor of the moment. The vast & more than Alexandrine Library of theological Controversies affords one continued
comment on and exemplification of this fact.—

In our conviction all the Texts of Scripture, appealed to by the
Pædo-baptists as positively commanding or even authorizing &
permitting infant baptism,—all without any exception, are made
to bear a sense in no wise contained in the Text or communicated *f50ᵛ*
to it by the context, and in direct contradiction to other positive
declarations of Scripture and to the Spirit of the whole ~~Liv~~ Gospel
History—so that as far as the question is an historical question, we
have not a shade of doubt in our minds, that the Baptism of Infants
was neither the practice or the purpose of the Apostles or the *Apostolic* Age.

P.S. More than this we do not consider as necessary to our
argument/and are far from joining with Robinson (Hist. of Bapt.)
in his assertions respecting the late origin of Pædo-baptism, as
commencing under, & at once condemned as general doctrine &
yet allowed on the grounds of particular Charity, & because Charity is greater than doctrinal Faith, by Cyprian; but as not becoming

a general or ordinary practice till after Augustine's controversial Heats with the Pelagians, and his diffusion of the Calvinistic Article of Original Sin & the Devildom of Infants dying *unchristened*. We reject this statement as rash & believe it to have been unanswerably confuted by diverse Pædo-baptist Divines. Without any pretence to determine, ⟨how, where, or⟩ at what time Pædo-baptism began, ~~to be the practice, of the Churches~~, we content ourselves with the negative assertion, that it did *not* begin in the *Apostles* and that it was not the practice of the *Apostolic* Churches.

f51

Item: Launcelot Wade coincides with me in the full conviction, that neither the ceremony of Baptism under any form or circumstances, nor any other *ceremony*, but such a Faith in Jesus Christ as produces conformity to his holy doctrines and commandments in *heart* and *life*, that *properly* makes us Christians: that in the strict sense of the term essential, this alone is the *essential of* Christianity, that the same spirit should be growing in us which was in the fullness of all perfection in Christ Jesus. Whatever else is called essential is such only because and only as far as it is essential *to* this as its means or instrumental, or *evidently* and practically implied in this.—

f51ᵛ

In this class we place all the express doctrines ~~in~~ of Scripture, namely, that Jesus Christ was the WORD made Flesh; that the Word was co-eternal with God, προς τον θεον, and was God; that the Word, and the *Son of the Living God*, are names of the same Person, and distinct but not divided from the Father ("My Father and I will come—and *we* will dwell in you) that the same Person became the Son of Man, i.e. the Messiah of the Jews, and the crucified Saviour, and Redeemer of all Men, Jew & Gentile; and that by him and thro' his mediation, including the mystery of his incarnation, passion, and Resurrection, ~~and~~ alone is the World saved; and that a regenerative Faith in the same is the sole appointed means for each & every individual Sinner in order to his Salvation/Whether in all instances this must be an explicit faith, if tho' implicit it be actual & effectual, we presume not to decide; but leave each man to be judged by his all-merciful Lord and Master, who alone can truly know the heart—tho' as rational creatures we may ~~venture to~~ humbly anticipate, that his opportunities of instruction & understanding will be taken into account in each particular

f52

case. If from the full and compleat coincidence of our inward experiences, the direct declarations of Christ, and the manifest spirit and tendency of the ~~whole~~ Christian Scriptures throughout, (attested moreover by the concurring testimony of all ages since the apostles & so interpreted as we now interpret them, while the Greek was a living language) we find ourselves incapable of conceiving ~~th~~ it as possible, that a Christian having the same mind as was in Jesus, and with both the dispositions and ⟨the⟩ predisposing feelings of a true disciple of Jesus, should reject and renounce ~~the~~ all belief in the ~~existence of a~~ Redemption from Sin, and in the necessity of any Redemption, should deny both ~~the~~ guilt and the *f52ᵛ* atonement for guilt, and thus receive Christ solely and exclusively as a merely human Creature, differing in degree only from the Prophets before him, and only by precedency and acquired privileges from his own immediate Disciples—and consequently should exclude from his scheme of Religion all but the doctrine of a future state as *taught* in words and evinced by a miracle, in addition to a pure system of Ethics—if we find this *inconceivable*, ~~in itself~~, and have found no sufficing proof ~~of its real~~ of its reality (nay, can imagine no proof in this present state that could *prove* it *real*, however inconceivable it might remain)—we are bound in Christian Sincerity to *declare this*—and yet do not make our powers of Conception the measure of God's Power, or of the divine Mercy. We do not consign a ~~Turk Unitarian~~ who calls himself a ⟨a Mohametan Unitarian who does not call himself a Christian⟩ to damnation, because we deny him the name of a Christian, but repeating the words of Scripture as the *Law*, we leave the administration *f53* of the Law in each individual instance to the omniscient Law-giver who alone is the Judge—. In like manner when we refuse to ~~call~~ a ~~Unitarian~~ Priestleian Unitarian who does call himself a Christian, that title—we judge not another, but simply abstain from the insincerity of equivocation, or (the sole alternative) from ceasing to call ourselves *Christians*/in as much as every contra-distinguishing Title must imply the believed Essentials of that from which the Title is derived.—While I hold the ⟨affirmative⟩ opinions of Mʳ Belsham to be no otherwise Gospel Doctrines than as every Christian is *a priori* a man, and *know* that Sᵗ Paul held every one of the doctrines, as separated from ~~the~~ historic events, while he

was persecuting the Christians, and that he not only does not admit
but disbelieves and earnestly contends against every article ~~which~~
f54   ~~I believe~~ peculiar to the ⟨⟨turn over to the next leaf⟩⟩ Christian
Scheme, and ~~now every~~ all the essential parts of the same, even
those which can not in so full a sense be pronounced peculiar to
it—ex. gr. the existence of a responsible Will, as the proper origin
of our moral acts/—how without the grossest hypocrisy can I retain
the name myself and yet concede it to him?—I will not be angry
if he refuses to call me a Christian—(let him call me, if he pleases,
an Augustinian, or Calvinist, or even a Platonist)—and let him
not be angry with me. We both soften our creeds by the common
concession. God alone is our Judge.

f59ᵛ   4751 24.106   Cottle's Psalms with morals of his own added
to each.—Diamond + Oxygen = Charcoal. Even so on the fire-
spark of his Zeal did Cottle place the King David Diamond (worth
a hundred Pitt, or even Great Mogul Diamonds) and caused to
pass over it ~~a~~ the oxygenous *blast* of his own ~~Ox (or Calf or ass)~~
~~ygene Genius~~—Inspiration & lo! the Diamond becomes a bit of
Charcoal.
N.B.—Oxygene, just as Homogene, Heterogene &c—i.e. of the
Ox genus: on which Jo. ought to congratulate himself, as it follows
perforce, that he is so far secure from blundering that he will
never make a *Bull*.—

f60   4752 24.107   Dʳ Crompton
                               ~~Dʳ Nº/13 Essex Street~~

4753 24.108   P. 128, 129 of Oken's Lehrbuch der Natur-
philosophie are worth reading as *the other side* of the question
respecting the adequate exponency of the external Characters in
Mineralogy, asserted by Werner, and defended by Henry Steffens.

4754 24.109
gn   ng
χ   w
k̲   v̲

Ϝοικος—simply softened would become soivos—
Vicus
Wick
κοιϙος
civis
hive
ive

4755 61.39   I draw the line between what a Christian may   *f37ᵛ*
ignore, & yet be a true & good Christian—if the causes & occasions of his ignorance be involuntary of blameless—
    Likewise, what a Christian may doubt—or disbelieve, or inter-
pret other than the commonly received Import. Ex. Gr. the infallible truth of every sentence in the canonical Books, or even of
every book—
    but then it will be objected—o men will *be indifferent.* The very
contrary! I reply. By removing slavish selfish *fear* we encourage
& cherish the love of Truth, the habit of delight in Truth—&
what a delight this is, & how far it extends, even into the minutest   *f38*
fibres of a thing. you may judge by analogy of men interested in
Nat Sciences (the anatomy of the Caterpillar &c) & which those
little know to whom Truth as Truth is nothing, & the *selfish* Cui
bono every thing. Ex. Gr. I believe Luther to have been as faithful
a Christian & as well-pleasing to God & as beloved of the Lord
whom he so dearly loved, rejecting or doubting the divine origin
of the Apocalypse as if he had been its Archaspistes—& hold Newton's ⟨Belief⟩ not a whit less a semi-demi- 32ⁿᵈ of Christianity on
account of his orthodoxy on this point, & yet I could *expend* myself
in defence of its authenticity.

4756 61.40   Mʳ T. Poole   *f38ᵛ*
                  Old (or *New*) Humours—
                  New if at Breakfast—./

4757 61.41   *Jaw*—provincially & in old Spelling, Jow—the
w = ch Teut. thro' the medium of gh—Jough, Jugum—as Pflug,
Plow—
    Thence Jaw-bone from, or =ᵈ *Joch bein.*—

4758 61.42   Corals, Polypi and Infusories are the only animals, that want the sexual organs.—The *female* first appears in the ascent of animal life, & the ovary to wit: as in Medusas & Muscles.

f39 4759 61.43   "Once when Mr Onkruydt was with the Second King alone (at Madagascar) while viewing from his window a great storm at sea, he said to Mr O.—I have heard from my Grandfather and from my Uncle, that all these things were made—did you ever hear that?" Campbell's Travels in South America, 1812, p. 14.—The sequel of this most momentous Anecdote evinces that neither Mr O. nor Mr Campbell entered into *f39^v* the true and full import of the word, made, in the Vice-roy's Sense.—"Made? said Mr O. to try him—Do you mean that the Sea made itself?—No! I mean, made by a its Maker. O yes, said Mr O. all white people know that. (!!)— Then He said—"I have told you who told me—now tell me—how YOU ~~only~~ know it how you *know* it—On which Mr O. informed him of the Bible!!—

f40   Now it is plain that the Madagascar King used the word "made" in 3 fold opposition. 1. to having been *always*, 2. to having been begotten, 3. to growth————ex. gr. an artificial flower as contradistinguished from a plant or insect. Now in the first only of the 3, and this the least likely to have been in the King's mind, does the Bible teach this doctrine—Namely, that God *created* (gave existence to Heaven and Earth)—For the rest, the Bible speaks of *f40^v* the *generations* of the Heaven & the Earth—and every where supposes an evolution from within, or Life—*No* where a Shaping by opposition from without—or a *Making*.

4760 61.44   It is not probable, that my friend, Elia, and I should differ in any essential on this subject—~~familiar~~ often as we have ~~chatted~~ conversed on the subject—and it was probably from delicacy that he did not elucidate his remarks by the stories I have *f41* so often related of my own experience/& which if I am not deceived, are even more lively than those which he has substituted—

4761 61.45   To the Students in Theology, the future Teachers, and to the better educated & riper Members of the Flock, the truths of the Mystery of the Tri-unity often & explicitly—to the flock some~~whatt~~imes, lest we should seem to hide any part of the Gospels, but whatever supposes & implies these Truths, constantly & always—

4762 61.46   Readers of Miscellanies, Even when more than *f41ᵛ*
miscellaneous Readers, and of course excluding, or all but excluding articles strictly scientific—

4763 29.62   Τὰ περὶ ῥηματων και λογων: or the Principles of *f39ᵛ*
Logic, ~~adapted to practical purposes, the Pulpit, the Bar, and the Senate~~ with their use and application in the acquirement & communication of Knowlege, with an especial view to the Candidates for the Pulpit, the Bar, the Senate,
? Επεα ζωοντα:
Discourse of Reason: or the Principles of Logic, its uses in the acquirement and communication of Knowlege, and its especial importance in the study of the liberal Professions, and to Public Speakers, whether in the Pulpit, the Senate, or the Bar: ⟨together with the History of this Science from Aristotle to Condillac⟩—To which is added a connected Glossary of Philosophical Terms, arranged in the order of the Thoughts; but with an Alphabetical Index; ~~and a brief sketch of the History of the Science of Conclusive Discourse~~
                              by S. T. Coleridge
~~Prefixed to this work is a brief Sketch of the History of this Science~~
For the use of the higher Classes in Schools, the Undergraduates at the Universities, and ~~generally~~ Students for the Liberal Professions in general.—. Logic: ~~comprizing the three distinct yet connected Sciences (or scientific Arts)~~, 1. ~~Common, i.e.~~ Logic properly so called, or (Syllogistic. 2. Dialectic. 3. Organic.)—~~With~~ introduced by a brief histori~~caly~~ of ~~Logic~~ these Sciences from Aristotle to Condillac. ~~The whole simplified by the removal of Subjects belonging to other sciences, of false or unprofitable Subtleties,~~ *f40* ~~and of barbarous or pedantic names which yet will be found noticed and explained, in the Notes or in the Historical Introduction. Annexed to this work is a~~ and concluding with a connected Glos-

sary of Philosophical Terms, arranged ⟨methodically⟩ in the order of the Thoughts; but with an Alphabetical Index. by S. T. Coleridge. Esq·^re

~~The~~ One great object of this book is to exhibit the practical importance of Logic ~~as the ground work of all~~ in the acquirement and communication of all other knowlege, & to restore it to its former rank, as an indispensable part of a liberal Education; but especially to evince the high utility of the Second Branch, viz. Dialectic (of which this is the first systematic Treatise, as applied to the English Language) to all ~~who are~~ educating for the Pulpit, the Bar, or the Senate, or ~~who are likely, in any rank, who~~ in any capacity may be called on to speak in Public.

§The whole simplified by the removal &c *ut supra*

Books enough there are, pretended systems of Logic, or pretended Substitutes ⟨for Logic⟩ by Book-makers, Scotch Professors, ~~who~~ the idly-laborious whom ⟨are honorably⟩ distinguished from their Brethren at Oxford, as *Búsy-dó-no-goods* from *Lázy-do-nóth-ings./*

Lambert's Organon & his other logical works are full of accurate Subtilties, & so far might be of service in sharpening the Understanding—But on the other hand, these are endless—every man in proportion to his Talents & to his close attention to any particular subject, distinguishes pro re natâ, and according as his *f40^v* Object requires, or as he finds conducive to the particular purpose which he has in view—and the only effect of such Books as Lambert's & of many of the School-men before him, is to fill a man's head with another's man's Subtilties, for which probably he may never find occasion./It is little better than as if a Painter should write a large Book on all the possible differences of Light and Shade which a Bunch of Grapes placed in different positions &c may exhibit. The progress in every science is to simplify, and by establishment of Laws to supersede this multiplicity of distinctions—or rather to enable the Teacher to leave them with safety & confidence to the Common Sense to enlarge the sphere of which, while its gives steadiness to its dicta, is one of the most beneficent Effects of all Science. The Scholastic must precede the popular— or what would there be to popularize?—unless indeed (as unhappily is too generally case) a popular work means one in which the

people are ~~to~~ taught their own errors, instead of having the ~~truths~~
results of the labors of the Learned adapted to the capacity & habits
of the Unlearned by presenting in concreto et per exempla what
had been discovered in abstracto et de genere.—The voluminious
Writings of the Sophists under the Empire respecting Grammar
~~which~~ of which in truth our common Greek & Latin Grammars
~~have amended chiefly by~~ are but servile copies in little, magis,
tolerabiles quia breviores—still retaining enough of the old lumber
to be a vexatious Burthen on children, at the knee, and like all
superfluity of *distinctions* that exist only in superficie leaving a general Indistinction in the mind to which it at length becomes reconciled & adopts as a habit—& by what we are now slowly beginning to acknowlege respecting Grammar, our posterity will
doubtless see in our present Botany, Nosology, & in a larger degree I suspect, even in the systems of minute anatomy of late/—
fashionable among our continental Neighbors, French & German.
    Let it be observed, however, that the preceding remarks apply   *f41*
solely to subtleties and hair-breadth distinctions in the *forms* of
knowlege, in classification, and nomenclature—ex. gr. Spur-
zheim's 36 Faculties corresponding to twice that num. of Convolutes of Skull-marrow. In singulis ~~verbibus~~ verbis we cannot be
too accurate—the reason is evident—every word that is capable of
being used for two different Thoughts is a lurking hole for a
Sophism, and a word $= a^{(1}$ cannot be used for b or for $a^{(2}$ without
conveying a falsity./

4764 29.63   The Syllogism being the universal form of all
mental discoursing implicitè vel explicitè, must of course contain
in it the form of all erroneous as well as of all right, conclusion—
and on this ground: that the whole strength of the conclusion being
derived from the major, and this again from the Definition, the
assertion makes the definition and affirms the Major with a fore-
knowlege of & with a view to, the Conclusion, while the other
party accepts both without either. In a book, where the Process
can commence anew, & the former admission be retracted, this
may appear of small consequence—& as to oral disputes in
Schools, they are mere sports.—But Experience has shown the contrary—the falsity in a definition may be revealed so slowly, the

earlier conclusions may be in themselves so reasonable, that before the faulty consequence is brought forward, the Definition has been taken for granted, as a fair demonstration, & the Reader looks every where, only not to the true source. From Aristotle to Wolffe there have not been wanting Philosophers who have taught us how to *proceed*; but few if any who have instructed us how to begin. Bacon indeed pointed out a part of the means; but not the Principle—

f41ᵛ   It is a truth not sufficiently considered, that Axioms themselves do not supersede Principles. The former are rather the first manifestations, ⟨simplest instances⟩ or immediate results of the latter— Thus, the Axiom: Two straight lines cannot inclose a space, is an instance that Space or the presupposition of the relations, Length and Breadth, is the constituent & so far the universal Form, of the outward Sense or Intuitio Co-existentium; but all the terms of the axiom subsist wholly in the outward Sense. Therefore, the assertion "can not" is not a mere appeal to the imagining faculty— not a mere synonime of unimaginability, but flows from the principle of *all* reasoning, viz. that of Identity and Contradiction—or A = A: and − A not = + A.—The *fact* of the demonstrative force of Geometry has been known from the beginning; but to Kant we owe the *insight* into the fact, the Διοτι in addition to the Οτι εστι.—

Such is the influence of words, that on reading Lambert's first Letter to Kant, I believed myself to have found an anticipation of & an authority for, my thoughts; but I soon discovered, that he used the same terms in the contrary sense, meaning by Form what I meant by Materia, & vice versâ.—in short, that Lambert had fallen into the same error with Condillac, in confounding impressions (the subject of Physics or Psychology) with Notions or Thoughts (Begriffe) the proper subjects of Logic.—

The custom of designating a composite whole by the principal or rather the more conspicuous part, is allowable & useful in ordinary Life; but it is of sad influence in morals & philosopher ~~when~~ that we say a gold watch when the case only is gold.—

Things throughout homogeneous, in relation to the point in question, are alone the subjects, ~~of~~ as of addition in Mathematics, so of Syllogy in Logic. Example.—all men are mortal. Socrates is a Man. Socrates is Mortal. 2. Omne rationale est immortale. Socrates est rationalis. Ergo, Socrates est immortalis.

The contradiction of the second to the first syllogism does not *f42*
lie wholly in the heterogeneous and double sense of the term mortalis in the ~~first~~ positive of the first and & in the negative of the second Syllogism, but in the false assertion, *Socrates* is a rational being, the *in parte* ~~axiom~~ standing here for the in toto, which latter must always be presumed in a syllogism when the contrary is not expressed.—Grammar, or the Canons of connecting words significantly; Rhetoric the art of discoursing persuasively; Logic the Science of disc. conclusively.

If, as I think we should do, we place Rhetoric or the art of persuading between Logic as the science of con~~vincing~~cluding and Grammar as the Canons of connecting words significantly, all the so called Figures, with exception of the first, will find their place in Rhetoric.

4765 29.64 De principio contradictionis: item, De. Pr. Identitatis. I question whether even these belong to common Logic or Syllogy. A *is*. By this Position I either assert necessary Being by right of Reason: and then it belongs to Metaphysics: or I speak of some *fact* in the right of my outward or inward Sense, and it belongs to History.※ But toto genere different is the question—What is A? To this question A = A or A)=(− A [†] would be no answer for these are implied & the same with the affirmation presupposed in the question. For "*what* is A? = A *is*; but *what* is it? The answer must be a Predicate of A as a *Subject*: & not A as ens absolutè positum, or that which is its own predicate, I Am that I Am—where the single term, Sum—or the single term, Ego—is

(※ in the widest use of the word as we say natural history, when we mean only Zöography, perhaps, or a description of animals, or Phytography. &c.)
[†] ⟨)=(with two horizontal lines means *contrary* to or precluding the possibility of: while)-(means opposite to. Thus
Bitter)=(Sweet
Sour)-(Sweet⟩

perfectly equivalent to the whole position. Hence the (improperly so called) Subject and Predicate are in the latter formulæ (A = A or A ⚹ − A, or the Principles of Identity and Contradiction) always *convertible* Terms. Example. Quid est Spiritus? Ens se ponens. Quid est Ens se ponens? Spiritus.—But let A signify Hood and B black then A = B is very far indeed from B = A—& such positions alone appertain to Syllogistic Logic. As to the famous Pr.

f42ᵛ Con. et Iden. if they mean anything quoad Common Logic, it can only be that the proper Subjects of Logic are λογοι, not ῥηματα; or φωναι, or ειδωλα, but λογοι suppose—the Λογος, or reflective *Reason*, of which it is a constituent known in the act of knowing its own being that it cannot at the same time & in the same sense deny what it affirms, or affirm what it denies.—The Principle of Contradiction is: Impossibile est idem simul esse ac non esse. Well! This is a good *Definition* of the Impossible; but a Principium? In the name of wonder, what is to *follow*? How can you arrive from this Negative to a Positive? Thro *another* negative? on the *grammatical* rule that two Negatives make a Positive? Whatever is *not* ens and non-ens at the same time, is possible? But even this is not to be done by you except thro' an intermediate principle, viz. the Contrary of the False is True. Both may be entitled axioms, but neither, methinks, a Principle. The rival Principle Pr. Identitatis, is in fact two positions—1. Whatever is, is: 2. Whatever is not, is not.—Now the first is merely a repetition per reflectionem of X *is*—the second is a metabasis εις αλλο γενος, or nonsense. i.e. It either means, A(= omne ens) non est Y, pro predicato ejus, & so belongs to the principle of Syllogy; or it amounts to, Omne Ens, quod non est ens, non ens est/How can *Non-sense* be be a principle?—. In short, the substance of these boasted Principles is a mere assertion, or as it were description, of the act of reflective Reason, i.e. Judgement—.or the assertion of Reason as the universal in all individual persons—If it be so judged by thy *Reason*, it is valid in *all* Reason. And even here, the negative part, the Reason cannot at one & the same time of one and same thing deny what it affirms, is borrowed from a lower derivative, namely, a form of *words* having a semblance only of meaning obtained by the habit of comparison—as ex. gr.—I am accustomed to see *jet*—& thinking of

f43 jet I find a piece of Amber, in almost all points alike, & I say—

but Amber is *not black*. But all these, with the principle of Alterity & Multeity, & whatever else may be supposed to give some meaning to the Prin. Cont. or Ident.—appertain to Metaphysical Ontology, and are as much pre-supposed in Common Logic, as Sounds are in Grammar.! Nay, after all that can be said, the nego here does not properly answer to affirmo—but is an incorrect ψευδο-synonimic for removeo)(pono—& have their rightful use in the doctrine of characters, as + and − .

Perhaps, the clearest way of stating the thing is this. It is a fact of universal Consciousness, that man possesses the power, ~~of~~ not only of beholding A and B, but of noticing that they are *two* and *different*—and hence if he reflects on B in immediate ~~to~~ succession to A, B coming while A is still present to his thoughts (which is Memory or the Condition of Comparison) he soon discovers an abbreviation for A = A: B = B—in the words A is *not* B—. This "*not*" having been in fact derived from some painful feeling occasioned either by himself looking for A = a Carrot, and finding B = a horse-radish, or some other person whom he had sent on the errand—. The gesture, motion of the head, or uneasily shrinking from, the object, and by those & corresponding motions in the organs of Utterance themselves, produce even in Infants a Sound, in which it is not difficult to discover the germ of the simple Negative—originally, perhaps, in all primitive languages being a dental, in infants ng, the Hebrew *Naing*, the roughest and primitive Digamma—. It is not therefore so properly an intuition, as a sensation connected with it in consequence of some other Intuition having been in the fancy, waiting for that increase of vividness &c, which its presentation to the series has been wont to give.—When by the frequent repetition of such occasions the sensation has become evanescent, the abbreviation still remains in use from its convenience, and the "*not*" becomes the mere sign or character of the above connective & comparative power which man derives from reason—i.e. Complex Perception. A & B at the same time yet as two & *pos*. different.

4766   29.65   φ 7 The scheme of ⌐ . . . ⌐ arranging the first   *f43ᵛ*
communication of Knowlege scientifically, so as to begin with that which requires or suppose no previous knowlege in order to its

ıntelligibility; much more the notion of teaching the Sciences *seriatim* on the same principle, were it even feasible in itself, what is more than doubtful, is at all events impracticable in that state of society in which alone the Sciences can be expected to exist.

In the infancy and childhood ~~both~~ of ~~States and~~ Individuals (and something analogous may be traced in the history of Communities) the first knowleges are acquired promiscuously. Say rather, that the Plan is not formed by the selection of the Objects presented to the Notice of the Pupil, but by the impulses and dispositions suited to the age, by the limitsation ⟨of the comprehension, the volatile & desultory activity of the attention⟩ of the faculties, and the relative predominance or earlier developement of one or more faculties over the rest. ~~If~~ This ~~or~~ is the ~~healthy fancy~~ the happy healthy Delirium of the physical, moral and intellectual Being, the Lightheartedness ~~and~~ as well as Light-headedness of human Life.— There is indeed "Method in it"; but it is the Method of Nature, thus storing the mind with all the materials for after use, ~~and yet having the freedom~~ by ~~means of the seeming~~ promiscuously, and as it were with a gay and motley Chaos of ~~Images & Experiences~~ Facts and Forms and thousandfold Experiences, whose origin lies beyond Memory, traceless as Life itself, & passing into a part of Life; & yet by virtue of this seeming confusion effecting her wise purposes without encroachment on the native freedom of the soul, and without precluding or superseding ⟨or overlaying⟩ the inventive, tentative, or combinatory and judicial powers.—

f44   4767 29.66   In the present *Fac*totum State of our Alogology or anti-philosophical Philosophy it is one of the Airs of Fashion, the Haut Ton of the Learned whether the Literate, the Scientific, or the Experimenting, (for all must now be Men of *Business*, clever Hands, men of solid Sense, and sound practical Utility) to speak of all the Disputes and Controverted Points in Metaphysics and Theology as mere Logomachies, the Dust-clouds of the Schools—the scholastic Logic being itself but a wordy art of wrangling de umbrâ asini, sive de tribus Capellis. Now deeply sensible as I am of the evils that arise from ambiguous Terms, I ~~can~~ am nevertheless persuaded that the ~~fact~~ case of two persons falsely supposing themselves to be of diverse opinions when they are really only expressing themselves in ⟨different⟩ Terms ~~actually equivalent but which neither had defined intelligibly~~ to which ~~each~~ they indeed had attached ⟨each⟩ a different meaning; ⟨but which are in truth equivalents⟩ is one of the least important of these Evils, & however frequent ~~it~~ such cases may be in ordinary Life, and oral arguings ~~among~~ between individuals, I am even disposed to doubt whether a single instance can be cited ~~in the history of~~ from among the philsophical Controversies of any considerable Duration or extensive Interest, of a mere Logomachy. On the contrary, far more common at present is the artifice of keeping out of sight real distinctions, nay, even essential differences, or of reducing those that had been hitherto acknowledged into a mere Difference of words by a Sophistical Synonomistic. i.e. by bringing forward a part only of the Meaning of the two phrases or sets of words as the whole, or by bold assertion of a figurative sense in the one, and other ways of cutting a knot which it is difficult or inconvenient to unty/an evil which in contradistinction from Logomachy has been aptly named Logodædaly—

4768 29.67   It is certain that a Government ⟨not a positive   *f44ᵛ* Theocracy⟩ cannot will for a Nation, what the Nation cannot without abandonment of its essential character as a human community, and of the final causes or moral end of all nationëity be supposed capable of willing for itself. A. Thus a nation is morally bound to attribute any injuries, measures, oppressive ordinances &c to want of correct information or mistaken views in the Sovere⟨i⟩gn, and this again to defect of Knowlege or Capacity or Courage or Integrity in his Ministers and public advisers, but never to bad Intention or a design of injuring his Subjects—but then no Sovereign can for this very reason will (i.e. consent to a Law) to prevent or discourage the Subjects from making known the nature of their complaints, or from taking the means of ⟨acquiring the needful knowlege & of⟩ informing their fellow-subjects/which latter right is implied as a Correlative to the Duty which every Subject is under of seeking into the grounds causes and occasions of such measures as he finds heavy or injurious—in order that he may not mistake ~~as injurious~~ hardships that are perhaps necessary for the good of the whole—& at all events not be tempted to make his

Sovereign the immediate object of his resentment or condemnation which yet would inevitably be the case if no New Object were placed within this permitted sphere. For who ~~can~~ dare & who can quench the sentiment of Injustice?—To prevent, nay even to discourage Petitions is a high misdemeanour—& to discourage the freedom of the Press is = to render Petitions as much as possible, worthless, as from ignorant, & dangerous or mischievous as from passionate Persons.—B. Thus too, No Government can will concerning any form of speculative Doctrines, or Points of Faith not indissolubly & indispensably connected with the Duties of social Morality that it shall never be changed—for as Progression is no less a final cause of a Nation or Community governed by Law, than Permanency, the Continuity of a State ~~being~~ consisting in the reconciliation of both, it would be for a Nation to will its own improgression—. For this reason, therefore, a Government or any Sets of Government officiaries, as a Bench of Bishops, cannot consistently assign (the mere dread of *innovation*, and the difficulty of stopping the progress of a Change once begun (for instance, Gibbon's cowardly & unprincipled advice to Lord Shelbourne to oppose the correction of any the most admitted Abuse, & the Advice of the Austrian Minister, Prince Metternich, to a South German Monarch published *officially*.) For this is but a repetition of the Outrage on the former Principle, B. The pretext, moreover, admits of an easy answer. If there be other changes, the necessity and advantage of which are equal and equally confessed by the great majority of all classes, why should they not be made? If this is not the Case, the difference applies the justifying reason for stopping at the given point—and History sanctions the safety of the procedure. Thus, our Revolution of 1668 changed the Law respecting the dispensing Power of the Crown, which Blackstone admits to have been legal in the *letter* of the Law, however unconstitutional in consequence of its contrariety to the Spirit—i.e. the object in the view of the Legislator. Before 1668, the ⟨Spirit of the Law as well as its Letter⟩ supposed the dispensing act rightful till the Contrary was proved. Since then, the Law supposes ~~the~~ every dispensation or suspension of the same criminal, till a sufficient exculpation has been substantiated by the responsible Advisers of the measure & admitted by the Legislature—and then the Law in its

f45

living Source (the Legislature, or King & Parliament) pardons
it—or rather strikes midway between Pardon and Acquittal by an
act of Amnesty & Indemnification—

4769 29.68   What a blessing Christianity has been to the   *f45ᵛ*
Jews themselves! Suppose their dispersion to exist when none of
the Nations, among whom they were domiciliated & whose several
Languages have become their native Mother Tongue, had recognized the divine origin and authority of the Old Testament? What
reason is there for supposing that in each Language the comparative Handful of unsettled and wandering Jews would or could have
made a Translation? Without the aid of Learning how long ago
would the Rabbinical Writers & the Syro-Chaldean Version &
Paraphrase have become as much a sealed Book as the original? If
even now, the Bible has been almost overwhelmed by Talmudical
Rubbish & the Tradition of Man, what would it have been, when
no confirmation were given, no ancestral pride awakened, by the
equal Faith & Veneration of this same Scripture avowed & da
weekly, daily, proclaimed by the whole *cultivated* World? It is
scarcely too much to say, the state of the Jewish Scriptures in the
generation before Ezra almost warrants us to infer, that Judaism
itself owes its Continuance to Christianity! If then the blessed Redeemer hath extended such Blessings to his Brethren according to
the Flesh, even while they reject and solemnly curse him, what
may we not hope for them in the day of their Reconcilement? Vide
Sᵗ Paul . . Romans.—

4770 29.69   I have reflected much and often of the verbal
translation into words of the ιερα γραμματα or hieroglyphic carved
on stone or painted on the Temple walls (for such I am more &
more persuaded it is) contained in the 2ⁿᵈ Chapter of Genesis.—
I apprehend the Document to begin with V. [*]—and to   *f46*
form a separate apologue, ⟨allegory,⟩ or poetic Myth—and that the
subject is not the creation of Woman, or indeed any thing *physical*
which in a poetic Myth (μῦθος) would be out of place & *keeping*;
but the institution of Marriage, as a *positive* Ordinance of Reli-

[* Coleridge's blank.]

gion.—I do not agree with my Friend, Hurwitz ⟨that—⟩—at least
I doubt whether the co-aggreation of the Beasts before the Man
has any reference to the origin of Language—I rather incline to
think, that "names" are here = essential properties, nomina quasi
νουμενα—& that thro' the comparison produced by this insight
Man was brought to see that in the mere coupling which was
common to him with the animals, there was an essential part of his
own nature left without a meet correspondent—. He wanted a
Mate, a Companion—the Trance (falsely translated, deep sleep) is
the trance-like State into which the ~~bold~~ Understanding is thrown
by the first fascination of a peculiar preferential Love—

Ὡς ιδον, ως εμανην, ως ες βαθος αλλομ᾽ Ερωτος!—During this one
of the Ribs, the permanent Bones that enclose and confine the region of the passions & affections, the Bone nearest the Heart—
one of the strengths of the Male is taken away (we still say, I have
lost my heart)—the Rib then is the ιερον γραμμα of an inclosure,
a confining Band, and the soft susceptible Flesh occupies the place.
This becomes the *Strength* of the Woman, and out of her God with
his own hands (i.e. a positive Institution enjoined by a divine Authority and with a sacred sanction) makes the Woman a Wife.—
Well does the man say—this Confining Bond is with my consent,
it proceeded from near my heart, but still it was not a creation of
my choice, or the result of conventional agreement from expediency but was *in* my original nature, whereby I am a *Man* contra-
distinguished from all other animals—Well therefore may I welcome it home again, & behold in the Wife an archetype of my
f46ᵛ   humanity realized and rendered objective—and hence it is too, that
inasmuch as the mere Begetting or Propagating, and consequently
the mere solitary Relations of the Impregnator & the Parturient
& the Youngling considered prior to or abstracted from the Moral
relations arising out of ~~marriage~~ continuous Monogony, is a part
of the *animal* nature and not of the *humanity* as contra-distinguished
from it, therefore the Conjugal Bond takes precedent even of the
~~the~~ Filial, in as much as the Conjugal was not only *before* the
proper Paterno-Maternal, but the cause and creator of the same,
elevating and ~~not~~ transubstantiating the ~~Param~~ Bringer-forth into
the *Mother*, ~~the spark livening arm~~ by providing the necessary
conditions under which the live-long Maternal Storgè can be sus-

tained & rationalized while the Father is wholly constituted by this relation—the mere Impregnator having naturally no connection therewith, and in man ⟨a⟩ co-existent with rather than even the animal substratum of the paternity.

4771 29.70   Logic commence with—1. The high expedience of drawing as sharp & distinct a line as possible around each several science, and rather than bring Heterogenes under the same head, to imitate the Botanists by creating a new class or genus, or species, as the occasion may warrant. Then, passage from Kant's Verm. Schr. Vol. 3. p. 107.—No where is the truth & force of this remark more strikingly exemplified· in the various works entitled Logic, by Watts, Duncan, Condillac & centum alii—. In some of them indeed the Common Logic, or Logic properly so called, first presented in all its essential perfections by Aristotle, & as the nature of the science brought with it, remaining unaltered to the present day—In science itself, I say ~~in which~~ what excellence one Treatise may possess above others in point of ~~Matter~~ arrangement, illustration, and the exclusion of irrelevant matter— in some books entitled Logic the Reader may find something about almost every thing, only not a word of Logic itself.

On the other hand from Φ. the seventh page ⟨to the Reader's   *f47* natural Judgement⟩ counted backwards

1. Then the Swallows ~~soaring~~ skim over the History of Common Logic—chiefly of 3 movements—1. the Organon of Aristotle. 2. Schoolmen. 3 the Reform of Wolff, co-ætaneous with the earlier eliminations, calcitrations, of the Sciences in ~~France~~ England & France by Locke (misconceiving Bacon) and Condillac, the Plagiary of an Hartley—. as a sort of propædia or ⟨athletic⟩ training of the Mind by ~~the~~ first appeal ~~to~~ & the consequent exercise of the Common-sense which proceeds by the same Rules as will be afterwards brought forward in the scientific treatment, but without any distinct conscious adverting to them, I give a review of Condillac's Tract— —

1st Chapter. Precognoscenda et predefinienda. Logos—Princ. Cont. et Id. See p. 10 or 11, ⌜counted⌝ backwards./The three ~~Sort~~ Genera, Canon or Syllogy: Criterion, or Dialectic. Organon or Heuristic. 11. Syllogy—. Critique on the Syllogistic Figures, and that they belong to common (as distinguished from oratorical) Rhetoric, or rather to an Art, forming the transit from Grammar, the Canons of connecting words significantly, to Rhetoric or the [*]   of connecting integral portions persuasively—& which therefore may be defined the art of connecting words, sentences, & periods, as constituents of Sections, so as to be moreost readily understood—and with the least effect, by imitating the order of the associative faculty—Synthesis)(Sunartesis? Or Grammar regulates the termin significant modifications of words and the order of Words belonging to the same sentence whenever (as in English compared with Greek & Latin) the order is the *necessary* substitute for such modifications—. The X gives the principles of the ⟨most *expedient*⟩ position of words & sentences & periods for the purpose of more ready of comapprehension, either in making so that the sequence of words correspondance either with the order or comparative importance of the Thoughts, or with their comparative proximity in point of connection & reference. The X, or intermediate Art, would give the most *expedient* position and sequency of both words & sentences, in order for the easier READIER apprehension of the sense intended purport, namely, so that the ⟨order of the⟩ words, may imitate the order of the Thoughts, Images, &c, according to the laws of Association, or = automatic Memory; or their comparative proximity of connection, & reference, according to the law Judgements of cause and effective or reciprocal influence anticipation and reference; or lastly, the comparative importance, whether determined by the judgement or given by the passion of the Speaker—and Rhetoric comprizes all the rules of art, derived from all sources & built on the experience of Psychol has for its subject the arts of persuasion, and for its object the reduction and generalization of the same into technical rules by aid of psychology generally tracing their operation to psychological sources, or deducing them empirically from psychological experiences.—Thus Logic is the Science of discoursing conclusively; Grammatic the scheme & instrument of connecting words significantly, the Meta-grammatic ⟨Rhematic⟩, the Doctrine of arranging words and sentences perspicuously; and Rhetoric the *art*

f47ᵛ

[* Coleridge's blank.]

of declaiming persuasively; and Logic the Science of discoursing conclusively.—Now all but the first Figure of Syllogy belongs either to Sophistic, as one unworthy subdivision of Rhetoric; or to Meta-grammatic.—

1. Grammaticè (Συναρτησις γραμματων)
2. Rhematicè (Συνταξις ῥηματων
seu Metagrammaticè
3. Rhetoricè (Συνθεσις πειθ
4. Logicè (Συνδησις λογισμων

Grammaticè

1. συναρτησις γραμματων

Rhematicè

2. συνταξις ῥηματων

Rhetoricè

3. συνθεσις πιθανων η πεισματων.

Logicè

4. συνδησις λογισμων.

The 3 first Arts—the 4th Science

4772 28.87   Advantages even of Freedom misused to a Government, exemplified in the Palace Yard, Smithfield, Spa Fields, and North Country Assemblages of the Populace. The opportunities of knowing their strength and purposes—of checking their schemes in detail—above all, of knowing such of the higher classes as may incline to head them (Sir C. W. for instance) and of wearing out the first impression made by such men appearing among the Malcontents. Let the Government be but tolerably firm and active, an Insurrection beyond a Riot is scarcely within the bounds of Possibility in a free Country, in which the Influence of of London acted, in calling out the *duties* of the House keepers, as extra constables.—But Lord Sidmouth is, I fear, the saintly Sycophant of Carleton House and the military Policy!

f78ᵛ

f79

4773 28.88   Being certain ⚹ feeling positive. How many errors, quarrels and mishaps would not the practical conviction of this simple ✳ desynonomization prevent.

P.S. In how very few instances can ✳ such a word (of 8 syllables!) be used in our Language without contravening the purpose of all languages! (It stops and insulates, of course, disconnects, the attention—and thus confuses under pretence of compression, and scatters the mind under pretence of bringing its objects close together, & compact, and co-instantaneous.)

4774 28.89   Great indeed are the difficulties of a true philosophy—not merely those of attaining truth or the intellectual vision (for this is a continued warfare of Life against Life, during the whole of our mortal existence; yet the fervor of the contest and the Joy of Victory are more than a † remuneration) but the difficulties of communicating the truth when attained. For first, we have to convey the truths of Reason in the language of the Understanding—(this of itself sufficiently formidable) and secondly, a language of the Understanding, 1. immature, not yet developed & fixed, 2. corrupted by the Senses and the Market, 3. solecismous from Ignorance & Carelessness consolidated by Fashion into Idiom. Lastly, an age in a will o' the wisp Dance after Metaphors—but in utterly incapable of, nay, abhorrent from the Symbolic.

f80

† such indeed that the vis poetica itself is taken up into it, and lebt und webt in a form not its own! such that the want of it (in the two fold sense, absence and instinctive craving) is the causa sufficiens of Gaming, War, an Sensuality and thirst of Wealth—all the *restlessness*, with all the means of employing or of stupefying it!

4775 28.90   Perhaps, of the numerous forms in which the ⟨cor⟩relative Natures of Time and Space are representable, the simplest is that which Steffens has given in the spirit of the Ionic School—viz.

f80ᵛ

SPACE = the form by which the ✳ Boundless is subsumed into the Bounded.

TIME = the form by which the Boundlessed is taken up into the Boundless.

✳ I prefer this to "the Infinite taken up into the Finite" on account of the general abuse of the term "Infinite" as = the All-perfect— at least, its constant association with Magnitude ⟨or *Maximity:*⟩ in short with EXCEEDINGness.

Tho' the phrase "taken up" or "subsumed" does not quite please me. If I think of it, I will transcribe the above, then place in an opposite column the following.

SPACE: in the generation of a Line that which supplies the   *f81*
Fluency.

TIME: the Fluent, or

In the generation of a Line, that which gives the continuity to the Point, is SPACE: that which superinduces the Point on the continuity is TIME: the Synthesis of both MOTION.—Sp: = the Base; T: = the Epibase; Motion, the ~~one~~ Act of Union; the Line, the Product—or lastly, The Fluent, the Fluibility, and the Fluxion— and ask V'ridè which *he* likes the best.

In infinito finiendo, τὸ Infinitum ⟨finibile⟩ est Spatium, το Finiens est Tempus, Actus quo finitur Infinitum est Motus—et το Productum est Figura.—All this is well—and good as far as it *goes*. But   *f81ᵛ*
Steffens will not stop there; but takes it up *pick a back* and carries it over the boundaries into another Country—from the quiet realm of Geometry ⟨in⟩to the Domain of Dynamics, and passes off a mathematical Theorem for a physical Idea, and so doing he ~~employs~~ draws with a slate pencil on the *Thought* of a Slate, and ties the members of a Syllogism together with with a real Whip-cord— i.e., His Time is actual, his Space a mere term for the power implied in the act, or his Time is a verb transitive with an O for   *f82*
its accusative Case.—But Space actualized must re-act, as the co-agent with Time—its antagonist as well as its Spouse—*lædit in amplexu*—subjected but not destroyed, and subjected too as a mother to her ~~Son~~, children, the common offspring of both, ⟨namely in Figure,⟩ ~~and~~ in whom both exist and continue to exercise a modified ~~power~~ influence, he as the Power of Figure, ~~in Her~~ she as the *Power* of the Figureless, i.e. ως το αντιμορφον.— he in the Lineal, she in the Globular. That these are the Twin offspring ~~from~~ of both in the mysterious Love-and-War-Embrace of productive Nature, implies that both Parents exist virtually in both the rival Twins; yet so that *this* (Tempus, ut vis Figuræ, nisus   *f82ᵛ*
figurativus, το επιμορφοῦν) ~~in~~ shall preponderate in the one (Linea, Longitudo) that (Spatium ut nisus ὁ αντιμο⟨ρ⟩φος ~~principi~~ Fugacitas a Longitudine) in the other (globus, σταγμα). And thus again in the second Generation, or offspring of the Lineal)(the Glob-

ular—in Breadth,—this predominant in superficial, this in dense, breadth; or Breadth with density. (N.b. Density is Depth + Breadth—for who would call a Spider's Web ⊗ hung perpendicular to the Ground, or the spokes of a slender wheel, dense?)—

f83 But Space actual must by the very definition actuate itself, i.e. be causative of its own reality—but as its Actuation was not by its own power, the self-actuation is itself an *effect*, the ignorance or denial of which is Schelling's and Steffens's πρωτον ψευδος, and converts Nature or the phænomenal World into a blind Godhead playing ⟨by himself⟩ at Cat Cradle with himself as the thread.—The Result, however, as far as our *present* argument is concerned, is the same—Space and Time are realized, but realized Space is Ether, realized Time is Light—hence a new series of Powers are ~~presented~~ brought into view, co-æval with the preceding and co-agents in their products—yet different from them by *successive* po-

f83ᵛ tenziations, the Ether as ⁽¹ vis continui, ⁽² fugacitas a Lineâ, ⁽³ ☉, ⁽⁴ ⊘, ⁽⁵ ⊕ /&c.—

and tho' the Lineal and the Globular are the primary ~~Powers~~ Forms or Formants, as *Subposita*, yet Surface and Density are the primary *Formates*, as re posita et facta—while the ~~former~~ Lineal & Globular first *appear* ~~among~~ in the successive evolution of Figures, ⟨according⟩ as the □ and > are potenziated in a threefold Polarity, 1 the Substantive, 2 the modifying, and 3 the ordinant. 1. □ = / and ∴ 2 > as .... and ∽. 3 □ + > as + ☉ and − ☉ (or centripetal and centrifugal.)—The Lineal domi-

f84 nating in the elementary forms of Chrystallization, the Globular in the integral Masses—according to the degree of their independence—Hence their motions elliptical &c.

4776 28.91   INTRODUCTION to the preceding. I am mainly solicitous, that on this stage of our ascent, which may be aptly termed our first great Landing place, and before we attempt the second Flight, = σζ ⁓, ~~φύτα η φυτοειδῆ~~ τὰ μὲν φύτα, τὰ δε τυχὸν και Φυτοειδῆ—we should have thoroughly mastered the elementary ~~or [?cosmic/common]~~ Natures, the primary physical Powers, the Divi et Numina Cosmoplastæ: and so, namely, that we should not ⟨only⟩ possess distinct conceptions of their genesis and proprieties, their hostilities and alliances, direct and indirect,

but by repeated presentation of the same in various forms, and
even in synonimes of language have rendered them *clear* as well as   *f84ᵛ*
distinct, in short manageable, alert and ready at the first call.

Now we cannot perhaps commence this Muster and Review better than by calling out the two Leaders of the File, who for a long
time past have not appeared before us in their own names—I
mean, SPACE and TIME. And this too will have the additional
advantage that it will recall and impress anew the ~~differe~~varince
between our system and the Schellingian; that the points, in which
we differ, are not merely momentary but essential, and that the
Difference therefore amounts to Diversity. Let me not, however
fail to declare that in the ~~different~~ several Works of Heinrich
Steffens, especially in his Beyträge zur innern Naturgeschichte der   *f85*
Erde, the Spirit within me bears witness to the same Spirit in
him—but that ~~he denominates his~~ ⟨it shows⟩ the Line of ⟨its⟩ Circumvolution was ⟨begun⟩ from a false centre and with too short
and undistended a Compass, forced ~~us~~ thereby usque ab initio to
close too early on itself, and thus ~~imprisoned~~ leaving ~~the~~ his familiar Genius ⟨imprisoned⟩ within the magic Circle of its own
describing.—Still among all the real or verbal definitions of Space
and Time, given by the Natur-philosophen, Steffens's seems to me
the clearest and most simple, and breathes most the spirit of ~~of~~ the
old Ionic School, the genial Spirit of Anaximander and Parmenides—. (*Then proceed from p. 07.*)

4777 28.92   Amid the ~~hardest~~ ⟨~~most prolonged~~ profoundest⟩   *f85ᵛ*
and most condensed ~~energies~~ constructions of hardest Thinking,
the playfulness of the Boy ~~and~~ starts up, like a wild Fig-tree from
monumental Marble.

4778 28.93   Steffens had an ahnung [*Ahnung*] of the anteriority of *a* scheme to the *celeste mechanique*—p. 28 of his first
manual-book. For if the Sun *goes forth* as Form from itself as =
Form + Essence, the First born (Sᵗ Paul) leaving the army of the
reborn, in the going, in the struggle of departure (& all struggle
in nature is productive Embrace, νικη αει ερως) there must have
been a product.

4779 28.94   A very interesting little article might be compiled by collecting the different ways in which great men have
disguised truths at variance with the ~~articles~~ prejudices, religious
dogmata, and political Institutions of their Age and Country, in
f86   cluding the necessary accomodation of the Gift (Donum veritatis)
to the Receivers—this last taken as the *casus rectus*, from which to
estimate the degree of moral defect in the others by an increasing
Series, from Socrates to Leibnitz—Incapacity of the whole Truth
in the Contemporaries. Q? Domestic attachments, Wife and Children, Friendships, Unwillingness to expose the Convinced to Persecution or the temptation to the denial of the Truth.—Mid point,
personal apprehension of Life, Liberty, and Livelihood.—1. Personal Ambition and Vanity, in matters of literary and intellectual
Distinction. 2. Selfish Truth-bartering, for worldly Honors and
Emoluments. The first right and wise: the 2nd the amiable over
f86ᵛ   balancing the weak and faulty—the mid point condemnable in the
abstract; but yet the degree of excuse so various, in different temperaments, that it ought rather to subtract from our admiration
than to call down our censure.—The first below is a great but in
regard of human frailty pardonable infidelity, where it does not
amount to a total abandonment of Truth. The last is utterly abominable.—

In the mid point lies Descartes' ~~un~~ *orthodox* assertion of the
immoveableness of the Earth, by giving a definition of Motion
which, as he well knew, applies only to relative motion—and then
tho' the atmosphere circumvolved, round the Sun, yet as the Earth
maintained the same relations of place to this, the surrounding
object, *it* remained fixed and stable!

f87   In the point below this, his quibble and metaphysical Riddle in
support of Transsub'n. which he was declared by the Jesuits to
have endangered by his axiom, that accidents cannot subsist of
themselves. The Church and Pope cared nothing about it; but
DesC. wished to remove all obstacles to his Philosophy having the
Lead in the different Catholic as well as Prot. universities, and to
baffle his rivals, the Jesuits.

The last we leave to those, who have only second hand truth to
betray—the M°In^shes. We scarcely hold it a possible crime in a true
Philosopher.

The 5 points may be ranked as Culmination: Descent: Level: Sinking: Sunk. and the facts arranged accordingly.

4780 28.95   Myrrdin, Merlin, fl. 560 A D, wrote the   *f87ᵛ*
Avallenau. Aneurin wr. the Gododin 540 Pictish Kings. Drust,
Son of Erp, died 451. Talorc, Son of Aniel 4~~80~~55 Necton Morbet,
Son of Erp, 480.—Elpin, Son of Bredei, d. 779 Cineoch, Son of
Luthrin, 636./⟨Scotish Kings.⟩ Kenneth MacAlpin, r. from 843
to 859, Donald MacAlpin to 863, Constantine II fr. 863 ⟨to⟩ 881.
Aodh the Son of Kenneth but one year. Achy and *Grig* jointly,
882 to 893.—Kenneth IVᵗʰ surnamed the Grim, the Son of Duff
995 to 1003. Malcolm II. S. of Kenneth IIIʳᵈ to 1033—In this
reign, Lady Gruoch (wife of Gilcomgain & then Lady MacBeth,
Maormor of Ross & Moray—Kenneth the III, (Son of Malcolm
I) who reigned 24 years from 970 to 994—while he suppressed
an insurrection in the Merns (the district between the Rivers   *f88*
North-Esk and the Dee) he put to death the only son of Finella,
daughter of Cunechat the Maormor of Angus and Wife of the
Maormor of the Merns—Kenneth, either in pursuit of the chase,
or in *pilgrimage* to the Shrine at Fordun, lodged ~~with~~ in Finella's
Castle, near Fettercairn & was assassinated—Finlegh, Maormor
of Ross and Father of Macbeth, murdered in 1020—Maolbride
⟨(must be the same as Boedhe)⟩ Maormor of Moray, the Father
⟨of⟩ Lady Macbeth & grandfather of Lulach, burnt within his
Rath with 50 of his clan, in 1032. (Boedhe, Son of Kenneth IVᵗʰ,
left a Son & a Daughter—the Son slain 1033 by the last orders of
the aged Malcolm—Thus a grandfather dethroned & slain—a
Brother assassinated—a husband with 50 of his clan burnt, & herself with her infant Lulach a fugitive and Macbeth himself had to   *f88ᵛ*
revenge the death of his Father, Finlegh.
    Vikinger, or Pirate Kings—Sigurd, Thorfin. ⟨War-cries—⟩
Craig-elachie, rock of alarm. Cairn-na-cuimnhe, the cairn of remembrance, even now the tocsin cry of Aberdeenshire—causing a
tumult in Fair or Market.

4781 28.96   864 the great magnetic period—1728 the yet
greater.—Qʸ Mem. To inform myself what is meant by the Magnetic Period, Equatic. &c—

4782 28.97   *Long* admits that the ancient Chaldeans held the true opinions of Comets, that they moved in Loops & were periodical—adding that they pretended to predict them "undoubtedly *f89* a vain boast, but the less to be wondered as they pretended to foretel Earthquakes also."—and as he supposes "on some fallacious rules of judicial astrology."—The conjunction of the two gives me a more favorable notion.—

4783 28.98   Loch Broom. Little Loch Broom—at the end of the magnificent Scenery of Dundonnel, on the South Borders of Sutherland and North of Rossshire, Pennant Vol. II, p. 379. The nigh mountain at the foot of which the House stands, pap-headed = round *cone*—the ridge or *Causey* on from which it rises, with six Gylls or Gullies, the last filled by a milk-foam Sike. The high STRADDLE Mountains, seen over the Causey, on the left of the Pass, serrated and needled ⟨and spiring,⟩ alders—birch groves, ⟨Wych-elms—⟩ Pines—Cataracts of all sizes, visible and only audible—Stags, Roes, and Black game—snowy glaciers. Squr-fein— Hills of *Wine*—Pen. proposes—shains of Wind. But the intoxicating effect of the Air on these summits gives a propriety to the former.

f89ᵛ "Detained with the good Family of Dun Donnel by a violent Fall of Rain which rendered the Waters impassible." *Cloud-berries* (Rubus Chamæmorus) as a Desert."

Loch-nan-niun, the Lake of Birds. Amazing mountain of white marble, smooth, glossy, a vast sheet of Ice—called Lecach. and strata of red & white marble to Loch Maree (Oak, ash, Willow, Hazel, and *enormous Hollies*—on the neat and gravelly shores of Inch-Maree, one of the cluster of Islets which crowd the (4 mile broad) Lake in its southward Bend—this the favored Isle of the Patron Saint of all the Coast from Apple-cross to Loch Broom. In the midst a circular Dike of Stones, with a regular narrow entrance—the inner part used for ages and still in use as a burial place. Druidical & taken up by the Saint, *as transfer is easier than abolition.* Devils if you like; but Venus, Cupid &c. must not be os.—The stump of a vast Tree an altar (recollect that at Stowey, with the Briar Flowers & Bramble Leaves, the Eglantine Arch, *f90* and the central Foxglove or Mullein—but above all the Well of the Saint, potent in Lunacy. The Patient is brought into the sacred Island, made to kneel before the altar on which his friends leave an offering in money—then brought to the well & sips from it— a second offering—then thrice dipped in the lake—and this repeated daily for some weeks. If the ~~lek~~ Well be full, St Maree propitious, if not, doubtful.—The common Oath of the country, the Saint's name. At St Maree's resting places no Traveller rests or passes without leaving an offering, but a stone, a stick, a bit of rag contents the moderate *Manes*. High Rock of short Precipices with shelves to each—and "self-sown Pines". The South Side of the Lake, *birch* groves—mountain bases not high but opening to disclose the skiey *Serras* beyond—. At the Headland wooded to its very summit the Lake suddenly narrows to the breadth of a hundred yards, so winds the Rapids with many a half-moon Bay for a mile, then discharges into a deep and darksome Hole (Pool-Eure) which opens into the large Bay of Loch Ewe Loch Maree 18 miles long. Potato gardens in the Peat Moor. The thin gigantic $f_{90}{}^v$ Hag with her Dog and withered child, Glasslich.

I find that Pennant is the source of W. Scot's Novels, the suggerent, I mean.

4784 29.203 Glossary. To begin † with the passage from $f_{128}{}^v$ Kant respecting Trichotomy, and vindicate Baxter's claim to the merit of this important remark & that of having grounded it in the necessary Idea of God, by quoting the passage, from his own Life.—Then explain the equality asserted by the Pythagorean School of the Tetractys, & the Triad—namely, that the former contemplates the Deity as unmanifested, or if we may hazard the expression or indeed any expression of the Inexpressible, as the Monad or Absolute One, not yet unfolded & still containing in itself the Triad:—while the Deity, as self-manifested, was contemplated by them as the Triad, in which the Monad was revealed as the ⟨first name or Xposition of the Three,⟩ source & principle of all.—I hope, I need not ~~hav~~ disclaim on the part of these ancient

† nay, rather begin with the two different possible modes of contemplating a line, either as formed by the aggregate of its points, or as a Point producing &c—,

sages the absurd intention of asserting the Deity as actually existing or differently in different times; but merely that such the order of Thought in the formation of the *Idea* in the Mind. According, the Monad is designated as the semper presuppositum quod nunquam ponitur, and the same Idea is expressed ~~by~~ in the Schools of Theology & by the philosophizing Greek Fathers of the Church as an eternal Generation.—It is ~~mentioned here~~ here introduced however, as the ground & reality, & so far therefore (as Baxter has ~~said~~ implied) the proper explanation of the universal, tho' long neglected, Form of Logic—the logical Tetractys, ~~or Triad~~ in which the Monad has its correspondent in the Prothesis, & the Triad in the Thesis, Antithesis, and Synthesis, according the following Figure.

Prothesis

Thesis   Antithesis

Synthesis

while in the logical Triad, or Trichotomy, which is the form of all manifestation—the Prothesis takes the name & place of the Thesis—a rule observed in classification generally & as it were instinctively.—Thus Metaphysics ~~as~~ in contradistinction from Physics, as the Science the evidence of which transcends the evidence afforded by the outward Senses & their appropriate Objects, *f128* includes the Science of the pure Intellect, and that of the pure Intuition or the a priori forms of Space and Time—Both are alike branches of Metaphysics, which may here be taken as the *Pro*thesis; but the name is specifically appropriated to the former and in fact the earlier, Science, which here answers to the Thesis— And if ever in the progress of Knowlege a Science should arise which combined both by contemplating both as acts & powers under a higher form, ex. gr. of the living & ⟨& as it was entitled, Dynamic&⟩ intelligential Will, we might represent the order in the same figure as above, viz.

1. Metaphysics (Prothesis)

2. (Thesis) Metaphysics   3. Mathematics (antithesis)

4. Dynamics (Synthesis.)

The evils of Dichotomy are endless; but the greatest & the original is that of seeking an opposite, or antithesis, or counter-position for that which *contains* the opposites as the germ of a Tree contains potentially the Trunk and Branches, but has none, it substitutes a *contrary* for an opposite, i.e. a mere negation or nothing, which of course can be opposed to nothing—Thus, to Reality they would oppose Non-entity—but Reality can have no opposite, and must therefore be placed thus

Real~~ity~~

Actual   Potential

The Truth, necessity, and immense importance of contemplating the Potential as a species of Reality (for instance, the quality (potentia) of rarefaction in condensed air) and as its negative Pole, as it were, the actual being the Positive, we may hereafter have occasion to show—(Here introduce in a note the passage from Mendelssohn's Morgenstunden)

Now—this same form under other names appears in all systematic Knowleges—Thus in Philosophy, the Prothesis we retain under the name of Identity, (whether Absolute, as in Theology alone, or relative Identity as in ~~Anthropology~~, any natural Philosophy or Physiology in its widest sense as the science concerning created $f127^v$ Nature, is determined by the Subjects—while the Thesis & Antithesis appear as plus & minus, or positive & negative, or + & − , or opposite Poles, and the Synthesis, as ~~combination~~ compound with predominance of one of the components (for instance, Water-acid lately discovered by the French Chemist,——: or with equilibrium, as Neutralization (for instance, Water as the equilibrium or mutual transpenetration of Oxygen & Hydrogen. (Put Neutralization first). But in Physiology there arises a fifth Form, differing both from Identity and from Synthesis, whether negative or positive, & which we have term, Indifference. It differs from Identity or the co-inherence of the Thesis & Antithesis contem-plat~~ing~~ed as anterior to their manifestation as opposites—& out of which as their pre-existing principle they are both evolved: and from synthesis, which is posterior to both, and ~~arises~~ is formed by adding the one to the other so as to produced a third different from both. But the Indifferent ~~contains indeed the~~ is that which may be either, & ⟨even⟩ both at the same time, but not in the same relation or to the same object. Thus Sulphuretted Hydrogen ~~is capable~~ acts as an Acid on the more powerful Alkalis, and as an Alkali on the more powerful Acids.——

But perhaps the most perfect instance & illustration of this is to be found in philosophical Grammar, as the purest at once Product & Correspondent of Logic ⟨⟨Here the whole passage on grammar from this Book⟩⟩ We should therefore ~~trace~~ commence with the ~~origin &~~ aweful ~~and~~ Supreme Reality, of which the radical forms of Speech are the faint types, or reflexes, with the living I Am, the eternal *Word./*

f126ᵛ   4785 29.209   Die Metaphysik ist ohne Zweifel die schwereste unter allen menschlichen Einsichten: allein ~~est~~ ist noch nicht eine geschrieben worden. Man hat Ursache sich nach dem Wege zu erkündigen, auf welchen man sie aller erst zu suchen gedenkt.

KANT.

4786 29.210   I ~~am~~ can never persuade myself, that the most indispensable of all Knowleges, There is a God, or what is but the same thing in other words, Our Reason is grounded in Reality, = has a real ground, would be in any serious danger, even tho' it should be without the support of deep metaphysical Demonstrations. A demonstration indeed, in the strict and scientific sense of the word, would at once remove ~~thesee~~ most important and pratical of all Truth from the Table of our Duties, and render the ~~Comm.~~ first Commandment as superfluous ~~as it~~ as a Command to believe the equality of the lines drawn from the center to the circumference, or any other demonstrated proposition in Geometry or Arithmetic. It is amply sufficient, if such ⟨rational⟩ inducements ~~of the Reason are~~ exist, as no rational man can withstand——~~if on the one side it be demons~~ the strongest arguments from all quarters unite ~~or~~ to enforce the belief, arguments that are ⟨all⟩ but demonstration, & which weighed in any but the Gold Scales of absolute Science would ~~by~~ with all men ~~be~~ pass for demonstration, while on the other hand it is strictly demonstration, that there neither does nor

f126   ever can exist any valid argument to the contrary. Besides whatever is incumbent on all men must rest on grounds within the apprehension of all men. And such in fact are the ~~grounds~~ reasons in erection of the ~~E~~ existence and attributes of the Supreme Being

and of the obligation to obey his ~~commands~~ laws written in our
Conscience, that it is necessary to be more than a Fool not to
acknowledge their force sufficient. The Disbeliever must be a Fool
in heart—a Fool of his own making not of Nature's. To make him
wiser we must commence by making him better.—But if it should
be asked—Yet why seek to detect the fallacy in the hitherto accepted Demonstrations of an article, the Truth and Necessity of
which you admit—I ~~ans~~ have already in part anticipated the answer
namely, that the intended ~~ally~~ Support, even were it really what it
purports to be, Demonstration, would be a mischievous ally, and
end in degrading a moral, fruitful and living Faith into a ~~devil's~~
mere heartless ~~and passive position speculative~~ Theorem of the
speculative Intellect. ~~What the sensational result (would be) of a
sciential certainly of that full and perfect (absolute and necessitated)
Assent which the Conclusion of the pure Sciences compel may be
fairly conjectured (by a fair analogy be more than conjecture) from
the results of that Assent were it not, like a destructive Ingredient
in pharmacy, incompatible with moral truth, and like destructive
ingredient in pharmacy~~ What the practical Results would be of a
sciential Certainty in Religion, of that absolute and necessitated
Assent which the conclusions of the pure Sciences confer, ~~may~~ were
it not precluded ~~from~~ in all *moral* truths, is a contradiction in
terms and destructive in *kind* of the essential character of the latter—but what the consequence would be, we are permitted by a
fair analogy to infer from our experience respecting that species of
Moral Assent which in its accompaniments is nearest an equivalent
to the state, ~~of mind~~ in which the mind is placed by the ~~simpler
truths~~ axioms and simplest Deductions of Geometry or Arithmetic.
How many thousands in former times, and in spite of the numerous ~~quacks [. . . . .]~~ Apostles and Missionaries of Disbelief in this *enlightening* Age, in spite of the zealous Candidates for
Martyrdom and a *Subscription*, obscure Scribblers and notorious
Publishers, even in the present time how many pass from the Cradle to the Grave without a single doubt, without a single suspicion
even of the possibility of a doubt ~~on~~ respecting the certainty of the
two fundamental Articles of Religion, and who ~~find a~~ would find
a suggestion of the contrary as strange, preposterous and incredible
as a disbelief in their Multiplication Table! ~~And Nor yet I here~~

f125ᵛ

~~speaking of uneducated worldly.~~ Nor am I here speaking only or principally of those, to whom this immunity from doubt has been giv~~ing~~en ⟨the⟩ Custom ⟨of their country⟩ and guaranteed by their own ignorance, and whose ~~belief Faith~~ Persuasion wholly destitute of Insight consists in a blind Acquiescence substantiated by a *sensation* of positiveness; ~~what I have been taking for granted their~~ but of such as being questioned, why they hold, That there is a God, & that they have a soul to be saved, would give, at once ⟨the same⟩ reasons for their Assurance, ⟨as the School-Divine could do, & perhaps more intelligibly, of those who⟩ and in the native soil of ~~their~~ Common sense ~~& find~~ growing at their feet as it were, ⟨find⟩ the best & strongest that the Hot-beds of metaphysical Speculation ~~have~~ ever produced— ~~that a Somewhat must have been always, in order for any thing to become that~~ that it is absurd to talk of a pendent chain, without a staple & the longer the Chain, the more glaring the absurdity—that it is nothing less than a wanton Falsification of the Common Sense & Understanding of men, to confound two such perfectly distinct conceptions as are conveyed in the words, *made* for and serve for, ex. gr. The sea-shell serves for a cup—or thi~~se~~ Eye of the Surinam Spider was *made* for the Insect to see with, yet *serves* the Naturalist for a microscope—& as for the second question the answer—Because I am a Man & not a Beast, comprizes and involves all that is really effective and solid in the arguments of ~~Socrates~~, the academic and Stoic Schools from Socrates to Cicero, and from Seneca, Epictetus, & Antonine to Clark, Wolf, and Mendelsohn.—and yet, I repeat, how vast a number even of these, who by the light of their common sense kindled and kept clear by the happy ~~accident~~ circumstance of their Birth-place possess ~~the~~ in *substance* ⟨the best results⟩ of philosophical Disquisitions, ~~while they are~~ unconscious of the difficulties & strangers to the Doubts which had caused or occasioned them, do yet ~~as Bishop Jeremy Taylor has too justly observed~~, notwithstanding, this their unclouded ~~Confidence~~ Assurance of a God and a future retribution, live (as Bishop Jer. Taylor has too justly observed)

f125

> tu stesso ⟨ti⟩ fai grosso
> Col falso immaginar, sì che non vedi
> Ciò che vedresti, se l'avessi scosso.
>
> Dant. Paradiso, Canto I. St. 30.

Licet illis qui in affirmativo sunt de Veris Fidei, per scientifica intellectualiter confirmare illa non autem illis qui in negativo sunt. Nam qui non credit vera divina nisi } persuadeatur ex scientificis, evincatur nunquam credet.

Now it has been my object to determine the ground of the Truth *in* rather than *of* this Remark: and by presenting the truth by itself deprive the falsity and priestcraft potentially contained therein of all ~~its~~ color and ductility

4787 29.204   περι αξιολογω Υσση τε—ου γαρ μονον εν τοις *f127* αρρητοις, αλλα και εν αδιαφοροις η ανελευθερια ενεργειαν ποιητικην παραλυει, και Ορνις συν πτερυγεσσι δεδημενοις, that cannot soar its natural pitch, flies heavily & awkwardly even across the Coartyard of its Master.

4788 29.205   Fennel Water, ounce & a Half
Solution of Subcarb. of Potash, twenty Drops.
Spirit of Nitric Ether, half a drachm
x Tinct. of opium from x to xx drops.
This draught to be taken x 3*times* a *day*!!

4789 29.206   Mucilage of Gum Acacia, half an ounce—
Fennel Water, an ounce. Spirit of Nitric Æther, half a drachm.
Tinct. of Opium x=xx drops. Syrup of Marshmallow (a Meæ) one Drachm. Mix.

4790 29.207   Dentifrice. Equal parts of powdered Catechu *f126* & Peruvian Bark, with one fourth the quantity of the powder of Myrrh.—

4791 29.208   ⟨Gum acacia, an ounce—olive oil, two drachms—to be mixed thoroughly in a marble mortar: then add of Spirit of Nitric æther, one Drachm Laudan. x-xx drops—Fennel Water, an ounce—a Draught/Stone—frequent injections of sweet oil, or of milk & water warm—⟩

f124ᵛ **4792** 29.211   Mʳ Jonathan Skelton—once broke a blood ves-sel—subject to inflammation of the lungs, in taking cold—cough—occasionally spits blood—finds Vinum colchici—a tea spoonful & half at bed time, & in the morning a specific, that has often prevented the necessity of *bleeding*—violent pain in the side & chest—

4793 29.212   If a modern Divine of the orthodoxy now in fashion, if a Toulmin, Mant or Doyley will explain to me what he means by *Inspiration*, & and what by inspired Writers, and what by inspired Books, by something more than synonimes—i.e. if he will explain his *sense*, and not merely (by help of Entick's English Dictionary) *construe* the words—I will tell him what I think of Behmen & of Behmen's *Writings*, as to the inspiration of the one or the other—& whether there is any portion of the latter which I regard as unassisted and partial *recollections* of Truths first pre-sented to him by *inspiration*: As such, Behman himself offers them to us. For when I have received the desired explanation, I shall have learnt, whether or no an antecedent Inspiration of necessity preclude all fallibility in the after recording of the same.—

f34 **4794** 29.54   On Time as connected with the Religions of the East, especially the Egyptian, & the post-homeric Greek as its derivative, & the connection between the former and the Mosaic institutions

The French Savants ⟨who went to Egypt⟩ in the train of Napo-leon (Denon, Fourrier, and Dupuis), have, it is said, ⟨trium-phantly⟩ vindicated the Chronology of Herodotus from documents that cannot lie—namely, the inscriptions & sculptures of those enormous Masses of Architecture, the gigantic Tomb-stones of the elder World—. It is decided (say they) that the present division of the Zodiac had been arranged by the Egyptians already 15000 years before the Christian Æra—. While according to an Inscrip-tion the Temple of Esne is ⟨of⟩ 8000 years' standing.—Now, first, I do not see the impossibility of an Inscription lying—or the im-probability of an Interpreter—misunderstanding it; or the ~~proba-bility~~ credibility of a ⟨n Infidel⟩ French Savant being free from either—The Inscriptions &c may be & in some instances very likely are, of later date, the Offspring of Vanity & priestly Rivalry—2. The relation of Moses, conveying, in perfect accordance with all we know of analogous facts, the vast progress in civilization & splendor from Abraham & Ahimelech to Joseph & Pharaoh, is worth a cartload of such inferences/—. It is almost universal to speak of the gross Idolatry of Egypt & an argument has been grounded on this assumption in favor of the immediate divine origin of the Mosaic Monotheistic Theocracy. But of this idolatry I find no decisive proof in ~~the~~ Moses's own writings—& regard the absence of any such as collate with the passages in the Prophets as an argument of incomparably greater value in support of the Age & authenticity of the Pentateuch—at least, of the documents from which it was formed.

There are three passages that appear to me of highest moment $f34^v$
in the enucleation of this problem—one from Herodotus, asserting the identity of the Gods of Greece with those of Egypt—& implying the chronologic or calendary Nature of the latter; & two from Homer—that of the Sacred Sheep & Goats in Trinacria; & ⟨that of⟩ the Journey of Jupiter with all the Gods to Oceanus & the Ethiopians.—The most convenient order of the discussion will be—1. What is the Homeric Oceanus?—2. What the Sheep & Goats symbolized?—If both 1 and 2 should prove to be measures of *Time*, civil or natural, then it would follow by strongest presumption at least, that the Gods with Jove at their head represented the Divine Power manifested in *"Time & Times & half a Time"*—& this Presumption or Inference would be converted almost to certainty by the passage from Herodotus.—Suppose the above satisfactorily established, the next question would be—Was the scheme originally polytheistic?—~~Then was~~ If so, did the Polytheism itself originate in a Pantheism (i.e. God = World + W = G.)—Or lastly & the opinion to which my own belief inclines, did it begin in Monotheism (World − God = 0. God − World = God + World) but ~~by~~ soon degenerated into Pantheism, & thence by means of the ἱρα γραμματα into Polytheism?

—Was it not the subordination of *moral* grounds to Physiology, & the *magical* study of Nature joined with astronomical & meteorological Observations as the grounds of Prediction, the cause & occasion of this degeneracy into Pantheism?

Whether the fact, that all cycles were divine, i.e. proofs & manifestations of Divinity, does not plead strongly for original Theism?—In what part of the Process Egypt was in the time of Moses?—Whether the restoration of the true order inverted by the Egyptian Priesthood, even by the discouragement of Physics, at least by the exclusive toleration of the mechanical, & the suppression of Egyptian Physico-theology, is not the right Clue of the Mosaic dispensation? If so, the Institutions of Moses will be 1. the eldest & purest part of the Egyptian Temple worship & Ceremonial—2. Original measures for the exclusion of the corruptions & the occasions of the same—. 3. Historical Ordinances, for the forming and sustaining of a National Spirit—. The Essay would conclude with the consideration of the Mosaic Sabbath and its relation to the Mendes of the Egyptians & Pan of the Greeks. 2. ~~With~~ Of the *sacrificial* Code of Moses, viewed in the light of *veiling* the idea, too glaringly symbolized in the Egyptian & Indian, of Incarnation & Redemption, so as to remove the idolatrous consequences by transferring the import from *the Past & Present* (which almost necessarily rendered it idolatrous) to the Future— from fabulous, or rather interpreted into fable, record & superstitions attribution to Hope & Promise.—Finally, the sublime character and *aweful* importance of the Mosaic Dispensation contemplated in this Light—the character divine, the importance mundane, i.e. commensurate with the human Race—for *us* therefore superseding the necessity of miraculous or accessory & superinduced evidence by its Truth & the God-inherency of this Truth, & yet at the same time removing the only obstacles to ~~our~~ the historic credibility of the Miracles by establishing their ab anteriori probability.—The Kind of these Miracles, ~~as~~ distinguished from those of the Gospel,—namely, as physical in subject and *providential* in import, so that the Natural Laws should work in manifest subservience to the Supernatural, & Aaron Rod (Cycle or Deity) should swallow up the rods of the Pantheistic Physiolaters.—The *necessity* of understanding the Mosaic Worship as *prophetically typical*, deduced from the End and Object of the Mosaic Dispensation, & its relation to the Religion of the then civilized World, & the preservation of the Semitic Faith & a pure Semitic Race—this in confutation of the anti-Messianic or psilanthropo-

ƒ35

messianic Jews—for if prophetic, it is of course but preparatory, if typical—ad futurum, it of course infers ~~an~~ *substantial* Antitype—that the Typee of all the Sacrificial Codes, Egyptian, no less than Mosaic, is to be found in the Idea of Incarn. & Redemption, *f35ᵛ* against the Deists & Unitarians: and the combination of both, as further illustrated by Christianity, as a mundane Phænomenon & the conquering Spirit of the Planet, against Dis-Mis- and Un-believers of all sorts.—

The Ωκεανος, the Author of Phamenophis contends, is the Civil Day (bürgerliche Tag) of the Ancients 1. from Evening to Morning & Evening. I cannot take it in so definite & particularized a sense; but while I think it probable that it expressed the diurnal Motion of the Earth on itself, or of the Sun, and thence probably a sort of imaginary horizontal Circle, cut twice in 24 hours at a different point by the Circle of the Sun's Motion, & thus dividing Hades (the Invisible = the supposed under Hemisphere, or Space equivalent, according as the Fancy represented the Earth as platter-shaped or globose; I yet consider the primary symbolic import of the Ocean Stream to be *Time*, not indeed, abstractly altogether a Time Universal; but Time relatively to the Earth & Mankind, as the *Total* anterior to & continent of the parts & special Measurements thereof, considered not as the component, of an aggregate, framing, & in order of Nature prior to, the Whole as their Aggregate—in other words, not as a generalization; but—as the offspring of this productive Antecedent, which remained still as distinct & self-subsistent, even as a Parent from his Children. I would therefore define Ωκεανος (*ab* ωκυς, ωκεος, *and* ενος, *annuus, vetus?*) the natural self-measuring Time of the ~~Polar~~ Earth, considered as the Ground of all other measures of Time, forensic & festal. Consequently, comprehending the whole *popular* Religion— the higher astronomical Cycles be~~ing~~longing to the sacerdotal & esoteric. Here I interpose a digression, rather a few digressive mementos—1. of that numerous class of Mythological Alogi Amythi (αλογοκ'αμυνθοι, i.e. neither Symbol nor Sense) who are to those *f36* philosophers who, like Leibnitz & Plato before him, relate the eternal truths & immortal Yearnings from the involucrum (pupa?) & sepulchre of ~~an~~ ancient Oriental & Egyptian Wisdom to Life, & Light and Love, Eye, Wing & seminative energy, the exact

opposite of what the Bees are to the Aphides—the Aphides convert
the rude natural Juices of the living foliage to higher life, & leave
behind them sugar—So did the Ancients—then come the Bees &
~~eating~~ feeding on the sugar convert it to yet intenser life (= more
distinct consciousness) into Honey, collect, store up & arrange the
same—So did Bacon, Leibnitz, & their Followers—But the gentry, of whom I speak, turn it to *Dung*—O! the Gods of Egypt,
Osiris &c, mean nothing more than that Corn &c grows only in
summer, & does not grow in *winter*. &c &c—
     Even the Zendavesta is to be either forgery of Alexandrine
Greeks, or exenterated in the same way—. Tho' the Ahriman &
Ormuzd be directly taught to be creatures, ~~derived~~ created by the
Zervana Akarene (Χρονος αχρονος, eternal) which would have
been equal; but that Ormuzd possesses by Birth-right the primæval
Word, Honover—i.e. the eternal Ideas, the Laws & the Reason
that are in Time but as free from Time. What can this mean, but
that most vital truth, at no time of more concerning Interest than
at present—that empirically & mechanically contemplated Apparent Evil & Good would be equal, but that in created Good there
is a something more than apparent—or that in Good alone the Law
is found—the consequence of which is, that Evil is in the ignorance or subjective absence of the Law—not *is*, except as it is held
to be—in other words, that Evil exists only in the defects of the
rational & the sins of the volent, Creature!—But that ~~by~~ still by
the Honover Ormuzd can preserve a pure self even in the com-
mixtion & seeming interpenetration of the Peetiare Ahriman? =
I can really find *no* essential difference between my philosophy &
the Zend Avesta the ~~act of the material creation~~ *Chaos* in both is
an Apostasy—the potentiating creation the Spirit & the Word—
the final causa redemptionis; & reascent to the Plenitude.

f36ᵛ   The six days Creation of Ormuzd with his Amschaspands (Jehovah Elohim) is *clearly* taken from Gen. I—I say, *clearly*: for it
a varies in *one* essential (& in one only) from Moses—viz. the
heavenly Bodies are created on the first day—while in Moses this
act intervenes between the vegetable and the animal. Now that the
Author of the Zend should be perplexed at Light anterior to the
Sun & that he should transfer the latter to the first day as one with
Light, is natural; but the contrary inconceivable.—

Light of the first day the only *real* substrate of the term, Nature—an idea, we cannot dispense with—& most observable it is,
that the word Bara = created is used twice only, first verse, &
then of Man. In Light God created all things potentially, only not
the Soul which made the last effort of Nature *Man.* Hence, too,
possibly, the use of *We*—*We* will create man &c.—

4795 29.55   *A place of vision* where all the dreams of youthful Poets under Trees by Brooks &c &c realized themselves, according to their co-incidence & unanimity—. Each additional
Shaping giving a new degree of increased substantiality & clearness to the edifice—& vice versâ, Hell or Purgatory formed of
the malignant willings, wishings, & fancies of bad men—

4796 29.71   The four Rivers, into which the River of Eden   *f48*
dispartsing became into four Heads, have exercised and baffled the
~~erudition~~ Learning, palæ o-geographical Researches and conjectural ingenuity of Commentators, Cosmogonists, and Interpreters
from earliest times, while the ~~T~~Mystics, ancient and modern, have
tumbled in rampant luxuriancy thereon like Cats on a bed of Val-
erian.—If I might venture to have an opinion at all on so obscure
a passage, I should not hesitate to interpret the passage of the four
main *Heads of Houses*, or primitive Races (Radices) into which the
Tap-Root divided itself—viz. Phison, = the Inhabitants of Minor
Asia, perhaps including Egypt—The part first inhabited—Q.̣
Spain? Q.̣ Phison by Saadias & in the Samaritano-Arabic Version
= Nile: and that this was a received opinion among the Samaritans
is proved by their Liturgica, in which, we are assured by Edmund
Castellus the following words occur over & over again—A malo
te salvum præstet Deus, *qui Moisen e fluvio Phison incolumem ser-
vavit.* May it not therefore in sensu grandiori mean the Mediter-
ranean & its Coasts—Phœnicians generally, with the Arabians.
The fine *gold*, the Bdellium & Onyx Stone, seem to be *commercial*
allusions. Q.̣ To seek for the root of Zowila or Howila.—2. the
African *Giho⟨un⟩* & *Nigritarum Terra* instead of Gihan and Ethiopia we find in the Samaritano-Arab version. 3. Babylonian, Median, Persian. 4. Tatar, Mogul, Chinese.—If so, what is *Eden*
itself? I answer: the first human Age or Race, that lived on the

Fruits of the Earth, previous both to Hunting, Pasturage, and Tillage.

f48ᵛ   In the VIᵗʰ Chap. of Gen. V. 2 and 4. The Samaritan & Samaritano-Arabian Version renders Sons of God, Filii *Sultanorum*, vel Nobilium—Filii Hominis,—Filii Plebeiorum, and in the 3ʳᵈ Vers. the *Sam-Ar.*, and Saadias ex parte juxta Pentateuchem Polyglottum Constantinopolitanum (instead of ~~our~~ non habitabit spiritus meus in homine usque in æternum, or of our—My Spirit shall not strive with Man.) gives it—non recondetur quasi in vaginâ donum meum in homine in perpetum—Saadias differing only in having Spiritus meus for donum meum—while the Scholion (says A. J. Silvester de Sacy) quod in utroque codice nostro versionis Samaritano-Arabicæ reperitur) vocem donum meum de animâ intelligendam esse docet, & that by *sheathe*, conjunctionem animæ cum corpore metaphorice innui.—That the text refers to Gen. II. v. 7 cannot, I think, be doubted—and a very interesting, & if my wish does not warp my wit ᵼ probable interpretation would result: "The Soul which I gave to man & by which he is a man in contra-distin~~guished~~ction from animals, whose Life as well as Materia Substrata is from the *Ground*, shall not remain always in the *animal* Sheath which *the Ground* (Nature, ⟨Natura Naturans⟩ Lux = vis distinguens cum Tenebris, = vi unienti abdita, ut natura naturata) conspired to produce as the receptacle of the Gift divine, the opus Dei proprium) shall not always remain sheathed in the Flesh—yet it shall have a period of 120 years wherein to prepare itself, as the pullet within the egg.—Of some interest likewise is the rendering of v. 21, C. 8.—of the Sam.-Arab. Version, viz. instead of our— God said in his heart—Deus dixit *familiari suo*—and Onkelos,

f49   cum *Verbo* suo—Versio Samaritana, *Secreto*—Septuagint-~~Dia~~ Διανοηθεις, like the δια NOY of Heraclitus, and Saadias, *Prophetæ suo*—which taken metaphorice, per Prolepsin, a re inferiori, as it must be in this passage, is equivalent to Sermoni suo—The *Logos*.

4797 29.72   On reasoning by Consequences. If the Consequences (which we will here abbreviate by the letter X, and the order of each by a figure attached, ex. gr. X ⁽¹, and the consequence of that X ⁽², & so on) are admitted by the Party attacked, there can be no doubt of the fairness of the Reasoning. Thus, from the tenet of Psilanthropy, or mere humanity of Christ, I may deduce the denial of the doctrine of Redemption considered as Atonement, and the efficient cause & necessary antecedent of Man's *Saveability*, and not as only one frequent occasion of the Salvation, i.e. Reformation of individual Men. For this is admitted and avowed by the Unitarians, ~~or~~ more approximately entitled, Psilanthropists, of the present day. And if this denial contain in itself matter of offence to Christians in general, & bring the deniers into Odium, this is *their* business not mine, who have only stated the fact as it is. But I could not have done the same, with the former Socinians: for these did not avowedly deny the Redemption by Christ, in a sense of personal efficiency peculiar to Christ, as our Redeemer. I might assert and attempt to prove the *incompatability* in reason of the idea, Redemption, and the idea of Psilanthropy, and thus the *logical* necessity of rejecting the former: and if I succeed I prove Socinian*ism* an anti-Christian Scheme, i.e. for all who held Redemption for an *Essential* of Christianity. Still logical is not necessarily actual: and still the Socini*an* may *be*, as well as believe himself to be, a Christian. The Unitarian, on the contrary, has, I admit, a Religion, which he believes to be the true Religion taught by Christ: but I cannot without palpable inconsistency admit it to be that which I mean by the word, Christian Religion. For Redemption *f49ᵛ* is the sine quâ non of the latter, to which all other parts show as means, to that as the end, or effect of that as the cause—& I might as reasonably allow a Triangle to be called a Square, because there are strait lines in both / Any pretence to the contrary would be as gross a Sophism, as if a Tolerationist should say—why such a difference? There are three strait lines in each—concealing the fact, that the *essence* of the former consisted in having *only* three lines.—

So far then of X ⁽¹—if only we add what we have indeed implied, that this consequence would not follow in the case of a Man or sect, who rejected the outward & visible signs of Baptism & the Lord's Supper—first, because these are not the *End* constitutive of Christianity, but two, among many, of the *Means*—& and as not the number ~~but~~ of the means, but the intensity, causes their efficiency, how dare I assert, that God may not bless the remaining means? In order to justify such an Assertion, I must shew, as in the former instance of the Divinity of our Lord, or as in the article of a disease in the Moral Will, that these are pre-supposed in the End, the one as a Mean, the other as a subject matter. Nay, the Means rejected may for Mankind at large be a necessary means of the conservation of the Knowlege of Redemption—even as the Ox- yds of Mercury, for the cure of a specific Disease, viz. so that without it *all* patients cannot be cured—& yet this cannot a priori be approved of any *one* individual.—Besides, this would fall under X $^{(2}$ or third—. Secondly, because what remains of the Christian System after the subtraction of the Sacraments is the *same* as before. Neither the Head nor the Heart have been removed—but two of the fingers, at most.—Or granting that the points rejected were = the two hands & arms! Doubtless, were this universal the whole human Race would perish; or could not have continued to exist; but it not being universal, it by no means follows, that Individuals may not exist, in sound health too, without hands and arms.—

f50 There is a clear example of this in the Quakers relatively to their doctrine of never taking up arms even defensively. Great Britain could not exist with the universal practice of this doctrine, but the Quakers not only may exist in Gr. Br., or any other great naval, commercial, and warlike insular Kingdom, but may be among its most useful Subjects—yea, useful even on account of this peculi- arity, as a check to the *excess* of the opposite feeling.—In their case the Many save the Few—and the argument all cannot—ergo, *none*, is a mere equivoque on the word "all", or a false statement instead of—*all* could not have been *so* saved, from which it does not fol- low, that none *can* be!—

Still however this mode of Reasoning may be both fair & weighty, used not [ad] hominem, but as a dissuasive a doctrinâ.— But when it appears as a non-admitted X $^{(2}$, X $^{(3}$, &c, it becomes very suspicious.—The most trifling ⟨error⟩ contains in its possible consequences all falsehoods! and from an error in fluxions, as that of taking, as Zeno did, the sum of an infinite number of infinitely small quantities as infinite, an acute Logician might finally deduce the denial of a God as Zeno actually deduced the non-entity of all visible Acts, and the delusion of all the notices of the Sense. The most useful formula in the Logic of Consequences is the following: an argument which would prove the falsehood of an admitted Truth, is no proof of falsehood in any other application. Let A

represent the argument: C the disputed position: B a position admitted true on both sides. A is adduced to prove the impossibility
of C; but A would apply equally against B.—but B remains true
nevertheless—so therefore must C, as far as A alone is concerned.   *f50ᵛ*
But even here many cautions are requisite to secure the formula
from sophistical uses. First, B and C must be subjects ejusdem
generis. Secondly, A in both cases must be ejusdem naturaæ et
gradûs: In B, it may present a difficulty only, & perhaps indicate
only the limit of our present knowlege: while in C, it may present
a positive contradiction to some essential predicate of C. A thing
may be intuitively irrepresentable, and yet intellectually conceivable—nay, a thing may be *inconceivable*, as the uninterrupted rectilineal progress of the rays of Light moving in all directions, and
yet not involve any absurdity—i.e. contradiction in the terms of
the position.—Of the neglect of these cautions we have striking
proof in King James's No Bishop, No King: & Dʳ H. More's,
Glanville's, & Jung alias Stilling's, No Ghosts, no God.—Applied
to B, the truth of which rests on proofs of its own, and the constituent ideas of which would remain even tho' the predicate attacked by A were left out, A sinks into a mere difficulty, at best a
partial Objection: while if applied to C, which has no sufficient
proofs of its reality, and only negative proofs of its possibility, the
same A would swell into ⟨a most⟩ formidable Objection, and in
certain cases into a full disproof, if not of the thing, yet of the
rationality of the belief in it. Thus, I may deny the reality of a
Ghost, or finite yet mere Spirit, & have a right so to do so as long
as I can demonstrate the groundlessness of the contrary assertion—
and I may fairly doubt its possibility—i.e. whether it is even a
notion & not rather a non-sensical Word, like a round Square—&
should laugh at the syllogistic figure—You deny the possibility of   *f51*
a Spirit—but God is a Spirit—therefore you deny the possibility
of a God. No!—What I̶ ̶d̶e̶n̶y̶ had my belief in an absolute infinite
invisible Spirit, whom no one at any hath seen or can see, to do
with my disbelief of a determined, figured, finite, visible Spirit?—
So likewise must C and B. express this same *relation*. The negation
of B may be a full proof of the non-existence of C; yet C, not of
B. An argument which disproved a God would effectualy disprove
final causes in Nature; but the denial of final causes might weaken

the feeling of faith but ⟨is⟩ by no means incompatible with the faith itself, final causes being indeed one of the most persuasive inducements but not the strongest, much less the only, evidence of an existing God.— ~~No there is~~ Had ~~James~~ Laud said, No King, no Bishop! & used it as an inducement to the dignified Clergy to stand firm by the royal prerogatives, there was much to be said for it—but No Bishop, no King! in James's mouth proved that he had neither the Spirit of a King, nor Logic enough for a Parish Clerk—. The fairest case in which the argument, C = B, if A − B = O, A − C = O or A cannot prove C to be − Y; for it is equally applicable to B, which is known to be + Y—is that ~~of~~ in which I have used it against the oppugners of the Trinity by shewing the ⟨equal⟩ applicability of their arguments to the Attributes of God admitted by them.

4798 29.73   Quod absque *ideis* intellectûs et inde † cogitationis nulla datur perceptio de quâcumque re. Swedenborgh . . † Theory i.e. *Ideas* or Laws evolved into Rules by which the Universal is applied to all *particulars*. This is exactly what I have

f5 1ᵛ   taught at large in the Essays on Method—Friend Vol. 3. Perceptio is here equivalent to what I call a legitimate *Fact*. That~~is~~ is, if I do not flatter myself, the preferable word—id videlicet, in quo idea sive cogitatum *factum* est—is realized. ~~An Idea~~ *Fact* as the ground or origin is false grammar—a verb passive ~~part~~ mistaken for a substantive, & that too a verb without a nominative case expressed or understood—

Quod verbum non intelligitur quam a *rationali* homine: nam credere aliquid absque ideâ rei et absque rationis intuitione, est modo memoriter retinere vocem omni vitâ perceptionis et affectionis destitutam / quod non est credere. Eman. Suedomontanus *De Verbo et ejus Sensu* p. 11

4799 29.74   ⟨√ means the root of, and this, = when *the Divine* is spoken of, is the same as the *Identity* of: in all else = that which *represents* the Identity. The × signifies, interpenetrating each other, *beget* a third, not constitute.⟩

Hints of a Letter to Mʳ Tulk.—Ever since our last meeting, chiefly perusal of, & constantly conversing with Suedom.—confident that this had been in no ordinary measure the case, many many years before I had ever seen so as to attend to S's Works, appear to myself to have obtained an insight into that Law of the Homo internus, of which S. is the fullest and most demonstrable, demonstrative, and exemplary instance; but as may indeed be shown from his own relations, not the first nor the only one. That this (Ὓπαρ = Ὕπνος ⁽² + ἀγρυπνια⁽² × aperitio interni Hominis, & deinde apparitiones spirituales, non autem idcirco semper vel necessario *rationales* sicut nec in omnibus hujus mundi communionibus: hoc verò in aperitione Interni pendet semper de statu morali et intelligentiali Recipientis. Falsificati falsa et vident et audiunt: at nihilominus verè vident et verè audiunt) is not necessarily confined to Men of Love & Faith such as Behmen & Suedom. tho' by divine mercy chiefly so—What an enlightened Member of the New Church is now called on to do. 1. To call no *man* Master & to prove this from Suedom's own express declarations. 2. That the same Ideæ Rationis (veritatis eternæ) may manifest themselves relativè ad sæculum et Individuum in several, more or less adequate, Ideæ Cogitationis, i.e. Theoremata, per quæ *Lex* aliqua discernitur in singulis et applicatur ad singula. 3. The important difference between merely *inadequate* & ⟨that which is⟩ mixt with heterogeneous, besides its inadequacy. 4. Of *venial* mixtures, such as discriminate (by their occasional occurrence) the works of good and even of highly-gifted men, & to whom extraordinary *Apertures* have been dispensed, from the works of Inspiration in its *highest* & absolute sense, & from those likewise in which f52 not all but all ~~for the~~ excepting morally indifferent admixture from the active powers of the Percipient, whereby the pure *re*cipiency can be modified, has been prevented by an especial act of the divine will—a distinction which Suedom. has himself applied to the Canonical Books themselves. Now these venial *Ab*verbs (a Verbo √ Boni et Veri divergentia) may, I think, be reduced under two heads—1. a Confounding of the Ideæ Rationis with the Ideæ Cogitationis, including the transfer of the affection or emotion arising out of the one to the other: i.e. When the Feeling, which a Dissent from the Truth could approximately call forth & not only sanction but require, is connected with a Dissent from the Form or Mode in which I have contemplated & conveyed that Truth. 2. The assumption of a Part (pars magna forsan vel etiam maxima) for the whole—a conclusion of the Universal from the General.

f59ᵛ   4800 28.57   Clearer than the inference of Heat and Light from the relative position of the Earth to the Sun, is this to me. A nation, that substitutes Locke for Logic, and Paley for Morality, and both ~~for~~ this and that for Polity, Philosophy and Theology, cannot but be slaves. But if this be the case with the Gentry, Clerisy, & the Learned in all liberal professions, it is so with the Nation— ~~and the consequence~~ or a Revolution is at hand.—

Without Principle *Unanimity*, or even a coherent Party, impossible—and Longanimity even so. For as every Month producing some new fact (ex. gr. the ministerial *majority* of 120, which being struck off, the Min. had yet 176 against 178!) it alters the per-

f60   spective of consequences—and as each mind may have & most will have a different perspective at the same time, so will each in May differ from its former mind in Janʸ—

4801 28.58   Guilty *Smiles*—ex. gr. of the H. of L. on Lord Holland's narration of the infamous Oppression of the Neapolitans—& the Austrian evasion.—a good Sonnet, entitled, The two Smiles.

Review the pledges, promises, oaths &c. of and from Kings, Emperors, Princes & Cabinets since 1813: and it seems as if we might dispense with the ill-mannered Words, Perjury and Subornation, the same sense being conveyed in Royalty and Vice-Royalty—or "the monarchical principle."

Fearful effect of voting not according to conviction respecting the measure itself, but for the ministry: I abhor A; but I vote for it—because the ~~tae~~ condemnation of A may lead to B = change of ministry!

f60ᵛ   4802 28.59   The Western Church ran in one stream from E. to W. till the 15th Century—tho' sadly lutulent from the swamps, it had oozed thro'. At that time it met a Rock, (Luther & compeers) and after violent impetus split into two streams, one running N.W. the other S.W.—In leaving the Rock, the N.W. precipitated a large portion of the mud and worse impurities, which the ancient River had contracted, from Cent. 3rd where it had ~~made~~ had a sad inflow from a Canal cut across to it from the vast River of Civil Power, & in ~~the~~ its further course it had deposited somewhat of the Remainder. Now (quoth the Rivales on the Banks of Riv. S.W.—Where was *your* River before Rock, Back-filth? Why, w[h]ere yours was, to be sure.

4803 28.60   The Queen's Prosecutors composed of Legalists enobled for their Effrontery & Brows of Iron ~~and~~ precious Keepers of the Royal Conscience. Priests, mitred for Hearts of *Nickel* (el for eld, & eld for Senior = Nick Sen?? or Diabolino, Nickelino?)—&c &c—but all happily enumerated by the far-famed Magisterial Bard in his Poem, entitled Propria quæ Maribus—

Dux, Illex, Hæres, Exlex: *a fronte* creata,
Ut bifrons custos: Bos, Fur, Sus, atque Sacerdos.

4804 28.61   Imitation of the passage in the Mids. N. Drm.   *f61* on the fatality of true Love—in reflections on the fatality of Genius, especially poetic Genius—either Poverty (Collins, Spenser, Burns, ϛΤΣ or the acquirement of Wealth ($\alpha\xi\iota o\rho\eta\mu\alpha$) or hopeless Hymen, or Disease.

4805 28.62   I grieve to have a moral charge to make against W. Sc. but the attempt to give a palliative gloss & an interest to the villain Leicester, whom the Novellist himself has shewn a 10 fold Villain—at this time!—When—but see the Debates in both Houses of P. on the Austrian & Lord Cast's. Circulars respecting Naples! Add this to the conduct respecting the Subornation & Perjury of the Milan Commission & its Ruffiancy.—*Lordly Smiles!*—

4806 28.63   In inquiries into so called Superstitions and   *f61^v* supernatural Influxes and Influences, so as to guard against the credulity of Disbelief from mere previous Habit and the dread of being supposed to believe, on the one hand; and the facility of receiving wonders from a secret partiality for the wonderful, or from a readiness to find an Idea of our own, an old speculative Possibility, realized, on the other—for ~~men of original Views are~~

one is right apt to welcome as found what ~~one~~ "it would not surprize me to find"—it is well to bear in mind, as often as we seem
to ourselves to have explained ~~the~~ an anomaly into some natural
cause, or as the product of some ordinary Faculty disguised by the
f62 Unusual in degree or circumstances, that ~~if X~~ if X = a, it is
possible that a = X. Exempli gratiâ: that if the zöo-magnetic influx be only the influence of the Imagination, the active Imagination may be a form of the Zöo-magnetic Influence—and whether
it would not ⟨be more⟩ expedient to consider both as unknown
quantities, XY = Z. The criterion must be this: First, will the
facts be less remarkable by reducing X to Y? Second, will X be
better understood by being reduced to Y—or Y by its reduction to
X—or both by reduction to Z?—Let Z represent the Volition as
the making power acting in the imagination, as one of its forms—
X, the magnetic influence as the result when the + and − poles
f62ᵛ of the nervous cycle are in two several organisms, the positive Pole
being the nervous System of the Magnetist, the negative being that
of the Patient: and let Y, representing the Imagination, be the same
in ordinary cases where the Poles subsist in one and the same Organism, + in the Cerebral, − in the abdominal, and the conducting and balancing point in the pectoral, Nerves.—This would
be analogous to Electricity ~~as~~ in its relation to Magnetism. And
remember, that the passion for the doing away of all wonders may
~~move~~ make the Theorist just as credulous, as the Love of the Wonderful makes the Plebeian.—

f63 4807 28.64   We are often told of the danger of playing with
Edge-tools. Through my whole Life I have found the most harm
from playing (aye, and working too) with dull tools.
       Improved Proverb. Do not play with Edge—nor work with
Dull—Tools.

4808 28.65   Moriæ Encomium, p. 229 Oxoniæ, 1668—
shews an acquaintance with the magnetic Epopsy, Vision, or Clear-
seeing—tho' probably induced by nervous derangement without
treatment ab extra. So Plato—So Sᵗ Paul, Corinth/

4809 28.66   It would be idle to repeat or reason on certain
magnetic Statements, says Dʳ Parrot, "because no Authority can

avail to give them the slightest *probability* in the eyes of impartial $f63^v$
men."—But what have we to do with *probability* in this case? Are
they *Facts?* Have they been attested by Eye-witnesses, & by whom
and of what competency? It is clear that by denying the former we
take on ourselves the obligation of explaining the latter—wherever
the attestation itself is not denied nor even pretended to be doubtful. This is the difference between contemporary and historical
Evidence. In proportion to the distance of the event, the loss of
documents, &c. the evidence and the asserted event are both in the
same scale, & cannot therefore, be weighed against each other.—
A doting delirious old woman may at different moments use contradictory words—as I may say—A. was black—& the next moment add—and but likewise all white. For what that is articulable
may not the Tongue &c articulate? But a logical *impossibility* no $f64$
one can *see* or *believe* himself to have seen. And improbability is a
relative conception,—the measure of which is in its Antecedent—
and the Antecedent is the previous Theory received as certain truth
by the Assertor of the improbability. For instance—the very circumstances, that determined Dr Parrot, a materialist, to reject a
statement on the ground of an improbability not counterponderable
by any possible evidence (an historical impossibility) had determined me to *anticipate* & predict the *fact*—i.e. to believe that facts
equivalent to that stated would be found to occur./P. will believe
on no evidence, and I believe without any—and even when I
disbelieved the evidence & its the occurrence of the fact in the
particular instance, in which it was asserted to have occurred.—
The term, Fact, must first be defined.—

I hold myself bound (says Ghert, P. G. van, Dagboek einer $f64^v$
Magnetischen Behandeling, Te Amsterdam, 1814) in speaking of
the *Far-seeing*, or Telescopy, of the Patient to add, that in this
point she often forgot herself, and gave descriptions of Places and
Persons that were altogether false and errant—which perversion
(Verkehrtheit) she always charged on the levity or distrust of the
Querists.—

Now this two or three failures of this kind would suffice with
the knowing ones, who do not even wish to *know* any thing, and
who ought therefore to be called the *handy* ones, and *all my eye* $f65$
gentry, to vault high-ringined into ⟨Tyburn Court,⟩ ⟨as the Roman

Gen^s into⟩ the triumphal chariot, with the carcase of detected, convicted and executed Clair~~icy vey~~voyance at the Tail, blowing the
Horns &c.—It would constrain the true Philalethist to *suspect*—to
look narrowly into the whole case—but he would not shout, Imposture! till he had convinced himself that the coincidences with
the truth were such as could with probability be accounted for by
the law of Chance.—It might well happen that not only the series
~~of~~ and number of actual Veridictions might leave an obstinate dissatisfaction in the mind with regard to this solution."—"chance
f65^v   hits" but a single one might consist of so many particulars ~~as to
shock the senses of Experience.~~ that the hypothesis of its being a
mere accident would shock the feeling of experience more than the
position of a correspondent power manifestable only under unusual
conditions & circumstances.—If so, any number of recurrences of
such cases in different Patients in different countries, and where
no collusion was possible—as ex. gr. when the same phænomena
have been noted at the same time at Milan, and at St Petersburg,
might oblige him to admit the Patients' own Solution as probable,
f66   and to cite Newton's aphorism, that difficulties are no objections
to the existence of a Law adequately proved by undoubted Facts—
That the Law has not been rendered manifest in X Y Z, may
warrant a conjecture that some other Law exists in these precluding
or suspending the former—but nothing more—supposing it satisfactorily proved in A.B.C.D. &c—

Compare the knowledge and experience which men had of electrical phænomena before and since the invention of the electrical
machines with the Zoo-magnetic phænomena before and since the
discovery of ~~its~~ the producibility by art, i.e. since Mesmer.

f66^v   4810 28.67   A pretty unintended Couplet in the Prose of
Sidney's Arcadia

> And sweeter than a gentle South-west wind
> O'er flowry fields and shadow'd Waters creeping
> In Summer's extreme heat.—

Nor did great Clerks disdain our Conference.

—rather by the working of the Sea than by any *Self-industry*

4811 29.75   N.b.—To seek for some light respectibi̶l̶i̶t̶yng   *f52*
fusion as disparate from solution—It would be easy indeed to reply
that F. = Solution in the Fluid of Warmth, S = ⟨Fusion⟩ in the
Warmth of Fluids—or that Fusion : Caloric: : Solution : Water.
But what is Caloric? + Dilatation? and Hydrogen?—Dilatation!—
Or is Caloric the sole Dilative? And the difference of F. and Sol.
in the different capacity of Caloric in diff. bodies? Still the ? re-   *f52ᵛ*
turns. What is Caloric? If it *be*, what is its Caloric? Would *melted*
Carbonate of Lime, for instance, placed o̶n̶ in a hollow sphere of
Ice melt a quantity proportionate to its comparative *Infusibility*: as
frozen Quicksilver does e contra? And how is it that the Alkalies
have so great a power of communicating fusability to Silex?—

$$\frac{\text{Gr.}}{\text{L}} = \text{C.}\ \frac{\text{L}}{\text{Gr.}}$$ Color—Oxydation.—contractive Fire?—and then

the transition of the Contractive to the Dilative, by the antagonism
of *Contr.* to *At*tract.—having as the result continuous Dilation?—
This would answer, I think, all the *facts*—& determine the Nature
of Hydrogen & its relations to Nitrogen, on the one side, and
Carbon on the other. But the Carbonic Acid requires stern inquisition.—Are not the precious stones, ex. gr. Diamond = Carbon,
Sapphire + Clay, &c. Proofs that the Stoffs have their essence
wholly in *the Powers*. The same or similar energies of Contraction
acting on similar basic energies of *At*traction constitute Clay &
Coal into the same or similar substances/And that Diamond become
Charcoal, & Sapphire Clay—this will be sunrise of Physics whenever a better reason shall be found than that the one *was* Carbon
& the other *had* been Clay.—

4812 29.76   Swedenborg, in his Prodromus Philosophiæ ra-
tiocinantis de Infinito et Causâ Finali Creationis: deque Mecha-
nismo Operationis Animæ et Corporis—Dresdæ et Lipsiæ,
1734—written therefore 16 years before that attack of Brain-fever,
in which his Unbelievers suppose his spiritual Epopsy to have
originated, at a time when his vigor of intellect & great scientific
attainments were attested by the Learned throughout Europe—
places as the *ultimum* inter demonstrationes, Infinitum esse causam
Finiti, et Deum infinitum/esse Conditorem Universi—tacitus, an-
imarum consensus, esse Deum et Deum esse infinitum. Now *this*

Consent he determines to be, in part, an assumption connate with, or co-essentially immanent in, the Reason, a postulate of the Reason itself and therefore a Postulate that involves the Confession— and in part, a conclusion of the Understanding from the order of the World—. This statement Sw. expresses with his wonted & *f53* characteristic happiness & precision—*curiosa felicitas*—"hoc dictari, inquam, partim ab animâ liberâ, (i.e. while the Reason is the *form* of the Will—ubi Voluntas Rationi subest) partim ab animâ ex effectibus diversissimis mundi instructâ et quasi admonitâ."— The following sentences of this, the § VI. (p. 83, 84) suggest a possible origination of this universal *Consent* or *Idea* from influences ab extrâ, of which we are unconscious, & which therefore appear to us spontaneous—that closely resembles Democritus's theory of the origin of the Belief of Deity. The Conclusion, however, p. 85, 86., of this §, is admirable—"Tho' this, I grant, will not stand the test of a strict philosophy," usque tamen non negari potest, quin in Homine (qualitercunque Homine, modo rationis usu polleat) sit illud quod agnoscat Deum Omnip. et Numen in omnibus præsens et providum, adeo ut videatur tanquam innatum, et Rationis non nimium per † ideas turbatæ aut perparum excultæ vis.—Vi ration⟨a⟩li sciverat homo, numen dari

† Be aware, that ⟨the Term,⟩ Ideas, here & elsewhere is used *laxè* et abusivè, as was the fashion of the age.—Strictly, for per *ideas* we should read, per cogitata discursiva, or per discursiones animi (mens being = Reason, Anima = the Soul, and Animus = the Understanding) or still better, per idola et discursiones animi

f53ᵛ   4813 29.77   ~~Oken~~ Notes on Oken's Natur-geschichte.—

Vol. II. p. 8. ~~Are then the Nerves of lessnecessity~~—("the $\frac{Darm}{Gut}$

forms itself to the Gut-sense (Darmsinn), The ~~Lungs~~ Tongue; The Lungs the L. Sense, Nose; Flesh & Bone to the Bone Sense, Ear; Nerve to the Nerve Sense, Eye.)—Are the nerves then of less necessity to the senses of Smell and Hearing than to the Sense of Sight? Are not these nerves (where any are) in all the senses alike the primary and sole proper Agents and Sentients? (I use the language of Psilo-somatism, and arguing with Materialists howl with the wolves.) Are they not at least that ultimatum in the visible Organism, to which all other parts are but the Stands, Joints, Beds, Channels, Tubes—& sometimes even, little more than the protecting *Cases*! Is it not a stubborn presumption against Oken's scheme, that the Eye appears in almost the lowest, the most nerveless Animals? And why? Take care, that you do not confound Feeling, as the mere ⟨*subjective*⟩ *sensation* of a present (locally immediate) Stimulus, the objective accidents of which are supplied by Association, with the *Sense* of Touch: and I will tell you, why? The Eye appears in the lower animals because of all the *Senses* it is the least *reflective*, the most superficial. Hence the number of Eyes in Insects, whose Life is a Life of *Irritability*, that is, of the electrical *Form*, the Power of Breadth & Surface. For Irritability may be defined—the *Objective Self-less* Sensibility as opposed to the *subjective*, or Sensibility properly so called.—The high dignity of *Vision* in Man is the source of Oken's Delusion. But *in Man* Vision is a *Language*, the meaning & substance of which has been provided by other senses, & by functions more than sensuous. The difference is as the words of a Book to and Diagrams of a Book of Geometry to a Book-worm ⚹ and to a Mathematician—. Another objection—viz. to the Lungen-sinn = Nase. Now Insects have neither Lungs nor Gills—yet their Smell is almost miraculous. R. Southey dipped certain Beetles, say half a dozen, in oil—half of them he placed on a Shelf or Table in One room, and the rest in another Room, under the same circumstances of Light, & Warmth, & Ventilation—To the former, lying lifeless on the *f54* Table, he brought a Female Beetle, & put in the midst of them—& within a minute or two, they were re-animated & briskly pursuing the female—Those in the other room remained lifeless, & died for good & all.—

  p. 12 Organic Atoms! *Wahre* Atome auch: i.e. right genuine *Atoms, composed* ! aye, Atoms composed of Coal, Water, Air and Light!! Fressende Puncte! Germ-Atoms! Life-Atoms, (p. 51. Hydra or Arm. polypus, of *Trembley*) "Das Wunder ist aber eben nicht gross." The Deuce, it is not! What causes these Life-atoms, these Milen or Milettes, always to make *Arms* at the same places? Why a mouth, and yet not an Anus? Why, a Mouth at all? The Quicksilver divides into endless Globules; but do these Globules arrange themselves? And *for* whom is it a Mouth? Does it admit the same Milbel or Milette, only as the ones already congregated? If so, what is there then to digest, what to spit out? And why should this living Globulage receive these accretions or rather ac-currents or adnatants from *within*? Again: *who* eats? Not the At-oms. *They* form the *Channel* only for the Food. Who digests? If each Point has the same Life as the Whole, the Whole (more appropriately, the All) can have no other Life or Instinct than that in each. If one ⟨seek to⟩ form a knot, all must form a knot. For of perfect Likes there can be no Subordination.—Finally, to Heighten the *glare* of the Absurdity, this Polyp is but one of very many *kinds*, each kind diverse yet all composed of the *same* Mul-bels or Life-Atoms—But what are Polypi?—All animals are but organised Mulbeln or Milen!! Ein Korallen-stamm ist ein Haufen Mile, der Menschliche Leib ist ebenfalls ein Haufen Mile!

The Clio Borealis (the snail which the whale feeds on) has Heart, Veins, Arteries, & Nerves, yet no Eyes.

f54ᵛ   4814 29.78   A slime, individualizable into gelatinous Warts, overskins the Carbonate-of-Lime Stem, or earthy Pipe; within & out of which is a gelatinous Pipe (Rohr) blossoming into an animal, or syngenesia! ~~The~~ a buds or ⟨a⟩ wart, either if sepa-rated, forms the commencement of a new Coral. It grows, and as it grows deposits ~~the~~ Carb. of Lime (∕ + ⋱. by ....) or subjugation of ⋱. to ∕c by the alliance of ∴.. with the latter. ∕ even as gristle becomes bone. What remains unsubdued, the yet balanced combatants, = the life, & ⋱. being the constructive Power or Denominator, animal life, that thus lives by dying—. Rightly, Zoophyte; for the *vegete* manifests itself by the detrusion of Lime, as the Blood of the Mammalia or *animate* extrudes Car-bon. The gaseous Form of the latter in Carb. Acid Gas from the Lungs marks the subjugation of the ∕c to the n⋱. . while the ∕ as *silicium adheres* to the Grass, as Epidermis of Silex—∕c under the dynasty of ∕. Q.ʸ Diamond of animal origin?—betwixt Iron and Silex?—found in eisenhaltigen Sand. In what other way can we originate its ante-chrystalline Fluidity? or Gaseity? The diamond sparkles ~~in Soda Water. It is hard indeed to say,~~ what the com-bined Powers of Heat, enormous Pressure & the attraction of me-

tallic Iron may not exert on the Silex, so as to compel it to excrete
the small remainder of Carburetted Hydrogen, or hydrogenated
Carbon which it had retained in its primary chrystalline precipitation: or not impossibly to accelerate that maturation of Granite
into Coal which Nature effects ⟨elsewhere⟩ in long series of for-
mations. It would be interesting to know whether any the least
difference either in magnitude, arrangement, or quality exists between the Diamonds found in ochreous Matrix, ~~or~~ & those in
irony Sand.—Still, however, my thoughts fly back, ⟨either⟩ to the
powers of Life in the *dis*animinated, or to the galvanic moment in
which the synthesis takes place of Magnetism and Electricity, under the predominance of the Magnetic Factor—i.e. Chrystalization—tho' we may admit the former Powers or equivalents as
causes of the extrusion of the Coal. But here we should notice the
distinction between the processes of gradual Maturation of likes
into higher likes, or the dying away thro' grades, in which however the mystery of Proportion, plastic Numbers, reveals itself—
& the continuity becomes *intellectual* solely, in order that it may
inferred at all—for by harmonious *Distinction* we infer the continuity of the Law—or the Lex Continui—in the Fluid & Aeriform
without *breach* of continuance, co-existent to the Light & yet not
combinable in the imagination—or conception; but in the Solid
necessarily separable.—Thus the Metals always found with Plati-   *f55*
num, which for the Metallic seems what the Gems to the Mineral
world.—Or, the presiliency, the predominance of the Repulsive
Power, projecting Opposites as Contraries—as the thin strata of
purest Flint between the vast Masses of Lime.

4815 29.79   Θεος ανθρωπῳ ου μιγνυται, αλλα δια του δαιμον-
ιου πασα εστιν η ὁμιλια και η διαλεκτος Θεοις προς Ανθρωπους.

Διοτιμα.

4816 29.80   Did you *deduce* your own being? Even that is
less absurd than the conceit of *deducing* the Divine Being? Never
would you have had the notion had you not had the Idea—rather,
had not the Idea worked in you, like the Memory of a Name which
~~I~~ we cannot recollect and yet feel that we have, and which reveals
its existence in the mind only by a restless anticipation & proves

its prior actuality by the almost explosive instantaneity with which
it is welcomed & recognized on its re-emersion out of the Cloud,
or its re-ascent above the horizon of Consciousness.—Sie wurden
[*würden*] mir dies ohne Mühe anders zu erklären [*wissen*] and
even [*bring*] my own facts on your side by *Words*: denn immer-
hat die tiefer liegende Wahrheit das Wortgewebe gegen sich: Es
ist der Instinct des Buchstabens die Vernunft unter sich zu brin-
gen, mit ihr umzugeben, wie Jupiter mit seinem Vater.

4817 29.81   Si propositio hæc Euclidis: *Tres Anguli Trian-
guli æquales sunt duobis rectis* utilitati eorum qui dominantur con-
traria esset, non dubito quin dudum, si non disputata, suppressa
fuisset.—HOBBES.

f55ᵛ 4818 29.82   Hear then, dear [Alsop] the ground and the
limit of my Tolerance. A form, a shape, or figure must all things
have, and to remove all shape from a thing is the same as to
annihilate it, to make the thing nothing. But still it is not the Shape
· that brings forth the ~~th~~Being, but it is the Being that in all cases
assumes a Shape, as the condition of its *Existence*: for de rebus non
apparentibus et non existentibus eadem est ratio. Thus it becomes
a *Thing*—i.e. ens apparens per formam quæ est a se et per aliud,
or ens formam sibi propriam habens et patiens. (A grain of Corn
is ens apparens: a Heap of Corn is rei apparentia.) Doubtless,
some Shape it must assume, and ~~such~~ a shape whereby it can manifest its being, et per quam se *ponit* et proponit: et quâ subtractâ,
solvitur. We dismiss the *figure* (id, quo figitur) in order to contemplate it in ~~the~~ its *principle*: ex. gr. the circle in a ~~strait~~ moving line
fixed at one point. All the different ~~Languages~~ Tongues that men
speak & have spoken, Indian, Greek, Latin, German, are so many
contingent forms, figures, (= fixtures) shapes, metamorphoses of
one and the same, Man-tongue, Lingua Humana. Each of all these
several Tongues ⟨or Speeches⟩ may become extinct: Speech cannot
die ⟨~~Great~~ Some one of these particular Languages, this or that,
~~or another~~, may be fitter than another, to present the Soul of Man
or ad extra, to propose the mind⟩ (and the species, that most partake of the immortality of their genus linguæ *gener*atricis quæ omnibus et singulis *sub*est, causa linguarum communis *sub*faciens (suf-

ficiens) are those that are miscalled, the Dead Languages, rightly to be named, surviving Speeches—Γλωσσαι αγλωσσοι, the Souls or Spirits of dead Tongues.—)

4819 29.83   A state of overgrown Wealth = a Sow too fat *f56* to move, with Rats that have eat into and nested in her Lard.—It is asserted, that these die of Swallowed Salamanders, or Land Newts—nay, that the mere Carrying of a Basket or Tray of Crabs thro' a Herd of Swine will throw them into mortal Convulsions.—

4820 29.84   A sentence of ΣFHδενβουργ (p. 216, De cœlo et inferno) of no novelty but infinite concernment. Assuescit Homo ab infantiâ amicitiam benevolentiam et sinceritatem præferre et suæ propriæ voluntatis cogitata celare; inde ex habitu trahit vitam moralem et civilem in externis, qualiscunque sit in internis. Ex illo habitu existit, quod Homo vix sciat sua interiora et quoque quod non animadvertat ad illa.

4821 20.21   Lord Grenville pro Papistis Britanno-Hiberniis *f8ᵛ* Tuesday Night, April 17, 1821—A Declamation of Combustibles and Common-places, and Confusions of Accidents with Principles, without an approach to a senatorial or even a dialectic statement of the true *Question*. He keeps out of sight of the points adhuc sub lite, and spouts away, like a Lead-gutter in a ~~Rainstorm~~, Thaw, on the points admitted on all sides, ~~and~~ or rather like a Kennel in White Chapel or Newgate Market, in a Rain-storm swells and sweeps onward the bloody offal, filth, guts and garbage, which the very Shambles and Butchers' Dogs had long disowned—Swift's Humane Project for bringing to the market, and salting for exportation, the young children of the Irish Peasantry, was scarcely better fitted to rouse and madden the vindictive Hatred of the lower orders in Ireland/Nay, one portion of his Lordship's long Oration seemed to have—at least could answer—no other purpose than that of recalling to their minds their perfect **right** of reclaiming the property, that had been confiscate, by acts which without even adverting to the antecedent Provocations, and Necessities of Self-Defence, without noticing the numerous points in which these acts were acts of Retaliation, Statutes passed by the Catholic Par- *f9*

liament a few months before, in which the names only were
changed from conquered Protestant to reconquered Papist, his
Lord'ship describes as monstrous unqualified Tyranny and Iniquity. Can Lord Grenville be ignorant that his supposed *Right* is
burning in the Heart of 7 out of 10 of the Irish Papists: and
needed only ~~the~~ its admission in toto ~~of~~ by Protestant Statesmen to
burst forth in act on the first opportunity?—I allude, however, to
this passage, and to others, of the same kind in the H. of Commons to contrast it with the panegyrics on the prudence, temper,
&c with which the Question had been debated, & the brow-beat-
ing, coughing down, nay, (see Mr. Canning's speeches) sharp in-
vectives against every man who ever dared hint his convictions
that Popery was still Popery, and that Popery did not consist in
the Pope but in a papal Hierarchy—Now just as fairly as Sir T.
Lethbridge & Mr. Ellis were charged with a wish to excite a No
Popery Riot, might Lord Gr. be calumniated with taking the fit
means to excite a new Irish Massacre.

Lord Liverpool's Reply is like all his other Speeches, sensible
and statesmanlike, but even he does not strike *into*, tho' here &
there he appears to strike *at*, the root of the Cause. If for *foreign*
he had said *alien* Influence, he would have hit the Eye of the
Target.—

f9ᵛ   Can ought be more senseless than for the two Branches into
which a Tree had disparted to squabble which is the Trunk?—

The (so-called) Catholic Question re-considered in its relations
to the ~~social~~ Duties and correlative Rights of the Subject, and the
Constitutional Interests of the State: in three letters to C. A. Tulk,
Esqʳᵉ. M.P. ⟨by S. T. Coleridge.⟩

1. Preliminary Facts ⟨and Principles⟩ ~~⟨with a brief statement of~~
~~the common⟩ and general Principles admitted on all sides, and in~~
~~the application of which to the present state of Ireland and the~~
~~question arises, and the difficulties of a satisfactory solution consist.~~

2. ~~A bad Solution the~~ A Pre-removal of certain Errors and Mis-
statements tho' respecting Facts of high importance in the solution
of the Problem ~~taken for granted~~ assumed by the one party and
admitted or not denied by the other.

3. The ⟨true⟩ *Root* of the ~~cause~~ Question: i.e. the actual Ground
of the Danger on each side.

4822 20.22   Mem:—Tho' I take for granted that I *have* done it—the Sophism a gradibus continuis, or the Horse-Tail Conundrum, as applied to the doctrine of *non-resistance*. What? you would not resist the Sovereign (James II) for patronizing a Jesuit, or because he has used a vigor beyond Law in controlling the Statutes of a quarrelsome College?—and just as well on the contrary side—Suppose a third or 4ᵗʰ generation, the first being a confessed usurper—You would not resist Cromwell IVᵗʰ in the 10ᵗʰ year of his reign—nor the 9ᵗʰ &c—therefore you have no right to resist Cromwell I in the first month of *his* reign.—Item—the Sophism of Sit pro causâ ⟨rei,⟩ sine quo res non evenisset ⟨& facta fuerat⟩. Your wife died in child-birth—Ergo, you are her murderer. Sophisma malitiosum.

4823 20.23   Prometheus—the *good* side of his Gift.   *f10*
    The Man alone, when all other creatures have ~~fled from~~ forsaken the altered World (Clime) and the whole living Nature ~~prepares (is busy in making ready) for Departure and when~~ has taken flight or but the last ⟨few⟩ scatterlings of the Rear ~~are taking~~ seen lingering in their last leave, the Man remains behind on the solitary Ruins: for Love and old Attachment beautify ⟨and humanize⟩ their stern ~~Looks~~ aspect. Other Creatures see the world ⟨but⟩ in its own natural charm; the Spirit of Men ⟨shall⟩ sheds ~~and superposes~~ suffusive over the decaying Nature a new lustre from its own glory. The Northern Nightingale, whose simply plaintive tones the Travellers † of former Centuries described, has disappeared from Iceland, ⟨together⟩ with the dark-green Forests and the bowery Rose-Thickets.—On the dreary Mountain-wastes to which Summer nai brings back no green Leaf, only Grass and a few adventurous yet timid Flowers, the Man, ~~as one~~ privileged sleepwalker all unaware of the universal Decay, still sings ever light of heart the old glad Songs of his fore-fathers, of ~~green sweet leafy & fragrant Bowers~~ leafy Spring and roseate Bowers, ~~that are gone and of~~ the deep green Woods and and the ⟨sweet, sweet⟩ Song of the Nightingale.—

† I am accurate; but I more than suspect, that the Bird which the earliest Norwegian Travellers named the Nightingale, was not *our*

Nightingale—but a Wood-Lark, or one of those night-singing sweet Shore- Sand- or Reed-Larks (Sedge-pipers), Birds of stronger wing than our Nightingale which has never been able to cross over from Wales into Ireland, or from the Elbe (where they abound) to the Humber.—

f10ᵛ   4824 20.24   *from the first leaf*
Of Subjects for Meditations on Broomsticks (for such they will appear & such will be their value, in the eyes of the Wits and Worldlings) I can think of none more fruitful in moral Symbols and Similitudes than the Caterpillar. A thoughtful man, of tolerable quickness in recognizing analogies, might spiritualize its history ab ovo ad imaginem.—Inter alia quam plurima what a peculiarly happy and appropriate illustration of the succession of changes in the Views and Moral Habits of a progressive Christian—have we not in the frequent Sloughings and Moultings of the Caterpillar, and not of *the Skin only*, but of the Jaws, palpi, antennæ, yea, the very Skull and the Spiracles, yet the vital principle, the Psyche and whatever in the Larva is essential to its Growth survives—of Christian repentance and Reformation posterior to the great *Metanoia*, and germ of another and higher Individuum.

Those that live in Society and have a common Nest (a church) retire thither, fixing the hooks of the feet, during this operation, firmly in the web of their nest—For it is a season of weakness and sorrow—& is performing by painfully disengaging all the vessels that conveyed nourishment to *the Old Man*—Yet still they will flow again ad extra tho' to a better, brighter, and less compressive & imprisoning coat—at each time more however will flow inward upon, assimilate to & unite with the Psyche—till at length the last & starved Coat is thrown off—lifeless & without successor.—

f11   It seems impossible that the ordinary and natural food of the Gnat should be animal Blood, when you think of the sea-sand and sun-moat Swarms in dank places where ~~no~~ few or no quadrupeds come—& yet not over pools or employed in dropping their eggs on them—But the Larva of the Gnat is certainly carnivorous. Qʸ A sudden recollection, a re-awakening of the old instinct?—

4825 29.183   July 11, 1821. Highgate—Mr Gillman's $f150$
View of the Absorbents, as found chiefly in the cellular Texture,
the Integuments, & generally in the lower vegetöid (= Bichats'
Organic & what the later German Philosophizing Physiologists
(Natur-philosophen) more happily name the Reproductive) System. The first and lowest manifestation, or *manifest* Power of Life
is *Contractility*—The second *Appetence*—and soon as the second su-
pervenes on the first, there arise, as the Synthesis of both, the
Absorbents, with their two-fold Function to take up what is wanting, and to take off what is superfluous.—The fluids thus produced
are for the most part colorless.—Color is first induced when the
fluids are *Contained*—in other words, proper vascularity is a previous condition of color—and accordingly in the Venous Blood the
Carbon, as Carbon, first manifests its existence. Mr Gillman proceeds further to consider what the Correspondent to Carbon is in
the scheme of vital powers—in other words, of what Factor or
Constituent of Life (since Life being a *Constitution* must needs
have Constituents, even as the Force and the Weight are the Constituent Factors of the Action of the Lever)—Mr G. I say, en-
quires, of what principle essential to Organic Life this Carbon is
⟨the⟩ representative—& he sees reason i̶n̶ for believing it to be the
Excitability in contra-distinction from the Energy, e̶x̶c̶i̶t̶e̶d̶ or the
action of Life on the excitement of the Former—Whatever therefore weakens this Excitability ought proportionately to *diminish* the $f149^v$
Carbon, and with it that peculiar Color which marks its relative
preponderance in the veins as compared with the color of the arterial Blood. Now the excitability may be weakened in two ways—
first, by the direct abstraction of the Blood as the proper Food and
Supply of both the Powers, but evidently of most importance to
the Excitability which in fact is the Life itself, that from which
the Energy goes forth—and into which it must return, or there
could be no sensation, but a total Palsy/. It would be easy to substitute a quantum of Stimulus equal to that contained in the Blood
abstracted, if the stimulant property of the Blood were the principal point—but we know, within how narrow bounds this is practicable—Secondly, by the direct action of Stimulus diminishing
excitability by expending it ⟨in⟩ and as it were transforming it into

Excitement.—Now for this there are 3 Facts in evidence—first, the change of the black gradually into ~~water~~ scarlet Blood during copious bleeding from the veins—2. the Blush effected in the small vessels—3. Nitrous Oxyd.

f69   4826 30.59   mercy of God, that beyond a certain point Guilt is too vast to be imputable to Individuals, and thus assumes the form of Punishment & becomes divine Justice.—In this sense I would *interpret* (n.b. it does not follow of necessity that I so *understand*) the text. Is there evil in the *City* (i.e. the State) & I have not done it, saith the Lord? = Instance. The utter non-performance of the ultimate & most essential Duties of Government & Church, & the consequent affrightful state of a *majority* of the Souls in Engl. & Ireland—

The late Queen's Persecution, with all the circumstances preceding, following & accompanying her Trial, with the Constituents of the Trial itself, I should instance as a Maximum of Guilt still imputable and personal.

f37ᵛ   4827 M.28   In ruder ages, as from the 6th to the 15th or 16th Century in Christendom the frequency of outrageous *Crimes*, of single acts of Atrocity, force on the minds of Men the belief of a Corruption in the nature of Man. But when Society has become better organized, & the necessity of *Character* to Interest is every where felt & acted on, an Age of outside Decency & *conventional* Morality commences.—Man becomes less criminal, ⟨in act,⟩ & more guilty in the principles of Action—& then some such Phænomenon, as the Calumniation & Mock-Trial of the Queen by a House of Lords, with a House of Commons condemning yet
f38   acquiescing—some such Displays as the ineffably base, blind, & brutal Advocacy of Perjury for the ruin of Innocence, as that of our Attorney General—Some such broad disclosure of high-born, at least high-titled Courtiers & Statesmen, some pandaring for the adulterous Lusts, and all pandaring for the unnatural Hate, of a Loathsome Tyrant, the compound of a Tiberius (but without his talents) and an Heliogabalus—is necessary to check the Spread of a shallow~~ing~~ Pelagianism, or self-complacent Materialism—to make as many as are capable of resuscitation known the aweful Truth, that man cannot be on a level with the Beast/Either im-

measurable above or below—either tending toward the Angels, or fast sinking into the Fiend.

This especially instanced in the contrast between the Religion $f38^v$ which these men *are* & that (viz. the Religion of the Bible) which they blasphemously profess.—

4828 M.29   Credit

higher κυδος in a fellowship—

⟨Comparative Advantage from Classical Lectures—⟩

Compar. Chance of Scholarships, Exhibitions, &c durante tutelâ/

Comparative Chance of Fellowships, private Pupils at College, Tutorships in high Families, or Episcopal Chaplaincies, &c after Degree—

4829 29.85   I am more and more inclined to prefer βη $f56$ $\triangle$ to the $+$ of the modern Teutonic Physiosophers (= Naturphilosophen.) The Pentad would comprehend both $\varnothing$: the ideal = powers, and the phænomenal = bodies: the former, Light and Gravity, each $+$ and $-$, i. e. 2 = 4) and the latter, or 2 + 1, by the synthesis of both: viz. Comburent, Combustibly, Combust: or Acid, Metal, Salt. In Man, as the summit of the Organic World (and according the Law of Polarity or Duplication followed in all the ~~high~~ nobler Organs of *Animal* † Life, in which Male &

† The organs that conduce to Perception and to Action ad extra $f56$ are called Animal, by Bichat, the Entrails &c vegetable. The Heart which in Man belongs to both systems is bilocular, 2 in One, as the Eyes are one in 2. The lower animals have two uni- $f55^v$ locular Hearts. Thus Beast have *four* Legs— ~~perhaps this~~ If we were forced to consider Man as Nature's chef d'œuvre, we should say, that in the Beast Nature had not yet arrived at her full power. But far rather say, that the Beast in its noblest form is the ne plus ultra of Nature, and that to mortify her presumption, she was permitted, after a higher Model had been presented by a Power above Nature, viz. the upright stature & the Hand, to try *her* hand—& she produced the Apes—quadrumanous, as her former Effort had been quadruped.

Female, Active and Passive, + and −. Positive & Negative &c
are represented by Right and Left, ex. gr. Two Eyes, two Ears,
two Hemispheres of the Brain, nay, the human Body is two Bodies
with a distinct line of Bisection as traced by Bichat = animal
duplex)—this Pentad is symbolized by the Right and Left Hand,
or the Decad. The Pentad is the Hand, the 5 fingers of Nature—
δεχεται, digiti, decas—

P.S. The Dyad is the essential form of Unity; the ~~manifested~~
integral *one* would be put half manifest, in a single Pole—the
manifested, i. e. realized One, therefore, ipso termino, *exists* in
and by self-duplication each duplicate being an Integer, and an
Alter et Idem—and the *real* Image of the other. But the duplication of the Dyad itself by mere repetition is the mark of weakness
either from strength not sufficiently matured or exhausted. It is
Copying as contrasted with Imitation.

4830 29.86   I should like to know, whether or how far the
delight, I feel & have always felt, in adages or aphorisms of universal or very extensive application, is a general or common feeling with man, or a peculiarity of my own mind. I cannot describe
how much pleasure I have derived from "Extremes meet" for instance; or "Treat every thing according to its Nature", and "Be"!
In the last I bring ~~in~~ all inward Rectitude to its Test, in the former
all outward Morality to its Rule, and in the first all ⟨problematic⟩
Results to their Solution, and reduce apparent Contraries to correspondent Opposites. How many hostile Tenets has it enabled me
to contemplate, as Fragments of the Truth—false only by negation,
and mutual exclusion—.

f57   4831 29.87   Δι' ενδειξεως = intuitive: αποδειξις = demonstration. Ενδειξις ⫴ διεξοδος or Discursive. The endictic or
intuitive, availing itself of composite visible Signs = συνθηματα,
may be either Symbolic, or Iconic (δι' εικονων): and a Whole
formed of either or of both is a Mythe or Μυθος. Ἐν δὲ τοῖς ποιή-
μασι διὰ μυθικῶν συμβόλων λεγει (Ορφευς) τὰς τῶν Θεῶν τάξεις τε
καὶ σειράς. The Mathematic or Pythagorean is iconic, the Discursive or Logical (Διεξοδος) κατ' επιστημην, as in Aristotle, or κατ'
επιπνοιαν, as the Sibyls.—

Συμβάλλειν, συμβαλλεσθαι, to cast together, to unite what had
been severed. ~~Conjicere conjecture~~ 2. followed by a Dative—to
treat with any one, to strike a treaty, bargain &c—3. conjecture,
conjicere, to compare, or collate one thing with another and thence
to solve, conclude, especially to decypher or interpret, ordinarily
applied to Oracles & Prophecies.—Συμβολον. First & simplest, as
used by Plato, Symposium, Cap. XVI. ad initium, one composed
of two. To break a tablet in two Halves, as our Sweethearts the
crooked Sixpence, was an ancient custom of the Greeks—The Half
was Tessera, & συμβολον, tessera hospitalis. Thence, whatever in
the progress of refinement was substituted for the tessera—and
thus, a contract, commercial Treaty, Law of Alliance &c.—
Thence, any Pledge as in buying & selling. Thence, eminently, a
Ring: that being the Pledge or Ticket given in pledge of the
Money contributed by each Guest in a Picnic or Common Feast;
⟨& thence the betrothing Ring⟩—Hence, the Tessera Militaris.—
The *Word*, Watch word = συνθηματα, or παρασυνθηματα in War.
+ and the *seal*-ring.—Lastly, by progressive Generalization
συμβολον was used as σημεῖον—and as a sign is antithetic to the
essence or thing itself, συμβολον became = a *word*, or words: & a
representative Image.—Finally, the highest sense of συμβολον rests
on the two first senses of συμβαλλειν—viz. unexpected Co-incidence, & conjectural Deciphering. In the manly faith of the ancients the communion of the Gods with men, and all the diviner
Truths might be interpreted or conveyed by analogies, & best of
all by the same Powers in their lower Forms and Dignities, but
could not be explained—or demonstrated. This Hinting, or Suggesting of the hidden sense is μαντεια.—: μαντεια thro' the Ear
is χρησμος, φημη, κληδων. (The attributing oracular wisdom to a
man's words or works constitutes his Fame, as distinguished from
his reputation. Quod putavit ille, nos iterum putamus.) Χρησμος,
= Oracle, and φημη, κληδων, omina de voce, especially, the cry of
Birds, are combined by the Athenians in Οττα, and poeticaly
ομφη.—Μαντεια to the Eye = φασμα, Vision, τερας, portent, and
lastly, συμβολον; but still with a notion of the unexpected accidental—as the ominous meeting of a Man.—Hence, Meteors, and
similar signs in the element of Air are συμβολα—and particularly,
the ominous or suspicious Flight of Birds. Hence, Aeschylus (Prometheus 486) combines the ominous Meeting on the Road (ενο-

f57ᵛ

διους συμβολους) and the flight of Birds.—Aristophanes calls the sacred Bird itself συμβολος Ορνις (Aves, 720)—and Symbolus occurs as a Masculine in Plautus.—

There is some truth, but in effect a falsehood in the form of a half truth, in what the Greek Lexicograph (see a fragment of his work at the end of Hermann's De Emendand. Rat. Gramm. Gr. p. 319) says: Εικων και ὁμοιωμα, is that which naturally and in the common apprehension of Men is what it expresses, as the icon or portrait of a Lion: on the other hand, Συμβολον και Σημειον are only conventionally representative—θεσει. This is so far just as it states the distinction between the κυριολογικον and the figurative; but it wholly omits the peculiar force of the Symbol, as omening the presence of the Divine, the sense of the inexplicable, or aboriginal—. That which unexpectedly, from the depths of Nature, started upon the Eye as Prediction or Warning, was Συμβολον, in the wider sense—& then, by philosophic Precision, that which was itself supposed to be one with, or a living part of, or having its constituent principle from, the higher somewhat, the whole of which it represented. Thus those Statues, Images, or Signs of a God, in which by having been magically constellated to the influence of the same God the God himself had a virtual & efficient Presence, were *Symbolic*—. τὰ δε γαρ ως συμβολα καθιερωται εξ αιδιου τοῖς κρειττοσι (Iamblich: de Myst. Ægypt)—and ~~by~~ these ~~the~~ are even contra-distinguished from the εικων, portrait, substantial Image, such as that in the Mirror would be, were it begotten and not merely reflected: were it representative adequately, and in *f58* toto, not of the surface alone—Hence the Cabbalists, and St Paul (Coloss.) appropriate the term "Εικων" to the only begotten Word, the Filial Deity, all other Words being at their highest dignity *Symbols*, often mer~~l~~ely σημεια, θεσει = conventional Marks, or αφομοιωσις, ομοιωματα, as Hush! Whisper. Clang.—The simplest use of Symbolic, and yet containing all the above-mentioned characters, is that of the Stoics, who distinguish~~ed~~ing ερωτησις, = asking (a question) and πεῦσις = inquiring, call the answers to the former symbolic, i.e. those which may be given by a nod, or a shake of the head, or a gesture. Is that a Line of Virgil's? Nod = Yes. This is an ερωτησις, the last word of which suffices for an *affirmative* ⟨answer to it⟩. In whose Works does that line occur?—

This is πεῦσις: and requires an additional term not contained in the Inquiry.—From the use of symbolic (taking care however to confine it to visible signs that are as natural to the body of Man as the Assent or Negation to his mind, and in part are in truth the same Act in a lower form, a living part of that the whole of which it represents. For talking on the Fingers would *not* be symbolic) we may observe another enriching of the term, viz. momentary co-instantaneous presentation of a meaning to the Mind thro' the Eyes, a union of the greatest possible simplicity, rapidity, and pregnancy—a Magnet in a Lady's Needle-case, the friction of a stick of Sealing Wax on your Sleeve, a Pewter Pot of Porter held by the Hand to the Lips of the person drinking, are *Symbols* to the Intelligent, of the whole physical powers of the corporeal world. Hence the Insight obtained from Symbols is appropriately expressed by the Greeks as προσβολη, a glance, θεα, θεασθαι, or a beholding of a Whole at once.—The propriety of the word in religious and ceremonial uses is apparent. First in Paganism— even Words of especial weight & containing a compressed solution of any problem of deep Concern are συμβολαια—See Herodotus V. 92, 7. . of the memorable Word which Periander received by means of the Oracle (Νεκρομαντεια) of Melissa. The Fawn-skin in which the Initiated were wrapt, the Grasshoppers worn in their Hair, the purple Carpets on which they trod, were all συμβολα, συνθηματα— & doubtless, many of the dietetic laws of Moses were grounded on the same *principle* with the ιερα γραμματα, the symbolic Birds, Beasts &c of Egypt.—Lastly and as culminant, and in which all the senses converge, the Σεβασμια Συμβολα of the Christian Church, or the consecrated Bread and Wine. For such *f58ᵛ* as affect to despise the painful investigation of Words upwards to their sources, their *Genui*neness (τὸ ἔτυμον) as useless, we might produce an instance to the contrary even in this very word. For the appropriation of the term, συμβολα with some epithet of honor or transcendence to the Eucharist by the Church in the earliest Ages suggests a full confutation both of the Romanists (i.e. since the Council of Trent) and of the Monkish and Papal Faction of in the Western or Latin Church after the persecution of Bellenden - rengarius, Scholasticis pæne omnibus invitè et quasi dissentienter assentientibus vel rectius Assentantibus; and of the Calvinists,

Zwinglians and ~~other~~ the Sacramentaries in general, on the other
hand. For neither to the notion of bonâ fide Transsubstantiation,
nor to that of the Signum merè significans, could the term, Symbol, have been attached without a gross ignorance of its specific
⟨religious⟩ import, with which we have no right to charge the
Fathers and Councils of the first five or six Centuries. ~~Bellenden-
us~~rengarius ~~who deserved a ⌈. . . .⌉ faith (or if you like, a better
fate than to fall under ⌈. . . .⌉)~~ asserts and vindicates the real Presence (and in the same words as ~~the~~ our Church Catechism) ~~with~~
as earnestly as he rejects the total changes of the corporeal Elements. Thus neither a Sound nor a primary Thought can be a
Symbol; but a Word may. Rhetorically we might say, A Word is
not a sound, or no longer a sound—& so the Fathers in their
Orations expressed themselves concerning the consecrated Bread &
Wine,—But in their didactic & controversial Treatises they place
beyond doubt their opinion, that the Word is no longer a (mere)
sound & cannot without irreverence & the risk of conveying an
heretical falsehood be entitled a Sound—because it is more and
other than a Sound, and other because more, and because the In-
fusum is of incomparably higher worth than the Base. For the
"sound" put the Bread and Wine, and for "the Word" put the
Body and Blood of Christ in the Lord's Supper; and it is evident,
in what sense alone the consecrated Elements could be called σεβ-
f59 ασμια ΣΥΜΒΟΛΑ—and thus Maximus in Schol. ad Dionys. Areop.
Cap. I. 58. αι των μυστηριων τελεται εν Συμβολοις θεωρουνται.—
The other interpretations of the Symbols in the Lord's Supper are
either mere secondary meanings of the word, or later than the
absurd Legend of the Creed = Symbolum or Symbola Fidei, as
the Pic Nic contributions of the 12 Apostles./

4832 29.88   Simile, Metaphor, Allegory, Fable, are of easy
resolution: tho' I have not met with any precise & adequate definition of all four in any modern Writer.—Simile. He is like a
Lion. Metaphor. Behold our Lion rushes to the Prey.—I.E. A
Simile by absorption of the particle of assimilation becomes a Metaphor.—A connected Series of Metaphors to one Whole is an Allegory—~~But~~ And where the Metaphors are adopted conventionally
by all classes of a society, so that the objects, to which the assimi-

lation is implied, are Symbols or partake of the Nature of Symbols, and are assured as already known & understood by the Auditor,—this Allegory, so qualified, is *A Fable:*, & this alone merits the name of an Esopic Fable.—The Ass, the Fox, the Lion, the Oak, the Wolf, the Lamb are all either συμβολα, or ως συμβολα; & these too και ες το παν ερμηνεως μη χατιζοντα. This last remark, for the tenability of which I dare pledge myself & which is fruitful in its critical inferences, is, I believe, my own. Heaven knows, to what extent even respectable Writers may carry the Licence of Misnomer. I have often seen Parables, and even Histories, nay, non-descripts entitled Fables †. But tho' every Fable, as a whole, whether the component parts be—Symbols or only conventional Metaphors received in ~~the~~ common discourse, is an Allegory, every Allegory is not a Fable. And our Instructors & School Masters might have learnt a practical Lesson from the true definition— namely, that Fables, rightly so called, are in their proper place when addressed to popular Assemblies, to Kings, or their Majesties, the Mob, to all in short, before whom it would be ticklish to blurt out the naked truth—as the oldest fable, that of Jotham, the true Esopic Fables &c—but least of all are fitted for Children— & as for many good reasons, so especially for this—that *Prudentials*, not *Morals*, are the End and Butt of Fables—the regulation of Self-love by Self-interest, including the dread of being laughed at & held in contempt, not the elevation of the Mind to a higher principle, which is or ought to be the one great object in the education of Children.—Hence the affinity between Fable and the

f59ᵛ

† Take as specimen two of Holberg's. 1. In the last Judgement a Vomit is given to every one, having this virtue that the Takers cast up the contents of their consciences instead of their Stomachs.— Moral. There is no conceal~~ment~~ing of crimes in the World to come. IInd Satan allowed a Furlow to a Malcontent Devil, to sojourn on Earth in a pleasant valley as long as he pleased, on one condition that he should keep a flock of young He and She Goats, perfectly chaste. ~~Before~~ At the close of the first day the Devil went back to Hell & hid himself for shame.—Moral. There are both Goats & Devils without Horns on their Heads. The fable shows, that Lewdness is very unmanageable!

f59

oldest (& only genuine) Comedy—see the Plutus, Aves, and Pax of Aristophanes. The Fabulist adopts Signs already stamped & current—the Comedian proposes certain Signs of his own making for currency to the People, & contrives to make them understood or to choose such as (he knows) will be understood.—

The Fable leads us to the Mythus, it being itself a species of the Mythic: viz. μῦθος πολιτικος, ⟨δημοσιος,⟩ η κοινος: as distinguished from those, the signs of which are conventional ⟨only⟩ within the pale of ~~any~~ some particular guild, or societas in societate, as the Priesthood, the Mysteries, &c—Μυθος φιλοσοφικος, = φιλοσοφημα. Μυθος ἱερος = Ιερευμα, ιερον γραμμα.—Μυστηριον.

Μυω = claudo. μνεω arcanis initio. μνζω, musso, clauso ore quasi per Nares loqui—the nasal twang of the fanatic Pulpit. Even μυθω had originally a sort of confidential secrecy attached to it—or rather in the ruder states of Society & thinner population all language was a *letting* you know—Iliad XVII. 200. μυθησατο προς ον θυμον.—The Esquimeaux at this day seldom speak but by equivoques, suggestions, dropping a hint (Southey's *Omniana*)

⟨Μυθος = Λογος ψευδης εικονιζων την αληθειαν. *Theon: Suidas*⟩ Λογος—Λεγω, I count, *tell*, number, reckon, count it *for*—. Hence Λογος, a Discourse—κυριολογικος, in proper terms, ~~or~~ definite positions, or determinate icons (εικονες):—the language of Calculus, the calculating Understanding, and of reasoning (λογισμος, αποδειξις.) Λογος, a credible Report)(Μυθος, a *rumour*. Hence ⟨λογος εν μυθω = the true Import of a Mythos. μυθος δημοσιος = a faction (cry, Shaks. Coriolanus) Μυθιητης Ionice, the Mouth or Speaker of a Faction, Head mutterer.⟩

Επος. απο. απω (in old Latin, apio: = fasten on to, adapt, connect) επω: επομαι. Whence by prefixing the sibilant lenis, as sex for ἐξ, septem, ἑπτα, and by the change of π into q, as ποιος, qualis, πεντε, quinque, &c, the Latin sequor, and in old Latin, sequo, insequo, for I say, I relate—and Livius Andronicus translated the Εννεπε in the first line of the Odyssee by "Insece"—. Hence, the Επος, i.e. a well-connected, well arranged Series of Events narrated—the *flowing Line* of the Epic,)(the circle, or line returning on itself round its own focus or center.

'Ρημα. ῥεω, fluo. Stream of words. Flow of Eloquence. Hence perhaps the German, ich rede, the old English, I areed—& ⟨our⟩

Read it to me, doubtless first used by those who could not *read*. =
Make it *flow* for me.

Τοῦ καὶ ἀπὸ γλώσσης μέλιτος γλυκίων ῥέεν αὐδή.

The possible derivation of Faba, the judicial Bean, from Fari, fatum; and then to *play* with counters or significants, by the diminute Fabula—while Fabulor, Fabulatio, Talking for amusement (the most common in rude societies, as in Turky & the East, is playing at Judge & Convict,) seems to partake of both. I merely throw upon the waters. It is worth noticing, however, that the Romans had *no* Μυθοι Αισωπικοι—~~as~~ for that the pretended Phædrus is a modern Work, for the greater part of Perotti's own composition, in the middle of the 15ᵗʰ century, I have not the least doubt—for tho' some Difficulties ab extra remain to be solved, yet these are outweighed by the difficulties & objections of the same class, to ~~their~~ hypothesis of their authenticity. The external & circumstantial proofs, & presumptions against the earlier existence of the Parisian Mss, discovered after the first edition by Perotti, are more—and stronger those ~~in~~ in favor of it: and the internal evidence of the Fables themselves appear to me decisive against their having been composed by a Poet of the age of Tiberius. Perotti's own conduct, expressions & concessions forcibly remind one of Macpherson & his Ossian.—This is worth mentioning, because it has tended to mislead our Critics as to the true Nature of the Μυθος πολιτικος η δημοσιος: ⟨the Αινος;⟩ i.e. the genuine Esopic Fable. The Roman Fabula is a mere Story; thence, ut Omnes pro Pluribus, a fiction, as we say, a story-teller: What stories you tell!—

In reviewing the above investigation of words, I see that I have one mistake to guard against. I believe myself to have given the true sense, according to the general usage in the best Greek Writers; but I do not assert that the words are no where found less discriminately employed. Demetrius de Elocut., I am aware, seems to use Symbol and Allegory as Synonimies. Much less do I mean to convey, that the highest and fullest Sense of Symbol, as distinguished alike from ειδωλον, from εικων, from ομοιωμα, from conventional Sign, and from Allegory, is the only sense of the Word. The contrary is implied by me in the history of the term, and in the opposition of προσβολη to διεξοδος: of which we have

*f6o*ᵛ

again an instance in Demetrius §. 243. Διὸ καὶ τὰ Σύμβολα ἔχει δεινότητας, ὅτι ἐμφερῆ ταῖς βραχυλογίαις. Καὶ γὰρ ἐκ τοῦ βραχέως ῥηθέντος ὑπονοῆσαι τὰ πλεῖστα δεῖ, καθάπερ ἐκ τῶν Συμβόλων.—I assert only, that "an essential part of that, the whole of which it represents" is the *peculiar* sense of συμβολον, and ought to be its philosophical and religious Use:—and this with the greater propriety, because my present main Object is the interpretation of the mythological Io, ~~as~~ in its connection with the most profound and venerable of all the Greek Theomythics (θεομνθιαι), the Æschylian Prometheus.—~~Tho'~~ For tho' I do not exclude the allegorical, ~~not even~~ no, nor the par~~mas~~onomastic, Exposition, even in this; & both see and acknowlege the indispensableness ~~both~~ of Allegory *f61* and both Metonomy and Paronomasia (i.e. the transfer of names from some ominous or auspicious Incident, as in the instance of Βουτρωτος, the name given by Helenus to the City founded by him, from the incident of the sacrificial Ox (Etymol. Magnum in βουτρωτος) or the accidental Coincidence of Sound—ex.gr. in the ~~event~~ stories told of Homer (in the Life of Homer under the name of Herodotus and elsewhere) all or the greater part of which are grounded in whimsical etymologies of, say rather bad *puns* on, the word 'Ομηρος—ex. gr. α non and οραω, video ergo, he was blind—Ομηρος, an Hostage—ergo, he was left as a Hostage—Ομηρευομαι, I sing in company, Concino—therefore he was at the head of an itinerant company of Bards &c in the interpretation of the φυσιομνθιαι, and still more of the geneological or historical, the πατροπαράδοτα μεμνθευμένα of Dyonis. Halicarn. & Strabo—and tho' these very incidents, & ⟨the⟩ co-incidencies of names & sounds are themselves (as I have already shown) συμβολα, or συμβολαια, in the simpler sense of the term & by virtue of the Etymon, συμβάλλεσθαι;—yet in the theologic Emblems, the proper Theosophems, the object of which is to convey and preserve the convictions of Ancient Sages respecting the Nature and Intercommunion of Man, God, and Nature, the Theme itself leads to the highest & peculiar Sense of Symbol namely, that sense, which remains, after all the narrower senses gradually developed during the evolution of the Root have been expressed, ~~by~~ each by an appropriate term, & which remaining sense must, of course, *contain* all the former, but with a something more & other peculiar to itself. And such is the Definition of Symbol already given: and it

may be observed, that D~~y~~emetrius does not say, ως συμβολα, but
καθαπερ εκ συμβολ~~εω~~ν—And it is in this especial sense that Plutarch
(de genio Socratis) remarks: Here the highest wisdom comes in
contact with the mythic poesy—and Julian—Many an earnest truth
has Plato taught mythically. The Mythe of Mars and Venus is a   *f61ᵛ*
physiosopheme and the Journey of Jove to the blameless Ethiopians
and the circling River Oceanos, are ~~prine~~ mixt Symbols, ⟨or Symbols grounded on allegory, & picture-words.⟩ The eighth Incarnation of Krishna or Vishnu, as Man, under the name Bhogovan,
in the Bhogovotgita, as translated by Fr. Schlegel, is ~~another~~ ✻ a
poetic Symbol, ⟨i.e. a personification in order to a Symbol. The
Caterpillar & Butterfly a real Symbol.⟩

   "Yet an other ~~Vishnu this~~ in me, a higher Essence ~~in me~~
     acknowlege then,
   "That which gives life to the Earthly, ~~and~~ that which the
     World ~~ere~~ preserves, and bears.
   "This is the Mother of Things, of all things the Mother,
     believe me, Friend!
   "Is there besides Me an Other and Higher?—O never, O no
     where, Friend!
   "I am the Universe' Well-spring, I the Destruction too!
   "I am the String of the Pearls. I, ~~the~~ God-man, am Center
     and Circle too!
"Hast thou seen me, Philip? Thou hast seen the Father?.—This
⟨last⟩ is the consummate *Symbol*, ⟨a Tautegory:⟩ the golden chain
in ⟨the⟩ threatning Speech of Homer's Jupiter, on the other hand,
is a pure *Allegory*. N. B. It will often happen, that in the extension
of ~~our~~ human Knowlege what had been an *Allegory*, will become
a Symbol. Thus: the identification, in genere, of the vegetable Life
with the animal life, as the same ⟨power⟩ in a lower dignity, would
raise the Homeric allegory or compound Metaphor of the Leaves
into a Symbol. But the Florentine Gem, in which Eros and An-
teros súpport a Globe, is neither Symbol nor Allegory, but picture-
language or single images in the place of general Words—the *lowest* form of which, however, as an Eye, a ⟨winged⟩ Boy with Bow

✻ and one of many examples, of the conversation of an *Idea* into ´ *f61ᵛ*
a *Fact* by an imagined first instance. "In Adam we all die." This
constitutes Symbolic *Poesy*.

& Arrow, and a Yew Tree = I love you, is not, I believe, without
an instance in the Egyptian & Greek Mythology.† In some in-
f62   stances the Symbolic and Onomastic are united—as in Psyche, =
anima & papilio.

The Butterfly the ancient Grecians made
The soul's fair Symbol and its only *Name*;
But of the Soul, escaped the slavish trade
Of mortal life. For in this fleshly frame
Our's is the Reptiles' Lot—much toil, much blame,
Manifold Motions, making little speed,
And to deform & kill the things, whereon we feed.—

As Natural Symbols, acknowledged as such by men in general,
are few, the Numismatic Art accepts as Substitutes significant
forms, ~~mond~~ and personifications which by these forms are made
intelligible, or visual Metaphors which in time become conventional, in the fine arts—Thus a dusky female with a Scorpion in
her hand, and a Head-dress of Elephants' Hide, was known to
every Roman to be *Africa*. The Lily between Joseph & Mary we
all know to be Jesus—and who would give the Virgin any other
colored garment than *blue*! ⟨Lorenzo's White, Green, Crimson for
Faith (Truth & Fidelity), Hope, and Love.⟩ In the treatment of
any grand and comprehensive Symbol, or Symbolic Mythos, these
happily chosen are the appropriate minor ornaments of the Temple; and the choice and gradation of these from the conventional
visual Metaphor to the συμβολαεαια or pæne-Symbols evince the
f62   *tact* of the Poet.

† The Fish (the Free-mason *Symbol* ⟨of the early Christians⟩ in the
lower sense as secret *sign*) is a case in point, and perhaps one of
the flattest of the onamastic Sort. Iησους Χριστος Θεου Yιος Σωτηρ
= IXΘΥΣ. Of the same sort & merit the *Abraxas* Gems & medals
of the Gnostics & Basilidians. The Cross at first, a simple Mne-
mosynon historicum became in the hands of the Mystics a Symbol,
as the Tau in far elder times.—a collection of all the Emblematists
so numerous during & in the first Century of the Reformation,
very desirable.

f62ᵛ   4833 29.89   Electricity⟨3 or Irritability⟨2 = Understanding.
The Thoroughbreak (Durchbruch, Perruptio, Διαρηξις) of the

U. in the Insect World, as the Representative of vital Electricity, or Irritability. See Huber on Bees: Ditto on Ants.—In the Mammalia wherever Nature seems to fall back a full step, so as to link a product of Life(6 with the uppermost extreme of Life(4, i.e. a Mammale with the Fish, as a line running *parallel* with the Birds, she of course sinks back upon or re-approximates to the predominance of the Irritable Principle, and its characteristic Functions are re-awakened. So it should be at least according to the Theory: and that so it is, the Natural History of the Beaver, the Sea-cow, the Dugong, Manati, &c. affords abundant proof.—& we recognize the social instincts, the Monogamy or monandrous polygamy, the constructive arts, the accomodations to varying circumstances of the Bird & the Insect, united and potenziated.

4834 29.90   I know of few more, among very many, striking proofs and instances of the effect & almost universal influence of the Mechanic Philosophy, the Doctrine of Death and cowardly yet boastful Despondence, than the Brunonian Physiology as the ground of a practical and theoretic Pathology. Dr John Brown was a Man of Genius, born and bred in an age and country, in which the Authority of Bacon, falsely interpreted indeed or drawn from those parts of his Works in which he was least himself—i.e. when he is no longer the Legislator of Philosophy, but a Handy-craftsmean in the Laboratory of a commencing Physiology—the imposing name of Newton and the plumbëian Despotism of Locke—had conspired to establish throughout Christendom as a fundamental and constitutional law of the Republic of Letters the Right and Obligation of taking Matter, Body, Organization, & Sentiency, including Sense and Sensation as *Data*, non *Intellecta*—and to which the Old Proverb, which forbids us to look a Gift-horse in the Mouth, was applied in its full rigor. John Brown was a Man of Genius, but not of that kind or in that extent as which could conquer the Spirit of his Age. He with all his Contemporaries and   *f63* immediate Predecessors begin with *taking for granted* and as primary Facts above human comprehension or so evident in themselves that to seek to understand them was to look into the Sun by the Light of a Rush-Taper, all the Phænomena that are worth looking into, and in assuming which we in truth have pre-assumed as given and insolvible every other problem and object of sciential research, that the World of the Senses can present to the Mind, or the Mind to its own Reflection. But he was too much the Man of Genius to ~~take~~ follow the Herd of his Age in their inconsequence. Having accepted the Boundary Line and abjured ~~all~~ both Right and Claim ~~to even to look over it~~ to all excursion into the Space beyond, as an airy Realm too thin to support the wings of a solid Philosophy, he scorned to supply its place with ~~po~~ substitutes.

f63ᵛ   **4835** 29.91   Of the vital Energies that are common to Man and the Animals below & nearest him—i.e. to Man as ~~an Ani~~ one of the Animals that possess a compleat system of Nerves in organic combination with an arterial, Muscular, Venous and glandular system.

1. The first truth to be deeply impressed and *seen into*, is: that a there are two kinds of Unity, the negative and the positive. And first of the *Negative* Unity. This, as the epithet expresses, is in all cases ⟨known to be⟩ that, which it is ⟨affirmed to be,⟩ because it is *not* something else. We call a boy John to show that he is not James, Henry, &c. a = a − b, c,——Z.—Of course, the subject of this negative Unity must be either an Individual ~~one~~ Fact or Phænomenon, or an Abstraction: and in the latter case, specific or universal.—Negative Unity = A − B. − C. − D. etc. ad—— Z. It is A = A because it is *not* A = B, *not* A = C, nor = D, &c. Secondly, the *positive* Unity, the One containing, and revealing itself in and by, the Many. In its highest Form, i.e. God, it is A = A + B. C. D.——Z: as far as the Relations or secondary Births are excluded from the contemplated. Ex. gr. A is not equal to B, as B is shorter, colder, ~~greater~~ slower, &c than C; but it *is* equal to B, as to that which constitutes B's capability of *being related*, i.e. to the *Being* ab ab of B, or as far B *is*, and in all relations remains same.

Now of this latter kind are all true and really subsistent Unities: while the former exist wholly as abstractions, representable not by any distinct image but by the ⟨abortive⟩ strivings of the Imagination, and the instant dissatisfaction, the immediate sense of the utter inadequacy, ~~nay, contradiction~~ of the representative Image to that which was to be represented. And whatever seems more than this is but a delusive, tho' too common transfer of the physical

properties of the *Word*, by which we recall the Abstraction to our
own minds or to those of others—and which, as a single *word*, is   *f64*
of course a definite whole.—To be convinced of the truth of this,
we have only to trace the process of the mind in the formation of
the Abstraction, Space. Not that that *unimage-ableness* is the distinctive of Abstraction or Negative Unity: for this it has in common with the real positive Unity. But the tendency for the Imagination to strive to produce an image, and the inadequateness in
the *quantum* of the Image, as distinguished from the utter *alien*ness,
the absolute nihil ad hoc, of Image *as* Image, which is perceived
when ever from an acquired bad habit of living in the senses
wholly we attempt to attach an *image* to a positive Unity—these,
~~or~~—I say—this innate tendency, and this *inadequacy* which yet is
not heterogeneity, are the first contra-distinction of the negative
from the positive Unities.—And the second is the barrenness, the
emptiness, the absence of all growth and development, which characterizes ~~all~~ every negative Unity~~ies~~, taken by itself. Try to produce aught out of Space, or to think of any forms of Space, abstractly—i.e. without first destroying the abstraction by uniting
Space with Time & both in some Positive tho' it were but a *Point*,
as Motion or a real Power moving. Without this we could not not
even construct for ourselves even the simplest Forms of Length
and Breadth, the Abstract Elements of Geometry—or the Abstracts
of the second power in the reduction of Abstracts to Realities,
Space, Time, and indefinite Power being the first & purest. We
might as rationally derive Tom's son from the Tom or *Tommeity*
of the Father, whose negative Unity in exclusion of Jack, James,
Bill, &c &c is represented by the word, Tom, as ~~e a~~ expect any
addition to ~~our~~ the quantum of our knowlege from a Theory having its first Principle in a negative Unity of any kind.—Abstractions (& all negative Unities are but abstractions) have done their
best when they add to the *distinctness* of our Thoughts—& make
us *know* that we know.—

Two things to be considered. First let the line $\dfrac{\quad A \quad}{a \quad c \quad b}$ *f64ᵛ*

express a relative Identity. It can disclose itself only by the Dyad,
a b, or its poles, and the motion of those must be either from a to
b, and simultaneously from b to a, in which case they approach

each to its minimum immediately thro' its maximum, at the common punctum Indifferentiæ. c: or they both recede from each other:—now in order for this to be conceivable, we must contemplate the Line a b, no longer as A, that is, the Identiy, or original Ground, but as itself a Product, a thing produced a~~n~~ Consequent of some higher A, which in the Line a-b is represented by the point, c. as A vice-gerent. Corollary. The Punctum Indifferentiæ is not ~~the~~ = A, or the primary Root or Involute of the Productive Power, in the sense of = as "*the same as*" but = A in that sense only in which a Son standing in the place of his Father at the head of a second Table in his Father's House is said to be equal to his Father. *The punct. Indiff. is the Representative of* THE PUNCT. IDEN-TITATIS.

To conceive then the recession or fleeing of a from b, and of b from a, we must pre-assume the point, c (= A) as producing (or expanding) itself on each side / a‾‾ɔ‾‾‾‾‾‾‾b, which of course is the same as a receding from b, and b from a. Now here two cases are possible. Either c a actually disparts itself from c b, and c the punctum indifferens become two, ~~a~~ each of which appears as the midpoint of a several bi-polar Line, the first of which, c a, is now the line a‾‾‾‾‾‾‾‾‾b, and the other, c b, is the line b‾‾‾‾‾‾‾‾‾a, the enduring relation of which to each other by virtue of the common or identical c, is expressed by + and − or Positive and Negative. This case the second in order of ~~nature~~ Thought we will consider first.—We have now two lines, + and − relatively to each other. +a‾‾‾‾‾‾‾‾‾b and −b‾‾‾‾‾‾‾‾‾a; but relatively each to its own poles, b to a in bca is positive to a, even as a in acb is positive to b, b in the former being *negative* to a, and a in the latter line negative to bc. Each line is for itself a bipolar Integral: tho' relatively to each other + and −. ⁺ +a‾‾‾‾‾‾‾‾‾(−b‖ ⁻ +b‾‾‾‾‾‾‾‾‾(−a.—Now this case is the Electrical

f65 Evolution ⌈. . .⌉ and the Manifestation of the Power of *Breadth* or *Surface* thro' all sensible (= phænomenal) Nature—and the aptest example & illustration is given in ⟨the⟩ Positive and Negative Electricities. Say rather, that *dynamically* considered, i.e. with exclusive reference to the acting *powers and forces*, as abstracted from the sensible products, this case contains the principle of + and − Electricity; but *phænomenally* considered, it states the nature and origin of Breadth or Surface, Electr. being to Breadth as Form (forma *formans*) to Shape (forma apparens.)—But this will be more evident, when we have considered the second possible case: or that in which + and −, or a and b, remain united.

4836 29.92   Argument with a very intelligent Lady, Miss Booth—Sept. 1821—& with an excellent heart, loving truth, but with her faith formed on the Arminian Pelagian Philanthropic notions of the dependence of moral evil on circumstances, in one word on temptations, instead of the true origin, a guilty temptibility. The great difficulty that I find in the treatment of this question is that of making persons so educated perceive & comprehend the difference between an individual Soul, to whom Salvation is open whether Jew or Gentile, where ever Christ is preached, and nations, communities, races, which are not persons tho' composed ~~of~~ *in part* of such, but *things*—just as a ~~Ladder~~ machine formed by men & shields in the Roman way of scaling the Enemies wall is not a man but a scaling Ladder—On the comprehension of this, and the truly Christian Faith that Christ died for *all*, ~~or~~ tho' he is not preached *to* all, rests the interpretation of St Pauls IX. Romans—and the equi-distance from the Socinian Scheme (and Arminianism is only inconsequent Socinianism) which evacuates   *f65^v* Christianity, and Calvinism (the modern at least) which fills it with Horror.—The difference between a Nation or Race (the Chinese for instance) and any one Individual, as an Individual, may be thus illustrated. Say that some epidemic Disease had extended over various Districts, involving a million of men in the same contagion—say, that a medicine had been discovered, an effectual remedy, but yet such that the Infected had almost without exception a deep prejudice against it—that this aversion was a part of the disease, a constant symptom of the infection, that took place even in those districts, in which the medicine was to be had in every street, and its infallible virtues announced by public Authority, and its administration provided for—how much more virulent & rooted then must we suppose this antipathy in those Districts, in which the Medicine was previously unknown, nay, forbidden by the Laws, & denounced by the Physicians of the District, as a Poison / ~~Now beyond and~~ while no effect, few & rare instances excepted, could be hoped for from the *Prescription*, ~~or~~ unless ~~those~~ persons, who understood it, were present to administer it.—Now we have but one other point to suppose—namely, that beyond the number indispensable for the more favored District there were enough for the hundredth part only of the infected—and you need only substitute the Preaching of the Gospel for the administration of the Medicine to see the truth as it actually exists. Every one of the Million is curable & yet it is none the less, that only one in a hundred can be cured.—

f66   The view is most important—for mutato nomine it applies to Revolutions.—what was holy & valid when effected by the Nation, is treason in individuals. Why! because a Nation is God either rewarding or chastising.

4837 22.160

f89   Here lies Sir ~~Williamy~~ Curtis, ~~Once~~ our worthy Lord Mayor
Who ⟨has⟩ left this here ward & is gone to that there.

f124ᵛ   4838 29.213   Faults on both sides: or an Essay upon the original Cause, Progress, and Mischievous Consequences of the Factions in this Nation, shewing &c &c. By Way of Answer to the Thoughts of an Honest Tory—Second Edition. London. 1710. I want to know who ⟨was⟩ the Author of this very able, sensible, & yet very artful pamphlet—Some one of Harley's Friends, no doubt. The §§phs from p. 37 to 41 exhibit an interesting specimen
f124   of the ignorance of the most enlightened men of the Landed Interest at that time respecting the nature & operations of money and credit, with paper money—And yet nothing more was wanting to them but a few simple Facts, or rather the being set right in a few erroneous suppositions which they had taken as premises—ex. gr. that Paper Money is mere convenience—that the Debtor must always *have* in his own possession whatever *money*, his Paper

amounts to—ex.gr. Banks &c.—Whereas the whole meaning of Credit goes on the admissibility of a Calculation approximating to certainty with the increase of the number of Depositors in the same Bank, that A will not want *the cash* till next month or the like— that during this time another representative of that *very* cash may be exciting productive labor which the original Capital of the Bank balances against the contingency that A should want & call for it.—Had they (the Tories) understood its true Nature, they would have at that time have made out a far stronger case against this Paper credit, which is evidently at the cost of all actual possessors whether of Land or of Cash who do not themselves *eat Onions*. For the nation, however, it is extending power of the Middle Class—greater Freedom of Thought & of Communication—⟨Rev- olution from Virtue & Hope—National Credit—⟩ Capital—in- tense Prosperity—Wars—increase of Population—Pauperism— Decay of Property—Monopoly of all Power by Wealth & Patron- age (i.e. Government) Sedition—Oblivion of all Principle & Ex- pedience substituted—Military Despotism—Inextricable Difficul- ties & Confusion in Finances—⟨National Bankruptcy⟩ Revolution from Vice & Despair.

4839 29.214   Egypt according to Herodotus was the Birth   *f123ᵛ* place and Nursery of the most and holiest Religious Rites & Ten- ets, Divinities & divine services, adopted and humanized by the Greeks and introduced into Greece by the Argive Colony. Peri- zonius de Orig. Ægypt. Cap. XVI p. 327. I find noted by me for a collection of the oldest and obscure traditions of the Inachidæ, Io, Epaphus—with the more distinct traditions of Danaus. The Αποβαθμοι, at which this Ægyptian Colonist landed with his chil- dren, remained a Memorable Place in the mouths of the Argives, as like as Pausanias. Corinth. 38. 4: who likewise speaks of the tradition of the Megarenses of Lelex, another Egyptian Emigrant & Colonist. Confirmations of Herodotus's Account from the Books of Moses may be found in our Spencer de Legibus Hebræor. ritualibus. Plutarch's Objections & Attacks are weak, with few exceptions.—It must not, however, be forgotten, that Herodotus derived most of his information from the accounts and traditions of the Priests of Dodona; & that these had an especial interest in

Egyptianizing the Greek Religion, and of course therefore of representing it as originally Egyptian—On the important connection
of foreign Religions, Oracles, &c. with commercial schemes &
interests the Gottingen Historian, Heerens, has written with
greater ability in his Ideen über der Politik &c.—I knew the man;
but do not possess his Works, which I know only by references to
them in other Writers.

    Thrace. Samo-Thrace—Thracian, & Samo-Thracian Colony.
This was very early the subject of keen Controversy, and Herodotus ~~himself~~ seems in one Book to contradict his own assertions in
another—.Thus, he talks of Orpheus, and other Teachers as the
Alumni or Pupils of the Egyptian Priesthood—and after him Dio-
dor. Siculus.—Yet elsewhere H. dwells on the religious instruction received by the Athenians from the ancient Pelasgi—who had
settled in Samothrace—Not only the Poets had an influence inasmuch as Thrace was their conventional Land of Savagery; but
there was a strong party who on historical grounds denied the
derivation of the Eleusinian Rites from Thrace, and affirmed the
sacerdotal Eumolpidæ to have been Joaones and among the original
Colonists from Ionia, who founded Athens.—The derivation of
f123   θρησκεια, ceremonial Rites, Cultus divinus, from Thrace has been
rejected, as a mere hypothetic etymology of the Grammarians, and
the etymon, θρεεῖν, θροειν, = to *patter.* Mum mum—mutter, as
in the confused sound of congregational or ~~pra~~ superstitious
prayer, has been substituted by Hemsterhuis and Lennep—most
forced & improbable, ως εμοιγε δοκεῖ.

    The Attic Colony. N. b. a most instructive & weighty passage
in Proclus, in Platon. Timæum. p. 30. containing the various
opinions of Theopompus, Callisthenes, and Phanodemus. The two
latter Historians derive the Saitæ, inhabitants of Sais in Egypt,
from the Athenians, while Theopompus asserts the Athenians to
have been ~~originally Saitæ~~ εποικους (Settlers) at Sais. Charax again
asserts the Athenians to have been Saitæ, and that Sais is the Ægyptian name of Athenè—and that this is evinced by the symbolic
Attribute of the Crocodile in the statue of the Goddess in the
Acropolis.—In national Tradition and the Legends of the Poets,
the Saitic, Cecrops, is the Representative of Ægypto-Attic Legislation & Culture.—

The Pelasgic Colony in Thesprotia—: the settlement of the Do-
donaic Priesthood—see Herod: II.54.—

My own opinion or rather my full conviction is that the Cec-
ropidæ and all the other Colonists from Egypt had themselves
emigrated from Minor Asia, Lydia, into Egypt—that they were
truly εποικοι at Sais, that the Greeks were all Japetidæ; that they
were in the service of the old Egyptian Kings of Egypt & without
a single trait of Egyptian Character or Person—. That when the
Colonists began to prosper in Attica, there is no doubt, that many
of these Naturalized Greeks, always restless & enterprizing, left
Sais & joined their fellow Ionians—& no doubt, brought with
them many customs &c learnt at Sais—In aftertimes the political,   *f122ᵛ*
commercial, and Sacerdotal Interests raised an Egyptian Party
throughout Greece—. "We are the old original Religion, say the
Roman Catholics at this day—& the pretense, tho' still idler than
that of the Priests of Dodona, has ever been & still is, the most
effective of all their arguments among the ignorant both of their
own sect and of the neglected Protestants.—Doubtless, there was
somewhat common to all the Branches of Heathenism/and in order
to determine what this is, we must in the first place ascertain the
River-Head or Source out of which the primary Branches diverge—and secondly, the points of Confluence of one or more into
another. The differences, nay, the contradictions not only of the
moderns but of the most ancient Schemes and Theories, with each
other, nay, as in Herodotus, the inconsistencies in each scheme,
afford a strong presumption, that the Greek Mythology is a stream
formed by confluences. This being premised, I seem to find a
distant but yet illustrative Analogy in the History of the British
Christians before the arrival of Augustin, and of the influx of the
gorgeous Ceremonial and multiplied Traditions of Rome, the
Rome : to Britain : : Egypt : earliest Greece. And yet yet the old
Cake was not wholly destroyed or trans-substantiated—it remained, not indeed as a fragment, but as a faint Ferment, leav-
ening the British and the Anglo-Saxon Church with a predisposi-
tion to the resumption of its original character in the form of
Protestantism.—Mem. The Welch Triads.—Wickliff—What
Simplicity in relation to *Truth* in the Ante-Roman Britain, that
Simplicity in relation to *Beauty* was to Ante-egyptian Greece—&

continued to reveal itself (the auxiliar influences of republican Habits and Institutions being at once cause and effect of this original or *genuine* Tendency) in its anthropomorphic, humanizing, reactions on the many-headed, many-armed beast-shaped Polytheism imported from Egypt. The decisive æra was when the Greeks recognized and established as the great criterion between Greek ἄν-

f122 θρωποι γνησίοι, and Barbarian in the sense of the significancy and transcendence of the *naked* and the Homogeneous. Thus, they refined and raised the allegorical ιερα γραμματα into the proper *Symbolic*, the Conventional and Local into the Universal and Permanent (i.e. that which is always the same & every where intelligible per simplicem Intuitum, under the same given point of Cultivation/ex.gr. the Jupiter of Phidias, the Apollo Belvidere &c) and finally, the Idolic (το ειδωλικον) into the *Ideal*, or perfect Symbol, in which the Shape is but the Translucence of the inmost or constituent Form—an Idea being the presence of the Whole under the paramouncy of some one of its eternal ~~M~~ and infinite Modes. And this excellence is purely and inalienably Greek, and fully acquits of presumption and national conceit the Greek-made distinction between Greek and Barbarian. Whatever of Egyptian Statuary or Architecture approaches to this Excellence, Belzoni and others have shewn to be later than Alexander, works of Greek genius, under the Ptolemies—ex. gr. the Temple of Tentyra.—

Of Comments or of Works suited to be comments, on the ⟨passages in⟩ second Book of Herodotus, there exist in the proportion of a large Volume to each single ~~page~~ Line of the Greek Historian—I might almost say of my own Reading, at different Periods of my Life—from Aristotle to Proclus, and from Vossius and Bochart to Gebelin (Monde Primitif) Banier, Bryant, Dupuis, Creuzer, &c &c &c: and as far as the apparatus eruditus, Facts, Authorities, Materials & Excitements of Thought extend, I consider my ~~time~~ self sufficiently repayed for my time & trouble. But ⟨as to⟩ the subject itself, the sources, dates and directions of the Greek Religion, mysterious, sacerdotal and popular, I came out of the Jungle-wood with little other recollection than that the paths

f121ᵛ were numberless, and that I had been bewildered. Creuzer, the latest and thorough Master of all his predecessors' labors, had still more important advantages. A true German in the depth & extent of his Erudition, he had first evolved his ~~mind~~ intellect—in that best of all Schools of discipline, the προπαιδειον of the Critical (= Kantean) Philosophy, ⟨and taught to seek the *radicals* of Truth in the *constituent Forms* of the Mind itself;⟩ ~~was soon taught~~ then learnt under FICHTE to rise above the point of Reflection & to contemplate the births ~~of~~ and genesis of things from the point of creation or production; was emancipated by ~~the~~ Schelling & the Physiosophists (Natúr-philosòphen) from the monkish Cell of Fichtean pan-egoistic Idealism, & especially fitted for mythologic investigation by the accurate & con-amore study of the Greek and Italian Neo-platonists from Plotinus to Pletho, and Marsilius Ficinus.—The Work of such a man could not be other than valuable: and as a vast Magazine of Materials, it is of indisputable value. But after a ~~first~~ Flash or two of sheet-lightning in his first chapter, he has left me as much in the dark, as before &—even in his first chapter the πρωτον ψευδος, and source of many other errors, is betrayed—viz—an undue estimation of Pantheism, and the Schellingian Scheme of considering the primary Heathenism, ~~not~~ as a congener of Monotheism, & not as a *de*gener—as venerable in itself, and one of the two essential and necessary Forms of Religious Truth.—Add to this an error common to Creuzer with the rest of the modern Mythologists—& which is well worthy of a Student's attention. I mean the being deceived by the admixture of Historic Names, Inachus, Cecrops, &c in the ancient Theomythics without duly considering the transfer & secondary appropriation of Hieratic Names & attributes to Men, and in each Country to a different Man (ex. gr. The numerous Brotherhood of Jupiters, and Herculeses, and thence the introduction of other celebrated men, Founders of Colonies &c, whom Tradition had made Contemporaries of the former—and gladly introduced by the Poets, by the Tragic Poets in particular, both for their ~~int~~ poetic interest, *f121* as giving an air of reality and credibility, an historic character, to ~~their~~ Drama, and as a Veil, preserving the ⟨Tragic⟩ Poet himself from the Charge, to which he was constantly obnoxious, of disclosing the Mysteries to the Profane.—

Not only historical Dates, but even relative Chronology, must be put out of the Question in every attempt to extract the radical sense of a Symbolic Mythus—they and the names that are supposed

to determine them, must be contemplated as the Costume and
Drapery in ~~the~~ Albert Durer's grand Scripture-history Pictures.
We might as rationally prose over the historic Names and persons
introduced or referred to in Shakespeare's Cymbeline, as over
those of the Æschylian Prometheus—The anachronism of Hector
who quotes Galen & Aristotle in the Troilus & Cressid of our
great Countryman is ~~not appear~~ in effect only & because most of
us "know better than that tho' ", grosser than the flourishing state
of the Mathematical Sciences, ~~with~~ or the Pythoness,—and He-
sione, & what not, as *anterior* to the προσπασσαλευtion of Prometheus to the solitary Scythian Mountain, ~~supposed~~ i.e. Caucasus—
from which however, Prometheus gives directions for Io's itinera-
tion *to* Caucasus, πρὶν ἄν πρὸς ἀυτὸν Κάυκασον μόλῃς.—

So much for the failures hitherto, ~~and~~ the causes and occasions
~~of~~ thereof and the precautions suggested thereby. The man on a
wide heath who knows he must not go South, nor East, nor West,
has learnt something, tho' there is abundant room for him to lose
himself & take as wrong a road, in the space between North-West
and North-East-by East. Up, however! & take our chance—/

And first, what are the signs of the right Track, at least what
are the marks of rational promise?—The most indispensable step
in our journey I have already mentioned. We must ascend the Hill
to the Fountain-head of the different streams. ~~However~~ To whatever extent Shem, Ham, & Japhet may have ignorantly misunderstood or wilfully contradicted, the πατροπαραδοτα of their common Sire, all will not have been rejected, some of the old stones
will be retained in the new buildings—tho' in each, perhaps, differently place[d], & often hard to recognize beneath the strange
f120ᵛ cyphers engraven & bas reliefs of clan history and junior traditions
carved out of them.—I can but *mention* it, however. To give even
a plausible scheme of the Λογοι εν μυθοις, much more of the με-
μυθεμενα [μεμυθευμενα] and συμβολα themselves that are common
to Greek and Barbarian Mythology, laic, templar and mysterial,
would require a large disquisition of itself, ⟨as far as the main
points of Greek Myth. are concerned, I *have* done this in my
letters to Hartley Coleridge in reference to the grand θεανθρωπο-
μυθeme of the Eschylian Prometheus.⟩ Suffice it for the present to
observe, that these common points must be *either* incidents of Tradition, whether facts of real occurence, or *first* instances invented

for the purpose of solving the riddle which Man as Man is for himself, & in which the problem at least must have been one and the same in all human religions—*or* metaphysical attempts at the solution itself, more or less disguised in mythical emblems, allegoric personifications, and ideal Symbols. To the former class belong the chaos, ~~and~~ the Fall or Degeneracy of Man, and the Deluge: ~~to the~~ in the latter the two noblest instances, A and Ω of Grecian Theanthroposophy, are the Prometheus and the lovely mythos of Cupid and Psyche—the one the glory of the Day-star ~~on~~ surmounting the Eastern Heights, the other the last soft rich gleam of the setting Orb!—

Supposing this first and weightiest Preliminary settled, there remain two other problems, the solution

4840 29.216   The want of a grasping, holding Faith in the   *f119ᵛ*
Heart, when it sighs for it, is, I am persuaded, reducible to the Wonder, the *Hollowness*—how any thing at all can *be*!—For the Soul can *substitute* nothing for the truths of Revelation—it cannot *make out* the plain Negative, much less endure to look at it. This is one ~~great~~ motive for dwelling long and often on the great preparatory yet fundamental, ever-accompanying Truth, the *Being* of God † A Xtn must be made to feel how insufficient his *Understanding* is in this respect—yea, and that his Reason is but the *sensorium*, which the Spirit must fill.

† no less than on the Truth of the *Existence* of the Supreme *Being*.

4841 29.215   The Chiefs (at East Cape, Lat. 68, 48, the   *f120*
point of Asia opposite to and once probably joined to Cape Prince of Wales on the American Coast) ["]The chiefs with some others came into the Cabin where everything seemed indifferent to them except the large Looking-glass before which they stood as if enchanted. With serious countenances and fixed looks they contemplated their images: and as one of them moved and saw his motion represented in the Glass, they were all seized with a shuddering and without speaking a word hastily left the Cabin.

※ ※ ※ ※ ※ ※

I have often had an opportunity of observing in my voyage, that the Northern Nations are afraid of a Looking-Glass, and the Southern, on the contrary, behold themselves in it with pleasure.["]

Kotzebue's Voyage. Vol. I. p. 246, 247.—Ditto. p. 219.—The green Island that proved to be an Ice-berg. "masses of the purest Ice to the height of an hundred feet, concealed under a rich cover of Moss and Grass—Mammoth Teeth & Bones exposed to view in the melting—the covering of these Mountains, on which the most luxuriant grass, is only ½ a foot thick—a mixture of clay, sand and earth—below which the ice gradually melts away, the green cover sinks with it, & continues to grow—in time, the Mountain will vanish & a green valley be formed in its stead. ["]

The striking & melancholy picture of the wretched Indian con-
f119ᵛ verts under the Mission in California—and ["] the rage of making Converts (i.e. Xtns before they are made men) the cause of bloody Wars—in the Friendly Islands—[. . .] The Coast of California inhabited by so many tribes that there are frequently in the Mission Indians of more than ten different races, *each having its own language.* [. . .] The Missionaries assured us, it was difficult to instruct them, on account of their stupidity; but I believe, these gentlemen do not give themselves much trouble about it. They also told us, that the Indians came from the Interior of the Country & voluntarily submitted to them—which we likewise doubted.— California is a great expence to the Spanish Government which derives no other advantage from it than that every year a couple of hundred heathens are converted to Christianity (i.e. baptized) who however die very soon in their new faith as they can not accustom themselves to the different mode of Life. Twice in the year they receive permission to return to their different homes. This short time is the happiest period of their existence, & I myself
f119 have seen them going home in crowds, and with the loudest re-joicings. The sick who cannot undertake the journey at least accompany their happy Countrymen to the Shore where they embark and there sit for days together, mournfully gazing on the distant summits of the Mountains, which surround their houses. They often sit in this situation for several days without taking any food—so much does the sight of their lost home affect these New Christians. Every time some of those who have this permission run away: and they would probably all do it, were they not deterred by their fears of the Soldiers who catch them & bring them back to the Mission as criminals—that fear so great that 7 or 8 Dragoons are sufficient to overpower several hundred Indians. ["]

4842 29.217   Presentation Copy of my Works to
Mrs. Agnes Ibbetson, that ~~singular~~ rare Union of feminine fineness of Intuition with masculine energy in combination and inference, ~~and~~ both consecrated to the worthiest and most appropriate
Objects by a Strength of Purpose and a Delicacy of Moral Taste
scarcely less rare—a Lady, whose Writings chastely and as it were
unconsciously eloquent present a model of Style for philosophic
Disquisition, herself eminently a Philosopher, impelled by the love
of Wisdom and guided by the Wisdom of Love—these Volumes,
~~are~~ as a humble testimonial of Respect and admiration, are submitted for her Acceptance

4843 29.218   [The Indistinction or Nature in its lowest]
dignity = Nature $^{(1}$ was as it were collected into that *sleep* in w^h *f118^v*
(we may suppose) a magnet would be while the magnetic powers
yet slumbered in the point of Indifference & before its *polar* forces
were awakened—i.e. before the magnetic *point* had expanded (or
produced itself) into the bi-polar *line* wherein the One manifests
itself by the *two* correspondent & interdependent opposites. This
state of trembling indifference Moses calls the *Darkness*, but a
darkness (in Hebrew the Container) *antecedent* to light as Magnetism absolute must in order of Nature be supposed anterior both to
its positive and to its negative Pole: or as a *point* conceived as the
productive power of the line, in the moment prior to its production
or elongation into a Line.—
    And now the Divine Word (see the Evangelists sublime com-
ment on 1 Gen. v 1. 2. 3. John 1. v. 1. 2. 3.) the coeternal
distinction in the absolute *indivisible* unity awakens the Duplicity
in the Identity. The pregnant point *unfolds* itself, to exist hence-
forw^d in its *poles*: the Darkness divides itself into light (lux lucifica,
the distinctive, manifestative, & unfolding power throughout nature & of w^h the light so called is *a* phænomenon, i.e. the *visual*
phænomenon—) and into Darkness 1. Tenebræ tenebrificantes,
σκοτος σκοτοποιον, the *Hider*, the Enfolder, the retractive and retarding power—in modern language *Gravitation* as the *unific*
power in the manifold—hence Gravit. Gravitation is the principle   *f118*
of all MASS and as far it acts, of all *indifference*, as light of all
difference. I need not, I am sure, point out the absurdity of sup-

posing the Mosaic Darkness to mean what *we* call Darkness—i.e.
that Moses sh^d gravely inform us that a *negation* (rather privation,
or better still absence, non-existence of light was antecedent to
light, and that light was divided f^m the non-existence of itself. Not
quite so absurd but woefully inadequate is the notion that by light
is intended the rays f^m a luminous body—w^h luminous Bodies the
inspired physiogonist has *most* philosophically evolved as the
products of a far more advanced period of the creative process—
even in the fourth of those aweful pauses or complete epochs in
the progression f^m lesser to greater evolution (= f^m evening to
morning) w^h formed the symbolic Days.—

 Henceforw^d Nature is no longer mere potentiality. The actualizing principle has been infused. Nature is now τὸ γινόμενὸν ὅ αει
γένεται. She is elevated into a servant of God, at once the material
and the instrument and the Hand-maid, or mechanical operative
working according to a pattern i.e. the divine Idea working in her
as her law. Thus Nature $^{(2}$ may be conceived first as the Identity
of light and Gravitation = Natura essentialis that w^h establishes
each of the two in the other, & coinherent yet each as modified by
& connaturalized to that to w^h it is subordinated. Thus light in

f₁ 17^v and subordinate ※ to Gravity is SOUND. Gravity in & subordinate
to Light is color: &c &c. Secondly Nature may be conceived as
preeminently existing in the active (= the contractive, expansive,
evolving & modifying) the objective or positive pole—in w^h sense
it is the same with the power of light, or lux lucifica. Thus taken,
Nature is well expressed by the Schoolmen as NATURA NATURANS.
The Sal ubiquitarius of the alchemists: or thirdly it is taken as the
negative or *sub*jective pole—The vis substantifica or corporifica w^h
acts by resisting action = vis inertiæ, striving to keep enfolded
and one what the natura naturans, or light, is striving to manifold
& thus forming ~~the~~ a fulcrum and base (*sensu Chemico*) or *subject*
for the Light or objectivizing power. In this sense in which Nature
is the same with the power of Gravity, Nature is = *Natura*
NATURABILIS. Fourthly & lastly, Nature may mean the sum of the

※ Hence the connection of sound with the hard & the Metallic w^h
are the especial exponents or representatives of Gravity in the
world of the senses: and I fear not to call sound the soul of Gravitation and color the body of light.—

Products and Phænomena of these the twin primary Forces, or opposite yet interdependent & correlative Poles of the one Power in their generative love-struggle & interpenetrative Synthesis, & thus taken Nature is = Natura Naturata κοσμος.—

4844   29.219   In the ~~two~~hree first ~~syllables~~ Words of the 4th $f_1 17$ of the following Quadruplet we have an instance of graduated Emphasis—

<u>Reas</u>	=	||||
<u>There</u>	=	|||
<u>is</u>	=	||
<u>on</u>	=	|

and so *in* the remainder of the line, *then*; *her*; and REIGN; have each a quantum of emphasis equal to |||, *reign* being distinguished from *then* and *her* by the grave or cadence, and those from "reign" by the acute or arsis, while *"gins"* = / and "be" = ½ / or ⌣. Q.ʸ Where is Reason? Answer.

> Whene'er the Self, that stands twixt God and Thee,
> Defecates to a pure Transparency
> That intercepts no light and adds no stain—
> There Reason is; and then begins *her* reign!
>
> S.T.C.

4845   18.327   The Reason in Man which sees only what is $f_1 68^v$ right under all circumstances (? without circumstance? independent of—?) and the Understanding of Man which comprehends only a poor fragment (? fraction) of circumstances, dictates ⟨perpetual⟩ Peace; but Nature, wiser than Man, & whose wisdom is the identity of Reason & Understanding, forces him into perpetual War— See Kotzebu's Voyage, Vol. II.—on the new-raised Coral Islands.—

4846   20.50   Hell? but whence came the descriptions of its $f45$ Torments? From the imagination? But who having experienced what can be suffered in distempered Sleep, will compare the imag-

inative *unsensational* power of the man awake with the imagination
that the Soul produces & suffers in Sleep?—One of the most horrible of these states of Morbid Sleep is the Sensation that counterfeits Remorse—& actual Remorse we know, when intense, ~~takes
the~~ realizes all the horrors of Sleep & seems indeed the identity or
co-inherence of Sleep & Wake, Reality and Imagination.—If then
Hell mean, & I know no more rational meaning, the state &
natural consequences of a diseased Soul, abandoned to itself or
additionally tortured by the very organic case which had before
sheltered it, and the force of the blows & blunted the point and
edge of the daggers—it must contain—& surpass all the description of Hell, that were the portraits of the disturbed imagination—
/—To consider the proper consequences an Act or Course of Action
is to consider the Act itself, and no way inconsistent with the hatred
of Sin for its own sake.

f44   **4847** 20.55   Diderot's Dialogue in Goethe's Works—ad finem to substitute for these §§phs the few words—
    A Bug! a loathsome Bug! the very Thought, the very Sound,
turns me sick.—And yet a Centipede, a Scorpion, is worse. Fang
in Head, and Sting in Tail and deadly poison in both—Yes! that
is ~~still~~ worse! But ~~worst of all is the~~ worse still, worse than Bug
or Centipede, is the Man who compares them in order to choose
between the two.

4848 20.56
LOVE.
    Argumentum a consequenti ~~κατα~~ ἐναντιόλογον κάτα τοῦ *ἀξιο-*
λογίκου δόγματος, ὡς ἔρως ἔστι ἐπιθύμια (τῆς σάρκος, ἠγοῦν) πρὸς
φιλίαν—i.e. nihil aliud ac Amicitia Libidine conjuncta in relation
to the same object—Ergo, Vir ανδρομανὴς ἢ παιδέραστος τόν φί-
λον αὐτοῦ ἐρᾷ—
    ⟨This, this most damnable abomination⟩ is in itself (ω καταρᾶ-
τον! *Verbo-digno* indignum!) the same emotion the very same state
and mode of being as the Love of Jacob to *Rachel*!—"Love a vehement appetite for an Object which is at the same time *esteemed*!"
f43ᵛ *Appetite* for a *Person*! *Esteem* for a *Thing*! Absurd incongruities!—
No wonder, therefore, that the Alumni ⟨⟨Nurslings⟩⟩ of this truly

french School of Morals find nothing more natural than to *love* half a dozen women at the same time! ~~Peace go with~~ Farewell to *such* as take the whole subhuman code of Gallic Ethics and Metaphysics

Words worth

en masse—~~but~~ they are not *Verbois digni*—! But those who pretend to far other principles ~~in the~~ on all ~~main~~ other subjects; and yet ~~and~~ entertain this degrading Faith; I wonder how *they* can bring themselves, without a sense of blaspheming, to speak of the "Love of God"—or speaking thus, how they dare use the same word to express *that* feeling and impulse, which ~~they~~ (and nothing more or other than which) *they* ⟨(according to *their own* confession)⟩ experience toward the Woman, they wish to marry—. Surely, the ~~words~~ Phrase *the Girl of my Liking; I am in liking with* (~~sti~~or still better, *of*) *that Girl*; would be far more appropriate and ~~decent~~ far more consistent. He who marries such or such a Woman because he loved her *the best*, never *loved* at all.—He merely *fell* into a *Liking* of Her. Even a ⟨the⟩ Liking *for* which our simple Rustics profess is a something nobler than his Passion.—A *Longing* after her—*pron.adj.* Elongatio veretri versus vaginam. Elong. Ver. (sc.   *f43* Estimantis) versus vag. (sc. Estimatæ)—this is all!—And THIS is—I recoil from the very thought of *writing* the word in this loathsome perversion of it—No! I would almost as soon use the term Communion Table for a Hogs-trough as even *write* ⟨it down⟩ that—This is Love!—Would to Heaven, however, that (in another sense) I could *write it down*! S.T.C.

4849 20.1

                          Scene 1.   *f1*

   Enter Luke (alone)
   Luke. (groan-grunting)—Aye! The more you do, the more you may—and the less is thought of it!—

4850 20.4

                          māxīmōs
$$- \smile \smile \mid -\ -$$
$$\mid \smile\ -\ \smile$$

4851 28.84   The advantages of Paradoxy—and first that it *is*   *f76ᵛ*
certain of fixing limits to itself—by the excitement of opposition

from so many different Classes/First, from the *one*, perhaps, who often deceived has learnt to suspect all Paradox as equivoque of two sides—Blank Truism and glaring Nonsense, the undistinguished Co-presence of which in the mind of the Hearer chiefly produces that peculiar feeling, that something between a sense and a sensation, which follows the Hearing of a Paradox.—This good as logical Discipline. But where it is αληθεια παρα δοξαν—then the old School—the grounds and Heel-taps of past respectability—
*f*77   the half-learned Beginners hot from the Lecture-room.

*f*77ᵛ   **4852** 28.85   Reformed Olio. Rump of Beef or Aitch-bone, ⟨Knuckles of Veal,⟩ Neats' Tongues, boiled and dried and Bologna sausages; having boiled them together two hours, add mutton, pork, venison, bacon, cut in pieces—turnips, carrots, onions, celery, and peas (green when to be got) pepper, salt, alspice. This done, in another pot boil a Turkey, a brace of Pheasants, or Capons, or both, partridges, & stock doves in water and salt. In a third vessel prepare a sauce of (white wine?) strong Broth, butter, chopt liver, bottoms of artichokes, with cauliflowers, bread, marrow, yolk of eggs and mace. Then dish it—first the Beef & Veal with Tongues &c round—then the Harico—the Fowl, Roots—& Sauce.—

*f*51   **4853** 21½.99   Archbishop Leighton's Works, in 4 Volumes Octavo, by Revᵈ Erasmus Middleton.
        Vol. IV. The beautiful passage extracted from Seneca, in page 82; on the identity of God and Nature, a sentiment in attacking which I foresee what offence I shall give—tho' it is clear that if Nature be the same with God, God must be the same with Nature—is clearly in contradiction with Leighton's own Convictions as finely expressed in a following Lecture (XI) p. 113—And this sentence again contrasts strangely with the very weak solution attempted in the next and concluding sentence of the §.—Insects and Animalcules Leighton will not derive from God's glorious Nature; but he has no scruple in deriving them from his "good pleasure"— i.e. his productive Will.—
        Every day brings me new occasions of seeing the vast and not only speculative but practical importance of the fundamental *Idea*

of my System, and the Conception thence deduced concerning the Chaos—.That contingent wills (the αποστατοι) formed † *Time* & then Eternity acted thereon.

† at least the conditions of Time, rendered Time possible as *a good* by being a less Evil—. The following § (113, 114) throws a great light on this but receives a greater a greater. The defect of Archb. *f51ᵛ* Leighton's Reasoning is the taking Eternity as a *sort* of Time—a Baro Major, A Baron of Beef or Quarter of Lamb, out of which and *off* which Time is cut as a Brisket, or Shoulder—while in even in common discourse without any design of sounding the depth of the Truth or of weighing the words expressing it in the Hair-balance of Metaphysics, it would be more convenient to consider Eternity as the Antitheton of Time,—as simul et totum to pars and successive.

4854 21½.100   'Αἷμα Χστ. ναι, κατα Λουκαν (πρ. Αποστ) ⌈αι⌉ αἷμα Θεου:—Χρστς agens = Jehova Memra Sol intelligibilis, Lux lucifica—but in all agency there is a ⟨form of⟩ passivity subordinated and the Cosmos (Sol) sensibilis, Lux elucens, are the *passive*, voice, Existence, the outmost *Body*, of the Agent, as far as they are one, entire, and indivisible—They are the Sermo *realis*, Verbum *phænomenon*, the Passive Voice, the Fit of the Facient—(fit et facit, creat et creatur—gemina natura. These to the *intellect*—and to the Χριστος patiens Thus too existence, Χριστος *agens* is = *f52* Anima Animans, Calor fovens.—

Χριστος patiens— = principium vitæ reproductionis in vitam in formâ passiva—Elementum, ut alimentum, vitæ. Vis assimilans *assimilationem patiens*—but in all passivity there is an *essential* activity involved—therefore Vis vitæ superioris assimilationem *patiens*, simul autem incitans ad actum assimilandi—Now what is the *proximate* food, as distinguished from the process and preparations? Evidently, the Blood. But what is the proximate *incitant* to the Absorbents? The Active Stimulus of the reproductive Powers? The Blood—. What ⟨but the Blood⟩ is the Mediator between the Fixed and the Fluid—the ⟨first⟩ recipient of the Spirit (aura vitalis per pulmones) which must *have been* & must *be* in order for the Spiritus *Confortans* to descend—but not incarnate, as the Blood?—(Al-

len & *Pepys* versus Priestley & Lavoisier de Oxygene non in san-
guinem permaente) It is yet not said to be Christ in toto, but the
Blood of Christ—or Christ as his Blood/*Ruminantia*—The Divine
f52ᵛ   Apis making an inferior life (grass &c) assimilable by means of
his own vital fluids—thenus *suffering* the inferiors to take *him* up
into *their* Being in order in the next process to take them up into
him—. But the Blood in the Scripture use includes all the fluids
essential to reproduction in any of its processes—serous, lymphatic, &c. The Blind Man (in S̶ᵗ̶ John) was saved by means of
the † Saliva.—The Blood of Redemption therefore I interpret as
the Indifference of the Vis Vitæ and the Principium Vitæ—the
which, both as Thoughts and as Terms, are so commonly confounded that it would be expedient to designate them as Vis vitam
ciens, and Principium vitæ excitabile—(capacitas vivendi, condi-
tione datâ?) Principium ortûs est et Principium statûs.

† Unusually great earnestness, intension and devotion to any one
thing in and for itself necessarily weakens ⟨or precludes the dis-
turbing⟩ the force of associations   Quarles, Withers, and others
have been unkindly under-rated on this account—their want of
Taste was from fullness of Appetite, their sound Hunger and
Thirst after religion/But old Fuller had not − but)(, not the a
deficiency, but the positively opposite, of this φιλοπρεπον—&
f53   would have given, first, an Edipus Ægyptiacus identification of
Hermes with the Logos, Mercury Χρισμα with the Χρστῳ—Salvation from Salivation, and conversely Salvation from Salve-ation,
in proper *gout*.—

4855 21½.101   The difference between Refraction and Dispersion is not clear to me, as yet—and this alone is wanting in
order to a full theory of LIGHT & WARMTH. Inflection, Reflection, and Refraction differ but as the Directions—or as a b and c
= a + b, i.e. the Median between both.

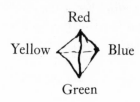

Red

Yellow   Blue

Green

Red the culmination, Green the Union. "As Red to White and
Black, so Green to Yellow and Blue", seems to be Oken's Doctrine. But I cannot assent. Black is for me an *absence* or inference
from the Absence—but neither an opposite, nor a contrary. But
Blue is a polar opposite or Antitheton of Yellow. An Equipoise or
indifference of the Causes or Conditions of *specific* Colors, occasioning any Substance to act merely as Substance, i.e. <u>αντιφως</u>,
gives us White = φως + the minimum of Anti-φως—the least   *f53ᵛ*
quantity necessary to the manifestation of Light. N.B. This is the
way and the only way, by which the Universals of the mind are
realized, i.e. find an equation, in Nature. And in this sense White
may be called *Color* in distinction from *a* Color. (Mem. the superiority of the English to the Greek—Gr. Θεος, ὁ θεος. Χρωμα, τό
χρωμα. Eng. A God, The God, God. A color, the Color, Color.)
But for the same Cause there must be a point in which there is the
least quantity of Light necessary for the manifestation of Substance
(as Antiphose). Blue, evanescent, not transitional—passing *out* of
itself, not *into* any other Color—this ~~of your~~ point of dissolving
boundary of Blue, you may if you please call Black—& thus preserve the old Black & White in the sense of *Opposites*—but then
the mere negation of White, the absence of the old Black & White
in the sense of *Opposites*—but then the mere negation of White,
the absence of †Color, we ought to call by some other name. Dark,   *f54*
for instance—& not Black.

I have not leisure at present to pursue the speculation. But in
memorand, for a future time, two curves, 1. Intensity, and 2.
Relaxation—or something better—

	Orange	Red	Purple	
White				Black
	Yellow	Green	Blue	

an Ellipse of Color—From White to Black, thro' the ~~higher~~ upper
curve, of Orange, Red, Violet, and from Black to White thro' the
lower, of Indigo, Green, and Yellow—
In short, the true theory of Colors, as of all physics, is but a

† For White is the preclusion of *any* Color, but not by the absence
but by the *presence* & equipoise of all colors.

position—special of the fundamental Relation, Extension and Intension as the two polar forms of Tension (*Spannung* of the late
German Philosophers, ενεργεια of the Greek—hence centrifugal,
centripetal; central, peripheric; Light, Gravity: S~~o~~un, Planet,
White, Black. Hence it is ad libitum, whether Color be referred
to the Light, which ~~it~~ is modified, and White be = Color; or to
the Gravity (Body, Material Substratum) and Black be = Color—.
In both Yellow, Green, Blue are the extensive acts of Color, Or-

f54ᵛ　ange Red, Violet, the intensive. The distinction, however, between
Black and Dark, if we employ one to express the contrary of, and
the other the opposite to, White, is of great value. Among the
numerous Sophisms and equivoques of the Newtonian Prism, the
confusion of two senses in the one term, Shadow, has not been the
least fruitful of bastard notions—the first sense, the privation of
Light, the other, the re~~st~~lative diminution of the same ⟨by partial
interception.⟩ In the latter, the Shadow is *something*—a + seeing,
in the former a nothing, a − seeing.—Now the Prism casts a
Shadow in the latter sense, as a dense and semi-opake Whole; but
it likewise casts 1. Color by ~~the~~ its total *energy*, as qualifying (not
intercepting) Light: i.e. the Prism generates *White* within itself—
and 2. it casts *Colors* generated within ~~the Prism~~ itself by the
polarising energies of its parts acting on the White.

　　Thus the Prismatic Spectrum is a highly complex
phænomenon—so that, in the present state of our knowlege, the
same appearance is susceptible of several Solutions

f55　4856　21½.102　　　The Plough Ox in the Thesmophoria Symbol of Marriage (συζυγια) forbidden to be slaughtered by Trip-
tolemus—in later times, when this Law was broken thro', still the
slaughtering Priest was obliged to flee, and to leave the sacrificial
Weapon behind, to be proceeded against according to Law—as the
Culprit.—Deodand?—Hereditary Priesthoods & Dign. Eumol-
pides, Butades (Buddha) Kyniden, Κηρυκες. Buddha : Pandu ::
Butes : Pandion. In each Demos (District) the High Priest originally the King—the different struggles of the Gods, different Religions—*Confusion of the Lip Babel.* Q͟—All of *Ham. and Canaan*,
originally—the faithless Shemites given up to the superstitions of
those, with whom they had intermarried—PERHAPS, *the nakedness
of Noah = Physiotheism.*

4857 21½.103   One of the very strongest arguments against the Unitarians is in effect their main bulwark & the strength of their Cause. Christianity (the Faith common to the Greek, Roman and Protestant Churches) is so unutterably awful and *concerning*, its radical truths and its permeating energies do so circulate thro' the whole living Body of its code, in every spray, in every leaf of this Tree of Life—and even to such parts as must of necessity, in & of themselves be common to every scheme of civilization and *f55ᵛ* social Intercourse, it ⟨so⟩ transfuses its own higher & peculiar life—that even a Heresy which retains the latter only, severed from & in scornful rejection of the former, yet retains it *as* Christianity, will appear to the unreflecting or rather will be blindly felt and admitted as holding these parts in the same spirit with themselves—& the parts themselves as the same—which however they are only as an amputated arm or an extracted eye is the same with the arms & eyes of living & unmutilated men. Hence if you expose in the true light the unspeakable worthlessness of the Unitarian Scheme, the pitiable weakness of the Evidence on which they ground their belief of *any* part of the Gospel, o̶r̶ i.e. justify their consistency in the non-rejection of the whole—other Christians are shocked/—they c̶a̶n̶n̶o̶t̶ have not powers of abstraction and imagination enough to d̶i̶s̶s̶ detach their feelings from the 1000 arms & retinacula of old and impassioned Association—and because a dry leaf is still *called* a leaf, and because the earthy vessels & Capillaries had been the Channels of the Juices of Immortal Life, therefore you must not speak of a feuille mort as no leaf at all—you must *f56* drive it before the gale of reason, and eddy it in the Gust of Indignation/—(a *fullerism*—or smile at them who make shoes & boots of the divine Caoutchouck which was given to them from the milky bosom of the Tree to *rub out* their sins from the Book of the Accusing Spirit.)

The only persons for whom Unitarianism could be a religion, would be the infra Mohammedan race, unhistoric—in whom humanity just dawns enough to have a glimpse of humanity as comparative divinity (as in Dogs)—but even in these it would in proportion as it improved the believers evolve itself into the Orthodox faith—i.e. it would even in its first be *implicit* Theanthropism— The ⟨Asa–man⟩ Odin would gradually be transfigured into the Odin Alfader.

4858 21½.104   Astral Spirits—with exception of the Epicureans & (perhaps) the Sadducees/in Palestine at least a mere
handful of rich men—the universal belief.—How unhistoric then
the interpretation that would make any thing out of Paul's Words,
only not that which ⟨alone⟩ his readers could possibly at that understand by them—I have often urged the same argument applied
to the Logos of John—and the water-blood at the Cross.—and yet
f56ᵛ notwithstanding the undoubted belief of all the Fathers of the
Church for the first 5 centuries, yet still true to grand Mundane
or world-historical distinction, even on the most trifling points,
the Church as obstinately rejected & anathematized *Astrology*—

Exquisite passage in "Of the Nature and Substance of Devils &
Spirits" written as a Supplement to Reginald Scott's Discovery of
Witches—. The poor simple People imagine they see ~~cloudy
shapes~~ shapely Clouds and meteorological Prognostics, where in
fact it is *only* these Astral Spirits—?—

4859 21½.105   The Cephalopodes want the Optic nerve
(Sehnerv.) No bad emblem of those that leap before they look.—

4860 21½.106   The extra ordinary Florency of Letters under the Spanish Califate in connection with the character ~~of~~ and
capabilities of Mohammedanism has never yet been treated as its
importance requires. Halim II. founder of the university of Cor-
dova, and of numerous Colleges and Libraries throughout Spain,
is said to have possessed a Library of six hundred thousand Mss,
the Catalogue filling 44 volumes. Nor were his Successors much
f57 behind him in zeal & munificence—that the prime article of
Islamism, the uni-personality of God, is one cause of the down-
fal—of the merely meteoric existence of their Litera~~tur~~ery Age, I
am persuaded—but the exclusive Scene (in Spain) suggests many
interesting views.—With a Learned Class Mohammedanism could
not but pass into Deism—& Deism never did, never can, establish
itself as a Religion. It is the doctrine of the Tri-unity that connects
Xty with Philosophy—gives a *positive* Religion a specific interest
to the Philosopher, and that of Redemption to the Moralist &
Psychologist—. Predestination in the plenitude in which it is =

Fatalism was the necessary Alternative & Succedaneum of Redemption—and the Incarnation the only preservative against Pantheism on one side & Anthropomorphism on the other.—The Persian (Europeans in Asia) Form of Moh. very striking in this point of View—.

4861 21½.107   Certain hereditary Tricks, in Dress, Attitudes Looks &c. *Stereotypes* of the Stage.

4862 21½.108   Instead of the inconvenient terms, Productivity, Irritability, Sensibility—we might substitute, the Phytic, Entomic and Zöic—or Growth, Existence, Being—or the Protonomy, Deuteronomy, Hypsonomy—or ~~Self~~ evolution, Life, Subsistence, Vegetative, Entomic &

4863 21½.110   That the colors of different seas from different proportions of Iodine—the Rio negros from Carbon & Hydrogen   *f57ᵛ*

4864 21½.109   ⟨What⟩ Humbold in his visit to the Cavern of Ataruipe relates of the enormous Balls (50 feet in Diameter) of Granite perfectly round on the summit of a Granite Mountain & which he ascribes to decomposition wholly, may be thought to favor the *globific* tendency of Granite, throughout. It wishes to be a planet of itself—perhaps, the Moon ~~be~~ may be such a Ball, which some Comet has played at Nine-pins with—and brushed off to its present distance—As probable as Sir H. Davy's Stones from Jupiter.

4865 21½.111   The difficulty of discovering the relations of the vascular system, and of the different parts of the Body generally, to the nervous system—and of the nerves themselves to the Brain, is aggravated by the polypus nature of every nerve—not only has it its proper as well as general relations to its center, but it contains a center in itself, potentially at least, and capable of being awakened—tho' our perception thereof must be in the Brain, perhaps as a perception of resistance and interruption—such a portion of nerve would be *a thorn* in the system, and acting in the

same way—: as in Tic Doloreux.—Add, however P.S. Not correct—or but partially. It must be a resistance of Life by Life—
f58   the thorn must be a *live* thorn. A mere "ne plus ultra" would not
produce the extreme pain: as is formed by the excision of the diseased portion of the nerve. It must be *contradiction*—contra-action,
I should say. It is not improbable that the effect of topical bleeding, as in the Temples, may work in this way, by exciting the
latent totality of the part—to which suddenness, a large Orifice &c
may contribute.

4866 21½.112   It is not by Individual Characters that an
Individual can derive just conclusions respecting a community or
an Age. Conclusions so drawn are the excuse of selfish, narrow,
and pusillanimous Statesmen, who by dwelling on the kindred
baseness or folly of the persons, with whom they come in immediate contact, lose all faith in human nature—ignorant that even
in these a spark is latent which would light up and consume the
worthless overlay, in a national moment. The spirit of a Race is
the character of a People—the Sleep or the Awakening of which
depends on a few Minds, pre-ordained for this purpose—and
sometimes by the mere removal of the dead weight of a degenerate
Court or Nobility pressing on the Spring. So I doubt not would
it be with the Turks, were the Porte and its Seraglio conquered by
Russia. But the Spirit of a Race ought never to be supposed ex-
f58ᵛ tinct—but on the other hand no more or other expected than *the*
Race contains in itself. The true Phænomenon Cause of the irre-
coverable Fall of Rome is to be found in the fact, that Rome was
a City, a handful of men that multiplied its Subjects incomparably
faster than its Citizens—so that the latter were soon diluted and
lost in the former—On a similar principle Colonists in modern
times degenerate, by *excision* from their Race—/the Ancient Colonies were *buds*—This I think, applies to the Neapolitans and most
of the Italian States—. A nest of Republics keep each other alive;
but a patch-work of principalities has the effect of excision by
insulation—or rather by compressure.—How long did the Life of
Germany doze under these ligatures—yet did we not despair
wrongfully of the People—The Spirit of the Race survived, of

which Literature was a part.—Hence I dare not despair of Greece; because it has been barbarized, and enslaved, but not split up into puny independent Governments under Princes of their own *f59* Race.—The Neapolitans have always been a conquered people— and degenerate in the original sense of the word—De genere, they have lost their race,—which what it was is uncertain.—Lastly, the Individual in all things is the prerogative of the divine Knowlege. What it is, our eyes can see only by what it has in common, and this can only be seen in Communities—Where neither Excision, nor Ligature, nor Commixture exist, ~~Slavery~~ Despotism and Su- perstition will not extinguish the character of a Race—in Russia for instance. But again, take care to understand that character, and expect no other fruit than the Root (Radix, Race) contains in its nature.

The rigorous superintendence over the preservation of Races in the divine Legislation before as well as after the Deluge, and in human in proportion to their wisdom is a weighty presumption of its importance, and its pregnancy in good & evil—the prohibition of intermarriages in the same family, and the confinement of them to the same Race, or (as an advanced bulwark, and perhaps for the maturation of distinct Powers in different portions of the same race) to the Tribe—are the ~~Peri~~Diastole and ~~Anti-peri~~ Systole of *f59ᵛ* Humanity.

4867 21½.113   Next to the inspired Scriptures, yea, and as the *vibration* of th~~e~~at once struck Hour remaining on the ~~old~~ Air, stands Archb. Leighton's Commentary on the 1 Ep. of Peter—

4868 21½.114   Nothing but evil can ensue from the doc- trine of the 3 Dimensions, or even from the triple 3—if it be not used chiefly as the basis of more special relations and oppositions. Ex. gr. Worse than vain would be the opposition of the Arterio- muscular to the Nervous or to the Veno-glandular powers, if at least equal attention were not given to the opposition in the Irrita- bility itself between the Muscles and Arteries, the firmamental and the fluid.—

4869 21½.115   The wretchedness of the Septuagint Version
of Daniel such that the Christian Church which retained all the
other books substituted Theodotion's Transl. of Daniel—Is not this
a presumption that the version of Daniel was among the latest?
~~translated~~ and probably not sanctioned by the Council of 70 in
Alexandria. The true meaning of Septuagint.
—The Pentateuch as the eldest (probably, the only one required
by & by the Sanhedrim delivered to Ptol. Philadelphus and Lagi,
so the best—next to this the Proverbs—Job with great poetic
spirit, but with more knowlege of the Language into, than of that
f6o   from, which it was translated.—The Psalms & Prophets only not
so bad as the Book of Daniel—or the Prophets all bad, Daniel
being the worst.—
    Now the Reading of the Prophets in the Synagogue commenced
⟨in Palestine⟩ about ~~160~~70 years before Christ—and here commences the most pregnant epoch for an inquiry into the *Messianic*
Interpretation.
    Next to the *Laws* would not the Oracles have most excited the
interest of the Ptolemies—as soon as their influence on the expec-
tations and therefore on the probable conduct of the Jews became
manifest?

4870 21½.116   Esdras with exception of the 3 & 4 Chapters
a free and in many respects a better & more faithful tho' less literal
Translation of the Canonic Ezra, ⟨with parts⟩ Nehemiah, and the
Chronicles. The source of the 3rd & 4th unknown—but certainly
not interpolated by the Christians; for this Book was used largely
by Josephus—besides the Aλη Θεια, or Ruach Elohim, which a
Christian Interpreter would have rendered Logos, or *manifested*
Intelligence, ~~Outerance~~ of the Divine Mind or Will—.—For had
~~the~~ a X^{tn} ~~Interpret~~olator meant the Holy Ghost, he would have
called it Sophia—and neither would he have attributed the κτισιν
η παυγενεσιν to it.—But the Spirit = 7 Spirits of God rest in
plenitude on the Messiah—& St John himself put το πνευμα, not
f6o^v   Logos, in our Lord's own speeches—This passage therefore, which
must have been extant before the Apostolic Writings settles the
sense of the N.T.—~~E~~ Εγω ειμι η Αληθεια and the Koran, which
borrowed much from Jewish Sources, declares Christ to have been

Ruach Jehovah—the Breath of God, αλη θεῖα— That it was not a
personification the whole passage proves—in which it is compared
throughout not with Wine even, tho' the Plan of this Amoibaian
Eclogue seemed to require—nor with arms ⟨or gold⟩ nor with any
abstraction, as Courage, Knowlege—but throughout with *persons*,
with moral and rational Beings—v. 35..37. 40—Sᵗ John's Epistle—.—But in truth nothing but consummate ignorance not only
of the only philosophy adopted or rather adapted by the Jews before and during the Apostolic Age, but of the genius of Hebrew
Poetry in all f former periods, could alone have suggested this
fancy of personification—A figure comparatively rare even in the
Greek and Roman Poets, and the more rare, the more religious
the Poet or his Age/Pers⁰ a substitute for Polytheism, as Pruden-
tius Psychomachia—Thus too at the æra of the Reformation, Emblems, Allegories, Symbols, became the Passion—. Besides, why
should Wisdom, or Truth, or the Spirit, be the only *Abstract* personified—if it be a personified abstract. Why should so many
Writers hit each on this one Quality?—

4871　21½.117　　　　N.B. Neither are Public Festivals always or　*f6 1*
of necessity Evidence of the Truth and Authenticity of Books professing to give or containing an account of their historic Origin
and occasion: nor the assertion in a Book of such an Institution any
certain proof of its actual existence—Proof—the assertion in the
Book of Judith (received even as canonical by ~~the~~ only not all the
fathers) of the Feast of the Deliverance of Bethulia from Holo-
phernes—the whole story being either a mere Romance, or a tradition so absurdly scened, dated, and trans-personed as to be of no
more worth than a Romance.—

4872　21½.118　　　　The Mosaic throughout a *State*-dispensation,
and for Individuals in relation to the State—Hence the frequency
with which the Nation and (after the schism of the 10 tribes) the
two Nations are represented by the Prophets as Individual *Persons*/
Jonas is in all probability an Instance. The Jewish State was as one
Individual—I deduce, first, the propriety with which Paul, a Hebrew, speaks of Christ as the Head and the Church as his Members—his Body—To a people whose associations had been all

formed under a Theocracy, nothing could be more natural or intelligible—.2. the superior suitableness of *Providence* ⟨to Miracles
as contra-distinguished from Pr.⟩ a series of striking Providences
all linking on in one Chain, the *Chain* tho' not ~~each~~ any separate
link—the *chain* and therefore every *link* in connection, every Prov.
as a link, having the essential character & effect of a Miracle.
Vindication of *my* view of the Plagues of Egypt in a religious
respect.

f61ᵛ   4873 21½.119   On the Schmen see my Marginal Note to
Thomson's Chemistry, Vol. I. p. 388. Third Edition—Roemer's
and Bradley's mensurability of Light no proof that Light is a
body—it is only necessary to take the subjects, acted on or called
into Action by Light, as bodies—. Thoughts are timeless; but
being successive, a series of Thoughts must be in time—and therefore in *some* time. If we supposed Light to be the result of an
action between the center or + and the periphery or − , and this
periphery to be one of asterisks with interspaces, or an asterisk and
an imaginary Circle (as if a Halo were to shrink up into one
Ball)—then the rectilineal Theory would follow, without any proof
of the Materiality of Light—& a just contemplation of Color
would alone be wanting to an insight into the phænomena of the
Rings &c from pressure of Glass Plates—In one case the periphery
becomes a point—in the other the Point either becomes or as a new
Center generates a periphery.

f66   4874 29.93   The extreme impolicy of throwing obstacles in
the way of the importation of Pictures, Statues, Books &c&c—
these being the very Mounds to Wealth which it is most desirable
that Wealth itself should create for itself.—For thus what would
be a demand or a power of demanding the Labor of so many fellow
creatures is thrown into suspended *Animation*, at least—& every
valuable Picture, as long as it remains, is pro Tanto a payment of
the National Debt—~~Suggested~~ Remarked to me by Mʳ J.H.
Green, 3 March 1822. Sunday—

4875 29.94   In + Roman, − Catholic States where Science
has forced its way, and some Light must follow, the Devil himself

cunningly set up a shop for Common Sense at the Sign of the
~~Devil~~. Infidel! S.T.C.

4876 29.95   Misattributing Fear, like women who scarce
heeding the wan Day Lightning are frightened to death with the
crack and roll of the Thunder—

4877 29.96   The 2 first Chapters of Vol. II of the Abi-   *f66ᵛ*
pones—the confident belief of Immortality compared with the utter
absence of the Idea of God. This in relation to the Mosaic Mission—

4878 29.250   Last Flower plucked in the garden of the Cot-   *f101ᵛ*
tage in Southwood, 23 March 1822—before the removal of the
Milne Family to Holly Terrace.

4879 23.35   Berberis = common barberry—the Stamens   *f33*
brought into contact with the Pistil by the stimulus given by the
Insects to the base of the filament.

This still more striking in the shewy Iris tribe. In these the true
Stigma is found on the upper side of a tranverse membrane (arcus
eminens of Haller) which stretches across the middle of the under
surface of the petal-like expansion or Style-flag—the whole of
which has been often but erroneously regarded as fulfilling the
office of a Stigma. Now the anther is situated at the *base* of the
Style-flag that covers it, at a considerable distance from the Stigma;
and not only so but cut off likewise from all access to it by the
intervening barrier of the Arcus eminens. The Pollen therefore
could never reach the place of its destination withou[t] extrinsic
agency—which in this instance is that of the Humble-bee. Led by
⌐ . . . ⌐ Instinct—not impossibly by one of those *Saft-maale*, or
Honey-marks (i.e. spots of a different color from the the rest of   *f33ᵛ*
the Corolla, which (Sprengel conjectures) are placed in many flowers for the purpose of guiding insects to the nectaries) the Humble-
bee pushes herself between the stiff Style-flag & the elastic Petal,
which last, while she is in the interior, presses her close to the
Anther, and causes her to brush off the Pollen with and on her
hairy back—and ultimately but not in the first instance conveys it

to the Stigma. For having exhausted the nectar she retreats backwards, in doing which she is pressed by the petal to the arcus eminens; but only to the lower or negative surface, which cannot influence the impregnation. It is now that she takes her way to the second Petal, and insinuating herself under its style-flag comes into close contact with the true Stigma, and impregnates it with the pollen of the anther first visited—and in this manner migrating

f34   from one part of the corolla to another, & from flower to flower, she fructifies one with Pollen gathered in her search after honey in another.—(a sweet simile or image of perusing books of entertainment, as Poems, Faery Tales, natural curiosities & the like, for purposes of illustration of ~~profoundest~~ scientific Truths—and the impregnation of the Pupil's mind.) Iris Xiphium often barren, where the largest kind of Humble-bees are scarce—these alone being strong enough to force their way beneath its Style-flag.

Aristolochia Clematitis—its mouse-trap for the Tipula pennicornis—which can enter the throat of the flower easily but not return—restlessly moving to and fro it deposits the pollen of the anthers on the stigma, which of themselves have no mechanism for this act—this effected, the obverse hair, which prevented the exit of the Tipula, shrinks to the sides of the flower, and little Penit gets his jail-delivery.

f34ᵛ   No less important are insects in fructifying the Plants of of the Linnean Monœcia, Dioecia, & Polygamia, in which the Stamens are in one blossom & the Pistil in another—as the Insects explore these for honey or for Pollen, the Pollen gets involved in their hair (possibly given them for this end) and is conveyed to the germen requiring its fertilizing influence—(This last would form a fine Simile for Revelation, as effectuating Reason—but not giving any thing different—.

4880 23.36   The vegetivorous Insects (as the Caterpillars) take ~~one~~ a Larva for instance weighing 36 grains, it will be found to void every twelve hours 15-18 grains of excrement, consisting of undissolved vegetable matter from which the juices only had been extracted—& expanding in hot water like our Tea—while the animal itself will not have increased in weight in the same period more than one or two grains.

Object . . Destruction simply.—

The carnivorous Larvæ on the contrary increase in weight proportionally to the food consumed. Redi found that the Flesh fly, maggots, of which 25-30 did not weigh above one grain, in 24 hours afterward weighed 7 grains each—having thus in one day *f35* & night become about 200 times heavier than before. Object— ~~Destruction~~ Remotion of the Destructed for the prevention of the destruction of higher life and nobler Organisms. No vital principle suspending and imprisoning under safe custody the pestilential chemical and chemi-zöic, or disanimate Zöic.※

※ Ex. gr. I should consider the ~~virus~~ vaccine and variolous virus as disanimate Zöic, in distinction from the ammoniacal Gases or malaria, as inanimate or azöic.

4881 23.37 A spider thread not thicker than a human hair = 16000 millions of threadlets—or sixteen thousand millions of the elementary lines of which the webs or nets of the more minute Spiders are composed, equal only to a single Hair of a man's beard—.

4882 23.38 Sir G. Staunton asserts that in the forests of Java Spiders' Webs are found of so strong a texture as to require a sharp cutting instrument to make way thro' them. Pity that he did not procure a specimen & bring them home with him. It woudd be pleasure to see a Sailing-boat rigged with them, twisting the larger threads into ropes and weaving the smaller into a sort of silk canvas—resembling the ⟨indestructible⟩ white cloth of the Arindy or Palma Christi Silkworm/

4883 23.39 The *Raft* Spider discovered by the Rev.ᵈ R. *f35ᵛ* Sheppard on the fen-ditches of Norfolk, sailing on a ball of woods held together by slight silkeny cords—and darting or rather skating out on the surface of the water as soon as it sees a drowning insect, which it carries home to its raft to devour at its leisure— & under this raft has a retiring hole or *hold*.—

4884 23.40 But in proving my scheme of the Insect = Instinctive = Irritability—and that this is = Understanding (¹— or Irritability (³— I mean to catalogue the adaptations of means to

ends of the Insect creation, and on a parallel table the machines &
other contrivances of the human Understanding.

N.b. not to forget Huber—Dozen Humble Bees put under a
bell-glass along with a comb of about ten silken Cocoons so unequal in height as not to be capable of standing steadily—to remedy
which 2 or 3 of the Humble Bees got upon the comb, stretched
themselves over ~~the~~ its edge and with their heads downwards fixed
their forefeet on the table on which the Comb stood, and so with
their hind feet kept the C. from falling—and when these were
weary, others took their places—In this constrained and painful
f36   Posture, fresh Bees relieving their comrades at intervals, did these
affectionate little Insects support the Comb for nearly three days—
at the end of which they had prepared sufficient wax to build pillars
with it—but these having accidentally got displaced, they had again
recourse to the same pedœuvre—till Huber, pitying their hard
case &c &c—

Understanding only means to an *end*—in Man Reason and Will
in the noblest instincts Storgè—~~Synthesis~~ Interpenetrancy of Will
and Reason in the *opake* state. As *Sense* to Reason, so Storgè to R
+ Moral Will—.

Self-finding = Empfindung—. When that, which is found, is
a *seeking*, it is an Empfindung der Sehnsucht, sensatio desiderii—
if *for* self, it is appetite—if ⟨a not-self⟩ *as* Self, yet wholly *for* Self,
it is Lust—if a not-self as a self ~~yet~~ but for a not-self, it is Love—
Love interpenetrating the vital energy, and acting with and on the
Life in the final organization, & along with the Productivity, independent tho' not ~~exclu~~ always or necessarily exclusive of or dis-
connected from the Consciousness,—is Storgè, Virgo Mater in
Metaphysics—.— Λογου Μητηρ τοῦ θεανθρώπου.

4885 23.41   I am not aware of any Language in which there
is an appropriate term for the pothos or desiderium as connected
with the memory of the having possessed that which is now
f36ᵛ   needed, in contra-distinction from the craving after a something
not yet possessed, unless it be our English miss—as "I *miss*" him
sadly—as differenced from "I feel the *want*" of such a one. The
Latin Desiderium is *more* often used for the former, the Greek

ποθος perhaps *more* often for the latter, but neither, I believe, idiomatically or exclusively.

4886 23.42   Q.ʸ—a momentary thought, 2 April 1822, the emotions ex. gr. of Rage, Anger, as of the Bees against the Drones—may they not be ~~occasioned~~ caused as well as occasioned by, nay, may they not consist in, a stoppage of the *Actions*, whether with or without the Motions and Doings consequent on these Actions and the Products of them? What if I translated my meaning into an allegorical eye-language, represented the Animus Substans, or Life⁽² = Irritability. or †το εντομöειδες, by the glutinous semi-fluid in the Spinner-teats of the Spider—the productive acts of this *Substance* or *Under-standing* by the nets and webs.—Now these suddenly checked or crowded back in upon the former so as to dissolve the *form* would convert the irritability into a restless Productivity—where there was nothing to produce, all the organs already existing and the productive energy, ⟨Life⁽¹⟩ their creatress, still working in them as their functions.—This repressed Irrit. Life⁽² can therefore only act on them as *stimulus*—and thus directing them ad extra. A confirmation of this I seem to find in the numerous common-traits between Anger & Lust—which latter I suppose to differ from the former by an awakening of the *Sensibility* in the Productivity/or ⟨in the higher animals⟩ of the Irritability in the Sensibility, by means of the suppressed or congested Irritability in its own ~~Dynast~~ Triarchy. Hence in Insects Lust seems scarcely to exist as *Lust*; but either as Destructiveness or some other *Act*/I mean not as *passion* in the way in which it exists in classes in which Life⁽³ or το ιδιοζωικον exists as a nervous *System*.

   I am aware that this is obscure & confused—but it is a first *Thought* in its semi-fluid or *matter*-of-light state—. *Sting* of the Bee a sexual organ—Death of the Male consequent on coition—. Hence then, perhaps, the rage of the Bees toward the Drones at the close of Summer from *sense* of Inutility becoming as it were a *sensation* of *Utility-checked*—the Substans in congestion.—

                                                                                              f37

† Instead of the vague terms Reproduction, Irritability and Sensibility, I would substitute, 1. το φυτοειδες; 2. το εντομοειδες; 3. το ιδιοζωικον.

                                                                                              f36ᵛ

f37   4887 23.43   How much better it would be to confine animal
to its generic ⟨meaning⟩ instead of using it in the all-common—
Plants, Insects, Animals. At present, it is both universal and gen-
f37ᵛ   eral—Assuredly, the exceedingly small number of Individuals appropriated to the functions of Reproductivity in the most instinctive & intelligent Insects as in the Ants, Bees, and Termites, is a
most noticeable proof of the predominance of the Zoo-electrical
over the Zoo-magnetic in these Primates of the Insect World.—
Add to the incessancy & peristaltic mode of the egg-production in
the Mother termite from a single Impregnation—how like the un-
intermitted discussion, and busy succession of Thought, and the
endless evolution of Thought after Thought, in the Understanding—an *Idea* once given, which is all-present and yet entire in
each, as the germinal power in each egg!—

  Mem.—The terms, Emotion, Passion, Appetite, Affection, are
in a s̶a̶d̶ woeful state of Confusion at present, and sadly want *aus-
einandersetzung*—and Unicuique-suum-appertiency.—

4888 23.44   Kirby and Spence, Vol. II. p. 187 mentions a
fact that seems to confirm my conjecture of the nature of Bee-
Anger—"When one Bee had thus collected its load (of quasi Pro-
polis, from a Bees-wax and Turpentine Tree-bark Plaister) another
often came behind and despoiled it of all it had collected. A second
f38   and third Load were frequently lost in the same manner, and yet
the patient animal (*Insect*) pursued its labors without any signs of
Anger."—The instinct of m̶o̶r̶e̶ a̶c̶c̶u̶r̶a̶t̶e̶l̶y̶ *means*—more accurately,
Instinct—i.e. Understanding considered abstractedly from Self-
consciousness, and the other datum of Reason, Ultimate *End*—was
not contradicted.—

  Even in speaking of the *smell* of Insects we are too apt to potenziate the faculty on an infusion of our own pāssĭŏn or sensibility.—
It is, I doubt not, more of the nature of *Light*—more a *motive*—
as the correlative of means—and less of fruition, o̶r̶ a̶t̶t̶a̶i̶n̶i̶n̶g̶ =
Being + *Having*, as the correlative of *end*.

  The want of this leading Thought is at the bottom of the false
reasoning in so many instances in Huber, Kirby (Vol. II. p. 198-
99—et passim) and all the illustrious Entomologists—who are for-
ever trying to refer the acts of Bees, Ants, &c to some painful or

pleasurable *Sensations*. That in each of the evolutes, A.B.C. the others are involute

4889 23.45   To Christ from Bernard—Nec mihi tua suffi- *f38ᵛ* ciunt sine te, nec tibi placent mea sine me.—N.b. This single Epigram—worth shall I say? O far rather—a sufficient antidote to—a waggon-load of Paleyian Moral and Political Philosophies!—

4890 23.46   On minute Teleology—or the hunt after final causes in detail, a la mode du Durham, Neuwentiet, Lyonnet, & other truly amiable writers—1. the gross of Sophistry. 2. the degrading conceptions of the divine Wisdom—ex.gr. cutting a round bit out of a rose leaf as exact as a Lackwit child could have done with a pair of Scissars—O the divine Wisdom manifested in the Grub! 3. The inutility—for unless you have already by better evidence convinced yourself of the Being, Existence, and Attributes of the Absolute Will-Intelligence-Wisdom, or Power-Light-Love—the final causes present a mere Quarrel of Purposes—Kirby & Spence II.223.—And if you have, they are superfluous. 4. The *f39* injury,—by preventing all pure Beholding (Intuitio, Anschauung) and by accustoming the mind to seek for that in a part as a whole, which can only be found in the Whole—as if a man should seek the entire solution of the Lungs in the Lungs, without reference to the Heart & Brain.—
5. or rather as a corollary of 2.—the ludicrous associations hazarded—Another———affords a *beautiful* instance of the Wisdom of Providence in adapting means to their end. Some singular Grubs, with a radiated *"Anus"*—&c and for what? to enable them to plunder the industrious Bees—with impunity✳—Well! and the sting of the Bees?—Oh! to enable them to punish the Grubs!—
One instance✳ that of the Serpent's fangs (only about a seventh part or less of Serpents venomous, yet the rest saved by the terror inspired by these—which I met with in Paley's Nat. Th.—first opened my eye to the absurdity of the reasoning.—The fact is so notoriously the contrary!—So the luminous Flies *scaring*—and the

✳ ⟨So too the terrific Ugly of Kirby's Stag-beetles, II.ⁿᵈ224–225.⟩

f39ᵛ   brilliant ones dazzling—as if the conspicuity was not ten to one more hazardous.—

Observe. These remarks apply exclusively to *final* causes—and ~~by~~ in no ~~means~~ respect to immediate *ends*—as the correlative of *Means*. This is not only a Contemplation most worthy of a wise man, but an investigation of indispensable value for a Scientific Man—tho' even this must be qualified by the higher Physiology, which teaches us to consider all Insects as one Insect—all Animals as one Animal—and ~~espec~~ often to find the proper end of *a* ~~in~~ as a part of B. either in b, as a part of C. retrospectively, or in c as a part of the superior D. prospectively. The Bones of the Human Ear furnish a remarkable Instance.—

Besides, it might be objected and not unplausibly—that such and such Tools are not in X because X is a Spider; but that X is a
f40   Spider, because it has such and such tools—In fact, both are sophistical, the one as much as the other—just as if I should ~~say that the~~ admire the final cause of the Letters D O G having been asigned to the word, Dog—or on the other suppose that D O G having dropt out of a chest of Types, the word, Dog, ~~had its~~ became a part of the English Language/which we have only to contemplate *a posteriori* to ~~read therein God~~ arrive at the knowlege of G O D—A fair specimen by the bye of Demonstrations of the Supreme Being a *posteriori* in general.—

4891 23.47   *Prolegs*! ! i.e. Forelegs—Dr. Gooch's hyperacute is modesty, in comparison, a blunder of my own. The compound is barbarous and mulish indeed; but Pro = Vice, in stead of, Lieutenant De Legs, not *Fore.*—*Pro*rex, *Pro*consul.—

4892 23.48   The Libellulidæ fly all ways without needing to turn their bodies—onward, backward, right and left—with more than Swallow-rivalling rapidity of wing, readiness of evolution, and indefatigable continuance.

f40ᵛ   4893 23.49   I cannot think that R. Hooke's conjecture as to the white Summer Clouds (mement. those brilliant Purissimæ of White so divinely pencil-shaded, every summer afternoon, about 2 o'clock at Rome—generally but *one* cloud—I never saw more than two) being agglomerations of Gossamer (God's Dame's Hair—Coma Matris Dei—der fligende [*fliegende*] Sommer being probably an unintentional Pun on a Frankish St *Mere*, like our Billy Ruffian = Bellerophon, or from Cymarr, or Samarr—a robe of floss Silk—or silken Veil) so absurd a fancy, as Kirby + Spence denounce it for.—The amiable Historian of Selborne seems to have been of my opinion.

4894 23.50   I have allotted the Musculo-Arterial to the Dynasty of Irritability, = Ins(tin̄)ctivity or τοῦ 'Εντομοειδοῦς—yet the Instinct-creatures, Entoma, Insects have no arteries. I will give my answer in Kirby's words/that the Trachei and Bronchiæ must be considered as their arteries, and the air be regarded as their blood.

Vol. II. p. 363.

2. Insectivity 1. Vegetivity. 3. Animality.

Hence, doubtless, the intensity of the Vis Irritibilitatis in the Muscles of Insects, its concentration. I ought, perhaps, not to leave unnoticed—delicate and obscure as the Idea at present is—the *naturiency* of the Sensibility involved in the Irritability, and which may, nay must, render the Irrit. in some Insects and in some functions & periods of some Insects as different from mere Irrit. as the Reproductivity in the Stamens and Anthers of some Plants are from ordinary reproductivity. The ganglia of Insects are possibly the *Apices* of such Functions. Or Respiration, which in the Mammalia is the Mediator between the Irritability and Sensibility = Heart & Brain, may be the Mediator between the Irritability and Productivity in Insects.—Or both may be severally true.   *f41*

4895 23.51   The merry little Gnats (Tipulidæ Minimæ) I have myself often watched in an April Shower—evidently dancing the hayes in and between the falling drops, unwetted or rather undown-dashed by rocks of water many times larger than their whole bodies. Ephemeræ and other minute but less minute half-transparent Insects do by their exceeding velocity of motion θεωρουντες θεωρηματα πραττουσι a happy and most exact illustration of the identity of the Act of the imaginative Intuitus (Anschauung reine) and its Product, in the mental Diagram.—Figure as the γεννημα   *f41^v*

of Motion.—Such must have been the imagined *strings* of Ephemeræ in articulate Triangles of Silver Lumen round the Torch—as described by Reaumur & quoted by Kirby & Spence, Vol. II. p. 370. ⟨Never⟩ Armillary ⟨Sphere with so many⟩ Zones ⟨as here Circles⟩ with the Flame for their center—crossing each other in all directions, and of every imaginable inclination ⟨—all more or less eccentric.⟩ Each Zone composed of *an unbroken string* (a ~~met~~ an optical deception) of Ephemeræ = a piece of silver lace formed into a circle deeply notched & consisting of equal Triangles placed end to end so that one of the Angles of the Angles of

f42 that which followed touched the middle of the base of that which preceded—.

Reaumur—born in France? If so, his Mother a Semele or Mʳˢ Amphyctyon—Alcmena. ⟨Item: Frenchman against all analogy of Language-Coinage. Man-french, man-frenches. as Horse-radish, Stag-beetle.⟩

Insects garrulous Mutes—incessantly noisy, and everlastingly *mute*.

4896 23.52
That Vegetivity = Zoo-Magnetism,
    Insectivity = Zoo-Electricism,
&   Animality = Zoo-Galvanism
we have proved. May not the Luminosity of certain Insects be a transitional act of Vegetivity into Insectivity—an interens between Magnetism and Electricity, like the Aurora borealis?—Hence so common in the softer Zoo-phytes—or lowest orders of Vermiform Life.—It seems evidently closely connected with the Productivity or Life.⟨¹, and yet with the Pr. in its connection with or ascent into Irrit. or Life⟨²—So in luminous Marigolds—

f42ᵛ 4897 23.53   Monday, April 9, 1822—I have been reading the ⟨first⟩ eleven Chapters of Exodus: and I cannot resist the impression left on my mind, that they are of a later ~~day~~te, a distinct Book, a traditional Life of Moses and his Brother Aaron, previously to the commencement of his Legislatorship—of far higher value indeed, but still analogous to the Gospels of the Infancy— ~~and~~ the first and second Chapters of our present ~~S. Matt & S. Lu~~

Umarbeitung of the Gospel of the Twelve Apostles = S! Matthew;—the first 3 Ch. of Luke—from v.4 ch. I;—and the biography of Daniel, I-VI.—If I were asked by whom compiled? I
should reply—Possibly, by the Rhapsodi, or Homereuomenoi, the
Bards or Prophets, to from whom we the Book of Jesher—or
Cycle of War Songs—the collection of Ballads, rudely organized
into the Historical Book of Judges, proceeded.—Who the Lycurgus, and Pisistratus of these Hebrew Homeridæ? Why not Samuel
& David?

Memento. Where is to be found the Proof, that not the Books
of the Laws of Moses only but the Pentateuch of the Two Tribes
was in the hands of the Priests of the Ten Tribes, at the time of   *f43*
their defection from Rehoboam? Their Book of Joshua was different from the Joshua of Judæa. When we reflect on the comparative
barbarism of the αναλφαβητου realm of Israel—where is the im-
proba⟨bi⟩lity in the supposition that during some one of the Alliances between the two kingdoms, the ruder ~~Kingdom~~ Nation or
its Hierarchy might have adopted the fuller, better arranged, and
more interesting Pentateuch of the more learned Sister Kingdom?—The more so, when the Mosaic Priesthood had always continued the Dominant and Established Church of Judea. Do we not
antedate the Hatred of the Jews & Samaritans?—Ha~~ves~~ not the
Scottish Presbyterian Church adopted the Version of the Prelatic
Church of England? How Many things have not the Jews taken
from the Christians!

4898 23.54   O qualia, O quanta irridentes potuimus ca-
villantesque depromere, si non religio nos gentis✻ et Literarum†
prohiberat auctoritas.
                              ARNOBIUS.

✻ common people
† the sacred Scriptures

4899 23.55   Characteristik der Alten Mysterien für Ge-   *f43ᵛ*
lehrte und Ungelehrte, Frey-Maurer und Fremde, aus den Orig-
inal-Schriften. Franckfurt und Leipsig, 1787.

This anonymous Work—written in opposition to the Extollers
of the Mysteries and the Setters-up of the same as a Christianism

before Christ, is not without its merits among the Surface Books
of the Common-sense Party—and may be read with great advantage after the ⟨mock-learned⟩ infidel works of the other Party who
without a grain more of Philosophy have no Common Sense.—
The Author, however, makes sad work of it in sundry places, and
strangely misrepresents Origen in particular—and this from two
mistakes or rather *nesciences*—1. the rendering Origen's μυθους και
γραμματα fables and letters, instead of symbolic Stories and sacred
Books—from not knowing the true import of *Mythes* or Philoso-
f44   phemes, which Sallust, the Greek Platonist, happily conveys when
he ~~speak~~ describes the Kosmos or material Universe as the Μῦθος
κατ᾽ εξοχὴν and the creative ~~Wisdom~~ Logos as *Myth*ologizing.
Thus too in Origen's belief the transgression of Adam and Eve
was a Muthos, εν γράμμασι ἑβραϊκοις—An Idea shadowed out in
an individual Instance, imaginary or historical—the truth remains
the same. It did take place—and the Individuals, in whom it first
took *place* (realized itself in space, & a fortiori in *time, place* implying both: for space cannot be particularized but in connection
with Time, as the sole measure of Space) were Adam and Eve—
"In whom it *first* took place: in this alone different from all other
Men and Women/—In the former the Individuality is rightfully
assumed—in the second, it is recorded—the Truth is the same in
both, and both alike are Mythic, and belong to Mythology.—2.
The Author is ignorant of the true sense of *the Gods* in the Mysteries and Esoteric Doctrines—viz. *demiurgic* Potences, the Plastic
f44ᵛ   Powers of Nature—Laws as we now say—but but in reference to
different Epochs of the System, some Cosmical, some Geological,
or planetary. Hence therefore in the Ancient Creeds of Paganism
as in the modern Roman, it behoves us to distinguish the ~~Dogma
or Hypothesis~~ Speculative from the Practical, the Dogma or Hypothesis from the Precept or Permission—The one may be ap-
plauded or ~~excus~~used, while the other is utterly condemned—the
belief, for instance, of the Communion of Saints, living and departed, from the Worship of Saints, or rather of individual dead
Men whom others have chosen to consider as Saints.—

4900   23.56   Nothing, however, can be better than Arnobius's Exposure of the Allegorizing of the Muthi into the common

phænomena of Nature—Jupiter = Rain, Ceres = the ⟨vegetable⟩ Earth, Proserpine = the Seed, Pluto = the Subsoil, &c as given in this work, p. 134. The only fair ground of complaint is that Arnobius, who knew nothing of the Mysteries but by Hear-say, and even this in their utmost degeneracy, does not at all [differentiate] the fabulous additions of poets and popular tradition, from *f45* the actual representations in the more August Mysteries, the Eleusinian, Samothracian, Persian and Egyptian, nor even from the Sacerdotal which held a mid-place between the inner Mysteries and the popular Legends. Origen, who had studied the subject, speaks very, very much more respectfully—& favors the opinion of those who regard the Original Doctrines of the Initiated as *refractions* of the Light of the ante-Mosaic or Patriarchal Revelation.—

4901 23.57   Varro's a quo = ex quo — and secundum quod—to which add, actio continua, or ipsa actio—we might apply better than himself

A quo—the Will

Ex quo—the Being. "O ων" of S[t.] John, or the Pleroma Realitatis.

Secundum quod—the Logos, Idea Idearum.

Ipsa Actio—πνευμα τρις αγιον, Love, Wisdom: under which last term the Hebrews before the Incarnation of the Word identified, at least united, the Logos and the Pneuma.—

(*Samothracum*) ~~Fidei~~ *Ecclesiæ* nobilia Mysteria eaque quæ *nec*   *f45ᵛ* *suis* nota sunt, scribendo expositurum pollicetur.

Varro, de seipso.

4902 23.58   Let any unprejudiced man conversant with the Canons of Criticism in respect of Authenticity, and especially of Autobiography or contemporary History as distinguished from compilations founded on Traditions and Inferences (ex. gr. Inventions of Harmonists for the purpose of reconciling contradictory Reports & Documents, among which the multiplication of the same incident into several separate events holds a prominent place, IV.2–9—with anticipations of events in the form of prescript or prophecy, III.22) read δ—and ask himself, whether this disjointedure or rather ~~fragment~~ succession of out of their places frag-

ments could have been written by the Pars-maximist himself?—
24, 25, 26 v.

f46   Take again the V.th Is it credible, that even a Contemporary, much ~~more~~ less than thant an Eye-witness, and that Witness a fellow-sufferer, but least of all that the Leader, Planner, principal Agent recording the particulars of his own Enterprize, and that so momentous as the Emancipation of a whole People and the Foundation of a New State (the only pure Theocracy and the Sun and open Eye of Monotheism on the World/

f66ᵛ 4903 29.97   6 July 1822. I have myself too often, of late, harrassed with ἀρτλι's idiocies, used the phrase "rational Self-love", the same as "enlightened Self-love".—& no more of this! What have Love, Reason or Light to do with *Self*, except as the dark and evil Spirit which it is given them to overcome?—*Soul*-love, if you please.—O there is more stuff of thought in our simple and pious 'Fore-elders' adjuration—Take pity of your poor Soul! than in all the volumes of Paley, Rochefacault and Helvetius.

4904 29.98   A Tyrant is only a Monstrous Phantasm upsteaming from the Grave and Corruption of the huddled Corses of the self-murdered Virtue & inner freedom of the People—i.e. the Majority of the Citizens of the State.

4905 29.99   Tuesday, July 1822—23ʳᵈ Day of Derwent's Fever!—God be merciful to me.—Turned a poor (very large & beautiful) Moth out of Window in a hard Shower of Rain to save it from the Flames!

f67 4906 29.100   Oft Jahre wie nichtig!—Augenblicke wie wichtig! Years in a moment & Years but a moment. Such difference is there between Man and Man!

4907 29.101   It seems to me, that the difference in the doctrine of the Holy Ghost as taught by the Greek and by the Latin Church, arose from the former contemplating the Trinity chiefly in relation to the World, natural and physical while the Latin or Western Church dwelt on it as the Self-manifestation of Deity,

without reference to the μη οντως οντα. Hence the Greeks presented the Νους as uttering in the same act the Logos & the
πνευμα, the word and the Breath.—But this is at best a very inadequate presentation, appears from its not containing any ground
for the distinction between filiation & procession, nor can it be
congruously said that the Spirit proceedeth even *thro'* the Son—!
—Se effundens + Effluens se refundens + the Unity of Ef. and
Re fundence—the one Result proceeding from both.—Forms +
Lux + Lumen = Sol. But the Lux lucifica contains the Radii
Luciferi—the Heavenly Host, Uranions, Ideæ deiformes, Veritates
eternæ Pleroma Actualitatum.—How art thou fallen, Lucifer,
Son of the Morning.—But as these, suppressing the Spirit (the re
fundence) evacuated themselves of their actuality, and became
merely *potentials*—even so thro' the Spirit of Love the Son suffered
the inanition of his *Divinity* (actus absolutus sine potentialit[at]e)
and ~~be~~ made himself *Man—.perfect Man*, i.e. a Being in whom
the Potential was subordinated to the Actual, in order that the P.
should ultimately be swallowed up in the Actual (& God be all in
all)—as the Luciferi became evil Spirits, the actual lost in ⟨or
transformed into⟩ the Potential.—

    To Θειον—wholly Actual—το πονηρον wholly potential, το αν-
θρωπινον $\dfrac{\text{actual}}{\text{potential}}$ or $\dfrac{\text{potential}}{\text{actual}}$; but in either case bi-polar.

4908   29.102   Dr Passavant (Frankfurt A.M. 1821) has enlivened and renewed my interest in the Magia Thelematica, The-   *f67ᵛ*
lematomagy, or Zoo-magnetism; but in other respects has left me
as he found me. My convictions are contained in the following
Articles of Belief. I am satisfied—
    First, that the Idea is legitimate and philosophical, both in re-
spect of the Agent and Patient. It is consistent in all its Terms,
and I see no reason precluding its reality. I find no impossibility
either in the human Will ~~becoming~~ extending its influence beyond
the visible outline of the Willer's own body; or ~~of~~ in the metastasis
of the sentient power from one part of the Nervous System to ~~the~~
another, as from the cerebral to the pectoral or gangliac; or the
energizing of the Mother-sense in the net work of the cutaneous
nerves into a higher, and more specific Sense; or lastly, in the

existing of a percipiency of the invisible Man beyond, and in certain states and under certain suspensions of the Activity of the bodily Organs, independent of theese Organs. And I have long been convinced myself, and before I became acquainted with the discoveries of Mesmer, that there is a recollective Faculty far higher ⟨than⟩ and altogether distinct from the passive Memory— and the latter alone is a function of the Organization and conditioned by the state of the Brain.

Secondly, that the argument from analogy, in favor ex. gr. the evident existence of a magical Energy throughout the Creation, and that it is the ground and pre-condition of the Mechanical, even as Gravitation is supposed in the Lever, Screw, and Pully; that *f68* this manifests itself most clearly in the Organic World; and more and more clearly, the higher and more complete the Organization is; that the more perfect and exquisite the Organization is, the more distinctly are the Revelations of a Power higher than the Organic Function, and that in the highest Organ, the Brain, the Organization seems to sink under its own power subtlety, and to becomes shapeless for the outward senses; above all, the Depth is not a form of *Space*, yet Length and Breadth are mere empty forms without Depth, and are in fact no other than the forms by which the Depth reveals itself;—these, I say and other arguments from analogy in presumption of Powers and Faculties affirmed to have been exerted and called forth in the processes of Zoo-magnetism, are numerous, weighty, close, and catenated—and I know of no tenable argument from analogy against their existence on the other side.

Thirdly, that the supposition of the truth of Zoo-magnetism enables us rationally to account for a series of Phænomena hitherto unexplained, or most unsatisfactorily explained away with Lies, Tricks, or the Devil, the Oracles of the ancients, Charms, Amulets, witchcraft, Prophecies, Divination, and extra ordinary Mem Individuals, as the Female who misled Montanus & thro' him Tertullian, Behmen, Swedenborg, & (according to his their own declarations, Philo Judæus, and Porphyry) and of a lower kind, Bleton, Aymar, Pedegache, Campetti, the Zahuris of Spain, & (still living) the Swiss Female, Catharina Beutler—. And that it is a special advantage of Zoo-magnetism that by the very same means, with which it is confirmed, it removes & answers before hand, the objections of the invalidity of human Testimony &c grounded in the assumed utter Falsehood and mere Delusion of all the Facts or Narrations above mentioned.   *f68ᵛ*

Lastly, the deep Moral Interest, which in every Moral Being is excited by the presentation of these Ideas in an historical form— the death-blow given by the philosophy of Zoo-magnetism to Materialism, Sensuality, and *Worldliness* on one hand, and to Superstition and Credulity on the other, ought to be considered as an argument of their truth, in the absence of all sufficient proof to the contrary. There must be Truth in that, which every good and wise man must wish to be true: nor need the strongest mind be ashamed of an argument which beyond all others weighed with Socrates, Plato, and Tully, in the belief of Immortality.—I am aware, that the Theory and Cases of Zoo-magnetism may suggest, nay already have suggested, to the Infidel, plausible grounds for *explaining down* the Facts recorded by the Inspired Writers and Inspiration itself into a mere Natural Magic—but in the first place, this attempt was made by the Contemporaries of the Apostles, and in fact by all Infidels who were not likewise Materialists & Epicureans, during the firstve first centuries of the Church, and was repeated by the Italian Paganists at the restoration of Literature. It cannot therefore be attributed to Mesmer or Mesmerism, tho' it may have & has been re-animated and made more distinctly intelligible—and in this secondly, it is a mere primâ facie plausibility, which not only disappears on closer view but leaves in its stead the strongest confirmation of the Divinity of the Christian Faith, by acquainting us with the summits of human nature, on which the Divine, as it were, alighted.—The legitimate *Theory* of Zoo-magnetism spiritual Intuition (clair-voyance, Hell-sehen, Inward Vision) every where *supposes* a Divine, above and free from Nature—& then presents and demonstrates the *Basis* in human Nature, the recipiency & the necessity of a Super-natural, in order to actuate & actualize the Base.—As well and as reasonably might the Qualities of the Marble or the Canvas be urged against the reality of the Sculptor or Painter, as the pre-conformity and pre-   *f69* established Suspiciency of the human Mind in its freest state be urged against its Inspiration actual Receipt of the Gift—. To show the inspirability of Man is one half of the Proof of positive Inspiration in some men.—

These are my convictions—and with such convictions, wherein
consist my Doubts? Of what do I complain.—I answer with perfect simplicity—that the Cases detailed and the Facts substantiated
of the most celebrated Clear-Seeers and Extasists do not *bear out*
the Theory—In no one of their Revelations, physical, physiological, or spiritual, have I found more than recollections of what they
had before heard or read or seen, blended with wild fancies—(I
am speaking now of *Truths*, not of Images or Persons.—Take as
instance their descriptions of the inward parts and structure, and
the particular appearances therein, of their own bodies or those of
others *in report* with them—Has Anatomy derived a simple addition of a Nerve, or a Mode of action of a Nerve? And what wild
stuff, of co-agulated Blood in the Vessels, Pimples on the apex of
the Heart, &c&c? Are not the Images clearly the Products of
Sensations explained by the Fancy as in ordinary Dreams?—

The final Impression on my Mind, therefore, is: that we ought
to begin at the other end—namely, from the individual Cases,
selecting chronologically such a number as that all the remarkable
Phænomena of Magnetized Patients should be found in some one
or other of the Cases selected.—and then drawing from each part
the fair inference, of which it is capable, or rather, simply generalizing their import. Wienholt comes the nearest to this—but
neither he, nor Kluge, keep faithful to their intention, too often
blending the facts with their Theory, and still oftener inferring
more than the Facts of Necessity required & describing them in
words, to which the Facts by no means correspond.

f69ᵛ 4909 29.103   Mem. Wednesday, 29 July 1822. Read Haliburton's Life—from his own account of his *"Outgate"* and Conversion or Birth of the Spirit, as from similar relations of others
who like Haliburton had been previously or even from Infancy
~~promising~~ engaged in religious thoughts, studies and struggles,
that this New-birth consists in a peculiar *state* of Being—that the
New Light is not any New Sense recognized in the words or truths
of Scripture, but as being otherwise affected and impressed
thereby, with a power of approximating the same to his own particular case. Hence it comes, I suppose, that there is no where

found in the so called *Experiences* of these good men any exposition of what they precisely mean by the *Blood* of Christ, it being evident that in many passages it ~~stan~~ is more than a mere Synonime of the Death of Christ. It is often difficult to understand them as not intending the visible and tangible Fluid, or rather that portion or portions exuded by "the Man, Jesus" in his agony, and shed first at his circumcision, and afterwards from the Thorns, the Nails, and the Spear or Halberd—and equally or more difficult to understand how it is possible for such men (such at least as some of these Writers unquestionably were, Archbish. Leighton for instance) to mean this. Perhaps, the true Solution of the Problem is that they never clearly and distinctly put the question to themselves—and that the phrase had its correspondent not in any Idea, or Conception but in the Feelings or in that negative Unity, or Allness which arises from the confusion & indistinction of a Multitude of Thoughts existing for the Consciousness only in the Common impression.—This, however, is little more than a matter of ~~course~~ curiosity, and at the utmost has only a psychological interest. Far otherwise is it with another Question—namely, what do the Scriptures, what did the Apostles, John and Paul, mean by the Blood of Christ? What did our Lord himself mean to convey, John VI? The redeeming Blood is here stated not as that which Jesus was to shed but that ~~of~~ which we are to *drink*, and of which whosoever drinketh not cannot be saved—and this, he explained, was a *spiritual* Substance. Now St John as an Eye-witness assures us that the Blood which Jesus shed on the Cross or rather which flowed from the wound in his side after his disanimation was not ⟨a⟩ spiritual but a proper corporeal & animal Blood consisting of Lymph and Cruor like that of all other Men.—My own opinions I have disclosed in part in a marginal note in the first Vol. of Leighton's Works.— *f70*

Haliburton is one of many instances of pious and learned Men, ~~who were~~ Searchers in good earnest, and not eristic or keen Players at the Game of Disputation, ⌐. . .⌐ who was after a full conviction of a consciousness surviving the Death of the Body were sorely tempted with doubts respecting the reality ~~of~~ and the actual existence of *a* Supreme Being, personal and super-mundane—and who at last found no satisfaction either in the ontological Proof (Om-

nibus dependentibus præsumitur independens) or in the physico-
theological a posteriori—i.e. from the established harmony of
things, with the former as an Heterozetesis, and not proving what
was wanted to be proved—(A is: but B + C = A. Therefore A
is.)—The evidence, by which they conquered, ~~were~~ was first
moral—the necessity of the Faith in order to morality, or the moral
interest—(the imperative of Conscience. and 2nd Spiritual—in Thy
Light did I see Light.—

f70^v   In like manner with regard to the written Word. The belief of
the Inspiration of the *Books* increased as the importance of the
~~Article~~ credendum diminished, and became compleat as the latter
became almost evanescent. For an insight into the moral and spiritual truth of all the contents of a Book, one of the contents of
which is that all moral and spiritual Truth is inspired by the Holy
Spirit, is an insight into the truth of the Inspiration of the Book
as the aggregate of the Contents. This ascertained, what consequence can it be whether the mechanical Act of putting ~~them~~ words
on parchment or paper or brass was or was not by an impulse
distinguishable from the ordinary co-operation of the divine Power
with the impulses and voluntary Acts of good Men? In all cases
but that of the Autograph, or ⟨first⟩ Reduction of the Words ~~to~~ of
the Dictator to characters, in the Transcripts, and Translations, no
such question is mooted.—But especially useful in the unripe &
struggling time of Faith is the reflection—that such and such positions are ~~unwritten~~ expressions (that these are true—eminently,
vitally true—and that their truth is not and cannot be at all affected
by the character of other passages—and the truth such that what
motive can I have troubling myself? Then comes the recollection,
in how many instances equal or greater difficulties have perplexed
me & after a time, ~~even when~~ not seldom, unawares, changed into
beauty & confirmations. For instance, in what way can my Assurance of the necessity, my faith in the reality, and my Hope ~~of~~
⌈ . . . ⌉ in true participation, of Redemption by the Incarnate
Word be connected with the Question respecting the six first Chapters of Daniel—viz. whether they form a proper part of the prophetic Book or are a biographical Preface to it, by a writer of a
later age.—and whether founded on documents or on popular Traditions?—The Bible is all Life—like the Polypus.

Smiles of the Soul that almost wasted Nature. Haliburton, p.   *f7¹*
193.—withered?—

The State of clear Vision (des Hellsehens) thus described by
Plotinus.—It is given to the Wise Man or Initiate—Ὁρᾶν δε εστιν
ενταυθα κακεινον (Θεον) και εαυτον, ως ορᾶν θεμις· εαυτον μεν
αγλαιομενον, φωτος πληρη νοητοῦ, μαλλον δε φως αυτο, καθαρον, κου-
φον, αβαρη, θεον γενομενον, μαλλον δε οντα, αναφανεντα μεν τοτε·
ει δε παλιν βαρυνοιτο, ως μαραινομενον.—

Psalm 82. v. 6. F. I have said, Ye are Gods: and all of you
Children of the Most high. But ye shall die like Men and *fall like*
one of the Princes. What can these last words mean? Princes =
δυναμεις η δυνασται εκ του πληρωματος αποστατai; Αεραρχοι;—

In the highest State the antithesis of Subject and Object ceases,
and with it ceases the ordinary consciousness, and the communicability (of the seen, των ορωμενων) by words or signs—Hence
(says Pl.) it was forbidden to attempt such communication in the
Mysteries—for it would be as vain as to attempt to communicate
to another one's whole Soul.—It would be more to the purpose to
say—that the Seer and the seen being the same, and (were even
tho' this were not the case, yet) the seen not existing in the world
of the senses—it cannot be presented anew as when I give a man
my sense of a Diamond by showing it—nor can it be conveyed by
words—for all words represent abstractions and generalizations
only—but here no abstraction nor generalization has place, from
the absolute simplicity of the matter to be represented. Only by
reproducing it—and for this are the Mysteries.

The most objectionable Particular in Haliburton's System and
Autobiography is the constant effort to bring all and each of his
Sins (i.e. every thought, wish, want of wish, all that he considered
as results & proofs of original corruption) in vivid detail into
distinct consciousness—Ah—how many would such a Forcing of   *f7¹ᵛ*
the Soul into a familiarity with Sins have led to Despair, or Ob-
duration, or Antinomian Licentiousness, or Spiritual Pride & Hypocrisy! To borrow a not too elegant image from his own book,
and which ⟨he⟩ was said told, had been used by Francesco de
Sales—who that had been brought by a gracious Ransomer, who
had redeemed ⟨him⟩ from the most abject Slavery and the filthiest

dungeon, to an aromatic Bath, & with a ~~pure~~ snow-white and beautiful garment on the margin prepare[d] for him after his purification, would stay to pick at, examine, and catalogue all the Lice, Fleas, and Bugs, one by one, in the old filthy rags—or afterward return to them for this purpose—nay, fervently entreat his Benefactor to help him, and point out any that might have skipped or crawled out of his sight?—The Moravian Doctrine in this point is incomparably both more Christian and more philosophical.—

fx79   Compare the 5 last lines of p. 19 and the 3 first of p. 20—with the two following sentences.—May we not suspect, that Haliburton ~~must~~ intended something ⟨more⟩ by Adam's Sin, or rather that he included or involved something more *in* the Sin of Adam, than the mere words express? If *with* Adam we all suffer the penalty, individually and personally—does not the parity of reason require, that *with* Adam we must commit the offence?—Must not ~~the~~ "in" contain the sense of the *"with"* not in respect of Time or Place—

fx79ᵛ   but of co-presence as to that which is wholly irrelative to Time and Space—and transcendent. Therefore, I do not say that *with* Adam we *did* commit the offence.—I have not sa~~y~~id—must we not *with* Adam (i.e. as well as Adam) *have* offended?

I am convinced that the main difficulty and perplexity respecting the admission of Original Sin results from the want of understanding and considering, that ⟨the Will and⟩ that the Acts of the Will are not *in* Time any more than in Space—neither *before* nor *after*—but *timeless*/even as Thought is *spaceless*.

f71ᵛ   4910 29.104   The incomparable Passage in W. Wordsworth's incomparable Ode—Our birth is but a sleep—Earth strews her lap—Abound even with something of a Mother's mind—And no unworthy Aim The homely Nurse—&c is prefigured in coarser Clay, ~~and~~ by a less mastering hand & with a less lofty Spirit, yet excellent in its own kind by Henry More, Stanz. 5. 6. 7. of his Poem on The Pre-existency of the Soul.

5
Thus groping after our own Center's near
And proper substance, we grew dark, contract.✻

✻ partic. passive

Swallow'd (up) [†] of earthly life, ne what we were
Of old, thro' ignorance can we detect.
Like noble babe by fate, or friends' neglect
Left to the care of sorry salvage wight,   *f72*
Grown up to manly years cannot conject
His own true parentage, nor read aright
What Father him begot, what Womb him brought to light.

6

So we as stranger Infants elsewhere born
Cannot divine from what Spring we did flow,
Ne dare these base Alliances to scorn
Nor lift ourselves a whit from hence below;
Ne strive our parentage again to know,
Ne dream we once of any other stock
Since foster'd upon RHEA'S *knees we grow,*
In Satyrs' Arms with many a mow and mock
Oft danc'd, and hairy Pan our Cradle oft hath rock'd.

⟨Rhea, the Earth as the transitory ever-flowing Nature—the sum
of ~~the~~ Phænomena or Objects of the outward Senses—in contra-
dist. from the Earth as Vesta/ = the eternal Law, from ῥεω, fluo.
Satyrs the sports and desires of the sensuous Nature. Pan = the
total Life of the Earth, the presence of all in each, Universal
Organismus of bodies & bodily Life.⟩

7

But Pan nor Rhea be our parentage!
We been the offspring of all-seeing Jove
&c

Whĕthĕr = whēthr in old poets frequent.—And the forcible use   *f72ᵛ*
of the verb, been, not as an Elleipsis for *have been*, but as a tense,
containing in one the force of are and were—or Præteritum adhuc
presens, or Præteritum continuum.

The renitence against ~~the~~ employing ~~of a word~~ in its ~~proper~~
general and primary sense, ~~when this has been~~ a word of frequent
and almost hourly occurrence in a secondary and particular sense—

† ⟨*Swal'd up*
⌣ ⌣ — for ⌣ —

for instance, Passion is simply the antithet of Action. More uses *perpession*. Q⸿—All ear, all eye—Sphere of pure Sense which no perspessions curb Nor uncouth Shapen Spectres ever can disturb. Stanz. 14.—

Our particle *fore* an unfortunate equivocalizing pseudography for ver (pronounced fer) having the force of fahren or fahren lassen—to make away. Kochen to boil, verkochen, to boil away—Reissen to rend, verreissen to rend away.—Thus foreslow their flight—to make the flight *slow* away, diminish into slowness.—In the common sound of forget, I *hear* that it was originally *fer*get.

Stanza 17—Asserting the same theory of earthly-minded Souls haunted their sepulchres and linger near Their wonted homes, and oft themselves they show—very ingeniously in

Stanza 18. Illustrates this by Somnambulists—there being no other difference than that the latter Souls have a ⟨dead-asleep⟩ body to lug about, instead of hover over.

> For men that wont to wander in their sleep
> By the fixt light of inward phantasie
> Tho' a short fit of Death fast bounden keep
> Their outward sense, and all their Organs tie;
> Yet forth they fare, steared right steadily
> By that internal guide: even so the Ghosts
> Of men deceas'd, bedewed with the sky:
> And night's cold influence, *in sleep yclos'd*
> *Awake within*, and walk in their forewonted coasts.

f73 This might be made phy~~soph~~siologically *plausi*ble by placing the difference in the total death of the sepulchral body—so that there is no life to serve as a copula or magic Hook, between it and the life of the Soul—whereas in the Sleep-walker, tho' the Idiozoic Life be dead pro tempore, yet the Zoë entomöides, instinctive, insectiform Life (the Irritability, or Arterio-muscular Life, and the Ζωη φυτοειδης, or vegetable Life (vis vegeta) or parenchymatous and veno-glandular Vitality, are alive—and in fact the idiozoic, with exception of the *aesthetic*.—Q⸿ ~~Thus:~~ In cases of proper Neurolepsia when the Body's highest Life is deprived of her lower instrumental parts, we find the secretions approach to simple & elementary natures—Gas, Water—But is not secretion = attraction? Analogia. might not the Soul be imagined to have the power of attracting air or vapor—or when not that, as too complex yet perhaps *auras electricas*—so as to produce visible motion tho' she could not produce visible forms?—Answer. O yes! you may imagine, what you look—not contradicting geometry—i.e. you may bring words together without perceiving their incongruity.

Were there no other operative causes, as there are many, for the partial diffusion and sudden decay of Platonism in the 16th and 17th Centuries, its obscure and in part erroneous exploration of *Matter*, and the frequency with which the Platonists confounded Matter with Body, would have sufficed. In Henry More who blended the Doctrine of Des Cartes (viz. that Matter is mere extension, and that Body and Soul or Spirit are h essentially heterogeneous, with his the Notions of Plotinus, which are built on the assumption of their being differences in degree, Body being the dying-away of Spirit into its last vibrations & echoes, this incongruity is especially prominent and revolting. Matter is mere Potentiality, Potentiality, mere Non-entity, & yet this non-entity makes a great plays the part of a most energetic Figurante in all possible forms, attracts and is attracted, exerts magic influences, bird-limes Spirits &c. In short, the πρωτον ψευδος of all those Schemes is that they commence with an Abstraction, that is, an *Object*. Hence whatever is in its nature incapable of being contemplated objectively, and which as the I, We, with all the Affections and Passions, are not explained at all, or with more than Stoical Bravado called Nothings, that require and permit no explanation— tho' in every Object these Subjects are supposed, in order to its being an Object.—Once again and yet from the same cause Explanations are endlessly sought for, in lieu of that insight which Ideas alone can afford—for no an Abstraction quoad Abstraction is necessarily incomplete, and supposes a something from which it is abstracted; but this again is an Abstraction, and so on ad infinitum.—This, however, is an evil common to the Pseudo-platonists with the Epicurean-Naturalists; but it is peculiar to the former, that their Objects being either properly subjective, as the Soul, or Transcendent, as Deity, their Explanations are all not so much suppositions or hypotheses, as *Suffictions* or hypopoieses—ex. gr. the eight orbs, Monadical, Intellectual, Psychical, Imaginative, Sensitive, Spermatical, Quantitative, and Hyle or coactive—And

f73ᵛ

yet the Attention of the Soul being throughout intentionally and professedly directed to her highest Interests, those Writers have cannot but have a charm for Minds, that feel and struggle up against the weight and witchery of Custom and yearn for an evi-

f74   dence and a reality beyond what the flux of the Senses can afford! and after all, if there be not some third better than either, it is nobler and perhaps wiser to dream about realities, than to be grave-awake about dreams!—

4911 29.105   Easily, I find by experience, may the Anti-nicene Fathers be misunderstood and misquoted by the Arians from the necessity of long experience in the choice of words so as to avoid the⟨ir⟩ unmeant yet possible meaning—the sense, of which they cannot be deprived, tho' it was altogether absent from the Mind of the Employer.—Thus: in revising my lucubrations on the Trinity, I find that I have repeatedly distinguished the Father and the Son, that as self-originant & self-subsistent, this as self-subsistent tho' originating in the Father—But of late I had occasion to state the position—Evil (or Sin) *is*. It is originant, i.e. has an origin, i.e. is not eternal. Even therefore it did not originate in God, who is the Eternal—and here I saw an inherent sense of the word, origin, which gave an impropriety to its application to the co-eternal/and for ~~not~~ "self-originant["] and "not self-originant["] I would substitute self-existent or self-caused, & not self-existent yet self-subsisting.—And yet my meaning was the same then as now—and my writings taken collectively would leave no doubt of my meaning—the particular sentences might be quoted in favor of a quasi creation of the Son—or that he had an origin, a first com-mencement—that he was not ἐν ἀρχῇ but απο τῆς αρχης.—

4912 29.106   Of the Measures of Time in Daniel, as a ["]Time, & Times & half a time," &c. I should not say with the Run of Commentators, that the numbers are not to [be] interpreted

f74ᵛ   with chronological accuracy—for that is to say, that they are false or inaccurate—and therefore irreconcilable with inspiration—: for why not make them accurate? If the Days were in fact ⌐ . . . ⌐ 1350, by what strange and perverse predilection for the Numbers,

1270, could these latter have been adopted?—But I should infer, that they expressed a measurement of Time proper to the Soul in the state of inward Vision, or the super-organic state—and what if one part of the Pythagorean Wisdom consisted in a *part* knowledge, & part seeking after the knowledge or principle, of this psychical Chronometry?—It is possible that it may not be commensurable with ordinary Time, or abstract succession of infinite moments in parallel Lines equal to one line. The Soul may have in the necessity of its specific finiteness alternate immersions ⟨in⟩ or relapses into, the Super-conscious & Universal, & emersions— these its nights, those its days.—And the Fulfilment may be according to the same, in its Spirituality—independent of the historical Manifestations or Symbols of the same in the Mechanism of the Sensible World.—

4913 29.107 The strong argument in support of the Old Testament Writings in general derivable from the palpable proofs given of the fallibility of the arrangers of our present Canon, and their want of Taste, Judgement, and competent Knowlege, in the erroneous Inscriptions of many of the Psalms & Oracles—and from the attachment or prefixture of Names (vide Eichhorn/—ex. gr. that of Solomon to Ecclesiastes.

4914 29.108 Two things I disapprove, the one in several of the Divines before the Restoration—the other in only not all of the C. of E. Divines since.—The first a boastful and exaggerated display of the Christian Mysteries, as so many conundrums seemingly in imitation of the Stoic Paradoxes—Ex. gr. Lord Bacon's Christians Faith—of these Voltaire & Volney are mere but mischievous Plagiaries. The Conundrum consists in stating the Transcendents of Reason, above or rather alien to, the Understanding, as contradictions to Reason—to that Reason which they *are*!—The other is the cowardly and unfair way of stating the arguments of Infidels— which with generous minds in youth is enough to make them infidels a priori.— *f*75

4915 29.109 *Most important.* In proportion as Religions are founded on the *Senses* (as the Romanist) or on the understanding in exclusion of the Reason, as the Unitarian & Mahometan, must be their tendency to *persecution*. Mahometanism, persecution justified by its followers on this ground—& the same with the modern Jews. ~~Th~~ We ask nothing but what every man must assent to, except from a diseased intellect or corrupt motives—Every man, who is not convinced by Priestly or Belsham, must be either a fool or an hypocrite: thinks the Unitarian.—For the same reason the Mystics have been always tolerant even to extremes. We have what the Many have not—God grant that their day may come—for our hearts yearn toward them.

4916 29.110   Why so outraged against Volney?—I read him, when young and exclaimed Shame on this slanderer of the Christian Faith! I read him a few years after & then sighed—
     Shame fall on those, who thus had taught it him!
     In other respects, the Ruines had as little effect on my mind as the Railings of a Pol Parrot over the door of a Wapping Bagnio.
f75ᵛ   And why? because I had never been taught ⟨to consider⟩ such doctrines, as ⟨parts of⟩ Christian Faith: ~~or be~~ Because I could safely laugh with the Author at absurdities that had never formed any part of *my* Christianity, or of the Religion which my Instructors in School, or in Church or by the Fire-side, had represented as such. For instance: I ~~ha~~ could laugh at the notion of the Son of God being *as old* as his *Father* because I had been made to see that to apply the term old or aged ⟨at all⟩ to ~~God and the~~ any *Eternal* Beings, ~~was for~~ was preposterous, and a contradiction in terms— ⟨but⟩ not more ridiculous when affirmed of the Son than ~~were~~ the comparative (older) would be if attributed to the Father—and I know that in the right sense & with the term actually used in the Christian Creed, the Christian says nothing more of the *adequate*, & therefore ⟨the⟩ *substantial*, Idea (or Intelligible) of the Supreme Mind than Volney himself & all his fellow-infidels who deny a time-beginning to the World yet admit a supreme Intelligent First Cause, must & do believe of the World—viz. that it is an effect co-eternal with its cause.—In like manner with the rest of Volney's Pseudo-Christian Creed (Ruines, Chap. XXI.)—either the articles or the terms expressing them were not to be found in my Bible or Prayer-book, or used in a sense haud ejusdem generis; or lastly,

the historical inductions, ex. gr. the co-incidences with the Zenda-
vesta, the Veda, ~~the~~ with Buddaism, Lamism, & the like, stripped
of their factitious drapery, unproved antiquity, and whimsical
most aribtrary connections with Astronomy (the mnemonic of
which presupposes the Mythic Fables, it is absurdly asserted to   *f76*
have given rise to & to form the meaning of) not only may be ~~as~~
safely admitted but must be advanced & established as an essential
part of the Evidence of Christianity, but its enlightened Assertors.—Such was the effect of Volney on my mind & such must it
be on all minds similarly instructed, but if the effect is the contrary, must it not be that the Reader was conscious that he had
hitherto ~~understood~~ believed the doctrines of Christianity to be thos
stated by Volney, and had understood them in the same sense as
Volney represents them—in short, if after reading or hearing
⟨heard⟩ read the passage ~~p.beg~~ commencing with the words—Et
tenant d'une main la bible, p. 159, and ending at *de se perdre*, l.
15. p. 160, if he have been bred a sacramentary Protestant, or at
des hommes six lines further on, if as a Romanist or a Lutheran, he
says—This is ~~what I~~ our Religion—This is what I have been
taught that it is my duty to believe.—The effect, ~~I grant~~ ⟨of such
a work as Volney's on such Readers will be likely to prove⟩ a
mournful and pernicious effect—but is it Volney's Fault or the
Preachers & Instructors of Volney & the Reader?—

4917 29.111   Mem.—Partial Decortication, occasioning the
production of Flowers & abundant Fruit instead of Leaf-Buds. Consult Darwin's *Phytologia*, p. 378—and confirmed by W. Spence,
Esqre, F.L.S. in Tilloch's Phil. Mag. June 1822, N°. 290, Page
439.—In the same number an account of the Fly, from whose
eggs proceed the Gooseberry Caterpillar—a Fly in all respects
(*transparent* wings) except in its metamorphosis which is not of the
Phalæna & Papalas genus—female just like the common Housefly,
only the body is yellow—Male larger, & thinner—body the size
of a common Pin—Both remarkably stupid & easy-caught.—The
remedy recommended, to stink off the Fly by reeds or Tow steeped
in Tar Oil. Tar-oil, twisted at the lower part of the Stem & among   *f76ᵛ*
the Branches—from the beginning of March to April—. The
Horticultural Society had before recommended the digging up &

taking away the superficial earth a few inches from around the Root
of the Tree & filling it up with quick lime.—

f103ᵛ   4918 25.98   Dress, Furniture, &c Elongations of human
Physiognomy—

4919 25.99   Mem. against the Physiocratic System—The
Land or Soil not the essence, nor the Substance of the *State*. How
should it be, whether it is not so of the meanest plant, that strikes
root in it. It is a condition, indispensable on the rule, tho' Tyre,
Sidon, Carthage, Holland, approach to *exceptions*. A mighty auxiliar—but it may be so mighty in itself, as to become an impediment as in the rank richness of tropical climates, in which man
himself suffers himself to be conquered by it, and sinking below
individuality to be incapable of State-Unity—a savage, or a herding
Barbarian.—A State, like a River, constitutes its own products—
*sub*sists in its own productive *Ideas*.—

4920 25.100   Mem. versus Canning's *additional* argument,
i.e. argument not borrowed from *The* FRIEND. In consistency you
(Reformer) ought not to confine Reform to the H. of C.—The
House of Lords must have equal demands to be reformed/. Answer. Why not? That the King is allowed to _make_ Peers ad libitum,
o egregious Reformers—The State can only declare, that such a
man *is* a Peer—.

f103   4921 25.101   All the inhabitants of a Country except the
Possessors and Cultivators of the Soil, the only proper *productive*
Class, are Aliens, to whom Protection is afforded, sold or bart-
ered—. The Land is the State—and these are Strangers in the
Land.—/ So say the Physiocrats to the Artists, the Artisans, the
Men of Science &c—& so (could it speak) would the Dung-heap
say to the Melons & Pine-apples, that grow thereon—and the
Night-man to the Gardener and Botanist.—

4922 25.102   The momentous Error of H. Steffens in his
Conception of the State, as an Institute for the mutual redemption
of Men—i.e. that the State is the Church, or that the Church

ought to be the *State.*—I have in part confuted this notion by anticipation in the Letters to Judge Fletcher—but the full confutation is contained in the right idea of the State as the − Pole, the Church being the +, & both the Thesis & Anti-thesis of the ⊕ or +o or + × −/Plus multiplied into minus—Hence the State = sum of *negative* Forms, formative by resistance of form ab intra, or *positive* forms—a continued production of good by lessening its own evil (*nature* of evil—S^t. Paul of Concupiscence), and this by *f102^v* equalizing not mechanically but by proportion to the forms resis⟨t⟩ed. The *Bee-hive,* as constructed by the Insects themselves, a beautiful Illustration.—The only plausible objections (see the Omniana, article Toleration) originate in the inadvertence to the principle, that the + Pole necessarily *comprehends* the −. Thus the *evolving* forms of th̶ each Bee becomes a *compressing* form to its next neighbour, and *contains* the property of repulsion. The *ultimate* end of every − must therefore be found in the correspondent +—the State in the Church. But as long as we speak of the *State* separately & or in contra-distinction we are to seek its *proper* end, its *own* specific finality, or causa finalis *pen*ultima. Consequences— The moral necessity of *Representation,* of Liberty of the Press—in short of an active *indifferencing* power of the Church & State—But still this o in the + o, becomes itself *polar*—and the Repres. Legisl. is the −, the Lib. of the Press the + pole.—Hence I can demonstrate the inherent unrighteousness & outward unrightfulness of all Censorships, so rashly admitted by Fichte & German Philosophers—

4923 29.220   When we *think* Body in the abstract, we call *f117* the result Matter: when we *imagine* Matter in the concrete, we call it Body: i.e. Matter is the abstract Notion, or το πανκοινον, *of* Body.—This is the best scholastic definition of Matter—But a more serviceable explanation and more consistent with the subjects *f116^v* and occasions, on which we might use the word, *material,* where we could not say either spiritual, or bodily, is this—that Matter is an abstraction (of the attention) from the substance (= *esse*) of Body to the appearance (= *videri*), or a Thinking of the appearance abstractedly from the substance. In this sense Matter is not a Universal or πανκοινον: for the appearance may be determinate or

indeterminate, seen or thought of (= Anschauung oder Begriff),
so that it be *appearance* only.—Thus: I might hold Light incorporeal, Lux = vis incorporea—but no one will deny, that the
phænomenon of Light = Lumen, is a material phænomenon.—
So the Rain-bow, the Reflection from the Glass, &c are not bodily
but yet *material*. I have only to add that by *appearing* as the translation of *videri* I mean a sensuous appearance, or an appearing to
the outward Sense.

f116ᵛ **4924** 29.221   One main Object of my Work is to establish
the difference of the Spiritual alike from 1. the Notional: 2. the
Phænomenal: and 3. the Carnal—and that it alone is the Truth
that verily and indeed is.—Now these three Non-spirituals comprize all the forms & sources of Heresy and False-doctrine: and
by one or other of these may we distinguish the Spiritual Christian
clearly tho' indirectly and by Negation. By the first (i.e. as denied
respecting him) we learnt to discriminate him from the mere
professional Theologue; by the second from the Visionary; and by
the third from the Fanatic and Extasist. Again: in the first, or the
Mistaking of the Notional, under which term I here include all
f116 the functions and products or reflexes of the unenlivened Understanding, Sᵗ. Paul's φρονημα σαρκος for the Spiritual, arise all the
errors, rejecting or exenterating the Doctrines of the Tri-une God
and Eternal Life; of Sin & originative Evil; Theanthropy; Incarnation, and Redemption by the Cross from Unitarianism upward
to Grotian *Verbo tenus*—and yet likewise the ~~errors~~ heresy of Modern & the inconvenient expressions of genuine Calvinism, cloud-
ing or deforming the Idea of God as God—In the second & third
all those aberrations, that consist in the declared hostility to Reason
no less than to the Understanding, and in the substitution of Excitements & Morbid states of the Sensations, and sensuous Fancy
for Spiritual Acts & Evidences—

4925 29.222   Even the Iagos must play a sophism on themselves in order to justify their principle of Self-interest—they must
project their *own* nobler Nature out of themselves & call it *Nature*—or God—"Each man for himself & God for us all".—How

come this *Each Man* to know of a Nature or God, and to know
that it cares or acts for the good of all, but by partaking of this
Nature or Divinity?—

4926 29.223   The Hour after the First Love, and the Love   *f115ᵛ*
at First Sight.

It seemed, the ~~whole Cope~~ Zenith of Heaven opened out as with
a start, like the Evening Primrose that in an instant mocking the
intent eye inverts (reflects) the Spring (Feder) ⟨at the base⟩ of its
compressing Calyx, that now ~~looking~~ed inward to the Stem is hid
beneath the full expanded Flower, all flaming golden Light, and
Fragrance ~~issuing~~ bursting round.—or simply bursts like a Flower
that hid within its Cup. Born in the moment of full growth./?
Full-grown ere born—/that coyly hides its growth/within its Cap-
sule tight comprest. Bursts in its full expanse upon the Light/; and
then describe the Even-Primrose Bush at Sunset, with the Sylphs
& little children watching—and there! there!—~~So seeking what
was and~~ Turns round to share the sight & and miss~~ing~~es both—.

A thousand times in thought & inward motion He spoke the
Name—and started ever & anon, thinking he had uttered it
aloud—or ~~fearing~~ starting at the Thought, what if he had! or
should?—

A music heard ⟨from distance⟩/~~as~~ he sits & weeps like one forlorn—all ⟨sweet⟩ Thoughts, all sensations of Sweetness, and yet he
pines forlorn, unutterably ~~alone~~ forsaken and alone.

That distant Music stealing on the air, Seemed the sole Motion,
seemed the only Life in the then Nature—He watched it o'er the
grass and when the aspen shivered and from the ~~zephyrs~~ skimming
Earth-winds sheeny Flit on the smooth Upland or o'er the bean-
field ~~from~~ the Zephyr floating ~~Streaming~~, dissolves in silver ~~as~~ in
its passing—she borrows visibility for Sound and blends the Eye
and Ear.

4927 29.224   A Paradise of Sound—in which the Brooklets
& Kittenracts & Falls actually flow & fall and eddy, with the tunes
& overtones of Mozart, and ~~with~~ in the vocal laughing tripping
skipping & vaulting mocking rallying tones of our prettiest Mu-

f115 sical Snuff-boxes—suggested by listening to a part of the overture
to Mozart's Tancredi, from a Musical Box brought by M^r. Gillman—Saturday, 16th Nov. 1822—Highgate—/

4928 29.225   The Truths of Reason, as distinguished from
Truths of History are all anonymous. There is no heraldry in
science—Not Quis dixit? but Quid dixit? is the question here.

f28 4929 23.34   Genesis and ascending Scale of physical Powers, abstractly contemplated.

Corollary. These assumed as finite involve the conception of Plurality—i.e. Powers, Spheres, Existences: and this again, as far the
several Powers are assumed as unigenous, or ejusdem generis, involves the conception of Relation or relative position.

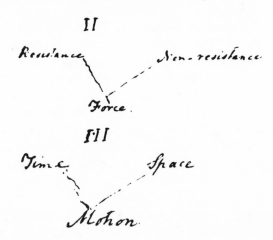

f28^v Corollary. Motion in its relation to the human perception, or the
Product of Motion as fixed and presented simultaneously to the
esemplastic and image-making Faculty (= the Sense) is FIGURE.—

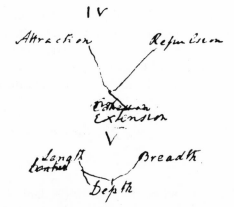

SCHOLIUM. The Schoolmen more precisely expressed this 5ᵗʰ Order by Length, Surface, and Body.

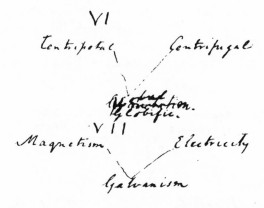

Corollary. In a globe (as the exponent of Gravitation) Magnetism *f29* is to be contemplated as the bi-polar Axis; Electricity as the bi-polar Hemispheric Line (The most beautiful Symbol is the Vertebra with the Ribs.) Thus we have four Poles, or two Pairs. First, *Magnetic* Poles: Astriction or Appropriative attracterion = Negative Magnetism, or − M. and Self-projection, Repulsion, Volatility = positive or + Magnetism. ⟨2ⁿᵈ⟩ *Electrical* Poles. Contraction or − E (negative Electricity:) and Dilation or + E (positive Electricity). Again: the product of the synthesis of the two *magnetic* Poles, in the series of their proportions is the Ground or Base of the Combustible (= Metallëity, or Metallic principle.) The two

Electric Poles (the + = Warmth, the − E = Light) constitute the comburent or combustive. N.b. Oxydation is to Light what Colour is to Flame, i.e. it is Lux ligata, fixa, absorpta, ⟨or⟩ Light under the predominance of Gravitation.

Hence we have another Triad, which dynamically contemplated is

[handwritten: Combustive ✗ Combustible / Combust:]

and contemplated as bodies, 1. Oxygen (+ Chlorine + Iodine) 2. The Metals + Hydrogen. 3. Oxyds, Acids Alkalies, and Neutral Salts.—I conceive a the same Metal = X, as to be the common base of Hydrogen and Nitrogen: that X in the state of Positive *Magnetism* becomes Nitrogen, and the constituent principle of Air; and ⟨that⟩ in the state of Positive Electricity ⟨it⟩ becomes Hydrogen, & the constituent principle of Water: Aërity being the *form* of + Magnetism, Fluidity the *form* of + Electricity.

f29ᵛ (margin)

[heading, handwritten:] VIII.

[handwritten diagram: Reproduction / γυΓ ο ειδΣ s — Irritability / εντοπιστΣες / Sensibility / Ιδιοζωικυ.]

[handwritten:] IX

[handwritten:] Vegetable   Insect

[handwritten:] Animal.

Scholium. Again, the Union of the 3 powers, all ⟨manifested⟩† in the VIIIth dignity, under the predominance of Reproduction is Fish; under the pred. of Irritability is Bird; under that of Sensibility is Beast or Mammalia.—

† I say, all three being manifested: for in the vegetable the irritability is scarcely ⟨manifested⟩ & only for a final moment when the Vegetable ceases to exist, & the Sensibility not at all. So Reprod. and Irrit. are manifested in the Insect; but the Sensib. is latent or obscure.

This is the ~~square of 3 = 9 and the~~ ne plus ultra of mere Physiology or Nature. A new, higher, & heterogeneous principle must be *added*, must *descend*. ("But Man we will make in our own Likeness: and there was breathed into Man a living *Soul* ") in order to the *Tenth*, the completing & unifying Decad.

P.S. Between the VIth and VIIth I should have inserted, at least as a Corollary to the VIth   *f30*

i.e. Wholes distinguished & distinguishable from other Wholes, ~~in~~ having a mutual relation to each other, as *parts* of a common Whole, ⟨but⟩ *parts* that are at the same time *integers*. The co-inherence or perfect Union of the Powers of Light and Gravitation can only be realized as the Sun, or Central Body of a System. But they may exist in synthesis or combination in a double order—viz. Light + Gravitation, in which the Light is the characteristic and modifying power; and Gravitation + Light, in which Gravitation is the modifying power, and determines the character and sort of the Product. Thus, Gravitation modified and transformed by (i.e. ~~part~~ made to partake of the nature or character of) Light is Sound: ~~Light~~ and on the other hand Light in the service of Gravitation is Color. Sound is Volatile Metal, Color is fixed Light: the one, the Soul of Metal, the other the Body of Light, or Light embodied. Call the principles akin to Light, Oxygen, Chlorine &c, photöid *f30ᵛ* (τὸ φωτόειδες).—We have a similar instance in Acids and Alcalis— both are composed of the same Elements, but in inverse proportions. Both consist of Metals and Oxygen. But in the Acids the Photöid is the predominant; in Alkalis the Metallic. Unite an Alkali and Acid, and by means of a double Attraction, the surplus

of the Metallic in $^M/_P$ uniting with the surplus of the Photöid in
$^P/_m$, an equilibrium takes place = Neutral Salts. But it is well to
observe, that in Nature, however ⟨far⟩ you may proceed in narrowing the arc of oscillation by the determination of distinct kinds,
as by subdividing the *Combust* into ~~Acids~~, Oxyds, Acids, Alkalis,
Earths, and Neutral Salts, there is still room for gradations and
distinctive Characters. The Earths, and the Neutral Salts are still
distinguishable into Alkalöid and acidulous Earths or Salts—Thus
the Clay is an Acidulous Earth, Lime an Alkaloid Earth—But
above all bear in mind, that in Nature, in real Things, all the
primary Powers are present in each Thing, and that in the co-
existence of A. B. C. and D., each product becomes that which it
is by the predominance of one & the order of the others: ABCD.
BAC.D. C.B.AD. DCBA. &c &c.

f31   The object, which I proposed to myself in the fore-going Scale,
is simply that of awakening and exercising in the Beginner's Mind
(i.e. in one who is weary of being whirl'd in the Round-about of
professional Routine, who wishes to walk in Light, and in his own
Light and to feel firm footing at each step) ⟨my aim, I say, is to
call forth in the student⟩ the faculty of recognizing the same Idea
or radical Thought in a number of Things and Terms which he
had ⟨never⟩ previously considered as having any affinity or connection; which he had taken, each by itself and insulated, or ~~had~~
if he ever had thought of two of them at the same time, had
brought them together by the conjunction disjunctive of Contrast
or Contrariety: Thus the common man would either never think
of the Gas Lights in the London Shops, and of Water in any
relation to each other, or only as Contraries, Fire and Water—and
such compleat Contraries, that he ~~instance~~ sports at their conjunction as an instance of difficulty that is humanly an impossibility.—
"He will never set the Thames on Fire"—i.e. He is no Conjuror:

f31   He will not work *miracles*—. Who ever attended a first course of
Chemical Lectures, or read for the first time a Compendium of
modern Chemistry (Lavoisier, Parkinson, Thomson, or Brande)
without experiencing, even as a *sensation*, a sudden *enlargement* &
emancipation of his Intellect, when the conviction first flashed upon
him that the Flame of the Gas Light, and the River-Water, were
the very same things (= elements) and different only as A *uniting*

with B, and A B unit*ed*? or A B balanc*ing* and AB balanc*ed*? "Thus,
as the Lunatic, the Lover, and the Poet" suggest.each other to
(*Shakespear's*) Theseus, as soon as his ~~thoughts~~ mind presents to
him the ONE FORM, of which they are but Varieties; so Water and
Flame, the Diamond, the Charcoal, and the mantling Champagne
with its ebullient sparkles, are convoked and fraternized by the
~~Chemists~~ Theory of the Chemist."—
(*Turn to the Friend, V. III. p. 174.*)
I remember a similar feeling when I first saw the connection
between Time, and the being resisted; Space and non-resistance—
or unresisted Action.—that if no object met, stopped, or opposed
itself to, my sight, ear, touch, or sensitive power, tho' it were but   *f32*
my own pulse rising up against my own thumb, I could have had
no sense of Time; & but for these or the repetition of these in the
reproductive Memory or Imagination, should have no Time.
Even when a something like this occurs, ex. gr. when listening to
a monotonous continuous Sound, or with the eye listlessly fixed on
a motionless, unvaried Sky, or expanse of Water, we say—I was
absent. I had quite *lost* myself. For in truth, Time and Self are in
a certain sense one and the same thing: since only by meeting with,
~~as~~ so as to be resisted by, *another* does the Soul become a *Self*.
What is Self-consciousness, but ~~m~~ to know myself at the same
moment that I know another, and to know myself by means of
knowing another, and vice ~~other~~ versâ an other by means of & at
the moment of knowing my Self. Self and other are as necessarily
interdependent as Right and Left, or North and South.—In like
manner, you will soon discover the *analogy* (or rather the common
radical) between Time and Hardness, Space and Softness, and further in a new Genesis, or step of progressive Realization, between
Time & the Ear, Space & the Eye—&c &c.
You have but to remember, that what in one dignity,~~as~~ say for   *f32ᵛ*
instance A$^{(1}$, is a *constituent* power, in the next dignity is the *Prod-*
uct, or *thing* constituted, $=$ A$^{(2}$; and in the ~~next~~ 3rd, it is ($=$
manifests itself as) the *property*, active quality or *function* of that
Thing $=$ a³). This is what the Greek Platonists intended by their
αυτοπατωρ, αυτουιος—its own Father, its own Son—. Thus attraction $+$ Repulsion $=$ ~~the Union~~ Extension as ~~the~~ a$^{(1}$ present
next to the mind the ideal forms of Length $+$ Breadth $=$ Depth,

⟨or a⁽²⁾⟩ and these, namely, the *Power* of Length and the *Power* of Breadth interpenetrating *produce* a third power, not as an Acid & an Alkali *become* a neutral Salt, but as Parents produce *another* without ceasing to exist in their own persons—and this third power is the *Power* of Depth. The two former constitute *matter*, i.e. ~~extension~~, *appearance*; and the third constitutes *body*.—~~When~~ The body now existing, the same powers re-appear as Functions—under the name of Magnetism, Electricity and Galvanism—and we know by experiment that neither + nor − E. acts by itself other than *superficially*; but as soon as they meet and unite, they penetrate into the *Depth*—become Galvanic.

f141   4930 25.68   No
                        Septʳ   1820, 42
                        Octʳ   1819   31
                        Octʳ   1821   56
                        Novʳ   1819   32
                        Janʸ   1822—50
          These Blackwoods contain Articles of mine—

f102   4931 25.103
                        Nöus and Antinöus: a dialogue.
ANTINÖUS. (contemptuously):
"Transcendental Logic—a parcel of German Mysticism!"
NÖUS.—Indeed? I pray you then of all courtesy, what would ⟨you⟩ call the practice of using words without knowing their meaning? Words connected with ~~sensation~~ no ⌐from Sense or¬ ~~Understanding~~ [. . .] ~~only definite sense~~ definite sense or determinate understanding but only with sensations or feelings—words therefore that ⟨in fact⟩ express only the Speaker's own inward state of liking or disliking, and yet *pretend* to ~~do~~ something else, and ⟨and to do a great deal⟩ more—that is, to ~~express the~~ character⟨ize⟩ ~~of~~ the *object* of ~~the Liking or Disliking~~ the Feeling or to tell *what* it is that *excites* or *occasions* the sensation—in short, to ⟨explain⟩ particular~~ize~~ly *what* he likes or dislikes and why? What name would you call such a practice by, Antinöus?
Antinöus. I do not remember—at least, I cannot recollect at present—any one word, that would express it. Do you?

Nöus. Not, ~~perhaps~~, I fear, any one that would exactly answer—; but perhaps we ⟨might⟩ get near to it—and hit the target tho' not the Bull's Eye. ~~First, however, what do how do you define~~ But by the bye, before we make the attempt, how do you define Mysticism?

Antinöus.—Oh! if you are for your definitions, good-bye. The moment a man asks me to define a word, I know, that he is ~~laying a plot~~ planning a catch for me. You will excuse me, Nous! for not giving you the amusement of seeing me flutter my wings in your logic-net.   *f1 0 1ᵛ*

Nöus. Why, surely, a man might have learnt his Catechism, and be tolerably at home with his Bible, & the Whole Duty of Man to boot, and yet have occasion to ask a friend, what Mysticism means—when that friend too had himself made use of it—especially since by the epithet *German* it seems to be an *outlandish* commodity.

Antinöus. O—doubtless! *especially*, such a *plain* homely Christian, as you!

Nöus. Jesting apart—~~if~~ and Sneering is not the most amiable species—~~if~~ shall I attempt to fix the meaning of the word? And if you find nothing to object to in my explanation, will you abide by it?

~~Phil~~Antinöus. Till I hear a better one. ~~I will listen~~ At all events, I will listen.

Nöus. You would not call a thing a square, or a rhomboid if you meant only that it was rectilineal—and if this was all, you knew or recollected with regard to its figure?

~~Phil~~Antinöus. ~~Certainly not—if I did—~~ I hope, at least, I should speak improperly, if I did.

Noüs. Properly speaking therefore, you would not call a thing Mysticism, when you meant only to say, it was not intelligible to you. You would not ~~at a Mathematical Lecture~~ in expressing your dislike of the higher Mathematics tell an Algebraist, that the Doctrine of Fluxions, or the infinitesimal Calculus, even tho' Leibniz alone had been the Inventor or Discoverer, was ⟨a parcel of⟩ German Mysticism? or that Landen's and Le Grange's Analysis of Functions was Scotch or French Mysticism? And yet the latter has ⟨had⟩ the unfortunate name of transcendental affixed to it, and is included in the Transcendental Mathematic?—   *f1 0 1*

~~Philo~~ANTINÖUS. ~~I should hardly have the courage~~ No—there are too many Mathematicians in ~~our circle~~ neighbourhood the club, and I should get blackballed—They might vote me Ignoramus + Self-sufficient = Coxomb.—But *jesting* apart (as you say), I should not do so, because I should ~~take~~ attribute the defect to ~~be in~~ myself, and ⟨regard⟩ the ⟨Algebraist's⟩ unintelligibility ~~of the~~ as an accidental of my ~~ignorance~~ own inconversancy with his Science.
NÖUS. Well! and our neighbor/Chaos's ~~Narrative~~ Detail ~~of the his~~ the ~~5 years'~~ Law-suit after his ~~in which five there were five Claimants beside himself to one intestate property on the ground~~ with the five Claimants to an intestate property—~~the~~ especially, when inflicted at Midnight after his third *Cheerer*.
ANTINÖUS. When ~~every seco~~ every second Pinch of Snuff traversing obliquely the point of his Nose lodges in the outward angle of his left eye—Spare me the ~~5 Claimants & their genealogies~~ Recollection!
NÖUS. Or Lee's rapturous Lines

f100ᵛ

O that my Mouth could bleat like butter'd Peas
Engendering Windmills in the Northern s[eas]
Coaches & Waggons rumble down my Nose,
And blue iniquity flow off in propse—
Then run full tilt at your Subjunctive Mood,
And fatten Padlocks on Antarctic Food—

~~I may~~ You may fairly acquit yourself of all share in the unintelligibility ~~or the wh~~ both of the ~~narrative~~ prose & the ~~p~~ verse—but you would not, I presume, designate either as *Mysticism?*—
ANTINÖUS. Granted!—and now to the point. What might I designate as such? What do *you* ~~make~~ call Mysticism—and do you use the term in a good or in a bad sense?
Nöus. In the latter only—at all events, as far as the present subject is in question/. When a man refers to ~~any~~ *inward feelings* or *experiences*, of which Mankind at large are not conscious, as evidences of the truth of any opinion, such a man I call a Mystic, and the grounding of any Belief or Theory on Accidents of individual Feelings or Fancies, and the use of words invented, or adopted and

appropriated, to express these peculiar facts or states, of interior
Consciousness, I name Mysticism—. Where the error consists   *f100*
simply in the Mystic's attaching reality, or the character of permanent Truth ~~that would reveal itself to others but for certain
obstacles or defects in their intellectual or moral Be~~ having an
existence in the divine Mind tho' revealed only to himself, or a
few similarly favored, & gifted, to these *idiosyncracies* and neither
expects nor demands the same faith in his neighbors, ~~this we~~ I
should call it a species of ENTHUSIASM. But where the Mystic is
induced by ambition or some other ~~Pa~~ selfish Passion, or ~~as o and
this is~~ as often happens is impelled by a lingering and uneasy doubt
in his ~~m~~ own mind, that seeks ~~for~~ confirmation in outward sympathy, to impose his faith ~~on o~~ as a Duty, on mankind at large,
and for this purpose asserts that the same ~~state~~ experiences would
be vouchsafed, the same truth revealed to every man but for certain moral defects and obstacles in his Will or unholy life, such a
man is a mystical FANATIC, and in certain states of the public mind
a dangerous Member of Society—in those, for instance, in which
Fanatics of older standing ~~set about~~ are allowed to persecute the
~~new Devil~~ fresh Competitor.

For ~~this Mysticism species of Fanaticism, tho' originating in
(and for the greater part consisting of,) anomalies of an individual
mind, is nevertheless contagious~~ under these predicaments Mysti-   *f99ᵛ*
cism, tho' originating in the ~~peculia~~ singularities of an individual
nature & ~~consisting of~~ in its very essence anomalous, is nevertheless highly infectious, and on the score of its possible effects therefore as well as of the ⟨Founder's⟩ temperament, ~~of~~ merits the name
of Fanaticism. ~~Liars and inquisitive folks are most commonly
credulous~~ What I have so often experienced respecting Liars, ~~holds
the   we are so~~ may with equal justice be said of the Inquisitive.
Curious folks are commonly credulous folks—. The man who has
trusted a Seer so far as to descend with him into the Cave of
Trophonius, will ~~soon~~ by straining his eyes in the Dark, & some
occasional rubbing to boot, ⟨soon⟩ produce Sparks and flashes of
Light, and these, ⟨with⟩ a ~~right   good will~~ susceptible Sensorium
for the work-shop, ~~a predisposed Fancy, and a right willing mind~~
and a predisposed Fancy, and a right good will for Work-fellows,

will gradually shape themselves into ocular spectra or a very imposing semblance & that may at length assume even a connected
& systematic Character.

f99 ANTINÖUS. This, I own, is sense at least, and contains a definite
meaning. You have only to shew me that it is the proper meaning
of the term, MYSTICISM. Mystes (μυστης) in Greek is, I believe,
an Initiate, one admitted to the secret Mysteries.

NÖUS. The use, which you yourself made of the word & which
occasioned this discussion proves sufficiently, that ~~you~~ we are seeking for a general and philosophical ~~meaning~~ sense, and not for the
historical meaning, in which the word was first used.

ANTINÖUS. So I understand it.

NÖUS. Well, then, ~~the Etymon or Radical of Mystic~~ I attach this
sense to the word, or (if you will) I appropriate this word to the
sense above declared, first, because I know of no other ~~appropriate~~
definite sense, ~~of which~~ that the word can be supposed to bear, for
which some other known and accepted term has not been already
appropriated in our language; and of no other word, that expresses
and comprehends ~~in~~ this particular sense;—and secondly, because
the primary import of the Root, or (may I say) of the *fontal* word,

f98ᵛ which is continued in the derivative in question, does suggest, and
(measured by the analogy of symbolical language in general) adequately correspond to the given Meaning. Are you aware of any
other or stronger grounds, on which the particular use of any disputed term can be rested?

ANTINÖUS. Of none—but to the ~~point~~ Etymon—

NÖUS. Muo, μυω μυσω (from whence mustes, musterion) signifies
to close, to shut, especially, the eyes, ~~or and the~~ mouth, or lips.—
Thus the Faquir, or Oriental Mystic, sits with closed eyes as ~~seek-
ing or~~ one who seeks or has found a Light not derived from the
common Source, and an inward world peculiar to himself, that
cannot be described or communicated ~~by~~ in the common language
or by terms intelligible to ~~oth~~ other men—But should a favored
Few have sought ~~the same~~ and found the same treasure in the same
mine, i.e. each man in the hidden depths of his own inaccessible
Individuality, the adepts must ~~reveal~~ communicate with each other
by symbols intelligible only to such as are familiar with the inward

and spiritual correspondents. Thus as the Light is to be sought for
& obtained *mysticè*, i.e. μετ᾽ ομμασι μνομενοις, with closed eyes,
so is it to be considered and even signified *mysticè*—μετα χειλεσι
μνομενοις, with closed lips. Antinöus! your ~~Love of History~~ predilection for the study of History is at least equal to your prejudice
against all speculative inquiries. ~~You are deeply~~ impressed with the
⟨mournful⟩ results of Superstition and ~~the Spirit of Unitarianism~~
dogmatic Enthusiasm on the peace, welfare, and progress of Nations—and ~~I can trust to~~ your own recollection ⟨of the numerous
and jarring Sects & Species of Fanaticism⟩ will supersede any attempt on my part to determine for you, ~~how~~ what portion of the
sum total of Fanatical

The sad results of religious Dogmatism, superstitious or enthusiastic, on the peace, ~~&~~ happiness and progression of Families and
of Nations ~~are~~ form a familiar ~~to your recollect~~ subject of reflection
with you, and stand distinctly grouped in your memory. You can
therefore determine for your self, ~~&~~ what and how large the portion of the sum total of human Fanaticism, of fanatical Sects and
fanatical Tenets, the origin of which ~~may~~ must be traced to MYS-
TICISM— ~~That is, to the mistake~~ which exists wherever the anomalies of an individual Subject are mistaken for ~~objects of~~ truths in
themselves; ⟨that is,⟩ for facts ~~and~~ or appearances of which all men
may be rendered conscious, and for Judgements binding on all ~~the~~
~~human race mankind in general~~ which ~~because~~ cannot without
grievous error be affirmed ~~of any but~~ except of such as result from
the constitution of the mind itself, ~~and~~ as far as it is possessed ~~or~~
~~to~~ by ~~be presumed of~~ mankind in common.

ANTINÖUS. In *sober Serious*, ~~as my Dame~~ now, as ~~a my~~ our old
Dame used to say, I *thank you*. I both accede to this Sense for the
word, and to the word for this Sense—and you do me but justice
respecting the high place, which ~~you~~ I assign to Mysticism thus
interpreted, in the catalogue of Mischievous Influences.

NÖUS. ~~And I am sufficiently acquainted as to my knowlege of~~
~~History, on which you compliment me,~~
And as to my historical attainments, they are at least sufficient —
and ~~your compliment on my historical attainments might be still~~
~~more beyond my~~ my historical knowlege, however incommensur-

f98

f97ᵛ

f97

ate with your compliment, supplies me with abundanť proofs of the high rank which the said Mysticism holds in the ~~pandemonium of Mischievous~~ Hierarchy of Mischievous Delusion.

NÖUS. Yet—delusion! ~~This is~~ A Tenet or ~~Sys~~ Scheme of ~~of~~ Belief is not Mystical merely because it refers to the inward Consciousness of Mankind, but ~~because~~ where it ~~gro~~ is grounded on an exception from the general rule, ~~when it has literally a degenerat~~ on a *singularity* of individual Consciousness.

ANTINÖUS. Even so. But to what are you leading me?

NÖUS. To nothing that need awaken your suspicions. No where are *singular* characters more frequent than in England; and no where is there a greater dread of appearing singular. ~~By~~ In this, ~~at~~ as in other respects, Antinöus, you are a true English Gentleman—in your aversion to Extremes, even from the Sense of the Ludicrous that attaches to them—& while I am in the Complimenting vein, let me add that you are a genuine Whig of the old School—and disposed to anticipate the reconciling power† of Reason and philosphic Insight by the Spirit of Compromise, ~~under the guidance of~~

f96ᵛ

ANTINÖUS. ~~I hope so.; But for an instance that brings it to the point in hand~~ NÖUS You would not, for instance, call the belief in a Conscience, in the existence of a responsible Will, or the conviction, that there is a difference in kind between Regret and Remorse—or even the homely Faith, that I have a Soul to be saved—you would not brand these with the name of Mysticism?

ANTINÖUS. ~~At ye the age of reason I assumed took on myself the Pledge, the belief that had been confirmed as well as christened~~ I have ~~been~~ not altered my mind since my Confirmation: and am not apt to be guilty of ~~solemn~~ wilful lying, on less solemn occasions.—

NÖUS. ~~I did mean it~~ My questions were ~~for merel~~ merely rhetori-

† By reducing Antitheses to some higher principle in which both are contained, ~~and exist as one~~ and thus contemplating the apparent Contraries as the positive and negative forces (or + and −) ~~minus~~ of the same power—reciprocally supposing & supporting each other.—

cal—and were meant to imply the answer. But ~~Messr~~ ——
~~whose have minds are secretions of the Brain assures his youthful~~ *f96*
~~Auditors~~ frankly confesses to his Pupils, ~~that~~ whatever may have
been the case with the Parsons, yet that he who, in all ~~their~~ his
anatomical and physiological experience could never catch a peep
of the Soul—or Dʳ——who has discovered, that the Mind is a
Secretion of the Brain—. It is *evident*, saith the Dʳ——the the
office of the Brain is to *secrete* MIND."
ANTINÖUS. Precious Coxcombs! I detest Jargon of all sorts——
and the Jargon of cold-blooded Sophistry worse if possible than
that of heated Imagination.—
Nöus. ~~The effects of both are mournful~~ If we could prevent the
latter, and how are they to be prevented? ~~How, I mean, What~~
~~means are~~ The man would deserve the thanks of Society, ~~who as~~
~~in the formation~~
NÖUS. If we could ~~prevent~~ remove the latter, we should take away
the main incitement to the former—: for it is the Jargon of Mysticism that tempts the ——s & ——s to the jargon of infidelity.
ANTINÖUS. ~~There may be~~ *Prevention* may be possible—if the attempt formed a part of a liberal Education. And the man who
should hit on the means of guarding the minds of young men
against Mysticism would deserve ~~the thanks of Society~~ a statue of
Corinthian Brass, tho' a ship-load of German Metaphysics should
be used in heating the furnace—
NÖUS. I have often amused myself with imagining a ~~crowding~~ *f95ᵛ*
miscellaneous Crowd collected around the Telescope of Galilæo,
and in succession looking thro' it—and then listning to the different accounts of the different individuals, as to what they had seen
or experienced by means of this wonderful instrument.—
ANTINÖUS. I hope, that honest Sancho Panza, ~~was among them~~
who gave so edifying an account of his Travels on the Wooden
Horse, after his return from the Empyrean, was one of your imaginary Seers & Reporters—
Nöus—. I would not have missed that veracious Squire for the
world—~~but~~ I will not weary you with the details—~~you~~ but leave
you to imagine for yourself the variety and discrepance of the Relations—. ⟨Insert from I to II overleaf.⟩

f95   Numerous ⟨were the⟩ Pretenders, ⟨each of⟩ who⟨m⟩ spoke of Objects which none had found but himself, in the first instance— but there were a Few, a small and scanty Band, who ~~professed to have seen~~ agreed with each other, ~~but from whom the vast majority~~

f95ᵛ and were laughed at for their pains by the great majority.⟩ At length, a quiet sensible-looking man employed himself in collating the~~ir~~ assertions one with the other, and discovered many in which all agreed, many from which a few only dissented, and those ~~pers~~ too persons, who (~~it was suspected~~) had refused to look at all, or

f95   (it was suspected) had looked with both eyes shut.—~~while of the~~ Having meditated awhile on this my quiet Friend, methought, set himself seriously about examining the Telescope itself— Galilæo, methought, came at this moment, & on ~~hearing~~ learning his purpose & motives, readily assisted him, in taking the instrument to pieces, in order ⟨first⟩ to examine ~~each one apart~~ each part by itself, and then ~~to make the composi~~ the putting together; and lastly the constitution and ~~powers~~ application of the whole, as one power—And thus employed I left them—Now what if by a similar collation of the assertions and judgements on which all men ⟨under the same circumstances should⟩ agree we ~~inf~~ should first infer ~~a~~ the existence of correspondent facult~~y~~ies ~~in~~ possessed by all men in common/and i~~ft~~ would not, I presume, be other than reasonable if we consented to take the sum total & unity of these faculties for the human Understanding *generally*, or the standard mind—just as Physicians form their Ideas of Human Health—or as we all form

f94ᵛ our criterion of a lawful Shilling or Crown-Piece—.

Antinöus. So far, good.

Nöus. But it would better still, methinks, if after this & in addition to it, the same man, with his powers of examining, comparing and generalized thus strengthened, ~~and~~ & his ~~mind thus sob~~ Thought at the same time sobered and disciplined, should by tracing the process of his own Mind and its results during the former operation, & then reflecting, as it were, on his own reflections, clearly ~~discover~~, and by necessary inference, discover these Faculties as constituting his own Understanding, and then from these Faculties deduce these Judgements, as the necessary consequences of such Faculties?—Just as in Arithmetic, we prove the accuracy of a Sum by reversing the process—Would not such an

undertaking be desirable & respectable? And supposing it to succeed, would not the knowlege thus acquired & communicated be
a most valuable assistance to every man, who felt it his wish &
believed it his duty, to attempt the fulfilment of the heaven-de-   *f94*
scended Precept, Know thyself—? Above all, would it not completely coincide with my friend, Antinöus's, favorite Motto—
        The proper Study of Mankind is Man!
The ⟨mystical⟩ Abracadabras and Abraxases of ~~Mysticism~~ might
still be stamped on Card-counters, and fancy-medals, but ~~its home
made~~ counterfeit coins ⟨of Mysticism⟩ or the forged notes issued
from the ~~Forger's own~~ private Top-loft would have a poor chance
with as many as had obtained such a money-guage from the Public
Mint, & had learnt the Bank-marks from a Specimen or Fac Simile, purposely magnified for his instruction.

ANTINÖUS. I can only wish, and if ~~that will gratify if~~ this I do
wish, that ~~such a Science~~ this portion of Self-knowlege ~~ha~~ were
systematized into a science & ~~then~~ I promise you my best thanks,
whenever you can ~~point out~~ bring our name to me the Book, in
which it may be learnt—.

Nöus. ~~On my word and hon~~ It is my firm and I trust firmly
grounded Conviction, that such a Science does exist—and the Book
I am about to place in your hands—

ANTINÖUS The title? the name?

NÖUS. The ~~name of~~ Science of Transcendental Logic, systematized by an English ~~Enemy of Mysticism~~ Lover of COMMON   *f93ᵛ*
Sense, for the ~~Prev~~ Cure and Prevention of ~~all~~ Mysticism, ~~Scotch,
German~~ whether ~~of human~~ native, or imported, Scotch, English,
or German.—

4932   25.104   Another error——is a Conceit, that of Opinions and Sects the Best hath still prevailed and suppressed the
others—N.b.—the English is so inferior to the corrected & enlarged Latin Translation that I had better re-translate it from Vol.
I. (Mallet's Edition) p. 43, last §.

Alius error (superiori affinis) est eorum qui omnium sectarum
et δογματων (= systems of philosophy) postquam excussæ fuissent
et ventilatæ, optimam semper obtinuisse existiment. Itaque putant,
si quis de integro institueret inquisitionem et examen, non posset

non incidere in aliquas ex rejectis opinionibus et post rejectionem recte et jure obliteratis—quasi verò multitudo, aut etiam sapientes ⟨hujus quidem seculi⟩ multitudinis deliniendæ gratiâ, non illud sæpe probärint, quod populare magis atque leve sit quam solidum et alte radices agens.—For the *Noetic*.

Alius error fluit ex nimiâ reverentiâ et quasi adoratione intellectûs quem singuli homines quisque sibi proprium habet. Cæterum præclaros hos *opinatores* et (si ita loqui licet) Intellectualistas, qui ⟨tamen⟩ pro maximè profundis et sanæ mentis philosophis haberi *f93* solent) recte Heraclitus perstringit: Homines, inquit, quærunt veritatem in microcosmis suis, non in mundo majori. Respuunt enim, quasi abecedarium Naturæ primumque in operibus divinis tirocinium/quod si non facerent potuissent fortasse gradatim et sensim post literas simplices et deinceps syllabas ad textum et volumen ipsum mundi expedite legendum ascendere. Huic vero obstat alius et finitimus error, nempe quod post singulas scientias et artes in classes distributas mox a plerisque *universali* rerum cognitioni et *philosophiæ primæ* renunciatur: quod quidem profectui doctrinarum inimicissimum. Prospectationes fiunt e turribus aut locis præaltis; et impossibile est ut quis exploret remotiores interioresque Scientiæ alicujus partes, si stet super plano ejusdem scientiæ.—

~~If the consequences~~ Such then are the advantages of of habitual accuracy in words/which as we have already more than once affirmed, are not words (λóγοι) without a correspondent accuracy of conceptions, ~~atque ideire~~ even as this supposes an answerable knowledge et rerum conceptarum et facultatis conceptricis.—But if the consequences are desirable, so are the moral causes ~~for~~ and pre-conditions honorable to the Individual. It is a symptom of goodness as well as an instrument of Power. Our ~~great~~ illustrious Verulam, himself a man of the largest and loftiest comprehension, the philosopher ~~whose~~ beyond all others ~~(if only Plato be excepted)~~ characterized by (if I may use a Painter's Phrase) a *breadth* of *f92ᵛ* Thought, and ~~with perhaps too little mitigation a Contemner and Persecutor~~ especially intolerant of useless subtlety, and wriggling vermicular cavillations—and with too little mitigation a Persecutor of the School-men, qui quæstionum minutiis rerum frangunt pondera/n.b. ~~neve~~ he, I say, ~~applauds~~ carefully distinguishes the ~~love~~ desire & habit of accuracy from this minute and captious scrupulosity (scrupulis et captatiunculis) and while he denounces the latter

4933 60.12   To notice Chandler's and Delany's et centum   *f21ᵛ*
ali̶iiorum mischievous attempts to palliate or explain away or (as
in Jael) even to justify the criminals in the Old Testament—who
are in any way spoken well of for their general conduct—or principles.—This too furnishes one striking instance of the ill-consequences of literal translation in phrases, which in the western Languages, Ancient & Modern, bear an altogether different sense—
Had the phrase—a man after God's own Heart—been rendered,
as it ought to have been—a man strictly orthodox in his religious   *f22*
opinions—i.e. a devoted Supporter of the Mosaic Institutions in
Church & State, in their utmost purity—this mischief would not
have happened. I am led to these remarks by a casual Looking into
Mʳˢ Trimmer's Sacred History, Vol. III. (*Seventh* Edition!—a
work in Six Octavo Volumes!)—and thus introduced into numberless Schools and Families—especially, tho' not exclusively, among
Serious Church People.

4934 60.13   The Italian Language the Ruin of the Latin the   *f22ᵛ*
Blocks remaining but with the greater part of the Cement dropt
out, or the Knobs, that joiced in to the correspondent Cups, worn
away—
    The Spanish the Latin orientalized by adoption of the Arabic—
    The French is a *neutralization* of the Latin with the other Com-
ponents—a tertium aliquid, the least powerful but most perfect of
the modern European Languages—As Brass to a rich Ore of Copper, Silver and Zink—
    In the English the Saxon and the Latin are still in antagonism—   *f23*
Hence the more numerous and more marked Varieties of *Style/*The
English can write worse (a la Johnson) and in certain kinds of
writing—better than any other Nation ex. gr. shades of feeling, as
well as of meaning not phænomenal: for in the Latin the Eng.
yields to the German—
    The German is the full-grown Gothic, which has here con-
quered and here denizened the Latin & Romanesque—the rough
Compeer of the Greek—.
    Qʸ. Whether we should, or rather which it would be more ex-   *f23ᵛ*
pedient and convenient to use the German for the Race, and the
Gothic for one of the Branches—or vice versa?
    The answer will depend on the extent of the generic term—

Steffens & Schlegel ~~hav~~ make the German and the Scandinavian
two kinds—and the Gothic a branch of the former—while I make
the Gothic the Radical, both of the German & Scandinavian as the
*Sub*genera/Perhaps, the North Iapetic for the Genus—the German
and Scandinavian for the Subgenera—would be best.

f24   But yet *Sweo*-gothic?—What if—
North Iapetic
Gotho-Scandinavian
Gotho-German

——

Gotho-German
Marcomanni
Alemanni
Gothi Occidentales
, &c

and the Franks, as already inoculated with the *character* of the
Gaulish Romanized Celts—where we first read of them, more ag-
greggative, mobile, impressible, ab extra—therefore ⟨more⟩ in-
constant, faithless, explosive: As the Conquerors of the Gauls, they
were already *protoxides*—proto-Celtides—& so gradually by dilu-
f24ᵛ tion of intermarriage, & dying away of the purer families, f about
the mid Reign of Lewis XIV, became as now perkeltides.—

f61ᵛ 4935 21½.120   Ψυχὴ the Scripture sense of—σοφια ψυχικὴ,
Sᵗ James. ανθρωπος ψυχικος, Sᵗ Paul— = συνεσις της σαρκος—The
human life—as a co-agent with the elementary Powers in the production and conformation of the Organs = Life, Vis vitæ; but of
all the co-agents it is the only one persistently *substant*—and over-
f62   flowing the products as their *function*, it becomes, ψυχη—and the
Substans considered with a view to its reappearance as a *function*,
and of course a schematic Function, would be ανθρωπος ψυχικος.
Still, however, something more than the *animal* life must be presumed in the *Substans* itself—The co-agency of the elementary
powers supplied *a* size, *a* shape; but *the* size, *the* shape, *the* ordon-
nance, must have been contained potentially in the Individual
Power—for in all psychal Natures the Genus is evolved out of the
Individual. A quality therefore must have been given to it, constituting the formative Nisus or Instinct a *Will*—and what can this

be but the *Law* spoken of by Sᵗ Paul—i.e. Conscience—and this we must conceive as having two sides, the one uppermost and receptive, the other undermost and influencive—the influence will be 1. Consciousness & Reflection. 2. Self-consciousness—and the Substans ψυχικον so potentiated becomes truly the Understanding/ The superior side = Reason, but this again not actualized except by an analogous co-agency, i.e. a *spiritual.*—To both therefore, to the ⟨ascending⟩ Spirit, which it *qualifies*, and renders human, and to the *de*scending Spirit it is a *Receptivity*—and hence we may aptly call the Reason the *sensorium* of the *Spirit.*—The inferences are clear—When the Man uses the Understanding, in *mastery* only for that which is below it, but in subserving as to that which is above it, as not comprehending it but comprehending *by* it, then ανθ. πνευματικο[ς] but when *only* for that which is *below it,* &   *f62ᵛ* winning the will over to the same exclusively the ανθρωπος ψυχικος, φρονημα σαρκος—lastly, when he uses the understanding in mastery over that which is above it, and pretending to comprehend ⟨it⟩ within its own limits & laws, which yet is impossible—it dreams itself to be that highest, refuses any higher, and assigns its own measures to justify its refusal—this is ανθρωπος διαβολικοςαιμονιωδης, σοφια διαβολικηαιμονιωδης.—(Sᵗ James.)

4936 23.59   [?Lacha/Lacka]—[?Lanchum/Larckum]—   *f46ᵛ*
clacker

4937 29.226   Wednesday 14ᵗʰ May 1823—The six Exhibi-   *f115*
tions ⟨of 20 £ each⟩ 3 for O, 3 for C. founded by the Goldsmiths' Company, for 5 years if residing so long—the same number for four years successively, when the six first will have become vacant, were decided—after a canvas of 4 months, by the majority of the Candidates, for the last 10 days of which I or my friend had known of the circumstances and yet, spite too of the non-arrival of the proper Petition from Derwent, he was elected—What? if it should be only a half year—yet 10 £ is worth having.

4938 29.227   Thursday 15 May 1823—Debate in the House of Commons on Mʳ Fowell Buxton's Motion for the Eman-cipation of Negro Slaves, whose speech, a something between a

College Declamation, and the opening Harangue of the Counsel
for a Prosecution at the Old Bailey, but sensational only according
to the Cut of the Deisidæmoniac Bible-and-all-other-goody-and-
inquisitional Society-mongers, M.P., was answered by Mr. Canning with his wonted ability and ~~dexterous argumentative~~ adroit-
ness. and likewise with his wonted Sophistry and dexterous Quid-
pro-quoism.—The following extract from the Report in the
f114ᵛ Morning Herald of Friday 16 May deserves a conspicuous place
among the examples of Multivocal terms, where one word plays
many parts, ⟨and of attaching a sense to other words, which they
were neither intended to convey nor capable of bearing—ex. gr.
repugnant⟩ in any Logical Exercises.—

"The Honᵇˡᵉ Gentleman stated Slavery to be repugnant to the
British Constitution and repugnant to the Christian Religion.—
but the Hᵒⁿ Gⁿ must admit that he had here stated a proposition
not *historically* true—and how can Parliament make a distinction
between what was morally true and historically false? (*I should have
thought that nothing could be more easy. S. T. C.*) With regard to
the allusion to Christianity in the Resolution, Mʳ C. confessed that
he always had a decided objection to the introduction of the Name
of Christianity in the debates of the House. (*In this I perfectly agree
with Mʳ C. Would that he had extended his objection to the Bench &
Law Courts! S. T. C.*) If it meant that ⟨in⟩ the Christian Religion
there was a *Spirit* under which Slavery could not continue (*Mark
this "continue" for "exist": and the equivocal "under" for "together
with which as existing in genuine Christians not accomplices in
Slavery: for in any other sense Mr. Canning* ~~presents it~~ *asserts what
he cannot prove or rather it is a mere petitio principii* S. T. C.), that
was also historically false. The Character of Christianity was that
it was adapted to all stages and situations of Life. It is true that
Christianity is the Glory of Freemen; but no less true that it is the
Glory of Slaves (*Exquisite!* Test it by the gl. of those who have
their money safe in the Bank—and the gl. of those who by forgery,
fraud, and arson are reduced to Poverty—ergo Forgery, Treachery
and Arson are consonant with Christianity, and can continue under
its *Spirit*! S. T. C.) It is true there is no permission in the Chr.
f114 Doctrine for the infliction of Slavery, but it was not true that there
was any direct *prohibition* of it. (MEM. *Winch's Defence of*——*and*

leaving the Sin offering in full fume on Bowyer's Desk "You know, Sir! You never forewarned it". S. T. C.)

Non meus hic sermo. They were not his opinions alone but were taken from one whom the House would consider as a good authority.

Here Mr C. read a long extract from Dr Paley—

I have declared with co-incidence with Mr C. on the introduction of the Name of Christ^y in the debates of a temporal Legislature— or I would have proposed a Compromise—I will give up the appeal to the New Testament; if Mr C. and others of the School of Expedience will give up their appeals to Paley—As soon as any other thing wicked and contrary to the direct Commands of the Law of God & Man is to be defended in the H. of C.—be sure, that out pops Paley—If perjury, if fraudulent Subscription, if addressing to the Almighty what we believe to be false 104 times, besides week Church days, in every year, and thus lying once to a Bishop by the pen and hand in order to lie to God ore pleno 50 times during every Sunday & Festival Day in every year—if Pluralities—if Simony—if Corruption in Parliament—are to be vindicated—still Paley—Paley—the perpetual advocate asserter of the Optimism in the present tense and Devil's Advocate in all Courts and Causes.—The Logical exposure of the equivocations in the passage above given I leave for the moment that I am to make use of this example.

4939 29.228   What says the tolerant and speculatively scep-   *f113^v* tical *Cicero*, speaking of those who deny either the reality of a Light of Conscience, ex. gr. ut neminem violem commodi mei gratiâ, or, et esse Honestum, et esse per se expetendum; or that is *binding*, i.e. who deny that is a Law of Conscience. Turn to his De Officiis, Book III. c. 6.

Quamobrem Hoc quidem Deliberantumium genus pellatur e medio (est enim totum sceleratum et impium) qui deliberant utrum id sequantur, quod honestum esse videant: in ipsâ enim dubitatione facinus inest, etiamsi ad id non pervenerint.

What then shall we say of those who pretend se non honestum de ullâ re videre posse, et discrimen inter malum et pravum; inter

bonum et voluptatem propriam omnino nescire? As of the former
I should say, They must be made better men before they can be
wiser; so of the latter I should affirm, they must cease to be beasts
before they can be talked to as men/—For if they are not lying in
the face of their better knowlege, the want both the contra-distinguishing Ingredients of Humanity, Reason and Conscience.—in
all else they differ from the Beasts in *degree* only. I ask what Right
can such a man pretend to the not being treated as a Beast & when
he denies that any Right exists? or that his Will should be ~~exerted~~
consulted who confesses he has no will for us to consult? or ⟨in⟩
what sense can he complain—save only that the not complaining is
just as senseless—vide Sibylline Leaves.

4940 3½.77
              IDEA~~L~~—Take an instance
f99ᵛ   1. That which is common to States of all times and all Countries
is, says Steffens, the Idea of a State. ⟨P.S. 1 not different from
2—I would say, 1 the ultimate End presented in the form of its
means.—⟩ 2. Whatever we have hitherto found ⟨the same⟩ in all
states that are and have been, ⟨i.e.⟩ as far as the Experience of the
Past and Present extends, constitutes the *general conception* of the
term, State.
         According to this statement the difference between the Idea and
the general Conception consists in the limitation of the latter to the
f100   Past. It is simply an Exponent of a Fact, and does not necessarily
imply any ground of insight into the same, or any principle by
which we are enabled to form a comparative Judgement of different states, as better or worse the one than ~~an~~ the other, or from
which we could derive a Rule of Guidance, directing us in the
~~anticipation or modification~~ amendment, improvement, or modification of an existing State. ~~much less any general Scheme,~~
~~⟨mental⟩ outline, or scientific Model, in the Min~~ As little does a
conception ~~so~~ formed in this manner by abstraction and generalization supply, of necessity, any principle of foresight, ~~for the~~ or
historic anticipation, or suppose any general Schema ~~an~~ or scientific
f100ᵛ Model in the conceiving Mind for the construction of a State,
where it does not exist (~~or~~ in a new Colony, for instance) or as far
such a thing is possible where it exists no longer.

If instead of a State or other product of human Effort or Concurrence we take any fact or phænomenon in Nature—for instance, the attraction of iron by the Magnet—. The general Conception will contain all the phænomena that had been noticed up to the moment of its formation, and these will determine the name of the property, to which the phænomena are too often attributed as to *the* cause of the same: whereas in ~~effe~~ fact ~~the~~ it is only a repetition of the effects involving the universal assumption of *a* Cause—or ~~as the~~ in the language of the transcendental Logic, the effects are re-expressed under the Categor~~y~~ic (= the ~~a priori~~ pre-constituent) Form of Causality. ~~No Light is, necessarily given, or any nay~~ No way suggested of ~~an~~ controlling or reproducing the phænomena ~~is~~ need be contained in the Conception, ~~or can be deduced as a necessary~~ immediately or as a necessary Consequence—No Light necessarily given for the explanation of the variations and apparent anomalies, or for the anticipation of such under given or preconceived Circumstances. *(Here quote the whole passage from the Essay on Method.)*—

f101

It would seem then, that if the practical character of an Idea, and one at least of the marks by which it is distinguished from a general Conception, is this—that it contains that which common to all particulars of the given kind—(ex. gr.)—that the I. of a St. contains that which is common to all particular States—*of all Times*—if this be granted, it would seem that the Idea must likewise contain some principle of *insight* and *positive* assurance in respect to what is essential—that it must afford, or itself be, a criterion of the essential, and indirectly therefore of the ~~merely~~ accidental likewise—and this independent of the historical fact of such or such characters having always attended every State hitherto—a fact, that ~~forms~~ argues indeed ~~the~~ a high probability of the essentiality of ~~such~~ the characters in question, and at once begets and warrants the anticipation, the expectation that so they will be proved to be—but cannot give the direct *insight* or certainty that they are essential—and therefore exempt from all the accidents of Time & Place. For that which must be true & can be known to be true, in *all* times, must needs be extra-temporal, and independent of Time—.—It follows then that the knowlege of the common characters, ~~or general conception, of a St~~ constitutes a general Con-

f101ᵛ

f102

ception, which may ~~be a~~ prove the way of arriving at the Idea, but is *not* it—and that the words so defining an Idea form an inadequate if not a false definition. We should therefore say that the essential characters common to all states of all times constitute the Idea, State.

f102ᵛ   But here again, we need only reflect a while to ~~be see~~ detect a double Flaw in this definition, ⟨1ˢᵗ. a deficiency & 2ⁿᵈ. a superfluity.⟩ First, the term, essential, requires to be itself defined and explained, as to its full, ~~and~~ proper and positive import in this particular position & application—. For in ordinary usage it sometimes means that which absolutely necessary to the existence of a thing—in which sense it may be said, that neither Legs nor Arms are *essential* to a Man:—or it may signify the ~~generic or most general Character of a Class~~, specific Character ~~of~~ common to an indefinite number of individuals, or the generic character common to several species, and where these form an ascending Series, in which each species perfects itself (i.e. becomes at once more complex and yet more individualized) as it ascends/The term, essential,

f103   The referring to a particular instance

N.B.
    The preceding pages are an exemplification of the process of seeking, groping after a truth/—But the first sentence taken from Steffens had put me on a wrong scent.—That which is common to all States of all times *may* be no more than a common *materiel* (ex.gr. a number of men existing under some common Law) and give the conception of a Negro Plantation or a Tartar Despotism. An idea is a Form presenting & presupposing an ultimate end, appropriately.

f104   4941 3½.78   Wie Gedanken durch Gedanken sich klar werden und verständigen in der Seele des einzelnen Menschen, so wollen sich Geister verständigen unter einander, und das in sich geschlossne, in sich klare Verhältniss aller innern und äussern Verhältnisse eines Vereins, ordnet und belebt und bildet den Staat. As the Copula, or that which pervades and is implied in, all the Thoughts, and which initiates and gives the direction to the motion of each, and yet is itself re-actuated and potenciated by the result or quotient of all (the true, living Multiplication, as opposed to the artificial implicit Addition falsely so called)—as this, I say, is the Mind of each Soul, so is there a correspondent common Consciousness, that in every age is the Mind of the State—This too, as in Individuals, is not indistinguishably continuous, in cycle or in stream; but evolutive, and revolutionary—It has its *Epochs*—& the Epoch not the Circumstances constitutes the true ground & principle of political Insight, and herein consists the main value of History & the distinction of the Historical from the recordless *f104ᵛ* Ages, of the Historical from the barbarous Nations, whether civilized (as the Chinese) or uncivilized as the Tartars.—The Chinese have *Records*—so a City would have whose Church yards were filled with Tomb-stones, ~~of all~~ from the trim New Comer of Yesterday to the weather-gnawed Sepulchre of remote Ages, all with the *Initials* of the Dead Men's Names. But what are Records, where there is nothing to record. The Chinese Mind has had no *Epochs*—and these and all else as illustrative of these, are the sole materials of History.

4942 3½.79   The Sovereignty of the People, ~~or~~ i.e. Nation, is like the Universality of Magnetism, true or false according as it is understood—if it mean the ground, or essential Power ever acting, then it is true that Magnetism exists wherever cohesive Lineality exists & according to the Cohesion—therefore in all Metals from Carbon to Ammonium—if it mean the Phænomenon, *f105* then it is false—for it exists naturally only in Iron, & in Iron only under certain conditions, as a certain *degree* of oxydation, heat, &c—So with States—the King is the Natural *Magnet*, and yet by a Scientific Balance of ~~the~~ Silver and Zinc, as the two metals that most nearly resemble the + and − minus Forces in the amphoteric Iron, a Magnet may be constructed/and so may a supreme executive Cabinet/.

4943 60.14   Das Gemeinsame, the All-common, ex. gr. of *f25* all the different Constitutions, Governments, Public Codes, &c, existing or recorded by History is *one* way of arriving at the IDEA, *State*; and an indispensable means of warranting & convincingly communicating the Idea—but still it is not the Idea, the universal

Type—otherwise it could be only co-extensive with the already known, & therefore no Criterion, it could supply no Ideal, for the Future—or any new form of State.

f28ᵛ   **4944** 60.15

| — / \ ∪∩ ⊂ ⊃ ○ Yes!
                                Yes

/ H Π Λ A Δ P

f132   **4945** 3½.112   Fallacia causæ non causæ—Kant's Vermischte Schr. 3. 315—Pleasures of Conscience—
——— conditionis pro causâ—Air to respiration—Sophism of the Materialists generally—
——— instrumenti sine quo non pro causâ. Eye and optic Nerve to Sight—the Brain to recollective Consciousness—
——— Comitantiæ nunquam non expertæ usque ad nunc pro causâ—Cum hôc: ergo propter hôc/.
    The Moon: Weather.—
    N.b. This, however, is a *Genus*, ~~contains~~ or rather a verbal generality, comprehending not only several but diverse Sophisms—ex. gr. A general term taken for ~~a~~ some *one* of the events ~~&~~ or phænomena, where these of necessity exist singly & successively. Thus the Weather = ~~for~~ all sorts of weathers, ~~change for~~ for some one sort—Change for some one change—. Now it may be with verbal truth be said, that the *Weather* changes with the
f132ᵛ Moon's Changes—for as the Moon is present, and *always* changing, how should it be otherwise. In order to prove any causality, it should be affirmable, that the Change of Weather from a to b regularly accompanies the change of the Moon from ~~one~~ some one determined phase to another—.
    Again: here is the Sophism of a μεταβασις εις αλλο γενος, or a comparison between Heterogenes—the Change of the Weather is a *reality per se*, the phases of the Moon a relative Appearance, not a change in the Moon, but a change of appearance relatively to a

Beholder on some given spot of the Earth—At all events, not the changed appearance but the something of which these are the necessary effects or at least constant accompaniments must be the true.—

The Sophism of a Co-cause that may become the determining Cause for the Cause sufficiens & proper efficient—or of a General Cause or Agent deriving its causal influence from the nature of the Subject in which the effect is produced. In this way a slight motion may cause a ~~fluid~~ fluid menstruum so to chrystalize when it would not or before it would otherwise have done so—And thus suppose tides in the higher atmosphere from the attraction of the Moon, it may occasionally ~~depend~~ happen that where the local, chemical, ⟨or⟩ electrical (~~or the great planetary~~ proper & immediate) causes are nearly balanced, the stronger or weaker attraction of the Moon according to its solar position & distance from the Earth may disturb ~~its~~ the equilibrium—   *f133*

4946 3½.113   When shall I find time & *ease* to reduce my Pocket-books and Memorandums to an Index—or Memoria Memorandorum? If—aye! and alas! if—if I could see the last sheet of my Assertio Fidei Christianæ, et Eterni temporizantis, having previously beheld my Elements of Discourse, Logic, Dialectic, & *f133ᵛ* Noetic, or Canon, Criterion & Organon, with the philosophic Glossary—in one printed Volume—& the Exercises in Reasoning as another—*if*—what then? Why then I would publish all that remained unused, Travels & all; under the Title of Excursions abroad & at Home, what I have seen & what I have thought, ~~and~~ with a little of what I have felt, in the words in which I told and talked them to my Pocket-books, the Confidantes who have *not* betrayed me, ~~and~~ the Friends, whose silence was *not* Detraction, and the Inmates before whom I was not ashamed to complain, to yearn, to weep—or even to pray!—   *f134*

To which are added Marginal notes from many ~~books~~ old Books and one or two new ones—

Sifted thro' the Mogul Sieve of Duty towards my Neighbor—
by Εστησε

21 June 1823.

4947 3½.114

Highgate

In two or three places of my Pocket-books, I forget which, I have noticed the striking analogies between the Reason and the Sense. Visio Idealis et Intuitio Sensibilis. As in the simple Sense the Image and the Thing, the Representation and the Presence, are one and undivided, so in the Idea the Thought and the Reality. This indeed is the final end of philosophy, to restore the Unity which *f134ᵛ* had been *entzweit* in the act of Reflection—to remove the Division yet retain the Distinction.

4948 3½.115   Captain John Franklin's Journey to the Shores of the Polar Sea in the years 1819, 20, 21, and 22.—

Not less instructive than interesting, and most worthy to appear as the Successor to Hearne's and Mackenzie's Volumes.—Instance of an Indian Husband's suckling his Infant, whose Mother had died in Child-birth on a Journey, in consequence of inanition.—

p. 188, 89.—I recommend these pages to the ingenuity of the physico-theological *minute* Final-cause men—. Their Teleology, I suspect, would have a hard job of it with the American Musquitos, *f135* and winged Bull-dogs, "that range in the hottest glare of the Sun, and carry off a portion of flesh at each attack["]. The goring Musquitos that retire to the Shades in the heat of the Day, and the plunder-flesh Bull-dog Flies, are the dire Dragons of the North, who keep alternate guard for the ⟨misanthrope⟩ Spirit of the Polar Region.

22 June 1823.

4949 3½.116   In medio *tutissimus* ibis—is not true either in Politics or Theology even where in medio tu rectior ibis—is the truth. Moderate men are crushed betwixt the extremes—"it faring with them as with the guest that sat in the midst of the Table who could reach to neither mess above or beneath him—

Esuriunt Medii, Fines bene sunt saturati,
Dixerunt Stulti, Medium tenuere beati"

Fuller's Holy State

Vide *Literary Life*—

4950 3½.1   At p. 90   *f1*
Look for the obsolete Words.

4951 3½.11   Entity informed = das Hineinbilden des   *f5ᵛ*
Seyns in das Erkennen = Education
  Lastly as it is implied in the very conception of Life. That it is
a power/—

4952 3½.86   "I am glad that the Inmates of Rydale Mount   *f108ᵛ*
discovered "an Amendment" in me. And truly in Self-manage-
ment, and the power of keeping my Eyes more, and my Heart
less, open than in the days of my Devotion and Simplicity, I *do*
believe that I am *amended*: tho' in innocence of Life and Purpose,
in the incapability of deliberate Selfishness, in detestation of
Treachery, Apostasy and (silent or suggestive) Detraction, in the
Love of Truth *as* Truth, and of Good *as* Good, it will be well for
me if I but remain what I was from 5 and 20 to the Hour that I
first sate ~~down~~ under this hospitable Roof.
  Amendment in Health, Manners and Appearance, I can cor-   *f109*
dially ~~set~~ put down to Mʳ and Mʳˢ Gillman—in Heart and Principle they would as strenuously deny any change for the better as
they would indignantly refute any change for the worse.—"
"Extract from a Letter to Mʳˢ Coleridge, dated 2 July 1823,
Highgate—

4953 3½.85   An excellent Epitaph for a good woman—   *f108*
N.b.—abridged from Flecknoe
          With softest temper & the mildest breast,
          Most apt to pardon, needing pardon least,
          Who scarce had any passion of her own,
          But was for others all compassion:
          Saint-like?
          A Saint she liv'd and like a Saint she died,
          And now is gone where only Saints abide.—

4954 3½.80   Strype's Life of Sir Thomas Smith—Instance   *f105*
of the calming and humanizing Recollections connected with Classical Studies in the *controversy* between Smith & Gardiner (then

Chancellor of the Univ. of Cambridge) on the Greek Pronunciation—and Gardiner's Protection nay, Patronage of Smith & As-
cham (both zealous ~~anti~~ operative & leading Anti-Romanists as
well as Anti-hellenists. See Chapt. III. Chapter V ad finem, and
Chapter VI.

Mem. Not to forget *the heat of fancy* Tetrastich in Strypes Life of
Cheke.

f105ᵛ "And indeed, *using Wisdom therewith*, Courteous and gracious
Speech doth much profit."

Secretary Cecil (Lord Burleigh) his Letter to Sir Thomas
Smith, then Ambassador at the Court of France.

Quere   Have Smith's Letters, ~~so~~ in Strype's time still extant in
the Paper Office in two bundles, been ever published?

full of Slanders and *Brabbles*.

The extent and accuracy of the secret information possessed by
Elizabeth's Great State-counsellors are as a proverb in our
mouths—~~at~~ but the rate, at which it was obtained, is scarcely less
wonderful. From 5 August to 3 Octʳ 1565, the heat of the Ne-
gociations that ended in Peace with France, Sir T. Smith's extraordinary Charges amounted to 103£, the greater part "spent in gratifying Spies and Intelligencers, Scots and French". The Sums
given ~~may~~ monthly varying from 4£ to 40 Shillings—and one of

f106 them, De Rege, received 6, 13ˢ, 4ᵈ, in August, and the like Sum
in October.—$\frac{£}{13}, \frac{S}{6}, \frac{D}{8}$ for three or perhaps 4 months' work.—
When we read the strong and repeated commendations of Eliza-
beth's Cabinet on Sir T. Smith/on the score of the quantity and
importance of the state-secrets procured and communicated by
him, we ought to call the circumstance admirable rather than wonderful—for Wisdom, penetration, persuasive Speech, and a commanding Spirit were the *Make-weights* in the so lightly loaded
Scale.—But Tricks, Deceit, Cunning, ⟨hollow Promises and
equivocal Phrases⟩ and the manifold Sleights & Stratagems ~~of Di-
plomacy~~ and double meanings of Diplomacy were perhaps the Ingredient, or at least entered largely into the composition, of this
lauded Wisdom & penetrative Spirit? In Leicester's policy, and in
that of his congenial Creature and Favorite, Sir N. Throgmorton,

Smith's Colleague in the Embassy, they did? And what was the
result?—Deluding and deluded, a shuffled Shuffler, he got himself
into a Prison, for his *over-business*, to his own disgrace & the
dishonor of the Queen, whose person he then represented, and
baited with gold to catch gudgeons, while the Fish worth catching   *f107ᵛ*
ran off with the bait—like the Shark's *Tooth-pick*, that when filled
with the ramenta ~~was~~ of the Monster's Meal, gets swallowed itself.
All "this was strange to Cecil, a plain-dealing man, and of no
turnings and windings, tho' a great and wise politician," and who,
notwithstanding he knew that his friend needed it not, gave this
advice to Sir T. Smith, that he should use all integrity in his
transactions with the French Negotiators, for that England was a   *f108*
Country, so strong and self-sufficing, that it was under no temptation to propose to itself other than just and noble ends—the seeking whereof by underhand and base means were a desacration that
not derivable from the nature of the ~~Object~~ Commission must be
attributed to the nature of the Commissioner/adding that the Testimony of a good conscience is the Rule, which God will exact of
all alike, and by which alone we can hope to be distinguished from   *f109*
the Goats.—

Sir T. Smith's ~~golden~~ chief Rules of Discretion were—
  1. Tell not all that you think, nor shew all that you have, nor
say all that you know, nor do all that you can.
  2. (Which I select, tho' rather common place, for the now obsolete use of the word "utter"—except in the law-phrase, uttering
of base coins i.e. *out*ering, getting rid of, putting a thing *out* of
your power—irrevocabile verbum). In other men's cases meddle   *f109ᵛ*
not too much, nor in your own enforce not time: for governing
you so, you may remain in the good estate you be, or else may
easily happen to *utter* what you were.
  3. Procure unto yourself such friends as will rather stay you
from falling, than such as will reach unto you their hands to help
you up.
  4. Bestow your patronage by your sense of Fitness and Desert,
not by your affections of friendship. For among your friends it is
lawful to *depart* your goods (see p. 90) but not your conscience.
  5. In what you counsel, be not affectionate—in what you dis-

counsel be not passionate. Whatever   advise, do   advisedly.

6. In ~~plain~~ evident cases *abide* not the counsel of others: and in doubtful cases determine not of yourself.†

f110 Strype has (intentionally, I fear) smothered & perverted the sense of an excellent sentiment of Sir T. Smith's—The original words are—

Ita homo sum, *vexari nolim quemquam*, quietos esse cuperem omnes mortales, *et liberé philosophari qui velint: ceteros* suam quemque rem agere. Strype translates the passage as if he had *read* ceterúm, and construed it ⟨as⟩ attamen, = nevertheless. Smith's meaning is this—As far as my own feelings and individual Judgement are concerned, I am as unwilling that any one should be persecuted on the one side as ~~I am desirous of general quiet on the other~~ that men's minds should be disturbed and the public peace

f110ᵛ interrupted, on the other. I would have every man mind his own business, and be free so to do; but I do ⟨not⟩ see why Philosophy, (or the attempt to find out the first principles of Things and to reduce things to their first principles) should not be a Business or ~~Profession~~ Calling for the few, to whom God has given the ability and inclination, as well as the production or preparation of other things useful or honorable to mankind—or why they should not enjoy the same liberty in the pursuit thereof.—"

To which he might have added:—~~As long as the~~ Let but the Philosopher follow the rules and ~~dictates~~ by-laws of his own Mystery, let him philosophize as freely as he will, provided he does indeed philosophize—the only danger is from over-jealousy that attracts the attention of the Many to his lucubrations and drags them before an unfit and incompetent Tribunal under the pretence of preventing it: ~~Thus~~ as when in the times of Darkness and Superstition, the Wizard-hunt~~er~~ing Inquisitor ~~unstopped the Phials & let loose the fuming Liquors of the Chemist, and thus *made*~~ the

f109ᵛ † "Neither is this second fruit of Friendship, in opening the Un-
f110 derstanding, restrained only to such Friends as are able to give a man (they indeed are ~~the~~ best;) but even without that a man learneth of himself and bringeth his own thoughts to light, and whetteth his wits against a Stone which itself cuts not. In a word, a Man were better relate himself to a Statue or picture than to suffer his Thoughts to pass in smother."—Bacon's Essays.

~~nuisance he sought to detect and punish~~ shattered the ~~Flas~~ close-
stopped Flasks and hermetically sealed Phials of the Chemist, and
letting loose the fuming liquors *made* ~~it~~ the nuisance, which he
sought to detect and punish.

4955 3½.15   Aye! your dull fellows of Lombard Street,   *f25ᵛ*
with their Plums and Surplums may boast of their Prose-perity—
mine is Poetry-perity.
     Pros-perous and Verse-perus

4956 3½.16   Mʳ G. complained of eating his Veal (pie) over
again—(rose on his stomach)—Aye! you are no friend to *R*evela-
tion.—

4957 3½.17   Mʳˢ G. versus Rhoda who went to Blackheath
Sunday Morning, 9 °clock, 12 July, 1823—& is not yet returned,
Monday Evening, 8 °clock, 13 July—
G.   I expected her back long ago—
STC.   You can't be disappointed then in not seeing her *face*.

4958 3½.87   In Lord Bacon's New Atlantis there is a sen-   *f111*
tence which ~~the~~ might have been quoted during the Debates on the
Marriage Bill by Lord Ellenborough or Canning—"Marriage
without consent of Parents they do not make void but they mulct
it in the inheritors: for the children of such Marriages are not
admitted to inherit above a third part of their parents' Inheritance."—

4959 3½.88   On Lord Eldon's speakingly slightingly of
Lord Bacon on some point—
     The learned Lord, ~~in looking up~~ standing near the footsteps of
his colossal Predecessor, looking up mistook his knee for his
Forehead, & swore that he was blinded & had never an eye in his
head—

4960 3½.89   P. Servilius medium se gerendo nec Plebis vi-   *f111ᵛ*
tavit odium nec apud Patres gratiam inivit. Well worth the attention of the Whig Party.

4961 3½.90   Full of sound and practical Sense is that Speech
of Zeuxis, in answer to his admirers—"Had I made the Boy as
lively as the Grapes, the Birds would have been afraid to touch
them"—In other words—It was not in the power of my Art to
make the paint-boy, the human flesh, features, and expression as
like the real Boy as ~~lik~~ painted grapes may be like real Grapes—
therefore, it was injudicious in me to injure the nobler part of my
picture by doing unnecessary justice to the meaner.—Or, Had the
grapes been less like, the Boy would have been more.—

4962 3½.91   an upright shoe may fit both feet; but never
saw I a glove that would fit both hands—. It is a man for a mean
or mechanic office that can be employed equally well under either
of two opposite Parties.—

f112   4963 3½.92   Mr Irving's error. ⟨To use⟩ Declamation (high
& passionate Rhetoric not introduced & pioneered by calm and
clear Logic) ~~I would compare~~ is (borrowing the simile tho' with
change in the application) from the witty-wise, tho' not always
wisely witty, Fuller) "to knock a nail into a board without wim-
bling a hole for it, which then either not enters, or turns crooked,
or splits the wood it pierceth".

4964 3½.93   Admirable Remark of Lord Bacon's on the in-
termixture of the Learning to swim by bladders (a facili ad gra-
vius) and to leap by loaded shoes—a gravi ad faciliora/p. 192–3,
De Augment.

f115^v   4965 3½.101   Collection—as they occur—
     Words now obsolete, or confined to technical use, or ~~used in~~
bearing a different sense from the present usage.
Incontinent = instantly, without *containing* yourself.
Utter = lose, get rid of
Depart = give away a portion of, portion off. Sir T. Smith. see
p. 78.
Abide = wait for. *Idem*
Huke—New Atlantis. Q^y—misprint?—some sort of cloak or attire
     . .
     "A Messenger, in a rich huke"—

4966 16.389   Strype's "Heat of Fancy" in his Life of Grin- *f₁22ᵛ*
dal above all.

4967 3½.95   Spirit, Edge, Sparkle—Starts of ~~witty~~ humor- *f₁12ᵛ*
ous wildness, like a wild lad that plays with his infant Sister over
the Mother's shoulder—These make the man that wins the hearts
of Princes/

4968 3½.96   Our Spirit strives after Unity in the system of
its Cognitions, and endureth not to have for each particular Appearance a several Principle assigned; but believes itself to behold
Nature there only, where in the greatest manifoldness of
Phænomena it discovers the greatest simplicity of the Laws, and
in the utmost prodigality of Effect and Products the utmost fru-
gality of means.

Every Thought therefore, that without confounding the distinctions in the Results proposes for its end the simplification of the
Principles, deserves attention, however immature and inadequate
it may be—if it answer no other end, but that of exciting attention
to the Idea, which is at the base of all Theory—namely, that the
discovery of the true ~~Principle~~ Cause, and the simplification of the *f₁13*
supposed Principles, coincide—& therefore that the latter is a *presumption* of the former, and the contrary a proof a priori against
it—and of supplying a new impulse & occasion to the Questioning
of Nature, to confirm or confute, it will have more respect from
the wise than whole Books of mere Distinctions for Distinctions'
sake, or to swell a Nomenclature. In a philosophers' Purgatory ⟨or
Ariosto's Limbo in the Moon,⟩ such men would be employed in
describing each several leaf of an Acre of French or striped
Grass—with the different positions, breadths, & shades which
each has peculiar to itself—

4969 3½.97   A certain Italian (saith Hollerius) by often
smelling to Basil had a Scorpion bred in his Brain.—Hoc appli-
caverim περὶ ἀξιολόγου temporibus erroris mei nunquam redi-
turis!—

f113ᵛ   4970 3½.98   Rue or Herb Grace a natural *Sycophant*, ⟨so⟩ delightfuling to grow near the Fig-Tree—⟨that it marketh it out⟩—at the same a great Destroyer of Toads, i.e. a Toad-eater, I suppose.—So saith Pliny: and veryily I have known so many ⟨human⟩ *Herbs of Grace* with rueful Phizzes, and who like in one other point resemble their vegetable Namesake, [which is said to be again a perfect Antidote to all Carnal Desire in Men, but yet worketh the very contrary effect in women.—]

— LibiCupidinis Oestumrum

Ruta Viris, minuit,   mulieribus auget
              ∧
Cupidinis Œstrum

Ruta Viris flagrans minuit, mulieribus auget—

that I am much inclined to credit his account, tho' his great Work is the very Africa of Natural History, monstrorum ferax.—

f114   4971 3½.99   ⌐I never knew why Southern wood was called the *old* Batchelor, till I found in Pliny that a branch of the Herb laid under the Pillow doth greatly move a desire to the conjugal venereal Embrace and is of force against all ⟨frigidities whether⟩ charms preventive of the Desire or suspensive of the ability—an experiment "to be made (sayth old Master John Swan) in the night of Sᵗ Jefferies Day—which is neither before Christmas nor after it"—⌐

4972 3½.100   An excellent specimen of Logical Conclusion—The αλυσσον, alyssum, lunaria, and in English Madwort, or Moon-wort, in Italian called: *unshoe-the-horse*, a herb in high esteem with the Alchemists in the making of Silver, and such like lunaries and lunacies—

Tis said Who to Du Bartas dare his faith refuse,
That Steeds, that tread on Moonwort, lose their Shoes.

f114ᵛ   Whence gets't thou, Moonwort? tell us—from what Smith
Hammer and Pincers to unshoe them with.
Sith the best Farrier cannot set a shoe
So sure, but thou with speed cans't it undo—
Now quoth the World's Specialist, Master John Swan (the 4ᵗʰ Edition of whose Hexameron or Speculum Mundi much enlarged & beautified was printed for John Williams, 1670): This secret,

tho' somewhat strange, is mightily confirmed by what Pliny writeth of the Wood-pecker, who by the means of a certain Herb draweth the Wedges out of the Holes in Trees, which Shepherds have driven in: Yea, Nails, or any other such like Clinchers, are fetched out by virtue of this Herb—of all which was assured to this wise Ancient by one Trebias, who bore witness of the same. See *Plin.* lib. 10. *cap.* 18.—Mʳ Gerard saith, that for its rareness *f₁15* it is sown now and then in gardens, but the Seed (saith he) is brought over either from Spain or Italy. *But why may it not grow in other places? I remember what a Friend of mine, of good credit, once told me, that his Grandfather had a Close, wherein it was a common thing to find their Horses unfettered in the morning, altho' they were fast shackled over night. He named also the place; but I have now forgotten it.* HERE DO I CONCLUDE, MUST HAVE GROWN SOME OF THIS HERB.

turn to p. 92
Celandine, Chelidonium.   *f₁16ᵛ*
   For Pliny writes (tho' some thereof make doubt,
   It helps young Swallows eyes when they are out!—
Cyclamen (Sowbread) dangerous for Women with Child to touch, take, come near, or stride over it. *"Without controversy"*, Mʳ Gerard affirmeth, who attributeth this effect to the *extraordinary natural attractive* virtue in it. "He therefore, having it growing in his garden, used to set sticks or bars around it, that such a danger might be shunned."

4973 25.4   Had I proceeded in concert with R. Southey   *f2* with "The Flight and Return of Mohammed" I had intended a Disputation between Mahomet, as the Representative of Unipersonal Theism with the Judaico-Christian Machinery of Angels, Genii, and Prophets; an Idolater with his Gods, Heroes & Spirits of the Departed Mighty; and a Fetisch-Worshipper, who adored   *f₁ᵛ* the Sensible only, & held no Religion common to all Men or to any Number of men other than as they chanced at the same moment to be acted-on by the same Influence,—as when a hundred Ant-hills are in motion under the same Burst of Sun-shine. And still, chiefly, for the sake of the last Scheme, I should like to do something of this Kind. My enlightened Fetisch-Divine would have been an Okenist + Zoo.-magn. with the Night-side of Nature.

*f*85   4974 25.54   + o. The Point.—The Punctual.—⟨The⟩ Puncturient. ⟨Ex. gr.⟩ In the effort or tendency to form materia nervosa—Return to the Point, which in the Line is l̶o̶s̶t̶ dualized in its production, which in the Plane is s̶e̶p̶a̶r̶a̶t̶e̶d̶ divided.
1. The Line. The Lineal. Stark, rigid, firmamental.
2. The Plane. As the Point ⟨is lost⟩ in the Line, so the Line in the Plane. The Principle of the Fluid.
3. The Body. In its propriety, the Semi-fluid.
+ − sub eâdem Copulâ = Magnetism.
+ and − sub desiderio Copulæ = Electrism.
    Magnetism and Electrism contemplated as *Acts* of a Self-constructive Power, and identified in this Power = Chemismus—. The transit from Elec. per Magn. into Chemismus = Galvanism.

4975 25.55   Quarles' Emblems—Even in the present Rage for our old poets, how much under-rated! B̶o̶o̶k̶ ̶I̶.̶ ̶I̶I̶.̶ N.B. Those of inferior merit, yet meriting praise, I mark by the numeral Cyphers—⋇ the numeral Letters
Book I.—IV.—5.—X—5ᵗʰ of 12—XIII.—
Book II.—III. IV.—V.—VI—(p. 93. 7ᵗʰ 11—18 line) XII. 1.2̲. (!!) X̲I̲V̲. XV. p. 122. the last 16 lines.
Book III. p. 125. *126* last 14 lines, erasing 9 & 10ᵗʰ. IX. very *spirited*.

*f*85ᵛ   4976 25.56   The Divines of the Middle age, Sᵗ Bernard, Hugo, &c—the great Store houses of Conceits, from whom not only Quarles but Young drew largely.—May t̶h̶e̶y̶ not the occasional use of them be excused on *mnemonic* grounds—as Hooks and Barbs of technical memory—Ex. gr. The Heart in the proper and metaphorical sense. "It is not sufficient for a Kite's Dinner, yet the whole World is not sufficient for it." Hugo de animâ.

4977 25.57   A weighty Answer to a weighty Objection grounded by the Jew & Pseudo-Christian on the promises of Pardon to the Penitent under the old Covenant.—True! God hath

from the beginning promised Forgiveness to the Penitent; but hath
he promised penitence to the Sinner? ANSELM.

4978 25.58   Id Numerus Numerans se non sibi substan-
tians, e̶t̶ ἀυτόνιος et in prole sive producto perditus = νομος.—
The l̶o̶s̶t̶ self-losing = γενεσιουργὸς λήθη.

4979 25.59   Genius = δαιμων καθολου συνακολουθὸς βιου
μυσταγωγος, νομευς θειος—
Summus hominum omnium genius communisque est ipse Amor—
Genii per turpem sui amorem falsamque prudentiam πτερορ-
μυσταγωγος, νομευς θειος—
     καλῳ, σοφῳ, αγαθῳ—τουτοις δη τρεφεται τε και αυξεται μαλιστα
του της ψυχης πτερωμα—
Wisdom the most beautiful, but Love is Love of the Beautiful.
Love therefore perforce a *Philosopher*.

4980 25.60
          Da mihi fræna, Timor! Da mihi calcar, Amor!   *f86*
The fear of the Lord is the beg. of W: but perfect *Love* shutteth
out F.—I love nothing without thee & nothing with thee which I
love not for thee!—

4981 25.61
          Peace, peace, my dear! Alas! thy early years
          Had never faults to merit half these tears.
          Come, smile upon me! Let thy Mother spy
          The Father's image in her Baby's Eye!
          Husband these$\begin{smallmatrix}\text{spendthrift}\\\text{guilty}\end{smallmatrix}$drops against the rage
          Of harder fortunes and the gripes of age:
          Thine Eye's not ripe for Tears!
                         Quarles' Emb. = p. 93.—

4982 25.62
          αει φιλοκαλος
Ερως εστιν το τ̶ο̶ν̶ καλον φιλεῖν
Των δε καλλιστων Σοφια
Ερως οὖν αναγκη Φιλοσοφος.—
               συλλογισμος Πλατονικος.

4983 25.63   ευσχημοσυνη)(ευθημοσυνη—or θυ the total
sum and symmetry of outward accomplishments, address, de-
meanor, mien, grace in movement, elegance in attitude, proportion in make and adjustment, expressiveness in Countenance,
expression in look and gesture, and intelligibility in all.—These
collectively form the ευσχημοσυνη.

The inward Realities, correspondent to these, and of which these
are the Symbols and and Sacraments, constitute the ευθυμοσυνη.

ποθοβλητος ψυχη. | εισπνήλης)(αἰτης
                     amans   amatus

f86ᵛ 4984 25.64   Strange oversight in Linnéus and other Naturalists who have represented the superiority of Man to the Ape as
an difference in degree and that an *historical* event—that they did
not see that the apparent approximations of the Simia to the Man
are (as far as they are not artificial and the work of Man) the
perfection of the animal, the fullest evolution of its possibilities
under the most favorable circumstances—whereas the Approximations of certain *Tribes* (N.b. not of Races) to the highest order
of the Simia are manifest *Depravations* of the Man, aberrations
from proper Humanity and in the literal sense of the term, Degeneracy.

Nor is this all. Examine into the particulars of the obtrusive
resemblances, and they will be found to be the necessary
phænomenal Result of the absence, latency, or partial suppression,
of the essential characteristics of Man: and that in this state of
inward mutilation or atrophy he resembles an Ouran Outang more
f87 than a Goat or a Bear is an accidental consequence of the quadru-
mane Form of the Simia kind, that are all fructivorous and made
to live in Trees, and who must therefore be made capable of looking strait forwards. Hence they have the foramen centrale in the
Retina—which with this exception Man only possesses. From these
two properties, both altogether physical and animal—viz. the four
hands, and the climbing prehensile powers and habits, an Anato-
mist with the position and direction of the Eyes rendered necessary
by the frequent necessitated (not voluntary) erect posture, an Anat-
omist might easily deduce all the other Semblances of humanity
and prove them to be resemblances of the animality of Man, that

which is common to ~~him~~ Man and Beast, and not of his Humanity, or that which constitutes him *Man* in contra-distinction from the Beast.

As the analogy which cannot be denied and as the chasm which $f87^v$ in spite of the undeniable Analogy can not be filled up or bridged over, between the granulation of Metals ~~and~~ or their Arborescence in the Galvanic process, and the formation of the Infusoria and the Conservæ; so neither can the Analogy or the impassable Chasm between the highest Orders of Animals and the Man. They are *Types* not Symbols, dim Prophecies not incipient Fulfilments. Their purpose for themselves is wholly diverse from the *meaning*, they convey, and which depends altogether on the alien Natures, *to*, and *for*, and in fact *by*, whom it is conveyed. They are the Lichen Geographicus with the substitution of a *real* for an *imaginary* coincidence: still however only a *coincidence*!

The Word *became* Man, and Man *is* a Word. All below are *used* for Words, unpartaking of that which they but *excite* and occasion. Thus, Ants are Anatomists, and give lectures in Osteology; but only for Anatomists, qui Legenda lecturi sunt. Withdraw the *read-* $f88$ *ing* Eye, and substitute the Clown's—and what is it then? The relics of a Carrion-feast.

The Vegetable Realm is Nature's Stomach, ~~the~~ one vast System of her digestive Organs. ~~The~~ Relatively to this purpose, the Animal ~~Creation~~ World are ⟨but⟩ her Organs of Rumination—the myriodontal Jaw by which she chews the cud, and the supplemental culinary Stomach, in which the food is ⟨drest,⟩ seasoned and flavoured.

The extensor-souls of the Muscles Phytoid—the flexor animal—. We stretch in sleep, stiffen in death—the Plants with stiff extended fibres *react* in infusions—the fibres contract into the first forms of animalcular life, the living millets of the Microscope—and then dying again extend into microscopic vegetation.—Theory of the Infusoria—the Wimmel and Schimmel of Oken.

Das Luft-leben bey den Vögeln von der Masse losgerissen bricht in Töne hervor, die als der lebendig-gewordene Blumenduft laut werden—daher verstehen sich die Vögel und die stillen Pflanzen—

daher der Contrast von dem Farbenglanze der Tulpen und dem verschwimmenden Grau der sussduftenden [*süssduftenden*] Nacht-violen wiederholt durch Papagayen und Nachtigallen.

f88ᵛ   At all events, Speech must have existed before it declared itself in Sound: for the Sound is to the Speech as the Effect to its Cause, and begins to exist, as Sound, in the living Ear; as significant Sound, in the pre-conformed Instinct; as intelligible Sound in the pre-possessed and pre-possessing Intelligence. ~~In~~ As the first, it is representable in the unreflected ray or line; as the second, in the horizontal pendulum; as the third, in the conjunction of the hori-zontal and circular. In this highest connection, Sound may be de-scribed as the *Phœnomenon* of a Diameter, the two peripheric Points of which are reciprocally Subject and Object, to each other: the Diameter in actu being the Speech itself, beginning ~~from Reason, in Reason, and as Reason,~~ and ending in Reason, and rightly there-fore named "Discourse of Reason" i.e. Reason *in discursu*, sive transitu, and differing from it only as ~~the~~ Lightening from Elec-tricity. Contemplated in its eminence and Absolute⟨ness⟩, Speech (Sermo, Verbum, Logos sensu infinito) denotes the essence of the filial Deity; but in its finite and derivative existence, it is the act, attributes, and in the most ancient languages the name, of the *hu-*
f89   *man* Understanding—i.e. the Understanding as distinct from Rea-son but not, as in inferior Natures, *contra*-distinguished therefrom. Divinely and in the fullness of Inspiration did the Evangelist af-firm—In the Beginning was THE WORD: and the Word, God of God, became the Mediator between God and Man, and the Re-deemer of Man. But as Man ~~f~~ finds his redemption from the Captivity of his own Will in the Divine Humanity, so (we are assured by the Apostle) does the whole inferior Creation, which fell not willingly, seek yea, yearn and groan (i.e. significantly, ~~not~~ tho' inarticulately, utter its desire) for ~~the unloosing~~ Redemption in the Human Animal. In Man is the solution of their dark Enigma: ~~in Man do all inferior Natures seek~~ for the Word, the Son of God, has become the Son of Man, the living Sacrifice, and the perpetual Sin-offering. They too await his second Coming, even as the Fathers of old waited for his first—the soundless Plants breathes forth their sacrificial Odors in lieu of the ~~utter~~ atoning Word—and as the utterance of their Yearning—the Murmuring

Stream, the pealing Thunder, the Storm with all its impatient, and ~~f89ᵛ~~ *f89ᵛ*
all its ~~mourn~~ lamenting and demanding voices seek but THE
Word. It sleeps in the Metal; and ⟨under the touch of Man,⟩ like
an infant, συνετα ασυνετως βazon, it awakes in the ~~Storm & under~~
~~the touch of Man~~tring and the Cymbal and the brazen Trumpet.
What may ~~we~~ the Soul dare hope—~~on~~ that hath carried Captivity
Captive, that hath seen the Vanity of the Vanity, even the Death
which the Life and living Process of the outward Senses throw off
as their Recrement, and deposit as the Caput Mortuum—the Appearances that the Ixions of Materialist would fain embrace as
Reality, yea, under the name of Nature as a female ~~God~~ Divinity,
but in truth the Apparition of Nature, the Superstition of the
Mind? Reflect on the Past, contemplate the Present! The Organic
Forms ~~of~~ animal life, evolved from the Mollusca to the Ape, each
in its kind the Product and Exponent of some selfish Appetance,
assailing or resisting, pursuing or escaping, ~~these and these lower~~
these that like single features and partial limbs taken separately and
caricatured, or like Fragments prepared for some harmonious
Whole that ~~impatient ere the~~ had burst into particular life, anticipating the Command ~~as~~ in a dream, and in still enduring Slumbers
Somnambulant, for whom Vision is no more than a Scent, and the *f90*
broad Day-light exists only in the single Ray that determines for
each its mysterious *Rapport*—all these in the human Organism are
reconciled and balanced into Subordination and Symmetry, and
understand one another. In Man, the Vowels have been found, the
hidden Letters have become Consonants—the Sound there of is
heard, and the interpretation is made. So is it even now in the
outward Man—but in the inward and in the World of History
which is its Phænomenon, Man is to the Idea Man as the inferior
Creatures to their Co-organization in the Human Frame—. What
when the ~~w~~ spiritual World shall be perfectly reconciled, the
~~World~~ Manifold in each Soul to the Manifold in every other, and
all to the Mediator as their common Head. ψυχων απασων δια του
Λογου και εν τω Πνευματι αυτου συνκοσμουμένων, what may we not
then expect, according to the known & experienced harmony of
the physical & moral Natures—whether *in* man or likewise *with*
him, we presume not even to conjecture. But this we know that
even in the elemental Mass the Spirit pleadeth to the Spirit with

*f9o*ᵛ　groans unutterable, that the whole Creation groaneth to be redeemed—and that the Spirit can g̶ not groan unheard.

4985 25.65　　　"The Progress of Infidelity", in the last Quarterly—*Hugh*! *Hugh*! E. Hugh ⌜usse⌝ Hussee!—But why an oto-
tatoi or a̶n̶! When the Stilts are worn out or lost, the Borrower
must stand on his own legs.—But he does not *stand*. Well—he is
grounded on his own bottom, and exempt therefore from all risk
of falling—"Miracles the proper, *only* and *irrefragable* Proofs of
Revelation". Quere. What is meant by Revelation? or by the paraphrase, which the Asserter of this position would substitute by
way of a definition? Is it, or is it not, itself a Miracle?—To the
f̶o̶r̶m̶e̶r̶ immediate subjects, he would say—It is an interior fact,
r̶e̶q̶u̶i̶r̶i̶n̶g̶ that may be merely subjective—& therefore requiring
an objective proof of its own virtual objectivity. Good!—but if the
first Miracle must be proved by a second, t̶h̶i̶s̶ does this second
require a proof? N̶ "The proof is in the eyes of the Beholders"—.
Nay, the eyes may prove the occurence of some visual
phænomenon; but cannot be a proof of its being a *miracle*—unless
whatever is (relatively to the Eye-witness) unusual in the
phænomena or in their order of succession is to be called miraculous. If a wonder (miraculum) be that which folks wonder at, you
have only to assure yourself of the i̶g̶n̶o̶r̶a̶n̶c̶e̶ ̶i̶n̶ ̶o̶r̶d̶e̶r̶ ̶t̶o̶ ̶t̶a̶k̶e̶ ̶t̶h̶e̶
e̶x̶i̶s̶t̶e̶n̶c̶e̶ ̶o̶f̶ sterility of the Soil, and you may take a plentiful crop
of such miracles for granted.—Something more than seeing a
thing is necessary even for a proof, that the thing was there to be
f9i　seen—ex.gr. ghosts—much more, that it was all seen—the whole
truth and nothing added or changed. Now among the necessary
proofs of the p̶r̶o̶o̶f̶s̶ aforesaid, the Rationality of the matter revealed = the doctrines is tho' negative & in most instances conditional only, stands foremost. Tho' only conditional, it is a conditio sine quâ non.—Nor is this all. The rationality (o̶f̶ i.e. Insight
into the possibility) of a̶ ̶t̶h̶e̶ *Revelation* itself independent of the
contingent matters in any particular instance revealed is requisite.
We must at least have c̶o̶n̶s̶i̶s̶t̶e̶n̶t̶ conceptions consistent, and distinctly appropriate of what is meant by the terms—T̶h̶i̶s̶ ̶a̶t̶ ̶l̶e̶a̶s̶t̶
s̶e̶e̶m̶s̶ ̶c̶l̶e̶a̶r̶ We will suppose this to be the case, tho' it is not quite
so simple a problem as the Grotians make it; b̶u̶t̶ ̶t̶h̶i̶s̶ and return

to the Doctrines revealed. It seems clear, that they must be such as the ⟨human⟩ Reason can receive and approve, and consequently judge of; and yet not such as the human Reason could have discovered or otherwise acquired. (I speak, of course, of miraculous or extra-experiential, Revelation.) Now if this be possible (and I am not disposed to deny it) it is itself a proof—and one too better entitled to the name of *irrefragable* than the Miracles of the Senses for Geometry assures us that Reason is one & the same in & for all men, while all experience evinces the direct contrary of the Senses, and the Memory, and of Testimony grounded thereon.— Miracles therefore are not the *only* Proof of a Revelation—that *they* (i.e. Miracles in toto genere) are irrefragable, amounts to the formidable assertion, that Miracles are Miracles—and if A ~~is~~ has been apodictically *proved* to be a Miracle, it cannot be proved to be otherwise—in short, that what is irrefragably proved is proved irrefragably. But we will content ourselves with having attracted notice to this confusion or co-inhesion of meanings, tantamount to—All men are Philosophers—Socrates, Plato, Zeno, Epicurus, and Aristotle I mean—Miracles, i.e. the Miracles recorded in the $f_{91}{}^v$ New Testament, are the proper, only and irrefragables proofs that the Doctrines ~~taught by~~ contained in the New Testament were miraculously revealed to the Workers of these Miracles—. Now, tho' I for myself ~~now~~ would as readily admit that they were & under the same of equivalent conditions still are, *a* proper (i.e. fit and expedient) proof—i.e. inducement to the acceptance—of the Christian Revelation, I need only ~~to remind~~ the two first Chapters of St John's Gospel to deter me from acceding to the assertion, that they are *the* proper (i.e. peculiar & exclusively or at least pre-eminently appropriate) *Proof*—i.e. co-ercive Evincement—of that Revelation.—That they are not the *only* Proof, has been already shewn— & Christ himself declares a Blessing for those, in whose minds it is superseded by other, & higher, and more certain evidences. Nay, the Writer himself afterwards enumerates several others.— And lastly, that they are irrefragable is a Petitio Principii, if Reasoning be intended—but if only matter-of-fact, the Position amounts to the assurance, that Hussee *thinks*, that the *certainty* of the Facts and of their miraculous nature has never hitherto been refringed, ~~or~~ and *believes* that they never will.

4986 25.66

Jack Snipe
~~Spews~~ Eats Tripe:
'This therefore credible
That Tripe is edible.
And therefore, perforce,
It follows of course
That the Devil will gripe
All who do not eat Tripe.

And as Nic is too slow
To fetch 'em below;
And Geffard, th' Attorney
Won't quicken their journey—
f92　　The Bridge-street Committee
That ~~swear~~ colleague without Pity
To imprison or hang
Carlisle and his Gang
Is the Pride of the City,
And tis Association
That alone saves the Nation
From Death and Damnation.

4987 25.67　　One of those Clergymen who find it more easy
to hide their thoughts than to suppress the thinking—and who treat
the Articles as the Whale did Jonah—i.e. swallowed him but could
not digest him.
　or thus
　It is to be feared that in the subscription of the 39 Articles too
many Clergymen imitate Jonah's Whale & swallow what they cannot digest. In one sad point, however, worse off than their great
Prototype, they gulp down what they are unable to digest yet not
permitted to *throw up*

f43　**4988** 20.57　　27 Aug. 1823. Charles Lamb's difficulty.
　We have *begun* to be: what stronger analogy can we have for the
belief, that we shall cease to be? That which ~~begins, may~~ has a
beginning may have an ending—nay, in all things, we know of
and as far as we know, have an end.—The substance, the prima

materia, is not this or that Thing—the Gold is not *this* Guinea—
the Guinea is gone, the Gold remains in this Breast-Pin.—
But suppose a pre-existence—still the analogy of our own unconsciousness of its mode of existence or its having existed in any
mode, is valid in presumption of a similar oblivion of our present
state on the supposition of a post-existence.—
Then the argument from the coincidence of the decay of the   *f42ᵛ*
moral & intellectual with the organic.—And lastly
The argument of non-inducement to the wish of so believing
the common belief from his individual feeling—I want that which
I am, have, or had, an of which alone I can form any conception—
(mem. equivoque of conc. for image) not a something for which
I have no organs or corresponsive faculties—and if I try to imagine myself with positively other organs, & faculties, it is no longer
myself but an Angel or other Non-descript with the name (and
even that is to be exchanged for "a new name") C.L. instead of
Michael or Rafael.—
All these I answered—and as I think, fully & fairly.—The last
arg. denied as a *fact* by C.L.'s own acknowlegement not the S.T.C.
now before him but the S.T.C. ten years ago, was is the object of
his Love—& such the S.T.C. of now will be 10 years hence—
Therefore even to him the argument from the child & Cake to the
Man & Sweet-heart is of valid application—Item—the World not   *f42*
a total present, like a circle in space—but a manifest Spiral or
infinite Helix in time & motion—Proved by Geology.—
Item—a gradation proved, but if so, a point of individual Cons.
must begin somewhere—. In what instance has an *instinct* been
found to lie? A craving for a state (as in insects whose instincts
antecede the organs of its realization) where no such state or object
exists?—Why the instinct for a future state in man? Cannot be
denied to be generic—and as universal, as any other instinct, tho'
wanting or undeveloped in Individuals.

4989 20.58   To secure to each the greatest sphere of
fre⟨e⟩dom compatible with the safety, the security & the unity of
the whole, this (it has been often asserted is the proper aim, &
true object of a state, & therefor contains the definition of the
word.—This is very plausible, it says much, and there was a time,
and that of many years continuance in which I thought that it   *f41ᵛ*
means all; but of late years I have begun to fear that it means little.

At all events more is conveyed to my mind & far more definitely in the affirmation that the true aim & object of a state & its implied definition is—by the restraint of all—to enlarge the ⟨outward⟩ spheres of the inly free, so as at the same time to increase the inward freedom of those, whose outward spheres it had contracted. The epithet "outward" as here used for the purpose of increasing the clearness not of adding to the meaning; for the sphere of free-agency is the ultimate definition of property, which can be no better explained, than by saying, that it is the sphere sacred to an individual within which he may realize his own free agency without disturbing interference from the acts of other free agents: for this is not only the best explanation of the word; but *f41* the sufficient and only justification of the thing. For it is well worthy your remembering that the only definition, which deserves the name, a definition namely in contradistinction from an explanatory paraphrase which defines a thing by a reduction of the same to its proper antecedence & ultimate ground or productive principle. This exemplified in the two definitions of a circle, the one from equality of the centro-perepheric radii, which is a mere diagnostic or criterion, & other from the circumvolution ~~of the extreme~~ of a straight line the one end of which is fixed, which constitutes the circle, & potentially containing all its properties is antecedent to, & the ground of all.—

f40ᵛ

4990 20.60   Description of an approaching Thunder-storm from the Zapolya (improved)
~~Casimir~~ RUDOLPH
        See, the Sky lowers! the cross-winds waywardly
        Chase the fantastic masses of the Clouds
        With a wild mockery of the coming Hunt.
CAS.
        Mark yonder Mass! I make it wear the shape
        Of a huge Ram that buts with head depressed.
RUDOLPH (smiling)
        Belike, some stray sheep of the oozy Flock
        Which, Poets tell us, the Sea-shepherds tend,
        Glaucus or Proteus! But my fancy shapes it
        A monster couchant
        ?(~~Stretch'd out recumbent~~) on a rocky shelf.

CAS.

Mark too the edges of the lurid mass—
Restless, as if some idly-vexing Sprite,
On swift wing coasting by, with tetchy hand
Pluck'd at the ringlets of the vaporous Fleece!

4991 30.62
Sion: Coll: Lib:—.   *f67ᵛ*
Burnet's Memoires. U.3.4.
Wharton's Hist. of Laud, S.9.28. 2 vol.
Kirktons Hist. of the C᷆ of S. S.9.33
E.B.1.4.—

4992 3½.94   A witty sweetness in Reproof, a tenderness that   *f112*
soothes and a humorous fancy that amuses—diverting from the
offender while it draws the attention to the offence, may be compared to the ~~magnet~~ Loadstone of Laurentius Guascus the Physician, recorded by Cardan, the needles touched with which were so
civilized that the wounds & punctures made by them were never
felt at all ⟨or at least occasioned no pain.⟩ Turn to p. 92
So the Loadstone preserved in the Salt of a Remora has power to *f116ᵛ*
attract Gold out of the deepest wells—Certainly (says Sir Thomas
Brown) a studied absurdity, not casually cast out but plotted for
perpetuity: for the strangeness of the effect ever to be admired and
for the difficulty of the Trial never to be convicted". (A good
specimen of that grave Humour that renders Sir T. B. so delightful to a learned Reader.) But doubtless it is an intended allegory—
attractive manners Cautious Delay & Tenacity &c.

4993 3½.102   10 Septʳ 1823. Wednesday Morning, 10 °clock.   *f117*
                On the tenth day of September
                Eighteen Hundred Twenty Three,
                Wednesday Mornɪɴɢ, as I remember,
                Ten on the Clock the Hour to be.
                ~~The Watch & Clock do both agree~~

4994 3½.103   An *Air*, that whizzed δία ἐγκεφάλου (right
across the diameter of my Brain) exactly like a Hummel Bee, alias,
Dombeldore, the gentleman with Rappee Spenser, with bands of

Red, and Orange Plush Breeches, close by my ear, at once sharp
and *burry*, right over the Summit of Quantock, ~~item of Skiddaw~~,
at earliest Dawn, just between the Nightingale that I had stopt to
hear in the Copse at the Foot of Quantock, and the ⟨first⟩ Sky-
Lark that was a Song-Fountain, dashing up and sparkling to the
Ear's Eye, in full Column, or ornamented Shaft of Sound in the
Order of Gothic Extravaganza, out of Sight, over the Corn-fields
on the Descent of the Mountain on the other side out of sight, tho'
f117ᵛ twice I beheld its *mute* shoot downward in the sunshine like a
falling Star of melted Silver—

Aria Spontanea

Flowers are lovely, Love ~~of~~ is flower-like,
Friendship is a shelt'ring Tree;
O the Joys, that came down shower-like,
Of Beauty, Truth, and Liberty—
When I was young, ere I was old—
~~O Youth, that wert so glad, so bold,~~
~~What quaint Disguise hast thou put on.~~
~~Would'st make believe, that thou art gone,~~
~~O Youth! thy Vesper Bell has not toll'd~~
⟨O Youth, so true, so fair, so free,
Thy Vesper Bell has not yet toll'd—
Thou always &c⟩
Thou always were a Masker bold—
What quaint Disguise hast now put on?
To make believe that thou art gone!
Ah! was it not enough that Thou
In thy eternal Glory should'st outgo me?
Wouldst thou not Grief's sad Victory allow?
Hope's a Breeze that robs the Blossoms
Fancy feeds ⌈on⌉ murmurs the Bee
                        embosoms
                        Poesy—

f130ᵛ 4995 3½.110   That in the year before Christ 1383 Ceres
came to Athens and taught the Athenians to sow corn; and that
only 27 years (1356) the Eleusinian Mysteries were instituted (or
first introduced) at Athens—I believe, the one as much as the
other—my faith in either being = 0.—

Troy taken 1184; four years after Jepththa's rash Vow.—

Of an obscure Writer or Painter or any thing with an illustrious
name—as celebrated as Homer Junr, the Tragic Poet, 263 B.C./   *f131*
contemp. with Timæus of Sicily, the Historian—
After Christ, 1625, 27 March, æt. 59, James the first died—
ascended the Throne 1603.—
  1638. Solemn League & Covenant in Scotland
  1641. Strafford's Exec.—the Irish Massacre—& Chillingworth's
      Death.
  —42 The Civil War began—Edgehill
  47. Charles delivered up by the Scots ⌐ . . . ⌐
  49 beheaded for Lying.
  1651. 3 Septr Battle of Worcester, Quakers.
  53. Protectorate.
  1660. May 29. Restoration/

Important Dates of Connection—
~~1578~~ From 1582 to 1452 Years before the Birth of Christ, including a space of 130 years—the following Events:
~~1582~~ 1. The Chronology of the Arundelian Marbles begins
(1582). ² The Birth (1571) and Death (1451) of Moses. ³ Cecrops
bringing a colony of Saites from Egypt founds the Kingdom of
Athens (1556) and ⁴ Scamander that of Troy (46). ⁵ Cadmus introduces 16 Phœnician Letters into Greece (1493)—⁶ The Am-
phyctionic Council established (1497) ⁷ and Sparta built by   *f131ᵛ*
Lacedæmon.—
  1007 Solomon begins his Reason
  907. Homer flourished

  884–864. Lycurgus—the Art of Sculpture in Greece—the
Building of Carthage by Dido—
  757. Isaiah—753. Rome built.
  600. Alcæus, Sappho, Pythagoras, Ezekiel.

4996 3½.117

I

Verse, ~~is a~~ that Breeze mid blossoms straying   *f135ᵛ*
Where Hope clings feeding like a Bee.

Both were mine! Life went a Maying
With Nature, Hope, and Poesy
    When I was young!
When I was young! Ah ~~was a when~~ woeful When!
Ah for the Change twixt now & then!
    This House of Life
And ~~this poor House~~, not built with hands,
~~This Body that does me grievous wrong~~
    Where now I sigh, where once I sung,
Oer Hill and Dale & sounding Sands
How lightly then it flash'd along—
~~Like dist~~ Like those trim Boats, unknown of yore,
On ~~Lake~~ winding Lakes & Rivers wide
That ask no aid of Sail or Oar,
That fear no spite of Wind or Tide
Nought car'd this Body for wind or weather,
When Youth & I liv'd in't together.

This snail-like House, not built with Hands,
This Body that does me grievous wrong.

                    2

Flowers are lovely, Love is flowerlike,
Friendship is a sheltring Tree.—
O the Joys, that came down Shower-like,
Of Beauty, Truth, and Liberty
    When I was young—
When I was young ~~ah woeful when~~ when youth & I
~~Ah for the Change twixt now & then/~~
In Heat or Frost, we car'd not whether,
Night and Day, we lodged together

When I was young—ah ~~words of agony!~~ woeful when
    Ah for the change twixt now & then,
~~O youth, my Housemate dear, so long, so long~~
~~I thought, that thou and I were one,~~
~~I scarce believe, that thou are gone!~~
O youth! for years so many, so sweet

It seemed that Thou & I were one,
That still I nurse the fair deceit
And scarce believe that thou are gone!
Thou always wert a Masker bold.
I ~~hear the Breath~~ mark the change in gait, and Size,
Those grisled Looks I well behold.
But still thy Heart is in thy~~ine~~ eyes
What strange Disguise hast thou put on
To make believe, that thou are gone!
⟨When I wa~~s~~ young—ere I was old   *f136ᵛ*
Ah! happy ere. ~~ah~~! woeful when⟩
When I wa~~s~~ young—ah woeful When,
Which says, that Youth & I are twain!
⟨Ere I was old
Ere I was old! ah woful Ere
Which tells me, Youth's no longer here!⟩
O youth! for years so many & sweet
Tis known, that Thou & I were one—
~~Tis but a gloomy~~ I'll think it but a false Conceit.
Thy Vesper Bell has not yet toll'd
~~I'll not believe,~~ It cannot be that thou art gone.
And Thou ⟨always⟩ wert ~~still~~ a Masker bold.
~~Some~~ What strange disguise ~~thou'st~~ hast now put on
To make believe that thou art gone?
I see th~~e~~ose Locks in silvery Slips,
This dragging gate, this alter'd Size;
But Spring-tide blossoms on thy Lips,
~~And the young Heart is in~~
~~The~~ And Tears take sunshine from ~~the~~ thy eyes.
Life is but Thought, so think I will,
That Youth & I are House-mates still.

                    3   *f137*
Dew-drops are the Gems of Morning,
But the Tears of mournful Eve:
Where no Hope is, Life's a Warning
                    me   *thee*
That only serves to make us grieve,
                    Now *I am* old.   thou art

f11   4997 26.13   Seeds raised without Soil, merely by carefully
distilled the Water; yet on burning the Plants, even a larger portion of Iron is discovered than in the same Plants that have grown
in an irony (eisenhaltng) Soil—Emblem of Original Sin.—

In the heights of philosophic Speculation, as on the summit of
the Alps, the Plants all grow into corolla—The Flower is often
larger than all the rest of the Plant. = Imagination.

A ~~plan~~ Gourd of the pumpkin kind, called Kora, in Egypt, will
if supplied with water produced pumpkinettes four inches long in
24 hours' time.—4 × 12 = 48. Might very well make a half-
hour Clock—nay, a ¼ ; for the 24th part of Inch may be made
distinctly visible.

Generally but most remarkably in Persia which is above all
countries subject to cold hell-blasts, *Brizes*, the Plants, smooth elsewhere, are cloathed with a thick wool, oftentimes a downright Fur,
and sharp stiff Thorns. Offence & Defence of the Nations of the
North & Mountaineers—God tempers the wind to the shorn
Lamb.

f11^v   4998 26.14   The Chemist holds himself to know a Substance
then first, when he has decomposed & by decomposition destroyed
it, as *that* Subjstance. He understands only what he has mastered.
Suppose, for instance, that a certain contagious miasma had Nitrogen or some Oxyd of Ammonium + ~~plu~~ Hydrogen for its constituent parts. By decomposing it, the now innocuous elements, ~~of~~
Ammonium and Hydrogen, would exist, but the *Contagion* would
be no more. Nor is this effected by Decomposition only. In some
instances, ~~the~~ an equivalent result follows the Transposition ~~or in-
version~~ of the Components, where two bodies are in question—as
the Sulphate of ~~Soda~~ Lime and the Muriate (Chlorate?) of Soda or
common Salt.—& we have Sulphate of Soda on the one side, while
on the other instead of "the Season of the Earth" we have a deadly
poison, i.e. Muriate of Lime.—In other instances, the reversing
f12   or otherwise altering the *proportions*. Thus Oil becomes a mad'ning
Spirit, the tastless Water a corrosive Acid.—Even so is it with
Evil, *materially* considered—with the Matter or Substance of Evil.
Regard it, as ~~only~~ a *Potence*, or as having only potential Being,
and it is the necessary and good Involute of the Will and therein

of the Personality of all ~~in~~ finite Intelligences. It is ~~the~~ an essential perfection of their Will, which without it would cease to be a Will, as long as the *Actual* will, or the Act of the Will, is to ~~negative~~ deny itself, to sacrifice itself, as a finite Will—and to use its *Base* as the condition of its own *positive* ⟨or +⟩, reality, which can only be in correlation to an opposite − reality. But what exists potentially, may become actual. This is an interpretation of the ~~word~~ term, potential, and not an inference, or any thing predicated of it. Suppose this to have taken place, and that the Will has given actual existence or + reality to the − real as the Potential in itself. Here two cases are conceivable—both ideally possible. Either, namely, the Evil Will avails itself of its Actuality to will itself *absolutely* and totally, ~~to continue actual & yet remain potential~~ ⟨to will no potential, in itself, but to be as ~~the~~ God, the Universal Will, who is Actus sine ullâ potentialit[at]e, and like him to be ~~baseless~~ self-based, ~~so~~—having the ground of its existence in the existence⟩—a contradiction indeed; but what else can be expected to proceed from that which is ⟨itself⟩ a contradiction to Him who is *all* Truth, who is the Truth itself, the source & substance of all possible truth?—⌐ . . . ⌐ (an impossibility indeed, and a Will necessarily self frustrative & impotent, but what else can proceed from that which opposes itself to Omnipotence?) What must the result be. The evil will has no power~~ful~~ to exclude the Good: for in itself it has no power at all, ~~much less power over the Good~~ except against itself, by its inherent self-frustration—much less can it exert any power over the Good.—It simply therefore *falls* from the Good, as a Precipitate. And here we have the abysmal Mystery of the Devil, the Evil One—the Contrary of God, absolute emptiness as God is the absolute Fullness, a ~~rayless Fire~~ mere Potence as God is a pure Act, wherein all is that actually is—a ~~rayless~~ hidden Fire, for ever seeking a base in which it may ~~mani~~ actualize & finding it only to convert it into its own essences, which is necessarily baseless: (for how can that *have* a Base which then alone truly *is* when it is itself a Base?)—and still, in the expressive language of Holy Writ, roaming about, like an hungry Lion, seeking whom it may devour. For it is indeed an eternal Hunger, and the very *Sting* of Famine. Eternal because below all Time even as God is eternal by transcendency to all Time—and unintelligible, be-

f 12ᵛ

f 13

cause ~~east~~ an Outcast from intelligence even as God incomprehensible as containing all intelligence. And lastly, Eternal Death as God is eternal Life. Repent it cannot—for the power of Repentance is potential Good: and the Evil Spirit is itself potential, and has its potentiality in itself & like the increase of Darkness (Νυκτι εοικως) can only be manifested by the remaining Light. Well does the Apostle name it the Mystery of Iniquity—the Enemy, whom Christ came not to reconcile but to put under his feet.—Hence it is greatly to be ~~fearful~~ed, that the Disbelief of the Devil is but a hollow Bravado—a boastful ~~Lie~~ No-meaning, ~~to give~~ for the purpose of giving to a Negative the semblance of a Positive. The unbelief, the unconsciousness of the Devil is the characteristic of our Age—and a perilous symptom of the spread of his Dominion. For the Mole houses in Darkness, and says not, It is dark!—

ƒ13ᵛ

Let us now turn to the other possible case—that namely, in which the Good is made potential, and the Evil Actual. *Tomorrow I will do well*—only today/⌈ . . . ⌉ but! it is hard never to indulge one's Self. In all other things I will obey the Command; but this Fruit is fair to behold, the Serpent has eat it, and has become my Equal—unless I eat it, and become (as by parity of reason I may conclude that I shall) equal to the Gods, I shall lose my relative rank—and surely, it cannot be so very much against God's Command when I do this to preserve the order and proportion of things which he himself established—and I will be sure to employ my new powers to do good.—Here then there was a temptation from without—and as evil was produced from without, in the ~~certain~~ center thro' and from the circumference, so it might be hoped that Good or the Remedy of the Evil, might likewise be introduced or affected by circumstantial & extrinsic influences.—But alas! how came it to be a temptation? That it was a temptation argues a ~~change already in~~ shifting of the Poles ~~or~~, an Indifferencing or Neutralizing of the One by the Other, to have already taken place—Or rather the Potential must have no longer been the *base*, the latent *ground*, of the Actual, the ~~een~~ hidden center to the manifest Circumference of the Microcosm, but the Will has shrunk into a radius, having the center as one of its Poles—into a bi-polar Line, the Potential Evil being the negative Pole, and the Actual good the Positive Pole, while the *Self* is the punctum indifferens

ƒ14

ƒ14ᵛ

between both. In this sense it we may understand and in this alone
we can justify Luther's Assertion, that the *free* will of Man supposes a previous illapse, and a present ⟨co-⟩immanence, of the Evil
Spirit, and that he who has (i.e. consciously, or actually) a choice,
has already chosen—and But observe—this is said of a Will that
Man's Will, of a Self-will, and not of the Will *in* Man which
prays, Not my Will but thine—let it *be* only as it knows itself as
a perpetual gift in order to a continual Sacrifice—and in this consists the περιχώρησις of the Divine Spirit in Man regenate, and in
the Spirits of M made perfect.—Now this Fall in the will, this its
falling asunder, constitutes the *corruption*/and this here is the Mystery, and hence the correspondent Mystery of the Remedy—of
which, however, our Reason can comprehend thus much—first,
that the Fall is different from that of the Devil, and presupposes
itself certainly as the ground of the Temptation, perhaps as a *condition*, tho' neither ground nor cause, of the Temptability. Hence
fallen Man may be redeemable (for tho' the actual Good has dis-   *f15*
appeared, it has not been excluded, or utterly fallen off from, but
only sunk & if I may so say degraded into the Potential—Man, I
repeat, may be an object of a subject of Rescription, tho' the Devil
was not: and he may be an Object of divine Compassion, and the
Idea of Man still contained in the Logos, or Substantial Idea of
God, & in this respect an Object of Divine Love—tho' in this
respect only—for "in him (the filial Word) alone God loved the
world".—But secondly, we may see—that Man tho' not absolutely
unredeemable, could yet be redeemed by that power only, which
could act at once *in* the Will and *on* the Will. But this is possible
only for a Power *Divine*. But this is not all—nay, compared with
that which is still wanting, it is easy to be understood. What remains to be shewn, I see indeed, or believe myself to see, in its
main Outline—tho' the line be dim and dissolving, my Eye traces
it. But I find it most difficulty to express myself in words: and for
the majority of my readers I almost despair of conveying my
thoughts intelligibly—How indeed should it be otherwise? Since
words are necessarily general and all reason⟨ing⟩ by *words*, all *discourse* of reason, is more or less a reasoning by analogy/er where
it is more than a process of concluding what we had before in-   *f15ᵛ*
cluded (as when having *in*cluded Socrates in the dates number of

Mortals we *con*clude his mortality—But the Will is unique/belongs
to no Species, or Class, and possesses no common or generic characters: nor can it receive explanation from any thing else, for it is
~~forever~~ necessarily antecedent, or it ceases to be a Will—~~it~~ and
how can aught be put before ~~it~~ that which is the first, to account
for it? And even if this were not the ~~cause~~ case, yet how can the
Will be accounted for? ~~either by any of the~~ Not by such things, as
receive their ~~name~~ class and name from the supposed absence of
the Will, & ~~can not be~~ their own incompatibility therewith? Not
by any part of the Problem, of which the Will is itself the Solution? Yet in ⟨the⟩ one or the other of these all the objects of human
Conception are comprized.—Well then may it be difficult to convey by words even the Conditions, under which a Will may be
conceived to be acted on and restored, without ceasing to be a *Will*,
~~and~~ i.e. a self determining Principle. But more than thes ~~requisite~~
Conditions no wise man, no man who understands thes meaning
f16   of his words will require or expect to have shewn him. Blest are
those, who know the truth experimentally, ~~tho' to utter it they~~
~~knew not "They stand in the *Secret* of the Lord~~ "who have stood
in the *secret* of the Lord" (Jer. 23.18) tho' to utter it they know
not. Nor ~~has it been without long and~~ is it without awe, and after
long and ~~repeated considerations~~ earnest meditation in solitude,
and frequent communications with ~~zealous and~~ Ministers eminent
for their zeal, learning and successful labors, of both the established churches of this Island, and ~~of the Dissenters others who~~
that I proceed to ~~do~~ contribute such further Lights, feeble & inadequate tho' they be, that have dawned upon me ~~I have oft~~ In our
preceding reflections we had arrived at the conclusion, that the
restoration of the corrupt will could ⟨only⟩ be effected by a Power
that could at once act *in* the Will and *on* it. But if this is to be
more than a ~~delusive visual visual~~ visual image misapplied, a confusion of a relative and arbitrary *inward* in *place*, as when a bottle
let down into the sea ~~fills~~ known to fill itself we speak of the Water
within, in distinction from the water without, tho' we know that
all relations in Space are necessarily outward, and that Matter, ~~as~~
*f16*ᵛ   ~~Matter~~ contemplated abstractly, ~~and as far only as it is a as a mere~~
~~phænomenon in Space and exclusive~~ of ~~whatever is not an Object~~
~~of, all ⌐ . . . ⌐ that is not an Object of our Sight~~ as a mere

phænomenon in space, and exclusively of all that cannot be *seen*, can be represented to the mind only as surface, and that ~~its~~ the thickness of a Body, abstracted from its weight, its repulsion & whatever else makes it a *body* in distinction from mere Matter, can be no other way trans~~lighated~~ into the language of Sight than by imagining a superposition of surfaces—even as in Moses ~~or in~~ *the faces* of the Waters" is an equivalent phrase to that of chaos—while real depth, and true inwardness are affirmable only of Life, Sensibility, Mind, Spirit, Power—in short, of Substance as opposed to Surface, Subject as opposed to Object. On the other hand, if the process of assimilation in a living body, or even that of chemical combination is different in kind from mechanical juxta-position, this difference, which is utterly unrepresentable to the Sight or Imagination, can be conceived in no other way than as an inter-penetration of ~~its parts~~ Substances, so that the parts are truly in-   *f17* ward to each other. Sedulously therefore guarding against all intrusion of Sight and Sense, and ~~purifying and preserving~~ all mixture of fancy with ~~our~~ the Idea, lest the identity in the names should seduce us into a confusion of the meanings, and lead us to overlook the utter heterogeneity of relative merely nominal Interiority and the real *In*~~wardness~~ness let us try to discover under what conditions the latter can be supposed to take place.—

4999 26.15   "Yet I never heard his enemies blame him for the common vices of Princes, except the two bastards in his youth, and his swearing in his old age. People generally think his greatest unhappiness was, he mistook wilfulness for constancy, his condescensions always coming too late, granting unprofitably to his people to-day that which would have abundantly satisfied yesterday; and the next day that which would have satisfied this day, but all out of Time.

Kirkton, p. 47.

5000 26.16   Mental Revolutions & Moral Epochs: or the   *f17ᵛ*
Sceptic's Pilgrimage—or
     The Sceptic's Pilgrimage: or the mental revolutions and moral epochs in the Life of a Seeker after Truth.
1. Birth & childhood. 2. Boyhood in a Metropolitan public School

⟨moral Perplexities⟩ 3. ~~Youth~~ Innocence Loss of —. Early Infidelity by force of the Ludicrous & Apparently absurd, with the charm of new knowledge—from Voltaire's Philosophical Dictionary—Cato's Letters: & Necessity.—3. Youth/—Paley—Arianism/ Despise Voltaire—strong hold of the Morality of the Gospel—but all Morality made to consist in Sensibility, generosity, and abhorrence of Meanness & baseness, with vindictive Indignation at all real or supposed Oppression/Negative Democracy—i.e. Intolerance of Lords, and Kings; but far more of rich men—& hence a purely *Ideal* Politician—So far good that it preserved the link between ~~my~~ politic~~als~~ & religion.—/4. University—platonizing Socinianism/&cc 5. Early Manhood—/ (henceforward the facts & characters fictitious/

f123ᵛ   5001 16.392   A Conversation to a young man of great susceptibility and *heart*, and fine Imagination who had been railing, reasoning & laughing at the notion of the *Spirits*—A lively picture
f124   of the various Vices or Habits, foreseen as too likely to befall *him*, drawn out poetically as so many possessions of evil Spirits, under all the wildest yet truest forms of Thought. Ex. gr.—In health seemingly—eye clear, pulse regular, the delight of all who heard him/in one moment the evil Spirit comes/*Opium*. He had sold himself to *Death* to escape Pain—& the Spirit comes regularly to *dun* him—
So of the others.

5002 16.393   Surenhusius—Mʳ Fr.—to be sent immediately

5003 16.394   A [?gab/job/fob] [?Curtsy/Curby] (Mʳ Q—

f2   5004 30.3   Why so earnest in the defence or palliation of the Statesmen & Nobles or Gentry who confederated with the Reformers in H. 8. and E. 6.—Scoundrels they were—but from Papistry in which they had born and bred must their Scoundrelism have been derived—and with many of them, as the infamous D. of Northumb. the making the Ref. odious was one of the devilish excuses to their own consciences for their robberies & other sacrilegious Acts. The like answer to the persecutive conduct of Cranmer.

5005 30.60

f67ᵛ

Of
or   at

Ramsgate
Autumn, 1823
while contemplating a sort of Dramatic Novel, or Tale in a series
of Dialogues; to one of the ⟨imaginary⟩ characters in which the
Thoughts, ~~and~~ Plaints, Heart-effusions &c. refer. This memento
is prefixed, ~~lest~~ in case by accident this or other memorandum
books should outlast their owner and fall into the hands of his
Survivors, and they should fall into the mistake of supposing that
they had found ⟨in them⟩ materials of actual biography—& the Vie
interieure of S.T. Coleridge.

5006 30.61   Intus ut libet, foris ut moris est—attributed to
Cremonini, a follower of Pomponatius, & was afterward the favorite motto of the Italian Aristotelian Infidels.—

5007 30.63   The celebrated Physician and Systematizer of   *f67*
the Aristotelean Philosophy, with which, partly as materials, partly
as tools, he fabricated a sort of Pseudo-Spinosism, held that the
Imagination was affectible by outward things without the outward
senses—and Pomponatius seems to have held a similar opinion of
an *active* Imagination capable of affecting the Imagination & thro'
it the Organization of other similarly organized Animals in certain
so *constellated* Individuals—and this is his solution of true Miracles.

5008 30.64   Sunday Evening, 12 Octʳ 1823.—Think of   *f66ᵛ*
writing to De Quincy—and to Charles Lamb.—*Thought.* A man
who once only in his Life, unknown to himself, undiscovered by
others, & having returned ~~and~~ re-undrest, & fallen asleep &
awaked unremembering, had somnambulized, & during the somnambulism said, & done, & went *so* & *so*—and committed such
an act,—Many & these his friends Eye-witnesses. Conceive the
state of that Man's mind during his whole after life—.The strug-

gle between testimony & his own inward unconsciousness & consciousness (we may suppose) of the utter heterogenëity of the act
to his habits &c.—

5009 30.65   The base Spirit of the ~~Quarterly~~ Laudite Faction in their literary Implement, the Quarterly Review. The English Clergy live & ~~prosper~~ flourish, God be praised, under the
order of Things brought about by Burnet & others—Yet their *spite*
against all the clerical adherents of the Revolution & Flattery to
Sancroft &c, the non-juring & Jacobite Faction—No spiteful
abuse of a contemporary Enemy ⟨of the bigot Court,⟩ but has Gos-
f66 pel insight with these Critics, who contrive to unite the interests
of Vanity & Cowardice—abuse the privilege & licence of anonymous publication, & yet to be publickly known as the Authors.—
The *we* gives courage & influence—the *I* sucks in the credit.—
The consequence of the passage of pretended literary criticisms into
political Pamphlets, & *original* Essays—a really *base* Jugglery.—
The superiority implied in the character of a Judge & the ~~vile~~ Evil
of a *Public*, as bribed by their own Envy, Vanity, and Ignorance
to admit every self-elected Pretender to the Bench—.

5010 30.66   Sunday Night. *Ultima* alarmingly affected in
her Head & Eyes, doubtless, from over-excited feelings of Distress & honest Indignation.

5011 30.67   Monday Morning, 13 Oct! Ult. had a good
night—& better. But this is usual for the first half of the Day.—

5012 30.68   *Thought*. The two errors—of concluding a man
bad as ~~an~~ private character from his action as a Statesman (Eliz.
James I, Castlereagh, Liverpool)—and that of holding him a good
man if his private life & conduct be such, however slavish &
despotic as a Statesman.

f65ᵛ 5013 30.69   Thought. Extraordinary occasions eagerly
brought forward by the Philo-despotists in excuse of the illegal
Actions of Kings & their Ministers—they alone are to be judged
by ordinary Rules whose very existence arises out of extraordinary

occasions, and who are striving at the imminent hazard of Life &
Fortune to establish Liberty, Light, and pure Religion.

5014 30.70   Christ's Kingdom alone *natural*. because Christ
is of superhuman Nature/(Corollary against the Psilanthropists) In
all other ordinances but that of Kingship, we feel and act on this
Principle—Judges for instance. 1. Laws & Customs of Court. 2.
Precedents. 3. Many Judges, or a Bench. 4. The Bar. 5. Publicity.—and yet read only the State Trials & the Trials of Writers
versus the Aristocracy (Earl & Countess of Sunderland, ex. gr.)
and ask—if even all this be not but barely enough—

5015 30.71   Am reading the Biographia Scotiana—published in 1816 & C. K. Sharpe's Publication of the Kirkton MSS
1817—the first attacking & deprecating religious Toleration, and
the second out-Heylining Heylin himself, or the Presybitero-Pre-
latico-ultra-papistical Parker, or any other Chaplain of Laud or
Sheldon! Extremes meet. One advocates Despotism over Mind
sure to end in Despotism over Body & Estate—the other Desp.
ov. b. & e. sure to end in Despotism over mind!

5016 30.72   Pretty Answer & ⟨almost⟩ too elegant to be   *f65*
credible in a Scottish Reformer, of Mr Patrick Simpson, who
being blamed for his study of Pagan Writers, answer—They were
Jewels he was borrowing from the Egyptians to adorn the House
of God with.—

5017 30.73   Thought. Truth self-possessing is serene, joy-
ous, a blue Heaven far above the Clouds of Doubt, the Growls &
flashes of Anger—. Can I then hesitate to interpret the irritable
Prudery of our modern Orthodox into the sense of Hollowness
where a bottom should have been felt? Do not attempt (says Leighton, most unworthily) to ~~represent~~ explain the Trinity—(No! to be
sure, not. How can the most simple, that of which are other
Truths are but the Folds, be explained—i.e. unfolded?—but he
means, *represent*)—Do not attempt to present the Trinity to your
mind by any notions (No! not by *notions*; but ideas?)—~~n~~either by
the adequacy of God's self-knowlege &c.—in short, attach no

meaning at all to the words collectively—just as if instead of the phrase, Son of God, divine Revelation had informed you that Jesus was a *Son* of a *Gun?*—a blasphemy!—Blasphemy? to against whom? against Job's Friends, who ⌈ . . . ⌉ *lie* for God & would have all other men do the same or be damned?—Am I blaspheming the Trinity by contending, that it is Truth itself, & Light itself—not

f64ᵛ

only not words without an apprehensible Meaning but the ultimate Meaning of all other other Meanings? And by exposing in all its proper depravity and absurdity the assertion of the contrary, as an absurd error coupled with the deforming Vices of Hypocrisy, Fear, Hate, impotent Rage & wilful Self-delusion? Is a Fool, a hypocritical Fool, to be privileged from the punishment of his Folly, because he has aggravated it by choosing the best and holiest ~~subjects~~ Truths for the subjects to exercise it on? ~~Or~~ Do Folly and Hypocrisy become sacred as a soon as they are exercised on sacred Subjects?

5018 30.74   The smaller & shallower the River, the apter to overflow & transgress its bounds—applied to petty offices./— The Ocean never overflows.

5019 30.75   Bad night.
    Tuesday, 14ᵗʰ—Not well—confused & with a sense of fullness in the head, so that I declined bathing. Qʸ The villainous Creature, Ramsgate Table Beer?—

5020 30.76   Thought. Mem. to make a table of the ill results of confounding the Ec with the En klesia—among others, the inevitable Dread of & angry prejudices against Truth if in the

f64

form of Change, when it involves the loss of some hundreds or thousands a year? & yet the Livings in a ~~Chur.~~ *Religious* establishment must be ~~de~~ connected with these & these points of Faith— Whereas for a Professor of Natural Philosophy, or of Metaphysics, it is only necessary that he should understand his Science—& every Change for the better (if he does understand it) will be a source of Joy & Triumph. Too sanguine rather than too backward. Ex. gr. Professor Blumenbach—the medical Profession generally on Dʳ Jenner's Proposal of Vaccination—Linnæus in the Botanical World—

Werner in the Geological—Hunter in the Surgical—Priestley,
Scheele, Lavoisier, Davy, in the Chemical—Compare with this the
imprisonment of Galilæo—&c to the end of the Book—.

5021 30.77   *A learned Plainness.* Inquisitous Scotice =
Curious.
P. 60, Bibliog. Scot., 157–60.

5022 30.78   The ~~Defence~~ Vindication of Cromwell's Ejec-
tion of the Republican Parliament grounded on mere Railings
against the members is the only Passage of Milton's Life or Writings which I find ~~myself unable~~ it impossible to defend; and (with
scarcely less anguish than if I were speaking of some dear Friend,   *f63ᵛ*
whose Bier I had just been following, do I say it) difficult even to
palliate. ~~Rather~~ I might indeed refer to Milton's political Principles, viz. that the settling of Liberty must necessarily be effected
by a Dictature, that Liberty consisted in the government of the
Wise and Godly—to his Confidence in Cromwell from the utter
incapability of conceiving how such a man should turn from so
full a Glory to the toys of vulgar Ambition &c. but instead of
~~making~~ a stammering excuse I will rather make use of this ominous Sun-spot as a Warning to Men, who have drawn down a
faithful *Genius* with them in their descent from Heaven, not to
sink from their fixed sphere of contemplation into the orbit of
wandering Stars & personal Interests—which their very Excel-
lences prevent them from understanding—for Likeness is the only
Organ of true Perception.

5023 30.79   Biographia Scotiana.
P. 13. Note—Abuse of Toleration-Principles and the Right &
Duty of Magistrates to extirpate Heretics by the Sword—this
being evidently the meaning of the Covenant—first insinuated, and
then justified by condemnation of the Contrary! 1816! See Southey's Life of Wesley, Whitefield.‖ Erskine.

5024 30.80   Mʳ John Scrimgeour who having (he being a
notable wrestler & ~~an~~ extraordinary familiar with the Lord, & his
favorite Daughter given over, notwith.ⁿᵍ his prayer) reproached

f63   God with unkindness & almost ingratitude—thou knowest how I
have served thee, & thou seest that I take pleasure in this child. It
is very hard, I cannot obtain such a thing &c—said his prayer,
but was told not to use the like boldness for the future, for such
particulars.—A similar story by Cotton Mather of a John Smith
about a lost Boat in New England—!

P. 125 and 131. a most interesting Contrast between the two extremes of ultra-Calvinism and the *Take it easy* gentlemanly Creed
of the infra-Arminian Bishop.—

f62ᵛ   5025 30.81   Wednesday 14ṭ5ᵗʰ—better—delightful three Dip
& a Swimlet Bath, the Sea just stirring enough to be lively. Mʳˢ
Gillman too evidently better, God continue it! But still her Flow
of Strength, the tiny Spring at the bottom of the natural Fountain,
requires careful *husbanding*—too much (and but a little is often too
much) must not be drawn at once from the Basin. Wait for its
own gentle overflowing.—

5026 30.82   THOUGHT. He who begins with loving Christianity better than Truth, will proceed by loving his Church (or
Sect) better than Christianity, and end in loving himself better
than all three.—
        Church Historiography. If a Writer, tho' an eminent Member
of their own Church, Burnet or Leighton for instance, honestly
let out a few unpleasant Truths, it is enough to say—For all this
we have but the suspicious authority of the prejudiced Burnet. If
you ask proofs of this Prejudice & Partiality, these very passages
are adduced. So if you support a charge against Laud by quoting
Bishop Hacket, it is enough to say, that Hacket was the Zealous
Friend of Archbishop Williams—when no other perhaps could
have come at the information. In short, every man is to be a Liar,
who relates aught which the Party do not like to hear—as soon as
a possible motive can be drawn from any one of the Relations in
f62   which the Relator must have stood in order to be a competent
Historian. But all this, mark you! on the one side only of the
Question—on the other even a Non mi ricordo is Gospel, an
Evangelist.
        Secondly—your modern Impartialist, & Balancer of Merits,

who has either no ⟨Principle and consequently no⟩ determined conceptions of any form or party—State or Church (Ὕσοι) or a determined contempt of all, as Hume—.

5027 30.83   Took a single Pill with my Gruel at 9 ?clock.
Had a quasi-sleepless inly waking night, without much pain yet restless.
Thursday, 15ᵗʰ October 1823. Agitated at Breakfast by the sudden *Upsetting* of two Letters over me, in the calomelitical & trembling equilibrium of my nerves—N.b. my own fault.—
Had a wretched day till near Tea-time & did nothing but doze over Warton's Edition of Milton's Juvenile Poems—a capital Edition on the whole; but this (the 2ⁿᵈ Ed.) infamously misprinted, the Greek and Latin quotations often unconjecturable. . . . Spite of Warton's eulogistic Compliments to Judge Jenkins, Milton plainly subjected to posthumous persecution in the annulling of his Will. Good heavens! What a melancholy picture of his domestic *f61ᵛ* state—as Jupiter to his least Moon, so M. to S.T.C.—as M. to S.T.C., so θυγατερες to ———/

Mem. Not to forget to preserve somewhere my Detection of Warton's & the general misinterpretation of Milton's first Latin Elegy. Strong proof of the perverting & blinding power of party prejudice, for the passage is even school-boyically false-construed by Warton. n.b. Warton's unfledged criticism, but it was quite as much as his Age could bear, & we owe ~~feven~~rvent thanks to him—.

5028 30.84   Friday, 17 Octʳ —Pretty well—mean, God willing, to bathe & hope, that the Sea-plunge will remove this feverish Lead-mist in forehead & eyes & sickishness at stomach. Utinam, modo semel—et ante prandium!

5029 30.85   Query. *Could* any creature but a Prince have perpetrated such an act as the Murder of Crichton? Vincent de Gonzague, Son of the Duke of Mantua. More horrific acts I have read of; but an Act of such princely Baseness never.—
Gowrie Conspiracy—Bishop Andrew's kneeling Request as related by Hacket. The most absurd of grave Humbugs.

5030 30.86   The difference between Whig & Tory at present not easily described; but the difference between a Whig Minister, acting on Whig Principle, & a Tory Minister seems to me to consist mainly in this, that the Whig Minister contemplates the King as an Osiris, Tibetan Lama, or Sacred Crocodile—worships what is represented, & does his best to keep the representative in good order, and well *drilled*—as well knowing that a divine Ox is still an Ox, and that a sacred Crocodile has a devilish plantation of Teeth./The Tory Minister, on the other, regards him as his Master to whom he owes a dog-like fidelity. The King and the individual Man are the same Being & indistinguishable—Nomen et Agnomen.—Lord Keeper Williams.

f61

5031 30.87   Story of Oran & St Columba—whose first Building on Iona fell down by machination of some evil Spirit— A human offering being required, St Oran offered himself, & was buried alive—but at the end of 3 Days St Columba wishing to have another look of his old Companion had the earth removed when up started Oran all alive & kicking—& began by informing them that all, they had been taught to believe of Hell &c. was a humbug—St Columba alarmed set to work himself & disciples in shovelling back the earth upon the Blab and in a few minutes put an end to his

f60^v *5032* 30.88   But it is my Birth-day.—And so I said— Bathed—& felt the benefit. The outward ~~& almost~~ or just *beneath* the surface, Aching across the umbilical region removed.—

Were I free to do so, I feel as if I could compose the third part of Christabel, or the song of her desolation.—

5033 30.89   *Mem.* Awoke from a dream-sensation of the intensest, deepest, bitterest agony of *Grief* respecting Derwent—a purer more condensed Grief per se Grief, without fear or anger, cannot be felt—and found in the instant of awakening a *heavy pain* across the umbilical region, probably at the pit of the stomach.— Now this (often have I noted it) this translation of pain into mental passion!——

5034 30.90   Advice from a truly Christian Bishop to a
Statesman. A̶l̶ Legislate & regulate for us collectively, as the
Priesthood, as if the Dæmon of Spiritual Priest, of Worldly
Grasping, of Persecution, of Interference with the Temporal Mag-   *f60*
istracy, and of employing the Laws as instruments of our own
passions and purposes, were our presiding and pre-disposing Nature; but to every individual Clergyman, in whom no proofs or
presumptions of these tendencies are found, as to a minister and
representative of Christ, dear for his Master's sake, and dear for
his own as a faithful Follower of that dear Lord, who so loved you
& all Mankind that became Sin that you might become Righteousness and Joy Everlasting.—In human Masses the Whole is a
different Being from the Component Parts, as moral Integers.—"

5035 30.6   Of the railers against the Covenanters & Cam-   *f10ᵛ*
eronians—You drive men frantic & then accuse them of frenzy!
You deprive them of every earthly Hope, of ⟨every natural,⟩ every
rational, support and then scorn them for seeking it in the unknown world, by supernatural channels, and in interferences unsanctioned by Reason. Even under their error was a deeper Truth   *f11*
than the Heart of the Scorner even knew—for their error was but
in the clothing—the substance was, the communion with the eternal in the spirit of Man, & thro' it with the Spirit of the Universe—

5036 30.7   One sure Criterion of a Government or a Party
Scheme—Is it founded on the Good, the Human, on Human Nature—& its object to aid it, call it forth, direct, & marshal it in
the extrication from & warfare against the *Alien*, the Evil—and
has it Faith in the Good collectively & timelessly?—or is it
grounded on the evil, does it commune with the evil, and attempt
to produce a hollow bastard Good by setting Evil against Evil—
& making it a scoundrel's Interest to be a Scoundrel of good repute?

5037 30.8   Apostacy of a man of Genius—of a Genius—is
this a mean grief? Think but of what would be done if all, all men
of Genius, W.S., W.W., R.S.—had united in unceasing Warfare

f1 1ᵛ for the Good!—One of the subtlest of the Devil's Sophisms is the introduction of the category of Magnitude into the moral world— the intense *littleness* of all that can be done in the ant-hill as if man were not the *presence* of all.

Whence the Swell as from an Abcess of Ocean when a Brutus strikes—It is not the mob called Rome,—but Man that has destroyed the Anti-human.

5038 30.9   Protestants, divided into 1. Reformers of the Latin Church—Renovators of the Christian Religion. The latter of course placed themselves in the same situation as the primitive Christians—& curious to observe, how closely they recommenced the steps of the Church, they had recoiled from—Theocracy— Communion with the Spirit—Infallibility—Intolerance—Two successive Kings in Scotland that were sincere Zealots of the Kirk, Davids, would have completed the Parallel!—Well sketched in W. Scot's Macbriar in Old Mortality, Vol. I, p. 156, 157.—

5039 30.10   N.B. The contrast between the Fanatics (Cam-
f12 eronians &c) in Scotland and the Enthusiasts in England cannot be carried too much into detail—(The concluding § *phs* of the Life of John Nisbit of Hardhill—the Editor (1816) supporting the same atrocious principles, p. 408 ⟨murdering the prisoners in cold blood at Drum Clog.⟩ Yet the ~~beginning~~ 3 first § phs of the Life of Robert Garnock p. 364–365—an excellent specimen of the *persuasive* influences of persecution.)—The Prophets &̶, with Daniel, were Old Testament Favorites of the English Enthusiasts; but still the contrast holds good that the Scotch Fanatics h̶ preyed like Hyænas on the *bones* of the Old Testament, ~~which~~ & we may carry on the metaphor, for Hyæna like, they dragged their Prey (Religion) backward. The Mosaic Law & the Historians, but chiefly the Stories of the Wars, in Canaan & the civil Wars in the barbarized kingdom of Israel after the Separation from Judæa—The English junketed on the Dainties of the New Testament, especially the writings of Sᵗ John, the Apocalypse included—The Epistles of Paul indeed might be said to be common to both Parties, yet even in these the difference is very striking. The Scotch sought every where for a new Theocracy, a religious *State*, a one adamantine Form of Government—in short, for *The Church*, Ecclesia

Phænomenon. The English for means of superseding Government—for Congregations as *Families,* an independent neighbourhood—in short, for Symbols & All in each Mikrokosms, of the Ecclesia Noumenon/

5040 30.11   In searching ~~for~~ Mr John Blackadder's house,   *f12^v*
he & Mrs B. being then at Edingburgh, Sir James Turner's men
endeavor to force the children to betray their Parents by making
preparations for roasting them alive at the fire—& having stabbed
the beds throughout the House, amused themselves by turning the
children out in the dark night in their shirts—

5041 30.12   One of the epidemic sect of Æolists, whose
fruitful imagination led him into certain notions, which altho' in
appearance very unaccountable, were not without their mysteries
& their meanings—
    furnish plenty of matter for such, whose converting imaginations dispose them to reduce all things into Types; who can make
shadows, no thanks to the Sun; and then mould them into substances, no thanks to philosophy; whose peculiar Talent lies in fixing tropes and allegories to the *Letter* and refining what is *literal*
into figure & mystery.
                                        Tale of the Tub. Sect. XI.

5042 30.13   Let ῩΣΣΕ ask himself whether the spirit-
blighting liberticidal effects of Pseudo-Catholicism can rationally
be attributed to those particulars, dogmatic or cerimonial, which   *f13*
Arch. bishop Laud continued to reject, and disown? Or not rather
to the points, as to which he was one with the papistic Divines,
and their Competitor in the race of Persecution?

5043 30.14   The new-risen Day that shines in on the Day.
                                        Dante Paradiso I. l. 60

5044 30.15   What so different as Illness (bodily) and
Wickedness?—How Hume shocked me by confounding them! &
still does—but by the choice, it must come to that with a reflecting
mind.—Illness Wickedness? or Wickedness Illness?

5045 30.16   Hephæstion and Clytus the original Tory and Whig.

5046 30.17   As I disclaim all necessity of palliating Shake-spear's supposed offences against morals (& an offence against *our* manners needs no defence) from the Times in which he lived—wēh is after all but the multitude of accomplices—so I hold Bacon's *f13ᵛ* mind in too great awe to dare offer him the benefit of the abandoned & despicable Court of James I.—His conduct under Elizabeth respecting the E. of Essex does not in my opinion deserve the harsh reprobation it has receive. The meanness of his behaviour resolves itself, I think, in the general meanness of his submitting to being a Solicitor at all—into the disproportion of vulgar ambition, and craving for court favor to such and so self-conscious an Intellect.—Far more difficult to bring within the bounds of moderate Reprehension is his Conduct towards Coke, his Letters of Advice to James, his promises of abject & treasonable servility in begging for the Seals, his correspondence with Buckingham &c. It is indeed possible that Bacon may have actually, I scarcely dare say conscientiously, held the opinion, that the Government & stability of the Realm required a remnant of law-dispensing monarchy, an occasional ipse volo—sit pro Lege regia voluntas & some thing might, in a less man, be conceded to that notion so universal in the age of the highest ministers of State being not the King's (i.e. State's) but the *Man's* confidential Servants who sustained the *f14* name & shew. of the never-dying & impeccable King—so that fidelity obliged them to pursue and uphold *his* (the individual's) interests, ex. gr. his power & revenue, even against those of the People, above all, against Parliament—while their virtue consisted in not carrying their Zeal to a degree hazardous to *his* safety or popularity—But after all, the letters are so very base as almost to embolden me to enquire whether I have not over-rated Lord Bacon's *Genius* (To overrate his Talents is perhaps not possible)—to meet boldly the Question, whether Lord Bacon does really prove the one only known exception to Baseness in union with a *first-rate Genius?* In order to this, we must begin by ~~stating~~ seeking in what the character of Bacon's intellect Generalization—a most active associative Power—an opulence in ramification—felicity in obser-

vation and the reduction of observances ~~within~~ to the + nimis &
– nimis—and of particulars to their comprehensive & interpre-
tative *Maxims*—N.b. seldom *Principles*—
These are the excellencies—The reverse of the Medal may be
described in two compart⟨ments⟩, his Deficiencies & his Defects.

5047 30.18   By the bye, senz' altro nostro povero sfortunato
Henrico insano ò giá è ~~or~~ sará ⟨diverró⟩. Se non é pazzo, é scelerato, anche sceleratissimo: ma ~~egli~~ non é scelerato: ergo, ~~egli~~ é   *f14ᵛ*
pazzo. All'ottima (ah troppo sollecita et divota!) madre questo mio
presentimento—anzi mia intera convizione) dirò?

5048 30.19
                  Faith essential to Regeneration.
For Faith is the marriage of the Will and the Reason: or shall I
call it the offspring of that Union? Where the Reason is the Eye,
and the Light of the Will, and the Will is the Substance and the
Life of the Reason—there Faith is.
    How is it possible that Faith, which includes Reason, should
contradict it? As well might the Sun be supposed to require to total
extinction of Eye-sight, as the Supreme Mind to have demanded
of us the sacrifice of our Reason.

5049 30.20   Note, that *we* have the whole Good of the   *f15*
learned Bishops in James I & Charles I. time as well nay more
distinctly & collectively than the evil, but the Compatriots of Milton only their foul flatteries, their *Villiers*, their persecutions/

5050 30.21   The moment of Death, how far of the nature
of a Vision, from the entire abstraction from the senses; and yet of
a more intense Awareness, from the concentration of the Powers
not as in sleep passive in order to be restored—Hence in the Good
whatever Germs & knots of Truth or Good had been in the soul,
opening at once—So Spinoza, as to the Will & Personeity—and
in like manner the horror of the wicked.—

5051 30.22   I meant (last p. of last L. but one) that Bacon
might have considered the British Constitution as hanging many

and various weights & remoras on the absolute power of the Crown: but not as intending to destroy the spring (Federkraft) or to preclude utterly all and every room for its play. He might regard, for instance, the High Court of Chancery, as a sort of loaded or strongly weighted Safety-pipe of the Royal Steam-power, that ordinarily distributed itself among the pre-conformed Channels, at once restraining & giving it effect, while the Star-chamber, as a court of High Police, could not in theory have appeared *f15ᵛ* an unplausible Part of a mixed Constitution, when no other substitute has been found for it but ⟨the occasional Suspens. of the Hab. Corp. and⟩ a Bill of Indemnity on the meeting of Parliament—And surely no one can censure a Statesman of the age of James for not hazarding ~~such~~ so violent an anomaly ⟨as the latter,⟩ at a time when an annual Parliament would probably have been ⟨still⟩ felt as a burthen by the Nation, and when there were neither a standing army requiring an annual Meeting Act, nor a National Debt, as securities for its convocation—.

—A well-balanced mind cannot, however, but contemplate with complacency the retributive justice in Lord Bacon's Fall—ostensibly punished for comparative Trifles, which explained and precedented, as it was in Bacon's power to have done, would have borne no proportion to the penalty—but really *for* his base and servile compliances with the King & his profligate Ganymede, & sacrificed by them as a screen for the latter. It is to be feared that Williams's sagacity saw, & that his Desire of binding the Favorite to him prompted him to suggest, that a far higher Victim than the insignificant Scoundrels, he names in his letter to Buckingham, would be required either to blind or to satisfy the Parliament./ Bacon must have been base indeed.

f16 5052 30.23   The two equal in evil & in error—those who confound, and those who separate, the True and the Good. Here there needs a clear and steady Eye, to distinguish between the holding of an Error from too exclusive attention to the portion of Truth, it may contain, & for the sake of that Truth; and the predilection for the erroneous in the Error. Instance of the latter in a Spanish Inquisitor, in whom not zeal for the Truth but hatred for whatever durst oppose *him* &c. In short, not the sincerity at a given moment, in the 50th year say of a man's life, but the origin, positive and negative, of this sincerity, is the criterion of its moral worth, & unworthiness/the aversions *from* Truth ~~from~~ thro' Love of any thing else or from a base selfish fear end in aversion *to* Truth, and as this state is possible only in a *tw[i]light* of Consciousness and is besides both painful & humiliating, such averters will soon contrive to construe it into Falsehood, & to interpret their own feeling as an enmity to Falsehood.—Well would it become an Irvine to lay bare to contempt and indignation the maxims, sanctioned even by Divines & Moralists (woeful misnomers!)—keep to *this*—it is the safest side—and you think it true, you know now—& why should you disturb your mind? And if it should be otherwise, yet while you think it true, it is true for *you* &c.—and therefore take no means of ascertaining the one or the other!—Gracious Heaven!—What means the Parable of the Talents? or are not Reason, the Understanding, the Affections, *Talents* entrusted to us?

ƒ16ᵛ

But—this may be very well for the *Learned*—What? has God given Reason only to the Learned? or made Truth an interest only to & for the Learned! If in any instance book-knowlege is indeed necessary, to what purpose have we a National Church? Why then ample Revenues? That they may acquire truths to be kept to themselves?—or have you ever tried to make your Flock understand the articles, ⟨of⟩ which you require them to profess the belief? If so & all have failed, then have two Creeds, one for the Learned & one for the Many.

ƒ17

5053 30.24   Dared we imagine a ~~Delegate~~ Plenipotentiary, or Board of the Planet Tellus, appointed by Heaven—it often strikes me as a difficulty that would ask all conceivabiliy ingenuity to settle—what to do with certain Folks, like IANE 'APΔINΓ for instance, whom no one could think of putting in Hell, & who yet would make a Hell of every other decent person's Heaven?—Make a Heaven, if you can, for people like her—Try—What is it to consist of? Music? She has no taste for that or for any other refined gratification? Truth? Reason? She is a fool & an obstinate, self-conceited one —It fairly pozes one. Religion! She has no religious Feelings? Sensual Delights? She is a sliced Cucumber, Vinegar &

f17ᵛ Pepper without Oil. The aptest, I can think of, for the Old Maid
that I have taken as example of the Species, would be, a perpetual
Whiz in the Tail of a Comet, ~~too~~ close by all the planets of all the
Suns, just so as to be able to put down the names of the *Arrivals*—
& with Automaton Squires, Baronets, & Lady Such-a-ones, who
should seem to be Fellow Travellers/

5054 30.25   ῬΥΣΣΕ ὑπο χαραμάτος Ἱστορίκου, <u>Ραλει</u>—και
αλλοι μεγιστοι—Any breeze or gust of memoir or libel of the Day
sets the wind-harp a piping to it. Injury of this—Excerpts from
acts & manners judged of by present feelings & associations, &
with no excuse allowed—then in another form as extravagantly
extended in excuse of a James or a Charles II—

5055 30.26   A wise & rightly feeling Historian will find it
hard to decide which on the whole was the more despicable &
worthless character, of the four Stuart kings—all cruel, all liars,
f18 all morally cowards, and two loathsome; but he will have no difficulty in deciding that no four succeeding Monarchs ever blotted
the English Annals before, or since. O favored Land! while other
countries date their ruin & degradation from the vices & follies
of their Kings, for thee they were the means & occasions of Greatness, Liberty and pure Religion! ⟨Inconsist. in Miss Aikins con- ⸗
cluding Chapter—James I the best of the 4, owing wholly to his
Learning, and Love of Learned men and learned Conversation.⟩

5056 30.27   It cannot and need not be denied that the Religion common to Luther and Calvin and—the exceptions being so
few, and these too doubtful, we may add—to all the *first* Reformers—is more favorable to Whig Ideas of Liberty, than the ever-
stretching Arminianism introduced into the English by the Court
Prelates of the first James & Charles in its stead, ⌜ . . . ⌝ not,
however, from the parity of the Ministry & the substitution or
predominance of the Presbyteries for ⟨or⟩ over the Bishops, but
from the Symbolical character of the former. But it is no less true
than in this country the Difference has lost its practical importance
from the entire change in the object of national & patriotic Jealousy—Instead of the elevation of the individual choice, Liking or

Dislike, of an Individual elevated into the Royal Will, and armed   *f18ᵛ*
with its power and privileges, the object of ⟨just⟩ Alarm before the
Revolution, our *Jealousy* is now directed to the alliance & conspiracy of individual Wealth & State Patronage; and our *anxiety* to the
over-growth of the Landed, or Major-baronial, Influence in the
House, wherein according to the Theory, or more truly the Idea,
of the Constitution the representative of the collective minor Proprietors ought to ~~b~~ exist as exclusively as ⟨consists with⟩ the nec-
essar~~y~~ity of their existing fit Subjects for the occasional Ascensions
into the Peerage, ~~or~~ of those who presént their own estate & constituent Heritage, and réprésent the Nation—and again the disproportion in the influence of those who represent the agricultural
Franklings = the element of Permance, which in the H. of C.
ought never to exceed ⅓, to the representatives of the Towns,
Cities, Sea-ports, Professions, &c. = the element of Progression,
in consequence of the Boroughs having fallen into the very Scale   *f19*
(the Control of the great Land-owners) they were intended to counterpoise.

On the other hand, the so called National Debt prevents us from
drawing any clear conclusion—especially when taken in conjunction with the periodical Press, ~~and~~ the prevalence of Education,
and the diffusion of Methodism—

5057 30.28   The 'Ussean Overrators of the Performance of
the negative Duties and the high tone they affect over those who
are in all respects as blameless in their lives as themselves, only
because they do not choose to write their ordinary notes, and
House-hold Accounts ⟨all⟩ in Large Capitals. Charles's personal
non-immorality had no effect ~~on~~ even on his Court & immediate
Followers/Profligacy being the general & most approved Mark of
Loyalty/⟨i.e. *Re Netto*-ism⟩/much less on the Nation.

The darker charges, that Bishop Hackett thought right to suppress—& the Letters to the H. of Commons which Sir E. Cokes
(one of the Committee of 22 appointed to read it) durst read but
a line & a half—& then sent it sealed to his Majesty, who read it,
threw it into the fire, & returned his thanks to the Committee-
men—all strange!

f19ᵛ   The rights of Kings—and the Kings of the World have a common interest—as one integral Interest, and that of the People or
Nation (i.e. of all but the King; & himself too morally) being the
other & the opposite of the former. Explain it, soften it down,
smooth it up, do what you will, it comes to the same in the end—
if once a King be allowed as the individual Philip Baboon or James
Stuart, to have an interest not included in that of the People, and
his interest only because it is the interest of the People.—The former opinion is at once so wicked and so absurd, that it could not
have been sustained without the aid of Superstition, by which a
sort of Jewish Dispensation or perpetual Miracle was presumed
with regard to Kingdoms, the character of the kings been exactly
adapted by Providence to the merits or demerits of the People.

5058 30.29   The S boasted Scheme, the darling of the loathsome Lack-wit, James I, and so much *lauded* to their indelible
infamy by his Prelates, for a Union of the Protestant & Romish
Pseudo-Catholic Churches, was mere plot for the old conspiracy
f20   of Despotism with Superstition—or as James's Theory justifies us
in saying, for realizing the blasphemyous Superstition of civil au-
tocracy by the less absurd & not more blasphemous Superstition
of Papal Hierarchy.—It is evident that all James would have required, would have been a renunciation of the Dethroning & reg-
icidal Right of the Pope, and little more than a few quibbling
qualifications respecting the Sacramental Mysteries and the Hyper-
dulia due to the Virgin would have satisfied the majority of the
Court Bishops & Arminian Divines. The Resistance even to the
Stake of the Scottish Presbyterians, and the abandonment of the
Reformed Churches in France & Geneva, were doubtless foreseen
with delight by the puritan-hating- & fearing Scot—who even
after his providential escape from Fawkes could not suppress his
Puritans *"worthy of fire"*/

f60   *5059* 30.91   One of the worst symptoms of the necrosis ec-
f59ᵛ   clesiastical to my feelings is the indifference of the Clergy in general to the manifest depravity of the lower orders—ex. gr. of the
thousands of female Servants in London without characters, and
the obsoleteness of any moral or religious communion between the

Parlour & the Kitchen. The Relation of Servant to Master or Mistress is reduced to the convenience of a Bargain, or Contract binding no longer than the Whim or supposed Interest of either party suggests. As to the relative Duties and the Virtues arising out of the performance, the Protection, the Courtesy, the ⟨religious⟩ solicitude, for not on one side, or the inward Obedience, the fidelity and *family*-sense, with the *reflex* of filial Reverence on the other—Virtues, by which tho humanity is emancipated, enriched and ennobled, and the Soul trained and disciplined, and the *f59* Inequalities of Society not only mitigated and made a light and easy Yoke for the inferior classes but actually transmitted into a golden Chain of Unity, elevating a people into a true Community—this, like Chivalry or the Crusades, is a *Tradition*, furnishing matter for Poets and Romance-writers!—In short, the more I think on the subject, the more forcibly does the Question press on my mind—Did Christ intend a Church? Are we to understand any thing real and historical when we profess, I believe in *the Catholic Church*, or is it a mere duplicate of the words that follow, and the Communion of Saints, this latter being understood exclusively in a *mystical* sense, as a something which God alone sees and knows— some law of action and re-action, or of reciprocal influences in the *f58ᵛ* Spiritual World, of which we in the present state are unconscious?—If it be admitted that the Church meant is a reality, an object of outward Experience, like the House of Commons, then did Christ, or the Apostles by *apostolic* Authority and not merely as ruling Elders legislating only for temporary exigencies, make *Discipline* an essential in the constitution of a the Christian Church? If so, our established Church is undeniably lacking in an essential point; and we do not take his Yoke upon us in any sense, in which it can be called *his* Yoke. For this is characterized as light & easy in comparison with that of the Jewish Church. Now surely our Lord did not intend that his Followers should be less strict and scrupulous in the performance of the *moral* duties as Individu- *f58* als.—No!—By this shall ye be known to be *my* Disciples, if ye love—mankind? their country? or even their Enemies? No. These indeed are *indispensable* in to the Christian character; but they are not, nor are they here assigned as being, the distinguishing *marks*, the outward and visible *Specific Signs*, of it. It would be hard to suppose that there were not both Jews and Heathens, that were philanthropists, patriots, and who, like Socrates, would not think any fellow-man his enemy—But—By this shall *all* men know you to be *my* Disciples, if ye love *one* ANOTHER! If collectively you constitute a loving Family, a Household of Faith. But how can

f57ᵛ family ~~and~~ Love, the relative affections of Parent and Children, of Brothers & Sisters, ~~be~~ exist without mutual watchfulness, inspection, advice, reproof, submission to fatherly checks for errors in conduct—in one word, without *Discipline*? O House of Shame and Sorrow! where the Mother must call in the Constable, the Father apply to the Police-office, and Brothers bind each other over to keep the Peace! Yet such and no other is the possible Discipline of our Church—it may go to LAW with and against its Children! Of the two Evils therefore it is honorable to the feelings of our Clergy that they have chosen the least—that is, no pretence to Discipline at all! But fearfully and widely injurious is this lesser Evil—a mortal Dry-rot in the beams and timbers of the Edifice!— And here I might expose at large the pernicious sophistry of Priestley, Price, and others who would have churches, & churchmen on

f57 the same footing with Shops and Shop-keepers—or (as they say) as Apothecaries, Surgeons, and Lawyers—let Men who want their services pay them, & find out for themselves where they may be served best and cheapest. But in fact, ~~the~~ no State (the immature American perhaps exception) has ever dared to ~~take~~ act on this advice even with regard to Law & Medicine./But the whole is false and shallow—arguing an incapacity of the Idea of a *State*, as a dynamic Unity. Go, Sophist! ⟨or still better, Psophist!⟩ and study an Ant-hill or meditate on the Natural History of the Termites and the Bees. Hüber and Smeaton might teach you, what a State is, and its antecedence in order of causation to the aggregate of the Individuals at any one time in existence.

5060 30.92   There are certain practical Errors so contrary to the plain Light of Reason, and so repugnant to the feelings of

f56ᵛ common Humanity, that however persuaded we may be that they were *conscientiously* entertained, and from sense of Duty with pain and sincere reluctance reduced to practice, there is a voice within us that forbids us to hold the Individuals altogether guiltless. I feel

this strongly in Archbishop's Cranmer's case with regard to the
burning alive of Joan of Kent, and Pare, and *forcing* the young
King to sign the Warrant—not to speak of his being an accomplice
in the similar not less atrocious, because legal, Murder of Lambert
and Mme Askeyw in the preceding Reign—. With all my affectionate and reverential admiration of Cranmer, I cannot help as-
senting to those who thought his own martyrdom no more than a
just retaliation—nay, I could add, an inadequate one/For of how
incomparably greater importance were his Heresies, if, as *his*   *f56*
Judges & Queen Mary fully believed, they were heresies, how
immeasurably more *conse*quential & destructive to the Roman
Catholic Church, than the fancies of a single crazy poor ~~woman~~
Girl, and the honest unitarianism (which even the red-hot Zealotry
of Tertullian speaks of with great indifference as a common *thick-
headed*ness among the Idiotæ, i.e. unlearned & simple Folks) of a
harmless German could even seem to be to the Reformed Church.
And poor Joan's heresy (which for aught the Appendices to the
first and third Gospels say, is not contra-scriptural) so evidently
arose out of an exceeding Honor and Veneration of Christ—nay,
might easily appear to many persons necessary the make the whole
narrative consistent, and so make the miraculous Conception an-   *f55ᵛ*
swer the purpose assigned for it.—This Confession my Judgement
and Conscience extort from me—and it ~~pres~~ was great and dis-
creditable weakness in Bishop Burnet (Hist.Ref.Vol.II, p.112) to
slur it over in a tone of *half*-condemnation, in language so flat,
tame and palliative—as if of Queen Mary and Sᵗ Dominic it might
not be said with equal truth, that their Burning their fellow-chris-
tians alive "was truly the effect of those Principles by which ~~he~~
they governed themselves." But I trust that "the *just* retaliation"
(just, I mean, relatively to the retributive Providence was likewise
an expiation of his Crime, and will be accepted thro' the mediation
of Christ as his answer to the Appeal of the Royal Innocent at the
throne of God.

5061 30.93   An excellent remark of Moses Maimonides in   *f55*
More Nevochim, Lib.I, c.71, p.133, 135—in which speaking of
the Medabberim, i.e. LOQUENTES, or Sermonizers (our *biblical*
philosophers, as Grenville Penn, Dʳ Coppleston, and the other

Oxford Parsons on tiptoe with Prof. Buckland's ante-diluvian Hyenas)

"Summa rei est, tam ~~Chr~~ primi e Græcis qui Christiani facti sunt, quam Ismaelitæ, in principiis suis extruendis non secuti suint vel attenderint ad ipsam rei, unde ea desumpserunt, Naturam; sed tantum viderint, quomodo res deberet esse comparata ad sententiam ipsorum confirmandam, vel saltem non destruendam: et postea, cum hoc perceperunt, audacter rem ita se habere asseruerint, *f54ᵛ* probationibus super hac re adductis, principiisque suis eisdem superstructis."

5062 30.94   The learning and Genius that existed in a succession of Individuals during the tenth, 11ᵗʰ, and 12 centuries, have been much under rated—The names indeed are few; but each must have had friends, and admirers—& what men were not Scotus Erigena, Berengar, his pious and poetic Disciple Hildebert of Lawarden, with Anselm, Abelard, his antagonist Bernard, above all, those two Platos, Hugo de Sancto Victore and Richardus de Sancto Victore—and then our Countryman, Palleyn, and Johannes Salisburiensis! O what a delightful Romance for a Scholar's Library might not S! Thomas Becket's History & Age supply!

—I ought not to have omitted Bonaventura (Johannes de Fidanza, born 1221 at Bagnarea, in Tuscany) the disciple of Albertus Magnus; but worth a host of such Magnitudes, the Spiritual Disciple of the two *de Sancto Victores*. Of such men how cordially could I repeat the last distich of the following sweet Lines of Hildebert on his Master, Berengarius (N.b. Try to procure the whole Poem from Bulæus (Hist.Un.Paris, I, 471)

f54

    Cujus cura sequi naturam, legibus uti,
        Et mentem vitiis, ora negare dolis,
    Virtutes opibus, verum præponere falso,
        Nil vacuum sensu dicere, nil facere—

      . . . . . .

      . . . . .

    Livor enim deflet, quem carpserat anteā, nec tam
    Carpsit et odit eum, quam modo laudat, amat—

      . . . .

      . . . . .

Post obitum vivam secum, secum requiascam,
Nec fiat melior sors mea sorte suâ!

5063 30.95   Query? whether the passage in the Acts of the
Apostles, on which the Pontificial Divines, taken in combination
with our Lord's promise of a perpetuity of the Spirit to the
Church, rest (and not without plausible reason) the main strength
of their cause—Sancto Spiritui visum est et nobis—might not be
interpreted—Contemplatione (id est, intuitu spirituali) postea item
meditatione et reflectentibus visum est nobis—   *f53ᵛ*

5064 30.96   O! if even now, at the eleventh Hour, the
Crown would permit and instruct the Convocation to sit—and the
Church would join heart and soul to establish and encourage a
Discipline; would acknowledge in the bonds of Brotherhood the
Orthodox Dissenters (orthodox at least with the exception of the
Aversion to Infant Baptism, which if heterodox is yet not heretical)
and sanction the Methodists, under certain conditions which might
be expressed in Negatives, ex. gr. that no individual dare affirm
Perfection of himself, or of any other person or persons by name
(even the Church of Apostasy delayed this act of presumption till
long after the death of the Beati) and that no other evidence of
Election shall but the fruits of the Spirit shall be declared *neces-*
sary;—and if by the Church itself would set the example by gradually restoring to the congregation ⟨(that part, which submitted to
Discipline)⟩ their just privileges of Assent and Consent, and the
Wesleyian Methodist Consistery could be induced to admit of Deacons & Lay-Elders for the to assist in the *moral* discipline and the
temporal concerns of the poorer Members—if, *if* all these *ifs* were
more than "pious fancies", how much might yet be effected.—   *f53*

I am convinced that it could be proved tho' not that the Persons
concerned could be made to see the proof, that the Land-owners
would not on the whole lose on property, nor the Crown in influence, by submitting to a modification of Patronage—and I am sure
that all in every rank would be temporally benefited by the gradual
Re-purchase of the Lay-tithes. But the Reform must begin in and
on the Clergy, whose week-day Duties ought to be first determined
by Canons adapted to the present state of things, and then en-

forced—and greatly expedient on this account it would be, that the *Church*-duties should be confined to the Sundays, except in Cathedrals—that a new Division of Parishes should take place, bearing some relation to the number of Souls—and above all, that in all large parishes there should be one or more Junior Clergy whose

f52ᵛ Duty should consist in superintending the *catechumens*, and if it were possible that a place of worship & religious instruction could be raised for children from 4 or 5 years old to 15 or the time of confirmation, with an appropriate service & appropriate Discourses—the effects, God's grace assisting, would be blessed indeed!—

Under *such* a dispensation the Schools might be detached from *religious* Teaching/

f20 　**5065** 30.30　　　It is far from my wish or intention to detract from the merit of those Divines who have sought to establish the Gospel as Fact of History by historical ~~evidence~~ Proofs: or rather

f20ᵛ perhaps by judicial and forensic argument, as if ~~the great Cause were on trial~~ ed ~~in a Law Court~~, a Cause under litigation, ~~which they had~~ to ⟨be⟩ defend⟨ed⟩ on principles of evidence ~~sanctioned by the practice~~ received ~~in our Law courts~~ in Courts of Law, and ~~suited to the Object~~ of approved Sufficiency, where ever (as in ~~human~~ Courts of Law must always be the case) the Advocate has no higher object than to establish the *credibility* of the Matters averred by him, directly or by comparison with every known Alternative . . . ~~An~~ Between an acquiescence in the credibility of the Gospel History and a stedfast Faith in the divine Truth of the Gospel there is indeed a wide interval; but it is well if the one open the outward gate of the Temple, that may lead to the High Altar within it. I do not therefore intend to question the utility of

f21 this forensic Defence, tho' I am inclined to place it in the prevention of Infidelity rather than in the removal. I regard Works of this kind (of which ⟨it is saying too little to say that⟩ no language possesses more or more valuable than our own) as an interesting and popular Form of Church-History, and entitled to form a part of the instruction of Youth in the higher and middle classes generally,—and at *all* times—⌈. . .⌉ And under particular circumstances, such as I had an opportunity of witnessing soon after the

publication & industrious circulation of the Writings of Thomas
Paine, I feel the strongest assurance, that abridgements of such
works, in Sermons & cheap Tracts, dispensed by the Clergy of all
denominations among ~~the~~ *all* classes and ~~the~~ with more particular
care among the lower orders in Cities, & Towns and Manufact.
Districts ~~were of the greatest~~ ᴨere followed by the most beneficial
results—and not only superseded the necessity of prosecution by
the civil magistrate, of the Deistical Works, but acted retrospectively on the Seditious political Pamphlets of the same incendi-
ary—the venom-bag was extracted. For ~~who~~ to persuade a poor   *f21ᵛ*
fellow that the same man who would have put his soul in the fetters
of Darkness, would have ~~be~~ made him ~~a~~ free in any sense, or that
he who would have made his state in the next world a Hell, was
likely to make a Heaven of the present, is more than Cobbett
himself can do—tho' not more than he has attempted.—
    I trust therefore, that I shall not be supposed to under rate these
Defences, when I say, that I place my main reliance elsewhere,
and that in the case of a serious and truth-seeking Infidel, or an
unresolved Christian, I should expect more from ~~a single~~ the clear
and distinct Conception of a ⟨single⟩ Gospel Truth, preceded by a
contemplation of Christianity itself as an existing Reality, ~~in the~~
~~world~~, as a *State* of Things and as a still working Power in the
World, and the sphere of which ever widening has every promise
of being commensurate with the Planet, than from all the forensic
Evidences from Grotius & Jer. Taylor to Paley and Bishop Wat-
son/.

5066 30.31   Dʳ. H. More, 368—Any inferior fellow   *f22*
may————very heart."
    This is the glory of Christianity, that it is the Spirit of Truth—
and therefore appeals to Reason, as a lawful Monarch appeals to
or refers his causes to his own ~~high~~ Courts, among which the
Court of Conscience is the highest in dignity & nearest to the
throne—but the Court of Reason is the King's Bench, to which the
Chancery sends for the previous determinations of the Facts as to
the Understanding in his Court of Common Pleas, to the Prudence
in his Court of Exchequer—The Laws are his Laws—both the
common and the *written* & is graciously pleased to command the

Subject to receive no Mandates as the King's which are not count-
ersigned by the Reason, and have not received the Great Seal of
the Conscience—

The Priestleyian, Franklinian, Anglo-American Dogma of the
Clergy = Shop-keepers, Attorneys &c. all Parties of the Reformers equally free from 368, 369—

f22ᵛ   5067 30.32   The Hierarchy temporal, just like the false
Dyionysius's celestial, constructed out of the plain simple moral &
common-sense admonitions of Paul, might almost suggest that
these Divines had possessed an Autograph of the Apostles, inter-
lined & the blanks filled up, with Lemon-Juice, which by the fire
of inspiration they had brought out/

Few things in which men are more different than in the way
& force in which *Evidences* strike them/What seems overwhelming
to A, B. thinks little of—Much of this difference is, I am convinced, constitutional—the Hamlet and the Man of Business/the
Lawyer & the Platonist/—more still, perhaps, to their *sorts* of
Experience/a Sir M. Hales and a Harvey mutually wonder at each
other's cred: & incred—/

Add the serious difficulty occasioned by the miracles &c of the
2ⁿᵈ & 3ʳᵈ Centuries—

f23   5068 30.33   Quakerism, or Familism consists (says More,)
in a resolved infidelity or stout Misbelief of the History of Christ
as far as it is miraculous; & a Dexterity in a moral Mythology
thereof.—I should say—in making the Facts of the Gospel *Mu-
thous* and in annexing the Epyimythia.

5069 30.34   Nay but it is hard to believe, that the Author
of the Gospel & of the Epistles under the name of the Apostle,
John, was the Writer of the Apocalypse. It would inflict a sharper
pang than the Loss of any other portion of outward Evidence, on
my mind, were I compelled to entertain a doubt of the Authenticity
of the 4ᵗʰ Gospel—or that it was not bonâ fide, with the possible
exception of the latter half of the last Chapter, written by the beloved Disciple—& not only like Matthew, *according* to him.

However, be it whose Vision it may be, the *scheme* & principle
of interpretation is sufficiently clear, provided that it is to be retained in the canon among the inspired Scriptures—viz. The το
αχρονον as the Eyes of Time—past & future. In this view and in   *f23ᵛ*
this only can I explain and vindicate the *prophetic* tone respecting
known History—down to the sacking of Jerusalem, shortly after
which event the Drama appears to have been written. I confess,
however, that from the Sea-monster which Eichhorn affirms to be
Idolatry but which I believe to be the idolatrous Roman Empire;
and the lamb-like Beast out of the Earth which he seems to consider as a mere ornament of the Vision, but which I suppose to
represent the pseudo-philosophical Religion of Egypt, Samothrace,
and the Mysteries generally, with Simon Magus and Apollonius
especially in the mind of the Visionist; from this Chapt. 12, I say,
I can find nothing but fervid conjectures (Harry! thy wish was
father to this Thought) respecting the horrid calamities that were
to befall the Roman Empire, previous to and occasioning the a
similar sacking and utter ruination of the city of Rome itself, by
the different Kingdoms & Provinces into which the R. Empire   *f24*
split; but which, the Visionist affirms, will nevertheless renew the
idolatrous Empire—till Christ himself descends and heading the
persecuted Christians will destroy them utterly—when a long interval of pure Christianity, a fifth Monarchy, will take place—
after which the unconverted Nations beyond the bounds of the old
Roman Empire will be stirred up by the awakening Power of Evil
against Christianity, and by their miraculous Destruction to give
commencement to the Resurrection of the Dead & the Last Judgement—I cannot see any firm ground for spiritualizing the Milen-
nium into *conversion*—It is quite of a piece with the rest—a platonizing Cabbala of a thousand years purgation of the imperfect
but yet redeemed Believers, and of especial reward for the Mar-
tyrs, Confessors, & other eminent Labourers in the Gospel—Let
Eichhorn say what he will, of the ταχυ, εν ταχει, being prophetic   *f24ᵛ*
language for *certain* fulfilment, yet taking the words in connection
with the known *persuasion* of the apostles themselves (Paul, Peter,
&c) and the impatient expectation and eager belief of the Christians at large in the Apostolic Age, I cannot doubt that the Visionist
deduced his anticipations from either the written Scriptures in

Matthew, Paul, and Peter as we now have them, or from the
(perhaps) exaggerated oral traditions of the words of our Lord &
of the Apostles, joined with the old prophets & their probably
numerous paraphrases by Jews, converted & unconverted. For it
strikes me as highly probable that many Apocalypses were written
by the false Prophets and Zelotæ of Judæa, inspired by their expectation of the Σημειον, their conquering Son of David & their
frantic Hatred of the Gentiles generally and of their Roman Masters in particular—O for a Luther on earth! To him I could appeal
f25   without fear of being accursed as a Blasphemer—whether from
beginning to end the evangelical Idea & true Character of Christ
are not so overborne by the red and glowing Marks of the Jewish
Spirit, that would have called fire from heaven, as to appear only
now & then, flittingly, as drops of Water in a Vessel of much Oil
and little Water, when the Vessel is shaken for the purpose.—The
Word of *God*, the *King* of *Kings*, ~~&~~ & the Power & Plenitude of
the Seven Spirits, i.e. the Messiah of the Cabbala, is united with
the vindictive and military attributes of the Messiah of the Zelotæ
and of the Palestine Jews & Jerusalem Populace generally—. To
attribute the work to Cerinthus was indeed an unlucky conjecture,
~~as~~ which Eichhorn has compleatly exploded—and we know too
little of the sectarian Opinions (antecedent to formed Sects) among
the post-apostolic Converts from P.C. 70 to P.C. 100, to substitute a better./I should place the composition at the end of Domi-
f25ᵛ   tian's Reign, nay, when I consider that Justin Martyr who died
P.C. 163, and who perhaps did not write his Dialogue with Try-
phon early than 150, is the first known Acknowleger of the
Work—& how easily ~~Men~~ Fathers of that Age took the Date of
the work from the pretended Date (which here is a necessary part
of the Poem) even as he took the Author's name from the name
personated,/I scarcely hesitate to place it in the first Đ or even
second Decennium of the second century, under Adrian/and suppose the Author to have been an Ebionite, & Refugee—

God forgive me if I am in error. It cannot, I trust (notwithstanding the tremendous Judgement of the Apocalypt.
C.XXII.18.19. which does not improve the impression on my
mind) be a very grievous or sinful Error that I share with so many
good & wise men, so many eminent & chosen Heroes of the Gos-

pel Truth! And I fear the less from the consciousness that my
Judgement has been warped, if warped it should be, by no worse
feeling, or motive, than the reverential Love of the Gospel of *f26*
John, and the desire to preserve the heavenly & spiritual character
of the Christian Faith free from Dreams of Worldly Events &
Wonders that are more likely to breed uncharitable thoughts &
idle curiosity than the proper virtues of Christians—Hitherto, the
book has clearly produced the one former effects in large overbalance, & it is no hardihood to affirm, that it does not seem to have
been blessed to a source of edification. Indeed, it was mainly on
this account, that no part of it *struck to on his heart & made a
response there*, the rousing or comforting Spirit of Christ did not
play billowing under the Garment coverlet or outspread Garment
of the Letter, that caused Luther to reject it in the first instance,
& to remain in doubt respecting it to the last. S. T. C.

5070 30.35   I question, whether *inter Theologos too much* *f26ᵛ*
stress has not been layed on the *Revelation* (outward rev.) in Religion. Religion *implies* revelation, and every religion that teaches
a *first beginning* of the human race supposes a *revelation* quasi ab
extra, but then it is most safely represented as the historical conditio sine quâ non of the fitness of the man for the inward r-/ As
in order to walk we must be moved on or *walked*.

5071 30.36   A speaking of *Homer* means a *book*. Where's
your Homer?
    B. using the same word means the Author of the Book.
    C and D. mean the same by the word as B. But
    C thinks of one individual Poet, who at different periods of his
life composed the Iliad, the Odyssy, the Hymns & the Battle of
the Frogs, while
    D. thinks of a Body or Order of Men, ὁμηρευοντων, concinen-
tium, having for their common Subject the cycle of the events and *f27*
heroes of the Trojan War.
    Now when it is asserted, that the Logos of the Evangelist, John,
is not the Logos of Philo, the platonizing Jew of Alexandria, it is
either intended that they differ as A and B—and in this sense I
utterly deny the assertion:

or as C and D or (to express the difference by a still more apposite example) as Arius and Athanasius differed concerning Christ, περι τοῦ Χρίστου—and in this sense I neither deny nor assent, ~~but~~ till the exact amount of the difference is specified.

Perhaps the argument would be stated more clearly, if I took the Word of God or the Word as my instance—A means the Bible; B. the Author or Inspirer; C and D mean the same as B; but C believes the Word to signify God as communicating ~~truth~~ his wisdom or uttering his will, the divine Agency spoken of collectively, in respect of its manifestation: while D. believes it to signify a distinct agent, not ~~one~~ indeed self-originalnt (for then it could with no propriety of speech be called a *Word*) but yet self-subsistent— E and F, again ~~agree to understand the term~~ mean the same as D—and agree in this that the Word is a distinct Agent, and not a mere Collectivum or Personification of an Agency, but they differ *f27ᵛ* respecting this Agent, as Athanasius and Arius respecting the Christ.—Now if it be asserted that John and Philo differ as A. and B, I deny the assertion utterly—or that they differ, as C and D, I in like manner deny the assertion—~~but~~ if they affirm, that John and Philo differ as E and F, or as Athanasius and Arius, I neither deny or admit but wait for the proof—and till then withhold my assent—./—But lastly if they mean that John differs from Philo, as the Truth and nothing but the Truth from the same Truth ⟨in connection⟩ with sundry impertinences, and without the complemental accessories—to this I fully agree, even on the supposition, that I should see reason to dissent from the former.

5072 30.37   The general doctrine of the Spirit inculcated by Seneca—& the resemblance of the passage to that of Sᵗ Pauls in Ephes.—not improbably the occasion of the Legend respecting the intercourse & acquaintanceship between the Apostle & the Philosopher, and of the apocryphal Correspondences. Cicero's clear statements of the diversity of Virtue (Honestum) and Prudence/—The *f28* occasion of the error in the confusion of Virtue with the virtuous Man—i.e. the same blunder as that ~~on~~ from which all the inconsistencies of the Stoics proceeded—

God has given man Reason—therefore he must ~~have~~ seek Truth for the Truth's sake/has given him the moral sense, and Con-

science, therefore he must love the Good for its own inherent
worth and loveliness—
   but likewise Foresight, Understanding, and Sensibility, therefore he must propose to him *views*, motives from the *value*—in
short, *prudence/*
   And with all these the consciousness that in all these he is an
imperfect creature, and the duty therefore, first of rightly subordinating these in his *regula maxima*, and in this order make them
subservient, ~~each to the other~~ the lower to the higher, & conducive, the higher to the lower—
   Distinction in Seneca between the Decreta, Ground-positions,   *f28ᵛ*
fundamental Truths, and imperative Principles—and Precepta—
Rules and Prescriptions for the specific application of these Principles—fine Remark of Epict. (Enchiridion, c. 51) 1. the application of the Precept, ex. gr. Do not lie. 2. The Proofs or Reasons,
that we ought not to lie. 3. The reduction of these proofs to the
~~ultimate Principle~~ supreme, i.e. most comprehensive maxim, and
thro' this to the ultimate Principle of Morality—Now the second
is good on account of the first, and the third for the security of the
second, but alas! men too often reverse the order./

5073 30.39   The injurious influences of patristic reading on   *f29*
the discourses of our Church Divines, of James I . . . to Charles
II. Vide Hackett's Sermons on the Incarnation, the Temptation
and the Transfiguration/

5074 30.38   12 Decʳ 1823.   *f28ᵛ*
   Mʳ Mence pleased and fully satisfied with my explanation of the
Temptation of our Lord. I pray, that I may hereafter be equally
successful in clearing up my present difficulty, the Transfigura-
tion, especially *Elias*.—My views of Inspiration /⸸ Revelation: :   *f29*
Πνευμα:Λογος and the deduction of *degrees* in the excellency of Inspiration, become daily clearer and more distinct.—May God graciously turn it to profit—and chiefly at this present for my own
Soul—for it, I am *sure*, wants it.

5075 30.40   O that I could quiet myself & light on a safe
way for others, for reflecting Believers, not strong enough in the

liberty of essential Faith not to be *startled*,—for the reconciliation of the Circumstances of the Conception & Birth of our Lord, with the critical Results of an investigation into M. 1 & 2. and Luke 1. & 2./The only Article of the Universal Church endangered by the higher Critique. Is it possible, that at a very early period, as early as A.D. 80 or 90, a poetic Romance, allegorico-cabalistic, a Christopædia, could have been written?—The Apocalypse is an instance of a Poem on the Destinies of Xtnty—I must procure Hermas, the Shepherd.—But the so early universality of the Belief, "born of the *Virgin* Mary," and this an article of a brief *Creed* of Essentials—only less difficulty than the Alternative, viz. the entire silence nay, evident ignorance of the N.T. writers & the infallible symptoms of popular legendary Tradition, M. versus L.—

f29ᵛ

How soon after Charlemagne might the Ariosto-traditions have been in circulation?—Archb. Turpin—Geoffrey of Monmouth, Alexander the great, his *Birth* as related by contemporary Historians, above all, Plato by his own Nephew—Life of Plotinus—Philostratus—*Hercules*; the Jupiter Amphitryon must have been a story of very early date. If we assumed that the Verse in Isaiah (A virgin shall) had a place in the Marks of the Messiah—or still better, that there were diffi~~cult~~erent Transcripts of more or less Contents of such a work, it would go some way toward explaining the rapid & wide Acceptance of the Tradition. We see a stanza of a War-Ode in Joshua converted into history. Lastly (may it not be sinful to permit the suggestion!) what if it had some foundation in words that dropt from Mary herself—her own believed recollections of certain Visions, or Trance—And yet if this had been the case, it is strange that John, with whom she resided, should not have alluded to it.—But perhaps it might have been related by some one of her children (if she had any as the Gospel seems to imply—and surely so striking a fact as that Jesus was her only son, and the Brothers the children of Joseph by a prior marriage would have been noticed) or it might have been a family secret that Joseph had been disquieted, absentibus forsitan σημειοις παρθενικοις τοις νομιμοις/ while the innocent Wife was certain that if not by J. then by a divine Spirit./But all this is needlessly offending the feelings & imagination. The only excuse, at least, must be derived from

f30

the existence of the Relations by Blood of Jesus, posterior to the f_{30^v} general reception of this Belief—I must look into Eusebius, whether the honest Gossip Papias had picked up any account of Mary's Family.

—Is it not possible, that the last & greatest Evangelist may have *implicitly* & covertly opposed this rumour ~~to~~ in giving another and more spiritual explication of the Title—The Son of the living God—and that the Tradition may have taken its rise with Tertullian's Idiotæ, the Converts of the Circumcision?

5076 30.41 Fire = disorganizing, a perpetual prevention of re-organization. Evil in potentiâ can only become *positive* Evil, evil in *Actu*, by borrowing a *form* of Good—or rather borrowing *Form* from Good. *To be* it must have a *form*; but it is conquered when it is reduced from Being to an ever-baffled Striving to be, in which striving as opposed to the victorious Baffling the Spiritual Life, & the Joy of Life and the Triumph & the Power may be grounded. God is a consuming Fire—but there riseth up out of the Fire & cloatheth it as with an outspread garment the lightsome f_{31} triumphing & dancing Flames. The torment and the tormented one? The evil spirits = the Fire—. The Soul *lost into Spirit, mere will* = Satan, the Evil Principle—that in division would be what alone the Absolute One can be—therefore intrafluent instead of effluent, destructive of reality instead of causative and hence the Contrary of God—this the Will by its own act causative of Being, Form (Intelligence) Life, and Love, that the Will by its own act stript of true Being, of Form, Light, Life & Procession. For pure Evil what is it but Will that would manifest itself as Will, not in Being (Ἑτερότης), not in Intelligence (therefore *form*less) not in Union or Communion, the contrary therefore of Life, even eternal Death.

The Will, whose other name is the Good, is the Absolute One pure of the Many, out of whom the Many eradiates as so many iterations of the One. The Will, which is *Evil*, ~~is~~ would be the Many utterly without the One; therefore *not* the Many but a striving to originate the Many by the destruction of the *One*/. But the One is essentially indestructible: even to destroy the appearances of f_{31^v} the One, it must be of the One in the Many, and therefore by the destruction of the Many in the One. It therefore contradicts itself, in one and the same Act (or rather strife) willing to originate & ⟨to⟩ destroy. Self-contradiction is its essence—it is a Lie & the Father of Lies from the beginning. Evil is antipathy to the One; but the One is the Being of the Many. It destroys therefore the possibility of its own Being—and ⟨Self-destruction *is*⟩ its essential Tendency. It is the *dark* Fire: and the Wrath of God is the Fire in the Holy Will against the evil Will of the Fire. It is the creaturely Will which instead of quenching itself in the Light and the Form, to be the Warmth (o̶f̶ = Life), and the R̶a̶d̶i̶a̶n̶c̶e̶ Procession (= Love); and so resolve itself into the Will of the One, it would quench the Light & the Form, and shrink inward, if so it might itself remain the One, by recoiling from the One—& find a center by centrifuge—& thus in the Self-love ⟨it⟩ becomes Hate and the Lust full of Hate—and in the striving to be the one (instead of

f32   striving after & toward the One) it becomes the infinite Many, even as the Power of Rust in the Metal, which is the Prince of the Air, who is nevertheless an *Angel*, a bond-messenger, of the All-good, the forced Pioneer of Form by destruction of partial Centers—of the *Mass* (the Mosaic Darkness; but not the Dark Fire) which partakes of t̶h̶e̶ Evil, but is not ⟨the⟩ *Evil* i̶t̶s̶e̶l̶f̶—for it is attractive & therefore acknowleges the Alterity & seeks the Communion; but *blindly*, and *for* itself—hence the mixed essence, a social self, which is social for itself—hence solidity, or the refusal to be in another, or to permit another to be in it.—As long as the *Mass* (the Antagonist of *the Spirit*) continues, so long will Evil find a *Being*—and the Logos (Forma Formarum) the subject of redemption. When that is utterly overcome & the Form is the Substance, the Evil becomes *eternal*, preventing all evil from *being*—the pledge that no evil thing shall be.

5077 30.42   Therefore, quod effari haud licitum est—Nay,
f32ᵛ   I will give it utterance lest by denying egress to Truth I should prevent her Ingress, and she pass by my Soul as by a House which t̶h̶e̶ her cowardly Host had made her Prison, thro' fear of the inhospitable Mob—. I have not read Jonathan Edwards' notorious Tract, The Benevol. of God demonstrated in the Eternity of Hell Torments; & am ignorant of the principles on which his position

is grounded. But I suspect that they are *Leibnitzian*, or a Theodicee on the hypothesis of a *best possible* World. Indeed from Edwards' Book on Necessity it is certain (unless he had recanted and reversed his whole system of Theology) that his World is a *Machine*: and that his Convictions and mine can have no other than an apparent and accidental Resemblance—daring as my Paradox may be deemed when taking up my last proposition I affix the concluding Link of the chain in a [*]

Therefore, Hell or the eternal Fire of Darkness is the ultimate Object and final Cause of the Creation, or the calling forth of the World from Chaos, as set forth by Moses, in the first Chapter of Genesis from the *second* Verse to the 28.th N.b. by ultimate *Object* I ~~mean~~ intend a *Means* to an *end*; but that *end* does not belong properly or peculiarly to the *Created* Universe, but as it preceded so will it survive the creation (*I Cor. 15. 28*) It is A and Ωμεγα. Hence I say that the Dark Fire and its Eternity ~~are~~ is the *final cause* of the World—because it is the pledge of the *Eternity* of the Light and ⟨the⟩ Beatitude, the A and Ω of the *Generations* of God, the sole Condition under which the Cycle of perfect Good is closed for ever, and the περιχωρησις of Joy proceedeth and abideth everlastingly. Boldly, therefore I repeat, that the Fire of Hell eternal is the last, deepest, and blessedest Mystery of Love! 'It ~~and Wisdom~~ is the Echo from the Depths to the Wisdom in the Highest. The Heaven of the Heavens saith, It shall be: and Hell answereth, It shall be. Eternity calleth to Eternity: ~~Holy, Holy, Holy~~! Alleluia! the Lord God omnipotent reigneth. And again they said—Alleluia. Amen! And the Abyss resounded, Amen! And the smoke of the Burning rose up for ever and ever!

f33

f33^v

5078 30.43   This so controverted Article (often with the Mouth, but a thousandfold more often in the heart) is therefore the seal of the only true theory of the Origin of Evil. Without it what shall ~~preclude~~ remove the *possibility* of a second Fall or preclude its actualization! Can the second State be better than the first! Annihilate the *Will* & it is worse—it is no longer God *All in All.* Or shall the Logos cease, and be longer comprehensive, the Idea

* [Coleridge left the remainder of the line blank.]

Idearum—but where the Eterotès is not, the Nous cannot be, nor
the Spirit of Communion, and God forbid! that so I should understand the mysterious words of the Apostle (I Cor. XV. 28) The
Son is, relatively to the Father, the Distinctity in the One: relatively to the S̶p̶i̶r̶ Sabaoth the Unity in the Distinctities. As long
as there is any Enemy unsubdued/i.e. any Distinctness, in division,

f34   so long the Father reigneth in the Son, through him & by him,
but when all enemies are destroyed, the Son reigneth in the Father.
THE ONE that embosometh the Distinct, reigneth—all in all. The
difference is, that during the epoch of Probation which is that of
Distinction (Matthew III. 12.) the Son is, Ὁ ὬΝ ἐκ του κολπου
πατρος. *After* the purgation and the gathering into the Garner, he
is ὁ ων ε̲ν̲ τοις κολποις του πατρος.—.

Having thus beheld das Böse, το πονηρον, we may with better
hope undertake the inquiry into the nature & credibility of the ο̲
πονηρο̲ς̲, the hypostasised Evil, the personal, the plurarchy—κακο-
δαιμονες? A Clan of Devils? First, do we derive the doctrine from
Revelation? Apparently *not*. There is nothing of the kind in the
Old Testament. It was introduced & took root, and overspread the
Jewish Church in the Intersilentium of the O. and N. Testament—

f34ᵛ   and at the Birth of our Lord had already a long time become the
popular faith, and passed into the popular Language.—But is there
any specific Revelation of the Doctrine in the New Testament? i.e.
any passage, i̶n̶ ̶w̶h̶i̶c̶h̶ purposely written in order to teach it? is
there any passage, the main and special object of which was to
impress and establish the truth of the Doctrine, and to sanction the
belief?—Thus the doctrine of Resurrection to retributive Justice
was the universal belief of the Jews, a handful of Platonizing Sad-
ducees excepted—and our Lord repeats the words in order to confirm the Belief./Can any such passage be adduced in assertion of
the existence of personal Intelligences, self-conscious Individuals,
utterly yet responsibly wicked & malignant, of a diverse kind from

f35   the human, and neither Men nor the disembodied Souls of
Men!—I know of none. The passages, in which the Devil and
Devils are spoken of anthropomorphously, are all subordinate to
some other doctrine or purpose which would remain ⟨in⟩ the same
strength, whether the Devils are understood literally or figura-
tively. (If there be any exception, it is in one of Paul's Epistles)

Nor would the force of this remark be much affected by the admission, that the writer or speaker probably used the words literally/For so, doubtless, did the inspired writers use the words, the Rising and Setting of the Sun &c. They might & probably many of them Apostles did believe as their Countrymen of the same rank with themselves believed—but they did not derive their belief from *Revelation*. For if they had, it must have been their Duty and their Object to assert the truth of the Doctrine in its own name and for itself—(Here I we have an instance of the use & impor- *f35ᵛ* tance of the distinction between inspiration and revelation, πνευμα and λογος.) Objection. But does not our Lord speak so often and so expressly of evil Spirits, wicked Spirits, as that it is mere Exinanition of Scripture Meaning to interpret his words as intended to convey nervous derangements, or wicked Thoughts & Impulses from men's own corrupt Hearts!—Answer. I do not so interpret the words. Something *more* than the Will, mind, life of the Individuals themselves is clearly meant, warned against, prayed against: and this more is *the* evil *Spirit, an* evil Spirit, and evil Spirits. But is the Spirit of Evil, are is an evil Spirit of necessity a *Soul?* or an intelligent Person? Is it a self-subsisting self-conscious Agent, and not an Accident, or Potence? The burthen of the Proof lies on him who asserts this! Even the Personality might well be *f36* deemed proper exclusively to the Holy Ghost—and this is a *transcendent* Personëity—and we apply the term, not by any authority of Revelation but because we after repeated efforts & trials the Church could discover no term that was ⟨not⟩ still more imperfect—nay, I will may without fear remind the Assertor of Cacodæmons, fiendish Angels &c., that the most learned Divines as equally Orthodox and learned have felt and acknowleged the difficulty of proving the third Person of the Trinity from express passages of Scripture, unaided by the philosophic Idea and by the *Analogy* of Faith. The passage in the Acts of the Apostles respecting the Disciples of the Baptist may be otherwise interpreted—and tho' the inference from the Baptismal Institution in Matthew is very strong, & indeed decisive as to a third Distinctity in the Godhead, yet there is a heavy doubt among the Learned respecting the *apostolical* age of this Text. And lastly, the Church itself by the dis- *f36ᵛ* tinction between the *begetting* of the Logos, the filial Deity, the

Son, and the *Proceeding* of the *Spirit* from the Father and from the
Son implies & as it were insinuates a *diff*erence, which Language
did not supply the means of expressing—a difference, which I
might be *marked* by the term, the *personality* of the Son, and the
personëity of the Holy Ghost. But be this as it may, yet surely by
analogy of faith we are bound to *appropriate* this perfection to the
Spirit of God, as an incommunicable Attribute. For dare we attribute personality, self-subsistence to any Word, of save the Word
of God? To any Understanding, or mental Discourse? How
then to any Wisdom save the Wisdom of God? (Sancta Sophia,
Σοφια τρισαγια is the proper name of the Holy Ghost in the writ-

f37   ings of the Fathers.) To any Spirit save the *Spirit* of God?—I say
this in reference to the *Spirits* mentioned in Scripture, & because
my opinion is confirmed by the frequent sequence of a substantive
in the genitive case, & only in proof, that the personal Being of
the Devil, and of Devils cannot be concluded from the actual existence of *Spirits*, and of an Evil *Spirit*.—On the other hand, I
dare not deny the possibility of a finite Person *willing* evil irrevocably and beyond the power of Repentance, & Reformation—
nay, the *Idea* is indispensable in Morality—or that this Finite Person, or Race of Persons, may have been invested with larger intellectual faculties, & more enduring and subtle Bodies, than the
Human Race.—But *what* or *whence*, we are not informed by Revelation, which alone could inform us—*that* there are such, is, I
cannot doubt, *supposed* in several passages of the New Testament—
but whether *imposed*, or a *Revealed* Truth, I dare not decide—

f37ᵛ   5079 30.44   In Porphyry first I find a Pneuma, or Breathing
as the ethereal Body of certain Dæmon-Souls—a self-substantiating
Effluence of the Soul's Powers—so that the Body is the continual
Expiring of the Soul, and Spirit = Body ἐν δυναμεῖ, a *living*
Body, which is the Medium (μεσον τι) between Soul and the Body
in re. In this most unusual sense (the first mention in the Alexan-
drine School of the imperishable interior or proximate Body or
Vehicle afterwards so favorite a speculation with the Neo-platon-
ists, and since in Christendom of the Cartesian Platonists (H.
More) and the Leibnitzians & Stahlians (Plattner) and even of the
Epicureans & or Materialists (Bonnet)) Spirit is taken passively,
as the *immediate* result, and therefore inseparable co-existent of the

Corporific *Act*—Body *actual*)(*real* Body. How many odd fancies
might be spun out of this fancy—ex. gr.—*Electric Fluid* the Caterpillar exuvia & corpora mortua of Dæmon-Souls—Item, *Apparitions* & *Ghosts*.

5080 30.45   Division of Speculative ~~Doctrines~~ Pursuits into
1. Philæsthesy—Epicurus   *f38*
2. Philology—Aristotle
3. Philonöy—Zeno
4. PHILOSOPHY—Plato
5. Philokrisy—Kant. = ⟨the pre-ponderative inquisition of the
Weights & Measures of the Human Mind⟩

5081 30.46   No competent Judge can have read Plotinus
without bearing away the full conviction of his extraordinary Genius, and Capaciousness—Well worthy of remark is it therefore,
that when the Wit and Wisdom of the World were engaged in
setting up *a Religion* against Christianity, they could find no other
first principles, and no other Aim & Object—Distinctities in the
Unity of the Godhead—Apostasis—Metastasis—Anastasis—and final Stasis by the All in All, thro' purgation as *by Fire*—and in
each of these they differed from Christianity by errors, the consequences of which are the frustration of the Object & Aim—ex.
gr. in the explanation of Evil while in the attempt to attain their
extrinsic & temporal Object, the retention of the names, & practices of Paganism, they confounded & falsified the whole scheme—
while the articles in which they are one with the Creed of the   *f38ᵛ*
Christians are, rather the plain reliques of Superstition in the Converts, on points (ex. gr. of evil Dæmons) on which no Revelation
was given, tho' from the belief not having been removed by any
special Revelation, & not incompatible with a mind under the
influence of the Holy Spirit we dare not dogmatically determine
their falsehood. Clearly is this shewn in the contrast between Porphyry's exhibition of his own Theosophy and his attack on the
Christian Belief (more truly, the Belief among Christians—In the
former good and evil Dæmons, Dreams, Prophecies, ceremonial
and theurgic Rites &c, and the apparent Dissonances in the (supposed) Sacred Books of Hermes, Zoroaster, Pythagoras, so many
deep mysteries for the veiling of their perfect Co-incidence from

the Profane, no critical principles applied in testing the Authenticity & genuineness of these Forgeries; but all Faith in Twilight! In
the latter an eager & industrious detection of contradictions &
inconsistencies—no prophecies or prophetic power coni̵nceded but
all resolved into Foresight, and Conjecture, or narration under the
poetic form of Foresight, and a personation of some famous man
f39 of past ages (ex. gr. Daniel by a Poet of the age of Antiochus
Epiphanes).—From the few fragments of this Work, however, or
Reports of the Fathers, taken in connection with Porphyry's acute
& enlightened Remarks on Magic (in such strange contrast with
his elsewhere assertion of its reality) ⌈ . . . ⌉ and with his letter to
the Egyptian Priest, Anebo, I judge that Berkley is not justified
in concluding against the value or rationality of the Books against
the Christians from the Follies, boasts, and gross Superstitions and
phantasies of this inconsistent, humoursome, vain and ambitious
Philosophizer—who seems (like Warburton and Horseley, not to
say Grotius and Huet) to have wished to have the appearance of
conferring an *Obligation* on the Religion of the Age by believing
it—⌈ . . . ⌉ when he could (and brings specimens in proof) have
brought incomparably stronger arguments in its Confutation than
any of its avowed Enemies had done.—

(P.S. Animal Magnetism with all its trumperies, Baquet, Amulets, Clare Voyance, ecstasies, Crises, Mantique, descriptively alluded to in this Letter—Most remarkable the co-incidence—Plotinus : Porphyry &c a̵s̵ : : Schelling : Mesmerism./So Identity
f39ᵛ = Græco-Persico-Ægyptian Paganism in vogue, Natur-philoso-
phie: R Catholicism!—& Prince Hohenlohe, &—the extinction of
all Philosophy? I trust, that the parallel will not extend so far/&
yet *for a Time* it seems too probable—Item:
In the same letter the Question, whether a man's Genius is not
his own Reason—and whether he who hath a clear Reason (i.e. an
understanding converted toward the Reason) is not the Man of
Genius, the ευδαιμων. I should answer this in Porphyry's own
words on another occasion/ ως μικτον τι γινεται υποστασεως ειδος
ἐξ ἡμων τε τῆς ψυχης και εξωθεν θειας επινοιας—.

5082 30.47   Sometimes the exaggeration of an evil turns out
to have been a comparative Good. In the Scottish Reformation the

Rapacity of the Nobles suffered no check from the power & interests of the Crown—they seized all, & returned so little that none
but zealous Protestants & popular with the congregations remained
in the cures. In England more than half the lower Clergy & a
considerable number of the Hierarchy were conforming Papists.
See Burnet's *Reform*. Vol. II. Preface, p. 10—Likewise, both
from the ~~oth~~ different size & still more populousness of England,
and from the important Reforms made in Henry's Reign, a very
much larger number of Clergy were absolutely & *legally* necessary
(among other causes, to prevent the rights of Patronage from falling) in Scotland ~~they~~ it was possible for the Reformers to prefer   *f40*
the doing no more than by sound Agents & Partizans could be
done, to the employment of rotten or suspicious Instruments—. In
England the Liturgic & Ceremonial, in one word, τα κυριακα, the
Church, were uppermost in the minds of the men in power—in
Scotland, the *Preaching*, the *Calling*, the *Church*—as answering to
the *Ecclesia*; the εκκαλουμενοι—In England the Church or Kirk
according to its etymology—in Scotland the Kirk by a metaphorical
rendering, that a *Kyriak*, kirk; this ~~ab~~ pro Ecclesia.—⟨Q.y But
what would Scotland have been had *she been out* of all influence of
England—deprived of an *En*clesia, even that Fragment hidden in
our *E*cclesia—⟩

5083 30.48   In the reasonings on Incest in the controversy
respecting Henry's Divorce there is a good instance, how regularly
Divines take hold of a Truth by the meaner Handles—Incest was
forbidden, they say, because without such a prohibition the great
familiarities between those of the same family would have brought
impurity &c into families—Now *I* say, that the precaution, which
would be necessary if Brother & Sisters were allowed to marry
would have prevented that intimacy, ⟨that true *Family*-arity⟩ &
consequently that ⟨*kindly*⟩ *Affection*, that *Loving-kindness*, which
makes them morally Brother & Sister. See my Oldest *Cottle*-Mem.
Book./

5084 30.49   The Nobility could safely trust to their immense Property for their Power—the larger their Property, the
greater & securer their Power. But this was not the case with the

Crown—less & less so, the more the Crown became the Majestas
Populi, and Central Unity of the Nation / Every attempt to the
f40ᵛ contrary as by Charlemagne & others, failed.— The ~~great~~ Feuda-
tories, or actual Possessors, were the effective Lords, sooner or
later. The Crown must have a power organized into the State if it
is to be a Crown-Power. This Elizabeth saw & therefore withstood
the advice of her Nobles who would fain have played the Scottish
Thanes with the Church, & feasted on the Gleanings of Henry's
Harvest.—But hence unhappily the Differences between the Re-
formators Ecclesiæ Latinæ & the Renovators of the Christian Religion passed into fearful political Factions & Questions of State.
They became, first, worldly Interests—these produced on the Faction in worldly power Threats, & compulsory measures—these ⟨on
the other party⟩ resentment, obstinacy (for they were Englishmen
who were thus menaced & compelled) and lastly, a disposition to
over-rate the importance of the Points in Dispute, to believe the
darkest of the ulterior intentions & objects of their oppressors—in
short, all the virtues with all the infirmities of the believer *Suffering for Conscience*. But they were Englishmen, and their civil
Rights were attacked—hence Jealousy of the *political* power of the
Crown, in all things, temporal & spiritual—& this favored by a
very weak King & a Bigot for his Prime Minister (Laud) over-
threw the Monarchy—& so perished the Samson of Puritanism.
Both Samson & the Philistines were, it is true, digged up alive
out of the Ruins, but the compound Fractures were never thoroughly re-knit—since when we have had *no Church* of England:
f41 For surely a number of Estates, held under the condition of reading or causing to be read a Liturgy & ~~prin~~ reading or causing to
be read a Sermon, on Sundays do not constitute a Christian *Evo-
cation*, or ἐκκλησία, or Unitas Fratrum ἐκκαλουμένων.—

5085 30.50   Mem. Define a Christian Church National.
The distribution of the Inhabitants of a Country: into a proportional number of Flocks or Congregations, each under a pastoral
Charge, so that either by co-ordination or subordination or by
means of both all collectively shall form one interdependent
Whole—Corpus ecclesiasticum, or Ecclesiarum Unitas.—This definition needs only ~~the~~ full exposition of the term, Pastoral Charge,

to be compleat: and for this see Burnet's Preface, p. 10-12, History of Ref? Vol. II.—

Elizabeth right in her first step—but afterwards by selfish & personal jealousy of her Prerogative relatively to her Parliaments by preventing the redress of undoubted Scandals & Poperies made the Disorder an incurable Disease, and was the Accomplice *before the Fact* in the overthrow of the very Monarchy, she imagined herself supporting—i.e. as long as she acted as the State versus the large Proprietors, as private, & at least *partial*, Interests, she did well and wisely, but far otherwise when she acted as a one Co- *f41ᵛ* factor of the State against the other Co-factors, and therefore against the State itself, = *disruptio ab intrâl*—But this was the κοινον ψευδος & calamity of that age, the equivoque of *the King* including the Powers Judicial, & legislative, Powers by common law or irrevocable Charters, and the ⟨King in contra-distinction from the Peers and the Commons; or (too often, during the Stewart Desynasty) with the ⟩ Person intrusted with the supreme *executive* functions.

The interests of the King both in the first and in the second acceptation of the term did indeed require James (& should have impelled Elizabeth) to protect & strengthen the Bishopsrics, & with these all the other Church Dignitaries dependent on the Crown by vesting the manors to the former & the tythes to the Latter—but instead of this he & the infatuated Bishops kept up their Ecclesiastic Courts with Lay Chancellors, an impudent Brommagem-brass Counterfeit of Church-Discipline, with even the white of the Blindman's Bell rubbed off, or with enough only remain to make it look *dirty*—which gave them no real diffusive *f42* influence as individuals, while it was yearly weakening the true power of the Episcopacy—Thus while James & his unhappy Successor was doing one right thing by halves, & so that the half remaining leavened the new half & ever rendered it an additional cause of Odium, they entirely neglected the other equally imperious Desideratum, as important in relation to the third Branch of the Legislature as the former was for the second, & with an ex-parliamentary respect more important than either, viz. the increase of the City & Town Livings, with the Foundation of Lectureships

&c by Act of Parliament—/—Elizabeth's Policy & Measures as
Head of the Church I regard as by far the greatest Draw-back
from the Glory of her Character & Government.—

Burnet says a great deal too much in favor of the C. of E. as
"raised to that pitch of Perfection (Pitch & Tar too!) which few
things attain in this world"—.when he can only mean the Liturgy
& Articles. Surely these do not constitute a CHURCH! Yet if he
means more, he contradicts himself/

f42ᵛ   5086 30.51   (Viridescent.) It seems of difficult solution, that
the first, lowest and rudest forms of Individual † Life, viz. the
Infusoria, should possess a faculty not only beyond the most perfect
Vegetables but still absent in the lowest forms of Animal creatures—the faculty of Loco-motion.—Qʸ Is there any sufficient evidence for the Ocularity of certain Animalcula, asserted (if I remember right) by Adams & other Microscopians?

Problema difficile solvi, Infusoria vim vegetabilibus et Zoophy-
tis pernegatam, (locomotricem ⟨dico⟩) præripere. I see no solution
less fanciful than that these Appearances are the transient *Objecti-
fication* of the internal motions, ex. gr. the Globules in the Blood.
I see a vast Flock of Sheep moving rapidly & all in contact between Hurdles.

These are suddenly removed, and the frightened Sheep scatter
hurry-scurry over the whole Field. The ⟨vital⟩ Copula and Organism of the Plant = the Hurdles; the Infusion or Dissolution of
the Organism = the sudden and violent Remotion of the Hurdles:
the Infusoria = the single Sheep. Hence their sudden disappearance, the Fluid becoming clear—& then a microscopic Vegetation.
f43   The seminal Tadpoles give their mite toward the plausibility of

f42ᵛ   † I do not approve of this word so applied; but I mean only a
Totum in Singulo; by Assimilation)(Totum in singulo by attraction or geometrical accrescence, or i.e. chrystallization.

this conjecture. It is at all events harder for the Imagination to think of a *one motion*, in a ⟨Leach or a human⟩ muscle, for instance, than of a *total* appearance from an aggregate of motiunculæ in *one direction*: and even the philosophic Understanding would be led by analogy to expect a perfect unity or the nearest approaches to ⟨that⟩ perfect unity, in which the molecular Parts so *indiffenced* themselves that the Whole beacomes a monad *in actu*, and a Total *in potentiâ* only—(i.e. a monad not per essentiam, but *per accidens*, et *sub conditionibus*, and therefore a monad only quamdiu duraverint conditiones)—the Philosopher, I say, would expect to find this in the higher forms of creation, and in proportion to the ascent; while in the *relapse* of the temporary Monad to a mere Whole (ex. gr. a dead muscle) and of this again to an indefinite *All* (as in a putrid muscle) he would look for an image ⟨and analogon⟩ of the rudimental products of animation. Now this really seems to be the fact in Oken's Wimmel, Flimmel, his Mihila, or Paulo plusquam Nihila &c ⟨In these Creations⟩ the power Phænomen of Space (the Auseinderander) and the Ph. of Time (Succession) by the existence are contemplated in the moment of *blending*—or of transition from ⟨a,a,a⟩ a = ɣx000 into A = 1.—It is by tracing the phænomena of organization that I learnt to master the idea of the *Indifference* of Space and Time—the potential Parts or (more plainly tho' less *couthly*) the Separable now non ⟨in actu⟩ separata, in one word, the   *f43ᵛ* Separtibilia, give their successiveness (= time) to the Whole, and the Whole, as a *One*, gives its co-existence (= space) to the Parts or Partibilia. The sensible appearance, or representative Image, remains, doubtless, under the antithesis or duality of Time and Space—how else could it be an image? But that the *reality* is as above stated, it is enough to reflect on what we mean when we say—He or I advanced with one *foot*, or took hold of the thing with one outstretched *Hand* = we never dream of saying, His Foot advanced, leaving the remaini Man behind—

N.B. To A Physiologist unaccustomed to think transcendentally, i.e. under the most comprehensive Terms, or the Genera generalissima, or primary Antithesis of the pentadic or quinquarticular Dialectic (Prothesis, Thesis, Antithesis, Indifference, & Synthesis) which from its ordinary application, as Thesis, Antithesis, and Synthesis has been called the Logic of Trichotomy—the common

f44

Physiologist, I say, will be surprized when he is told that the Problem here set forth is the same with the old controversy whether the sensation is in the parts in which the imagination places it, or in the Brain—and that it is solved by shewing, that one is true as the other, and that the Proposition involves a quid pro quo—i.e. a *partibilia* pro *partibus*: inasmuch as the nervous system *dynamically* is a monadic Whole, that has only *relative* space, space in relation to other systems or Things, but has no differentials of Space in and for itself in the way that a Whole by aggregation or composition of has, a Heap of Corn for instance, or a Skeleton, or the Mass of the Brain & Nerves after Death. In like manner, it has only relative *Time*, i.e. Succession, as *differenced* from Space/But that which has no Time by difference from Space, and no Space by difference from Time, is of course the Indifference of Time & Space—Q.E.D.

P.S. Tempus in numero singulari non sine Spatium, vel Tempus sub formâ Spatii.

Spatia in numero plurari non sine Tempore, vel est Spatium sub formâ Temporis.

Co-instantaneitas = Spatium ⟨cum⟩ negatione Temporis anticipati, sive imaginati. Ponatur enim, necesse est, ut negetur—ergo, imaginatione tantum ponitur. Ergo, co-inst. semper & necessario
f44ᵛ *intuitiva* est—in reflexo desinat esse, et fit pluraribus successiva. Pluraribus autem ipsa haud potuisset esse nisi per Tempus *antecedens*—*esse* subjectivum volo, vel videri—to be AGnized it must be *re*cognized.

Plur

5087 30.52   D. Scotus held it possible to give a strict proof, & seems to have been satisfied that this proof had by himself been given, of a *first*, a *perfect and* a *final* cause, tho' really it is very difficult to distinguish the proof, he has given, from a proof of there being *no* cause, *no* finality, and no intelligible perfection, the Cause being one with the Effect, the end one with the beginning, and the perfection having no measure or relation. In other words, his proof is that what *is*, *is*. And that he must himself have seen that something very like this is the case, seems plain from his full confession, that neither the Life, or Goodness, or Wisdom, or Justice of a Supreme Being can be *proved*. His great Scholar & *f45* *seeming* Antagonist, W. Occam, speaks out. The Existence of God is an article of Faith, inaccessible to Reason, underivable from Experience. I agree in toto with Occam, & likewise that if the Argument from the necessity of a first cause is valid & capable of being *concluded from*, and not a mere Twirl round on the Toe with out progress, ~~thus~~ then it would have greater *evidence* by taking a sustaining or conservative ~~one~~ Cause, than a productive one, for a conservative Cause carries with it far more plainly the conception of a difference of the Cause from the effect, than a productive Cause,—at least, where the latter is supposed an infinite Power, and acting therefore with an infinite velocity. By what means then is the effect to be distinguished from the cause but by a petitio principii in the Terms A Cause & B effect.—

So too ~~the~~ with regard to the evidence of the Unity of God. Not *f45ᵛ* to seek in many what can be sufficiently found in one, is indeed a binding and evident maxim of *prudence*; but it is far enough from being an Insight into the impossibility of the former. If they were Gods, they must be supposed all good—and a Hive of Bees may make one Comb, by unity or harmony of Instinct. It is true, one God would do as well as many, but unless it can be made certain, that he would do better, it is no less true that many would do as well as one. That it would be silly to choose the latter, may be readily granted: for this implies, that it is a matter of choice— ergo, not impossible—

Item—neither ⟨the⟩ infinity (a word that might be expediently dismissed in speaking of God, more properly the Measure of Infinity as Plato well observes)

item of Intelligence—& here Occam makes a very sensible distinction between the impossibility not to be *convinced* of a truth, *f46* and the impossibility of thinking the contrary—the former is the result of the whole Man, moral & intellectual—it may be the consequence of an innate *Idea*, analogous to the impossibility of not seeing a face accidentally presented to my sight—it is a fact, not a conclusion: But if it be asked, what is the use of these nice distinctions—whether it is a demonstration or ~~neither~~ ⟨is as⟩ good as a demonstration. Of no use, I reply, as far as the Belief of God is in question; but of very great use when a disbelief of other scarcely

less important articles of Faith is justified on the pretext, that they
are ⟨not⟩ ~~strictly~~ *demonstrable* by the scientific Reason. Then it is
most pertinent to shew, that the belief of these articles is derived
from the same or equivalent Sources with that of the Exist. &
Attrib. of the Supreme Being—&c—

-f46ᵛ

f47

5088 30.53   Occam asserts the existence of *Ideas*, which he
considers as *Patterns*, Idea est aliquid cognitum a Principio effec-
tivo intellectuali, ad quod Activum aspiciens potest aliquid in Esse
reali rationabiliter producere! It is plain that Occam had only a
striving conception *respecting* ~~mo~~ Ideas, not ~~an~~ the *Idea* of them/
This resulted from his oppugnancy to the reality of the Universals,
of Genera & Species—& his inability to find any third between
this and the absolute singleness of whatever really is. Scotus was
nearer to the truth; yet Occam greatly served the cause of Philosophy by dissenting from ~~an-as~~ yet obscure Truth. The main force
of Occam's Reasoning is drawn from the assumption of Individuals, as Individual, in vero et primo Esse—& then calls on the
Realist to account for his *superinduction* of the Universal. Had his
Adversaries instead of granting his Postulate asserted that in the
very constitution of an aliquid in Esse reali the Universal was as
essential a factor as the Individual, they might have challenged his
utmost skill to prove the contrary/The petitio principii would fall
as fatally on him as on them. Hence however his very Ideas were
all *number ones*—of course, *Things*—& what is gained by calling
them Patterns, Exemplars, Models—. Raphael's Madonna is a
Model of fine Painting—but it is a Picture that therefore itself
required a Model—& so on ad infinitum. But the strangest of all,
& yet ~~it~~ in strict consequence with his first position, is that he
~~repeats~~ asserts & re-iterates the assertion, that the Divine Ideas are
not of the Divine Essence—and that they are all always rerum
singularium, and are themselves res singulares et distinctæ. "The
Ideas in God are not his Essence, they are not subjective in him
and real, but merely objective, as models of the divine Power
according ⟨to⟩ which it (the divine Power) produces them themselves, and therefore different from all things in themselves."—
Here there is so evident an absurdity—for if the Ideas which are
singulares et inter se Distinctæ, even producible without anteced-

ent Ideas, why not every thing else? But I suspect, Tenneman has
mistranslated the passages—Occam I. sentent. dist. 38. q. 1.

5089 30.54   If any ⟨one⟩ of my learned Readers should be   *f47ᵛ*
discontented with this scheme as unduly limiteding the sphere of
religious Inquiry, and inimical to a reasonable Faith: I would entreat him first to ask himself, what he precisely intends by ~~one~~ the
word, reasonable, what by Faith, and what by the combination of
the two and in order to this, let him ascertain for himself, in what
sense he employs the term, *Reason*. Does he mean by it aught
distinct from the Understanding? And if so, ~~does he admit a sim-~~
~~ple~~ he assume it simply, as the source of those universal Principles,
or Truths connected with a sense of their being universally, and
necessarily true, which tho' not the proper growth of the Understanding, are yet the condition under which alone the conclusions
of the Understanding obtain *scientific* evidence ~~that is~~ i.e., not only,
that so it *is*, but that *so* it *must* be? on which therefore, as Ground
and Antecedent, all logical Exercise of the understanding (*Discur-*
sio intellectualis) depends, and by which the discursive Faculty (~~the~~
~~nam~~ so the elder Logicians designated the Understanding) becomes   *f48*
"Discourse of Reason?" Or secondly, does he mean by the Reason
a yet higher power, or the same power with ~~an~~ other & yet higher
attributes ?, namely, as the source of *Ideas*? Ideas, I mean in the
~~total~~ Platonic sense, alike contra distinguished from Notions, Conceptions, and Images. Or lastly, does he use reason as a mere
Synonime of the Understanding—as the faculty by which we reflect on the notices given by the senses and sensations, and thus
form *conceptions* of the ~~Objects that have been presented — *respond*~~
corresponding Objects? The faculty, in short, by which we *under-*
stand what we see or have seen?—
     If he use the word, Reason, in the second of these three senses;
and if his *Ideas* are more than ~~high flying~~ high words, or vague
fancies, the creatures of a drowsy Eye, half sight half dream; there
can be no dispute between us. ~~The only difference Then the Belief~~
He expresses in Platonic Language the same convictions which the
Spiritual Christian conveys in the language of John and Paul. He
must know, that Reason in this unusual sense is not, and cannot
be, a merely speculative or intellective faculty, in distinction from   *f48ᵛ*

the Will, and active principle; and ~~he will needs will no outward informant to teach him~~, how far the preceding Remarks are applicable to *him*, he has in himself the means of determining. And here it will not be impertinent to observe, that what the eldest Philosophy called Reason (Nous) and Ideas the philosophic Apostle names *the Spirit* and *Truths spiritually discerned*: while to those who in the pride of Learning and Philosophy deny the doctrine of the Spirit in man and its possible communion with the Holy Spirit, as vulgar enthusiasm, I recommend the perusal of the following sentences from a pagan Philosopher, a Nobleman & a ~~director~~ Minister of State

f49   Ita dico, Lucili, sacer intra nos Spiritus sedet, malorum bonorum que nostrorum Observator et Custos. Hic prout a nobis tractatus est, ita nos ipse tractat. Bonus vir sine Deo nemo est.

5090   3½.69

f82ᵛ

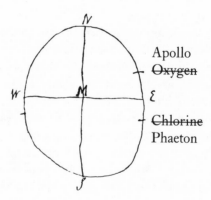

Apollo
~~Oxygen~~
ε
~~Chlorine~~
Phaeton

Tellus is an organic Part of a System, the Solar, which itself is probably but a part. Tellus therefore has no actual N.S.E.W.—or rather it has a threefold ⟨topo-⟩ tetractys/ 1 the magnetic Axis & the electric poles—. 2. relative to its own spheroid—3.—Solar.—We will take it as imaginary.—and thus

N = Estia   E = ~~Idion a~~ Horizon
S = Aphesti~~ona~~   W = ~~Catholon~~ Apeiros

The real powers would then be   *f83*

   NM = Estia Prosestia

   M.S. Estia Aphestia

   ~~E.N.~~ ʃ . . . ˥

   ~~E.N~~ ˩ . . . ˥

   N.E. Estia P. Orizomene

   N.W. Estia P. Exorizomene

   S.E. Aphestia Orizomene

   S.W. Aphestia Exorizomene.

+ Aphestia Exorizomene Phætosa would be Chlorine Gas—

− ~~Pros~~ Aphestia orizomene Phæboumene Oxygen Gas.

+ means Aphestia S.S.—Aphestia S.M.

+ Proestia N.N.—Prosestia N.M.—that is, verging to the Meson ti, or Equator.—So + HᶜOrizon—E.E.

− Horizon E.M. + Apeiros W.W.

− Apeiros W.M.—

But all four must ever co-inhere—we must take Degrees of Long. & Lat.—Estia ½ Aphestia 1½ Orizon 1⁹⁄₁₀—apeiron ⅟₁₀ = 4. Tetractys Chlorizon—

But Chloros is a kindly Accident—to form a name on—

Orud; Odur; Duro; Rudo; Doru; Rodu; Udor.   *f83ᵛ*

Let Oxygen be Puriphosphoros and Chlorine be Puriphlegethon. And I doubt not, that we shall discover some Gas that will shew in a similar Relation to Hydrogen, as Chlorine to Oxygen or as Oxygen to Chlorine ~~+ Aphestia (Ορἱζομενη) Puriphlegethon.~~ + Aphestia (− Orizomene Puriphlegethon, would in *f84* Chemical language be *Air* in the minimum of incoherent Metallity, or Azóte—Azote, in the Hyphydroguret state, or with the minimum of Hydrogen, contracted by the South Oxygen, or Puriphlegethon = Chlorine Gas.—Shorter but uncouth would be Phostopyr for Oxygen, and Pyriphos for Chlorine.—

     N   S   E   W.

   Estia: Aphestia.   Oros.   Hydes

The prior syllable marking the predominant the Greek Hydōr admirable states the méson tí—and not the Quaternion/Υ (ψιλον) = aer tenuis Δ (δεω) it binds: Ω (the stabile Spheröid) Ρ (ρεω) it makes flow.

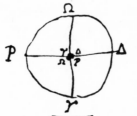

to the West Orud or Horus
To the East Odur or Hodur
E.S. Duro
E.N. Doru
W.S. Rudo
W.N. Rodu
S.E.N.W. Ὕδωρ

f82   5091 3½.68   Innocence ✳ Wisdom :: Start ✳ Goal or as the
Præteritum perfectum to the conditional Future
      Innocence far out of Sight in the remotest East, still travelling
Eastward, and Memory is the Shade, she casts behind—
      While Hope, a singing Pilgrim with girded Loin still westward
throws her Shade before, a giant shadow ~~whose~~ that ever as she
f82ᵛ   moves Beyond the ~~Horizon~~ ⟨change last line⟩ of the Eye stretching, presents its bust & head, wreathed with a glory ~~l~~in the horizontal Sky—~~&~~ and this is Wisdom

f30ᵛ   5092 3½.23   Abthu Abuth Thuba Thabu
f31   Let ✳ Bathu express the centre of the Globe.—or the point of
junction in the cross contained

      Abuth = North − Magnetic Pole
      Uthab = South + Magnetic Pole
      Thuba = E. Contractive
      Thabu = W. Dilative.

But taking the Surface, let Udor represent the Mid-point—& see
p. 26
      N. Duro   — E. Orud
      S. Rodu   W. Odur
Or to maintain the analogy with Ὕδωρ = Water, as the Surface
Power, instead of βαθυ, take Chrūs for Χρυσον = gold:—
      N. Chi   E. Rho
      S. Sigma   W. Upsilon

5093 25.95   —/xxx‑v‑↗ compared to Itching on the Toes   *f106*
or the Soles of the Feet—the Pruritus is intolerable, while the
Scratching gives no pleasure and but little relief.

5094 25.97   The Stoic and Academic Schools treated Logic   *f105ᵛ*
as a part or branch of Philosophy ⟨or Metaphysics:⟩ the Peripatetics
considered it only as a Mean, Instrument, or Tool = Οργανον.
Both opinions may be supported—each depending on the definitions of ~~Philosophy~~ Metaphysics and Logic. The former, however,
appears to me the more natural, the more consonant with the etymology of the terms, ~~(Metaphysics and Logic)~~ and of much
greater conveniency. The main difference consists in this, that the
Science which ⟨alone⟩ Aristotle entitles Logic, I include in Logic
as the technical part or Canon = Ars et regula formalis ratioci-
nandi.—The simplest Division is ~~the oldest   viz.~~ into Speculative
and Practical, in the words of Aristotle, Αληθεια καὶ Εργον—and
the Speculative we may either subdivide into the Pure (i.e. exclusively mental) and Empirical, or abstracting in the first instance
from the impressions on the Organs of Sensation (or the ~~Senses~~ as   *f105*
variously acting on, ~~on~~ in combination with, the Sensations excited
by the material and extrinsic causes) Speculative would be equivalent to Metaphysical, as the universal term for all kinds of Knowlege which seek an evidence transcending the evidence of the
Senses—and the arrangement would stand thus:
          Speculative   Philosophy
                    or
          Metaphysica (sensu generalissimo)
     Noetics ~~or~~ (Metaphysics κατ᾽ εξοχην). ⟨the Laws & Axioms of
Reason.⟩
     Logic or the forms and functions of the Understanding.
     Mathematics—the Forms and Constructions of the Sense
and Logic would be subdivided into   *f104ᵛ*
     1. the Canon, or Syllogistic
     2. the Criterion, or Dialectic
     3. the Organon or Heuristic (ἑυριστικὴ)
the last being the uniting Link of Logic with Noetics, and then of
Noetics with Mathematics—and of all as one to Nature considered
as Power—or the Application of Reason as Idea to Reason as

Law——. Now when the Ideal is realized in Nature, and the Real idealized in the Mind, there is the sum and ~~end~~ content of SPECULATIVE PHILOSOPHY.

Even so to manifest the Reason as Will or productive Power, and the Will as Reason, and the ~~free~~ Constructions (these being acts of Freedom) necessary in order to such manifestation, is *Practical* Philosophy—& this too has its Noetics, which here includes the Intuitive, the analogon of Mathematics, and its Logic—or Judicial Ethics.

The Sum of both is properly *Philosophy*, as distinguished from Philalethy, and Philagathy—& the identity of both—& Philosophy is the Transit to Theosophy, or Religion.

f106   5095 25.96   The Church Episcopalians under the Stuart Dynasty took the worst way of defending Episcopacy; first, jure divino, by Scripture—in which they made out nothing—and 2^{ndly} by Church Antiquity and the Authority of the Fathers in which they either made out nothing to their purpose, i.e. Diocesan Prelacy, or presented vulnerable Points to the Romanists and exposed themselves to the charge of inconsistency from both parties, Papist and Puritan. Had they supported their cause by the Right of the State to make use of its learned Body and ~~the~~ its public Instructors in the manner best suited to & most congruous with its Constitution, as a particular State—and then challenged their adversaries to shew cause, what should deprive the Sovereign Power (in England, the King & two houses of Parliament) as the representative, and in the right of the State, being themselves Christians, from choosing the Pub. Instructors & the members of the permanent *f105^v*   Learned Class from Xtn ministers—or obliged or even permitted these ministers to refuse compliance—the Puritans would have been entangled & silenced by their own doctrines of the Right & Duty of the Civil Magistrate to interfere with Religion.

f5   5096 30.4   Extract from Berkeley's Minute Philosopher, 2nd Edit: Vol: 1st—Dial: 4.

Euph: No wonder, we cannot assign a time beyond our remotest memory. If we have been all practising this language, ever since our first entrance into the world: If the author of nature constantly speaks to the eyes of all mankind, even in their earliest infancy, whenever the eyes are open in the light whether alone or in company: It doth not seem to me at all strange, that men should not be aware they had ever learned a language begun so early, & practised so constantly, as this of vision. And if we also consider that it it is the same throughout the ⟨whole⟩ world, and not, like *f5ᵛ* other languages differing in different places: it will not seem unaccountable, that men should mistake the connexion between the proper objects of sight & the things signified by them, to be found in necessary relation, or likeness: or, that they should even take them for the same things. Hence it seems easy to conceive, why men, who do not think, should confound in this language of vision the signs with the things signified, otherwise than they are wont to do, in the various particular languages formed by the several Nations of Men—

Alc. I propound it fairly to your own conscience, whether you *f6* really think that God himself speaks every day & in every place to the eyes of all men? Euph: That is really & in truth my opinion: and it should be yours too, if you are consistent with yourself, and abide by your own definition of language. Since you cannot deny that the great mover & author of nature constantly explaineth himself to the eyes of Men by the sensible intervention of arbitrary signs, which have no similitude or connexion with the things signified, so as by compounding and disposing them to suggest and exhibit an endless variety of objects differing in nature, time, & place thereby informing & directing men how to act with respect *f6ᵛ* to things distant & future, as well as near and present. In consequence, I say of your own sentiments, and concessions, you have as much reason to think the universal agent or God speaks to your eyes, as you can have for thinking any particular person speaks to your ears. Alc. I cannot help thinking that some fallacy runs throughout this whole ratiocination, though perhaps I may not readily point it out. Hold! let me see! In language the signs are arbitrary, are they not. Euph: They are. Alc. And consequently they do not always suggest real matters of fact. Whereas this natural language, as you call it, or these visible signs, do always *f7* suggest things in the same uniform way, and have the same constant regular connexion with matters of fact: whence it should

seem, the connexion was necessary, and therefore according to the
definition premised it can be no language. How do you solve this
objection? Euph. You may solve it yourself by the help of a picture, or looking-glass. Alc. You are in the right. I see there is
nothing in it. I know not what else to say to this opinion more,
than that it is so odd and contrary to my way of thinking, that I
shall never assent to it.

5097 30.5   De potestate maritali.—This solution would be
prematurely attempted, without first determining, whether the
Question is put morally & ~~to~~ respecting persons under Christian
f7ᵛ obligations; or legally. For these are not merely distinct, but re-
motive, each of the other. The former supersedes the necessity of
the latter; and the latter supposes the non-existence, or failure, of
the former in the husband or the wife or both.
     First then, morally & evangelically. Love, MUTUAL Love is
here the Prothesis, or Punctum Identitatis, or One potentially involving two: or Two *in* One, as one Reciprocal ~~loves are~~ is the
bipolar Line into which the Point = Mutual Love, *produces* itself—Of the two Poles the Husband, by superordination without
breach of Parity, ~~and~~ nay, *in order* to the equality of both, and as
the indispensable Mean and condition of their Cöincidence, the
Positive Pole or Thesis; the Wife the Negative or Antithesis.
(N.B. You cannot too early be guarded against the misconception
of the term, *Negative*—which does not mean, *nihilitive*, or the
mere absence of the contrary, mere privation; but an *aliquid* cor-
relativum, or the correspondent Opposite of the Power first *put*
(= a contraction from posited, posted, post, put), from whatever
reason this priority may have been determined, or with no other
f8   reason than that where two are to be severally mentioned, ~~the~~ one
must be put first.—Thus, it is indifferent whether I say that Oxygen and Hydrogen, or Hydrogen & Oxygen are the Constituents
of Water. But if I say the latter, then because Hydrogen is the
Positive or Thesis, *therefore* Oxygen becomes the Negative or Antithesis. ⟨P.S. + signifies Thesis or Positive; − signif. Antithesis
or Negative⟩
     The whole Duties of the Marriage State may be easily & beau-
tifully unfolded by pursuing this simple Correlation into the detail

of its application to the Sexes. We have only to construct in the mind a scheme, first of polares, or correspondent Opposites, of the same Line; but secondly, ~~not of~~ the Line not ~~be in~~ having an horizontal direction, in which case it might be arbitrary which of the two Poles was deemed +, & which −; but vertical, the Thesis therefore being Positive: in Superposition, the Antithesis negative in Subposition, i.e. voluntary, or self-subjection "Wives, be subject to your Husbands!" St Paul—Tho' the former word, Supposition, is the more apt & appropriate—for it is a self-position, The Wife must *suppose* herself in subordination to the Husband. In this the whole character of the Duty is implied—The Husband is not to be the Overly Water forcing the Wheel (the Woman) onward—but the circumference, which in moving moves the nave with it, both motions actuated by the same power. As soon as the Wife is driven by a force ab extra, she is no longer a Wife but a servant—the Christian Yoke is gone, & the Law comes in its place. *f8ᵛ*

As the Head to the Heart (in strict language) as the cerebral Nerves to the Pectoral, or the Brain to the Ganglion (Plexus Solaris) in the Breast, so the H. to the W.—Even in the Individual, the H.'s Brain should be in his Heart—the W's Heart in her Brain—and to venture on a more delicate point, in the inferior system the Husband desires the Wife, but the Wife rather desires his *Desire* than directly desires him—i.e. she desiderates, misses, *wants* ~~rather~~ his want of her/*his* Desire of her is more to her, ~~than~~ is more consciously the *object* of her Soul, than the Fruition common to both.—But let us return to the first—the Head to the Heart—i.e. the distinct Understanding to the Emotions, Affections, & *sentiments* in the philosophical sense of that expressive, indispensable & yet almost universally abused word. You have only to consider, in what relation a wise man, at equi-distant from ⟨the⟩ Stoic ~~Pride~~ Super-human & the Epicurean Infra-human, would have his Feelings & his conscious Understanding, to know what the functions of a Wife should be to a Husband, what the directive Power of the Husband should be toward the Wife—Thus unfolded & illustrated in detail—not omitting the feelings which are to be resisted, but how? not imperiously—that would be vain—but by endeavoring to call up some other Feeling or Emotion *f9* arising out of the Motives that had determined the Understanding. So the Wife—not to make blind Feeling have the sway, ~~or a~~ the U. in abeyance, but to warn, to modify, to make pause, always with & under the Understanding—Often, O how often will the Understanding receive the first tidings of its error from a repugnancy on the part of the Feelings. In short, the similie almost goes on all fours: it is so unusually correspondent & adequate.—Item: it is the *Understanding* that is her Husband—the *Reason* is the punctum Indifferentiæ.

f9ᵛ　Such are the rightful Powers of the the Husband who reveres in Marriage the *great Mystery*.—Now for the *Legal* Privilege of the Husband—which may be reduced to this—all the above being presumed to be absent in the internal principle, then to produce ~~as~~ a sufficiently tolerable outside shew of those parts of the same as are in immediate connection with the public peace & the division of Families, the security of Inheritance &c. as Law acting on animal feelings can do—& for this purpose Law gives no privilege, but only recognizing certain prerogatives of animal nature in the Male limits them so as to preserve for the Female those Rights to which she is entitled as a member of the social state, as far as can be done without altogether suspending & annulling the natural prerogative of the Male—not that this would be not right or not desirable but that Law is too coarse & too imperfect an instrument to effect this purpose, & therefore leaves the Task to the progress of Civilization, Pride of Rank, Sympathy & with it Solicitude of Character. First therefore, to apply to the Law at all—i.e. to exert the Rights which Law suffers—is certain infamy for one or other

f10　of the two parties—& in all but the so rare as to be scarcely imaginable circumstances a necessary Stain on the Husband, even supposing the Wife to be ~~an~~ irreclaimably no better than the Female allotted to him, & he forbidden to seek another—

Here comes the Gordian Knot of *Divorce* for other causes beside corporeal Infidelity—

But where the Husband cannot prove the Wife not to be a *Wife*, the Judges, of late times, very wisely interpre~~ting~~ the Law according to its *Spirit*—& non-suit the Husband—& grant a separate maintenance to the Wife. In order to avail yourself of the Law, you must prove that you are under the circumstances on the assumed existence of which the Law is entitled to interfere—.You must prove that you are out of the sphere of the Moral Law & consequently within the legal sphere. You must prove that this Woman relatively to you is a *Thing* not a *Person*, & then the Law will justify at least, give you an immunity from itself, if you treat her as a Thing—But with these limitations, first, she is a living Thing, & so falls under Mr Martin's Act of Parliament against Brutality to Brutes—secondly—tho' not to you, as a Husband, she may be a *Person* to others, & at all events she appears so & cannot be outrageously treated otherwise without the commission of a Nuisance to the Neighbourhood.   *f10^v*

Still it must be confessed that the Law retains the character of the barbarous age, in which it was made—& that much ampler protection might & ought to be afforded to the Wife in her natural & moral claims—especially, with regard to the possession & disposal of the children, in which the Law secures her no voice/

5098 30.1   = equal to. N.b. I have elsewhere noticed the   *f1* insufficiency of this sign, except in mathematics. In philosophic reasoning we want three signs.

1. the mathematical or
      = equivalent to
2. = one with ⊃? or simply ⌢?
3. = the same as ⌒? or simply ⌣?
   ⊁ antithetic to, opposite
   ⊁ contrary to
   + added to: or positive, plus
   − less by: or negative, minus

5099 30.97   Monday Night, Jan. 1824—a close compact   *f52^v* Halo *mob-capping* the Moon. Ask~~ed~~ myself—Does this omen Snow, or change—the Day having been so fine & Frost-like tho' not a frost, & remembered I had asked the same last year, & wished, I had kept a weather-book—

5100 30.98   Tuesday—A fine glorious most exhilarating Hoar Frost, & the Ponds Frozen—& this evening, from 4 to 5, such a Sunset as I scarce ever beheld, in respect of yellow-greens, yellow-reds and orange-reds & Blues indescribable!

*f*5² 5101 30.99   On Thursday Noon, however, (a Thawishness on the Night preceding) Snow came on. Q̣Y Did the Snow-chrystals exist on higher up in the Atmosphere already on Monday Night and cause the Halo? ~~Has~~ Will the Diameter of the Halo ~~be~~ indicate the height in inverse ratio to its length—i.e. the distance of the outward circumference of the Halo from the Moon?

5102 30.100   Swedenjburg's Appendix to the White Horse, from my excellent Friend, C. A. Tulk.—But surely the Doctrine of Symbols or Correspondences should first be proved, as a Science—i.e. its Principles should be established: then its Canons deduced, and its Classes (its Ordinates, Subordinates and Co-ordinates) unfolded & exhibited—Lastly, a Vocabulary of the Symbols hitherto determined, ~~and~~ in consonance with the Principles, Canons, and Classific Characters, previously ascertained.—*Then* if by the application of these to the Sacred Writings, a worthy and coherent Sense should be successively and *articulately* evolved, this would be, no doubt, [at once Exemplification, Confirmation, and Test. . .]

*f*5¹ᵛ 5103 30.101   ⟨Simple⟩ Arithmetic is founded on *three* rules, the rule misnamed Multiplication being only complex or involved Addition. ~~These Rules are Position, & Counter-position (Distribution).~~ A. like Geometry begins with Definitions, or determinate Intuitions (and here comes the question whether *Number* be a mere *Intuitus* like Lines or whether it does ⟨not⟩ partake of a Noumenon) the superinduction of the mind's unity on any plurarility, ~~at once or~~ simultaneously or continuously contemplated, and so as ~~at~~ in the same form to express its relations and comparative quantity to all other plurarity-faggots. The Unitarian Notion ~~are~~ mere confusion of Terms—the number *one* confounded with ens ~~simp~~ absolutè simplex—. Strictly speaking 3 is the first number, ~~one~~ 1 and 2 being reflexes or after-bounds of the mind. There lies on the Seabeach a Limpet & a Pebble—no reason exists why I should connect the image, L. with the image, P. or vice versâ, rather than with ~~a~~ ⟨any one of a⟩ thousand other neighboring objects—but if I add

another Pebble, then the two pebbles re-stand in a relation to the
Limpet:—, and I can draw Lines inclosing a space—or say, that
two Limpets referred to each other in consequence of there being
no more of that sort, then the *collective* circumference, or the in-
terjacentce forms a third.—If for a triangular I suppose a circle—
still the centre, the circumference, and the combining radius are
the tri-une/After the Definitions come the Postulates—and these   *f5 1*
are, Position and N̶e̶g̶a̶t̶i̶ Remotion. (Negation is but imaginary
Remotion—)

The ⟨3 first⟩ Rules themselves are the Axioms, with the way of
presenting them—and should be called Addition or S̶u̶p̶e̶r̶ ̶I̶m̶ Apposition, Subtraction or Deposition, and Division, or Decomposition. Multiplication is merely complex or involved Addition, or
perhaps it may be better described as a mode of Addition, viz. the
determinate ⚹ to simple Addition, as indetermined—& thus it
might be retained and the 4 Rules stand, ⁀Indeterminate⁀
Apposition, Deposition,
⁀Determinate⁀
Composition and Decomposition In order to compose I must first
put a *ratio*—in order to decompose, I must likewise determine by
what *ratio*—all *quality* being abstracted from, and decomposition
in simple quantity being infinite.—

5104 30.102   I humbly pray, that it be no want of *Christian*
Faith, of the Faith that saves the Soul, that I cannot at present find
any other way of interpreting the 6, 7, and 8ᵗʰ Chapters of Genesis,
but as records of the Fact as it appeared to the Arkites themselves,
with their knowlege and their notions and no-knowlege of the con-   *f50ᵛ*
stitution of this Planet—It is plain, that of the two sources of the
diluvial Water mentioned by the Historian the p̶r̶i̶n̶c̶i̶p̶a̶l̶ ̶&̶ ̶l̶e̶a̶d̶i̶n̶g̶
first & principal place is assigned to the Rain—and that this was
Rain in the ordinary sense of the Word is clear, for but treble the
force and density of the Tropical Rains, and a Vessel like the Ark
must have been submerged—and yet that 40 days continued Rain
should have been the *principal* cause of Waters five miles high over
the whole Earth, or even 2½ is inconceivable. Then the

5105 30.2   *f2*
                          Achmates
                          Artemidorus

f49ᵛ 5106 30.56   Monday, Jan. 26, 1824—Derwent's arrival *from* Cambridge/one hour's conversation with him/

5107 30.57   O heaven! I have passed my life in over-rating every body, but myself ⟨in posse;⟩ and *there* I have erred still more mortally, for from hour to hour I have dreamt—thro' life over-rating the *Velle*, the strength of the Will to effect, the "Hoc Age!, which I had promised myself to perform—

f49 5108 30.55   On Perspicuity and Obscurity—Compare a Metaphysician and for yet undisciplined Readers a Logician, to a Bauer or other eminent Microscopic Experimenter/Even Sir H. Davy found himself unable to make use of Baker's Microscopes left to the R.S., and gave it up as requiring too long an apprenticeship. Mem. my Remarks in a former Mem. Book. The difference is that the words representing shape and color do not depend on the size of the Objects, nor is the clearness of the descriptions of things once distinguished affected by the difficulty of distinguishing them—the Fancy is a magnifyer that every man can use without effort. It is far otherwise where in order to distinguish we must abstract, and remove; where the preparatory process is principally abnegative, and the final Product is a *mental* result *f49ᵛ* of which words carefully deprived of their original visual import are the only—not representatives; but counters and substitutes or proxies—where the *act* of the Teacher must be repeated by the Learner, and the Product of the Act is not, as in Geometry, a construction, but a fertigkeit, a readiness and facility in repeating the act with the same result in the Consciousness, in others, a conviction.—Hence the necessity, ~~of~~ in the commencement of philosophic Inquiry, of reading the whole Book or at least Chapter, in order to the understanding, of the first pages.—In short, the Baur's *seeing* is here involved in the Student's understanding of his Plates & Descriptions.

f50 5109 30.58   It is a most important Question which I have never seen properly stated, of course not answered—Is any Demonstration of an Ultimate Truth possible without admitting an *Interest* of Truth as a casting vote. Suppose for instance I come to a

point when the Road splits into X and Y, and the one is as inconceivable as the other, and both modally considered (i.e. in reference to the reasoning Subject, or the mind) involve the same or
equal difficulties. Is it not an *argument*, and an homogeneous part
of the demonstration, to m ⟨be⟩ made known, that one of the two
must be the truth; but that if I take X, no Truth is obtained but I
remain where I was at the beginning; while in Y, tho' I may not
obtain an insight respectivè ad ipsum Y, yet I obtain a great increase of insight with respect to A. B——W—and therefore a
conviction of the Truth of Y.—This is an important instance likewise of the substantial meaning of A = A—:Truth is to be pursued for its own sake means the same as—Truth as its own *Interest*.
Therefore there is an *Interest* of Truth which is one with Truth.

5110 29.229   1. N. B.—Tuesday, 27 Jan^y, 1824. Grove,   *f113*
Highgate—The red Mem. Book marked Ramsgate X on the red
Cover was this day filled—Of *this* Book there are 36 Leaves
⌈ . . . ⌉ still blank, this page not included, or 73 pages, this included. I therefore page them anew, under the title of, Sequel of
Ramsgate. Should I live to fill these with Memoranda, I will then
proceed to the blank Leaves of some other of my Memorandum
Books having blanks, under the title of Sequel of the Clasp-Vel-
lum, from p. 73—.
    Of Kant's only possible Demonstration &c I have given the sum
and exposed the Quid pro Quo in the blank leaves at the end of
his Tracts, Vol. II. (Mr Green's Copy) viz—"Something must at
all times have existed" for "A some one and the some Thing must
always have existed. In order to the proof absolute of the latter,
⟨either⟩ the absolute *impossibility* of a Regressus ad infinitum must
be proved, the feasibility of which I doubt; or the utter unreason-
ableness of preferring a thing must be held equivalent to the impossibility of the thing—And *then* the existence of a necessary
Being might be *enforced* vi Postulati; but it could scarcely be called
a Proof a priori.
    In p. 105 K. affirms his proof to be perfectly a priori, neither
pre-supposing my own existence, nor &c. Surely this borders on
a quibble—. His argument implies the knowlege & the knowlege
implies the thing. What is necessarily implied in the *use* of a Term

f_{112^v} is implied in the Term so used: for the distinction between the Causa sciendi (seu Causa quod scio hoc esse) and the Causa essendi (seu Causa a quod hoc est) is scarcely applicable to Existence and the Consciousness of Existence. A stronger, at least, a more intelligible objection is, that Kant's Existence is but a generalization, or nomen collectivum, clearly pre-supposing the existents, his own existence included, from which it had been generalized. Where an indefinite multitude of perfect Equivalent (~~in respect~~ equivalent in respect of a given relation) exists, A : a = B : b = C : c, there results the logical Numerus Indifferens, which being expressed by the grammatical Numerus Singularis has ~~deluded~~ led many a Metaphysician on to mistake it for the exponent of a *single* Being, and to hypostasize the παγκοινον into a real Unity, an Ἑν καὶ πᾶν or Universal One—If Kant could have shewn ~~a~~ some *one* eternal *Possible*, he might then doubtless have demonstrated the necessity of a *one* eternal *Actual*, who would of course be the Necessary Being— but possibility *generally* only supposes Existence *generally*. So vain is it for a mind filled with multitude ever to arrive at unity or rest.—Weary he falls asleep on the Road, forgets his journey and dreams of other things suggested by his appetites and sensations.

5111 29.230   The Oracle—mist, and intoxicating vapor— yet an Oracle & truly. *Mem. mem. mem.* ω π μ

f_{112} 5112 29.231   "Few die of a *broken* Heart: and these few (the Surgeons tell us) know nothing of it and dying suddenly leave ⟨to⟩ the Dissector the first discovery".—Ah—this is but the shallow remark of hard and unthinking Prosperity/Have you never seen a Stick broken in the middle and yet cohering by the rind?—The Fibres half of them actually broken and the rest sprained and tho' tough unsustaining?—O many many are the broken-hearted, for those who know what the moral & practical *Heart* of the *Man* is!—

5113 29.232   Mem. of the æra of Phil. Necess. with me ~~the~~ my true Lehrjahre. The World, man included, not the object; but God i.e. Good, Truth, Beauty + a Power limited only by its identity with G. T. and B.—Such was the beautiful half-truth that deceived & saved me. But D. & his Perverters!—O!—

5114 29.233   *Mem.*

Kant's einzig m.d.—is most worthy of being amended & perfected: and it is at this time highly expedient—chiefly for the idea,
of the essential inherency of Order in the very possibilities of Existence—which is the true & too-good answer to La Lande's Nonsense, of Dead Letter Boxes—

5115 29.234   *A good heart*—There is in Abbt's Essays an
attempt to determine ~~at leas~~ the true sense of the phrase, at least to
unfold (*auseinandersetzen*) what is meant and *felt* by it—I was
⟨much⟩ pleased with the Remarks, I remember, and with the counterposition of Tom Jones and Sir Charles Grandison. Mem. to
look for it.—

Qỵ Luther and Calvin? 2. Made less noticeable by ~~the~~ its co-
existence ⟨with⟩ and sometimes real, more often apparent, subordination, to a fixt conscious Principles, & thus less characteristic/
Parson Adams ⚹ Dʳ Harrison in Fielding's Amelia—3. Suppression of the g.h.; the Substitution of (α) Principles, (β) Motives for
the g.h.—Ex. Laud and the whole race of conscientious Persecu-
tors/—the Virtues of the Inquisition. A G. H. ⚹ the Pharisaic
Righteousness—This last comtemplation (videlicet, the Pharisaic,   *f111ᵛ*
the Opiniatres or Dogmatists, and the Rigorists in toto genere)
serves to reconcile one to the fewness of the Men who act on fixed
Principles. For unless there exist intellectual Power to determine
aright ~~and~~ what are the Principia jam fixa et firmata, and unless
there be the Wisdom of Love preceding the Love of Wisdom, and
unless to this be added a Graciousness of Nature, a Loving-kindness—these Rigorists are but Bigots often to Errors, and active,
yea remorseless in preventing or staying the rise & progress of
Truth: and when bigotted adherents to true Principles, yet rendering Truth unamiable & "*forbidding* little children to come there-
unto." As Human Nature now is, it is well perhaps that the number should be few, seeing that of the Few the greater part are
prematurities.

The number of those who act from *goodhearted* Impulses, ⟨a⟩
kindly & cheerful mood, and the play of minute Sympathies continuous in their discontinuity like the Sand-thread of the Hour-
glass, and from their minuteness and transiency not calculated to
stiffen or inflate the individual and thus remaining unendangered

by Egotism, and its unhandsome ~~Disguise~~ Vizard, Contempt, is far larger: and tho' these temperamental Pro-Virtues will too often fail and are not built to stand the storms of strong Temptation, yet on the whole they carry on the benignant scheme of social Nature, like the other Instincts that *rule* the animal creation.—~~Of those Lastly~~ But of all the most numerous are the Men, who have evermore their own dearliest beloved Self as the~~ir~~ only or main deliberate Goal or Butt of their Endeavors, ⟨strait and steady before their eyes,⟩ and whose whole inner world turns on the great Axis of Self-Interest. ~~The~~ These ~~number is greatest of all~~ form the majority, if not of Mankind yet of those by whom the business of Life is carried on.—And ~~how could it be~~ ⟨Most expedient it is— then so it should be; nor can we imagine any thing &c⟩—better contrived for the advantage of Society.

f111　　For these are the most industrious, orderly, and circumspect portion of Society, and the actions ~~exerted~~ governed by this principle ~~the only ones and~~ with the results 1. The only ~~calculable~~ materials on which either the Statesman, or Individuals can safely calculate/for ~~it may be confidently presumed that the still more numerous Aggregate (if we count only without weighing)~~ There is indeed (if we count without weighing)—a still larger number— the Aggregate rather than a Class, consisting of those who are below Self-interest, who live for the moment, and act (if actioning it can be called) from Liking, Appetites, Passions, ~~and who in their pure animal selfishness~~

There is indeed another Sort (~~of~~ a Class they can scarcely be called) who are below Self-interest, who live under the mastery of their Senses and Appetites, and ~~in when~~ whose Selfishness is an animal Instinct, a go~~o~~ad *a tergo*, not an attraction and ~~intention rath~~ a re prospectâ, or (so to speak) from a Projected Self. In fact, such Individuals cannot ⟨so properly⟩ be said to have *a* Self, as to be ~~the Slaves of~~ Machines for *the* Self of Nature: and ~~have themselves readily~~ are as little ~~in~~ capable of loving themselves as of loving their neighbours. ~~Few~~ Such there are. Nay if were to *count* only without weighing) the Aggregate of such Persons might possibly form a larger number than the Class preceding. But ~~it~~ they may, be safely ~~presumed~~, taken up into the latter, for the main ends of Society as being or sure to become ~~the~~ its Materials, and

Tools. Their folly is the Stoff in which the sound Sense of the Worldy-wise ⟨is⟩ at once manifested and remunerated—their ~~their~~ Idleness ⟨of the one⟩ with the Passions, Appetites, ~~and~~ Likings and Fancies which are the ⟨~~natural~~⟩ ~~weeds the~~ its natural growth. The *weeds*, of ~~Idleness give~~ give direction and employment to the Industry of the other./~~and the Wants~~, The Accidents of Inheritance by Birth, ~~are counterpoised~~ the accumulation of property in partial masses, are counteracted, the *aneurisms* in the circulating system prevented or rendered fewer and less obstinate—and ~~merely~~ Animal Want the sure general result of Idleness and its accompanying vices, tames ⟨at length the⟩ ~~and~~ *Selfish* ⟨Host⟩ into the laborious ~~Servants~~ Slaves and *Mechanic* Implements of the Self-interested. ~~Wh~~ Thus, without public Spirit, nay, by the predominance of the opposite quality, the Latter are public benefactors, and giving ~~consistency~~ stedfastness and compactness to the whole *lay in the ground* of the ⌈ . . . ⌉ Canvas, on which minds of finer texture may impress Beauty and Harmony. Lastly, there is in the heart of *all* men ⟨a working⟩ a principle, call it Ambition, or Vanity, or Desire of Distinction, ~~which is~~ the inseparable adjunct of our individuality and *personal* Nature, and flowing from the ⟨same⟩ source as Language does, the instinct and necessity ⟨in each Man⟩ of *declaring* ~~our~~ his particular existence, and thus of *singling* or singularizing himself. In some this principle is ⟨far⟩ stronger than in others: ~~and in some~~ while in others its comparative dimness, may pass for its non-existence. But in his Thoughts at least & secret fancies there is in all men (Ideocy of course excepted) a wish to remain the same and yet to be something else and something more, or to exhibit what they are: or imagine they might be, somewhere else ~~pr~~ and to other Spectators. Now tho' this Desire of Distinction, when it is disproportionate to the powers and qualities by which the Individual is indeed distinguished, or when it is the ~~ruling~~ governing Passion or taken as the ~~Maxim~~ Rule of Conduct, ~~in but intimating and anticipating (as a Phantom) a Familiar Spirit to haunt and disquiet Whisper directing the voiceless Ghost of a that Narcissus surviving but in a Whisper the convincing familiar Narcissus Whisper pining for an Echo~~ is but a haunting Whisper, the poor ghost of Narcissus now pining for the absent Echo; yet as a subordina.

f110ᵛ

f110   ~~it~~ is but "a knavish Sprite", yet as an attendant and subaltern Spirit ~~it has it its function and purposes in the General its uses and purposes and works~~ it has its good purposes & beneficial effects: and is not seldom

———sent with broom before
To sweep the dust behind the door.

~~For by this secret~~ Tho' selfish in its origin it yet ~~cou~~ tends to elevate the individual from Selfishness into Self-love, under a ~~more~~ softer and perhaps better form than that of Self-interest, the form of Self-respect. Whatever other objects ~~the~~ man may be pursuing & with whatever other inclinations, he ~~st~~ is still by this principle impelled and almost compelled to pass out of himself in Imagination, ~~in order~~ and to ~~contemplate~~ survey himself, at a sufficing distance in order to judge what figure he is likely to make in the eyes ~~of other~~ his Fellow-men. But in thus taking his station as at the apex of a Triangle, while the Self is at the one angle of the Base, he makes it possible at least that the Image of his Neighbor may appear at the other, ~~in form triangular by the associative Link of Likeness and Difference~~ whether by spontaneous association or placed there for the purposes of comparison, and so both be contemplated at equal distance. But this is the first step toward Disinterestedness; and tho' ~~the~~ it should never be reached, ⟨the advantage of the appearance is soon learnt, and⟩ the necessity of avoiding the appearance of the contrary.——~~is taught~~ But appearances cannot be long sustained without ~~sources~~ some touch of the reality. ~~As some good~~ At all events, there results a Control over our Actions: some good ~~fruits~~ may be produced, and many a poisonous or offensive fruit ~~be checked~~ will be prevented. Courtesy, Urbanity, Gallantry, Munificence, the outward Influence ~~in~~ of the (Law shall I call it? or rather Fashion?) of Honor—these are the handsome ~~offspring of the~~ Hypocrisies that spring from the desire of Distinction. ~~Even the merest Worldling who has observed A man need not be~~ I ask not the genius of a Macchiavel, a Tacitus or a Swift. It needs only ~~the eye~~ Worldly-Experience of a Cassius—and an observing Mind, to convince a man of Forty that there is no medium between

f109ᵛ   the creed of a Misanthrope, and that of the Gospel. A Cassius (quote the passage from Shakespeare in a note) will be as orthodox as Paul on the doctrine of *Works*. First set aside the large proportion, ~~of~~ that have their source in the constitutional Temperament, the merit of which, if any, belongs to Nature not to the individual Agent—and of the remaindering number of *the Good Works* nine ~~may be traced to~~ are derived from Vices for one, that has its origin in Virtue. ⟨I have often in looking at the ~~giant machines~~ waterworks and complex Machinery of our Manufactories indulged ~~in fantastic my Fancy~~ in a *humorous* mood by fancying that the hammers, cogs, fly-wheels, &c were each actuated by some appetite or passion—Hate, Rage, Revenge, Vanity, Cupidity, &c—while the general Result was most benignant, and the ~~wh~~ Machine taken, as a Whole, the Product of Power, Knowlege & Benevolence.—Such a Machine does the Moral World, the World of Human Nature, appear and for those who seem overmore to place the comparison and the alternative between Hell and Earth, quite overlook the opposition between Earth & Heaven, I recommend this meditation.⟩

5116 29.235   Noah—Νεον, Novem, Novum—the 9ᵗʰ from Adam and the Second (New) Proto-parent—. The more often I read, the longer I meditate on, the different fragmentary Documents in Gen. VI–IX, the less I am able to form any quieting judgement. The clean and unclean, ἱερα ~~or~~ καὶ βεβηλα, after the Law, or at least in Egypt.—Of the substantial Truth, however, of the Narration I have not the least doubt.

5117 29.236   X *a necessary consequence* of Y, Y being granted; can never be brought in disproof of Y—on the contrary, if any thing, it must be regarded as a presumption of the reality of Y.

Answer. X may supersede the necessity of the hypothesis Y, and therefore by the Canon de Causis non sine causâ multiplicandis disprove it.

Retort. Aye—under 4 conditions, that there exist no other reasons for Y—2. that Y be a mere Hypothesis.—3. that X be a truth of objective reality & commensurate application with Y—and 4. that X does not involve Y or affirm the same thing under another name.—

5118 29.237

f109 ON INSPIRED WRITINGS

Is there any medium possible between the hypothesis of *Automaton*-writers and that of a pure Heart in communion with the Universal Spirit, and proved by the fact to have been under a providential Guidance and the actuating influences of the H. Spirit on the moral frame, and thus preserved from ~~the~~ such errors as have their origin or first (tho' not perhaps their immediate) cause in passions that weaken and adulterate the Love of the Good and the True, yet not necessarily exempted from imperfection of Knowlege, or the mistakes and prejudices consequent on imperfect Knowlege, and in no wise countervening the specific Object of the Writing? Observe: that this latter hypothesis does not in the least stand in the way of the same person having received supernatural information = the Word of the Lord; but this having been received, there requires only the same Veracity to record it, that there would be required to record any other fact. Am I asked, by what criterion I am to determine the fact of a ~~Book~~ Writer, having written this or that book under this actuating Spirit, I answer— Tell me your criterion of a Book's having been inspired in your sense—i.e. *dictated* by the Holy Ghost to a passive Amanuensis: and then I will tell you mine. So much however I may say beforehand—that my Reply would be given in the words of the Fathers of the Church during the 3 first Centuries/

5119 29.238   If I should ever meet with Mr Greenough, I should ask him—wherein has the geological (chemical or mechanical) impossibility, or weighty improbability of a Mass of Water (or of the elements of Water) being or at an earlier epoch of the Planet having been, under the Crust, called Land, and perhaps under the Channel or Bed of the Sea which may be considered as a continuation of the same crust?—Might not the Sea under a vast pressure act as a Syphon, "breaking up the fountains of the Great

f108^v Deep" under the Land, into thousands of vast Geysers?—How do we know what ~~they~~ proportional the quantity of Solids and solidifiable Gasses diffused, dissolved, ⟨or⟩ simply suspended, in the Mass may have borne to the water itself? The diluvial Gravel may have been the last and perhaps irregular Precipitate. I cannot read

the Mosaic Narrative without the strongest impression that the Writer at least supposed the Rain-bow to have then first taken place: and it is not yet proved that Nature has not ~~the~~ and does not exert even now the power of converting Hydrogen into Nitrogen, and vice versâ. If Hydrogen ~~should~~ and Nitrogen should be, that prot-, this the trit-, oxide of the same Metal; or rather if Hydrogen should be Nitrogen + Positive Electricity, Nitrogen = Hydrogen + Positive Magnetism, our present Atmosphere may contain a large portion of the diluvial Waters, the superfluity of which our philosophising Noachists are so puzzled how to get rid of.— Where Knowlege = o, Fancies that pretend to be no better than Fancies, are something, a sort of + o at least.—

5120 29.239   I was once asked by a Unitarian, What God made Atheists for? Answer. To cure Deists and Unitarians; or counteract the contagion at least by showing their shallowness and inconsistency. Arguments that if valid would disprove an admitted ~~mistake~~ position, cannot be brought in disproof a controverted one: or the Negative of a true Affirmative is necessarily untrue.

5121 29.240   A young man from 3 to 5 + 20, of sound and reflective mind, and commencing the Study of Theology in good earnest and with conscientious as well as professional views—to such a student (an Import, I fear, from Botany Bay, with the Ornithorhyncus—a black Swan!) I do not recollect any Book that I should more strongly recommend than the Volume of Des Cartes' Meditations with the Objections (those of Hobbes, Gassendi and Arnauld more especially) and Replies. With these or next to these he might read Des Cartes' De Methodo: then my "Elements of Discourse" and the Discussion of the three fundamental Questions—1. Is Philosophy (i.e. Speculation περὶ ἀρχῶν) possible without Ideas, these being ⟨negatively⟩ defined as Truths or Forms of Truth having more than merely subjective Validity? 2. *Are*   f108 Ideas? 3. How are they to be *positively* defined? *Then* Bacon's Novum Organum.—~~These~~ Lastly the Articles in Brucker's Hist. Phil. on Plato; Zeno and the *Greek* Stoics; and Aristotle (N. B. I would gladly substitute the four first Volumes, (octavo) of Tenneman, if I could presume on a knowlege of the German—)—These

I should call the προπαιδευτικον of Theology. So accoutred let him begin his Church-History, and his Biblical Studies, as soon as he may.—The ⟨preparatory⟩ Reading here recommended might be honestly got through in a year, and without neglecting his Exercises in composition, and Pulpit Oratory.

5122 29.241   Nothing—I put these words in the mouth of a supposed Antagonist. Would, it were my lot to meet with such a one!—Nothing like taking the Bull by the Horns.—Clap the whole difficulty in the form of an undisguised Contradiction, or avowed Circle in Argument, boldly in the Definition of fundamental Postulate—and every thing must follow—For what will not come out of Plus ~~will~~ must come out of Minus—and you have got both at hand in the postulated incomprehensible $+\overarc{\text{o}}\,-$, the Identity of Finite and Infinite.—Answer—But what if the Contradiction and the Circle were of Nature's *putting*, and that I only *found* them there? ~~On~~ This I assert to be the case in *my* system which however is not what *you* have ⟨well⟩ described as $+\text{ o }=\overline{+\text{o}\,-}$! (*Antag.* Your *Causa sui* is just as bad!)—And in the truth or falsehood, proof or no-proof, of this assertion my System stands & falls—And as to the Infinite I am half inclined to say with Gassendi, Quapropter qui infinitum quid dicit, attribuit rei, quam non capit, nomen quod non intelligit.

5123 29.242   Feb. 11. 1824 (Or first year of the compleated DEVOLUTION)—. Consigning to deserved Contempt and Abhorrence the contemptible and loathesome ~~Slanderous~~ and slanderous Gossips of Bigots pagan or christened—the spirit of which is so alien, so utterly abhorrent from Christianity, that I need my phosphorous † mark to preserve me from excommunicating the Cal-

*f*107ᵛ

†Many years ago, impressed by an incident which I wish to forget, I wrote on two places of my Book Room, at each end of the Arc described by turning my head as I sate, with phosphorus the words, Judge not, lest——and (my bed being in the same room) every time I awoke, I *gazed* on the letters:—by this means the first thing I do on entering a room, is to *imagine* these words in some two places of the Room.

umnist, who as in the instance of Cumberland's unnatural Assault
on Socrates indulges this Vampire Propensity—I know of few
things more honorable to human Nature, than the Lives and Characters of the Philosophers from Pythagoras to Kant and Fichte.
Man perhaps never approached nearer to a moral harmony, than
in the instance of Benedict Spinoza. Scarcely less amiable does the
character of GASSENDI appear to have been. Animated by a sincere
love of Wisdom that still guided and tempered his passion for
Truth, sceptical in behoof of Religion, and adopting but at the
same time adapting and purifying the Epicurean Scheme of Philosophy in the conviction that it was of all the four Systems the
most reconcilable with the Gospel, and the ~~best~~ likeliest to predispose reflecting Minds to a glad and thankful Acceptance of Revelation, Gassendi united the most exten~~ded~~sive erudition with classical Taste, and profound Mathematical Science with a talent for
Observation: and is worthy to stand second only to Bacon among
the Founders and Promoters of Experimental Philosophy. Of the
Moderns, he has a right to be considered as the main Spring or
Fountain-head of the Atomistic & Mechanic Scheme—while ~~yet~~ if
you restore to him and Hobbes all the feathers that belong to them
there will remain of Locke's whole philosophic plumage the one   *f107*
or two feathers only which his Followers have been unanimous in
the wish to pluck out (ex. gr. his general Triangles &c—See Berkley, Hume &c—) Grant me Gassendi, Hobbes, Des Cartes De
Methodo, and Spinoza's first Tract/Principia Cartesiana more geo-
metrico demonstrata: and I will undertake to produce a duodecimo
volume containing in a connected form every principle of the Essay on the Human Understanding, the whole sum and detail with
exception only of Locke's Admitted Errors—nay, all that has been
since added by Locke's Followers, on Association, and the application of the same to the principles of Language and of general
Conceptions.—Now it is most worthy of notice, that in his first
work Exercitationes Paradoxicæ, written ~~by Gassendi~~ in the vigor
of early manhood and with just so much of the venial pugnacity
and intolerance of youthful Genius as fitted it for its intended purpose, that of shaking the pillars of the Scholastic Edifice and the
Superstitious Submission to the Authority of Aristotle, Gassendi
~~was~~ utterly rejected and exploded Logic as useless ~~in~~ for scientific

inquiries and rendered superfluous in all other respects by experience and common-sense.—But when after long intercourse with all the greatest minds of his Age, and long experience in the methods of acquiring and communicating Truth and solid Knowlege, he undertook the honorable task of replacing the False by the True, and of establishing the most probable means and methods of acquiring, arranging and extending the latter—in short when in ~~the~~ full and ripe Manhood, ~~if when with~~ the undiminished vigor of ~~mind he formed~~ his Genius combined with *robustness* of Judgement and Symmetry of Talents and Attainments, he brought forth his *f106ᵛ* Syntagma Philosophiæ, he openly and earnestly retracted his former opinions respecting Logic,—~~not~~ declared it a necessary Pre-discipline (προπαιδευτικον) of the Understanding, and a not less indispensable Organ of the real Sciences than the Mathematics themselves; the study of which exclusive of Logic he pronounces injurious to the finer and more judicial exercises of the Reasoning Powers, tending to render the mind alternately rigid and lax—rigid ~~in~~ by the expectation of mathematical evidence where the subject seemed tho' only *seemed* susceptible of mathematical reasoning, and lax from the ignorance of, or unusedness to, any other criterion & canon where the Mathematics were too evidently ※ inapplicable—Not only does he restore Logic to its right~~ful~~ of place but allows a scientific as well as forensic use and value even to the Aristotelean Dialectic. (In fact, in the latter and larger portion of Gassendi's own System of Logic, the superior method and the greater precision of ~~expression~~ Language with the aptness and felicity of the examples and illustrations belong to himself; but the rules themselves, and the *matter* generally, are borrowed from the ~~Orgenon~~ Analytics & Topics of Aristotle.) Nothing can be better or simpler than Gassendi's Definition of Logic—that while in Ethics and all the real Sciences we see the Truth in the Things, ~~in~~ Logic ~~we see it wholly in the~~ has for its object the ⟨Right⟩ *Thinking*

※This is strikingly illustrated by the fact, that the major number of the Commentators on Daniel and the Apocalypse have been more or less celebrated Mathematicians. The late Dʳ Waring's mathematico-theological work is another, shall I say humorous or melancholy instance.—

⟨in⟩ it itself. ~~The object of Logic is then to think aright~~. With the same propriety he distinguishes Logic into *pure* (abjuncta a rebus) and *applied* (conjuncta cum rebus)—and had he remained faithful to this Distinction, he might perhaps have superseded any further attempt in the exhibition of this Science. As it is, and as long as   *f106* the hypothesis of the tabula rasa (that the mind is a blank sheet of Paper gradually *written thro'* by the Senses) remains the predominant as it certainly is the most popular and most easily comprehensible way of representing the facts, and therefore perhaps the best way for those who require only a connected view of the Results of philosophic Analysis, I am acquainted with no Treatise on ~~Logic~~ the discipline of the reasoning powers that I could recommend in preference to the two first Books of Gassendi's Syntagma Philosophicum, in the first Volume of Gassendi's Works in Sorbiere's Edition published in 6 Vol. Folio at Lyons 1652—or which more perspicuously teaches the rules & assistances bene imaginari (right apperception) bene proponere (der richtige *Ur*theilen, the right placing of a thought before the Mind in its *original* or primary component *parts*, of Subject and Predicate) bene colligere (right conclusion, we shall say, I *collect* from you, that &c) and bene ordinari (right arrangement, disposition, method)—Hence Gassendi divides his Logic, into four sections, De simplici rerum imaginatione (which clearly belongs to rational & empirical Psychology) de propositione, de Syllogismo, de Methodo./

5124 29.243   I do not hesitate to avow that the argument from the universality of the Belief in all civilized Tribes and Nations adduced by Barrow and others in proof of the existence of an intelligent, and all good Supreme Being appears to me neither in point of fact, or consequences or logical conclusion nearly so strong as the same argument brought in proof of a Future State.

5125 29.244   Differing as I do so widely ~~from~~ and in ~~so~~   *f105ᵛ* ~~many~~ such momentous points from the System introduced by Gassendi I feel a pleasure in raising this humble monument in honor of the Man, who completed the downfall of the Aristotelean ~~Dogmatism~~ ⟨while he retained the most valuable part in a better & more intelligible form—⟩Philosophy, and *layed* for ever the gigantic Phantom of the Schools which by a misapplication of one Organ of Science ⟨(the Dialectic)⟩ and this strangely cumbered with extraneous annexments, had for ages usurped the ~~name while it precluded the reality~~ throne of Philosophy, and assumed the title while it prevented the ~~existence~~ growth of all other ⌈ . . . ⌉ Sciences.— the man who ~~more than any other Reformer~~ at once vindicat~~ed~~ing & exert~~ed~~ing the Freedom of Thought yet more than any other Reformer of equal celebrity kept the mean between Freedom and Licentiousness or who checked ~~&~~ the dogmatism & ~~emancipated Prescription~~ exposed the nakedness of the Cartesian ~~Speculations~~ Rationalism & Ficta-Rationalia on the one hand, and ~~layed bare before~~ precipitated the contagious Miasma of Enthusiasm and Mysticism on the other—/

(*This to be re-composed*)

5126 29.245   The two Extremes on the *ground* of the Xtn Faith, as usual nearest each other—

1. ~~The~~ Ultra-protestant. The Old & New Testament = the Bible the *sole* and *sufficient* (of course therefore necessary) Ground of the Xtn Faith—excluding Tradition.

2. Ultra-Catholic = not the only, not sufficient, and not even absolutely necessary—in as much as Tradition and the Church by virtue of Tradition supersede the *necessity* of the Bible—and are themselves necessary to determine its authenticity and inspiration, to settle its interpretation, and to limit and direct its use.—

Both therefore agree on one point—that a Tradition necessary for the Bible must be capable of being its Substitute—

f105   The first urges triumphantly and (I think) irrefragably two arguments—First, that in the very nature of things, in an age and state of civilization like that of the Roman Empire during the first Century all that was valuable in oral Tradition must have become Scripture, inspired or uninspired—2. They challenge their adversaries to prove the existence of any Tradition of any import in matter of Faith, not found in the New Testament and yet not originating at a demonstrably later period.—They probably ridicule the stretch of the word *Tradition* to mean the belief of the age of ~~the~~ a book; that determines its own age (Cicero's Letters for instance)—where there is no assignable ground or reason for the

contrary. The Fathers who as Tertullian, Ireneus and Augustin, who speak loudest of Tradition, what do they refer to it? Simply when when any one quoted a text against *their* δοξα, or gave a different explanation to a Scripture which they had cited, in lack of better arguments they boldly asserted that predecessors had all interpreted it as they ~~did~~ did/And by what Tradition is the Tradition to be proved? The other-minded (Heterodox) appealed likewise to the Tradition of their Churches (ex. gr. Marcionites—And prima facie their being heterodox is no proof they were not orthodox. But the Tradition to answer its purpose must be *universal*. This was too evident—and to cut a knot that was not to be untied, the first precious consequence of this Tradition scheme was the bold assertion that a Part was the *Whole*—*the* Church—& all other Christians Babeldoms, to be blown up toward their Master, the Prince of the Air! But if this meristo-Catholic, this partial-universal, is not to be a phantom, it must have some Focus. This too was undeniable; and hence the second consequence, namely, *Infallibility* some where, and thence a known *where*—/a tenet which has no $f104^v$
sense or application except in its most monstrous Form, namely, the Papal Infallibility—this however a Paradox so revolting to Common Sense & so irreconcilable with History that the Jack-o-lanthorn flits about to this very hour between Pope, Pope + Cardinals, General Council, General Council convened & confirmed by Pope & Cardinals, or General Council the Decrees of which have been acknowleged and adopted by Catholic Christendom— who shall fix it?—But lastly wherever it might be placed, one thing became very clear to the Hierarchy—namely, that it exceedingly inconvenient to have this Oracle too often questioned concerning the universal Tradition of the one only Apostolic and Catholic interpretation of Scripture: and the third ~~Consequence~~ Result which as being the immediate and proper logical Consequences of the Tradition-scheme, they might as well have begun with, was to ~~loc~~ put the Scriptures under Lock & Key, and ~~substitute~~ put the focus or concentrated Essence of Universal Tradition in their stead. For as foolish Mothers are apt to have thankless and ungrateful Children, so in this instance Apostolic Universal Tradition—conferred all & more than its own Authority, with the abiding enactive power of the Holy Ghost in all its original Apostolic

Force on the Church, i.e. the Head of the Church, Council or pope as the latter happened to be weaker or stronger in courage, talent and alliances with the Monarchs of Christendom/—& thence forward ~~Tradition~~ the want of an ab-original Tradition was no impediment to Dogma, or Discipline or Ceremony. The Church had enacted the one, had declared the other—against all Tradition the Cup was taken from the Laity, Marriage denied to the Clergy, Purgatory proved by Visions &c &c.—For answer to those protestants (chiefly Oxford Doctors & Laudites) who would qualify the Doctrine and admit of ~~an importuning~~ use of Tradition as opposed to a possible but novel interpretation of Scripture—for instance—Suppose a Quaker had wit or learning enough or cared enough about the Scripture-grounds of his Persuasion to urge, that by Christ's Second Coming the Destruction of Jerusalem was intended, and that the institution of the Lord's Supper was meant only for the Jewish Converts as long as they lived among their Brethren & joined in the Paschal Supper & that accordingly St John who wrote his Gospel after that event makes no mention of the Eucharist, other than spiritually in the VI Chapter, it would be decisive to urge the universal practice to the contrary, including St John's own Churches at Ephesus—In answer to such reasoners it is quite sufficient to say, Who I beseech you, being in his sound Senses ever thought of rejecting the Light of History in the interpretation of any author; but to what rational man did it ever occur to call a few known facts of History by the name of oral Tradition, or Tradition of any kind—~~History~~ Successive History, from the Monkish Writers to Hume, and his continuers is indeed one etymologically proper Sense of the Word—and Treason is another— and Capitulation is a third—and for aught I know, in this age of fine words, the Tread-Mill may be a fourth/~~sense of Tradition~~.— The weakness of Tradition as used by Protestants, i.e. its utter impotency when not supported by an admitted legislative & judicial Power of the Church, is strikingly exemplified in the Presbyterian & Episcopalian Controversy. None of the former party every denied the *historical* fact of Bishops from the Apostolic Times—well! What then? It naturally arose from the mode of the establishment and the circumstances of the Churches, while yet Christian Churches co-existed with Heathen Temples &c.—A

f104

f103^v

Parity of Presbyters better suits the present circumstances—and
what *authority* can an historical fact possess for perpetuating itself?
All that Tradition can say is, that when there was but one Pres-
byter, he was called a Bishop (over his Flock)—When many met
in one Church or in one City, one of them took precedence/. Can
it, the Tradition, prove that the Apostles by divine Authority &
for all ages made the Custom obligatory & a permanent Component part of Christianity? If so, with what face can you pretend to
the Romanists that the Bible contains the whole of the Christian
Religion? And how is this Tradition to be proved? Divine Right
is an opinion, not like the existence of Bishops an historical Fact.
That some men thought so, they knew not why, is no proof that
all did.

5127 29.246   Little dialogue on *Quidditas—Pig-Tail* Tobacco—Guineas—*gold* the *essence*.

5128 29.247   I hold, it it true, that all the demonstrative
proofs of a God either prove too little, as that from the order in
Nature, or too much, viz. that the World is God, or presuppose
the truth to be proved as the hidden Ground of the Proof (as by
the word, first *Cause*: while all of them presuppose the Idea or
Conception without being able to legitimate it or give account,
whence they had it.—Likewise I hold that the most natural and
convictive Proof, viz. the Cosmological, supposes the Ontological.
If the latter can provide a God, the former will prove his Wisdom
and Goodness.—All this I hold; but I also hold, that this Truth
the ~~least possible~~ hardest to demonstrate is the one which of all
others least needs to be demonstrated—that tho' there may be no   *f103*
⟨conclusive⟩ demonstrations, there are so many convincing reasons
for it, within and without, a grain of sand sufficing and a Universe
at hand to echo the decision, that for every mind not devoid of all
reason and desperately conscience-proof the ~~Being of a God~~ Truth
which it is least possible to prove it is little less than impossible ~~to~~
not to believe, only just so much short of *impossible* as to leave
some ~~place~~ room for the Will and Moral Election, and to preserve
it therefore a truth of Religion, and a Commandment . . . ⟨so
render it possible for a Fool to make a monster of himself⟩—On

this account I do not demand of a *Deist* that he should adopt the doctrine of the Trinity: for he might very well be justified in replying that he rejected not the doctrine,—not because it could not be demonstrated or on account of any difficulties & seeming ~~metaphys~~ contradictions & incomprehensibilities, which might perhaps be urged or rather by Atheists & Pantheists ha~~d~~ve been urged with equal force against the Idea and Attributes of a God at all; but because he had not the same reasons and moral instincts for the one as for the other. But the case is quite different with a Christian, who refuses his Assent to the plainest declarations of Scripture & explains the words into metaphors *because* the literal sense is absurd & contradictory to Reason. He is bound therefore to shew that it is so in any sense not equally applicable to the Texts declaring the Being and Attributes of God the Father/Meanwhile the doctrine of Redemption supplies him with reasons of a moral nature far more *concerning* & coercive subjectively than all the theoretical inducements that can act on the Deist *objectively*.

f102ᵛ   5129 29.248   First reflection of one who⟨se Belief⟩ is attacked by an Infidel.—Is the evidence demanded appropriate and proportionate to the subject in question? Has not Metaphys, or Mathem. evidence been required for a point of History? Absolute evidence instead of ⟨adequate evidence⟩ a satisfying overbalance tho' consisting perhaps of reasons for the belief as well as proofs of the Truth?—

Second—from an effect to a Power a poor inference—not ⟨to⟩ a Person. Ex. Magnet.

Third, to remove the confusion, into which Kant himself has fallen, between Limit by Negation, or defect, and Limit by Position & as an essential Perfection? applied to the ? of Will and Intelligence in God!

4ᵗʰ—whether the argument a non possibile, non, or the predicting of Mathematical Necessity concerning the Order & Fitness of Things is not greatly qualified by the assuredly *contingent* Fact of the Human Mind possessing the correspondent power of Insight? What would the Object avail without a rational *Subject*? And of this argument *in* toto, is it not m~~or~~eost startling at ⟨its⟩ first presentation? If the ~~Reason~~ Order in Nature be = Mathematical Necessity; and ⟨is not⟩ Mathematical Necessity ~~the~~ = Reason in Man? ~~would it not be true in conseq~~ and does it not therefore follow— that the Order in Nature is identical with the Reason in Man? And what more does the Theologian want? He has no interest in confounding the terms, Reason & Will—& there will still remain a necessary place for the latter, in the *application* of Reason, and the ⟨bi-sexual⟩ harmony, viz. the position of the subjective R., i.e. Reason + the Understanding and Sense, correspondently to the Objective R. i.e. Reason + self-constitutive & productive Power.—

5. But deeper & for prepared Minds dissipative of this whole colored Mist in the Slant Beams of the Dawn of philosophic Insight, is the essential posteriority of Reason—If I draw and when I have drawn a circle, *then* by necessity of Reason it is equi-radial &c—still the *past* Tense—It could not *have been* otherwise—but f102 the Circle contains in itself no causa sufficiens, no explanation, of its being at all, Cum sit Circulus, est e sua ipsius necessitate tot et tantarum Proprietatum.

5130 29.249   One means of contra-characterizing the Philosophy of the Lyceum relatively to that of the Aca~md~æmic Grove/ is: That Aristotle can give no definition of Philosophy, ⟨as⟩ distinguish'd from Science—the ειδεναι εκ τ~α~ων πρωτων αιτιων, η του Δια τι, i.e. Knowlege from *Grounds*, or To know a thing ~~by~~ in and thro' a knowlege of its necessary Antecedents which A. gives as the Definition of Philosophy is at least an *equally* proper Definition of Science. With Plato on the other hand Philosophy is the system of ~~th~~ Truths ~~that~~ having their sole and proper Source in the ⟨Pure⟩ Reason, ⟨moral and contemplative: or it is⟩ ~~or~~ Knowlege of and by IDEAS—~~or~~ an Insight into the Truth of Things by contemplating them in their essential (or constitutive) Ideas ⟨or simply, Essential Knowlege, neither theor: nor practice singly but both in one.⟩ From this alone we may conclude the falsehood of Tenneman's 50 times repeated Assertion, that Plato attributed a *regulative* function only to the *Ideas* of the Pure Reason. Had this been true, the difference between ~~the World's two Philosophers and Philosophies~~ the two philosophic Monarchs and the two Philosophies of our Mundus intelligibilis would indeed be little more than a Dispute in Words, and the Syncretists and Harmonizers would have an easy task.—Mem. The Reason, as at once moral and intellective, = the Light in the Life, is named the Spirit by St Paul.

The first man of Science was he, who looked into a thing, not to learn whether it could furnish him with food, or shelter, or weapons or Gold or ornaments, & or play-withs—but who sought to know it for the gratification of *knowing*: while He, that first sought to *know* in order to *be*, was the First Philosopher.—I have read of two Rivers passing thro' the same Lake, yet all the way preserving their streams visibly distinct: and if I mistake not, the Rhone and the Adar

f101^v   ⟨20 Feb 1824⟩

thro' the Lake of Geneva. In a far finer distinction yet a subtler Union such for the contemplative mind are the streams of Knowing and of Being. The Lake formed by the two streams is Man and Nature as it exists in and for Man: and up this Lake the Philosopher sails on the junction line of the constituent streams, still pushing upward and sounding as he goes, towards the common Fountain-head of both, the Mysterious Source whichose Being is Knowlege, whose Knowlege is Being—the ADORABLE I AM IN THAT I AM

5131 29.251   In Wonder, the offspring of Ignorance, Philosophy begins: ~~in Admiration it proceeds and~~ in Wonder, the Parent of Adoration, it ends: and ever-waxing Admiration is the Line of Transit.

or

In Surprize, that wonders, Philosophy begins: in Wonder, that adores, Philosophy ends: and Admiration is the line of Transit.—

or

In Wonder Philosophy begins: in Wonder it ends: and Admiration ~~is the Line~~ marks the interspace. But the first W. is the Offspring of Ignorance: the last the Parent of Adoration: that the struggling Birth of Knowlege, this its Euthanasy and Apotheosis.—S.T.C.

5132 29.252   A Knowlege for the sake of Knowlege is Phi-   *f101*
losophy, says Aristotle—Δια γαρ το θαυμαζειν οι ανθρωποι και νυν
και το πρωτον ηρξαντο φιλοσοφειν—ωστ' ειπερ δια το φευγειν την
αγνοιαν εφιλοσοφησαν, φανερον οτι δια το ειδεναι το επιστασθαι
εδιωκων, και ου χρησεως τινος ενεκεν. Metaphys. I. c. 2. Item Plat.
Theatetus p. 76. But this is evidently Philology or Philepistasy,
not Philosophy: the pure Love of Science nor the Love of Wisdom. Knowlege for the sake of Knowlege is pure Science: Knowlege in the faith that the True is likewise the God, is Philosophy—
or that the True is the Offspring and Constitutional Image of the
Good.

5133 29.253   Nothwendig aber ist nur das Allgemeine: =
but only the Universal is necessary. Thus but without due authority Tenneman renders Aristotle's φανερον αρα, οτι οσα καθολου εξ
αναγκης υπαρχει τοις πραγμασι—i.e. it is evident then, what what
applies to the whole ⟨scheme⟩ must apply to all the particulars. I
mention this, however, as a memento, how requisite it is to explain
the different senses incident to a scientific term, before it is introduced in a scientific proposition. I should have contented myself
with saying in the first place, that the Necessity of a thing is *evident*
in proportion to its universality: or that whatever is necessary, is
universal within the sphere of the conception.—I would explain
likewise, that this is merely a logical position, a canon of discursive
Thinking: & does not apply to the necessity by causation. Apply
it to God, for instance. Here is a Subject, the essential idea of
which is that it is necessary and has its necessity in itself—but
surely, I cannot say that it is universal, all-common, unless I turn
Spinozist or an Anima-Mundi Dreamer.—
     So too I think it wise, to begin indeed with the definition of an
Absolute Demonstration as a conclusion followingly necessarily
from Premises the truth of which presupposes no other truth—but
I should then shew that except in Mathematics the greater number
of Demonstrations are ex hypothesi, or a concessis, or a monstratis:
and that it would be a more useful and generally applicable Defi-   *f100ᵛ*
nition, that a Dem. is a legitimate conclusion from true Premises,
to the evidence of which no other needs be presupposed, and that
when this is effected by means of a middle term, it is a logical
Dem. or a Syllogism.

1. Mem. The heinous oversight in many Books of Logic, the includeding reasonings truly mathematical (i.e. matters of intuition) in logical reasoning because the terms are *words*, and not Lines, or Numbers and then trying to force them into enthymemes, or *interpolate* them into absurd Syllogisms. Example. If that is the Right Hand, the other is the Left = take one from two, and there remains one—A and B. being alone given, ~~take~~ remove A ~~from B~~ and there remains B.—Now for ~~a~~ the Syllogism—All men duly ~~proport~~ limbed and proportioned have two Arms, the Right and the Left.—The Emperor of Morocco is a man duly limbed &c—Ergo, the Emperor of Morocco has two arms, &c—The other ⟨Arm⟩ corresponding to the Right is the Left Arm.—But this is the Emp. of Morocco's other Arm, corresp. &c. Ergo, this is the E. of Morocco's left arm.—

11. Mem.—I am strongly induced to put the ?, whether the term, universal, might not with advantage be done away with in the terminology of Logic, and the term, *formal*, or essential, be substituted. In affirming the equality of the Rays of a Circle I affirm an essential form of *the* Circle or rather the Circle as a total (i.e. seclusive) Form, and the equi-radiality as a component (i.e. included) integral Part.—Even the phrase, true in all cases, is preferable to Universal: for *"cases"* does imply a previous limitation or sphere, within which the ~~Real~~ individual Subjects or Instances fall. Its truth is commensurate with the (rightly-used) Name of the Subject. At all events, *"Common* Truths, or Truths common to many, are alone demonstrable", seems to me more intelligible and less likely to be misunderstood than the Axiom, the Universal alone is a Subject of Demonstration. Then would *f100* come the proof, that: no predicate can be common to an indefinite Number of Individuals, that is not *formal*, i.e. having its ground and necessity in the laws or forms of the Faculty, by which the Instances are perceived and understood—which we may name generally the cognoscent faculty, comprizing both the intuitive and the reflective Power, or the Sense (αισθησις) and the Understanding (λογος).—Relatively to the form, this is what Aristotle means in the words, και γαρ αισθανεται μεν το καθεκαστον η δε αισθησις του καθολου εστι.

But I find a confusion in Aristotle's use of the term of the term, αρχαι, which sometimes means, Principles or Truths evident a priori, which of course (the doctrine of Ideas being rejected) can only be the laws or forms of the Mind itself—and sometimes means admitt primary Facts, resting on the evidence of the Senses, and the concurrent testimony of Mankind that the perception is not referable to any anomaly in the Senses of one or more Individual—αναγκη γαρ και την αποδεικτικην επιστημην εξ αληθων τ' ειναι και πρωτων, και αμεσων—sometimes only *Admitted* Facts—εξ γνωριμωτερων και προτερων και αιτιων του συμπερασματος, as the grounds of the particular Conclusion. Now of "αρχων" in the two latter meanings only can it be truly affirmed Διο τας μεν αρχας τας περι εκαστον, Εμπειριας εστι παραδουναι—Analyt. prior. I. c. 30.—which yet Aristotle seems, tho' not constantly, to extend to all three, in compliment to his mistaken Dogma, that Experience is the source of all Knowlege, instead of all knowlege of particular Objects. The simple Rule is—whatever is natur relatively to the human mind contingent in Place or Time is so far a Subject of Experience: whatever can be affirmed, abstracted from all contingency in Place and Time is a Subject of Demonstration: and lastly whatever can be affirmed, independently of Space as well as Place, and of Time as well as of any Time, is a Truth of Reason—*Veritas eterna*—whether it be exclusively of, or only severally from. Thus: the Idea of God is exclusive of Space & Time: the moral Will is to be thought of severally from Space & Time.—Again—those Subjects that are alien from Space yet not from Time, as our Thoughts, successive Emotions, are Objects of inward Experience by means of the Interior Sense./ *f99ᵛ*

I I I. *Mem.* In my Elements of Discourse after the etymological chapter to insert the Essay on Noumena and Phænomena as a separate Chapter—and not to forget the Noumena Statica et)(hypostatica—then the History (excluding the biographical details) of the famous Dispute between the Realists & the Nominalists—this hist. sketch introduced by and brought in proof the ill-consequences of the Aristotle's *Universals*, as shown in the preceding Leaf—and the confusion of Abstractions & Generalizations with Laws and Forms of perceiving noticing and thinking, whence followed the confusion of Ideas with Categorical Conceptions (Urbegriffe). In short, as there was the same neglect of της προπαι-

δειας in Aristotle r̶e̶s̶p̶ as so long after in our own Locke—Ar.
grounded a̶l̶l̶ *knowlege* on Experience, and Locke's Work is in fact
an Essay on Human Consciousness—and yet no where has Aristotle given a distinct and *genetic* definition or explanation of Experience, or the c̶o̶n̶s̶t̶r̶u̶c̶t̶i̶v̶e̶ ̶G̶r̶o̶u̶n̶d̶s̶ ̶o̶f̶ ̶h̶o̶w̶ process of Thought
by which he arrived at this fundamental Dogma, that all knowlege
is derived from Experience, as Source & not merely as occasion—
And no where has Locke d̶i̶v̶i̶d̶e̶d̶ ̶i̶n̶t̶o̶ ̶t̶h̶e̶ given a constitutive
Definitio (Def. realis ⚹ verbalis) of Consciousness, or any insight
respecting its elements or its conditions.—It is v̶e̶r̶y̶ ̶l̶i̶k̶e̶ possible,
that the nature of Experience may by a Reader who is already
acquainted with it from other sources be deduced from particular
sentences in the Analytics, Metaphysics, De Anima: but I do not
⟨know⟩ any t̶r̶u̶t̶h̶ position, however frequently and systematically
contradicted elsewhere, that might not be deduced from some sentence or other in so voluminous, multifarious, and i̶n̶t̶ difficult
(obscure from excessive compression) a writer as Aristotle.—To
this add Aristotle's Passion of detracting from his great Master—
his gross m̶i̶s̶i̶n̶t̶e̶r̶p̶r̶e̶t̶a̶t̶i̶o̶n̶ almost inferring *wilful*, misconception,
of Plato's Doctrine of Ideas, which he first confounds with the
altogether different Doctrine of Innate Conceptions ⟨and thus
makes a mish-mash of both that is true of w̶h̶i̶c̶h̶ neither of them
o̶f̶ ̶c̶o̶u̶r̶s̶e̶ The latter⟩ therefore fall under the same interdict—and
are controverted by the same misinterpretations, as the Cartesian
phrase Innate Ideas, was assailed by Locke, and the ⟨Leibnitzean⟩
Doctrine of Constitutional Forms, Aptitudes, or Pre-dispositions

f99   of the Human Mind under the † name of Innate Ideas was by
Locke's Followers. The Result, or rather the *Consequence*, is obvious, as $2 - 1 = 1$. The mind itself excluded as an active principle, w̶h̶e̶t̶h̶e̶r̶ and neither its productivity admitted nor even its
formative power—the Subject, I say, being denied to be the source
either of t̶h̶e̶ Stuff (Ideas) or of Form (Categories of Sense or of
Understanding, are nothing r̶e̶m̶a̶i̶n̶e̶d̶ but passive receptivity admitted) Arist., I own, is evermore implying an active or spontaneous recipiency; but how is this comprehensible, consistently with

f99ᵛ   † not indeed happily adopted: but it was the language of that Age
& continued to be the L. of the present.

the denial of Innate Forms, or even cogitable, I am unable to conceive/—nothing of course remains but the outward Nature, or Aggregate of Objects.—Whatever just and necessary Conceptions exist must therefore have their correspondents in Nature, must express outward Realities—But the so called Universals. ex. gr. Classes, Genera, Species, Height, Depth, Thinness, Largeness, Heaviness and other Exponents of Relation and Comparison, are just & necessary Conceptions—Ergo, ~~they~~ each must have ~~their~~ its origin in a Counterpart, in Nature—And hence the Realism of the Schools—a strict & legitimate consequence of Aristotle's nihil in intellectu quod non prius in sensu/

But perhaps ~~the most~~ there does not occur in the Hist. of Philos, a more remarkable instance of the Warping Power of Rivalry and Ostentation of Originality, with wilful Opposition as their Familiar Spirit, on the one hand; or of the impossibility of grounding universal & necessary Truth on the Principle of Experience exclusive of ~~the~~ Innate preconceptions ⟨in the Understanding,⟩ or the Absolute without admitting the Eternae Veritates, or unconditional and self-originated Dicta of Reason, on the other, than Aristotle's *Salto Mortale*, in deriving an objective, ~~or~~ real Catholon *from* (not only *by*) Abstraction, i.e. the power of attending to one part of a Complex Impression to the exclusion of the remainder; and the unspeakable grossness of locating a Necessary and Permanent *so* obtained *above the Moon*, under the names of *Corruptible*, com-   *f98ᵛ* prizing all *sublunary* (in what Plato in the spirit of philosophic Good Sense had called, Sensible) Objects, and the Incorruptible, the incommunicable Attributes of all BODIES (!!) above the Moon—φθαρτα και αφθαρτα.—To these Blunders annex the attempts to render the incogitable conceivable by the fiction of Species (vide Occam) and the Consequences, ex. gr. The plump Realism of the Schoolmen before D. Scotus.—In conclusion, however, observe that these Errors affected the *Dialectic* only, i.e. the legitimation and determinating of the *Premises*, or the Rules and the Criteria of true Affirmation (the Principles, by which what is affirmed may be known to be truly affirmed) and not the Science of LOGIC itself, as *Canon* of Legitimate Thinking, and an Organ for *distinct* Consciousness of the connection of our Thoughts abstractly from their contingent Objects.—

Surely there must be some worm or canker of falsehood at the very root of the Empirical Philosophy when even the ~~genius~~ practiced Subtlety and Acuteness of so an Intellect so vigorous, capacious, and richly stored as Aristotle's could not preserve it from such unsightly knots & Excrescences, or ⌐ . . . ⌐ prevent him from engrafting on its inconsequences, obvious even to the hastiest Revisor—of which let the two following be instances. Της ουσιας και του τι εστιν ουκ εστιν αποδειξις. The Existence of No Substance can be demonstrated but must be pre-assumed on a Datum of the Senses. (λαμβανουσι δε το τι εστιν, αι μεν δι' αισθησεως, αι δε υποτιθεμεναι.) And yet he afterwards gives (professes to give, at least) a Demonstration of a Necessary Being. II. The ~~truth of the~~ Mind's Affirmations & Judgements are true in proportion as they truly ~~copy or~~ represent the impressions and order of impressions received from the Correspondent Objects. ~~Or all~~ Truths are true Copies of sensible experience—εμπειριας δι' αισθησεως.—And yet in the face of this he lays it down as a true ~~Ob~~ Judgement that the Thing Acting is prior to the passive, and therefore the Objects that correspond to our Sensations & Perceptions would exist tho' there were no sentient Subject.—From what impression of the Senses did his mind copy when it affirmed Perception to be an Impression? Where did it find the interval of time between seeing and the sight? Above all, whence did he derive the assertion of a τι κινουν, a mover, that was not itself τι κινουμενον—i.e. of an originator of Motion? All that his senses could have presented was a succession κινουμενων. Or whence the assertion, that the percipient power is τι πασχον, or passive—and the Stone or res percepta is a τι ποιουν, an active power?

f98

While I charge the System of Aristotle as far as it is a System & his System with these defects, I am perfectly aware & most willing to acknowlege that in very many sentences & ⟨single⟩ passages of his Works far other Opinions are expressed and may be legitimately derived from a still greater Number—that not only a Reason is acknowleged but acknowleged as the source of Principles, as a steady Light in which alone the permanent and the necessary are seen, and that there is a Morality ~~of a~~ higher in kind than Prudence, ~~Moral Common~~ and a Law beyond what can be abstracted ~~from~~ by the Understanding from the Experiences, of the

Sense—&c—But in the first place the most striking and unequivocal of these Passages occur in the larger Ethics, and the Ethics to ~~Nico~~ Eudemus, both which are considered by the best modern Critics as spurious, ~~in imit~~ and of those that remain ~~the far greater~~ occur chiefly in his metaphysics which are believed on strong grounds to be interpolated, and tho' the matter in substance is for the greater part genuine, yet that the order and arrangement is the work of meaner hands—; and in the second place, they are but flashes, ~~as without the Author have not been~~ of which the Author makes no further use in the correction or modification of his proper system, nor (which would have the best possible use) suggested to him the necessity of beginning with the cognoscent Subject and submitting the subjective conditions, under which any knowlege is possible for man, to a critical examination and analysis.

There is one passage, for instance, in the Book De Memoriâ *f97ᵛ* (shewing that tho' we cannot reason *without* an image of Sense (ανευ φαντασιας) yet we do not reason *by* it, ⟨but rather as it were in spite of it:⟩ as in the accidental *Quantity* (το ποσον) of a Triangle by necessity of Sense (~~wh~~ of which, however, the reason takes no notice, but it is present as if it were absent) so remarkable that one would thought it impossible for the Author not to have seen the inference, that sometimes more than Abstraction is concerned in this process—and that the Reason must be following some rule or law of its own Constitution, and some act or product in the Mind itself to which *the Diagram* is but as ⟨the⟩ picture ⟨of ~~Eolus~~ Boreas to the North Wind⟩ to prevent the senses drawing off & distracting the attention, and as an implement of technical memory, necessary only in proportion to the weakness of the Person reasoning. But No!—Here as in almost all ⟨similar⟩ cases, ~~of~~ a double-meaning word intercepted the dawning Light/. Abstraction ~~wou~~ did every thing: tho' in this instance the Reason had never directed its attention to the Quantity, and therefore could not have withdrawn it, and the *Sense* ((i.e.) the Eyes) *could* not abstract from it, but rather in another rendering of the word abstracts it from the ~~substance~~ tangible substance.—And I pray of what *experience* are breadthless Lines, and depthless Surfaces the offspring, or Impressions? Grant (what is not very probable) that I had seen ten or so right-angled Triangles of different sizes at the same time—I might certainly abstract from the difference of the Quantities, ~~the tho' not from Quantity which yet I do~~ to take any one of the 20 by hap-hazard as a perfect representative of the remaining 19 can in any but the laxest sense of the word be called Abstraction, but not from Quantity altogether. And where is the original Triangle *general*, by which I learnt to ~~contradict~~ nullify all *particular* quantity? To perceive that one particular Quantity will do as well as another, is *f97* surely no act of Abstraction. If I told a Servant to bring a Log of a Wood, or a Shovel of Coal, or a Peat—either will do equally well—~~would~~ would a Peripatetic ~~might explain~~ say, that I abstracted from the Wood, the Coal & the Peat, and gave admission only to the Species, Combustibility?—But alas! If Aristotle had followed up the light that was ever and anon starting up in his mind, he must have admitted some pre-existing Moulds in the Sense itself and the same in the Understanding and these again would not have been sufficient, scarcely in theory especially the θεωρια των ἀφθαρτων but wholly inadequate in Ethics, without certain Exemplars or Patterns in the Reason—& he must have fallen back into ~~the~~ an upper boy of Plato's School/—It is probable that A. never thoroughly understood his divine Master's Doctrine of Ideas: and it is certain, that he took pains to *mis*understand it. The unsteady Notion concerning these Ideas that fluttered between the two—represented them to his own mind as useless & inapplicable in the investigation of Nature, which was still the paramount object of his Studies, and to which all his other Labors were more or less pro-pædetic or preparatory—and yet to this very Circumstance is it owing that neither the Stagirite himself or his ~~School~~ Followers and ~~adherents~~ Devotees ~~in~~ ancient or modern ever made any one great discovery in Natural Philosophy, or established any one Law of ~~the~~ Nature; but on the contrary hindered the progress of ~~Natural~~ Physics & Physiology far more by the dogmatizing Spirits of his Philosophy, and the fanciful hypotheses consequent on the realism inseparable from his System than it did service by his School's undeniable merits in the principles of arrangement and in the ⟨invention,⟩ distinction and appropriation of Terms and Descriptions.—It is most interesting & at first sight curious, that, [to] the Pythagoreans & Platonists whose attention was chiefly directed ad intra we owe the greatest discoveries of the external Nature—

while to Arist. and the Peripatetic School, who acknowleged no
original Source, no proper Spring-head, but Experience, we have *f96ᵛ*
received the greatest improvements in the disposition and connection of Thoughts & Words, Logic, Rhetoric, Forensic Discussion,
and all the forms and exponents of the world within, the busy
Microcosm of Human Nature—.

Aristotle's a philosophy in the *Spirit of this World*—what so evident (N. b. *certain* is quite another question), so common-sense-
ish, so useful and profitable and level to all capacities, as the Beginning—Use your Senses—remember what they have told you—
then by your understanding observe wherein they agree & wherein
they differ, and arrange in your mind accordingly.—The Sense
itself helps you in abstracting—put the least abstract at the beginning, and end with the most—which therefore will be the most
universal—and this is the highest—i.e.—the *emptiest*! So it is with
the allurements of Wealth, Luxury, Power—.

E contra, Plato begins with ~~surface in conflict,~~ hard Discipline,
a Drill of most difficult acquirement, Watching & Immurement
in the Citadel—proceeds to War and Conflict—but O! in what
transcendently substantive Possessions does he end!

There is no reason to suppose that the disposition to reconcile
the substantial intent and import of Aristotle's Opinion on the
more concerning and fundamental Questions of Philosophy with
the ~~Spirit~~ Doctrines of Plato/commenced with Ammonius, Plotinus ~~and~~ the Founders of the Alexandrine, Eclectic or Neo-pla-
tonic Schools and it cannot therefore be deemed ~~altogether~~ improbable, that ~~the~~ among the successive Editors, Compilers and
~~Rhapsodist~~ Arrangers and Correctors of the Long-hidden and ill-
preserved Aristotelean MSS, some may have been influenced by
this spirit, to add marginal Glosses, which others may have afterwards adopted or from oversight have suffered to slip, into the
text. But it does not seem to me altogether improbable in itself and
irreconcilable with the uniformity and the characteristic *Aristote-
leanism* of the style, that ~~it should~~ these burrs of alterations &
interpolations should have sufficient numerous or import, to ~~either
justify some doubt~~ affect the genuineness of the Metaphysics and
I am the more confirmed in this persuasion, that the ~~only ground~~

one argument assigned for doubting it is built on the presumption
that Aristotle had formed a compleat and consistent Body of Phi-
f96 losophy, a System of harmonious and interdependent ~~Divisions~~
Parts each having its determined station on defined boundaries—a
phænomenon that in the then ~~in~~ infant state of the Sciences and ~~the~~
Knowlege of Nature ~~would without~~ means we may safely pronounce morally impossible, and even as a Miracle, anomalous, and
a Species consisting of one individual; ~~and of which I can discover
no ground or confirmation in the~~ and were it not so yet the presumption of its reality in the present instance I find nothing to
justify in the works themselves—to be knocked away therefore, as
a remnant of the Idolatry of the Middle Ages—& as the Hypothesis of the Spuriousness of the Books entitled Metaphysics rests
altogether on this position, it must fall with it. The Poetics and
the Rhetoric are perhaps exceptions, as far as freedom from ~~the~~
Heterogeneo~~us~~ities and Inconsistencies is concerned; but ~~even~~ of
his other Works even in the Logical, on which after all the Sta-
gyrite's strongest claims on the admiration and gratitude of Mankind ~~must be~~ are grounded, there is a confusion, & that not in
terms only (for the word, *Logic*, is not found in Aristotle) between
Logic and Dialectic, and of both with the Science not yet named,
lying between Grammar & Rhetoric, and for which as being
ρηματων συνταξις I proposed the title of Rhematic, sive Grammaticè Superior—while psychological disquisitions are interwoven
with all. Nay, if I take the Treatises in the order in which they
were probably written, judging by the references found in ~~the~~ one
to others, I should not hestitate in drawing a two-fold conclusion—
1. That Aristotle (and who that considers his multifarious Pursuits
& not long life can wonder at it?) never revised his writings, as a
System: & 2. that if he had ~~(not a few of) his earlier Writings
would have been qualified in~~ many & those leading Positions in
his earlier Treatises would have greatly qualified if not retracted—
and that especially in his Categories (the immortal Trophy of his
Genius) he would have considered the Mind as a Kaleidoscope
rather than as a *Filter*—

f95ᵛ 5134 29.254   28 Feby 1824. In reading S. Wortley's answer
to Mr Abercromby's weak*ish* Speech for the Edinburgh Petition

for Ref. in its Repr.—I was struck with the instance here given of the *consequentness* of the human Mind.—Mʳ Canning & others first teach the House to justify the present state of the Repres. on the Expediency of it—that it works well—Ergo, Reform would be an Evil.—Well this is repeated as in the case of the Miser and the Guineas, which at first were dear because they conferred comforts, independence, and power & ended in being dear for themselves, nay, to the exclusion of all comfort, indep. and power, the Antecedent, Ergo, or οὐ ἕνεκα, is left out of sight, and the *Conclusion* becomes a self-supported Premise, a Major Maximus—an Axiom.

Next comes Mʳ Abercrombie and affords glaring and damning proofs of an infamous Total of Representation, a huge Bundle of Old Sarums, an ~~Squab~~ Apple Pie made all of old Sarum Quinces, and shews there how many and disgraceful ways it *works ill*, most villainously—Aye! quoth Mʳ Stuart Wortley—so it may be in Edingburgh—but it is still worse in Glasgow—& therefore from Edng. you must go next to Glasgow—but it is just as bad at Paisley—& there is no stopping—so that at last it would end in a Reform of the Representation—But we are all convinced, that Reform of Parliament would be a fearful Evil—Ergo, you must not reform the Repr. for Edingburgh/I have described Abercrombie's Speech as weak*ish*: but his reply was worse than weak. Never did advocate give his opponent so thorough a Lift as Mʳ A. in his assertion, that whatever the Majority in the House may wish or vote, the Public Opinion always decided the matter—the Will of the People was always obeyed—/

So the influence of Phrases—Court of Chancery/The Subject *f*95 may go if he likes to a Court of Law: if he goes to Chancery, it is a favor—. He is a Suitor; and the Lord Ch. has a right to say & see that he shall be deserving of it.—This applied to Lawrence & Piracy—. I do not know, which of the two, the *Favor* or the *Pure Hands* (i.e. an arbitrary assumption of the Chancellor to prejudge a Fellow-subject by busying himself with what he had no business) is the more compleat Specimen of Lawyers' Slang—. O these Law-Maximus—how many of them ~~were~~ are mere representations of a certain number of experienced Consequences, and remain after a larger number of weightier Consequences in the opposite scale, and are thus False Totals hastily abstracted from a Part of the Sum, needs investigation most lamentably—& philosophical investig. in the first instance.—Bentham on the Law Taxes & on Paley's Defence of the present System has supplied a very valuable contribution to such a work.—

Exercitationes Logicæ.—I might throw a number of Crackers in upon sundry legal & political Abuses (Law Precedents, for instance) under the name of Doubts & Queries—as Subjects for *Discussion*—

1^v-136^v 5135 26.97   [In *SWF* in connexion with Notes towards a Greek Grammar.]

$f136$ 5136 26.98   Euripidis Orestes.
General Character of Euripides—Of all the Greek Tragedians pre-eminent in pathos, and the representation of the Feelings and Sentiments common to all men, as men—replete with maxims and reflections, moral, prudential and political, therefore more in the mouths of the People than any other writer—in style easy and unaffected—
Faults—too apt to sink below the dignity of Tragedy by bringing in his characters in rags, or abject physical distress—passes too often into individual traits of character, & into sneers & satire better suited to comedy—makes too great a parade of his philosophical Sententiosity—& is singularly loose and inartificial in his plots and the conducting of the story, *cutting* the knot by the interference of a God ex machinâ instead of untying it.—
$f135^v$ λευσίμῳ πετρώματι. 442 and once before. A stoning of Stones— a Hebraism
    των σων δε γονατων πρωτόλεια θιγγάνω,/
    ἱκετης αφυλλου στοματος εξαπτων λιτας–383—
Hebraism. Calves of the Lips—Blossoms of the Mouth—Isaiah.
    κουρα τε θυγατερος πενθιμῳ κεκαρμενος. 458.
—with the shaving of Lamentation/
εξαμιλλωνται σε γης—fully (pity that we must add, *vulgarly*) expressed by our "hustle you out of the country["].
Maxim. Never content yourself with the general meaning of a word, or with the equivalent senses too frequently given in the

Lexicons as *the meanings* of the Greek Word: as if one word could
have more than one proper meaning: tho' one meaning (that is,   *f135*
one and the same visual image) may have ~~been~~ many applications,
and occur under different or even opposite circumstances. Board
her! cries Jack Tar, speaking of an enemy's Ship. Board her, my
Lad! cries Jack Tar to his ⟨bashful⟩ Shipmate, speaking of the
Latter's Sweetheart—

In calling the Words given in the Lexicons *Equivalent* Senses I
pay them a compliment, which they do not deserve. In a good
writer, above all, in the Works of the first-rate Greek Poets, Homer, Pindar, Eschylus, Sophocles, Euripides, Aristophanes, Theo-
critus, the *very* word is chosen, and chosen because it alone expresses the precise sense which the Poet wished to convey.—Now
to discover this, seek the etymon or root of the word—find out the
primary sense, the original visual image, or if I may borrow a   *f134ᵛ*
metaphor from colors, do not rest satisfied in rendering Cæruleus
Blue, but find out what sort of Blue/i.e. find out the *shade* of color
intended by the word. Now in rendering this your own Language
will help you ten times more than the Latin, which is but a poor
and meagre Dialect of the Greek. Instance this in Λαμυρος,
marked in Scapula as facetus, facundus, petularus, impudens, for-
mosus, terribilis. (Mercy on us! what an unconscionable Stuffing
for one poor Word! A perfect Scotch Haggis, or Devonshire
Squab-pie!) and applied to a Jester, an Orator, a Parasite, a Har-
lot, a Lion's Teeth, the Breakers of the Sea in a Storm, and a calm
Lake in moonlight—Of all the Latin words not one even approaches to the true meaning, which in a Greek & English Lexicon would occupy but a Line & a half—Thus: Λαμυρος, properly
flashing: metaphorice, flashy. N.b. the latter always in a bad sense,   *f134*
as the correspondent word in English.—and this might be signified
by the letters, *m.s.* (malo sensu) so that less than a line would have
sufficed: and the word, flashy, would convey more information
than a Note a page long. ~~Unfort~~ Only, imagine this done throughout a whole Lexicon! What an abridgement in the size of the Book,
what an enlargement ~~in~~ of the Information! What a Removal of
choice-perplexing uncertainties!—Unfortunately, we have no such
Lexicon. You must therefore try ~~to~~ in each word to do what the
Lexicographer ought to have done—and above all, never give the

least credit to the Latin Translation of a Greek Writer, least of all, in poetry. It may assist you in difficult passages as to the *position* of the words, or the order in which they are to be construed; but as you wish to be more than a mere School-boy Construer, never never let it tempt you to leave a single word not *looked out*, the precise meaning of which you do not know. Be assured, this Plan *f133ᵛ* will *spare* you trouble in the long run: for he, who has once thoroughly acquainted himself with the *history* of a word, its Birth, Parentage, Kinsfolk, Travels (& from the World of the Senses to the moral & intellectual world, or from the physical & what ~~the~~ Grammarians call the *proper* sense to the metaphorical Meanings) will be almost sure not to forget it.

The preceding Pages with the supplementary notices which will follow, will have you rendered you a master of all the Cement of the Building (~~per~~ significant Letters, and Syllables, positions (= Cases + Tenses) prepositions, Conjunctions,) but the *Stones* themselves you must acquire by your own industry and perseverance.—

But how can this be, as long as you take no pleasure in Reading? And with the *now and then* exception of a Novel, never fly to Books as a resource, or even as a refuge from Vacancy and finger-quirl- *f133* ing? You may say, that you never did like Reading: that naturally you have ⟨no⟩ taste for Books—The greater then (I answer) will be your Merit in acquiring it. And acquired it may be, like all other Habits, good, bad and indifferent. It would be hard indeed, if a Youth not deficient in Understanding or Ability should have it in his power to acquire a *taste* for Tobacco, but not for Shakespear or Milton? And for *what* have you a Taste? Do you not deceive yourself? And would it ⟨not⟩ have been more correct to say, that you never did like Trouble of any Kind? That you had a natural Dislike to exert itself, and ~~bend the~~ make your inclination bend to your Reason!—Alas, ⌜. . .⌝ this is but saying that you belong to the human race! To be forced to do what we ought to like, whether we like it or no, ~~or to suffer~~ is our common lot— the difference between men is, that some *foresee* it, & ~~are~~ do not suffer experience to make them feel it.

f95   5137 29.255   1 What radiates is near: The Planets radiate— ergo, The Planets are near. *Causa Sciendi*.

2. Luminous Bodies that are near radiate. The P. are l.b. that are near. Ergo the Planets radiate. Causa Essendi.

3. What is near, radiates. The Planets radiate. Ergo, the Planets are near.

The third is a false Syllogism. The Minor is not *included* in the Subject of the Major—& the Predicate is applied or participated but cannot *include*—Hence no *Con*clusion—& no necessity—for from near things radiating, it does not follow that nearness is the only cause of *radiancy*:—

5138 29.256   Mem. Sensibility in its nascent state—defini-   *f94ᵛ*
tion of in one or two lines—

5139 29.257   Aristotle says there are four Problems—& so many knowleges—ζητουμεν δε τετταρα, το οτι, το διοτι, ει εστιν, τι εστι.✻ I do not clearly see the difference between the 1ˢᵗ and the 3ʳᵈ. Are there Eclipses of the Sun?—and Does God exist? seem to me to differ only in the Subject—viz. that in the first I ~~have~~ know both the terms, & I ask concerning the fact of their combination.—In the other I ask whether a conception of my mind has an outward correspondent—or whether there is any real meaning in a given word.—~~Is~~ Tenneman in the German as we in English is obliged to render all ifs by ob, whether?—Now is there any difference between asking—whether there is a God? and I ask you, if God exists?—~~Are~~ If there be any difference, in these, there are many more than four questions possible—? Has not T. misunderstood *οτι*? May it signify, What?—& the 4 Subjects of Enquiry be—What a thing is? Why it is, or what is the ground of it? Whether it is? And what its properties are? There is a difference between What is that?—Answer—A Cloud—and—What is a Cloud? But surely all this is trifling—Why not—Where? and When? and in what relations?—/

✻ I would read ζητοῦμεν δε τετταρα· τα ὁ τι; διοτι; ει εστι; τι εστι; at all events, ὁ τι; = *what* any thing is:

5140 29.258   Mss. Notes in Jer. Tayl.—
Liturgy—P. 2. On the 3 sorts of Prayer—P. 4. On the overrating the importance of the dogma of Inspiration—. In p. 7. a

melancholy proof of the ill effects of confounding the *Spirit* with
the *Word*, especially in combination with the Grotian Scheme, that
Saliva mortificans Mercurium ~~Evangelicum~~ Fidei Evangelicæ—

f94   5141 29.259   Of the ~~perm~~ Duration of Infusoria??—Spiders
(transitional)—Final Causes (Spinoza cogent versus Understand—
o versus *ideas*/Type/

5142 29.260   The Distinction between Genius, i.e. The
Light and Darkness of an Idea which because it is Light $\times$ Darkness (N. B. not merely L $\pm$ D) is therefore generative (vera sui
multiplicatio) and that Pseudo-genius, which is not distinguished
from Genius as Talent is, but consists in a restless and fervid
activity of Intellect acting on itself—without any proportional *Capacity* which with the power of appropriating and applying the
knowlege derived ab extra is the definition of Talent—whence ~~Tal-
ent~~ this Pseudo-genius is ~~equally~~ no less *opposed* to Talent ~~as~~ than
Genius is, the one by defect, the other by excellence. The distinction between these, I say, is strikingly exemplified & illustrated in
the characters of J. Hunter & J. Brown/viz. Hunter's an Idea, &
in what sense simple—Brown's a mere reduction of multiplicity to
paucity, by leaving out or crushing together. N. b. this a most
important Remark.

f19   5143 26.17   Thursday Afternoon, 8 April 1824—(the day
after my return to the Grove, Highgate, from Mr Allsop's)
        A very ~~important~~ original & pregnant Idea started and pursued
by Mr Gillman afforded me a highly gratifying proof that I had
not idly attached so great an importance to the fundamental Schema
in the Logic of Trichotomy (Vide the larger vellum parallelogram
Pocket-book)—viz.

Prothesis
Real

Thesis   Antithesis
+ Actual   − Potential
the + Real or Positive Pole, and the − Real or negative Pole
being two forms of the same Reality, the latter no less real than
f19ᵛ   the former—just as negative Electricity is as truly Electricity as
Positive Electricity.

Now Mr Gillman's Idea may be expressed in this Position, &
in his own words—
Organization, every Organ, and ~~the~~ each total Organismus or
organized Body is *Potential* Life: Life *Actual* has no organ. The
act of organizing (as in the Fœtus) is the Transition into the Potential—a vital Fluxion—a *becoming* potential. Hence Thought can
have no Organ—no, nor yet proper Sensation. Spite of the contradiction to this in the phrase, Organs of Sense, ~~we~~ Sense has no
Organ—& in strict propriety we should say, Organs from the
Senses. Those so called are indeed only organs for receiving, &
preparing and conducting the *conditions* of Sense—the Cerebral
Lobes, or proper Brain, is the Organ—not *of* Sense—but as far as
the *organic* form and life are meant, and not the mere Carbon, *f20*
Azote, &c, it is itself *potential* Sense. Now hereby flashing a full
Light on the nature of Consciousness, and in all finite beings (for
herein their finiteness consists) of the Potential to the Actual: &
Consciousness is the immediate reference of an Actual to its Appropriate Potential. Hence God (Actus ~~pur~~ absolute purus, sine
ullâ potentialitate) is the only incorporeal Being. As Consciousness
is the passing of the Actual into the Potential, and therefore at a
given moment the Indifference of both (N. b. The Will alone is
the Identity) so Memory is the passing of the Potential into the
Actual—and all Potential, as necessarily referring to an Actual,
has an analogous nature to Memory. (Hence the feeling of Memory connected with sweet & pathetic Music—)Sensation + Sense,
Sensation *tending* to pass into Sense, the nascent quantities, as ex.
gr. of muscular function—when we seem to fly in our Sleep (&
vice versâ), the Sense rapidly becoming *transitional* into the Potential, which Transition is Sensation—Now this Mr Gillman means *f20^v*
to apply in detail to the explanation of Inflammation, as an undue
Actualization of the Potential, carefully distinguishing the sequents
which are in fact the correctives of Inf. from the Inflammation
itself, for what are the Thickening, Induration, effusion of coagulable lymph &c but so many forms of potentializing the Actual,
~~and~~ in reducing it to potentiality?

5144 26.18   Every generic Definition—or character of a
~~Class~~ Genus (kind) is the specific Definition of the lowest species
of that Genus or Kind. The lowest only can have only that which

is h̶ common. What is above the lowest must have some mark distinguishing it from the lowest, and which therefore does not belong to the lowest. But what does not belong to the lowest, is

f2 1 not common to all—& therefore no part of the definition of the whole Class. Our Conceptions are empty in proportion as they are comprehensives.—T̶h̶r̶e̶e̶ Two or more things having their essential characters in common, a̶n̶d̶ ̶(̶h̶o̶w̶e̶v̶e̶r̶)̶ ̶d̶i̶s̶t̶i̶n̶g̶u̶i̶s̶h̶e̶d̶ ̶f̶r̶o̶m̶ ̶e̶a̶c̶h̶ o̶t̶h̶e̶r̶ ̶b̶y̶ ̶d̶e̶g̶r̶e̶e̶ ̶a̶n̶d̶ ̶c̶i̶r̶c̶u̶m̶s̶t̶a̶n̶c̶e̶, are said to fall under the same general definition. Whatever falls under one and the same general definition, a̶r̶e̶ ̶o̶f̶ ̶t̶h̶e̶ ̶s̶a̶m̶e̶ ̶k̶i̶n̶d̶ however strongly distinguished from each other by *degree* or circumstance, are of the same kind, or homogeneous. E converso, that which i̶s̶ does not c̶o̶m̶p̶r̶e̶ fall under this definition, t̶h̶a̶t̶ ̶w̶h̶i̶c̶h̶ but requires an essentially different definition, is diverse from each and all of the things comprized

f2 1ᵛ in the former.—T̶h̶i̶n̶g̶s̶ ̶c̶a̶p̶a̶b̶l̶e̶ ̶o̶f̶ ̶b̶e̶i̶n̶g̶ ̶d̶i̶s̶t̶i̶n̶g̶u̶i̶s̶h̶e̶d̶ ̶w̶h̶a̶t̶ Difference in *degree* supposes sameness in kind; and vice versâ, Diversity in kind precludes distinction from difference in degree— much more, when that which thus diverse in kind is incapable of degree, such as the ideas of *Certainty*, of a mathematical Circle, of Deity, & the like, compared with the conceptions of *Strength*, Power, Wealth, Tallness.—Apply this to the terms Reason & Understanding.—The first is used in two senses, intellectual (or Scientific) and practical—in the first, in which sense it might be more conveniently named Light of Reason than Reason itself, the term expresses the power of concluding necessary and universal ⟨*formal*⟩ truths from contingent & particular Appearances—Reason here is the conclusive power of the human Intellect. In the second, it stands for the Source of Ideas, or such ⟨*objective*⟩ Truths having their evidence in themselves & undeduced become in their conversion to the Will ultimate *Ends*—such as God, Holiness, Beatitude, &c. ⟨In like manner Understanding must be distinguished into intellectual & practical. In the first, it is the faculty of r̶e̶d̶u̶c̶-

f23 i̶n̶g̶ferring particulars to classes. i.e. of generalizing & thus giving *names* to things. It is "the Faculty judging according to Sense". In the second, it is the power of selecting and adapting means to proximate ends, according to circumstances.—Now these Definitions are all diverse—therefore, R. & U. are diverse.⟩

T̶h̶e̶ ̶q̶u̶e̶s̶t̶i̶o̶n̶ ̶w̶h̶e̶t̶h̶e̶r̶ Of the Principle of Heat, i.e. the exciting Cause of the Sensation, heat, which we have every reason to identify with the immediate cause of the enlargement of Bodies and other physical phænomena,. ~~and which, in distinction from the sensation Heat~~ This principle, ~~Lavoisier~~ named Caloric, ~~or vis calorifica~~—in which he has been followed by Chemists and Naturalists almost universally. And yet the rightfulness and even the expedience of so naming it may be doubted. ~~If as far as~~ The propriety of distinguishing the Excit~~ing~~ant ~~Cause~~ from the sensation excited is ~~concerned, it~~ indeed beyond doubt, still more, that of distinguishing a Cause from a ~~synonime~~ subject that is only *one* of its effects. And if the new term did this & nothing more, all would be well. ~~But a~~ no Philosopher could object to the phrase, Vis sive actio calorifica. But Caloric implies according to the use & analogy of Language that the subject is a *thing*: for we give *substantive Proper* Names only to supposed Substances, or Self-subsistents, expressing powers, properties, qualities &c by Abstracts conformed with a distinctive adjective or Epithet, or by ~~Substantatives~~ Nouns *General* formed from Verbs or Adjectives—As Gravitation, Cohesion &c—. The term, Caloric, therefore, prejudges a question ad huc sub lite: and those, who have habitually used the term, are insensibly & unconsciously predisposed in favor of one side, alterâ parte adhuc inauditâ. ~~It is literally prejudicial~~—The term, however, has been received & naturalized—and instead of a fruitless attempt to eject it, we will endeavour to avail ourselves of its convenience without its prejudicial influence by referring the question ~~to the definit~~ from the word to the definition of the word, thus:

By Caloric are we understand a Quality, Property, Function or particular modification of some higher Power (Repulsion, for instance)—or a distinct kind of Matter, a peculiar Fluid for instance—or for our present purpose it may be sufficient to say—Is Caloric a thing, in the sense in which Water is a thing, or a mode in which ~~other~~ a thing~~s~~ exists, as a Wave? Or we may state the question thus—Is Caloric the Cause of Repulsion, or a Phænomenon indicating its degrees? Or—is Caloric an immediate Consequent of internal dilative Motion, or the Antecedent Motor?—The answer will, I imagine, greatly depend on the answers given to the same question put concerning Light? Nay, concerning Weight, i.e. positive Darkness.—I am most thoroughly aware that

f23ᵛ

f24

the Bible was given for other & higher purposes than to make us Naturalists: that God never intended to supersede Industry by Inspiration, or the efforts of the rational Understanding by the Revealed Word. Yet I am not ashamed to confess that I am strongly disposed to regard the first Chapter of Genesis, as in some sort an exception: as providing certain Truths a priori, as the supposita et postulata, vel potius jussa et præfinita of Physiogony, which could have ⟨been⟩ ascertained ~~from any~~ by no lower authority. Such are: first, that the Universe of Finite Existences began, & is not a co-eternal Effect of an Eternal Ground & Cause, a creation, not an

f24ᵛ emanation—Consequently, that Will is no less a real & essential Principle of Things than Reason, yea, that the Will is deeper than Reason, and is to Reason as the spring & basin water of an artificial Fountain to the Salient Column = the former representing Will = Will, or Will in its own essence; the latter, or Column, representing Will = Reason, or Will in the form of Reason.—. The second is that the World proceeded from the less to the more perfect, from indistinction to Order thro' ~~an~~ numbered ascending series of distinct ~~and~~ evolutions—i.e. the developement of the *Cosmos* (ornate construction) from Chaos.—Beneficial Results of this exemp. in Kant's Himmel-system, as developed by Le Sage & La Place—/—. Hence I feel more confidence in attaching a proper *scientific* worth & value to the Mosaic Antithesis of + Light and + Darkness—and greatly preferring the term positive Darkness, or the principle of Opacity, to that of Gravity or Gravitation/

Now on the same ground, whether ~~of~~ by right of Reason or by

f25 necessity of Sense & sensuous Imagination, on which we assume a matter, or universal common immediate product or self-realization of + Darkness, a ponderable Mass, I do not see how we can refuse to assume a ~~material~~ specifica minime ponderabilis, as the immediate inseparable Product or self-realization of + Light (Φως δυναμικον) and since Heat (Calor dynamicus) is not the Synthesis of + Light and + Darkness ~~both~~ut the Indifference (Color is the Synthesis in the *real* pole †as Sound ~~in~~ is in the *Ideal*), and there-

† i.e. Color is the synthesis of phænomenal Light, and Darkness, the Synthesis of the immediate Products; Sound the Synth. of dynamic Light & Darkness.

fore an indecomponible Unity (ἕνας), an Henad, there seems no reason for denying it *its* Calorique.—or Fluidum primum et essentiale. The Blunder consists in representing it as atomic—the ⟨absolute contrary of which is⟩ very postulate, ~~of~~ which the ½ truth of atomic Matter necessitates in order to its completion!—The precious Logic is this: ~~A is~~ X Y Z ~~are~~ form the Problem to be solved. Atoms will solve X Y, if a direct opposite to Atomic be granted as a Co-factor, namely, an absolutely Continuous Ergo—an absolute Continuous is necessary.—~~Aye~~ Well but (quoth Pleuronectes with *f25ᵛ* both eyes on ~~one~~ the same side of his Nose, & both squinting full on his favorite Atom) What is the Continuum made of? Why, of Atoms to be sure! Only let them be quite round, ~~wide~~ slippery smooth, & devilish little—the *leetlerst tiny* things/it is quite wonderful how *leetle* they are!—But Seriously, I do not recollect among a score instances of the utter stolid unthinkingness of the modern corpuscular Psilosophers any so palpable as this. By the mere mechanism of the human Understanding they are driven by the manifest ~~fragmenty~~ dimidiety of one Pole to the assumption of the opposite—& then, *forgetting* this, *convert* the 2ⁿᵈ into the first & by so doing *annihilate* it. ½ is $= 1 - \frac{1}{2}$. Therefore, $\mathsf{x}\lceil \ldots \rceil$ $x - y = \frac{1}{2}$ is *not* $= 1$. What a pity! that sweet dainty $x\langle -y\rangle$ on which my very heart is set—is there no help?—Why, yes! add $\langle y\rangle - x$, which counts likewise as ½, and as every whole ⟨in⟩ Nature is the Balance of two opposite yet equivalent Factors, you will have

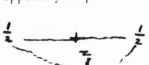

So said, so done; but then this ~~minus~~ y minus x, or *Anti-x*— *f26* What *is* it?—The opposite of x, to be sure—. O no! I can bear no opposite to my dainty favorite x—anti-x is nothing but xxxxx = X—& you may take away your Y −, as soon as you like!—and instead of ½ + ½ = 1, I will have ½ + ½ − ½ = 1—i.e. I will eat my Cake & have it—which when I was in pettycoats, instead of being a Corpuscularian full grown Philosopher, I was hummed into believing to be impracticable. But to what purpose is Modern Philosophy, if it does not emancipate us from the Su-

perstitions of Priests and the Axioms of the Nursery? Ex. gr. ½
Subtract ½ from ½ + ½ = 1, and there remains 1. the Deuce
there does.—O Sir! You are one of the Mystics—& there is no
use of disputing with *you*!—

f26

5145 26.19   The circulatory System elliptic with its Solar
Focus, = the Heart, and an imaginary Focus in the indefinite =
the Air of Respiration/The nervous System an Hyperbola?—or an
endless multitude of Lines from a Reservoir, fed by a double current so that the same line adduces & re-
duces?—*Nonsense*!—

f66ᵛ 5146 28.68   24. April 1824. ⟨n.b. composed extempore,
without taking my pen off the paper. Qʸ Will they stand a second
Reading?⟩

    Idly we supplicate the Powers above!
    There is no Resurrection for a Love
    That unperturb'd, unshadowed, wanes away
    In the chill'd heart by inward self-decay.
    Poor Mimic of the Past! the Love is o'er,
    That must *resolve* to do what did itself of yore.   ⟨mistaken⟩

f67   Item
    Desire, of pure Love born, itself's the same:
    ~~The~~ A Pulse, that animates the out~~ward~~er frame,
2. ~~The~~ And takes ~~an impulse from~~ the impress of the nobler part
1. ~~And~~ It but repeats the life-throb of the Heart—

5147 28.69   Monday night, 12 o'clock—26 April, 1824.
Just heard the Nightingales, from *my* Room window—and tho'
no~~t~~w sitting at the Table, with the Casement shut, still heard them
loud and distinct. N.b. a chill breezy dark night.

f67ᵛ 5148 28.70   I have so great a reverence for the gift of Language and attach so high a value to its cultivation, that I dare not
deny that to go thro' a well arranged Museum of zoology or a
series of accurate engravings translating each successive appearance, ~~of~~ of each animal and of the several parts of each animal,
may not be a laudable and profitable exercise—and something of
this sort, in respect of Minerals and the natural Orders of Plants

Rear view of 3 The Grove, Highgate, the home of James and Ann Gillman, showing the roof raised for Coleridge's "Bed and Book-room"

See 5147 and n.

has been recommended by my ingenious friend, Mr S. T. Cole-   *f68*
ridge, of Highgate as a part of ~~an~~ a liberal education, in the higher
forms, as an excellent Schooling, introductory to Logic, and forming a transition from Rhematic to Rhetoric—at once supplying a
copia verborum, a stock of distinct images, and a facility with the
conversion of Objects into correspondent words—in short, an apprenticeship to the two great Arts of Seeing and Expressing.—But
tho' I approve highly of this ~~Scheme~~ proposal, I do not think a
Lecture the best way of carrying ~~on~~ into practice a scheme, the
advantages of which depend mainly on the Pupils' ⟨learning to⟩
constru~~inge~~ each Lesson by himself with less and less dictation
from his Tutor, as he describes Diagram by Diagram on his own
Slate, and learns to enumerate without book the several steps of   *f68ᵛ*
the construction—And after all, when this is all, the Appearances,
whether total or component, will have no great Hold on the mind.
They will want the hook and barb of causative connection, and
intelligible dependency—and weak are the impressions of *Relation*
left by the mere impressions of the Images themselves when the
latter are held together only by the accident of their co-existence
~~in the same sphere of vision or~~ within ~~the~~ one same outlines.

5149   26.84   Henry Taylor Esqre   *f159*
                4, Kings' Street
                      St James's

5150   29.261   20 May, 1824   *f94*
    Before we inquire what there is of Nature in plastic Life it
would be well to learn what there is of Life in plastic Nature. In
the first, we ask for the object in immediate *connection with* the
Subject; but not as *contained* † *in* the Subject. In the second, we
ask for a Subject not the same as *this* Subject, but appertaining to,   *f93ᵛ*
or the polar Thesis of, the Object transiently ~~in~~ connect~~ed~~ion with
this Subject. O + SY.)(O = SZ, or still more plainly OZ +

† i.e. identical or sub eâdem Prothesi, with it; but polarized or in   *f94*
Antithesi. The Object so taken is the Self in Self-consciousness.
But taken as connected not involved, it is what I mean when I say
my Body.

SY ~~and~~ or Nature as my body $\mathbb{)(}$ OZ = SZ, or my Body, as
Nature, the Desideratum SZ being the Natura Naturans, or Ζωοεί-
δες τὶ. Now in this investigation we must begin with separating
as much as possible the positive phænomena from the noumena,
ex. gr. the uses and purposes; and then from the *degrees* of the
universal phænomena, Time and Space, ex. gr. rapidity, order of
succession, relative direction & co-existence. In this way we shall
best determine the actual sum of our materials, the alphabet that
we have to articulate.—Then comes the great problem of the *Multiplication* of Powers in Nature—, the generative Multiplication,
I mean; of their progressive potenziation, A $^{(4}$ being as truly a
Unit as A$^{(1}$, and the latter together with A$^{(2}$, and A$^{(3}$ remaining
and co-existing with A$^{(4}$, as a Father may survive the birth of his
Grandchildren. Now the possible advantage of this is evident—
For supposing such an ascent, in each each successive power repeats
the former with an addition, or in a higher dignity, to be a Law
of Nature, we ~~we~~ shall be justified in supposing such an aliud et
majus, vi ipsius Naturæ and independent of the peculiar Subjectivity of Life, at the moment or grade of the Ascent, in which it
is capable of being rendered an immediate instrument of Life, and
at which the Subjectivity of Life is superinduced—just as in a yet
far higher point the evolution of the triple Power of Organic Life
is sufficiently completed, and the Forces sufficiently centralized,
co- and sub-ordinated, to become the Base of a *descending* Humanity (Gen. I.26.) Assume, for mere illustration's sake, that Contractility (I do not mean in Bostock's most injudicious application
of the term to Haller's *Irritability*: but the property so called by
Haller & others in the Cellular Texture & Membranes)—assume,
I say, that Contractility as the Aliud et Majus of Elasticity were
such a power. We might perhaps compromise the dispute respecting the existence of distinct vital powers, haud ejusdem generis
with those of Nature, or the so-called mechanical and chemical./

f76ᵛ   5151 29.112   Before the art of Healing can be made a matter of Common Sense, the Common Sense must have been itself
enlightened by the conclusions of Science & the ~~Fruits obtained
from experiment & observation~~ Results of ⟨Experience &⟩ experimental Philosophy.

5152 29.113 Damp on walls papered cured by lining the damp part with sheet lead not thicker than that used in Tea Chests, & fastened with small copper nails—weighing from 4 to 8 ounces only the square foot—Hutchinson & Co, Pately Bridge, Yorkshire.—

5153 29.114 4 June 1824—That it is the *evil*, the selfish, the vindictive, the inveterate party-spirit that makes us *weak*—It is true, that all these when common to any collective number, to any party, when the selfishness is unnaturally socialized by either abstraction (as when a whole Club of Jews shall enjoy the toast, Every man for himself—& leave his Neighbour to God—because ~~he does not expect~~ the image of his advantage over some ⟨absent⟩ Neighbour is more vivid than that of his fear of the *Toast-giver's* cutting his throat)—it is true that those evils systematicaly operative against *half in half* goodiness (see Friend) is Napoleonic but by the power of what is good—viz. system—. These thoughts were forced on my mind by Blackwood's Magazine for the last year or 10 months—with the same quantum of Talent, had all been as good & what is real, powerful, aye & felt as powerful by the public, is, it would have removed mountains—

4 June 1824. I see more & more the advantage of the attempt   *f*77
to exhaust the conceivable forms in every problem.

                                        lb. oz.
5154 3½.118   A kilogramme (= 2. 2) of Chloride of   *f137ᵛ*
Calcium (*olim*, Muriate of Lime) is to be dissolved in 60 Litres (126.8 pints) of water. The ground intended for experiment is ⟨to be⟩ watered with the solution—the Seeds are then to be sown or the plants to be set in the ground and ultimately (i.e. from this time to their maturity) the Watering with this solution is to be repeated a third or fourth time at considerable intervals. The stimulant "electro-organic" power of this Solution is stated to be wonderful—on flower- & fruit-trees, on Flowers, onions, potatoes &c causing them to more than double their height, size, & weight,   *f138*
without injury to their flavor or nutritive qualities.

The great Sun-flower, which on ground watered in the ordinary way, did not rise more than from 6 to 8 feet has by means of this Solution been raised to 12 or even 15 feet—producing seeds, with oil half the weight, &c—It is to be regretted, that in Brande's Journal no mention is made of the *extent* of ground, to which the 16 Gallons of the Solution are sufficient.

5155 3½.119   Instantaneous Lucifer. The extremity of a fine platina wire rolled into a spiral form is dipped into ammonio-muriate or muriate of platina, until about 2 grains are taken up—after which it is to be heated red hot in a spirit Lamp. In this way

f138ᵛ a minute quantity of spongy platina is formed which fixed on ~~the~~ a jet-pipe so as that a current of Hydrogen passes over it, instantly inflames it—or a mixture of Oxygen & Hydrogen.—

Dobereiner's

N.b. Berzelius has proved that pure Hydrogen gas is inodorous— owes its usual odor to impurities, especially to an odorous volatile oil which may be separated by making the gas pass thro' Alcohol.

My suspicions respecting Cyanogen, and the Cyanic Acid, re-ceive *furtherance* from the discovery that the fulminating Metals owe this property to the presence of an Acid & that this Acid is the Cyanic/. The extremes or embodied Poles of the Metallic Se-ries seem in this singular substance to have been coerced into re-

f139 luctant combination by induced electric attractions—and it would be well to try every possible proportion of Ammonium, or Nitro-gen, with Carbon in the purest form, under various states & cir-cumstances/and under various influences of magnetic, electric and Galvanic or electro-chemical influences—If ever the composition of the Metals should be decyphered, it will probably be effected by something like this—Not that I adopt—e contra, I unhesitat-ingly reject—Steffens's hypothesis that Carbon & Nitrogen are the constituent elements of the Metals. ⟨First, *bodies* are *components* not *constituents*. Secondly⟩ Carbon & Nitrogen are doubtless Metals themselves—& we must first learn what are the elements of Car-bon, & what of Nitrogen or Ammonium, before we can offer even a Guess. Carbon in its purest form is assuredly N. by E/and Ni-trogen S. by W./. Now the dynamic or ideal *Constituents* of the

Metals must be expressed by ⊙ = Centrality + N.S. or polar
Length/In Cyanogen the ⊙ is wanting. Thus in the different Met-   *f139ᵛ*
als the differentials are not only the different proportions of the
N. or Negative Magn. to the S. or Positive Magnetism—but and
especially the intensity of the ⊙—& with this the assumption of E
and W.—Aqua Centralis/—/i̶s̶ out of which arises the varying
phænomenal proportion of *E* to *W*. as expressed by Neg. & Pos.
Electricity—.—Steffens paid too great and almost exclusive attention to the two points of fixity & volatility—

5156 3½.120   Many a Star which we behold as single, the
Astronomer resolves into two, each perhaps the center of a separate
System—Oft &̶ are the Flowers of the Bind-weed mistaken for the
growth of the Plant, which it chokes with its intertwine. And many
are the unsuspected Double-Stars, and frequent are the parasite   *f140*
weeds which the Philosopher detects in the received opinions of
men: s̶o̶ ̶p̶r̶o̶n̶e̶ ̶a̶r̶e̶ ̶w̶e̶ ̶f̶r̶o̶m̶ ̶j̶u̶x̶t̶a̶-̶p̶o̶s̶i̶t̶i̶o̶n̶ ̶t̶o̶ ̶i̶n̶f̶e̶r̶ ̶a̶ ̶n̶a̶t̶u̶r̶a̶l̶ ̶c̶o̶n̶-̶
n̶e̶c̶t̶i̶o̶n̶,̶ ̶a̶n̶d̶ so strong is the tendency of the imagination to identify
what it had long consociated. Things that have habitually tho' perhaps accidentally and arbitrarily ⟨been⟩ thought of in connection
with each other, we are prone to regard as inseparable. The fatal
Brand is cast into the fire, and therefore Meleager must consume
in the flames. To these conjunctions of Custom and Association
(the associative power of the mind which holds the mid place between Memory & Fancy) we may best apply Sir T. Brown's remark—that many things coagulate on commixture, whose separated natures promise no concretion.

5157 3½.122   Could a man conceive himself and another   *f143ᵛ*
fellow-being existing, with our now faculties and impulses, and all
around a chaos of indistinction, or (to render the supposition im-
ageable) a limitless objectless Surface—I and my Fellow-man live,
we know not how—or the viewless Air nourishes us—. We know
each other's presence tho' we do not yet see each other—e contra,
our communion consists in the reciprocal knowlege o̶f̶ in the generation of an I by a Thou. And then let a single Tree rise up in
the vast plain—we perceive new Presences, common to I and
Thou, *third* Persons—. Who shall blame if we adore the Tree,

whose attraction has made a center—. The growth & revelation
(as of a *Cloud* into a Form) of human Countenances by the emotions & thoughts excited by the succession of Images, Genesis C.I./
A pregnant Subject.—which (N.b.) I dare say, I understood when
I wrote it, how many years ago, I do not know. But what it means
now? *Latet*

f144   5158   3½.123   Demonstrationers and Defencers of Christi-
anity versus Infidels and Assailants, Messrs
—BRAG, BRAY, and BRIMSTONE Council for the Defencers, &
Messrs, SCOFF, STENCH and SKIN-DEEP for the Prosecutors—be-
fore the Worshipful of the Quorum, Justices
SIMPLE, SLENDER, SHALLOW, BARDOLPH, PISTOL, and Dame
Quickley. Foreman of the Jury—M^r WE-ARE-ALREADY-AGREED.

5159   3½.124   It is not that Hume, Gibbon, and the French
Encyclopædists have perverted the words into a Sneer ~~and~~ or a
prudential Mask—the Mask and Dark-Lanthorn of a Stabber—
that I will either conceal the truth or be scared from using the
words, which a succession of Divines and Philosophers from Tertullian & Origen to Bacon and Leibnitz have rested on—namely,
that the full, *positive* and satisfying Evidence of Christianity is by
Grace and the influence of the Holy Ghost—and that a Theologian
f144^v   has done all that he can or should wish to do when he has repelled
~~all~~ the pretended proofs of the falsehood of the history and doctrines of Christianity. That it is *false*, neither my Reason, nor my
Conscience, nor my understanding nor ~~the~~ recorded ~~of~~ History
compels or permits me to presume—that it is true, I believe thro'
faith, and in the light of an incommunicable Experience./
     There is much that my whole heart echoes in Lessing's Bruch-
stücke Vol. 5 & 6. P. *20*.

5160   3½.125   The Idea of God—so apt and proper to excite
the noblest most elevating emotions—an honest pride and sense of
the necessarily high rank of the Beings that could ~~com~~apprehend
God—this made use of by the Prelatical Priests & Crown Divines
under the Stuarts to justify in themselves the most abject servility
to a wretched Man with a bit of metal imagined on his head—

One of the prison drawings by Piranesi

See 5163 and n.

5161 3½.126   The Reading of Arnold's Great work did not   *f145*
shake but rather confirm the opinion, I had deduced from the
Scripture, and have since then found in Bucer's Exposition,
printed in the Appendix to Strype's Life of Cranmer. But if I had
known no other scheme of the Eucharist but that of Transubstan-
tiation, and the scheme of Bishop Hoadly and the modern Sacramentaries, I could not have hesitated in preferring the former,
spite of its ~~apparen~~ logical unstateability. I take the earliest Fathers,
and find no graduation in the terms by which the Eucharist is
described. From the very first it is το φρικτον μυστηριον—the
tremendous Mystery. Grant that the expressions were metaphorical;
yet the number of metaphors, all possessing a common character
of struggle and striving, and the constant use of figurative language, prove irrefragably a something meant that overfilled and   *f145ᵛ*
stretched the Writer's Mind, and by its transcendence suspended
the functions of the logical Faculty.—

5162 3½.127   First Creation = Incorporation of the Logos—1. The polarization of the *potentialized* Actual into Light and
⟨positive⟩ Darkness. i.e. the containing, constringent, and retractive Power—or Light and Mass. 2. The Polarization of Light into
Life and Warmth (Vegetable Life)—Life and Light, with Warmth
as the Indifference (Animal)—of the divine Noumenon or Lux
Intelligibilis into Understanding and Law (νόμοι φυσικοὶ) with
Reason as the Indifference (Man).
    New Creation = Incarnation of the Logos—polarization into
divine Life and Light with Faith as the Indifference (John 1.).
The Will of God—subjectively, as Holy Will; objectively, as redemptive Wisdom/copula, Love.

5163 3½.128   I wonder that no Historical Painter has been   *f146*
struck with with the passage, Nehemiah, II. 12–15.—What a glorious subject for a Remblant! Nehemiah, leading the Beast (Ass or
Mule) over or in among the Ruins, with torch or lamp—the
Dragon Well, the ruins of the Walls. &c—/—In fact, there might
well be 3 or 4 Pictures, in the manner of Raphael's Bible Gal-
lery—O if the Spirits of Rembrandt and Piranesi like two Planets

would shoot coverging Rays

f124ᵛ   **5164** 16.395   Wedn. Night. 29 Septʳ 1824. Θε/ξπλᾶνᾶ/τιον
ην αυτεμ ο φοβος του την λυπην διδοναι εποιεν μειον η ημισυ.
Ονειδος περι τῆς επιθυμιας—. Τα πρωτα τῆς <u>τοτε</u> ἐρωσης μᾶλλον
ἠέρωμένης φιλήματα, ἐγέιρειν ἐπιθυμήτικον πάθος, η μη εγειρειν,
εδει;—<u>ει</u> δη εγω επι πινος ετερης, ως αυτη επι Πανσόφου; ἡ εθυασα
ουδεν; Ερως ανευ θυσιας δυναται ειναι; Videri, non esse, hoc est
esse γυναικεῖον.—
Thursday. 30 Septʳ, 1824.
ΓΝΑ συν β̄ρ̄Δ̄ και Δυεννα εις ΑΠΙΕΤΙΣ Θυραν.—

5165 16.396   Now the Breeze thro' the ⟨stiff &⟩ brittle-be-
coming Foliage of the Trees counterfeits the sound of a rushing
stream, or Water-flood ⟨suddenly sweeping by⟩. The sigh, the
modulated continuosness of the murmur is exchanged for the confusion of *overtaking* sounds, the self-evolutions of the *One* for the
clash or stroke of even commencing Contact of the *Multitudinous*—
without interspace by confusion/—the short Gusts rustle, and the
ear feels the unlithsome dryness before the eye detects the coarser
f125   duller ~~green~~ tho' deeper Green/deadni̶n̶g̶ed, and not awakened into
the hues of decay, Spring's echoes from the sepulchral Vault of
Winter—Nature's Palinode—the memory of the aged year, conversant with the forms of its Youth, and forgetting all the interval—feebly reproducing

f77   **5166** 29.115   "It pleases me to think that she deserves to be
remembered by all that knew her. But after 40 years' acquaintance
with so amiable a creature, one must needs, in reflecting, bring to
remembrance so many engaging endearments as are yet at present
enbittering and painful. INDEED WE MAY BE SURE THAT WHEN
ANYTHING BELOW GOD IS THE OBJECT OF OUR LOVE, AT ONE
TIME OR OTHER IT WILL BE A MATTER OF OUR SORROW—"

Lady Russel's Letters: Letter 117 (supposed)
to the Bishop of Salisbury.

N.B. Read this fine sentiment at Ramsgate, 20 Octr 1824, the
evening when I saw dear Mrs Tulk's death announced in the Morning Herald—after a more than usually cheerful Birthday—& on
Thursday 21st Nix ista teterrima spes nostras et fidem sepelivit!—

5167 29.116 ⟨⚹ = opposed to⟩   f77^v

The Sum of the Philosophy which I receive as the only true
Philosophy may be thus exprest. 1. Cons*cience* is not a Result or
Modification of Self-Consciousness; but its Ground and Antecedent
Condition. (*Conditio sine quâ non.*) 2. The Act of Self-consciousness
contains in itself (ponit et imponit) the highest and ~~universal~~ most
general *formula* of all real Science. A = A is the Key of Universal
Nature. But A = A ceases to be an identical proposition (*pigra
ejusdem repetitio*) and becomes an object of distinct Conception (*po-
sitio verè synthetica*) on this assumption only: S = A. And O =
A. Therefore S = O and O = S. That is: the Act of Self-consciousness implies a Subject that is its own Object, or 1 = 2, the
2 ~~being~~ remaining = 1. COROLLARY. The Magnet is the
Phænomen of Consciousness—or Magnetism is the *Symbol* of Self-
consciousness—therefore, according to the philosophic sense of
Symbol, Self-consciousness is Magnetism in its highest dignity, its
Δυναμο-δυναμις.—

As the Actio Magneticia expresses the Thetic in Science, ~~si~~ i.e.
simply Affirmative or Negative, answering to the Principium
Identitatis et Contradictionis in Logic; so does Electricity (+ ⚹
−) express the Antithetic with all tentative and analytic Science,
and Galvanism the Synthetic, and Constructive Magnetism in Nature is the Shadow of approaching Life. Hence, the Life of the
Blood dies off (*elanguescit*) into Iron = negative Magnetism.—

5168 29.117   Sensibility—an inconvenient term, as the sci-   f78
entific name of the third Form of the vital principle, or the Power
supposed to be especially manifested in the Nervous System. It is
objectionable on the score of its inexpediency. For the word being
of such very frequent occurrence in common life, and *always*
meaning a high & marked *degree* of the Power, and most often

including the reflex consciousness and moral associations, with which it is accompanied in ourselves, it requires an effort to keep this popular use of Sensibility from blending with the strict physiological import of the term, so as to think of the *physical* power only; and of this too, in *kind* exclusive of *more or less.*—To abstract from all Degree—i.e. to fix the thought on the *kind* without reference to the quantity, intensive or by extension, is indeed one of the first, and not the least, difficulty which the Student has to overcome, in all philosophic inquiries, whatever the subject may be, and in all departments of ~~Sen~~ Science. It is easier to expose ~~a~~ the defect of our present Nomenclature than to discover a Substitute, not liable to equal or perhaps heavier objections. I should myself be inclined to propose, in the present instance, the term Centrality, or the Central Force.

Nearly as great objections I find to the term, Irritability, as expressing the musculo-arterial life. Q: *Instinctivity*! It would be a *f78ᵛ* serious convenience, could we get over the ludicrous effect that would for a time be produced by the introduction of the verbal Noun without the preposition compounded with it, so as to distinguish two modes or relations of this second power, *stinctive*, and *in*-stinctive—the utility, at least conveniency of which, first struck me in the examination of Flourien's Experiments.—

Productivity; the last & least objectionable of the three—yet even this does not entirely satisfy. At least, I should prefer the more modest, and less hypothetical, term, Vegetal or vegetive *Life.*

Life ⁽¹. = Productivity, Reproductivity. = το φυτοειδες
Life ⁽². = Irritability = Instinctivity = το εντομοειδες
Life ⁽³ = Sensibility = Centrality = το ιδιοζωικον

5169 29.118   Nov. 22 1824. Ramsgate.—I am more and more sensible of the difficulty of ~~under greater~~ solving the problem of the 4 Gospels. I find it hard to determine on which of the different hypotheses the greater number & weight of perplexities press.—That each Gospel was intended as a complete History of Jesus in his Messianic character & during the period of the Messiahship from his Baptism to his Ascension, independent of ~~any other~~ the other three, and with or without any knowlege of their existences—. Even tho' this should be granted of the three first,

John's must, I think, be made an exception. Or were the so-called Mat. Mark, and Luke Expansions of a Proto-evangelium? Or Excerpts from a more voluminous Biography, each Evangelist excerp[t]ing according to his particular views or the needs of his Mission or Church? Or were they compiled from smaller separate *f*79 Monograms, ex. gr. the Infancy of Jesus. 2. The miracles of Christ. 3. The Parables of Christ. 4. The Sermons & Sentences (γνωμαι) of Christ. 5. The Sufferings and Resurrection of Christ— . To instance one of many perplexities. If each Gospel was considered by the Evangelist as a sufficient History, d̶i̶d̶ were the *doctrines* of Christianity comprehended in his purpose? Could the necessary doctrines at least be learnt from either Gospel—so that what is omitted in any one i̶s̶ may be true, but is not to be regarded as of universal necessity?—If so, what would become of the Roman Catholic Doctrine of Papal Supremacy, which is mentioned only by Matthew, and either unknown to Luke or purposely omitted by him—. Could *either* have taken place, if the doctrine had been true—for if *true*, its importance is immense, and how strange that Paul in his Letters to Timothy and Titus, the main purpose of which is to declare and establish the right constitution of a Christian Church should not have left a single hint of the duties of obedience due from all Bishops to the Bishop of Rome—not a hint concerning the CENTER of Unity, the Unity of the Churches as of so many Units?—But if the one Gospel was to be supplemented out of the others, how are we to account for the *Repetitions*—nay, the evident variations & in a few instances apparent contradictions?—

Or take another unique passage, the 17 & 18 verses of Mark XVI—. The *traditions* of the third century form indeed a full comment, & an ample fulfilment of this prophecy—But does the credible *History* do so? Does even the canonical historical work (the Acts of the Apostles) bear it out? Is there the least proof of a miraculous power of speaking unknown languages? Is there not proof positive of the contrary in S*t* Paul? Has not the 17 v. a strong appearance of having been written by some one who had misunderstood Luke's account, Acts C. II*nd*?—Take the instances in which the conversation of our Lord is recorded by all 4, or by all *f*79*v* the three properly historical Gospels—would not a perfectly un-

prejudiced Critic infer from the very great differences in the
words, that they were all *hearsay* reports? What is the prominent
figure, the very *pith* and *purpose* of the discourse in one, is taken
no notice of by another—. Was this possible if each had either
been present or had had it *dictated* to him by an ear-witness?— On
the other hand the authenticity of the Gospels (namely, that they
are of the apostolic age, & possessed a peculiar sacredness at a very
early period) throws still greater difficulties and improbabilities in
the way of every supposition that would explain, or account for,
the preceding—ex. gr. that the Gospels were Traditions committed
to writing, and not written Testimonies.—

5170 29.119   What is A Mystery! that which we apprehend,
but can neither comprehend or communicate—a truth of Reason
which the Understanding can represent only by Negatives, or contradictory Positives.

5171 29.120   Heart— an Analogon, nay a rudiment of—in
the Rain-worm & Leech; while in the far higher rank of Insects,
there is only a very remote analogon, viz. an oblong Bag every
where close (in seinem ganzen Umfange verschlossener Schlund)
between the Skin of the Back and the Intestinal Canal, from head
to tail—. Q.y Is it not more truly an Analogon or rudiment of the
Spleen—or amphoteric? May we conjecture, that greater muscular
power is intended and required in Insects, generally, or at least in
relation to their total frame and its materials? The whole Earth-
worm, & (in a *very* striking manner) the Hirugo Officinalis is a
Muscle per se. Hence Nature may have wanted the total quantity
of Irritability (rectius, *instinctivity*) for this muscle, and so according to her usual plan give way for a step & leave the vascular
systems as a dropt stitch to be taken up again in the next Round
of the Organic Ladder—accordingly this is done in the Arachni-
dea—where from the same Bag vessels are sent off on each side.—

f80 5172 29.121   Had there been a Proto-evangelium in Paul's
time, is it possible that he should never have referred to it? Is not
this a convincing argument against the common interpretation of

the passage respecting Luke? And yet what should be the probable Interval between the date of Justin's Genuine Works and Irenæus who so familiarly discusses the reason of there being 4, and so many & no more Gospels?—It is a most perplexing Subject—and Eichhorn very unsatisfactory. The writer of the article "Abendmahl" in the Proto-Heft of the Ger. Encyc has ~~given~~ unwarrantably rendered Just. Martyr's δια Λογου Θεου, by the divine wisdom. It evidently refers to John's Gospel, and must be rendered, thro' or by means of the Logos of God, if not rather: the Logos God. If any inference can be drawn from these words, it would be that Justin had understood the Logos of John to be only the Greek Equivalent of the *Palestine* Ruach, literally grecized, πνευμα, i.e. that the πνευμα and the Λογος were one and the same. In the Apocryphal writers before the Christian Era they are plainly so—.

Possibly, it was not till the half century preceding the Council of Nicea that the Church generally had perfected the terminology of the Articles & distinguished Λογος and Αληθεια = the Son, from πνευμα and Σοφια = the H. Ghost/. That the Corpus et Sanguis νουμενα in the Eucharist ~~was~~ere actually the food and crescific agents of the immortal Life, may, perhaps, be found first in Irenæus, but cannot have originated in him—. In this Irenæus erred, in not making the Eucharist the *Symbol* of the Consubstantiation of the Ground of personal identity with the divine Life, but ~~the~~ *exclusively* the act itself. The multiplication of the Loaves & Fishes was, I doubt not, a symbolic Miracle—i.e. Christ wrought this stupendous Miracle in order that there might be an historical Envelope and Conservative of this most vital Doctrine of Xtnty.—The early Ages, whom the ⟨Pseudo-⟩ Catholics follow in the *dogma*, erred in making the Church everything: our Dissenters and even our *liberal* Clergy in making it nothing.

5173 28.71   Memo. The use, made by Gay Lussac & the   *f68ᵛ*
Experimental Chemists & Naturalists generally of the word, Law
and Laws (ex. gr.—that compounds, whose elements are gaseous,
are constituted either of equal volumes of those elements: or that   *f69*
if one of the elements exceeds the other, the excess is by some
simple multiple of its volume)

5174 28.72   The obtruding sentiments that belong to us as men, in our professional & individual characters no good sign— Modesty in all deep affection & Sentiment—Who trusts his intended wife in a Tavern?—Pleuronectæ—Soles, flounders, &

f69ᵛ floundering souls; both eyes on the same side/It is with those ~~splashing and~~ floundering Souls as with soles and Flounders and other flat fish/The eye of Religion and the eye of Science—why may we not even close the one for a moment to look the more steadily & and effectively with the other.

5175 28.73   In Insects the motive Organs, so dim or null in the most of the worms?/molluscs—and the vascular System the reverse.—Qʸ Since the former are intended to devour, the latter to be devoured, must not this be so? Can a Law be abstracted from this?—

5176 28.74   A campaign of the Duke of W. consisting wholly of the visual & auditual phænomena? So a Nat. History.

5177 28.75   Vital Power ⟨im Bildungsgeschäfte⟩ elucidated by ⟨plastic⟩ Instinct. Intr. Bee.‡

f70   1. Slime and Globules. 2. Flues or Lengths (Fasern) Patches or Breadths (Platten. 3. Skins or Membranes. 4. Tubes and Vessels.
The Flues or ultimate Fibrils of the Muscles, and yet more of the Bones, not composed of Globules or grains but of an homogeneous substance. This holds good of most of the Plates; but the Mucous Membranes manifestly granular. N.B. No determinate connection between the Organ and its ultimate constituents—ex. gr. in all the structures in which the Dimension of Breadth predominates. This depends on the ever-present Finality of the invisible Architect. The Law of *Zweckmäss!* What we have deduced

f69ᵛ   ‡ The possibility that a man may be a Hive, a myriad of men in each man, every one of the Myriad holding himself & held by others, to be *the* man. n.b. This was one of the strange whims & confusions that haunted me when a child, on merely numerical difference.

synthetically from the Idea of Life, the very same results we arrive
at analytically by abstracting the characters peculiar to animated   *f70ᵛ*
Nature. In the former (the synthetic process) we assume the possibility of a Law, or Power, acting in ~~such and such~~ certain directions, and with a certain tendency predetermined by the Idea, or
essential definition, of the supposed Power—& ~~then deduce~~ to
which we give the name of Life. From these premises we deduce
what the common characters of living bodies must be, if any such
existed—what the distinguishing characters, i.e. what the genera
generalissima, which we might expect to find—and the order of
ascent, under the principles included in or evolved from the I
original Idea, ex. gr. finality, multeity, succession of Grades in
the co-existence of All &c. And lastly, seek for the confirmation
of these subjective constructions in outward Nature—and accord-   *f71*
ing to the correspondency decide whether our schemata were
dreams from Jupiter Stator, or from Momus. In the latter we
presume that every man knows what are living things in their main
divisions at least—& passing by what they have in common with
⟨the⟩ lifeless seeks, first, what ~~th~~ more than these they have, common to them all—& then, what each of the great natural divisions
have, in negative or positive distinction from the others/—and
these we abstract & generalize under certain names, which we call
the Laws, Powers, Properties, or Principles of Life—Now by
both processes we arrive at the same results. ~~Demon~~ Look at the
Vegetable, the Insect, and animals with circulating blood and a   *f71ᵛ*
nervous system ~~trans~~ in more or less subordination to a center.—
1. Common to all three, growth ab intra with a predetermined
sphere always as to form, and within certain limits as to magnitude—& so on. In Plants, Irritability in the form of assimilation
&c—&c &c

5178 28.76   The wise ordinance of Nature in the Sea—   *f71*
which sets a bound to the evolutions of life & the types of Life.
In the atmosphere wild & grotesque forms are checked & hence
the chasms or rather interspaces in animated Nature, that as in
setting precious stones add to the charm. Ex. gr.—in the tropics
where water abounds, but for this we might expect monsters between Plants & Reptiles &c.

f72 5179 28.77   As soon suppose no intercourse between Hamlet & Hamlet in a low-civilized country, and no Passengers, because there were no roads or regular pathways, as no nervous Power from the absence of nerves.

5180 28.78   Harlots' Progress, Rakes' &c.—elucidations of Succession with co-existence.

5181 28.79   Why not Hypozoa, Entomozoa, Catholozoa— as the first broad Inter-distinction of the Genus generalissimum, Organizomena—in the same way, as the eye first divides the Rainbow into three colors—& then adds four as distinct and yet transitional and intervenient. The *Entomaozoa* I would give a larger sense, so as to comprize the Polymerea in contradistinction from Cathola.

5182 28.80   LAW. That Nature leaves nothing behind.—
f72ᵛ The exceptions apparent only or such as confirm the Rule. Memo. Apply this law to Chrystallization ÷ Life.

5183 28.81   No single Classification perfect or fitted to all purposes.—or The kind and degree of Abstraction, a the broader or a narrower Generalization intended must be determined and the Class. made accordingly—Ex. gr. for the purposes of *Type* the following is sufficient & the best I can think of—
    1. Ζωαι rectius quam Ζωα/—
f73   Stœchæa (στοιχεῖα), seu Elementa/et Elementigena.
            First ⟨Lowes⟩ Classis Infima
    1. Pro-organismata, vel Ζωο-στοιχεια
    Ord. 1. Elementa—vel Monozoa Monomorpha
    Ord. 2. Elementigena—vel Monozoa Polymorpha:

                    1. Intervallaria:
    2. Classisis Penultima
        Organismata Panzoa—Sc. Regnum Vegetabile
                    2 Intervallaria.
    3. Classis Antepenultima
        Organismata Entomozoa
                    3. Intervallaria.

4. Classis Suprema
   Organismata, Catholozoa.

5184 29.262   3 Jan.ʸ 1825—Jacob & Rachel—or the   *f93*
[*] &c. Youth and Age. Third Stanza—Estrangement.
Indifference of [?Eromere/Grσmere]

5185 29.122   ⌐Thursday, Janʸ *f8o*
. . y¹ !

5186 28.82   *f73ᵛ*
  1. Cupid and Psyche (Roger)
  2. Pastoral Apollo (The reproductive power of the flowing
                     Lines—the thoughtful Shepherd)
  3. Bas Relievo—close by the seat of Sir Thomas Frankland
     symbolic of [?twin/two] Sisters
     Sᵗ Michael *the Flaming Globe*

First, Resignation. Thy will be done
Sec. Deliver us from Evil
3—For thine is the Kingdom

Faith—Mem. The connection of the Head Drapery [?formed] by
the Robe
An ancient Feast—Bas Relief   *f74*

Clergyman instructing his youthful flock—contrast of the two Boys
& the intermediate Girl—
Bosanquet's Parting scene:
Ditto Mʳ Clowes ∧

Charity—the two children—(Dowager Lady Spenser/

5187 29.263   Analogies of/the Uterine : atmospheric : : at-   *f93*
mospheric : future Life.—Mem. to beg my honoured friend to
procure Tiedemann's Anatomie und Bildungsgeschichte des Ge-
hirns.

[* Coleridge's blank.]

5188 29.264   The weight and counter-weight at the ends of a Lever: Excitability and Resistance—in the former the same property in different subjects, in the latter opposite properties in the same subject.

5189 29.265   In adynamic Fevers the most frightful ravages of inflammation without pain—nay, instances when the consciousness of Illness has been subsequent to or commenced with the perforation of the Intestines. Acute forms of Peritonitis without pain, tension of the belly, and Alteration of the features with a small wiry pulse being the only Indicants. Q? Will these facts warrant the conjecture that there are fevers in which the Sensibility is sunk and lost ~~in the~~ and latent in the lower Life of Irritability/—and would Sensibility on this hypothesis appear to be the connecting link or conductor between the organs and the perceptive power—or between the Percipient Ichheit, and its Organismus?—

Or is the sensation still present as the vita propria of the organ affected, which is by loss of the Copula a Vita Monadica—& the man's entrail in the same relation to him as an Intestinal Worm?

Or lastly, may the το πασχειν, the passivity, the res fieri, of the Central Principle, the recovery from which is action, require a finite time in order to become Sensation—i.e. in order to *find* itself (Emp-*find*ung)? And may not in certain diseases the alternation be too rapid? Dʳ Woolaston's Experiments on the compound character of all muscular acts seem to favor this notion. May not this be one cause of the rapid death of each organ after the extinction of the co-organizing copula, that the action and re-action, a centro versus peripheriam, is no longer retarded by its production or procedure into other organs? that the Center becomes peripheric, or in all parts at every moment—so that the whole ⟨action⟩ is superficial, molecular, chemical—consequently, destructive, ? An indifference of pati et agere? Are there not in the lowest forms of Animal Life detachments from the Life of the Planet (or Nature) so imperfect that the Center is external, to them, Light, Air, Electricity &c being their Brain & Nerves?—Whatever of this puddle-dark Querification applies to Sensation as dependent on determinate time applies to Time itself—& therefore moves in a circle, & explains nothing. And so at an end to this Squirrel-frisk, and rotatory

f92ᵛ

climbing, the only use of which is perhaps, to suggest a reconsideration of the Position, that Excitability is *always* directly as the Power of Resistance, viz. whether in certain morbid affection the Resistance may not quoad *efficiency* diminish the dissipation or dissection—spent by being split into multiplicity of successive acts like a rocket star that splits itself & is all *rays*. Between the affection of Excitability and the re-action a pause or interval must be supposed, as indeed is implied in the term, Resistance,—(& here the analogy peeps out between Life and Will), otherwise the Ray from the Periphery to the Center & the Ray in the same line from the Center to the Periphery would take place in the same moment—i.e. in a distance of time infinitely small—& consequently, present the same phænomenon as a painted or motionless Wheel.—

It is at least worth thinking about, whether Pain e converso does f_{92} not suppose a lengthened interval = contraction, spasm. If so, what is Pleasure? That in *Substance*, in the *Stoff*, it is the same as Pain, we have good reason to believe—the orgasm answering to the Spasm. We know too, that in many instances the Maximum of Pleasure passes into Pain—which seems at first sight to prove that Pleasure is not the Maximum of Sensation, but a mid moment between Pain and Indifference.—But Pain does not pass into Pleasure in its transit of descent into Indifference. Besides, it is far from satisfactory—the reduction of a quality to degrees of intensive *Quantity*.—Shall we seek then for some modification or composition by which a certain degree of Spasm becomes Pleasure? To say, that Pain and Pleasure are primary passions in the Mind or Soul or living subject is but staving off the question, from the effect & ground to the act and cause. Why does Spasm y excite pain & Spasm z excite pleasure? If I assumed in the latter case the *Power* of resistance exerted in withholding the *act* of resistance to the excitant, the Excitability remaining, according to the Law, Ex^y = Res^{nce}—In which case the Excitant would be in inverse ratio to the *Act*, & not to the Power of Resistance—Yet this pre-supposes the thing to be explained. For *why* does this Analogon of Will in the Life, or the Will of the individual, withhold the resisting Act? Fichte has some valuable remarks on this point—viz. the differences between the interest of the Life and the Organization. But may not the case supposed overleaf, an approximation, I mean, to

the ~~rapid~~ number and rapidity of successive acts into which ~~the~~ a
Quantum, only, equal to a Single Act, split itself, have something
to do with Pleasure? ~~May~~ Is it not produced either by a multitude,

*f9r*ᵛ of single excitements simultaneous over a given space, or rapidly
successive in one and the same point—the papillæ of the Palate,
&c—while in Pain there is concentration or convergence. Hence
on the one side Titillation, i.e. a succession of ~~puny~~ twitchy resistances to puny excitancies—on the other, the Tic Doloreux, i.e. an
abnormous center in a conducting nerve—a false Focus in a conductor of Sensation! Is it not by concentration that Pleasure passes
into Pain?

f1 5190 20.2
Enigma

I $\overset{M}{m}$ultiply$\overset{me}{you}$ by 2, ~~and~~ add nothing within Something: and a
Universe shall be the Product.

9 Febʸ 1825—

5191 20.3   Aids to Reflection = an Egg with a unusually
large Yolk, and ~~Lard~~ Butter, Salt, and Cayenne Pepper for the
White.—Rose.

*f82*ᵛ 5192 29.126   21 Febʸ 1825.—My dear Friend
      I have often amused my ~~fancy~~ self with the thought of a Self-
conscious Looking-glass, and the various metaphorical applications
of such a fancy—and this morning, ~~I~~ it struck across ~~my~~ the Eolian
Harp of my Brain that there was something pleasing and emblematic (of what I did not distinctly make out) in two ⟨such⟩ Looking-
glasses fronting, each seeing the other in itself, and itself in the
other.—Have you ever noticed the Vault or snug little Apartment
which the Spider spins and weaves for itself, by spiral threads
round and round, and sometimes with strait lines, ~~in~~ so that its
Lurking-parlour or Withdrawing-room is an oblong square? This
too connected itself in my mind with the melancholy truth, that as
we grow older, the World (alas! how often it happens, that the less
we love it, the more we care for it; the less reason we have to value
its Shews, the more anxious ⟨are⟩ we about them!—~~and~~ ⟨alas! how
often do⟩ we become more and more loveless, ~~the more this~~ as

Inopem me copia fecit. 48

Francis Quarles: *Emblems, Divine and Moral* (1736)
Book I No. XII.

See 5192 and n.

Love, which can outlive all change save a change with regard to itself, and all loss save the loss of its *Reflex*, is more needed to sooth us & alone ⟨is⟩ able so to do!)

What was I saying:—O—I was adverting ⟨to⟩ the fact, that ⟨as⟩ we advance in years, the World, that *spidery* Witch, spins its threads ~~closing~~ narrower and narrower, still closing in on us, till at last it shuts us up within four walls, walls of flues and films, ~~and~~ windowless—and well if there be sky-lights, and a small opening left for the Light from above. I do not know that I have anything to add, except perhaps to remind you, that *pheer* or *phere* for *Mate, Companion, Counterpart*, is a word frequently used by Spencer, G. Herbert, and the Poets generally, who wrote before   *f83* the Restoration (1660)—before I say, that this premature warm and sunny day, antedating Spring, called forth the following

Strain in the manner of G. HERBERT—: which might be entitled, THE ALONE MOST DEAR: a Complaint of Jacob to Rachel as in the tenth year of his Service he saw in her ~~and~~ or *fancied* that he saw Symptoms of Alienation. ~~N.B. The Thought and Images being modernised and turned into English.~~

    All Nature seems at work. ~~Snails~~lugs leave their lair;
    The Bees are stirring; Birds are on the wing;
    And 𝖂𝕴𝕹𝕿𝕰𝕽 slumb'ring in the open air
    Wears on his smiling face a dream of Spring,
    ~~But~~ And I, the while, the sole unbusy Thing,
    Nor honey make, nor pair, nor build, nor sing.

    Yet well I ken the banks, where ✳Amaranths blow,
    Have traced the fount whence streams of Nectar flow.
    Bloom, O ye Amaranths! bloom for whom ye may—
    For Me ye bloom not! Glide, rich Streams! away!
    With unmoist Lip and wreathless Brow I stroll:
    ⟨*?Lips unbrighten'd, wreathless* Brow⟩   *f83ᵛ*
    And would you learn the Spells, that drowse my Soul?
    WORK without Hope draws nectar in a sieve;
    And HOPE without an Object cannot live.

✳ *Literally* rendered is Flower Fadeless, or never-fading—from   *f83* the Greek—a *not* and maraīnō, to wither.

I speak in figures, inward thoughts and woes
Interpreting by Shapes and outward Shews.
^xWhere rising still, still deep'ning
⟨Side answering Side with narrow ⌈. . .⌉ace⟩
And *walling* ~~in an ever narrowing Space threads in a about me~~
The World her spidery Lines ~~in Circles~~ on all sides spun,
    ⟨A wall'd ⌈. . .⌉ Room with a Straightn'd Space⟩
My FAITH—(say, I: I and my Faith are one!)
Hung as a Mirror there! and face to face
    ⟨For nothing else there was, between or near⟩
(For not a thing between us did appear)
One Sister Mirror hid the dreary Wall
                        ‡⟨bright Compeer⟩
But *that* is broke—and with that only   pheere
I lost my Object and my inmost All—
Faith *in* the Faith of THE ALONE MOST DEAR!

                            JACOB HODIERNUS
[*Lines written on a scrap of paper super-imposed on lines 15–24:*]
X-*f83*^v   Where daily nearer me, with magic Ties,
What time and where (Wove close with
Line over line & thickning as they rise)
The World her spidery thread on all sides spun
Side answ'ring Side with narrow interspace.
My Faith (say, I: I and my Faith are one)
Hung, as a Mirror there! And face to face
(For nothing else there was, between or near)
One Sister Mirror had the dreary Wall.
But *That* is broke! And with that bright Compe⌈er⌉

f84   ^xCall the World Spider, and at fancy's touch
Thought becomes image and I see it such.
~~Skilled in light~~ With viscous masonry of films and threads
It joins the Waller's and the Weaver's trades,
And see a twilight tent enclose me round
A dusky cell!—but hush! for all too long
I linger in the [?preamble/precincts]

f83^v   ‡ Mate, Counterpart.

With viscous masonry of films and threads
Tough as the nets in Indian Forests found
It blends the Waller's & the Weavers's trade
And soon the tent-like Hangings touch the ground
~~A Chamber'd Call!   But I digress~~
Hush, Muse, thou loiterest too long,
~~And (Cease) the preamble, & begin the~~
A dusky Chamber that excludes the Day—
But cease the prelude & resume the lay.

5193 29.127   *f*84
Jeshurun—Strait forward

יְשֻׁרוּן

5194 29.128   To compare the World (Europe, at least) to a
Skull on the Scheme and principles of Cranioscopy (Gall and Spur-
zheim's)—France, Austria, Russia &c—

5195 29.129   In the plausible passage in Paley's Sermons respecting Sacrifial Atonement—&c—'We may hope to learn what
it means in a *future* state! We *may* then PERHAPS see how true it
is—tho' at present it is, it must be confessed, sad nonsense!!—This
will, however, be popular—1,0001 of good sober pious Christians
will echo the words & adopt them as their Makers faith. Why? it
is feeble—& who ever is feeble favors mental indolence. It is   *f*84ᵛ
feeble: and feebleness in the disguise of confessing and condescend-
ing Strength is always popular. It flatters the Reader by removing
the apprehended distance between him & the ~~celebrated~~ superior
Author—& it flatters him still more by enabling him to transfer
to himself and appropriate this superiority, and to make his very
weakness a mark & proof of his strength. Aye—or a ⟨sighing self-
soothing⟩ sound between Aye and Ah.! I think with the great Dʳ
Paley &c.

5196 20.29   Australis and Caledon, frequent in breeding   *f*13
and multiparous.—

f14 5197 20.30   Bliss = the Soul's self-finding in its own state, primary Signature and proprium spatii—5 as 5, 7 as 7.

Happiness = the Soul's self-finding as modified by and in harmony with her Relatives and Circumstants.—

f13   Pleasure = the Soul's self-finding ⟨more accurately—they are
f14   the Self-finding of life *relatively*⟩ under the sense of Resistance
f13–f14 overcome, ⟨or overcoming, jam, jam victurus!⟩ so that for the moment she floweth onward in all directions. Hence the sense of Dissolving.

Pain = Contra-action against a conquering Resistant—hence *contraction*; and action consumed in Passion.

f14   ‡ As no thought can climb above Self-consciousness, so neither can it delve below Pleasure & Pain: which are the Analoga of Self-consciousness—⟨sub formâ vitæ.⟩ i.e. Pl. + Pain : Life :: Self-con. : Mind

Ingenious; but not satisfactory—unless the appetence (ut in æstûs primo et medio stadio concubitalis) be itself resolve into a succession of resistances overcome partially, or in that sensible interval renewed.—Imo! Hoc satis facere videtur. Still however, these are but the conditions, occasions and concommitants or Consequents of Pleasure & Pain. Pl. and P. themselves remain, like Gold, unaffected by the analysis. No metaphysical Alchemy can give them as products. See above‡

f13ᵛ 5198 20.31   Mem.   ⟨p 24⟩   Book I. C. 16 St. 23.

One of those witling Critics who in scorn of Spenser's verse would read with a grin the two last lines of the 23ʳᵈ Sᵗ as if he was reading a Newspaper advertisement, thus: To fetch a Leach who had great Insight in that disease of griev'd Conscience, And well could cure the same. His name was Páshence.—Senseless of the Effect on the whole scheme of the Harmony of the Canto, and too obtuse to penetrate the Poet's intention, that of drawing the Reader's mind to the weight and allegoric import of the Names.

f16   5199 20.32   like an earth-quake rends the massive wall of an old Belief which instantly closes again nor leaves a mark of its

brief ⟨dis⟩ruption, but yet in the brief moment let in a Light on my Soul, which—
sometimes like a favorite dog, that I caress & occasionally give a *pat* to and then make it, & go on with our Play—

5200 20.26   To a modern Rationalist (Lucus a non lucendo) Church Arminian or schmismatic Unitarian, who admits no meaning in the influences & graces of the Spirit but the ordinary dispensation & disposition of circumstances, his very virtues are snares—"I have *this* virtue at least"—"I have such and such conditions of future Reward"—instead of considering all these as gifts & workings of another, that renders the remaining sin yet more sinful.

5201 20.27   I transcribe the following §ph from the Epistola Responsoria I of the celebrated Sydenham, p. 300 of his Opera Universa, Lugduni Batavorum 1726—notwithstanding its length: it presenting a clear and faithful statement of the philosophic Code of enlightened Empiricism, for which term whenever it is used in a good sense it would be desirable to substitute Empīry, the penultima long = the diphthong ει, as *I*sland, Germanicè Eiland, Iron, Germ: Eisen—or ⁿerhaps still better, Historicism.

5202 20.28   Heylin's "Necessary Introd. to his Life of *f12* Laud.—
P. 3.—"No regard had to Luther or Calvin"/What does this mean? Did any one of the Reformed Churches profess to look otherward than to the Bible and the Example of the past ages? or will it be pretended by the Modern Heylins, that the Founders of the Reformation and the Framers of the Articles in England did not learn their faith from the earlier Reformers in Germany—did not correspond with them, hold their names & writings in Reverence & consult with them on all momentous matters?—
"But the Archbishop knew the man"—Where is the *Proof*, what shadow of evidence had H. to assert this, that Cranmer a held Calvin in other than reverence. It is a mere shameless retrojection

of his own political and theological Hates on an illustrious Name of the Age before him.—

P. 4. all Plausible—but how are we to ascertain wherein & at what time Rome had departed from herself, but by the Scriptures? Or if another authority be admitted, viz. that of the Roman ⟨*turn*

f13ᵛ *to p. 24*⟩ ⟨from p 21⟩ Church itself, at what particular date did this authority cease to be rightful?—But so it is, as Leighton Senʳ (Sion's Plea) observed—Against the Papists the Eng. Prelates used the Puritan's arguments, and against the Puritans the Papists— from the same staff, which they themselves had used as a Rod (i.e. against the ~~Reformed Church~~ Romanists) they fled from ~~in the hands~~ when thrown by the Puritans, as from a Serpent.—Is it not notorious that the favorite arguments of the Pontifical Divines (no wonder! they are their only plausible ones) are drawn from inconsistencies of Prelatic & Ceremonial Protestantism in Germany Luther! Confessionals, his Saints' Days & his Quirks of Consubstantiation & the ubiquity of Christ's glorified Body, &

f15 in England from the pretence of the Hierarchy to a positive Power in *significant* Ceremonies? and which therefore involves an equal power in matters of Faith.

But this was in truth the great, but perhaps the providential, oversight of the First Reformers. The Corruptions of the Papal Church were so gross, that all who had received but a gleam of Gospel Truth into their hearts, were alive to the contrast between the forms and purposes of Scriptural Christianity and the nominal Christianity then enforced.— ⟨These they all condemned by con- clamation.⟩ In the compleatness of their unanimity respecting this cluster of wild grapes they forgot to question each other whether in ~~the principles on which they had severally grounded their con- demnation, were as concerdant as the condomnation~~ the principles, on which they severally protested against these gross abuses, ⟨they⟩ were as concordant as in the protestancy itself they were unani- mous—or whether they were as concordant in the grounds, as ~~they were~~ in the act, of hostility.—On the Continent the Study of the Fathers was chiefly confined to the adherents of Rome.—Luther held them in small reverence; but in England the Universities produced a large number of great Scholars, men of extensive Learning—who adopted the Protestant cause but were not willing

to ~~let~~ leave their superior ~~gifts~~ acquirements behind them—which
they considered as ~~artillery~~ great guns conquered from the enemy, *f15ᵛ*
and which it would be their honor to turn against them—But in
order to this, it was necessary that they should be re-instated in a
portion ~~of~~ at least of their former authority, and reverence. But
how was this to be done without detracting or at least retracting,
from the plenitude and all-sufficiency of the Inspired Scriptures?
At the first, the solution was obvious—and to the Learned and
Sober-minded among the Reformed not alone satisfactory, but justifying the claims of the Antiquarian and Patrician Divines (πα-
τριζοντων θεολογων) to a high Rank in the Church-Militant.

There were a large number of Texts in the Canonical Writings,
to which both Parties appealed, but each according to a different
interpretation. Nay, there were in what for ages has been vulgarly
entitled ⟨Canonical⟩ & generally received as inspired Writings,
sundry Books from ⟨and against⟩ which the Reformers appealed,
but which the Romanists contended to be equally unappellable with
those acknowledged such by their opponents.—In both these respects, it was ~~evidently~~ an argument of great force to prove, that
the Protestants were indeed and literally *Re*formers, & in no respect Innovators or Subverters—that they interpreted the sacred
Scriptures, as those had done who lived nearest the time of Men *f16*
who taught their true meaning by an infallible Light, and while
the Language in which the more important Half of the inspired
Scriptures, was a living Language—and that to the Books in dispute they both gave and denied exactly what the best informed of
the first ages of the Church, and the Church (i.e. Christians collectively) were unanimous in giving or denying.—~~There~~ This was
and it could scarcely be otherwise generally satisfactory—tho' even
from the beginning there were many unlearned & a few learned
Protestants who were afraid of Weapons that had been in familiar
use with the Enemy—They feared the Wooden Horse tho' dedicated to ~~a true~~ their own Minerva/

5203 20.25   It is clear to me that Sᵗ Paul commences his *f11*
Reason with the most general sense of Law, as the correspondent
opposite of the Will, in contra-distinction from the *Nature*, of an
Agent—in *its* most general sense, as comprehending pure and cor-

rupt in rational agents—and again rational and infra-rational. In the last, as in animals, the Will is absorbed in the Law—or the Law constitutes the Will. In the former, viz., in the pure or un-fallen Nature of a rational agent the Will constitutes, is identified with the Law—(we may say, constitutes the Law—for a Will identical with the Law is one with the *Divine* Will)—In the fallen Nature both are *separate*—even when in the reascent from the Fall *f11ᵛ* the Will is subordinated to the Law—Still it is a subjection to an imposed Governor.

f12ᵛ   continued from l. 1. of the page before last—

Now whether this Governor delegated *ab extra* quoad *animum* makes known its prohibitory commands (for herein consists their essence, that they are prohibitory not directly impulsive) by a silent voice, an unwritten word, = the Conscience alone, or likewise by a positive Law—i.e. by a sensuous external record of the Law proclaimed and historically accredited at a particular time and in accompaniment with particular sensible manifestations of Power &c, makes no difference in essentials. In the former (as in the case of the Gentiles) there exists the Law, no less than in the latter—and in the latter equally as in the former the Law subsists apart from the Will—Both alike therefore evince a Will capable of, i.e. identifiable with, the Law—Ergo: both alike evince a fallen, & by their actions, have given proof of a *corrupt*, Nature—and thence are alike under condemnation. Sᵗ Paul's argument has nothing to do with the ceremonial *Orders*—which are Law only in ordine ad Legem—as appointed means of its preservation, publicity, its *f13* being kept in mind & recalled &c—delegated *ab altero*, and quoad *animum* existing ad extra.

f16ᵛ   **5204**   20.33   2 May, 1825. began to read Giambattista Vico's Autobiography—born in Naples 1670. The original Discoverer of the true Theory of the Ὅμηροι vice Ὅμηρος, & of the character of the ancient History of Rome.—The work in 3 vol. which Dʳ De Prati has lent me, contains only his Principi di Scienza Nuova D'intorno alla comune Natura Delle Nazioni.

Plato, Tacitus, Bacon, and—Grotius! li quattro Autori, che egli ammirava sopra tutt' altri. Vico had written comments on the first and half of the second Book of Grotius's De Jure Belli et Pacis, "della quali poi si rimase sulla reflessione, che non conveniva ad

uom Cattolico de Religione adornare di note opera di Autore Ere-
tico["].—Striking instance of the bigot-izing influence of the
Romish Superstition—even on the noblest Minds.—

P. 60. Vita di G. B. Vico.   *f*17

Omnis divinæ atque humanæ eruditionis elementa tria, Nosse,
Velle, Posse: quorum principium unum MENS; cujus Oculus Ratio, cui æterni Veri lumen præbet Deus.

5205 20.34   Zoroaster for Hither East = Semitæ : : Her-   *f*17
cules : the West = Iaones. the Founder of Sacerdotal (διογενῶν)
Aristocracies. The members of this Hierarchy were Chaldeans—
the Plebeians were the Assyrians, who headed by a Marius or
Cæsar (= a military Jacobin, a Ninus tho' no Ninny) made a
revolution which, partly a radice (probably a mongrel Race of the
Semitæ with the Hammonitæ) inclining to Slavery & Indistinction, partly from their numbers and the vast and fertile Plains,
they occupied, passed into a Sultanism or Military Monarchy.—
Zoroaster slain by Ninus—i.e. the Sacred Patrician Order did not
survive as in Rome under the Cæsars, but were utterly extirpated.

5206 20.35   O the notable chain of such *Dand*elions as grow
in the garden of Morpheus—The Fallen-out teeth of the old Lion,
Tempus edax! ~~pipe stems of Piss a beds To diuresis dear of Piss a
beds whose diuretic~~ or in homely but more appropriate English,
smooth glossy Links ytwist of P——a-beds,

Whose stems, to Diuresis dear, transform   *f*17ᵛ
The couch of dreaming Thought and make it wet and warm!
that the learned Sons of hoar Antiquity,
The Philægyptian Races have finger-forged!—

Zoroaster or——astes initiated and indoctrinated Berosus for
Chaldea; Berosus performed the same office on Mercurius Tris-
megistus for Egypt; M. T. quick-silvered Atlas for the Salivation
of Ethiopia; Atlas communicated ~~Morbus sacer~~ the ⟨Sacred Gift
(Teutonicè = Virus sive Pus atque venenum)⟩ to Orpheus for the
~~in~~ vaccination or iodation of Thrace; which Orpheus ⟨& his Dis-
ciples⟩ finally founded Schools throughout Greece!—Whether the
Missionaries travelled by Mail Coaches or Steam-boats is not ascertained!

O monopoly of my intellectual vision! All my Eye and Betty (I

beg her pardon! Eliza) Martin.—And these Chaldean Sages—
What do we learn from the recorded FACTS of History, as opposed
to the fancies, the putamenta, of Theorists that they were Fortune-
tellers, who practised divination by the trajectory of Shooting
Stars, and after a time improved this trade into the noble Science
of Judicial Astrology!—

5207 20.36
f18   Vico. 1. p. 135.
     Sacra i.e. secreta—a capital stroke of Jesuitry in an *uom di reli-*
gione—It would not surprize me to see it shot off against the Irish
Bible Society.

     Mem. Compare and collate the romantic tales and exaggerations
imported into Europe by the Chinese Jesuits, & again magnified
by the Solar Microscope of the Infidel Katterfeltos of France, with
the stories of the Greek Sophists & (not improbably) the Priests
from their enmity to Philosophy, the true *Religion* of Greece, respecting Ægypt and Scythia—. Again—the same trick played off
by Aristobulus—and again, at a later period by Tricksters of the
Same School, from rivalry to Christianity, by Iamblichus, Porphyry &c—/
     Mem. The Science of comparative History—Comparative AN-
THROpotomy.

5208 20.37   Qᵞ The Law of Connubia extorted by the Rom.
Plebeians from the Patricians, not intermarriage with the Patri-
cians tho' this might be one of the consequences, but legitimate
Marriage among themselves—Collate Negroes in West Indies—

f18ᵛ 5209 20.38   Exclude Utility? No. My System of Moral
Philosophy neither excludes nor rests on it: were it for this reason
only that it includes it. The Utility of a thing consists in its fitness
as a Mean to an End.—As far as Act, Motive, and Purpose (in
one word, *Conduct*) are founded on Reflection† I am willing to

f19   † N.B. The Understanding in its most general sense is the faculty
of selecting and adapting fit means to relative ends; and the *human*

admit, that they proceed in the first instance from Self-love— *f18ᵛ*
Amour propre/or that Self-love is the initial principle of human
action, and that on this stage the man pursues only his own interest,
or Utility. Hence the single Savage is influenced ⟨solely⟩ by the
principle of Self-preservation. He takes a woman, begets children,
who remain with him. Habit, Appetite, the Services of the
Woman, gradually form a part of the ~~complex~~ confused reflection,
or mental Object, which he calls himself, and he then seeks the
safety of his Family—.Families become Neighborhoods, and these
Tribes—and he seeks his own safety in the safety of his Tribe.
Tribes are influenced by ~~War~~ Conquest or Alliance, and became
fixed.—he seeks the interest of his Town, ⟨or⟩ City. By increase
or war many small States unite into a Nation, having the same
name, & perhaps language. He ~~tries seeks~~ blends his interest with
that of his Country—finally, in the progress of civilization, in the *f19ᵛ*
spread of a common religion, in the extension of Trade & Commerce, and with the growth and general diffusion of the Science
of Political Economy, his ~~fond~~ Self-love expands into a desire for
the welfare of the Human Race. (Now quote from Pope's Essay
on Man) All this is true as far as Conduct depends on the Understanding: ~~not~~ The mistake consists in taking it, either as the adequate description of *Human Nature* of the entire Man, on the one

---

understanding, considered abstractedly in relation ~~to the operation~~ *f19*
~~function~~ thinking to *Thought* is REFLECTION. In other words, Reflection is the *name* for Understanding, when ~~thus is~~ we speak of
the latter in its *intellectual* function, or in reference to *Thinking*.—
in the same manner as Housewife is the name of a Woman regarded singly in relation to her domestic duties and employments,
~~the~~ and as you can not always say, a Woman is a Housewife, but
can always say, a Housewife is a Woman—so you cannot assert
universally, that Understanding is Reflection, but may universally
assert, that Reflection is Understanding. Therefore, I say, R. is
the *name* of Understanding in one of its functions—not the definition. The definition of Reflection, or of Understanding contemplated exclusively as *cogitant*, is, the Faculty of judging according
to the Senses—i.e. of concluding from the impressions made on
the Senses a real external *Object*, as the cause and correspondent.

hand, or as the ground and rule of Morality on the other. For the
former it is too high, for the latter too low; for the former it is
flattery, for the latter detraction. As applied to the whole man, and
to men in general, the scheme implies an ignorance, of the qualities, properties, and tendencies which man has in common with
animals, neither differing in kind nor in degree, but only *in specie*;
and likewise an ignorance of ~~these~~ their powers & tendencies, ⟨be-
sides the Understanding⟩ the diff~~ence~~erence of degree of which is
so great as to appear & almost to form a difference of Kind—the
Fancy for instance/and which great difference, entitling these pow-
f20   ers (of which the Understanding is *one* but not the only one) to be
considering as distinguishing Characters of Humanity, tho' not
absolute~~ly~~ contra-distinctions, ~~as~~ is mainly ~~attributable~~ owing to
their co-existing with the ipso genere diverse, and properly con-
tradistinctive Attributes of Humanity. See Aids to Reflection, p.
240, §. 2.—But again as applied to Morality, this scheme demonstrates an ignorance both of the ~~essential character of moral~~ true
meaning of the word, the essential character of the thing meant,
and lastly a pitiable unacquaintance with the Man in the Man,
Reason, ~~Arbitrament or responsible Will~~ or Free-agency, Conscience, Personality, Love and Faith.—

Then exemplify this—first in rude man, in children, in the
common people even in civilized countries; in short, in all that are
below Self-interest—then in the Showy Characters from the abuse
of the Will as above the understanding (Napoleon), of the Imagination as co-ordinate with it—and from both deduce the possibility
of substituting the reason for the individual Will/the true as true—
~~the Conscience~~ Love or the desire of the Good as Good, the Conscience, the hatred of Sin for its own exceeding Sinfulness—&
Faith or the Love of God above all—

And thus deduce the rightful and legitimate sphere of the Love
of Prudence, and the Doctrine of Utility i.e. Self-love raised into
f20ᵛ   an enlightened Self-interest by force of the Understanding in its
function as Reflection, its importance & indispensableness as midway and the link of the Animal & Spiritual; but its degrading
influence taking singly or as paramount (ex. gr. the Chinese, and
Malthusians) and its impracticability and self-contradictory nature.—For Utility is mean to *end*. What is the end? Either animal
pleasures, and then the higher (viz., Unαerstanding) is servant to

the inferior/or to the Mind of the Agent, and then the first Precept
of the Code must be to have itself ~~thrown into the fire or~~ destroyed
or forgotten—thrown either into Puriphlegethon or Lethe—
See the old red Cottle Pocket-book.

5210 20.39 AIDS TO REFLECTION. The Scheme of Argu- *f21*
ment from p. 200 to p. 242 (subtracting the interposed aphorisms
from 228 to 234) may be thus presented.

The Position is—the Diversity or Difference *in kind*, of the
Understanding from the Reason.

The Axiom, on which the Proof must rest, is, that

Subjects, that require essentially different General Definitions,
differ *in kind*.

(*I call this an Axiom: tho' it is rather, perhaps, an identical proposition. At all events, it is a Self-evident Truth.*)

Now Reason must be considered, either in relation to the Will,
or the Moral Being, when it is termed the ✳ PRACTICAL REASON
= A:

or relatively to the Intelligence and as a Sciential Power, when
it is termed THEORETIC or SPECULATIVE REASON = *a*.

The Understanding, therefore, in order to be compared with
the Reason, must in like manner be distinguished into

The Understanding as a Principle of ACTION, in which relation
I call it the ADAPTIVE Power, or Faculty of selecting and adapting
means to proximate ends = B.

and the Understanding, as a faculty and mode of Thinking,
when it is called REFLECTION = *b*.

✳ This alone *is* Reason in the full and substantive sense.—It is *f20ᵛ*
Reason in its own sphere of perfect Freedom. Reason as the Source
of Ideas, ~~and~~ which Ideas in their conversion to the responsible
Will become *Ultimate ends—Ends* in the alone proper and adequate
sense of the word. On the other hand, the Theoretic Reason or
Reason as the Source of Absolute PRINCIPLES, the Universal &
Conclusive in Logic, is properly the *Light* of Reason in the Un-
derstanding which therefore, as now in a lower sphere, that of
Time & Place, must needs appear as Necessity & Universality, in
contrast with the Contingent & Particular, the *Indigenae*.

f2 1ᵛ   Accordingly, I give the General Definitions ⟨of these four:⟩ that
is, I describe each severally by its *essential characters*; and I find,
that
The Definition of A differs *toto genere* from that of B: and
The Definition of *a* from that of *b*.
~~But~~ Now Subjects, that require essentially different general def-
initions, differ in kind.
But U. and R. require &c.
Ergo: U. and R. differ in kind.

Q. E. D.

A more positive *insight* into the true character of Reason, and a
greater evidentness of its diversity from the Understanding, might
be given—but then it must be *synthetically* and *genetically*. And this
I have done in my larger work, in which I commence with the
Absolute, and from thence deduce the Tri-unity, and therein the
substantial Reason (Λογος) as the Ὁ ὤν—ὁ πρωτογενὴς.
But in Aids to Reflection I was obliged to proceed analytically
and a posteriori—in which way it is not, I believe, possible to give
a clearer proof than is given on the pages referred to.

S.T.C.

f22   5211 20.40   At first the Patricians and Plebeians stood in
relations far more nearly resembling those of the Planters and the
Negroes in our Colonies than the Litterati who receive Livy for
Gospel would dare imagine. The Polish Gentry ~~with~~ and the Serfs
would be nearer were it not that the latter are *allowed* to be Christian.—By degrees the Plebeians, availing themselves of the dependence of the Patricians on their services in the Wars (whence
the aversion of the Patricians to War) extorted the Jus bonitar-
ium—a right of property in their Victual-Grounds. (Black Regi-
ments in the W.I.—Jealousy of the Planters respecting them.—
Still however all rights of Citizenship were refused—At length
they obtained the Tribunate—and lastly, the jus connubiale, the
right to contract solemn Marriages. (N.B. *not* intermarriages with
the Patricians)—During this period Patrician (qui ciere *patrem*
poterat—nam nuptiæ demonstrant patrem) and the Plebeian were
f22ᵛ   the same as Noble & Ignoble & at a certain age every Patrician

was called in the Senate Roll, when the Censor saw no blot to exclude him—It was Fabius Maximus, who introduced a new constitution, as the only means of preventing a violent Revolution—
and distributed all the Romans into 3 classes, according to their
property—Senators, Knights, and Tribesmen.

5212 20.41   The boasted merits of the Romish Clergy in
attending the sick and dying in pestilences—Let it, however, be
remembered that the need, which they relieve, is of their own
making—and the comfort, they administer, derived from the superstitious terrors & vain god-dishonouring hopes & fancies, they
had themselves infused. ⟨You take the Catholic sick his Priest at
his Bedside; but carry your imagination a step backward & take
him before the arrival of the Priest! Poor wretch! the desolate
Godless solitude—His God has not arrived & no eye to behold &
pity him, &c.⟩ If the Protestant Clergymaen does not dally with
Suicide in this way, they haves previously armed his Hearer with
a just confidence in his own spontaneous appeals to the Mercy
of God thro' the mediation of Christ, and in the meantime are
usefully & more humanely employed in rousing the Rich &
Healthy to contribute abundantly the means of medical relief,
&c—

5213 20.42   What do I mean by a Socinian Spirit in the   f23
Clergy of the last generation?
    This: When a man professes to believe the Trinity, the co-di-
vinity of Christ & the Incarnation, I ask myself what the natural
consequences of such a belief, if sincere, would be—what would
be its influences on the Believer's other opinions.
    In like manner, I take the denial of all these doctrines & suppose
myself to believe the simple Humanity of Christ, as a great
Prophet sent to give a sensible proof of a Resurrection from the
dead—& ask myself, what the influences of this scheme would
be—or rather, what they had been on my own mind.
    Now if I find the opinions of A on all other points, excepting
the Trinity, exactly those of B, in substance, & merely with the
quantity of disguise, which the profession of Trinitarianism had
made necessary—I infer a Spirit of Socinianism

f23ᵛ   5214 20.44   Henry   Ancient Geography
The complete Works of the late Revᵈ Philip Skelton, with Burdy's
Life of the Author—

Baynes, 1824

f23   5215 20.43   The diversity of the U. and R. I hold of great
Value; but the determination to abide by the plain dictates of the
Conscience & Moral Sense against and even in contempt of any
seeming conclusions of the Understanding from general principles, alone indispensable. Yet surely it must be both a comfort and
a support to see clearly, that these general principles imply positions, which are true only in application to objects of Sense—and
that to apply them to Supersensual Subjects is at best arbitrary, and
on this account alone sophistical; But if any obeisance be due to the
f23ᵛ   word of God in Scripture, or to the Law written by God in the
heart, or if any credit be due to the Suffrage of the best & wisest
men of all ages, and to the feelings and common sense of all Mankind, as proved in the very structure of all human Languages,
such application is not alone arbitrary but false, and not only sophistry but wilful falsehood.

2. Again—it is alone indispensable to a Christian that he should
believe & feel that nothing out of himself, and which exists for
him only by means of his outward Senses, will avail to his salvation
without a correspondent principle within, call this inward something what you will, Conscience, Faith, Grace, the Spirit &c.,—
But surely to the Man, who is to exercise the functions of a Teacher
& Spiritual Guide, it cannot be otherwise than convenient & serviceable, to see the *ground* of this great truth, in the very constitution
of the Human Mind, and to be able to generalize and manage this
ground in fitting terms under a brief and perspicuous formula.

~~Object~~ Subject)(Object; but if the)(is to signify a correlative
opposite, and not an incompatible Contrary (for Contraries can exist
in no connection & therefore not act on each other), then there
must be conceived an Antecedent.

Subject = Object, i.e. the Identity of S. and O. or a Subject
which is itself the Object to and for itself.—And this antecedent
f24   we find in the Fact of an I Am, or *Self*-conscious Being./Thus in
the Science of Grammar

$$S = O$$

Verb. Substantive

O		S
Substantive		Verb

or Substantive = Verb produces itself into S ⚹ V as its two *poles* or correlative opposites.

And when in addition to this the Student has further mastered the corollary—namely, that all antithesis consisting in distinction not in absolute division, the Subject is such by the predominance of the Subjective, and the Object is an Object by the predominance of the Objective, not in either by exclusion of the other; and that therefore the strictly accurate Form will be

$$S = O$$

$$\frac{S}{O} \quad \maltese \quad \frac{O}{S}$$

he will have possessed himself of the Universals and universal Organ of a truly philosophical Logic, with which he may set at nought all Heresies, from Tritheism to Socinian Materialism.

In like manner I cannot but regard it as interesting & desirable for a Clergyman to see a way of preserving the mystery or doctrine enshrined in the Sacraments, yet preventing the Shrine from being perverted into Superstition & an Idol.—And this I have attempted in my disquisitions on Baptism & the Eucharist—viz. to retain the truth symbolized, so as to guard the Symbol from being rarified into a Metaphor—and I know no other way of effecting this double purpose. But if any one, first according with me in the *f24ᵛ* indispensable Articles, thinks he has discovered another & better scheme—candidus imperti!—I speak as a Dogmatist in none of the preceding points.

But these, my dear Sir! form a very small part of the Volume: and it is respecting the following that I put the earnest question, *Should* not every Christian, *ought* not, is it not the most awful *Duty* of every Minister of Christ to believe understandingly each and all of them? And is it *possible* to do this on any other views & premises than those in this Volume stated? More ~~lucidly~~ forcibly expressed, more lucidly arranged, more logically, more popularly, propounded, illustrated, recommended they may easily be; & grateful am I for every suggestion of a more intelligible phrase, most grateful should I be (yet God knows! not ~~an~~ as an Author

solicitous for his literary reputation, but as a Christian who, if he
be a Christian, must be anxious, yea, distressed respecting every
obstacle to the effective communication of the Truth in Christ!—
& most thankful should I be to the Reader, who should underline
the Sentences which he had not understood, and the obscurity of
which he, after he had understood them, could attribute to the
wording. (For this is the only fair test of reprehensible obscurity—
*f*25   can the meaning, when understood, be conveyed with equal fullness & precision, in plainer words?) Lastly, from what you know
or reasonably apprehend, concerning the present state of men's
minds & opinions—especially the Clergy—do you think an exposition of these momentous points *superfluous?* The moral responsibility of man, and the truths implied in this, either as presupposed
or necessarily consequent. 2. the Personeity and the *Holiness* of
God?—3. The Pauline Ethics resulting from the admission of the
1. and 2.? ₃ 4. From the *fact* of moral Evil and N°. 3. the reality
of *Original* Sin?—5. The removal of this by the incarnation and
Cross of the Son of God, as the *only possible* Redemption, thro'
Faith as the only possible means of appropriating the boon in each
Individual redeemed?—I affirm that each of these five, and each
in the full and literal sense of the words in which it is stated, and
that all five collectively, are *essential* to Christian Belief—and that
no one point, as for instance the Redemption by Christ's Assumption of Humanity as the unique, sole possible means of Salvation
which is denied by Archb? Magee, can be denied or doubted without the annulment of Christianity *in toto*—It becomes Mahomen-
tanism, Mono-idolism, or what not—Christianity it is not—and
in the name of Common Sense and common Honesty what chance
is there of establishing the Gospel in the hearts & souls of men, if
*f*25*ᵛ*   the Religion is represented as a set of words used only to be explained away, or at the best as arbitrary positions, having no
ground in the necessities or constitution of the human Soul, a mere
sic Deo placuit—an while the natural Retort, At Deo placuit? is to
be answered only by historical arguments, i.e. related relations of
human Testimonies.—As if a narrative of the circumstances of a
Revelation could constituted the Revelation—as if it was not a Revelation of Truths in themselves so divine and gracious that the

Redeemer reserved his especial Blessing for those who received them on their evidence, without the suspension of their inward freedom by the astoundment of their outward senses.

The Miracles of the Gospel have a fourfold potency—1. as ~~ful-fillment~~ completion of prophecies which delivered of one Man in one Man were all fulfilled. 2. as proofs of the Mercy and benefi-cence of the Worker. 3. as credentials of his Mission from God. 4. and of perpetual Benefit as a synopsis of the Precepts, Doctrines and Mysteries of the Religion in the universal & most remember-able Language of Action and Event.

In all these points the Miracles are the subjects of the warmest Gratitude & Admiration; but I doubt whether for us who now live they can be ~~called direct~~ classed among the outward evidences of a Belief, of which themselves form a part. They are either ~~Obstacles~~ Weights to be over-balanced, or constituent parts of the Self-evi-dence of the Religion. *f26*

The great moral importance of negative Knowlege and Belief in Religion. In this way only can the process of unsensualizing the Soul and purifying the temple of the mind from Idols in order to prepare for the Epiphany of the Ideas.—On this I have written a loose sheet: which consult.

But generally speaking, the Negative, the insight into the not-truth, the not-possible of A. B. C. D. and so on S.T.W. is all that the ablest and most gifted Reasoners can help others to. The Positive, the X Y Z they must find for themselves, or meet in themselves. All Ideas are *Felicities*. The most that can be done by Volition of Thinking, is but like *bringing out Stars from* the blue sky or ~~between~~ in the rifts between the sombring Clouds, on a Summer Evening.

5216 29.123 The full applicability of the characteristic Test *f80ᵛ* of an Idea, given in Note p. 226, Aids to Reflection, hidden from the Nos numerus of our half-reasoning Literati and Philosophists by the exceeding dimness of their Reflexes, as in a Glass at the interior wall of an horizontal Cavern, or in a room at late twi-light—. Long-nosed Tom, and Snub-nosed Bill, and Jack without a Nose may pass across it, and it might as well have been their

Ghost or Souls (as they Soul is commonly image-abstray'ed) for any distinction in the dusky dark shadows of the reflections—So Attraction and Repulsion—the Centripetal & Centrifugal Forces— = two insects with their tails linked or intersheathed. Hic et hæc—(Now the first as wanted in the direction upward or toward the acute point of the Leaf—and thither crawls Hic, & drags Hæc after him—now downward or strait toward the pedicle—and here Hæc has the better of it, & drags Hic after her—in short, a temporary Amphisbæna!—All this is exceedingly conceivable— i.e. picturable—and moreover very conceivably absurd—. For how is it possible not to see that if the Forces are assumed as two several Powers or Subjects, that Hic = Hæc = O—that they nullify each other—and that if they are not equal, the result must be either Hic − Hæc, or Hæc − Hic.—Aye, if on the same level line; but if Hic moves so | and Hæc so————, then the result will be a O! But pray, what put Hæc in a *central* Relation, & by gave it the competent superiority in Mass & attractive power?— Must not the same powers, *both* be supposed in each particle, to make the central mass a solid Circle (= Globe). What was is the necessary condition of the *Orbit*, is no less so of the *Orb*—. As Conceive therefore, or rather try to conceive, A and R, as two forces of the same Power, or two Powers inherent in one & the same Subject, and you will find that it is an IDEA, and as such capable of expression only by contradictory positions, *both* of which are true, and neither true of itself.—/Each singly is easily conceived, but it is false—both as one is inconceivable, but it conveys the truth.—

f8 1

5217 29.124   The connection of the Sense and Organ of *Smell* with the vis reproductiva projectrix—compared with Taste. The immediate object of Taste the common or universal properties of things—i.e.—contractive = pungent, peppery ⚹ dilative, dissolvent, mucilaginous, gum Arabic—/ smooth with disolvent + pungent, in synth. of predominance, Sweet, from starch, finely levigated charcoal, cream, sugar, honey ⚹ pungent *lineal* (⚹ pung. punctual) = cutting, sharp, + ⟨oxyd. or⟩ dissolvent = Acid.— when Pungence punctual, Rust, oxyd.—It is N. B. in the Bitter, as the central, that Taste passes into, or presents an Analogon of,

Smell.—But smell transports and renders sensible (objective) the *qualities*, the subject, of Objects.—It does not melt away into, & blend with, the Recipient, as the *Taste*, therefore the Adjunct of Assimilation; but excites to an functional Act, and this of a peculiar kind. sc. *similific*, an absundering or ecarceration of the Form from the Mass—Hence it is, that generation can never be conceived other than as a *power*, a specific Act—and refine the vehicle as subtly as you will, suppose the visible Sperm the entangling retiary involucrum of an electrical *Aura*, still as long as it is corpuscular & space-filling, it can only be imagined, as preparing the organic structure for the *Act*—and what is the *Germ*, the animal punctuale *futuriens*? *Figureless*—the negation of all *forma formata* in the for dimensionless globe—i.e. the only possible way, in which the *forma formans* can be presented by itself to the sensuous Imagination.   *f81ᵛ*

Of course, proportional relative Magnitude of Animals, and the component Parts of Animals is the most important consideration. But yet positive Magnitude ought not to be passed over—Ex. gr. the Skull in Birds *proportionally* larger in relation to the countenance (Antlitz) than in Amphibia—. Now in what sense shall we interpret the *positively* smaller? both Skull & Countenance in Birds compared with several Amphibia?—

The more my knowledge of facts increases, the more plausible does it appear to me, that the Brain ⚸ Nerves : : Excitability ⚸ Excitancy—and that is only indirectly the Cause of the intellectual or even the sensuous faculties.

Qᵧ—Let a number of Hens be highly foddered, and kept in a Coop or better still a latticed Aviary (in order to give them the power of exercise) within sight of a Hæram Farm yard Hæram with its usual Stock of Cocks & Hens—Then when it is probable that the Egg will be formed, to try at how late a Date the Cock being admitted will impregnate the Egg—/

Inattention to the impossibility of graduating per ascensum the classes, orders and genera of Organized Individua under any one form of Abstraction, or for any single point of view, is the true cause of the controversy between Oken & with the elder Naturalists on his side, and Meckel, Spix, Schweigger, & Goldfuss, the   *f82*

followers on this point of the French Naturalists, Cuvier, La-
marck, Dumeril & Blainville. Doubtless Oken is in the right—
in the main, because he uses more the *unseen* Eye.

Appendages of the great Operations, ex. gr. the pleasure of Lust
& Lust of Pleasure in the continuance of the Species.

5218 29.125   N. B. To draw up in Robinson Crusoe's fashion the reasons for Complaint and Satisfaction with my lot, as a
poor man, not as a man; and therefore I am to exclude those
whether boons or bales that would probably been as they are, tho'
I ~~had~~ were possessed of Wealth.—And again, n.b. that by Wealth
I mean any sum, not *to be* obtained, ~~or~~ not dependent on my immediate exertions that would enable me to have or procure what
would, in my own opinion, make me more comfortable, ~~and~~ set
me more at ease than I now am: and which (~~so at least~~ such at least
is my present belief or fancy) would directly and indirectly enable
me to exert and transrealize my powers, moral and intellectual, to
the best purposes, singly and continuously, without distraction or
disturbing events & calls—/. Mem. That in all my long life I
have never a rich man attach himself to a poor man, of similar
rank or education with himself—nor one, after he had become
rich—

f84ᵛ 5219 29.130   Vico, 7 May 1825! O what a heaven of a Day
and so Monsieur Champollon or what else the name is—the Pupil
& Completor I mean of Dʳ Young's Key to the Egyptian Hieroglyphics has decyphered a series of Kings, the last of whom was
elder than Adam ! I do not care A Dam' for the Hieroglyphics or
the Decypherer—. they are Stones, of which I cannot make Bread,
and for which I see no cause why I should make my *Wine* (whine).
Do⟨es⟩ not the ~~open~~ first Book of the Pentateuch prove an acquaintance with the contemporary state of Egypt in anno mundo 2490;
and do not the other four contain irresistible evidences of an intimate acquaintance with the custom, & religious rites of the same?
Have we not every (rationally postulable) reason to believe the
historic assertion that Moses was learned in all the Learning of the
Egyptians? Is it not, to say the least, a highly probable supposition

that he had himself initiated into the Secrets of the Priesthood—?
And can it be supposed, that he could have been ignorant of the
existence & meaning of the hieroglyphic Stone-history, had it existed at that time? or that without Motive & contrary to the crav- *f85*
ings for a higher & higher antiquity common to all Nations, he
should have shortened the period, ~~of the~~ assigned by the general
Tradition, and established by authorized Writings.

5220 29.131   Scales, Stipulæ, Chaff, from the bases of the
leaves of the Beech Tree in May 23, 1825, on the ⟨rich dark⟩
green Moss-carpet—
    The glossy Scales that gay as living Things
    Dance in the Winnow of the Moss-bees' wings
    That hovers ⟨o'er the Moss beneath the Beech⟩
    Then renews his *routing* toil
    Delving & tearing up
    With head & *sturdy* thighs—.   Bombyx Muscorum.—N.b.
What do the humble-bees do in those small hollow funnels, they
make—Often they put their hind Half & orange plush small-
clothes in those funnels, and move backward & forward—? clean-
ing their clothes from any thing sticky, from nectarin, or honey-
dew—or ovi-position. I, however, could never find any the least
speck even with a glass in the bottom of the funnel./

5221 29.132   Monday 23rd. *Times*. Infamous Attack on the
Reformation in the old *lie* that our's was the innovation, their's (or
the Romanist's) the old Religion/and the Editor a Clergyman

5222 29.133   To every *metaphysical* verity of religious import there will be found a correspondent *moral* idea. The most
important speculative Theorem in the theology of a Christian is
beyond doubt the Personëity of the Godhead, & the consequent
Personality of the Father, the Son, and the Spirit: and the moral
correspondent of this is the *Holiness* of God. Holy! Holy! Holy! *f85ᵛ*
    It is the neglect of taking this as the *foundation-stone* of Divinity,
the not-*stapling* the catena theologiæ to the "I AM," and ~~One Holy~~
I am the Lord the HOLY ONE, and with it the mind and faith of
the Student—("the knowlege of the Holy is Understanding,"

scientia quæ cæteris omnibus *sub*stat, it is that which *substantiates* all other truths in Divinity) that has occasioned the spread, has caused the the general susceptibility for the contagion of *Utilitarian* Doctrine/—

5223 29.134   Religion C. England attacked by Unit. & Roman—Evident that on these points the House of Commons do not represent the feelings of the Mass of the Population—Nor *is* that their function/but if they take up religious subjects, they ought to have a reform on the plan of universal Suffrage.—an important idea in *Church*

5224 29.135   Of all parts of Theology that, ~~on~~ which the Divines of the last 150 years have chosen as their favorite theme, many of them reducing Christianity to it, presses on my mind as the most difficult, and intimidates me as the most delicate—the Miracles, I mean.—I cannot clearly understand, how my Faith in Christ should be one & the same Act of my Soul with the judgement, my understanding is induced to form on the question respecting the Writers of the 3 first Gospels & which if it be a *f86* *judgement* and not a mere resolve to ~~use~~ articulate half a dozen words. ex. gr. "This Book was composed by S! Matthew"—and to declare every man a Miscreant, who does not echo them/must depend on the Data on which the judgement is grounded. And surely there must be some difference between the judgement, the Datum of which is—So I have always been taught to take for granted—or even the more solid Datum—It is the received opinion, admitted with scarcely any exception by the Learned—& as I know nothing to the contrary, I receive the Book as S! Matthew's—Surely, I [?say], there must be some difference between such a judgement, and that of a man who has carefully examined all the original authorities, on which the Learned have grounded their opinion, had studied the Gospel in the original language, which by his former studies he had been rendered competent to examine, in respect of internal & external evidence. But as the foundation of the Belief in the authenticity of the Narrative, so must be the Belief of the events & facts narrated—And of the Miracles inclusively, considered as this or that *particular* Miracle. If the former

Belief resolves itself into a mere opinion of this or that Learned Man's or learned Class of Men's, judgement & veracity, the latter can be no more or other than this, & "I believe such a Miracle" means only "I believe such a Priest"./The Romanists therefore have at least the credit of consistency when they resolve all their faith into the one all-comprehending Article of their implicit faith in the Church. And if only they had kept firm se to the Jesuitic & Italian Concentration of the Power & Authority of the Church in the one Person of the Pope, no charge could be brought against them on the score of consistency. We should know what was meant by *the Church*: whereas with the so called liberal Catholics, it is any thing, every thing, and nothing—the Pope; the Pope in ex *f86ᵛ* cathedrâ; the Pope with the majority of Cardinals, assembled in sufficient number to form a legitimate Conclave;—a general Council; a general Council convened by the Pope; a general Council convened, & having its decrees confirmed, by the Pope; a general Council, convened by the Pope with the consent of all the Sovereigns & Governments of the different Sees, having its decrees confirmed by the Pope, & *received* by all the Churches of the Catholic Church/—which last is a Magnificent O O O O O O O O = O!—In short, every remove from the Infallibility of the Pope, personally & exclusively, is an advance in absurdity. A general Council of 300 Bishops, not under the guidance of the Holy Ghost; but after the most indecent Clamours & disgusting Intrigues 170 decide + a, & 130 − a/. The former Decision is inspired by the Divine Spirit & infallible; consequently the 130 must have been inspired by the Evil Spirit: for what is contrary & in active oppugnancy to the Good, must be evil.—But what if the 130 were men of known Learning & unsuspected Piety; while 50 or more of the 170 were notorious Creatures of the Court of Rome, infamous for ignorance or profligacy or both?—Is this an impossible Case?—Read the Histories of the Councils, and say Yes! if you dare!—And what will a Romish Disputant *not* dare!—

Far otherwise is it with the belief of the Miracles generally; with the entire faith in the proposition, that Christ came with Signs & Wonders.—The man who has by moral evidence received with his whole heart the Incarnate Word as his Saviour & Redeemer, takes this position implicitly or by necessary consequence.

*f*87   5225 29.136   [A heavily deleted passage of ten lines]

5226 29.137   Mem.—Alas! what use *will Mem.* be? The
fullness, but much more the *undesigningness*, of my mind, the habit
& incapability of having any co-object with the point, I am arguing, totus in illo, et mei et audientium immemor, make it of no
use—Nevertheless, *Mem.* not to allow myself to be

ʔ7ᵛ-89 5227 29.138   [Notes toward a Greek grammar: in *SWF*]

*f*89   5228 29.139   I have ⟨myself,⟩ heaven knows! conflicts o̶f̶
m̶i̶n̶d̶ ̶e̶n̶o̶u̶ ̶—enough to exercise me. I speak not now of the struggles to unite the life of my Will with the convictions of my reason
& conscience. (Yea, the h̶u̶m̶a̶n̶ very Will, which is the dark and
hidden Radical of the bodily Life, must be mastered and inclosed
before the Belief has perfected itself into that fullness of Faith,
which I dare not deny to be possible, since the words of Christ
imply the contrary, tho' since the apostolic James I know no sufficient evidence of its having been realized—the power of miracles
being the only & indispensable proof, as it would be the immediate
consequence of such faith—. But that union of the Will, in which
our Salvation *is* concerned, and which every Christian is bound to
a̶s̶ struggle for, to attain to a possession of this to any sense or
fruition of comfort is enough to employ our best energies & prayers!—But never can I suppose that any doubt can be rightly
dreaded *as subtracting* from or in any other way affecting the Faith
by which we are saved, that Faith which in the Individual is the
subjective Correlate to the Incarnation, Death and Resurrection of
Christ objectively, which (Doubt) relates neither to the necessity
of t̶h̶e̶ Redemption, nor to the sense of that necessity, nor to the
Conviction of its Reality both historically as an Event, and spiritually as a continuing Cause, nor ⟨to⟩ the consequents in Affection,
Maxims and Conduct. Still less, when this Doubt is in great part
grounded on the Apprehension & Belief that the point questioned
has proved injurious to the Faith, and is calculated still to injure
it.—Let it be, for instance, a doubt respecting the apostolicity of
the Evangelia Infantiæ prefixed to the Gospel of Luke, and con-
corporated with our copy of the Gospel for the Hebrews, κατα

Ματθαιον. I cannot see that Lumen Spiritûs Dei resting on the ƒ89ᵛ
same which the Fathers made a criterion of Inspiration—I miss
the analogy of Faith, ~~the harmony and~~ ~~Ομοπνευματι~~ την ἁρμονίαν
καὶ ὁμοπνευματιαν with the other Scriptures, especially those
known certainly to be Apostolic or of the Apostolic Ages; much
less do I meet with any confirmation—& when I look for the last
presumptive test, viz. its effects and influences on the Christian
Church and the hearts and understandings of Christians individually, what meets my mind's eye but blasphemous Parthenolatry,
and indecent, nay, obscene controversies!—Under these circumstances, I cannot but be struck with ~~two~~ three very momentous
direct Counter-weights—the first, that ~~but for~~ had the Chapters in
Luke not existed, I cannot for a moment doubt, that the very
contrary belief must have been ~~assum~~ deduced from the τι μοι και
σοι, γυνη; & the "Who are my Mother & my Brothers?—2. The
absence of all allusion (except in the one word "supposed", which
the Marcionites affirmed not to be in ⟨Marcion's⟩ Luke's Gospel,
which that it was not intentionally corrupted or mutilated by Marcion, Eichhorn has, I think, unanswerably shewn) in any part of
the New Testament; but as perfectly inexplicable on the supposition
of its having formed a part of the original Gospels (which all began
with the Baptism of John), the absence of all allusion to the fact in
S! John's Gospel, ~~and~~ or the Apocalypse, and in the Epistle to the
Hebrews—the common object of all three being to establish the
superiority in kind of Christ, the Son of the Living God, to all the
Prophets from Abraham to Moses, and from Moses to John. It
seems to me impossible that neither Peter, nor Paul (both of whom
layed so great stress on the fulfillment of the Prophesies in Christ)
should not have referred to the verses in Isaiah, Behold, a Virgin
shall bring forth, &c. had both the Jewish Church previously interpreted these words, as conceptio ~~cum virginitate integra et sine
viro~~, virginis sine viro, and himself ~~to ap~~ suppose them, or in this
sense, to have been accomplished in the Mother of Jesus.—~~Lastly~~
Thirdly, ~~as a minor consideration, and yet not without its weight
on my mind~~, the existence of the admitted characteristics of popular rumour-grounded Traditionᵃˡˢ)(authentic Historical Records—viz. The widely-different way in which the same fact is
particularized—so as to need the identity of the proper names, or

f90 it might be supposed to be two different events spoken of./Do but compare the Differences between the *N*arration in the first with that in the third Gospel, of which even the figure ⏜ᴹ₁⏜ᴸ. is an extenuated Cypher, for even the ⟋ splits (in the Genealogy, I mean) with the trifling variations in the four Narratives of the Resurrection.—Lastly, as a minor consideration and yet not without its weight in my judgement, the striking circumstance, that from these Chapters the Socinian derives his only even plausible explanation of the attributes Son of God + Son of Man, belonging to one and the same Person, while on the other hand the Catholic & orthodox divine is perplexed by finding Christ, in seeming opposition to the whole course of the New Testament represented as the Son of the Holy Ghost—and not ⟨*then* of Man, as before & from eternity,⟩ of God the Father.✹

These concurring arguments would compel me to declare my Scruples: if I had a Christian Public, for my Readers. But alas! the vast majority, the only not all, of the Christened World, knows so little what they know, that they may aptly be resembled to Heifers, that start back with affright from their own Stall, if only the Stable Door should be painted ⌈ . . . ⌉ anew, or the same novelty of appearance produced by cleansing it from the coats of dirt or bad paint, to which they had been accustomed.—

It is a momentous question, how far and for whom ~~the~~ a merely *implicit* knowlege of the Truth is *safe*. That for the Doctors of the Church it is not seemly, that for the appointed Dividers & Expounders of the Word it is not consistent, is, I think, out of all question. *They* at least ought to know what they know—to know both the constituent Members of the Body of Faith, and their connections & inter-dependence.—Be it that the Faith is as the Impression from a Seal—all simultaneously—and that the Parts can be understood aright, only in relation to the Whole! Yet it is no less true, that the Whole must be understood in each part, or it ceases to be contemplated as an harmonious Whole—& becomes

f90 [✹] Besides, how could it be called a *Sign*—when every means were taken to conceal it, by her marriage with Joseph? How were the Jews to know it? It is certain, that they neither knew or suspected it.—

an indistinction ~~imprison~~ outlined by its own extent, like a
Shadow, or a History Piece hung so high, that you see the Frame, *f90ᵛ*
and that there ⟨are⟩ a number of Figures: ~~but~~ and nothing more.
Only you have always understood, and will live and die in the
assertion, that it is a capital Picture, none in the world to be compared with it.—Or perhaps, you go farther—and believe that as
~~you~~ long as you keep it in the House, and look at it, once a week,
bare-headed and exclaiming aloud—O rare Picture! wonderful
Work of a transcendent Master!—Good Luck will attend you. Is
this an exaggerated ~~statement~~ view of the state of knowlege &
Belief of Myriads of nominal, yea, of Church-going Christians
respecting the Christian Scheme, and their Bible.—A series of
propositions, that have *never been translated out of words into distinct
conceptions, will be to me no proof* of the contrary, however fluently
they may be uttered. As the Miser rests on Gold, so do the Many,
even of the educated Class, rest on Words. They should be transparent, or seen only as the Glass thro' which we see; but for the
greater number they are opake as ground Glass; for others translucent, but not transparent; and for ~~the~~ too many, of a higher order
of Intellect, they are colored Glass, that spread Frost over the
vernal Landscape, or the Glare of a Conflagration over Ice and
Snow.

5229 29.266   Mem. Not to forget to ask Mʳ G. for a ticket *f91ᵛ*
for Mʳ Stutfield.

5230 29.267   Where in confidential ⟨letter or⟩ tete a tete
with an old and most intimate friend & ⟨Partner in weal & woe,⟩
known to be perfectly acquainted with ~~the thing as it is or~~ Things
as they are or were, ~~a~~ persons ~~do uses of~~ the language, and ~~seeks~~
begin to ~~play~~ *act the part* of ~~a~~ Self-cheaters. I can never, never
have any reliance on ~~that~~em ~~hence~~ afterwards. They *make* what
they would undo; and ⟨by seeking to overlook they⟩ *find* what un-
sought *would* not have existed.

5231 20.62   Query. Whether there is any ground, on our *f40*
present scheme of Science, for Vico's postulate, that for some centuries after the Deluge Thunder was unknown. Vico's reason,

drawn from the soaked Earth's not exhaling the hot material of Lightening, is of course obsolete. In the vast always partially & for months in every year universally inundated Plains of the Oronooko, Maranha &c, are Thunder-storms more or less frequent & violent, than in the dry Plains of Africa in the same latitude?

f39ᵛ 5232 20.63   Isaac Perey or Pereyus *Historia Pre-adamitica*, who, & at what time—G. B. Vico speaks of him as an Apostate from the Catholic Faith, and attributes it to the assertions of the Chinese Jesuit Missionaries respecting the antiquity of the Chinese Annals—& their books printed before the Christian Æra.

Michael di Ruggiero and Martini, Jesuits, were the main sources of the notions respecting the Adam-swallowing antiquity of the Chinese—but the delusion was or ought to have been dispersed by Niccolo Trigaulzio in his [*De*] Christianâ Expeditione apud Sinas, who fixed the true date of Confucius about 500 years before Christ, and Printing barely two centuries earlier than the Germans—and at the same time demonstrated the meagre & popular character of the Conf Philos.—& the infant state of civilization deducible from the mystery & importance attached to a few physical facts blended into a mass of blunders & childish sensuosity.

The best record of the Egyptians seems to be their division of chronology into the Age of the Gods, to which they attributed the invention of the Hieroglyphic characters; of the Heroes, to which Sh. att. inv. of the Symbolical; and of Man, to which S. a. inv. of the epistolary or popular characters—corresponding to Varro's Obscure, Fabulous, & Historic Æras.

f39 Varro's Opus Grande Rerum Divinarum et Humanarum—Ah! that is a Loss!

De Nationum Jactantiâ communi & ingenitâ. Mem. To quote the original words of Diodorus Siculus as my Motto to the Races viz. that o barbare o umane si fussero, ciascheduna si è tenuta la più antica di tutte, e servare le sue memorie fin dal principio del Mondo.—

Tests of Tradition—1. That which least flatters the two characteristics of all rude States of Society—Tribal & National Vanity and Indefiniteness of Imagination or the childlike Rivalry in *big-*

ness—a mile high! *My* Giant was a hundred miles high—Our Joannes Giganticida lived a 1000 years agon. Po!—*Our* Jack the Giant-killer married King Olim's Daughter a million years ago—Ergo, this Hebrew chronology is the more probable.

2. that which coincides with the actual State of Mankind & the tillage & urbage of the Earth, so that the years may be filled up, without long strings of mere Names. Ergo—ditto.

3. That which best harmonizes with our own experience, ex. gr. of America, New Holland &c. Ergo—ditto.

4. That which corresponds with the science of Nature or Physiography—ex. gr. the formation of Coral Reefs & Islands—Ergo—ditto.

5. That Chronology in which the Nation itself occupies the least disproportionate space and rank. Ergo- -the Hebrew.   *f38ᵛ*

6. That in which there is least of the *Marvellous* and the Marvellous least of the gigantesque character. Ergo—the Hebrew.

7. That which is most *individualized* and *ordinary* human. Ergo: the Hebrew.

~~9~~8. That of which the remaining Documents appear most original—History and not mere Copy and Echo—Reports in late & perhaps speculative Times by Theorists of assorted Reports—or references to Books not existing or which more sober Literati hold spurious—/as Porphyry & Iamblichus's Citation of Pythagoras/—Ergo: the Hebrew.—

~~8~~9. That which has fewest of the *common* to all other nations—ex. gr. Varro counts forty Herculeses, of different Nations—how many Joves—Dianas—etc.—This ~~argument~~ fact has been hitherto historically interpreted instead of anthropologically & psychologically, as it should have been—& hence the argument applied to the opposite conclusion.—But I have not the slightest scruple in adding here too as in the former ~~7~~8. Ergo: the Hebrew—

10. That which tho' most unlike all the rest will yet, if admitted & layed down as the ground, best explain all the others, when taken in conjunction with Anthropognosy & Psychology—Ergo: the Hebrew—

I hold myself that eo in its double sense of subject-object, *am*,   *f38* and of subject active, do, send, and the modification of both, in *go*—is the ground work of all the verbs, & the greater number of

the conjunctions and prepositions which are but old verbs imperative—and these constitute the *language*, the nouns being imitative
sounds, and for a long time not sounds but pictures, gestures,
σηματα—
     I am not, however, unwilling to begin with the children of
Noah—and these I agree with Vico, are
     Sum, as the root of all supersensuous terms, sto, of all terms of
rest, eo, of motion, do, dico, facio, of action—and that the imperative mood is the original of all, except the first—i, sta, da, dic,
fac.

5233 20.64   Pleroma in the Idea—and the Birth of the Distinctities, the Forms, the Infinite in the Finite—yet having their
primal essence in Will, the possibility of the Finite willing to be
in itself? Willing to be in the Absolute Will, and not in the Idea;
to pierce deeper below the Light into the Fire, to ~~shape~~ control
the form by the essence & thus to be suicausal—I ~~will~~ would to
be that I shall will to be—Apostasis, Chaos—Condescension.

f91ᵛ 5234 29.268   Wed. 3 August 1825 Times—Cath. Aristocr
leave the whole to B. Connell & two or 3 Barristers—3 or 4 silk-
gowns & a Seat on the Bench all the result of Cath. Em.—O
insidious Falsehood!—No—a whole Island with all its rich Church
Lands & Revenues wielded by a Romish Hierarchy—Can we
wonder at the neck & nothing activity of the Jesuits in Ireland—
O Canning! Canning! Dupe or Traitor! There is no third possible.—

f36 5235 20.71   19 August 1825.—Yesterday morning having
been the whole preceding fortnight unusually even for me sick &
sad, I awoke like Nebuchadnezzar's Idol—an Image all gold.—In
my 17ᵗʰ year I had the Jaundice—never since till now. Alas! that
the main obstacle to the restoration of the Liver to its right func-
f35ᵛ tions, which I have neither strength of Body ~~or~~ enough, nor Fortitude nor Grace to overcome or effectually to cope with, should
be the main Obstacle to the willing Calmness with which I might
but for this possession look forward to a fatal result! Miserere mei,
Deus Salvator! Miserere me, Verbum Dei, in quo est Vita, qui

Caro factus es! The *Will* of my Life is poisoned.—I seem to see that for every finite moral Will, für jedem endlichen Ich, there must a Suppositum, in a Life, which in fallen Man is a blind tho' plastic Appetence, which may and too often does undergo a yet deeper corruption into a *Lust*, but cannot rise into Love—What other redemption for the rational self-conscious Will but the sub-position of the Life, that is Light in whomever it abides, & a creative, generative, & hence a re-creating regenerating Life?—In my affliction I see more clearly, how all the Truths of my mind conspire toward the view, that has been vouchsafed me, of the VIth Chapter of St John!—Ah! shall it have been vouchsafed in vain, for myself, like a Torch in the hand of the Blind! O! if but for others, that the Time may for a while be deferred when no man worketh! Mercy, Christ! Mercy and Faith!—

5236 29.140   I have reflected a good deal this afternoon (6   *f90*^{v}
Sept^r, 1825) on the Ideal Beauty of the Grecian Divinities—and the result, tho' not quite satisfactory to my mind, may serve as the Ground-plot for a future Lucubration—First, there seem to me certain aboriginal Ratios or determinate Propositions of Form, analogous to the harmonic concordances in Music, & both having their Radix in transcendent (Pythagorean) and their illustration in   *f91* common, Arithmetic. Not improbably, the Metals from Carbon to Nitrogen may be a chain of such primary proportions of ~~two~~ the two antagonist powers, Attraction or Fixity, and Repulsion or Volatility.—Relatively to Forms, these are discovered by the Fact. A combination is produced which reveals itself by its instant co-incidence with the Idea, and empirically by the discovery that no change can be made in any part without destroying &⟨or⟩ trans-muting the effect of the Whole. And those primary Integers (like the 2, 3, 4, 5, 6, 7, 8, 9 in Arithmetic, only that Nature has a myriad instead of a Decad, her ~~2 3 4 5 6 7 8 9~~ 23456,789, being exprest in a single proper cypher, ⟨a Planet for instance⟩ no less than a 5 or a 7) are distinguishable ¹· by the entire absence of all *Interest* ~~by~~ or reference to *uses*—(the Swan is beautiful without a thought of the instrumentality of its long Neck in Fishing—) and 2. by their incapability of being explained. They are true *Ideas*— each its own evidence, and self-grounded—Tho' doubtless an

accessional pleasure, & a refined sort of Interest, may flow out of certain consequents of the Forms/as the commanding Survey and facile obedience to every Volition in the high ascending-flexile neck of the Swan, and the division (or distinct residence) of the Guiding Power from the Mass of the Body—the S̶w̶ invisible Swan being the Noumenon which we actually mean when we describe its *Acts* of voluntary Motion.—The like I seem to myself to find in the Grecian Deities—and the consequence is a q̶u̶i̶e̶s̶c̶e̶n̶t̶ repose of the comparing Power in the quiescence of fruition, still as sleep, a̶n̶d̶ y̶e̶t̶ but with the stillness of concentrated Attention.—The second operative influence I find in the difference from the beautiful Human Forms & Faces actually produced in Nature—in the difference itself, I say, τῷ ἀλλογενεῖ as causing a negation, in perfect

f91ᵛ suspension of the comparing Power relatively to other faces. Look at a fine Portrait, or observe a *portraiten-massig* [*mässig*] Face in an Historical Picture—& you immediately begin to ask, who is it like? or whom have I seen like it? It is *an* individual of a G̶e̶n̶u̶s̶ Species. But in a Mercury it is indeed Individual; but it is *the* Individual that as itself constitutes a Species. Thirdly, the absence of all conscious direction of the Spectator's reflection to the finality of any part—the complacence is wholly intuitional. The forehead of the Apollo is not *reasoning*.—Lastly, the facility & effect of *Expression* are great in proportion to the *Balance* of all the Features.

f1ᵛ 5237 29.1   Dʳ Macculoch's Descript. of the Western Islands of Scotland—

5238 29.2   ʹΥ./προ ηττον. χαραγμα——2 αυγ. ᾳ ω.κ.ε.—last but 5 leaves of the this way writing.

5239 29.5
= the same as, equal to
+ the act of B. and C. mutually interpenetrating
× the *offspring* of that act. n.b. not the Compound of B & C.
V in the Deity the identity or Prothesis of: in all else the *substitute* which in that particular relation & subject *represents* the Identity or Prothesis, as the correspondent Image or Likeness thereof.

5240 20.45   A most memorable Remark of John Wesley's,   *f26*
and worth a Waggon-load of his Fanfaronades against Election &
Reprobation & Absolute Decrees, is that in Southey's delightful
Life of Wesley, Vol. II, p. 67, of his congregation at Monk-town
Church in Pembroke, composed "of *genteel* people. So I spoke of
the first elements of the Gospel. But I was still out of their depth.
O! how hard it is to be *shallow* enough for a polite Audience!" But   *f26ᵛ*
this is eminently true—so I have ever found it—of your sensible
classical Oxford and Cambridge Clergymen, such as you meet at
Rivington's or at Bartlett's Court, or the R. S. of Literature.

    Give me a Mother of a Family, who has read the History of
England & Milton, & Shakespear, in part at least, in addition to
her Bible and a few Sunday Books—or a man, that has begun to
read his Bible from a *Concern* rising in his mind, & all whose
other knowlege is of his Business or from conversation with his
religious neighbours—and I meet with no insurmountable difficulties in making myself perfectly intelligible—nay, not seldom to
my own surprize, most readily on the most *subjective* points. The
difference in the *educated* Blair-Sermon People, or the Clergy,
with Evidences, Natural Theologies, and Bishop Prettyman alias
Tomkins or the like on their Library Table with the last Bampton
Lectures, & the Bishop's Charges, ⟨the Quarterly⟩ & the Christian
Advocate's Answer to Jeremy Bentham or the Edinburgh Reviewer, is explained at once as soon as a man can understand the
Synthesis of exclusive Objectivity and Unrealness in all their
thoughts, and notions. The Species, or Effluvial Onion-Films of
Democritus, αναιμοσαρκες, people their mundus intelligibilis.
Without a *Soul* there can be no *Spirit*—and without Flesh and   *f27*
Blood ("for the Blood is the Life) there can be no Soul. And
therefore till these men feel that what is *substantial* must be *subjective*, invisible and therefore *unimagineable*, there can be nothing
done with them or for them. They approach to Reality as they
descend. ~~The lower they sink~~ The Reality deepens, nay, that is not
the right word—it thickens, as they sink from the Human into the
Animal Parts of their Being. From the Understanding to the
Fancy, from the Fancy to the Ear, from the Ear to the Eye, from
the Eye to the Smell, Taste, and sense of Contact, and recognize

their own Subjectivity fully in pain and pleasure—i.e. concentered Sensations—Who shall teach them to reverse the process? The Father alone when he shall *lead* them to the Son.—Peter Boehler & the Moravian Confederates in Fetter Lane may have, & probably did, caricature the principle, & apply it amiss & in a dangerous extreme. But a truth it is, and one, the truth & practical momentum of which I yearly see more & more plainly, that the οι πλειονες of even of our most respectable young Clergy begin where they should end, in their schemes of being *useful.* It is a fearful Hysteron Proteron to set about planning what they shall *do* before they have learnt what they *are.* ~~Statues of desert sand~~! "They busy themselves in building conduits, of which they are to turn the [?Cock/lock], dry themselves as Pillars of Sand, yet thirstless as the podgy Swamp—instead of waiting for the opening of the Wellhead within, that out of their belly might flow rivers of living Water—But how can this be unless they first *thirst.* For this is the condition, under which the invitation was given by Christ. *If* any man thirst, let him come to me. These schemes of utility are the most ruinous of prolepses (των προληψεων κακισται)—They overlay what they antedate—and accelerate by abortion. *Be*! When this is secured, then be *useful.* Nature herself gives the lesson—There is a uterine previous & indispensable to the atmospheric life—The Mother's Breath must vitalize the Blood & teach it its thousandfold channels, & till Life becomes a *Habit*, a Lesson passively learnt by heart, the Mother's Life is the Life of the Child. Its Brain is nourished by the Heart, in stillness & meek subjection to the Blood which is the Life. When this is perfected, ~~&~~ then comes the Birth into outward & all-common Light—and then the Lungs begin to play, and the Brain to act on the Heart, & to control the organs of motion & speech—& ascends a legitimate throne, & reigns there as long as it is still quietly sustained and nourished by the Blood from the central Spring—In the Heart it began, by the Heart it must be continued—let it but be the Heart that was in Christ! For in it is Life, and the *Life* is the *Light* of Men.—

On some future occasion, my dear Sir! / (ˣthe Revᵈ Blanco White I may offer a few observations on another doctrine of the early Moravians—viz., respecting the instantaneity of ~~the~~ what they call the New Birth. For here too I seem to see a great psy-

*f*27ᵛ

*f*28

chological truth working like molten Gold or Silver under the
dense surface-scum of Dross. Q.ʸ Whether all revolutionary Acts,
which can be revolutionary only when they are total and focal energies of the Will, ~~nec~~ must not of necessity *appear* to be the opus
operatum et perfectum of a single Moment. Is there any other
form of Time in which the *negation* of Time, its transcendency to
Time, can be revealed—What the preparations may have been is
another question—to which may be applied much of what I have
said respecting the Obstetrication of Ideas.—I feel certain, that
tho' Love is not always & even not often Love at *first* sight, yet it
is always Love at *one moment*. The analogy may be extended further—to the *diagnosis* of the regenerative Spirit. Thousands may
think themselves to *love*, & no such thing; but no man really loved   *f28ᵛ*
& could be ignorant of it, even by its essential diversity from that
state which he had before called by its name.

The part of your work respecting the blasphemous Parthenolatry
of the Romish Church ~~was~~ gave a fresh push to the Pendulum of
my Mind respecting the 〈"To〉 print or not to print"—respecting
the Fragment from some first Century Evangeli~~a~~um Infantiæ, ~~pres~~
interposed between the Dedication & the Beginning of Luke's Gospel, and the Fragment from some other Evang. Infantiæ concor-
porated with the Hebrew Gospel by the Translator whose Revision
we now have. Surely, never was the diagnostic Criterion of floating
Tradition from regularly authenticated History—namely, that in
the former every man feels no scruple in telling the story in his
own way, and modified by his own notions of likelihood, than in
the strange difference of the same ground-work in the 1ˢᵗ & 3ʳᵈ
Gospels.
   I am not ashamed to confess that I think highly of the old Test
of Scripture, that satisfied the old Divines—the lumen Dei apparens—and the subjective Miracles worked thereby—/i.e. the
blessed effects of the Scriptures & the inward witnessing of the
Spirit to their procedure from the same Spirit—in one word, the
recognition of the Spirit by the same Spirit!—Now when I apply
this to the whole story of the Miraculous Conception, and the
Angel's Promise to the Virgin—& compare these with our Lord's
words in the beyond all doubt & genuine authentic Gospels, τι   *f29*

μοι καὶ σοι, γυνή; &c—and when I reflect that it is these 54 or 5 Chapters, that have alone given the necessity & which probably gave origin, to the disgraceful contortions & snaky lubricities of the Harmonists—& lastly, that these chapters supply the Socinian with the only plausible defence against the name, Son of God, at once in distinction from, yet union with, Son of Man; these Results, so utterly unlike those of the Scriptures generally, have a great weight in my mind—and then the Narrative of Speusippus respecting his Uncle, Plato, ⟨so⟩ honestly preserved & so whimsically answered, by Origen—add the Devil's having been permitted by divine Providence to impregnate Rhea, in order that the Romulidæ (Romans) might not be able to reproach the Christians with their venerating (I ~~almost~~ shudder while I transcribe the nonsense!) the son of an Incubus!—

In a much, a very very much inferior degree, does the consideration of the mischievous, the senseless, disputes respecting Episcopacy & Church Orders, give a lene clinamen to my judgement respecting the actual Paulinity of the Epistles to Titus & Timothy.—

But of the yet more momentous Question, the since Chillingworth Watch-word of the Protestant Theologians—Scripturæ per se non modo sufficiunt, sed omnes alias fontes *obcludunt*—is not Milton's lately recovered & published work a Memento?—Exclude all Philosophy! Extinguish all Ideas! Hold in contempt all Church Tradition, even that which deserves the name, the successive Traces being extant in the Books of each successive Generation from within a few years of the Apostle John's Death—~~&~~ in short, depose at once Reason & the Church from the Chair of Interpretation, & I am not the first man who has ventured to think, that the Arians will reap the harvest.—It is very humiliating to think of a Milton seriously representing the Deity as making a Creature out of his own *Stuff.* (for Substance can here mean nothing more than *Material*, as Wool is the *Material*, of which Cloth is made!) As if M. had literally understood the Mosaic account of *God's Train* or *Skirts*!

f29ᵛ

5241 20.46   It follows from the essential character of Ideas, so often asserted and explained in my writings, and it will be found to be the fact, however such fact might be accounted for—that the terms of most frequent occurence on Theology have a two-fold meaning, a negative and a positive—and where the former is meant but the latter understood, there arises a confusion & sense of perplexity in the mind. Thus in the Scholastic and Cartesian phrase, Eternæ Veritates, Eternal Truths, the force of this word, eternal, is simply, having no relation to Time, i.e. it expresses a *f30* negation of Time—But when I affirm, God is eternal, I mean the total possession of his Being unsuccessively, so that ⟨there is⟩ nothing which is possible that is not ~~real~~ actual—which answers to the Schoolmen's Definition—Deus est Actus Absolutus ~~sine~~ absque omni potentialitate purissimus. Now my fundamental position is:

Religion differs from Philosophy (= Eternarum sive ἀχρόνων Veritatum Summâ) on the one hand, and from History on the other, by being both in one. (= the identity of both, or the coinherence of Philosophy in History, of History in Philosophy.— All its Truths are Facts; all its Facts eternal Truths.—And as my fundamental Position, such is my pervading Aim—viz. to give to the Truths of Religion the Life, Power, and Actuality of Historic Events, and to its historic facts the universality and evidence of philosophic Truths—to remove from them the imperfection of Contingency & Accidentality, and yet retain the immanence of *Will*.

Now when you consider, that the very contrary is the Plan adopted by Divines generally, that they have studied either to reduce Christianity to a system of Catena Logica of ~~abstract~~ Principles, abstract Positions, ~~deduced~~ and Deductions or—ex. gr. the School-men & the (so called) Systematic Divines ~~among~~ in the second generation of the Reformers, or to convert the whole into a series of contingent Actions & Events, under the common for- *f30ᵛ* mula of, "So it happened: and it happened so, because X, or Y or Z happened to *chuse* so"—(N.B. not the Arbitrium in Ratione ut fons in imo fonte subspirans; but the *pro* ratione Voluntas!)—can you wonder that the mass even of well-educated Readers find a difficulty in understanding my lucubrations, which they had not been conscious of in the treatment of the same subjects, nay, & sometimes in the assertion of the very same positions, in Burnet, Porteus, or Tomlins (he that was Prettyman, I mean—

I was particularly struck with a passage in Southey's delightful Life of Wesley, in which Wesley totidem verbis, as myself, asserts the diversity of Reason & Understanding, & that the former, not the latter, forms the difference *in kind* between Men & Brutes. Had I gone no further, no one would have complained, because every one would have fancied he understood me—But when I had proceeded a page or two further, I found that Wesley himself had never sought for the essential characters of Reason & Understanding, universally; but had satisfied himself with a single mark by which one might be drawn from the other, as Hemlock from Parsley by so many black specks on the stem of the Hemlock—& what is the consequence? A theory of a future state of Retribution for animals as well as men, in which from ignorance of the character & conditions of Self-consciousness, Wesley had confounded imperishableness of Substance ⟨ὑποθεσεως ψυχικης⟩ with immortality, and an imaginable metempsychosis with the Survival of the Ειμι αυτος, which if it had existed to survive, the Brutes would have no Brutes but human Quadrupeds, or four-footed Men.

*f*3 *1*

I will close this apologetic exposition of my Attempts & Aims by bringing the whole ~~question~~ cause to one question. Granting what I am not prepared to deny or affirm, that there is an implicit Faith, a Faith by simple adhesion of the Will, obedience in act and the state and habit of Feeling consequent on Prayer, yet is this a *desirable* state for any?—Supposing opportunities of Light to have been vouchsafed, by which the Believer might have known *the Reason* in the Faith of Christ (& how otherwise can he give a Reason for the faith in him or be assured that it is *the* faith?) is it even a *safe* state? ~~Does it argue an~~ Is it compatible with entire Love and Reliance on Christ, to remain content with a Faith that is the creature of *accident*—accident of Birth, or Country?—Lastly, even tho' it were granted, that such state is desirable for some, and safe for most, yet is it either desirable, safe, or becoming for a Minister of the Gospel, appointed to divide the Word—or for the Rulers of the Church, and the Watchmen on the Tower?—I appeal to *Paul* for the answer—1. Corinthians C. 11, v. 6–16. Titus 1.9.

Because our eyes would have been given in vain, if no Sun had risen—Shall we make no use of our eyes in beholding the Light?

*f*3 *1*ᵛ

The Eye itself, it may well be, would have been weak and blear,

had it been strengthened & nourished by the Light & other invisible eradiations of the Sun—the greater cause therefore for directing and exerting its utmost powers in contemplating its gracious
Fosterer./—For the Eye read the intellectual Powers, for the Sun
Revelation, and for the Light the Light of the Gospel.

5242 20.47   Sept. 1825
Of the Gospel Scheme objectively, as it exists in Idea and in the
Scriptures I have hope, that I have found firm land—but of the
individual appropriation of the same, and of clear views as to the
precise sense of *perishing* everlastingly, and of the consequence of
not being saved, to the individual Person—alas! I am in twilight.
And I feel the want & necessity of enlightening Grace to remove
the perplexities which the study of Luke's Acts of the Apostles, &
Peter's Discourses, compared with the Gospels, especially the 4th
Gospel, raise in my mind—Ex. gr.—the application of the words
of Moses, which judging by the context I must have understood
of Joshua, to Christ—Would it have been possible for Peter's
Hearings to have inferred the Divinity of our Lord? Or not to
have inferred the contrary? Is it permitted to assume, that the mind   *f32*
of the Apostles themselves was led into all Truth *gradually?* God's
Holy Spirit enlighten me!

5243 20.48   Some unknown Person, soon after the publication of the Aids to Reflection, sent me Relly's Treasury of Faith
(See Southey's Life of Wesley, Vol. II. p. 315) whething imagining a resemblance in my tenets with his, I know not. If so, the
Sender must have been a very careless reader—(the actuality of
Sin—) "the exceeding sinfulness of Sin"—and the its essential in-
communicability—being my foundation stones/and the conversion
of Sin into Disease or Calamity the error of errors, against which
I cry out. No less expressly have I declared the nature (τό *quid et
quale*) of the Redemptive Act, and the subsumption of the Humanity by the co-eternal Son of God, an incomprehensible Mys-
tery/to the belief of which we can *intellectually* supply one indirect
argument, viz. an exposure of the Absurdity of every comprehensible Substitute, for that has been imagined.
Nevertheless, there are certain Appertinents, for which we have

the authority of Redemption—for instance, that the fallen Nature, which Christ was born into, was capable of acting on his Will—and that this is a concerning truth is evident from its being recorded in each of the three Gospels.—And there are, I believe, certain Positions, in such apparent harmony with Scripture Declarations, & which, if admitted, would intelligibly connect all the various declarations of the Scripture into a Whole, that they may *f32ᵛ* be innocently and profitably set forth—provided that it be done modestly, as an aid to individual conviction ~~not as a substitute~~ respecting the doctrines of Faith, not as an addition. Such I hold the two following—that a finite Will can become personal, an I am, only under the condition of the Eternal Logos enlightening it, or that we call Reason is the Light or Manifestation of the Divine Intelligence; and that the finite "I" can exist really (or actually)(potentially) only as it has a ground or Base of existence in a Life or Nature; and that this Life or Nature is not individual & imparticipable in the sense in which the "I" itself is; but *generic*—or a Common Nature, so that each man speaks of his Nature, as a somewhat with which he is united but not identified, as mine not I, as *mine* & yet *our*; it being the incommunicable Perfection of God to contain in himself the Ground of his own existence.

Further, that the finite Will may by a responsible Act sink into a lower Nature, or infect its Base and commute it into a false yet sympathetic Life—(tho' I incline to the former as more agreeable with the words of the Apostle Paul)—and that from this Nature it cannot by its own act detach or liberate itself, tho' as long as it retains its susceptibility of the Divine Light, as long as the Light *f33* vouchsafes to be present *for* it, it will more or less distinctly be aware of the contradiction and disharmony between its spiritual essence and its generic Base (Romans VII. v. 4–25)—Lastly, that the end of Redemption is to give birth to a Spiritual Life as the Base or Supposition of the Self-conscious Will—and that during the Process the Holy Spirit acts, as it were vicariously, in ~~in~~ administering the impulses, supports, comforts, sense of reality; i.e. Faith the *Substance* or subsistence of Things hoped for, the *evidence* (not merely the conviction of the certainty) of things not seen—which the spiritual or heavenly Life, in its full development &

maturity would have done,—and that this new & spiritual Life is ejusdem generis with the Life of Christ, the Mediator.—

All these Tenets I believe to be orthodox, and accordant with Scripture, so as not only to be compatible therewith but capable of being *probably* inferred therefrom; but I do not raise them into Articles of *Faith*. My ⟨inward⟩ Creed, as a Christian, remains without substraction or addition as it stands in the Aids to Reflection—189–191.—My outward Creed is the Apostles' as expanded in the Nicene,—save only with regard to the former, I find a difficulty in receiving as an *essential* of Faith the words "born of the *Virgin* Mary"—seeing that there is not even an allusion to any such Belief as taught or required by the Apostles in any part of the New Testament, tho' I receive it as a *point of assent* on the authority of the Church, and the certainty that it ~~is~~ was as old as ~~the~~ our copy of the first Gospel./But it would not be worth the discussion, but for the support it gives to the Romish Parthenolatry.   *f33*ᵛ

5244 20.49   Alas! the desolation from the languor of my faith in the application of the Faith to my own Soul; the want of a realizing sense or Feeling of God personal, of God as the Father of our Lord and Redeemer; and the far more deep and clinging reality of my Fears from the Law than of my Hopes from the Cross, tho' I can feel the latter vividly and affectionately with regard to others, even to the Enthusiasts converted to Methodism;—these throw a gloom over the Light that continues to ray into my mind concerning the grounds & substance of the Redemptive Act, objectively. It does not directly diminish the Light; but it quenches the lustre of its Joy.—Thus it is a great opening to me, made this evening, Thursday, September, 1825—that the *immediate* operation of the Incarnation is not in the Will or imparticipable Eιμι of the individual Person but in the generic Life, or common Nature, which is the Base and Ground of the Spirit— [and in what sense may it be that here too all is in each—the whole Human Nature numerically possessed subjectively, and yet one and the same objectively—And this, may it not in the fallen & unregenerate the Master the Spirit, & shape the *Soul* (the *Soul* ⨉ Spirit, what?) as a particular Product or *Pipe* ad per-sonandum?   *f34*

And may not the Spirit thro' the Soul affect the Nature, according to its power & freedom? And Christ, the whole in himself, & theseus the whole in all as the whole, tho' not immediately the subjectively appropriated & fragmental.]

N.B. The Sentences within the Crotchets mere shapes of Truths *advancing*, or Shadows cast before them in Twilight, and not to be confounded with the preceding Sentence—/which supplies whatever was wanting to the perfect *Morality* (i.e. compatibility with responsible Agency) of the operation of the Incarnate Word.

f34ᵛ   Important remark on the arbitrariness, & unsubstantiality, and incontinuity of the common Grotian & even Calvinist notions respecting justification, and forgiveness—drawn from a human Judge, who directs an acquittal or produces the King's Pardon. These men forget that in the effectiveness of this process in a Human Justice Court, God is the realizing Power, Copula & Continuum. Just as the Mechanic Theorists forget that the mechanism of the Watch supposes the unmechanic agency of *Gravitation*. With this view, next to the Personeity, and Holiness of God, we ought to press on his attribute of Ens realissimum—the Supreme *Reality* of God!

f41   5245   20.59

For he dwelt at large,
As gay and innocent as the pretty shame
Of Babe, that rising to the menac'd charge,   aim
With wily shiness & with cheek aglow   large
From its twi-clustringed hiding-place of Snow   shame
Tempts & eludes   charge
                                                               glow
                                                               snow
                                                               kiss
                                                               miss
                              -cove?   targe
Of Babe, that from its hiding-place of Snow
Twy-cluster'd, rising to the menac'd Charge
Tempts and eludes the happy Father's kiss
Which well may glance aside yet never miss
When the sweet Mark emboss'd so sweet a Targe

5246 20.61   I am well-pleased to ~~know~~ discover that I ~~think~~   *f₄0ᵛ*
~~and act~~ have thought or acted as men of eminence hundreds of
years before I was born—tho' I should not go as far as the Hon.
R. Boyle, who thought it necessary to justify himself for publishing (he not being a Physician)—a Book of Receipts for Poor People by the authority "of Jubar King of Mauritania, and another
King named Nechepsos."
    Mem. To *have* transcribed the interesting account of his own
lamentable state of Health in the latter half of this Preface—in
answer to the anticipated objection—Physician! why can't you cure
yourself? Add to this the similar narration of R. Baxter & then
blush & mourn at the comparison—/Power of mind over body.

5247 20.65   Of the surprizing proportion of Oxalate of   *f37ᵛ*
Lime in a variety of Lichens—ex. gr. those resembling patches of
coarse white-wash on decayed Beeches.

    the equally surprizing *Electric* Powers of Oxalate Lime = Life/
= Elect. Fluxion of organic action.

    Macculloch's Facts in favor of Matter being a product of Life.

5248 20.67   There are positions hateful to Bigots, and Lim-   *f37*
pet-Believers that will remain Truths tho' the Devil himself should
have subscribed his hoof to them. Such is Hume's remark to Gibbon respecting Macpherson's Ossian/
    When a supposition outrages common-sense, any positive evi-
dence of it ought to be disregarded. Men run with great avidity
to give ⟨their⟩ evidence in favor of whatever flatters their passions
&c! Indeed, it is incredible to me how any one who values his
character as a man of sense, should rely on testimony without or
against a priori probability, after the testimonies published in favor
of Macpherson's stupid Forgery!   —S. T. C.
    De Canone Novi Testamenti—
From Lapland to Naples were the Poems of Ossian received,
within a space of 30 years!

5249 20.66   As the Absolute Will, essentially causative of all   *f37ᵛ*
Reality + O. The Will, causative of its own Reality I = The

Father, Contemplative of all Reality in itself and in the contemplative generative II = the adequate Idea, the eternal Alterity, the Son. ~~The~~ In the mutual affirmati~~ve~~on, the Love proceeding from the Father in the eternal pouring forth into the Son, and the Love flowing forth from the Son in the eternal attribution of his Glory, even all Glory, to the Father, the circulation and choral eddying of the ~~eternal~~ Divine *Life*, the eternal Act of Communion III =

f34ᵛ + O. The ⟨Continued from 3 leaves forward, the last line of the page fronting the 3ʳᵈ leaf, the book turned—⟩ in the reverse order.—1. The Love as the prevenient Spirit. 2. The filial Alterity as the Word.—

The Will of the Chaos—its dark disactualizing, clinging ⟨Self-⟩ Contra~~diction~~riety suspended, and forced asunder to become actual

f35 as opposites—Light and Gravity. Yes! this supplies the link that was missing. Now the Life of the living Thing opens on me— what it is—and its necessary union with *Mass*—The clinging wrestle, the ~~war~~ old war-embrace of Light & Gravity renewed, but no longer in *indistinction*, but in distinct union & indivisible!—Yes, except by the return of Life to its potential state, ⟨universality⟩ and of Mass to Multeity—These are but Glimmer—the Sky-blink.— But I see that the inward Light to preserve itself distinct in its union must draw perpetual recruitage from the universal Light, which again must be united with Gravity in order to have affinity with the Mass—Light particularized—Electricity, & Negative Electricity/ − E + Carbon = oxygen Gas—. The Life of Plants— the Tides of Light, and the centro-peripherical system ⚹ Animal Life.— : : Sun : Heart. Parts resolved to one Whole. The Whole in the Part./The in-striving of each. = an eddy of all. And now the *living Soul*—what was the Life of the Adam? This is still below the Horizon for me.

Mem. I do not know any one position, even of the apparently abstrusest & most metaphysical, in my system, which has not a direct practical consequent. Ex. gr.—The WILL as incapable of being *causatively* determined ab extra = the consciousness may be removed, & the Will become *potential* only; but it must *originate* its own acts, its own state: or it is not ~~a~~ Will. Hence its oneness

with the *I Am*, as the Verb Substantive./So too, the deep and fonti-
fontal Mystery, the Antecedence (in the Idea, αχρονως) of Will to
Being—
five leaves forward, from the last line upturned   *f40*
    In this alone can we see the necessity of the eternal *possibility* of
Evil, and that its reality must be a contingency, admitting of no
other proof than the fact itself—because identic with the Act, and
thus being itself its own Antecedent, and Accountant or propter
quod. I̶d̶e̶n̶t̶i̶t̶y̶ ̶a̶n̶d̶ In ordine ad scientiam the Idea of the Fall of
the Angels, and wherein it differs from the Fall of Man is a most
fruitful Contemplation, nay, indispensable for as many, as may
not consent to rest in *implicit* truth. Lucifer would have h̶a̶d̶ ̶W̶i̶l̶l̶
taken the absolute ground up into his Will, and that his Will
should be βυσσος αβυσσου. He strove to soar above the Light, and
to have the Light under him. The Adamic Man sought to have
his Will as his Life—to *enjoy* his Will, and to u̶n̶d̶e̶r̶s̶t̶a̶n̶d̶ know
his Life. *He* was *tempted*—i.e. his fall was not purely & totally
the birth (τοκος αμητωρ) of his Will. He might be aided—As he
submitted compati, so he might will co-agere in se collevando—   *f39ᵛ*
Mem. An angel ?, in what sense Adam was perfect, he needing a
Law ab extra?

5250 20.68
    Ad Blancum Album.   *f37*
    Remember! the question is: not whether a tenable or faulty, a
refined or a vulgar, theory of an Article of Faith shall be exhibited—but whether the Doctrine, which *is* Christianity, not merely
included in it, shall be justly assailable as immoral, blasphemous,   *f36ᵛ*
and subversive of the very foundation of all morality, all religion?—For in no gentler terms can you truly describe the Dorpian
Dogma of a Bargain between m̶ God, the vindictive Creditor and
Christ, the V̶o̶l̶u̶n̶t̶a̶r̶y̶olunteer Debtor & vicarious Undertaker &
Security for the payment of the Debt.—The question, I repeat,
must be: Is there a tertium aliquid between the denial of any Redemption by Christ—for to explain the word into a metaphor is to
deny the a̶r̶t̶i̶c̶l̶e̶ doctrine—and such a sense as outrages Reason &
the clearest most unquestionable Dictates of Conscience?—

5251 20.69   Never was the law of retribution more signally displayed in a succession of events, than in the history of the Presbyterian Party in England & Scotland. Their ⟨Papistic Principle,⟩ more than Papistic Spirit of Persecution, prevented the establishment of a constitutional Monarchy under Charles I.—of a constitutional Commonwealth during the Usurpation and of a free government at the Restoration. And for each they were the main & under Charles II their own Eléve, unpitied Sufferers—The same intolerant Spirit in Scotland inclined William & impelled the Ministry of Queen Anne to force the rights of Patronage on the Scottish Church, as the only known antidote & counter-weight to the fanatical Intolerance of the Clergy & Elders—but such an antidote as Sugar of Lead to a burning fever, which it exchanges for a Dead Palsy.

f36   *5252* 20.70   Two ways, one broad, open, smooth & safe, the other foul, full of pits & chasms, & at the end narrowing & winding off into a private by-way, lie before an Historian of the C. of England. The first, the proving that the follies & remorseless cruelties of the prelatic party under the two Charleses were vices of the Individuals armed by the common errors & prejudices of their age—Persecution and the Pursuit of the Phantom, Uniformity, for the Substance, Unity—& that there is nothing in the structure or constitution of the Church that requires or even favors these evils—this is as easy as it is honorable—the other to justify the acts & extol the Characters of the Individual Agents by reviving all the party-passions & exploded principles of a past age— The latter may be the way to rise in the Church—it is a sinfully bad way to defend it ⟨raise or even to preserve it at its present height.⟩

f159   *5253* 29.181   [In *SWF* in connexion there with Notes towards Greek grammars.]

f156   *5254* 29.182   1. Physiography, or ~~an arranged~~ methodical Description of the ~~inanimate substance~~ lifeless Bodies of the Planet, Earths, Metals, Minerals, and Fossils, ~~with the (so-called) Elements of Water~~, with the ~~simple (i.e. hitherto uncompounded)~~

~~Substances~~ elementary Substances, fluid, aeriform, or imponderable, with a popular ~~Explanation of the Theory of Chem~~ Modern ~~Chemistry~~, Display of the ~~action~~ laws by which they act on each other in composition and decomposition—i.e. the Theory of Chemistry, with an history and description of the main experiments, by which it is demonstrated.—For the higher classes of Commercial Schools ⟨; and generally for those who~~extend seek~~se views require only general yet accurate Information on these subjects, or an introductory Work as the groundwork & preparative of of more ⟨Instruction or⟩ minute Research demanded for Lectures, or Profess. Purposes.⟩

2. Phytography, or methodized Description of the Vegetable Creation, ~~its~~ its Properties, Uses, Climates, &c.—and the relation of the V.C. to the lifeless and the Animal C.—with a brief statement of what is known of Phytology, or the matter and organization of Plants & the Laws of Vegetable Life.—Ditto.

3. Zöography, or Meth. Des. of An. from the infusoria or apparent Molecules to to the ~~Home Sylvestris~~ Oran-Utang and Homo Sylvestris.

4. Anthropo~~graphy~~logy, in two parts. Part I. Anthropography: or a Description of the different Races, and Varieties of Men, the effects of Climate, and Civilization: ~~to which is added as~~ Part II. Anthropogony, or the Origin of the different Races as far as Facts and just Analogies render the same ~~the subject of~~ ascertainable or the subject of probable Conjecture.

5. History in Outline of the ⟨Egyptian,⟩ Asiatic, Greek, and Roman Empires, to the Dismemberment and Partition of the Western or Latin Empires—in numbered § § s and references to the best Works & Authorities on each particular æra.

6. Ditto of Christendom considered as one federal Body, & consisting chiefly of the events effecting the interests & development of the Whole.—

f155   7. Latin ⟨Tutor⟩ (Domestic Lessons)—!

8. The principles of Universal Grammar illustrated & exemplified in a Grammar and accidence of the Greek and English Languages. Part II—Greek Lessons, methodically selected and arranged.

9. Logic—1. Logic or Syllogy. 2. Dialectic. 3. Organic or constructive & heuristic.

10. Introduction to the construing of Homer and Herodotus
⟨11. Ditto----------------Theocritus, Bion, Moschus; with changes of Style & Hexameter in the Alexandrian & yet later poets.⟩
1+2. Ditto --------------Xenophon & Herodotus
1₂3. Ditto --------------Eschylus, Sophocles, & Euripides
1₃4. Ditto --------------Plato, Demosthenes and the Greek
                                            Orators.
1₄5. Ditto --------------Thucydides
1₅6. Ditto --------------Pindar and the Lyric Poets
1617 Ditto --------------Theocritus, Bion, Moschus / with critical
                         Notices of the Alexandrian & yet later
                         Greek Poets
17. and which ought to be the very last; if indeed read at all at Schools——Hellenistic Writings, Septuagint, and New Testament

Addenda. English Grammar, from 5 years old to six, supposing, the Child begins to learn at his Letters between three and four; in the form of a Tale, entitled, The Infant R. Crusoes or the Deaf and Dumb Nurse.—
    N. B.—On paper of the width A—B, 24 of my MSS lines = 32 of Octavo, the heighth of which is equal to the breadth of the vellum Cover below, and the width from A to X.
A———————————————X—————————B
so that 384 of my lines 384 of my lines make a Sheet c512

f154   Qʸ. Has the influence of Letters, i.e. a written Alphabet and Books composed of from 20 to 26 shapes in interchange of Positions—on Languages been sufficiently considered?—

5255 29.143
Mʳ G's ⟨20 leaves onwards.⟩ *f171*
List of Desiderata in School Books ⟨14ᵗʰ Leaf from this end.⟩

5256 21½.121   *f62ᵛ*
⌐Ab⌐ *Postulate*
WILL
DEFINITION (verbal)
Will is the xyz or + o, the Ground of Being, the Suppositum,
Timeless but in the Order of Production and Conception, the nec-
essary Pre-suppositum
Or more briefly:
Will is that which ✳ originates.
Definition (real)
Will is the Subject, the sole predicate of which is to be essen-
tially causative of Reality.

COROLLARY:
Therefore and *in origine* causative of its own reality, the essential
might abiding unexhausted, indiminishable.

                                                              f63
Position
I.
The Absolute Will.
Synomines or Appellations: Abyss βυσσος αβυσσος. Τὸ Ὑπερούσιον.
*Ase*itatis principium ineffabile. *Natura* Dei. Identitas Absoluta.
Prothesis absoluta.
Position
II.
The eternal Act ~~and~~ of Ipseity, or the Self-realization of the
Absolute Will. Synonimes. Asëity. Personëity. *Alfader* (in the
Gothic) The Father Almighty. Identitas εν Θεσει. Mens absoluta.
Position
III.
The co-eternal *Act* of Alterity, or the Begetting of the Identiety
in ~~the~~ Alterity. The causati~~on~~ve Conception and Utterance of THE

✳Verb active transitive.   *f62ᶻ*

WORD—or adequate Expression of the paternal Personëity in the Person of God, in the ὁ Ὢν ~~εν τῳ κολπῳ~~ εις τον κολπον του πατρος— in the which Act the Father ~~as~~ likewise is from all eternity personal, and the Word the only begotten Son of God. INTELLIGIBILE πρωτογενες realissimum et hypostaticum Absolutæ Mentis: quód si hypostaticum sive ⟨in se⟩ self-subsistent, ergo et Intellig in ~~an~~ which, and for which, and with which the Father willeth to be τὸ

f63ᵛ Intelligibile Intelligentiae Filialis.—Thus the filial Word is Intelligibile et Mens altera—The Father = Mens et Intelligibile reciprocum. (as the Father knoweth me, even so know I the Father.—)

Synonimes. Αληθεια, και Ο αληθης. Λογος. Intellectus communicatus, communicativus, et se communicans. Deus Alter et Idem.

Scholium. If the Hebrew Word, which our Translators render Wisdom in the Proverbs, *demands* this version—we must say that before the Revelation of the Word of Christ, the Word was known only in the Spirit or Efficacy proceding thro' and from it—~~and~~ i.e. as *the* WISDOM of God, the Appellative which after the Incarnation was appropriated

f2   5257 F°.7

1 November, 1825

Semina Rerum,
viz.
Crudezze

Audita, Cogitata, Cogitanda, of a Man of Letters friendless, because of no Faction:—repeatedly and in strong language inculpated of hiding his Light under a Bushel, yet destined to see publication after publication abused by the Edingburgh Review as the Representative of one Party, and not even noticed by the Quarterly Review, as the Representative of the other—and to receive as the Meed of his Labors for the Cause of Freedom against Despoty and Jacobinism; of the Church against Infidelity and Schism; and of Principle against Fashion and Sciolism; Slander, Loss, and Embarrassment.

f2ᵛ   5258 F°.10   [11 lines "hatched" out.]

5259 F°.11

Dewdrops are the Gems of Morning,
But the Tears of mournful Eve:
Where no Hope is, Life's a Warning
That only serves to make us grieve

5260 F°.12   Clinging by exploded Points in theology & for-
tifying them anew comparable to erecting a fort in the middle of
the Strand as an outwork to the present Metropolis.

Reasons for not answering *objections* would furnish a more convincing & valuable discourse than the most ingenious answers to
them./

Six first Chapters of Daniel—I value not at a farthing the *faith*
of the man who can believe them. In fact, such belief arises from
the want of faith—missing the inward streng[th] the giddy or
drunken man grasps at and clings to a Wig-block.—

5261 F°.13   νεφερ σαυ αυι γοοδ κομ οφ δεσπονδενς—κἁμοιγε
⟨ιν αυι σωρ καλαμιτι⟩ νο κονσολατιον σο κορδιαλλεσς ας θε βωστ οφ
ἀφινγ φωρσην ιτ. ιφ ιτ πλῆς θε αλμῖτι το ϖ Fιστ με Fιθ αν ἐFFι
ἀφλικτιον, I Fουλδ σῆκ κομφορτ φρομ ἱς μερσι, νοτ μι ων Fανιτι.

5262 F°.14   Let the first Sentence be of God:—were it but   *f3*
to record my grief for the low estate of his Church forced on my
recollection by the Critique (in the last N° of the Q? Review) on
Milton's late-discovered Summary of Theology—in which Milton's ante-dated Swedenborghianism and crude anthropomorphy is
extracted with too evident approbation—for so only can I interpret
the epithet "striking" under the absence of all hint of censure. I
really shuddered as I read it. The Reviewer was, no doubt, a
Clergyman/⟨N.B. It was the Revd Millman.⟩ Could he be ignorant
that such a notion that would at once elevate the Deism of a
Shaftesbury or Lord Herbert into a necessity of faith is incompatible with the Idea of the Trinity—the sublime perfection & prominent Object of which is to effect what in no other way can be
effected, the union of ~~the~~ Personeity with ~~the~~ Infinity ~~of~~ in the
Godhead? Could he be so ignorant of of the common Analytics of

Logic as not to perceive, that Milton's words are ~~either~~ *nonsense* as applied to an Absolute Being, ⟨and at the same time⟩ a daring Contradiction of Holy Writ—which declares the *essential* invisibility of God, ὄν ουδεις (= *no* being) εωρακεν ουδεπωποτε—that as the Absolute Will, the eternal *Ground* and *Source* of all Being, God is necessarily *super*-essential?—That Fear, and Grief, like Legs, Arms, and members in organic juxtaposition, derive their *existence* from negation and limitation?—The whole passage taken in conjunction with the eternity of Matter is a strange mixture of Arianism in its crudest form with Behmenism, Spinosism & the Idolism of Swedenborg. ⟨Reduce it to any scheme of connected reasoning, by taking any one of the Positions, as a for instance First.⟩ Assume the anarchy (unbeginningness) of Matter, and Spinosism is demonstrable, with an evidence fully equal to that of Geometry, and Milton's personal God ~~is~~ becomes a Poet's fancy, utterly arbitrary, & as to which no reason can be imagined, why there might not ⟨be⟩ ~~an~~ Myriad such. But the very thought is ⟨the Shriek of a⟩ Delirium! It is curious that ~~a~~ similar Assertions have been within the last Decennium brought forward by Schelling, the reviver of pantheistic Atheism with Romish Pseudo-Catholicism for its mythologic Drapery, in lack (as he himself avows) of a better—i.e. till the Governments of the World shall be ⟨sufficiently⟩ enlightened to re-established the Theology of Pagan Greece & Rome!!—

⟨Is *Matter* one *substance*—& Thought another? If not, M. must either be an accident of T. or T. an accident of M. Which of the three will you choose. In the first, to make can only be to impress a Shape on a given portion of Matter—which may account for a *Table* or a Stone but not for a Man, no nor even for a worm. The supreme Thought might make a *Statue* that might represent the Thought's Thought of an Arch-angel, but not the Arch-angel. Is this a permeation of the Statue by the universal Thought? This might *exist* for other Angels—but the *Thought* is supposed already to know itself—& for the Arch-angel it would have no existence except as the Arch-angel knew itself to be God & not an Arch-angel—and meantime, the whole ~~difficulty whole~~ problem is presumed as solved in order to its Solution—For whence came the multëity of Thoughts in the infinite Thought? Is the latter a mere

f2ᵛ

aggregate? A mere resulting Total?—But a Total supposes a Focus in which all becomes one. If the infinite Thought is antecedent & gives birth to the several Thoughts—what is this but ⟨either⟩ *creation*, or generative Power?—Or does it divide itself into infinite Thoughts?—What becomes of the Dividend? Can the Tree divide itself into Planks—and yet be both Tree & Planks? Be split and yet remain entire?—And in the meantime what does the *matter* do? Palpably, nothing.

5263 F°.15   The longer I think, the more clearly and mani-   *f3*ᵛ
foldly do the advantages open out to me of the distinction between the *E*cclesia and the *En*clesia. Among other results, it strips our Sectarians of every pretext for the charge of Persecution. The Supreme Power of the State has determined, that there shall be Buildings in which certain Prayers &c shall be recited, for *all* to attend *that like it*; and has sanctioned certain Articles of Faith for those to subscribe, *who like*. If James or John had the will & the wealth, they might do the same/and to the extent of their wealth, the Methodist Consistory actually do so—and who withstands or blames them? Is there any Tyranny in the Parliament's *doing* what every indivdual Subject is allowed to do?—. This applies as far as men are considered as *individuals*; and as a Religionist every man stands ⟨κατα τουτον κοσμον⟩ in no other capacity than that of an *Individual*.—But as a *citizen*, a member of a collective Body, and in relation to *civil* rights, and temporal privileges, he stands on a different ground. But neither in this respect has he any right to complain, as long as the Sect, to which he has attached himself, is not numerically greater than the sum total of the Members of the *endowed* Establishment. To class all the Sects together into a multiform Unit under the name of Dissenters is a glaring Sophistry. There are certain Objects which the State for its own safety and welfare is bounden to see realized—whatever is oppugnant to these, which remain the same under all revolutions of Religion, at once disqualifies † the oppugnant party, be their comparative number what it may—but these being secured, the functionary administration ought to be conjoined with that scheme of positive Religion, which counts the largest number of the Population among its adherents—⟨nevertheless, it is an error to extend the National

Articles even of the positive Religion beyond the doctrines common to all the established Churches.—ex. gr. the Greek & Latin,
and in the latter the Romish & Protestant. A self-founded Sect, of
recent origin, & whose characteristic Tenet ~~was never~~ is exclusive
of the Universals of the Church from the beginning, is not a
Church/⟩—Suppose, there were A = 7, B = 5, C = 4, D = 3,
E = 1, F = 13—the endowed Church belongs of right to F, ~~to~~
tho' ⟨to⟩ the total number it is but as 13 to 33—& in England, I
presume, it is more nearly as 12 to 20.—The Preamble to the last
Bill for Catholic Emancipation would, beyond all controversy,
have conferred on the Irish Romanists a *right* to the Revenues &c
of the Irish Church—

f4 † This is most strikingly shewn in the effects of the contrary where
the unhappy circumstance takes place that ~~its~~ so immense a majority of the population as to constitute a virtual whole profess a religion oppugnant to the great principles of *a State*—as in Spain &
Portugal. Hence too the stationary Barbarism of Ireland/⟨Even ~~for~~
of the theological Clergy of a National Church Subscription should
be required, only to Articles of Faith common to all Churches—
but of the other departments of the Nation's Clerisy only the absence of disqualifying Tenets, and the Belief a future state, as necessary to the civilization of the Subjects.⟩

5264 F°.16   The History of a Belief another thing from the
Evidence of its Truth quomodo creditum *fuit* from the proofs of
its *credibility* And yet how often are they confounded in our modern *Apologies*, & Defences of *Xty!*—A man exhibits power not
possessed by, and wholly unparalled in the experience of his Countrymen & Contemporaries. He assures them, that this power is
not innate in him or acquired by his own ingenuity, or taught him
by any other Man; but ~~that it~~ says to them: A Being had made
himself known to me, and bidding me do, as I have done, promised me that I should perform the wonderful things which, you
see, I have performed—and then assured me, and commanded me
to assure all other man that ~~if~~ it was he who created them, and
who could in a moment destroy them, &c &c—for that he was
eternal, all-wise, all-good and all-powerful/—Now this is a very

natural & satisfactory *Cause* of the Belief in the existence of God;
but surely not an adequate Proof of the Proposition itself. Should,
however, this Belief with the Commands, Threats, and Promises
conjoined with it, act both indirectly and positively on their moral
& intelligential capabilities, to the happy development of both, it
would have been the occasion and first Cause of its *proveability*

5265 F°.17   Nothing, but the ~~consciousness of my~~ sense of
the probability of Data existing which I have overlooked, would
prevent me from asserting the incompatibility of a Trade & Commerce indefinitely increasing with cash payments—and on this
ground, I should hold that the late Speculations in Companies, and
those in Cotton are rather to be regarded as the occasion of the
present distress~~eses~~ ~~&~~ by chilling the feeling of confidence, and
preparing men's minds for a Panic—this Panic being the ~~active~~
power that sets the true cause in action.—Known Indiscretions of
Over-trading, dishonest Gambling in Shares of Bubble Companies
with great Heads of Firms, Members of Parliament, and Peers
for Directors & Accomplices, ~~sudden &~~ Defalcations & Forgeries
in men of the most confidential Professions, as Solicitors, Bankers,
&c. joined with the natural tendency of the Human Mind to contract instantaneously from the maximum to the minimum, from
the hot to the cold Fit, had produced a general fore-boding, which
it needed only a single great Failure to condense into a Panic. The
foreboding itself by impelling ~~i~~ a multitude of men at the same
time to provide against an approaching demand, produces this
Link by suddenly depressing the Funds.—Whatever A fails to
answer the demand, causes an increased pressure on B C D on to
Z—and this increases in a geometrical proportion—with every suc-   *f4ᵛ*
cessive Failure.—But still these are all occasions of the incapacity
to answer the demands being *known*, they are sufficient causes of
the *demand*, but not of the incapacity itself to answer this demand—. The preceding Terms (over-trading, gambling, defalcations) are the Flint and Steel—the Panic struck by them is *the
Spark*—but what is the Gun-powder?—Now this I find in the evident contradiction between a transferable Property = 2.00, and
a legal Representative equal only to 5.—If every quantum of bonâ
fide property transferred had its ultimate Representative, Failure

could never take place but by forgery or fraud; but if the representatives of 200 must in order to be effectual represent the 5—either the 5 must be subdivided into so many parts, and a guinea be worthy 40 or 50 times its value, and remain unaffected by its co-existing representatives in paper, which is impossible—or the ~~re~~ wealthiest man quoad bonâ fide valuables as subjects to ruin on any run as a comparative Pauper. For the Panic makes it tantamount to having 200£ to pay, and when the Creditor comes, you find that 195 of the Sovereigns are base coin & no longer current.—

It is possible that the act allowing the Country Banks to issue one Pound Notes may have prevented as much gold from being imported as would otherwise have been/still this can go but a small way ~~to~~ in answering the question—Are the precious Metals adequate to the representation of all the property transferred—. In short, the Gold will do very well, turn and turn. My neighbor owns a Tree, valued at 10£, and I take his note of hand for thirty Shillings—because I know, that the Time will come when the 10 Sovereigns will pass into his hand in the course of their circut/—But what when no man will wait for his turn? ~~When~~ Can the circulating Gold become omnipresent?—

5266 F°.18

Fungus

The fleshy highly nutritious substance, obtained by Braconnot by washing off the soluble ingredients of Mushrooms (Q? of all sorts?) in alkaline water, and which in the results of putrefaction, the disengagement of Ammonia & Azote approaches so near to animal substances—joins with the πρωτοζωα in proving the priority of Animal Life—or rather that Life is radically animal.—

Bismuth + Acetic Acid = Sympath. Ink, blackened by Sulphuretted Hydrogen

The juxta-position of Gold in fusion & melted Bismuth, in separate vessels, deprives the former of its ductility. ~~What~~ How will your Corpuscularists solve this?

f5   5267 F°.19   There are times when I could wring my hands in anguish, and ~~gazing on the~~ seeing wherever I turned either the

Arminian or the Calvinist, cry out—O take from me all—only, only leave me *my God*—the holy, loving God—and again to the Grotian & Socinian—O leave me the Reconciler—

5268 F°.20   From the earliest time I can remember, I discovered I lived with my Thoughts, as my fellow-creatures. Consequently, as must be the case with every man who is governed by self-less Thoughts, Thoughts acting in their own strength and vividness without any addition or modification from ⟨his consciousness of their⟩ being *his* Thoughts, and not by *Motives*, I was an *out-of-the-way* Being—& every thing, I did or was supposed to do, was noticed & remembered. Hence tho' to my certain knowlege I was of all my fellow-collegiates of any note, the *least* disposed to Sensual Vices—tho' I had a natural aversion—yet thousands have heard of me, as a wild Debauchee at Cambridge—In my abhorrence of pretending to be better than I was, I was afraid, or rather made a sort of *slap dash* ~~election~~ inward refusal, to appear better than *others*, of whose *hearts* I thought well—& so consented—alas! thro' the greater part of my life have at least submitted—to appear *worse!*—In Southey I first saw the dignity of setting an example—; but I should not have recognized it, if Southey had not then avowed himself a Deist and a Republican—& therefore (according to my belief) uninfluenced by any worldly or self-respecting Interests. &c

5269 F°.21   *Davison*—P. 145–155—.Not so satisfactory as the rest of this excellent Volume—.—~~On~~ For the *surface* of the Mosaic Code ~~th~~ assimilate & compare Moses & Lycurgus, the Jewish Theocracy & the Spartan Republic—The immediate object the same in both—intensity of State—the individual = O, all individuals = 1.—
    Mem. If Sacrifices were Types, the Anti-type could not be a *Sacrifice* in any other sense than as the proper name of the Type is continued into the *metaphorical* name of the subject typified. Thus Light is a Symbol of Intelligence; and Intelligence is itself called a *Light*.—. But I utterly deny that strictly speaking the Jewish *Sacrifices* ~~were~~ represented the Death of Christ; tho' they were the Shadows that mutely pointed to it—their *immediate* import was the ~~sa~~ necessity of *offering up* and (in so doing) *hallowing* (*sacra* faciens)

the *animal life* & law—the law of the Flesh. It is true that Christ did this in respect of his own nature: for he had taken on himself our infirmities—& for us all—so that he was truly both the High-Priest & the Sacrifice; but yet the High Priest was his especial ~~Anti-~~Type—the proof of this in Melchisedek, who offered no Sacrifice (Ep. to the Hebrews.) But let it not be forgotten that all then are but Pauline Metaphors of Johannonian Proprieties. How could the Conscience be more [?intangled] in one Sacrifice than another—if both actually the same?

f5ᵛ   5270 Fᵒ.22   Qʸ?—Is the condition of human vision—viz. that we can see only by *not* seeing, can see A = a Leaf of a Tree, only by not seeing α, β, γ, δ &c = the gaseous bodies that fill the interspace between it and the adjacent Leaves, and form not merely a *continuum* but an energetic, co-organized Continuum—is this Law of our Imperfection aidant to the general tendency of Man to rest in a desired *End* without enquiring after the *Means*—or else to resolve them into the *magic* of a *Will* or a *Word*, tho' this Will, this Word is for them nothing more than a written O = O that being nothing makes a *shew* of something, and blunts the craving for distinct Conception, ~~and~~ intermits the *feeling* of vacancy, and filling the air with links of Air builds a rain-⟨bow⟩ bridge for the Fancy to pass over?—But no where is this frailty displayed more glaringly than in application to that Supreme Being, whose Will from all eternity goeth forth in the Word which it begetteth and in the Spirit ever proceeding—and whose WORD is substantial, O ων, self-subsisting tho' not self-originated—and whose spirit is the Spirit of Truth, *very* power, *very* act,—το περιχωρουν the intercirculating Catena Divina of all that verily are—⟨*Essential*⟩ *Communion!*—Yet instead of adoring the perfection of the Logos, the Plenitude of Being, in whom υπαρχουσι παντες οι λογοι we make it a pretext for dispensing with all Reason, all Νομον λογικον—Of the adequate *Idea* of the Supreme Mind, ~~in~~ whom calleth ~~all~~ the Host of living Ideas his own, his *Angelos discurrentes*, to supersede all *ideas*—in short, the Order, which is the source, ground, *sufficiency* and disponent principle of all order, of the whole Harmony of means and ends, is blindly profaned into a ~~pretence~~ justification of an—I ~~I~~ know not what—confused notion of an arbitrary reasonless ~~form of~~ state and mode of Being, according to which a corrupted Will, a bedimmed Intellect, and a guilty Conscience ~~made only~~ ceases of itself, or ceases to be evil, as soon as the *name* of the Individual is struck out of ~~one~~ a Book/ and further proceedings stopt in a Court of Justice—In other words, the human incidents of a Caitiff receiving a pardon from the King at the intercession of a favored Courtier is applied, nay, say rather it is without modification *repeated* of the Salvation of a Sinner—in defiance of the whole Gospel of John, of every word *f6* relative to our Redemption recorded to have been uttered by the Saviour himself—which declares it by its strict analogy to a process which of all others is the very plentitude of means following means with ~~an infinity~~ succession that measures time and space by infinitesimals, ⟨fills what it measures⟩ and distinguishes infinitely what it *fills*.—These reflections were suggested to me while reading the noble passages in the 52 Psalm—"For thou desirest no sacrifice, else would I give it thee; but thou delightest not in Burnt Offerings. Wash me thoroughly from my Wickedness, and cleanse me from my Sin. Lo thou requirest truth in the inward parts, and shall make me to understand Wisdom Secretly."—O! would the Jew & the Unitarian say—We have only to *repent* (μετανοεῖσθαι) and God has promised to *pardon* us!—As if a μετανοια, a transmentation, were but the holding up a finger, or a nodding of the Head—the immediate consequent of a self-produced Volition/—O if these men did but reflect on the complexity of the mechanism, of the Marvellous Organism of finely linked and ⟨nicely⟩ adjusted Means necessary even to the holding up of a finger or the nodding of the Head—.—Just the same Error in the opposite extreme of Calvinism—of the Literalizers of half a dozen metaphors addressed by the wide-hearted Christ-filled Apostle, who became all things to all men if by any means he might save any, and addressed to men whose imaginations were shaped & colored by the Legal Ritual, as Insect ~~on~~ by the Leaves, on which they live and feed—the *Bargain & Purchase* Theologians—Do I start back from such men because they attribute all to the *Absolute Will of God?* God forbid!—but because while they *talk* of the Will of God, and an absolute Will, they mean nothing better than the capricious enslaved dependent Wantonnesses of *human* Choice—determinations

pre-determined by the appetites or at best by the ignorance of the
Agents, and the narrow limits of their Agency/—

5271 F⁰.23   Dʳ Davison has threshed over again the bruised,
and chopped Straw of the ? respecting the compossibility of Prescience with Free Will; but setting aside the passage borrowed from
(at least, pre-existing in) Phil. Skelton, without beating out a single additional Grain—a mournful proof of the incommunion with
IDEAS in the ablest men of the present Age.—Yet methinks, even
f6ᵛ without the Idea an acute Thinker might have seen that the difficulty lies in the antithesis ⟨(= opposition)⟩ Knowlege ⚹ Will,
which is rendered a catathesis (= contrareity) by the predicates Præ
⚹ Post—i.e. by ~~mak~~ supposing Will posterior to Knowlege. Now
if *Pre*science is a predicable of God, ~~it must~~ this objection must
hold equally good of the Divine *Will*—~~but for~~ but if ~~this~~ Prescience with respect to *this* would argue an imperfection in Deity,
why not in the case of the *human* Will.—Can the imperfection of
the Object ⟨known⟩ affect the perfection of the Subject knowing?
But if omniscience, the necessary perfection of the Eternal, remain
omniscience under the form of Eternity whatever the Object may
be—is it not evident, that the whole difficulty resolves itself into
the impossibility of *expressing* the Idea, Eternity, (i.e. presenting
it in the forms of the Understanding or Discursive Faculty) except
by two contra-dictory Conceptions?—Now this is only saying, that
Eternity is an IDEA, not a Conception—for it is the common characteristic of all Ideas.—But the truth lies deeper. The ~~true~~ real
contrariety consists in Will = Object, i.e. in making *Will* an
Object at all. A Deed, a Thought, *are* possible objects of a knowlege relatively anterior—and from the Deed, the Thought, the
Will may be certainly known. The mistake lies in supposing Contingency to be the necessary character of ~~Free~~ Will or *Free* Agency/
for if so, God could not be *free*. Are or are not, all things simultaneously present to God—Is, or is ~~there~~ not, his knowlege always
~~and~~ equally certain? If so, and if God knows his own Will & yet
that remains free, why should his certain knowlege of *our* Will be
incompatible with its freedom? Its *presentness* to God is not affected
by its finiteness or evil Nature—.—There is an Equivoque in the

term, or rather a confusion in Man's Notions of Necessity—God's Will is necessarily free by virtue of its own absoluteness—the Devilish Will necessarily bound by force of its own predestinating self-determination. Properly speaking, Freedom of Will is one and the same with co-incidence with the Will of God—as far as it is ⟨one with this,⟩ it is known with all its products in the same Light in which God knows his own Will and Works—as far as it is not, it is a necessitated Will, the necessary tendencies of which are known to the Omniscient in the absoluteness Will of itself/but the direction is given by the Machinery in which & by which it is permitted to manifested ⟨itself⟩—but this is of God alone—. Consequently, its products are equally capable of being pre-calculated as the movements of the Planets. In either case therefore God's knowlege & (relatively to our conceptions of ourselves relatively to God) his *Fore*knowlege is certain—in the one case, as the Will is known as the *Subject*, in the other ⟨fore-known⟩ as an *object*.—The question—but how is it fore-known that Herod or Judas should ⟨be⟩ the Individuals whose Will was evil—is senseless.—The evil Will constituted itself Judas here and Herod there.—Finally, the Disputant will complain that I have not enabled him to *understand* the *f7*
matter better than he did before—And that is very true. I cannot enable him to smell Music or hear a color. Eternity and Eternal Things are not Objects of Understanding Conception—but pass all understanding./

5272 F°.24   For the instruction of a large School, on certain days of the Year, Experimental Lectures are appointed by the Founder, to give the Scholars an insight into the Laws of Statics, Magnetism, Electricity, &c.—Now in process of time a crazy School-master, utterly ignorant of Physics, taught the Boys to suppose that ⟨to⟩ these *particular* Experiments the Power of Gravity, or of Magnetism, was confined—. That Gravity Magnetism, ex. gr. *meant* nothing more than this ⟨one⟩ most marvellous and super-magical Manœuvre, monthly repeated before their eyes/and if the Manipulator had not said, Hocus Pocus, even this would not have been what it is.—This is a coarse but just elucidation of the Romanist, (alas ! not alone the Romanist's) management & notion of the Eucharist ! ~~What~~ As the Mariner's Compass ~~is~~ to the Law and Theory of Magnetism, so the Texts of Institution in Matt. Luke, Paul to the VIth Chapter of the Gospel according to John.

5273 F^{o}.25   Mem. With delicacy to urge on Mr Hurwitz the utter, the monstrous improbability that such an event as that of Christianity and Christendom, an event so intimately inwoven and co-organized with the dispersion of the Jewish People, should have formed no subject of Prophecy—which yet, if the Christian Interpretation of the Prophets be false, ~~might~~ will be the *fact*. Yet what were Nineveh, Babylon, &c compared with this event?

5274 F^{o}.26   MEMENTO. ⟨Hints of Thoughts⟩ for an Epitaph on Wordsworth for whoever capable and worthy therof shall survive him—long, I trust, after *my* interment!

As the virtue from the Apostle's soul passed to his shadow, and consecrat~~eding~~, gave healing power to, ~~his~~ the meanest robes, ~~let this and as the rent and battered Banners of ancient Victory &c~~ so let the dropt Vesture, the prophetic Mantle of the Vatis abrepti remain honored and undisturbed like the battered & rotting Banners of ancient Victors, ~~nor and~~ and disappearing yet communicated to the *fixed Spot* ~~a~~ holy influences—*Memorial* needs he none— He in ~~our we~~ his works survives. Not to the *Earth*—that too will pass away—but to the *place*, the sole immortal Attribute κ' ἀσωμα-τον τῆς σωματικης φυσεως—and in the utter perishing of all recall to the thoughtful Bard the imperishable Life of THOUGHT and sacred Song—of all Emotions that these to belong—& the immortal *Superstitio* (survival) ~~with~~ of all lovely *things* in the Imagination!—

f7^{v}   5275 F^{o}.27   Poor—embarrassed—sick—unpatronized, unread—/~~Yet~~ But (replied the soft consoling Friend) *innocent.*—I felt only as one that recoils—& sinful dust and ashes that I am— groaning under self-reproached inproaches!—*I* innocent?—.—Be thankful still! (repeated the same so sweet Voice) you are an *innocent* man—Again I draw back but as a little child from a *kind* Stranger,

but without letting go of the Stranger's hand/—"You have the child-like Heart.—Ah but even in boyhood there was a cold hollow spot, an aching in that heart, when I said my prayers—that prevented my entire union with God—that I could not *give up*, or that would not give *me* up—~~a snake~~ as if a snake had wreathed around my heart, and at this one spot its Mouth touched at & inbreathed a weak incapability of willing it away—/—Never did I more sadly & sinkingly prostrate myself in sense of my worthlessness—and yet, after all, it was a *comfort* to me—/My innocency was a comfort—a something, for which that was the name, there were which I would *not* resign for Wealth—Strength—Health—Reputation—Glory—/—Hence I learnt—that a sinful Being may *have* an innocence/ ~~but not his own yet not so innocent~~ I learnt, that the Skirt of Christ is nearer to a Man than his own Skin! For that *spot* ~~upo~~ in my heart even my ⟨remaining &⟩ unleavened *Self*—all else the Love of Christ in and thro' Christ's Love of me!

S.T.C.

5276 F°.28   As rationally might I ~~ackn~~ assert a Tree to be a Bud, as Bp. Berkley ~~that~~ Perception ~~is Sens~~ to be Sensation—which is itself but the minumum, lowest grade, or first manifestation of Perception. In the covers & blank Leaves of my Copy of Schelling's System des Transcendentalen Idealismus I have proved this succinctly yet clearly—But the occasion of the error deserves notice: for it applies to many other Schemes besides the Berkleian—Instead of resting at the *real* Minimum, it was carried downward by the imagination, or rather by an act of the will, to the extinction of all *degree*—and yet thought of as still *existing*. The true Logic would in this Case have been, Perception diminishing from its Minimum (in which it is called Sensation) into an absolute O, Sensation becomes = O—but no!—this hypothetical *sub*minimal Perception = O is still some*what*, viz. an ens logicum; and this, ~~by a common trick~~ the proper Offspring of the unitive and substantiating function of the Understanding is ~~taken as~~ by the imagination projected into an *ens reale*—or *still more* truly ~~as~~ a strange ens hybridum, betwixt real & logical and partaking of both—namely, it *is*; Yet it is, not as this or that but as *Sensation in genere*, Sensatio *per se*. i.e., the Perception surviving its annihilation† borrows the name, by which ⟨in⟩ its *least* degree it it had been distinguished, and commences a new *Genus*, without Species or individua—

⟨N.b.—The error here noted is only one of a host, that necessarily arise out of having but *one* starting point—viz. the lowest, instead of descent from the Highest & Ascent from the lowest, at once—⟩

f8   Berkley does at last but transplace the Subject. By little and little he familiarizes his fancy to the contemplation of himself, as a Soul, & this Soul as a Canvas, a recipient of an impressive power from without—& therefore, as an OBJECT.—But ~~if in~~ in this process ~~the~~ and relatively to the contemplative faculty both are *without*, X the impressed no less than Y the impressor—both are *Objects*—the true *Subject*, which contemplates both being the very I, which was to have passed *out*, ~~of~~ and for which the *Soul* answered, Here I am I—like the Bean on the Fire in the Faery Tale of the Bee & the orange-tree—but not an inch had the true Simon Pure stirred—for this plain reason, that it could not pass out of itself!—

Here we have a striking proof & instance of the difference between the ground and the condition: The *ground* of Consciousness, i.e. that which every act of Consciousness supposes, is the Identity ⟨or Indifference⟩ of Object and Subject; but the indispensable Condition of becoming conscious is the Division or Differencing of the *Subject* and *Object*—. When we say, that I = Subject-Object, we mean only, that I is that ⟨which⟩ polarizes into Subject ⟩⟨ Object—just as the Electric Principle is that which manifests itself in the two opposite yet corresponding Forces of Negative and Positive Electricity.—So that the Principle is *antecedent* to both, and contains both a priori—and not as a compound of both, the *result* of the union of − with + , or the quotient of the addition of the one to other.—

† or—Perception, which in its narrowest sphere and in its minimum of energy is called *Sensation*, sinks below *this* & becomes = O; but surviving its own annihilation borrows its last agnomen, or *Degree*-name, takes it for its proper Surname & commences a Genus per se—

5277 F°.29   The Error, which 20 years ago I noted in Warburton's Alliance of Church & State, prevails generally in the theological reasoning of that & the preceding Age— It may be thus
stated—The balance of the Pro and Contra dipping in favor of the
Pro, I receive X as the more probable—and I am disposed to
believe—Well, then! (says the Divine) if X be true, then Y must
be true—and if Y, then Z—Stop, Stop!—this will do where X is
all, absolute & certain Truth—& where Y is either false, or likewise unmixed & absolute Truth—It will do in *Mathematics*—but
not *here*—
  Ex. gr.—If the Proofs that God dictated every syllable of the
Bible had been mathematical—*then* it would follow, that we had
no right to trouble ourselves further than simply to understand the
meaning of the *Words*/to believe & as far as they are practical, to
obey. Tho' Even so I do not, I confess, see how we should have
advanced a hair's breadth in *faith*. For I began with the full belief
of the Veracity of God—& if in the words dictated by him there   *f8ᵛ*
is contained a Position, to which I either attach *no* meaning, or an
apparent contradiction—when I say, I nevertheless believe it—
what more can this mean but that I believe that God cannot and
will not deceive—And such must often be the case between a du-
tiful Child & his Father.—. But alas! the *Verity* (Supreme Reason)
is no less an attribute of God than Veracity—and the absence of
contrariety to reason was *presumed* by me, as Condition & a component part of the evidence, on which my Belief of the divine
dictation of the Book rested—In short, the so called plenary inspiration of the Canonical Writings neither is, nor possibly can be, a
mathematical axiom, or equivalent thereto—but the expression of
a Balance—
  Pro = 10
  Contra 6
  _____
  Balance 4.
  4 〈—10 to six〉 represents the Belief—/not true ⚹ false—

5278 F°.30   Compare the new London with the London of
Shakespear: and *then* compare Shakespear's

How London doth pour forth her citizens!
The Mayor & all his brethren in best sort
Like to the Senators of th' antique Rome
with *our* associations with the L.M., Ald. & *Common Council*!—

5279 F°.31   ⚹ correspondent *opposite of* ⚹ *contrary to*

5280 F°.32
SENSE.

Allow me by a *fleaing* (or flaying) Abstraction, ⟨and Sky-like Grasp of⟩ ~~the~~ generalization ⟨to reduce⟩ ~~the whole world of human Consciousness to the Participle Active and Passive of the verb Percipio, Contemplor, Ago: two Classes or kinds, opposed (as Correlatives) or Correspondent Opposites~~ all things, the whole *Tot* of the Universe which may be expressed by the Active and Passive Participles of Percipio, ~~Contemplor~~ Cogito, Ago/~~and or the like. Whatever I think of, as either Ens percipiens, Ens Contemplans, Ens or Agens, or Res percepta, res contemplata, res acta (i.e. acted on)—or more briefly either *ns* or *um*.—Ens Contem. Or more briefly, whatever I think of, is either *ns* or *um*—. Ens contemplans ⚹ Ens Contemplatum—or~~ ⌐. . .⌐—~~the former—~~
We will unite the two first, viz. percipio & cogito in the verb Contemplor—and the ~~part~~ active participles Contemplans, Agens in the term, Subject, the two correspondent passive participles, Contemplated, Acted on, in the term *Object*.—

The whole World of human Consciousness is ~~as far a~~ Subject or Object—and as ~~the~~ each is the Correlative or Correspondent Opposite of the other, we obtain the formula—World = Subject ⚹, Object.—~~New But it will~~ ⟨Here perhaps you will remind me, that⟩ it may and often does happen, that A and Z, ex. gr. Bride & Bridegroom are reciprocally Objects to each other. The Subject A is an Object to Z, and the Subject Z an Object to A. Whether this be so or not, we ~~must waive~~ shall see hereafter. ~~& for~~ For the present, We are considering the abstract relation alone: and in order to facilitate this, ~~we will enforce ourselves to for the former in the singular number yet,⟩~~ put the position thus ~~For each Individual Contemplant, the World is Subject ⚹ Object—/..~~ we will take A in the singular number exclusively, while Z may indif-

f9

ferently stand for Object, or Objects— ~~The Position may and may~~
so that our Formula thus qualified will be—For each Individual
Contemplant the World is A $\times$ Z, i.e. Subject $\times$ Object or
Objects./—/.

This premised, I say that SENSE consists in thinking of the Subject in determinate reference to ~~th~~ Objects, and of Objects in the
like reference to the Subject— ~~or and consequently~~ which of course
implies a Comparison of the one with the other. Now before ~~A~~
~~can be any thing A (the Subject)~~ any thing can be compared with,
or opposed to, another ⟨ex. gr. A ~~the Subject~~ to Z,⟩ it must have
been *distinguished*, i.e. ~~seen and considered~~ looked at by itself, ~~or~~
and contemplated severally —: ~~The Sub~~ And that which is contemplated is ipso facto an Object—& therewith no longer in correlative opposition—: The solution of this difficulty is—that for A to
be opposed to Z, it must be previously an Object & so far = Z;
But an Object for itself alone. A to and for A is A = Z; but ⟨in
reference⟩ to BZ, CZ, DZ, EZ, FZ, &c ad infinitum it is simply
A. Thus ⟨we have⟩ A, ~~which the~~ a Subject, which may be an
Object to itself, & consequently a Subject-Object, but ~~in a Subject~~
in all other relations, a Subject exclusively/— ~~It is therefore Now~~
~~such a Subject~~ —The Subject rises into ⌈. . .⌉ Mind—i.e. a Subject that ~~consists~~ is capable of becoming an Object to itself while
the Act, by which this capability is realized, and ~~the Mind so~~
~~acting~~ is expressed by the words, I Am; and the Mind so acting is
an *I*.

N~~ot~~either the Mathematician absorbed in the contemplation of
geometrical Diagrams, or ~~of~~ (that I ma~~d~~y add the ⟨~~outward~~⟩ tangible *outwardness* to the visual, and substitute the ocular for the
intuitive) not the ~~for~~ ardent Botanist, or Mineralogist, *totus* in illo,
on the one hand; ~~and~~ not ⟨on the other⟩ the Devotee or Pietist
brooding over and with psychological subtlety watching and recording the process & movements of ~~his~~ the self-conscious Being,
he calls his Self—is the Man of *Sense*. Neither character is what
we mean, when we say of this or that person, he is a Man of *sound*
Sense/ ~~&~~ or when we commend a line in a poem, or a remark in
Conversation/—There is SENSE in that !—or it is marked by strong
Sense./

The *Subject* must be contemplated in a determinate reference or

relation to an *Object* or *Objects*, & the Object observed and scru-
tinized in its existing or possible relations to a Subject (it is indifferent, whether it be the Contemplant's Self or others of which this
is the Standard & index—in order to *Sense*.—This is in fact the
true import of the Word:—for the human ~~Subject~~ "I Am" ~~when~~
as known in the act of Self reflection, is expressed in the formula,
I affirm myself—*Ipse* me pono—the *I* representing the Subject, &
the *myself* the *Object*, ~~&~~ while the Ειμι, or Sum, is the Identity of
both/Now as the I is the perpetual & universal Nominative, so is
the myself the universal Accusative (Categorical, Objective) Case
of the primary and only *Substantive*—all other Objects being but
f9ᵛ   so ma~~g~~ny *Adjectives*, or qualifications, & modifications of this *primary* and Substantial *Object*.—And bear in mind, that ~~I~~ the phrase
"all other Objects" includes all other Subjects. Strictly speaking
these are not perceived but *inferred*—but were it otherwise, yet for
the I, the Percipient, they would be Objects.—Conceive the primary Object as a Proteus, modifiable into a thousand forms, and
each form an exponent, a representation, of a somewhat that is *not*
myself.—Or if you can, conceive, a self-conscious self-sentient
Looking-glass, or plate of Wax—by and ~~of~~ in itself it would come
to the knowledge of, or to speak with severe accuracy, to an inevitable sciential *faith* in, forms that were not itself. This is *me* but
not *of* me, is the ~~common~~ logical Premise of every Conclusion, or
~~progress~~ advance in the whole progression, ~~of~~ and enlargement of
our Experience. Now the conversion of the Subject (= I) to the
Objects represented as if they were the Object represent*ant*, and
thus to contemplate the former in the place of the latter—and then
to compare them with the Subject ~~(that is the) containing identity
of Subject & Object~~ that includes the Object, that is, with itself—
these two Acts constitute *Sense, in kind*—and when correctly performed, *Sound* Sense, *good* Sense &c—/—1. ~~I con~~ Having contemplated myself as them, I compare myself with them—2. I compare
them with myself—He who does this aright, is a Man of *Sense*.

P.S. The term "myself" is used, and of necessity, in two
Senses—the first, the artificial & philosophic, that which few are
capable of, and which can be obtained only by an act of the will
and an energy of the productive Imagination—I must abstract
from all impressions, and leave only the attribute of impressibil-

ity—from all perceptions, and leave only percipiency—& so on till I obtain an idea of myself, as the Subject, Substance, Natura gemina quæ fit et facit, format et formatur—infinitum semper finitum, Finitum fines suos nunquam non affirmans et denegans, ponens et sublevans.—Second, the myself as modified by the circumjacent Objects irremoveable, and of closest proximity—organic body, language &c—Yet even of these we do not, when we task ourselves to speak precisely, say—They are *I*, or myself—; but they are *mine*.—It is my body—this is my Voice—my language—/—

Finally, all the preceding Disquisition is *no* proof of Sense—/ —For *Sense* would have made me see that simply to have said that "Sense consisted in thinking both of yourself, and of all other things, for a~~determined~~ some practical purpose suggested and determined by comparing your wishes and intentions with the Objects, in or by which they are to be realized—& both with your powers & your ul~~tima~~terior ends—/ is all, that your Hearers or   *f10* Readers want or would listen to—.—

α. Reflect on your powers, and seek to bring your wishes and aims into distinct Consciousness—

β. in reference to & comparison with (~~and~~ = in their possible relation to) the Objects, on which those powers may be exercised, and in or by means of which those Wishes and Aims may be realized.

γ. Vice versâ, contemplate & then distinguish for closer consideration & investigation the Objects in their actual or possible relations & proportions to your powers, opportunities, aims, duties and aspirations.

~~To~~ α taken singly, characterizes the Psychologist or the Devotee of Quietism: γ (i.e. the contemplation & investigation of Objects) ~~taken singly~~ taken singly ~~&~~ or in reference to the *universal Subject*, the Reason (i.e. for the purposes of Science) constitutes the Naturalist.—

But α, β, γ, ζ taken conjointly gives the Man of Sense—Knowing for the sake of Knowing (or Knowing having Knowlege for its end & final Cause) = Science: ~~Knowing for the sake of Being, where the Being (in relation to that) which concerns or~~ where ~~the interests of the latter~~ determine ~~and direct~~ the kind and degree of the former

~~in reference proper to to the essential concerns of~~ In short, Knowing ~~for the sake of K~~ having knowlege as its final cause is Science.
Kno~~wing~~ ~~when the~~ for the ~~purpose of true~~ sake of Being, in exclusive reference ~~that~~ to ~~that which concerning~~ all *personal* Being
~~(concerns the individua~~ i.e. the concerns common to all men, as
Men

In short, Knowing for the sake of Knowing is Science: Knowing
for the sake of Being ⟨is Sense.⟩ If in exclusive reference to ~~your~~
the responsibility of *personal* Being, it is the *Moral* Sense—to the
peculiar interests of the Individual, it is what we call good Natural
Sense—The perfection of human Nature arises where the first is
allowed to be an end but yet in subordination to the second, as the
alone *ultimate* end, and where this second ~~elevates~~ existing in combination with the third elevates ~~it~~ & takes it up into its own class
by the habit of contemplating ⟨both the common &⟩ the peculiar
Interests of *all* Individuals, as far as they be within his sphere of
influence, as his own individual Interest—Here we have the Man
of ~~Principle~~ practical Rectitude, ~~in whom~~ with right Principle pre-
scribing the Rule, Discretion determining the Objects, and Judgement ~~appli~~ *applying* guiding the application. ~~If~~ He seeks his own
happiness, and he seeks the happiness of his Neighbors, & he seeks
both in such a way and by such means as enables him to find each
in the other.—

Pass the Subject into ~~the~~ an Object— = Objectivize the Subject
so as that the Object shall reflect the Subject = Subjectivize the
Object. See yon Block of Marble—What is *to me*? An unconcern-
ing Alien, a mere ~~not me~~ negation of myself, that ~~send repelling
the~~ *out*~~ward light from its surface sends unmeaning Messages to
my eyes but~~ *Like* ~~in repelling sends refracting~~ sends the Rays of
Light ~~sends them as mute messages, to that my eyes, & whose only
messages so~~ with the unmeaning message of their own repulsion
but absorbs and stifles ~~the~~ every ray from the mind!—

Behold yon Statue!—It is Phidias's Jupiter!—See yon Marble
Bust! It is Chantrey's Wordsworth!—~~Shall I look at it as an~~ Who
is he that gazes on it? A young Artist—The delight, the admira-
tion, the entire Complacency in the work awakes aspirations in his
Soul, that ~~yield~~ reveal to him the potential *Chantry* in his own
Being!—And the ~~p~~ Youth beside him?—A youthful Poet! What in

f1o^v

that profound Forehead, what in the ~~artistic~~ spiritual Breathing from the whole Countenance does he find less than his own Soul in its inmost Communion with the Heights & Depths of ~~Humanity~~ Nature & Humanity—The surrounding Shell of his accidental individuality becomes transparent—the ~~fair~~ divine Form from within his shone thro' it—& he beholds it reflected here as from a mirror!—Is a word intelligible of itself, or only ~~in deference to~~ by virtue of an idea in the soul of him that hears it, & which the word awakens?—A lovely Child contemplates his form in the Mirror & believes it another—& even so thro' Love & Self-oblivious Admiration of ~~the~~ Excellence without, we have sought the existence of the excellence in ourselves, & in what it consists, & ~~how~~ where to ~~distin~~ seek for it & how to recognize it.—Nobly & exquisitely has Plotinus represented the Actual Soul as the Sculptor, and our its potentiality as the Marble, rising imperceptibly into the majestic Statue, in which as in a mirror it may first behold & then adorn itself—/ ~~a looking-glass of such~~ Still as it works, the material gives way & hides itself, till at length it becomes a mirror of such magic fineness, that the reflecting Surface is ~~invisible~~ lost, & the reflection alone beheld—

~~For surface the Subject is to an Object, and the Object shall return it with itself~~

Chantrys of Wordsworth :: as when a Musician sings the words of an inspired Poet ~~blended with~~ to music of his own composition—we have two Poesies in one.

Sense, concluded from p. 16.   *f1 2ᵛ*

If then *Sense* ~~consists in~~ in its excellence consists in the duly proportional reference of the Subject to an Object, and of Objects to the Subject, what is it that leads the Subject to refer the Object to itself *reflectively*. A pre-existing specific excitability in the Subject, to which any given Object stands in the relation of Excitant, would produce Appetite, not Sense. The Subject would transfer itself into the Object, would be *lost* in the Object/and one of the Co-factors would disappear—& since neither exists, as S. or as O., but in opposition to, and therefore under the condition of the Co-presence of the other, both would disappear. Nor yet would a   *f13* general Sensibility, a high degree of *Life* as Self-finding: for here the Object would be lost ~~in~~ or be dimmed in the Subject/But yet there may be a general susceptibility, conceived as the consequent of a specific excitability during the latency or dormant state of the Excitement—(ex. gr. the State produced by Puberty, and the permanent sympathy of the whole nervous system, of the entire Organismus, with the *potential* Appetite, or the excitability of the specific Organs). Now the Susceptibility even, when actualized, must not be in so high a degree, as to become itself an object of reflection/nay, while it is strong enough to awaken the mind to the Subject generally, yet originating in a specific excitability conducted and as it were pointed, toward an outward Object by specific Organs thereto appropriated, it can only be satisfied by a reciprocity of reference—and the Sensibility itself, tempered & diffused, will not attract attention to itself but simply, like a medicated Atmosphere, predispose the Mind, ~~where there one is presented~~ whichever of the two Object or Subject, be presented, instantly to reflect ~~in the other~~ it in reference to the other—. And such a Sensibility would be the condition and antecedent Ground of *Sense*.—

COROLLARY. The mere *Man of Sense*, and who is at all times the Man of Sense, would be a thriving Banker, a useful Homme d'Affaires, the Executive Trustee, ~~for~~ where the Rule & Scheme had been predetermined by higher minds, but leaving a discretionary power for the application/in brief, he will be a person whom all judicious men will greatly *value*, but whom none will love, admire, or honor.

f11   5281 F°.33   *Mem*

The *healthful positiveness* of compleat polarity, instanced in that chasm between the Subjective and the Objective, which *visual* sunshiny Outness in the latter gives.—Hence the importance of the *Historical* in Revelation, the Contingencies of Time & Place, Miracles &c./—Hence the pernicious effect of Convents & all the daily from year to year Routine of Religion—By unvarying Custom it so bedims the Outness as to end in removing the oppositeness of ~~mental~~ common & determinal Space, to mental, of impressions to thoughts & dreams.—Whence the uninjuring sanity of Mathematics, and in Mathematics the superior Sanity of Geometry but that the diagram on the paper or slate is a sufficient represent-

ative of, & identifiable with & therefore substituable for, the
mental intuition—while the contrary is the case with the metaphy-
sician/—

N.B.—The preceding in the mouth of a partizan of the Mant
& D'Oyley System/—it is the Truth on *one* side. The answer to
it, as far as it wants an answer, is contained in the term, *polarity.*
To preserve the HEALTHFUL Outness of the Objective there must
be an answering intensity of the Subjective. *Objective* Virtues (ex.
gr. the substitution of Utility for Honor & The Awe of the invisible) not less unhealthful & more pernicious than Subjective images: and with regard to actions the mischief is equal, whether
wholly objective (i.e. without inward impulse and principle) or
wholly subjective—i.e. the struggles of a Faquir or Animal
Magnetist to act on himself productively.—

Query. Whether more confusion, than is compensated for by
the occasional Convenience, does not arise from the ~~use~~ application
of the term "subjective" ~~for~~ to the illusive accidents of individual
Sensibility ~~They may be defined as effects the Causes of which are~~
~~either in cases where Effects of Causes existing in the same subject~~
~~Individual or acting on that~~ as Cases, ~~when the Cause exists in and~~
~~effect co-exists in the (same) Individual as well~~ as the *Effect*—or
where Effects ~~of Causes exist residing~~ in the ~~same~~ I—or the anomalous Cases, where ~~the~~ Causes† ~~Effect co~~-existing in the individual
produce effects, ~~exist and b for~~ ordinarily and regularly produced
by outward and general causes.

† The operation of which is confined to the Individual—whether
in his ~~Organs~~ Body, as in the case of ⟨Phantoms from⟩ turgescence
in the Blood-vessels of the Brain, or out of the Body as where
Colors & Shapes arise from a Blow in the Eye.—This therefore I
would denounce as an erroneous application of *Subjective*—& injurious inasmuch as it interferes with a connected evolution of the
right Senses from the primary Sense—For as soon as the Subject
~~is an~~ive ⟨is spoken of the peculia of⟩ this or that Individual, there
is no use in the word at all—/—Except the Object which is one
with the Subject, & therefore properly *subjective*, all others are
mere distinctions of this side & that side of the Item, in relation
to the metaphysical Subject all equally extrinsic. But what the Sub-

f₁ ₁ᵛ ject-Object, independent of and antecedent to all modification ab
extra, can only be inferred by the properties common to all Subjects of the same Genus—i.e., to Mankind at large ~~and the~~,. For
tho' each *I* must be assumed as essentially individual, essential Individuality is a Transcendent, and not the subject of Thought.

5282 F°.34   I consider the Syllogistic Logic as essentially
empirical in respect of its Preconcessi et Presuppositi—i.e. that it
takes for granted the facts of ~~A~~ Unity and Multëity, Singular and
Plural, no less than the principles of Identity and Alterity.—Consequently, instead of saying with Schelling that in the Position
(*Satz*) Tygers are brindled, the Subject *Tygers* represents the Object, and the Predicate "brindled" the Subjective, I should say that
the I (= Subject-Object), the *individually* self-felt (tho' not at that
moment ~~self~~-adverting *to* its *distinctive* individuality) Ego may attribute to that which it assumes as *really* existing and yet existing
as *non*-ego, its own Subjectivity yet not its egöity (i.e. Subject
objective for itself—)—. And that accordingly Tygers is ~~the~~ a
presumed Subject rendering itself objective by the Predicate
"Brindled".—Schelling's error is ως εμοι δοκει that he includes the
Logic, the ratiocination, the *formal* science, to the MAJOR—Now
the Major is the mere *Rule* generalized from the Particular Fact,
by the Understanding—/—The *Minor* the application of this Rule
to a Particular—But the *Logic*, the *Reason*, is in the *Ergo*, and in
the Form of the whole—Clusion, Inclusion, Conclusion = Logic/
But ~~the~~ neither the Clausure, nor the Included, is logical when
taken singly.—
        P.S.—. This is not intended to deny that for the Scientia
Scientiæ, or ⟨Science of⟩ Transcendental Construction, the Logical
Subject & all other Subject but the pure I must be regarded as the
Objective ~~derived~~ included in ⌈. . .⌉ the ~~true~~ *object* which the Subject *is* for itself.—The Transcendental~~ist~~ I *gives* its ⟨own⟩ Objec-
tivity by ⟨the same⟩ imaginative projection, ~~whic~~ with which it
constitutes the Space, the *Outness*, that it peoples ~~in~~ therewith.—
The Logical Subject accepts an indefinite multitude of co-existing
Subjects, and then predicates of each that by which it renders itself
objective generally, and that particular Object for the ~~Logic~~ Pre-

dicator, and the particular Subject which it is in itself. Every Object, fo of which reality is affirmed, supposes a *Subject*; but not necessarily a Subject that is an Object for itself.

A very faulty *Syllogism* may be an excellent Guess, and a very *f12* rational ground for Belief. Ex. gr.—All Tygers are brindled:—This beast is brindled: Therefor, this Beast is a Tyger—is a lame Syllogism—To be cogent it ought to be, All brindled Beasts are Tygers: this Beast is brindled—Therefore, this is a Tyger—Nevertheless, if I had never seen a Tyger but heard that it was a large animal, brindled, & therein different from the Leopards that are spotted—& then saw an Animal pass by that was brindled—I should have good reason for *conjecturing* that it was a Tyger—

5283 F°.35   A vast difference between man & man is exprest in saying, that for A I am = I is an identical or analytical position, while for B it is a synthetical, and presupposeds an I)(I, i.e. I as thesis and I as Antithesis.—A Is this a barren *scholastic* refinement?—Then one the difference between the Unitarian & the whole Catholic Church in all its denominations, Greek & Latin, Romish & Protestant, is a barren refinement/For the whole difference is reducible to this, that the Unitarian confounds & the Orthodox distinguishes the terms *Same*, and *one*.

An analytic position is A = abc: for a b c is what I meant by A.—A Synthetic always supposes a previous antithetic position—viz. A)(B—or Object = B is the Antithesis of Subject = A.—But A = B = I Am is a Synthetic Position—viz. Subject is opposed to Object; but in the Synthesis, I" Subject = Object—or I as Subject is one with I as Object.

In the ordinary man the I is exclusively a Subject, the Object being always diverse or a *not-I*.—a Table, a Tree, a Neighbor &c—In the Philosopher the Subject by a mysterious Act of self-construction becomes an Object for itself—All men are Conscious: few Men truly *self*-conscious.

I do not yet see into the force of Schelling's reasoning—which with all his disguises renders limitation succession, sense of imperfection in each present act essential Conditions of an *I'M*. Methinks, I have the same right & far better reason for climbing a

step higher, and from his transcendental to infer a transcendental
Absolute Will, as the Identity of Act and Agent—in whose supreme Reality Actual & Potential are one.

5284 F°.36   Weakness of the Argument in defence of Popery—not to judge of the Church by the Vices of Men—for here
the Church is not as in Scripture, the Religion but the Hierarchy—/

f12ᵛ   5285 F°.37   29 Novʳ 1825. A selfish character—as Colonel
Delmour in the Novel, called, the Inheritance—o̶r̶ I see in this,
and in many other excellently drawn Portraits what it is; but I do
not yet see, *how* it is, or in what it consists. A direct conscious
reference to themselves, as *them* in distinct contra-distinction from
others, as as this or that but nakedly as *others*, it cannot be. Is it
that which being interpreted would be this: but which yet is that
which it is, only because it is *not* interpreted—⟨not brought⟩ into
consciousness?—How does it begin? In fear? in a *strangeness* of the
Objects to them, as utter aliens which nothing within themselves
goes out to meet—& which therefore repel them or the̶i̶r̶ blind
feeling or complex o̶f̶ & habitude of image & feeling which constitutes their *Self* for them/the sight of their limbs, the sensation
of their body &c—? I do not understand it: but I suspect, that this
is the Clue. Never acted on by the Objects & Persons without,
they a̶r̶ have no *Subjectivity* for them/they are ever more & more
Objects, to the exclusion of the true *self*-consciousness, in which
the Subject becomes an Object for itself—. They are objectless
Subjects; even as the "All others" are subjectless Objects for
them—. Selfishness implies the want of Self-consciousness. *Test*
this by living over a Colonel Delmour in your own imagination.
The very phrase—What an Object!—Yes!—the *dread of becoming
an Object*. In splendour and high Fashion I *act* on others—they
Contemplate me as *acting* on them. I am the *Subject* of their admiration—not the Object of their pity or contempt or even of any
attention which originates in themselves—as a common-place
thing, that they turn their attention to—. But the *Betty* in Mʳˢ
Bennet's Beggar-Girl—will my theory apply to this—?
    In short, we do not think of an Animal as selfish—nor of an

Angel as having the Virtue opposed to Selfishness—It lies somewhere between the Animal, ⟨as he is,⟩ & the Man as he should
be—more than the former, short of the latter.

5286 f°.38   "Das Ich empfindet indem es sich selbst als ur-   *f13*
sprünglich begränzt anschaut. Dieses Anschauen ist eine Thatig-
keit [Tätigkeit]; aber das Ich kann nicht zugleich anschauen und
sich anschauen als anschauend." Schelling.—But may I not ask
Schelling, why he calls das Empfinden Anschauen?—I feel a pain,
I know not where, only I find myself in pain. What has this to
do, ~~with~~ and I mean has it in common with the Act of *looking at*,
or *beholding* a man writhing to and fro, which motion having been
~~a concomitant~~ increased & accompanied by Pain in my own experience, I interpret, as the expression of Pain generally?—Where is
the *proof*, that *die Em[p]findung* eines Objects, the affection of my
Sensibility by an Object, yonder Rose for instance, constitutes my
perception of the Same? It *may* excite and divert my Attention to it;
it may give vividness, and magnitude to the perception, and yet
be wholly heterogeneous from Perception!—An act that *cannot* be
united with Consciousness must surely be different in kind from   *f13ᵛ*
the conscious contemplation of that Act. I know well that by Consciousness we most often mean the consciousness of having been
conscious—and that we may often with certainty infer that we had
been conscious, tho' no memory of it remains—as for instance of
my steps when I walk strait for 3 or 400 paces, tho' I could not
walk 20 paces strait when blinded—but a consciousness of having
been *unconscious*—a beholding a past unbeholdable Act ~~this seems~~
of beholding—this ⟨seems⟩ strange!—And after all, what an arbitrary novelty of language is ein productives Anschauen! What has
Anschauen, Looking on, to do with production!—How incomparably more simple to begin with the Will. At all events, according
to Schelling himself, Sensation (das Empfinden) is a *perception* of
Self; and what greater incomprehensibility is there in the perception of another? Or rather what a vague term this *Self* is—! Can
it have any tenable Meaning but *Life* in distinction from *mind*?
Who ever *feels* his thoughts—. Let us boldly look into the
phrase—I contemplate myself. If it does not mean my body, or a
series of thoughts—is there any thing really *objective* in the "my-

self"—is there any real synthesis, aught at added to the single word, *I*? Is not the *I* a perfectly simple intuition sui generis—& therefore only impropriè and for the want of a fit term to be called an *intuition*—and as unfitly a Sensation. Even that *Life* is an essential of the I, is by no means self-evident. ⟨Perception & Sensation instead of being *degrees* of the same Act are Antithetic always in inverse ratios.⟩

Finally, in the beginning was the WORD, coeternal with the WILL, and the Life proceeded from the Will and from the Word. The Distinctions are as primary as the Unity—and equally irreducible, either into either. Hence the moment Schelling comes to the *Distinct*, or in his language proceeds from the Begranztheit [Begränzheit] überhaupt to the bestimmten Begränztheiten, he exclaims—"~~This is the~~ Das sie das unbegreifliche und unerklärbare der Philosophie sind—This is the incomprehensible and inexplicable of Philosophy—" a disguised confession, that his genesis of Intelligence ~~adm~~ requires & supposes an Intelligence already perfected as the ground of the possibility of "the ~~former~~ absolute I" which was to be the first.

5287 F°.39   Daniel, in the 4ᵗʰ year of Jehoiakim—i.e. about 6 Centuries before Christ—a Contemporary of Ezekiel who repeatedly mentions him, transplanted with other Hebrews to Chaldæa by Nebucadnezzar—/educated & instructed in the sciences requisite for the service of the Court of Babylon, even as the young Slaves are at the Ottoman Court under the institution of the Janisaries—. Three years after he entered into the service of Nebucadnezzar, & in the 4ᵗʰ year had been promoted to the office of first Minister or Grand Visier of the Babylonian Emperor—. He *f14* was alive in the third year of Cyrus.— This is all the Biography that can be deemed historical.—The rest, collected by Carpzovius in his Introduction V.T., p. 231 & seq. & elsewhere, are either empty guesses, or legendary traditions, or unwarrantable & forced Inferences from particular Texts.—The Book of Daniel consists of two parts—the Prophecies beginning at Ch. 7. and a biographical Preface. The latter independent of its most questionable contents is proved ~~of~~ the work of a far later period by the Lingua franca in which it is composed, and which could not have been in use till after the Conquests of Alexander the Great—. It is evidently a fragment of the same work, which contained the blind stories of Susannah & the Elders, Bel and the Dragon, in the Apocrypha— We will therefore dismiss the Preface, as in no way affecting the ~~the~~ Prophecies themselves, or entitled to influence our judgement for or against their authenticity and intrinsic worth. ~~As later d~~ Add too, that whoever the Biographer may have been & whatever his æra, the ~~Preface~~ Biography contains nothing that can interest us as Christians, or as inquirers into the truth of Christianity—except indeed the interest which in the former character we may have in the remove of half a dozen Chapters which present more temptations to disbelief, more and more primâ facie improbabilities, than all the rest of the Old Testament collectively.—Now then for the Book itself.—

That such a person, as Daniel, existed, and that he was a man of ~~eminence~~ great distinction and celebrity, we have the best evidence, the incidental mention of his Name by a Contemporary Prophet/that he was a noble Hebrew Youth, selected from the Hebrew Captives to be trained up for the service of the Court of Babylon, and under the name of Belshazzar raised to the rank of Grand Visier, or first minister of State under Nebucadnezzar, and survived the subversion of the Babylonian Empire by Cyrus, there is no reason or even pretext for doubting. The first question then must be—Does the Book correspond to these ~~known agreed circumstances of~~ particulars? Is it in language, modes of thinking and of cloathing the thoughts, in imagery, colors of style, &c such a Book, as ~~a~~ Daniel might have written? Supposing~~e~~ him to have received the gift of Prophecy, is it such a book, as ⟨might be expected from⟩ a Prophet of the known Age and Circumstances of Daniel?—To this question in all its particulars we may confidently reply in the Affirmative. Its entire freedom from every thing of a contrary character is not the least ground for suspecting the Chapters prefixed. ~~In~~ But in proportion ~~therefore as it~~ as the Book proves the inauthenticity ~~of these, these must tend to confirm~~ of the Preface, the inauthenticity of the Preface must tend to establish the Authenticity of the Book—which by the bye gives to the former a far higher value, than could be fairly assigned to it on the supposition of its genuineness. Its most serviceable Office is that of a Foil—

The utter ⟨and striking⟩ unlikeness of the Book to the rest of the Hebrew Canon, and the fact, that the few exceptions are found *f14ᵛ* in in Ezekiel who had likewise sate by the Rivers of Babylon, and in Zechariah who ~~in all probability had returned~~ doubtless had come from the land of the Captivity to the new Colony in Jordan, ~~from the Captivity, and~~ and not improbably might have imitated the ~~ө~~ elder oracles of Daniel,—the fact, I say, that the resemblances ⟨to Daniel⟩ in the ~~two~~ only Books, that contain any resemblance, are in proportion to the similarity in the circumstances of the Writers, furnish another and stronger presumption of its Authenticity. "In Daniel" (says a learned German Biblist, ⟨whose germanism I purposely retain in my translation⟩ quite a new World opens on us. ~~Let a man have~~ However familiar & intimate ac~~quaintanc~~eed a man ~~be~~ ~~might~~ay have made himself with the other Prophets of the O.T., however deep~~ly~~ he ~~might~~ay have *studied himself into* (i.e. *however thoroughly he might have mastered*) their spirit, their language, their ~~modes~~ ways of representing and poetizing (*the* ~~peculiar~~ *distinctive character of their style and poetic drapery*) he will here find all strange, and (meet with) Truths, which not Palestine but a wholly foreign Soil must have pushed forth."

Every where indeed we find traits of the native Hebrew, intimate with the History and Sacred Writings of his Nation; but in all ~~the~~ his references to these there is a tone & coloring ~~given~~, ⟨Lights and Shadows,⟩ which no untravelled Inmate of Palestine could have given. ⟨In common⟩ with Moses & the elder Hebrew Writers, Daniel calls the Stars, the Host of Heaven; but he names God "the Prince of the Host, and after the manner of the Chaldeans every Star is inhabited by its ~~guardian Angel~~ ruling Spirit, and he assigns to every Realm its own proper Guardian Angel.— So likewise the elsewhere unexampled Measure of Time—⟨now⟩ "a time, two times & half a time;"—⟨now⟩ two thousand & three hundred Days—now "one thousand two hundred & 70 days— when all the oldest & most judicious Commentators admonish, that the numbers are not to be interpreted with a punctual exactness.— It is highly probable that ~~this~~ the origin of this Chronometry is to be sought for in the astronomical or astrological Sciences, in which Daniel as a Pupil of the Chaldean Sages had been initiated. Need I add the Dreams & Visions, which tho' ~~not~~ in all countries ~~or~~ held in regard, yet find in Chaldean their especial World, their sphere of intensest influence—~~and~~ where likewise the Interpretation formed a Science of itself, and its Cultivators a peculiar & highly privileged Class/~~or~~ of Magi.—

This so perfectly natural under the circumstances of Daniel is the more striking, in that the whole of the Laws & Institutions of Moses expressly discountenanced ⟨~~the~~ all regard for & consultation concerning Dreams⟩ and indirectly but most powerfully tended to preclude this and all other superstition by accustoming the imagination of the people to external Services, broad day-light religion, and public Oracles.—The great change therefore in the revelations to Daniel may well be thought to augur a coming revolution, ~~and~~ *f*15 ~~in their~~ in the divine dispensations—and that Dreams, Visions, and the Symbolical Genus generally, ⟨having their source invisible & their seat in Individuals,⟩ form a step, a transition to an inward and spiritual Faith, the evidences of which ~~required~~ were in ~~the individual~~ each Believer's own ~~spirit~~ Heart & Mind.

5288 F°.40

Imagination

The infinite tendency of the I to be for itself, ~~or~~ i.e. the inseparability of the εıμı from the εγω, or rather the identity (for in the self-position the I consists) of knowing and being in one and the same act—this constitutes the primary *Bound—the end—finem* primarium.—Now in this first sentence we have a memento of the inadequacy of words, the creatures, instruments, and immediate Objects of the *Understanding*, to the expression of *Ideas*. What is expressed, delivered, must have been conceived. But Ideas are not *conceived* but contemplated. They may be apprehended but cannot be comprehended: a fortiori therefore, not expressed. In order to appl~~oy~~y the logical process to these spiritual intuitions, and to produce a mental *object* for the Understanding to reflect, we are compelled to decompose the truth into two contradictory positions, the first: affirming what the second denies. And yet the whole is mentally affirmed. Not that any actual Synthesis takes place. The Idea is ἕν καὶ ἀσύνθετον: and cannot be composed or decomposed. But the words, the Thesis and Antithesis expressed, may excite the mind to the intuitive act, or produce the inward assurance that the Truth had been contemplated—even as the simple enunciation of the 97th or any other Proposition of Euclid gives rise to ~~the~~ an assurance in the Mathematician's Mind that ~~it~~ he has ~~been~~ demonstrated it, ~~by him~~ tho' the demonstration itself is not distinctly present to him. Hence it follows, that to reason on truths that can only be spiritually discerned, or on any subject that cannot be referred to the Senses, or *reflected* in the Understanding, to a man without ideas, is as hopeless an undertaking as to discourse with the deaf respecting Music. Nay, more so: for between the harmonies of sight and sound there is at least an analogy; but Ideas and Conceptions are utterly disparate, and Ideas and Images the negatives of each other. Plato could make nothing of Aristotle himself, that intellectual Son of Anac, that Goliath in Understanding.

f15ᵛ   Now to apply this remark to the point which suggested it. I said, that the act of self-position, the I, is one and the same with the primary Bound—/i.e. that the latter is not the Consequent or Product of the former; but that the Bound rises out of the I, and the I rises out of the Bound. The identity of both (contradictory positions, p. 25. l.18) must be affirmed.—But what *Bound* is this? A bound that is no bound—that is a Bound by not bounding/—applied to which Milton's line is no mere play of words, but by a curious felicity of accident expresses the unique Act, here referred to. In very truth the I
    Does at one bound high overleap all bounds—
~~I fortified~~ Not content with the term I sought a substitute in *End*, and seemed to find the Latin *finis* more satisfactory. But for the Man who cannot contemplate that which is meant when he says, I am—who cannot consciously attend to the Act, in which he is for himself—for the Man (I might say, for the countless Many) who attaches no import or substance to the assertion—I am in that I know myself to be, and I know myself to be in that I am—all three words, Bound, End, Finis, are alike empty—no better than articulated air—Let me, however, suppose or dream that I have "fit audience found tho' few—and so re-commence my disquisition.—
    The I is its own *End*. Se ponit dum sibi finem ponit.

5289 F.42   ⚹ opposite to   Sweet ⚹ Sour   *f₁6*

⚹ contrary to   Sweet ⚹ Bitter

5290 F°.43   It seems probable that in certain subjects of dy-   *f₁6*
namic Physics we must admit a Heptad, i.e. Pentad between its
two constituent Antagonists. Color, for instance, between Light
and Shadow, as the ⟨only pure⟩ representative of Mass or ⟨Dark-
ness (i.e.) Gravity,⟩ ~~in its relation to Light, as its necessitant and
resist~~ as the dynamic Opposite of Light. In other words, Umbra
⚹ Lumen: or Shadow, Corpus merè phænomenon)(Lumen, i.e.
Lux phænomenon. The Color therefore, in which as the ~~material~~
Creature or Birth of Light and Shadow ~~o out of~~ both two Powers
exist in the maximum of energy ~~compatible with the existence of
the other~~, I would call the Zenith or Culminant Color—or Color
κατ' εξοχην—⟨and which as *phænomenal* and relatively to the
Phænomena ejusdem generis as to be taken as Identity.⟩ And this
no doubt is RED.—The Opposite (n.b. not the Contrary) I would
call the Nadir. As in the former ⟨Darkness (i.e.) Gravity, as the
Unific inhibitive Power) at once hides and represents itself in a
Form of Light, as the distinctive exhibitive Power; so in the latter
Light penetrates the Mass—to lose yet represent itself in a form
of Darkness.—
      I. Σκοτος παπμπρωτον—the Potential Identity of Light and
Darkness. The *all in each* ~~or~~ (Tohu Bohu) of Moses.—Chaos.
      II Σκοτος δυναμικον, Vis Tenebrarum, Vis *Massifica*, or
Gravity, as the Positive Pole of ~~the polarized firs Identity~~ Creation.
      III. Lux Lucifica, Λογος λεγομενος, the distinctive manifes-
tative Power—⟨whence⟩ Utterance, Song, Articulation ~~of~~ in Nature—the Negative Pole. ~~of the produced or polarized Identity~~.
      IV. Corpus, Tenebræ substantiatæ, Gravitas γινομενος.
      V. Lux materialis—ρημα εκδοτον.
      VI. Lumen seu ~~Lux~~ Forma Lucis et Phænomenon.
      VII. Umbra, seu Corp~~us~~oris Forma et Phænomenon—The
pure phænomenon of Body, as far as it is not Light.—

I have assigned Red as the Zenith, Culminant or Vertical Color—
and primo auditu it ~~would~~ill sound strange that I name Black as

the Nadir. If Black be the Nadir, White (it will be said) must be the Zenith. Let it be remembered, however, that I am speaking of *Colors*—and tho' ~~the form is very far from~~ I ~~am~~ have come to a very imperfect degree of Clearness on the subject and ~~cannot~~ it detain me too long to give intelligibly the little, I do seem to understand, yet the present result of my Reflections is, that White is a peculiar antithet to Green, ~~having~~ occupying the ~~same~~ punctum indifferentiæ negatively which Green occupies positively, or that ~~White~~ Green is the Indifferent Color in the maximum Affection of Light ~~&~~ (V) by Body (IV)/, and White the Indifferent Color in the minimum affection of V by ~~B~~ IV.

~~Th~~ The Processes of vegetable growth, in the passage from White to Green, and from Green to White, the radical fibres— Snow-drop to the Stem and Leaf, from the Leaf to the Petal favor my view—the whole being produced in the first instance by the feebleness of the contractive Act, a certain energy of which is required in order to the affection of V, and in the second by the intensity of the contractive Act, favor this View—and perhaps I may find some confirmation in the facts of Metallurgy—If by bisecting the line of Color, and producing the right hand or neg. pole we formed a line commencing with Green as its Positive Pole,

f16ᵛ   ~~so that~~ Green   Blue   Grey   White this would in
          + —————————————————————————————— · – ,

some measure convey what I mean if only the symbolic line be understood *dynamically*—i.e. not by transition, or as if Blue differed from green by grade of *dilution*, ~~but~~ and not by overlooking the polarity of Blue, as the relative − of + Color (all in which Umbra et Lumen are co-actual are + Color; but of this Y is the + and B the − Pole) but simply that White by increase of ~~&~~ VII may be conceived as ~~passing~~ rising thro' Grey and Yellow to Green; and Green by decrease of the same as descending thro' Blue and Grey to White—/ Mem. in a former Mem. Book my remarks on Tripolarity in Nature, when A ⟨the⟩ Punctum ~~of~~ Indifferens of B and D/is at the same time the positive Pole both of A and E

          _ A . . . B ————————— C ————————— D . . . E _
                            +   ⊙

But I must return to my Pentad or Heptad.—

Products of (~~Red~~) (VII.) Umbra + (VI.) Lumen.—

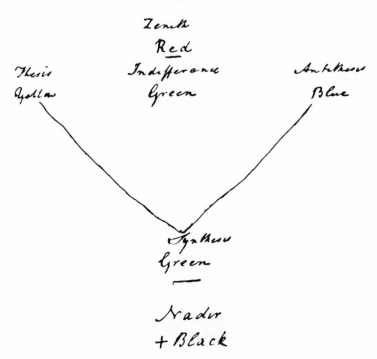

⟨N.b. The synthetic Green is decomponible/and by this alone distinguishable from the primary Green, as the Indifference of + & −.⟩

− Black = 0. mere Non-ens, neither Light or Shade. White is the Indifference of Light − Shade: Green the Indifference of Light + Shade. From this scheme we may understand the harmonious Effect of Red and Black in the Pictures of the Bassani.

P.S.—It is impossible to reason on the Genesis of Powers without feeling the impropriety and inadequacy of the terms, Negative and Positive, − +. Thetic and Antithetic, (and), would be less objectionable. But better still would it be that the relation of Antithesis should be presumed, as common to all—and what the terms of Antithesis are, determined for each particular subject—Thus—in the present analysis the Terms of Antithesis are, Subjective ⋇ Objective—or—in this disquisition the T. of A. are Ideal ⋇ Real—or—Real being the term of Prothesis, the Antithesis is Actual ⋇ Potential—&c.

Allon ⚹ Metallon: a serviceable names for φως δυναμικον ⚹ Σκοτος δυναμικον. Light ⟨Lumen⟩, the visual Form & Representative of *f17* Allon, and Shade ⟨Umbra⟩ of Metallon, the Metallon = Mass, Body being Σκοτος *substans*, Shadow Σκοτος phænomenon/vel Corporis *per* se, ⟨sed relativè ad lucem,⟩ *apparitio*, sub formâ Lucis— (Apparitio φωτοειδης)

1. Σκοτος προκοσμικος = Potentiarum in potentialitate suâ Omnëitas et Indistinctio. Chaos.

2. Chaos polarizatum = Natura, + − O −—⟨If Nature be expressed by + O, it is the Identity of + and −, the Ideal & Real.⟩

~~2~~3. Το αλλον = φως δυναμικον, Natura evolvens ab intra, evocans ab extra, et omnimodo se exhibens. Ideal or Subjective Pole of Nature.

~~3~~4. Το μεταλλον = σκοτος δυναμικος, Vis Massæ, Gravity. Natura se inhibens. Real or Objective Pole of Nature.

~~4~~5. Lumen Forma et Phænomenon του αλλου, in special relation to Space. i.e. Vision, lux phænomenalis Light

6. Umbra, forma et phænomenon του μεταλλου, in special relation to Light. (5.)

7. Colours, the Births or Creatures of Light (5) and Shade (6.)

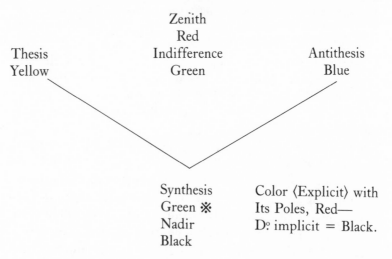

Zenith
Red

Thesis   Indifference   Antithesis
Yellow   Green   Blue

Synthesis   Color ⟨Explicit⟩ with
Green ⚹   Its Poles, Red—
Nadir   D? implicit = Black.
Black

f17   ⚹ as composed, so decomponible

Thus, the indecomponible Green is the Indifference of Yellow and Blue—and so far the Indifference of Light + Shade − But White is the Indifference of Light − Shade. And therefore it is represented on Line 11, p. 28. as

$$+$$

− White   Yellow   Green   Blue   White −

in which Green is the positive pole of White, in the scale both of Increase and Decrease, while it is the Indifference of Yellow and Blue.

RED : Black : : objective intensity : subjective intensity. i.e. the visual power *exerts* the same intension in presenting Black, a mass of ebony for instance as it *suffers* in beholding a crimson Cloud at Sunset. Hence it is that the Percipient or ~~Ob~~Subject engrossing the Activity to itself reduces Mass to mere form, or Capacity of Mass. It remains an *Object* indeed because Space is essentially objective, as the common (allgemeine) form of all objectivity—and the Mass becomes = Space, but as it is bounded by colors that express *Substance* i.e. an active power in the Objects, the Mass is = definite Space, ~~under the~~ with the dimensions of Space applicable thereto—In all respects it is the *abstract forms* of Body objectively presented, or beheld as outward. Thus a strong Shade on a rock will represent a Cavern. But if by any means an *exponent* of active power, or substantive Activity can be combined or identified with the Black, then as ~~it~~ the substantiality of the Object is made known—as it is ascertained that ~~it does~~ a power is in action, it follows that the power acts in retracting, restraining, compressing, i.e. as a negative and introïtive force—in short, that it is the *Vis* Massæ as the ⟨opposite & the⟩ antagonist of the *Vis* lucifica—/. It marks the intensity of the Metallon—and hence expresses Solidity, density, hardness &c. Now the only means, by which this can be effected, are by combining the expression of the repulsive force of the ~~Mass~~etallon, as the Antagonist of the Allon, with the expression of its retractive ~~force~~ introïtive force as the *opposite* of the Allon. It must have more or less of *Lustre*, or *Sparkle*. ~~But, I mean~~ This, I say, is the only pure *objective* means of substantiating black surfaces. *Subjectively* the Artist can produce the same effect by outlines that convey intelligible or known forms—by Shape under circumstances that preclude Shadow.

*f*17*ᵛ*

But whether Black represent the negation of Objectivity by possessing *the forms* only of ~~Light~~ Visibility & being consequently
Subjectless in itself and existing only ~~in the percipient Subject~~ by
virtue of ~~&~~ its circumscription; or whether it represents the contrary—the intensity of objectivity by virtue of its proper *Subject* or
Substance—its harmony and correspondence with Red are alike demonstrable—in either as ⟨the⟩ Penetrante and the Penetrable in the
Lightning-flash thro' the Darkness; or as the Inter-penetrated (=
co-inherence of Light and Mass) and the Resistent impenetra-
ble.—Red, penetrant)(Black, ⟨a resisting penetr⟩ penetrable

Red, interpenetration)(Black, impenetrability—as in the red
flesh of the Water-melon with the black shiny flat Seeds.—The
beautiful effect of the ⟨Dark⟩ Shades upon Reds, the folds of Crimson Curtains

NOTA BENE. Let me not be understood as if I supposed the
Complacency produced by the op- and juxta-positions of Black and
Red to be derived from the Beholder's associating the preceding
thoughts with these Colors. No!—The Law, ~~of~~ which these
thoughts endeavor to describe, produce at once the qualities of the
two Colors, and the Complacency in the mind of the Beholder.
Not because I *think* of Red, as the mutual interpenetration of Light
and Shade, but because it *is* so.—

5291 F°.44   ~~The~~ It is one great Objection to the ordinary
Antithesis of Soul and Body, that we necessarily bring the former
under the same Law of Cause and Effect with the latter. The
moment, I admit that the Soul acts as a Cause on the Body and the
f18 Body as a Cause on the Soul, I make them both subjects of the
same kind of relation to this Law. Now it is demonstrable that this
Law is altogether subjective/i.e. a mode of conceiving, not a form
of Being; and that it applies therefore exclusively to *Phænomena*—
i.e. to the Things as they appear in and for the mind of the Percipient. Consequently, we habituate ourselves to think of the Soul
as a *Phænomenon* which we describe by repeating the predicates of
the Body in other terms, just as the elder Phytolog~~y~~ists ~~predicated~~
assigned to vegetables the sexual Organs of the Mammalia, ~~under~~
~~the~~ altering the terms Veretrum & Vulva into Stamina and Ger-
mena—. What was impact in Body was *Motive* in Soul/& *Bumps*
~~were~~ designate Faculties; ~~and~~ because Faculties cause the swelling

of the Convolutes of the Brain which by pressure on the adjacent Skull cause Bumps. But then the Convolute of the Brain and its relative magnitude compared with the remaining Convolutes, and its positive magnitude compared with the same Convolute & Bump in other men's Brain & Skull. Things cause images, images excite tendencies and appetites; these reproduce the image, which now becomes a Thought; and a Thought associated with a tendency or appetite constitutes a *Motive*, which goads the Volition which sets the ~~abstract machine~~ nervous System, the galvanic fluid-generator in action, which moves the Muscles which move the bones which grasp the dagger which stabs the Man! Genius, Virtue, Piety are all *results*—nay, results of disproportion/The Man himself is no more—Thirty-six Faculties all in one Bone-casket are called a Man, just as thirty-six Sticks within the same Cord are called a Faggot. The Man is nothing different from the constituent Faculties, neither Antecedent nor Consequent, neither Principle nor Product. For the Understanding it is a mere ens logicum, signifying the Whole abstracted from the parts; for the Sense, an apparent Unity, from continuity of outline and Surface. Nothing is immediate: no where a center, and much less a centrific Power.— And ABSOLUTE indeed is asserted, for no better reason than that the Assert~~ion~~or is weary of counting the links & sees no use in going backward for ever; but it is always at an infinite distance and accounts only for an unknown unrecorded First, for a Somewhat that has ceased to exist, and it is difficult to say which is the more inconceivable, a first ~~caus~~ secondary Cause, or an Absolute, that is only a first Cause—whose functions were exhausted in ~~the~~ producing the *a* or commencing Link of an endless Series.

Now it is evident, that the Soul represents merely the unintelligible parts and stages of the process, which unintelligibility we hasten to remove by repeating those laws & phænomena of component Nature which ~~our~~ we suppose ourselves to understand (ex. gr. Impact, weight, stimulus, impression & the like) by ~~repeating~~ asserting ~~of~~ these, I say, under other names of the Soul, so that the Soul is but a duplicate of the Body, of the same stuff, and the same pattern, only woven *thinner/*—a sort of Body-*lining*. Well for him, to whom it has been vouchsafed the contemplate the *Spirit* of the Man, ανθρωπον τον αυτοτατον, of which Body and Soul are two effluent forms, the potential and the actual—for what can the

f18ᵛ

Body be, as distinguished from the Soul, but ɪ its potential Being, το αει γινομενον—its *Natura?* A thought, a perception, a sensation—all these are admitted as predicates of the Soul—in other words, whatever we actually are and immediately know.—

Identity or Prothesis

Real

Thesis	Antithesis
Actual	Potential

5292 F°.45   Mʳ Channing begins his profession of a sort of Arian Unitarianism with the words, *God is a Person*—. Now this is, ~~not even good~~ to say the least, slovenly Logic. Even Existence is no quality, property or attribute; but the *Position* of qualities, properties or attributes.—Much less can Person be either.—Neither is Person a generic term, expressing a *genus*—as Man, Sheep, Fish—as when I say, Neddy is an Ass.—The only right use of the words would be—The Person, who is and is named, the Father is *God.* The Person who is and is named the Son, is God. The Person who is and is named the Holy Ghost, is God.—Now here ɪ you have only to ask what is meant by the predicate, God? And it will be sufficient for me to reply, by a negative definition, viz. that the Idea, God, excludes all the qualities and characters of Body, and Matter—as limit, outline, or shape, multëity by division (as 100 guineas by division of a mass of Gold) and sameness by indistinction (as Water, or White from the confusion of Colors.—it is enough I say to do this, in order to shew, that the Persons cannot be divided/i.e. are essentially inseparable; and that they must be distinguished—i.e. that they are inconfusibly three Persons and indivisibly one God—or rather Three indivisible Persons are = God.

     A unity that excludes distinctity is a mere negation of multeity—
f19 Thus the Unity of Space—. One, one, one, one as constituting four, a one, b one, c one, d one—who does not see, that a (say, a shilling) is *one*, only as far as it is *not* b, not c, not d—&c but is this the Unity of the Absolute Will, which containeth all reality in itself, in whom all the Worlds and all the Hosts of Heaven live and move and have their Being?—The mystery of the tripersonal ONE—[or tri-personal GOD: for Unum and Deus in the positive and † dynamic sense of the former, are the same—and it declines

from the truth to be expressed to say, Deus est unus/instead of
Unum est Deus, et in omnibus unitis Deus est _το_ UNUM, το κατα
παντα τελειον, ἕν ἑνόποιον] the doctrine of the Trinity is not the
great or chief difficulty of the Christian Philosophy. A far steadier
Intimacy with Ideas, a larger grace of that spiritual discernment,
which, the profound Apostle assures us, can penetrate into the deep
things (or depths) of God himself, is required to the right apprehension of God manifest in the Flesh. The Idea and the *Fact*, the
Event, of the Theanthropy, that the Eternal became *historical* and
the ⟨focal⟩ Center of all History—this is the inmost Soul, the individualizing Principle, of the Christian Religion. This is the μεγα
ευαγγελλιον, the Great Good Tidings, Peace on Earth/ = the reconciliation of the Finite with the Absolute, and in this the concili-
ation of the Finite with itself, all warring Opposites being resolved into Symbols of Identity, that no longer rush against each
other to recoil from the Shock and ~~endless~~ renew the Strife but in
the very conflict mutually penetrated die into a higher Life—This
is indeed the ~~Bapto Mythus~~ mythic Hymeneal of Death and Love!
The Adam and Eve vanish in the Embrace, and the Angel Man
~~is found~~ rises ⟨remains⟩ in their place.—This is the GOOD WILL
to Man—τουτο εὐχαριστοῦμεν ~~εὐχαριστουμεν~~ Baptism is the initiative Light of Christianity, the Eucharist the *Life*, and the Light
in the Life!—

†Thus the *quality* of Brittleness in Arsenic is the *property* and
Power of Brittleness relatively to other Metals

5293 F°.46   ~~Should but~~ Let me by all the labors of my life
have answered but one end, if I shall have only succeeded in establishing the diversity of Reason and Understanding, and the distinction between the *Light* of Reason in the Understanding, viz.
the absolute Principles presumed in all Logic and the conditions
under which alone we draw universal and necessary Conclusions
from contingent and particular facts, and the Reason itself, as the
Source and birth-place of IDEAS, and ⟨therefore⟩ in ~~the~~ its conversion to the Will the power of *Ultimate* Ends, of which Ideas only
can be the Subjects; and if I shall have thus taught ✳ as many as
have in themselves the conditions of learning the true import and
legitimate use of the term, Idea, and directed the nobler and loftier   *f19ᵛ*

minds of the rising generation to the incalculable *Value* of Ideas
(and therefore of Philosophy which is but another name for the
manifestation and application of Ideas) in *all* departments of Knowlege, not merely technical and mechanic, and their indispensable
presence in the Sciences that have a worth as well as a Value to the
Naturalist no less than to the Theologian, to the Statesman no less
than to the Moralist— in Philology, Organology, ~~Philo~~ in Psychology ~~and~~, as *subjective*, and in ~~Anatomy~~ physiological Anatomy
as *objective*, Analytique, in Chemistry as the constructive Science
de Minimis and Astronomy as the correspondent Science de
Maximis I shall have ~~a rep~~deserved the Character which the fervid Regard of my friend, Irving, has claimed for me, and fulfilled
the the high Calling, which he ~~changes~~ invokes me to believe myself to have received.

f19   ✻ Negatively—i.e. what is not an Idea, and what ⟨the term,⟩ an
Idea, does *not* mean, for *all* who have sufficient power of Thought
to ask the question; but positively for those to whom it is given,
as the *occasion* of their turning themselves toward the East.

f19ᵛ   5294 Fº.47   The unsatisfyingness, the *felt* insufficiency, of all
Finites in themselves, and the necessity which the Understanding
feels of seeking their solution elsewhere—i.e. in an x that is not
finite.—It would therefore *derive* the Finite from the Infinite, the
Condition from the Absolute! But alas! by what intelligible ~~process~~
Diminuendo can the Infinite pass into the Finite. ~~Once assume
them as Opposites, and there is a chasm between the two~~, Once
separated and to separate them, ⟨(i.e. to contemplate the Finite as
subsistent et seorsum subsistens)⟩ is the genius of modern philosophy, which is well at ease as long as it can trace phænomenon Z
to Phænomenon W, and W to X and X to Y, which linking if
Finite to Finite is called *accounting for things*—Once separated, I
say, there lies a chasm between them, which no Industry can fill
up, no Imagination over-bridge.—Here the Ideas intervene, as the
Reconcilers: for herein ~~are~~ is it an Idea, that it ~~contemplates~~ presents to the mind the Particular in the Universal, and ~~contemplates
the Universal~~ is itself but a particular Form of the Absolute.

Hence is the mind raised above the Concrete, and refuses to receive as Axioms of Necessary Being, or Criteria of Truth and
Reality, the positions generalized from the imperfections and ne-
gations of the Concrete which does not exist there, because it exists
here, which exists only partially in this point of space because it
exists partially in another, but totally no where, and no when. The
Trinity is indeed the primary Idea, out of which all other Ideas
are evolved—or as the Apostle says, it is the Mystery (which is
but another word for Idea) in which are hidden all the Treasures
of Knowlege—But for this very case it is the example & representative of all Ideas—~~the~~ it is the common Attribute of all, that   *f*20
the Absolute exists ~~entire~~ in ~~all~~ the plenitude of its eternal Forms,
entire in each and indivisibly one in all. As a Mother listens with
tender smiles at the Child that striving to repeat makes nonsense
of her words, so does the Philosopher regard the attempts of the
Understanding to express the Ideas of the Reason, ~~were~~ which it
reflects and refracts in two contradictory positions—nay, demands
this as a negative test of the eternal truth intended.—Not, I mean,
that two contradictory positions always express an Idea; but that ~~an~~
~~Idea~~ what the Understanding, what Words which are the products
& sole immediate Objects of the Understanding can convey by
simple uncontradicted Affirmation, can *not* be an Idea.—
   It would be strange, if from the Unthinking any silliness ought
to appear strange—/~~that to learn a man~~ that a philosopher should
be expected to *put* into another man's Being and Consciousness by
the instrumentality and thro' the medium of general terms the definite knowlege of a *kind* (whether of Being, or of Knowing), with
no one particular or individual of which he professes himself to
have the least acquaintance. ~~And yet I have been required (far)~~
~~oftner and by more persons (than it is pleasant) to remember and~~
~~by persons who call themselves Metaphysicians, both from the~~
~~(English & Scotch) Schools, of Followers of Locke, *Helvetius*, &~~
~~Condillac, &c and from that of the Disciples of Reid and Dugald~~
~~Stuart~~ And yet, far oftener and by more persons than I find it
pleasure to remember, ~~and some this~~ ⟨and these too⟩ Professed
Metaphysicians, ~~of both the Schools, Scotch and Anglo-gallic~~—
Disciples some of ⟨the Anglo-gallic School⟩ Locke, Hume & Con-
dillac, some ⟨of the Scotch School⟩ of Reid and Dugald Stewart, I

have ~~received a request~~ had questions put to me, ~~that~~ which could be no otherwise understood than as a request that I should give them an *Idea* of an Idea. They would ~~smi~~ laugh at the man who should ask them for the Image of a Flavor, or the odour of a ~~Musi~~ Strain of Music/and to ask for the *Conception* of an Idea, is, if possible, yet more irrational—~~for The term word Idea,~~ What meaning I attached to the *word*, Idea, I had already declared. The *term*, Idea, I had already defined, ~~by~~ in the only way, in which the name of *any what*, that really or actually is, can be defined— viz. first, negatively, by contra-distinction—i.e. by determining what an Idea is *not*—2. positively by some character common to all Ideas—ex. gr. that in all ~~obj~~ we contemplate the Particular in the Universal, ~~or~~ the Universal in the Particular, the Qualified (or determinate) in the Absolute, and the Absolute in the Quali- fied. This, however, is not *the* Idea—which is *the* Form, in which the Absolute distinctly yet entirely and indivisibly is realized and revealed. This is that which cannot be *generalized*, on which the mind exercise no modifying functions—that which can only be *contemplated*—that which is deeper than all intelligence, inasmuch as it represents the element of the Will, and its ⌈ . . . ⌉ ~~anteced- ence as~~ essential inderivability. Thirdly by referring to some In- stance—as to the ~~law~~ *Ideas* of Kepler, the Correlates of the Law of the Planetary Orbits contrasted with the Conceptions of Ptolemy

f20ᵛ   who began with the phænomena, the apparent motions, as *data*— & then sought so to take them as that he might take them all together—i.e. *concipere, capere* hæc *cum* illis—and this *Conception*, or Synopsis of a plurality of phænomena so schematized as to ~~es- sence~~ shew the compatibility of their co-existence, is THEORY—a product of the Understanding in the absence or eclipse of IDEAS, or Contemplations of the Law, ~~or neces~~ and hence necessarily con- ditioned by the Appearances, and changing with every new or newly-discovered Phænomenon, which ~~the~~ Theory always follows never leads—while ~~it~~ the Law being constitutive of the phænomena and in order of Thought necessarily antecedent, the Idea ~~or~~ as the Correlative and mental Counterpart of the Law, is necessarily pro- phetic and ~~productive~~ constructive—et Solem dicere falsum Audet, and turns the contradiction of the Senses into proofs and Confir- mations of its truths—But take any fact, which the Senses do not present and which the Fancy cannot resolve in a series of images, or any position of Physiology which the Senses contradict or refuse to recognize—and see whether the Understanding can go a step further—whether our conception is not equally defective or oppugnant as our perceptions! Take for instance the fact of Chemical Combination as contra-distinguished from mechanical juxta-position, Chalk and Sulfuric Acid from Magnesia and Water—or the Penetration of Substances, ~~or in~~ the facts of Secretion and Absorption and try whether the Atomic Theory—if the hypothetical atoms are assumed as real entities and not as the $+$, $-$ ~~in~~ &c in Algebra for the purposes of Calculation/will help you to conceive the first and whether what is by misuse of language called conceiving does not consist in referring the fact to *Ideas*, of numbers representing powers ~~generally connect~~ essentially united with proportions, dynamic ratios, ratios not *of* powers, but ratios that are Powers, ~~Pythagorean Numb~~ αριθμοι Πυθαγοραιοι, Numeri numerantes— ~~Or~~ Try whether the doctrine of Pores will enable you to conceive the latter—or rather whether they are themselves utterly inconceivable ~~by falling below the Understanding~~ by virtue of their absurdity, as the Ideas are inconceivable by their transcendency to Conceptions, both equi-distant from the Understanding, the one below, the other above it.—How then can you require me to furnish you with a conception of an Idea, when its inconceivability is a ~~necessary~~ essential character of an Idea, and at least a negative Test?—

5295 F°.48   ⟨~~The man a, Be he naturalist~~ Whatever be the   *f2 1* Object of Pursuit, physical, moral or theological, the Man, who employs ~~the~~ his Understanding exclusively, is at ~~best~~ the highest but a Lexicographer—and few indeed are they whose Understandings are sufficiently capacious, and their Reading sufficiently extensive, to rank them with the Constantini, Stephani, & Ainsworths!—The greater number are but Index-makers of this or that ~~Preface~~ Volume—I contrast with this then the ~~philosopher who~~   *f2 1ᵛ* Dialectician in the platonic sense of the world—who uses his Understanding for the ~~utterance~~ wording of Truths known in a higher light—as an auxiliary—a go-cart of the infant Reason. And if in the following ~~illustration~~ similitude I pass from Illustration into

Instance, the nature of the Subject justifies me—for ~~in~~ what instance that would illustrate the superiority of Ideas (= the beholding of the Particular in the Universal, indivisibly) could be other than an Idea itself?—

f20ᵛ   I am studying a noble Dithyrambic in a Language, I am not perfectly master of—I turn therefore ever and anon my mind from the pervading Spirit of the Poem, from the unity to fix my atten-
f21   tion on this or that word or phrase detached from the context, and this I trace thro' its changes and relations, and treat it as if it has a sense of its own, and independent of connection; but I soon return to the inspired work, and the greater my progress, the less often do I turn from it, and believe myself then first to understand the Poem when I have *entered into its Spirit*, and ~~been~~ seated myself beside the *Charioteering Genius*—& this I have not attained till the words ~~are comprehended~~ lose their detached being, even as the various and manifold nerves, muscles, humours, ligaments are seen implicitly in the eye, into which they are co-organized, yea, and the eye itself as the symbol of the living Power, whose organ it is—And again even as I find, that it ~~can~~ would be ⟨a⟩ vain ~~to~~ attempt to solve the problem of the Eye ~~by~~ as a *result* of the ~~addition of this next to that, and form~~ component parts, taken severally—that a successive presentation of each, as a thing in itself, one by one, thro' the whole number, ~~the~~ would as little suggest an Eye, as the Syllables a, cre, can, de, de, di, do, et, fas, fer, mam, mum, ne, ni, per, pre, prop, pu, re, re, ri, sas, sum, tam, vi, vi, ven, suggest the Sentiment that expressed itself in the Sentence,
          Summum crede nefas animam preferre pudori,
          Et propter vitam vivendi perdere Causas.
In both alike I see with noon-day evidence that here the Spirit, the *Mens* Poetæ (or may I not say the *Mens* poeta, there the Vis Vitæ organifica/the silent Artist working after a pattern) is necessarily pre-supposed. Even Aristotle ~~to whom the Ideas of his great Master were a stumbling block, was yet~~ whose Understanding (i.e. the reflective, ~~and~~ anaytic and generalizing (categorical) faculty) was as a Cloud between him and the Ideas of his Great Master, availed himself sufficiently of the Light, that pierced thro' the Cloud, to ~~admit~~ establish two Wholes, a whole prior to the Parts, and a

whole resulting from the parts—the unity of *Form*, and the *Unity* of *Shape*—and the former is of necessity pre-supposed in order to the latter—the latter unity, or WHOLE (θολον τὸ ὅλον) resulting and constituted, the former (principium Formæ, vis formatrix) antecedent and constitutive. Now if this be named the *Ideal Unity*, it is well—but then let it be remembered that it is at the same time *actual* and constitutive, and that therefore the term, Ideal, must be opposed not to the *Real* but to the *Phænomenal*.

5296 F°.49   Note to p. 36, last line but 12.   *f21ᵛ*

Ὅδε περὶ θεῶν Πυθαγόρα τῷ Μνασάρχω, τὸν ἐξέμαθον ὀργιασθεὶς
ἐν Λειβήθροις τοῖς Θρακίοις Αγλαοφάμουω τελετὰς μεταδόντος· ὡς
ἄρα Ὀρφεὺς ὁ Καλλιόπας κατὰ τὸ Πάγγαιον ὄρος ὑπὸ τᾶς ματρὸς
πινυσθεὶς ἔφα· ταν Αριθμῶ ωσιαν ἀΐδιον ἔμμεν, ἀρχὰν προμαθέστα-
ταν τῷ παντὸς ουρανῶ, κὰι γᾶς κὰι τᾶς μεταξὺ φύσιος. ἔτι δὲ κὰι
θείων κὰι θεῶν κὰι δαιμόνων διαμονᾶς ρίζαν.

                    Iamblich. de Vita Pythagoræ.

I should read το εν αριθμῳ—i.e. not that the Being of Number is eternal, but, that an eternal Being resides in Number, or that there belongs to Number an eternal reality or substantive Being—
την Μοναδα ἄρχην απαντων λογων,—συ

Mem. On the dignity and lofty Hope of the human Being on the hypothesis of *Ideas*—εν ταις γαρ ιδεαις ουσια αιδιος ενεστι, αρχας προμαθεστατας—1826—alas!—

5297 F°.50   1 John v.7.—Had the Apostle John Theology been ever ~~understood~~ apprehended, which in age without ideas is impossible—had even a gleam of the Apostle's Reasoning in this chapter penetrated thro' the dungeon of modern Dogmatism, the ~~7ᵗʰ verse~~ true character of the 7ᵗʰ Verse could not ⟨for a moment⟩ have remained doubtful. It would have been detected at once as an intrusive Alien—dividing the Argument, like a word-screen between the Ray of Light and the Prism/like poor dear Hartley's Mʳ God Almighty win, when about three years old, in accosting God-win—

This text with the Jonas Text in Matthew (& I shrewdly suspect, 3 or 4 more) are perhaps the earliest fruits of that miserable imbecil totalization of the attention on single texts and sentences, during which the pious Dullman is ever on the alert to be thinking of something somewhere else that is like it, or which it recalls to his recollection—before he has seen what the sentence itself means, and its dependency on the context:—whether the Trinity as now received by our Divines, in which the Father is O ΩN, and personal in the same sense as the Son, without any distinction between the person*ëity* of the former, and the person*ality* of the other was at any time present to St John's Mind, I will not pretend to determine; but in this Chapter most assuredly he was thinking of some-

*f*22   thing else, and so intensely engaged in enforcing the great & pregnant Idea as to have no room for another and wholly foreign Subject/not to mention the palpable and blundering efforts to *make*, to force a parallel by the repetition of the ⟨Apostle's⟩ phrase "bear witness", which is justly and fitly applied to the two great Symbols of Christianity, ~~Baptism, and the Eucharist~~, Light & Life, with the Spirit as the focal Unity of both—these both outwardly, in the Sacraments and in the Gifts of the Spirit, and inwardly by the correspondent Grace and growth to the Believer's own Mind, did truly *bear witness*,—but lose all meaning when translated to Heaven & applied to the Persons of the Godhead—Are there any Sceptics or Infidels in Heaven?

1 The *personëity* of the Father, the Reason in the Will, and the Will—

2 The *personality* of the Son, the Will in the form of Reason, as the ουσια προτογένης—the Being, ο ων, and as the ο ων, the *Person* of the Father.

3. The *individuity* ⟨Actuity? i.e. the Identity of Will, Reason = Being, and Act in the form of Act?⟩ of the Spirit, which (if I may without offence venture to refract the ineffable thro' the turgid medium of Words) stands to the ~~Father~~ Absolute Will as the Logos,—ω ο ων, and to the Logos, the ο ων as *the Will*—proceeding from both, and ~~containing~~ actualizing both in the identity of its own Form (Idea, Αριθμος). Hence in the spiritual economy of the Church on earth the Father potentiates (*leads*), the Son realizes, the Spirit actuates.—Such I believe to be the φιλοσοφια Johannensis.—

⟨3. *Surprising*. I can not recall the view in which I wrote this; but it seems to me erroneous. If the H.G. be to the Father *as* the Logos, what is the L. to the F? Is it a case of double Vision?⟩

P.S.—Nota bene—I by no means oppugn the doctrine of the three *Persons* in Bull's & Waterland's Sense—in which Person is synonimous with an *I Am*.—But the two senses ought to be kept distinct, and the Divine ought to be aware that the word may be & has been used in two meanings, and to premise in which of the two he purposes to employ the term. I From the neglect or ignorance of this ~~the~~ Emanuel Swedenborg was induced to believe himself an opponent of the doctrine of three *Persons*, and to hold himself bound to reject it by Christ's own Assertion & the ~~Apostle John's~~ Evangelist's preceding declaration—Θεον ουδεις εωρακεν ουδεπωποτε—the Son is the Person (i.e. manifestable Form of the Father—which he who saw had seen the Father. Here if Person be used, it must mean ~~manife~~ representative Form—as we say of a well-formed Individual—He is a fine *Person* of a Man—from *personare*—per quod sonat Mens, sive Homo interior.

5298 F°.51   The directing Idea of History is to weave a Chain of Necessity the particular Links in which are free Acts—or—to present that which is necessary, as a whole, ~~without~~ consistently with the moral freedom of each particular Act—or—to exhibit the moral Necessity of the Whole in the freedom of ~~each particular Act~~ the component: the resulting Chain is necessary, each particular Link remaining free. The old Chroniclers & Annalists satisfy the latter half of the Requisition—Hume, Robertson, & Gibbon the former half. In Herodotus & Thucydides alone both are found united. In Physiology (Natural History, the history of Nature) the same Elements are found, in the reverse order— the moral freedom, the self-determining Will is to be the principle of the Whole, in the necessity of the component particulars. Now this is no otherway possible, but by the antagonist Factors, of which this combination of Freedom with Necessity is the product, shall be antithetic, correlative Opposites, to each other—not contraries.   *f*22*ᵛ*

It cannot therefore be Free-Agency ⚹ blind Compulsion or Fatality—but Will ⚹ Reason, and these as the polar points of a Line which in all its parts is both Will and Reason—which supposes a Prothesis, as the Identity of the two. And this is one of the cases in which the Thesis retains the name of the Prothesis—just as Metaphysics is the generic name of all the sciences, ~~that~~ the evi-

dence of which transcends the evidence of the *Senses*. It comprehends therefore the ~~Senso~~cience of Sensible Intuition, or the Construction of the pure Sense, as well as the Science of Ideas, and
pure Conceptions. But the latter as the Thesis takes the appelation
of the Genus—

Prothesis
Metaphysics

Thesis   Antithesis
Metaphysics   Mathematics
So here

Prothesis
Will

Thesis   Antithesis
Will   Reason—

So that in every creature there is that which can be resolved into a
Law of Reason—which yet does not exclude the Will. We cannot
say it follows from the Law, therefore there is no *Will* in this. For
a Law of Reason exists for the Mind only as an *Idea*—and an Idea
~~is~~ supposes both. But in every creature there is a something, an
individuality, that cannot be *accounted for*—i.e. deduced from a
Law of Reason. But we cannot affirm, This is *not* reason; but
only—this ~~can~~ is not reducible into the *form* of Reason—It does
not stand under that *pole* of the common-Line. ~~It~~ Tho' it does not
mark the Will in the Reason, it yet marks the Reason in the
Will—It lies *deeper* than the *Form* of Reason—even in that which
contains reason essentially & potentially, the Absolute Will—Illustrate the Will-pole by the water in the Basin of a Fountain—
the Reason or Ideal Pole by the water of the salient Column. Consequently as the Moral Necessity arises out of the *Law* or Form of
Reason, and the Freedom is the phænomenon or representative of
the *Will*—and as the Reason is itself Will/i.e. has its substance &
f23   reality in Will—the Necessity is a necessity of Will. But as contraries cannot be predicated of the same Subject, the Necessity cannot contradict the Freedom. Absolutely taken, each must involve
the other. It must be a free Necessity, a necessary freedom—which
our Liturgy sublimely expresses in the words, "whose service is
perfect freedom—

The Will is *felt* in each, the Reason becomes manifest in the Whole—. This may be rendered clearer by considering, that every Organism (organized Whole, or a Whole evolved from an antecedent Unity) is the realization (the utterance, i.e. outward making, and *ex* pression of an Idea. Consequently, the realizing itself cannot be the Idea—Hence the ~~more~~ finer and more lively the *Expression*, the more evident the *Individuality/*. The ⟨individual⟩ *Experiment* discloses its Accordance with *the Kind*, its generalizable or common properties & qualities. But that which constitutes it an Individual lies deeper than this, and remains as the ungeneralized, ungeneralizable, Self. In revealing its accordance with the forms of Reason, the Will reveals itself as the power antecedent to Reason—

Ἰδεα, ηδε Αριθμος νοερος, οὐσία εστι προμαθὴς. ~~το~~ και το μεν, προ εγγινεται απο του θεληματος του μεν αναγκῃ και ἀει πρὸιοντος.

The Idea has its attribute of prescience and predocence ~~as a Birth~~ by the Might of the Eternal Antecedent, and Immanent, and as a Birth or Offspring of the Logos, as the Absolute Form of the Absolute.

⟨The Absolute Will essentially causative of Reality (οὐσίας) Almight = Θεος. Θεὸν οὐδεὶς ἐώρακε πώποτε:

The All-Being, ο ων, ο λογος, the Eternal Son = Ο υιος. Ὁ μονογενὴς Υἱὸς, Ὁ ὢν εἰς τὸν κόλπον τοῦ πατρὸς, ἐκεῖνος ἐξηγήσατο.

The Life and Eternal Act—the Eternal Procession = τὸ πνευμα. The Absolute as containing the Son and the Spirit = Ο Θεος, Ο πατηρ.—

Hence the Father and ο Θεος have two senses in Scripture/first, The Father as comprehending the Word and the Spirit, as his Word, his Spirit, the tri-personal Godhead = God

Or in distinction from the Son or the Spirit—and in these passages the Father always represents the Divine *Will*, the Absolute Will SELF-REALIZED in its own form, as WILL.⟩

Nevertheless, the Power (as the representative of the Will) must be contemplated as distinct from the Idea—and by consequence of Idea as a *Forma* ⟨Altera⟩ supervening to the Form (or Idea) itself—even a Shadow takes a *form* from the surrounding Light/. The Idea is the unalterable Quantity—the Power the variable Quantity—. Hence the Synthesis—/—viz. when the Idea acts only with the *f23ᵛ* power, which by the immanence of Will in all real Forms, it possesses essentially as an Idea, we call it an *Idea*. But when the Power as Power exists in the same proportion as the Idea, and both become one/the Result is a Law. But the adequation of the Power to the Idea can be known or revealed in no other way than by the Manifestation of the Idea *Objectively*. This is evident. For the moment we place the Object in antithesis to the Law (ponderable Mass for instance to the Vis Gravitatis) the Law is conceived as the Subject—i.e. as ~~the~~ an Idea. But it is injurious to the mind to accustom itself to such modes of thinking—far better to contemplate the Law, or Self-objectivizing Idea, as the Noumenon ὑπο-στατικὸν, and the Object as the Phænomenon.—In order to this, however, the Mind must have emancipated itself from the thraldom of the sensuous Imagination, which perpetually craves an antecedent *Matter*—a self-subsistent Appearance—in short, an *Apparition*.—The first exercise in Philosophy is *facere* non *dare* materiam/or Matter is a result not a Datum—not τὸ, ἀφ᾿ οὗ αι δυ~~αν~~ναμεῖς, but ὅ ἀπο των δυναμεων.

5299 ꜰᵒ.52   Religion is: Ideas contemplated as Facts. Remove the symbolic character—the Speculative Truth that is represented—and the Religion becomes mere History, real or imagined. "There is a God" is a philosophic Dogma; but of itself not a Religion. But that God manifested himself to Abraham or Moses, and sent them to make known that he *made* the World, and formed Man out of the Ground, and breathed into him a living Soul—this is Religion. Hence Religion necessarily consists of *Traditions*. But then these are but the one ingredient. If the doctrine be as temporary & partial as the ꜰᴀᴄᴛ/ex. gr. the unlawfulness of Wine = the fact of the Pigeon conveying it from Paradise to Mahomet in a Cave—it is a false, illegitimate Religion—a Counterfeit in which a mere Conception or Notion of the Understanding is substituted for *an* ɪᴅᴇᴀ. The "Religion" ~~is~~ must still refer to *the Universal in the Particular*—viz. tho' the Idea ~~is~~ should be disguised in a Conception, ~~and the Law represented in a Fact~~, yet the Conception must still have ~~the~~ an Idea as its true import. Ex. gr. *the Idea* of the Eucharist in the Roman-Catholic Conception of Bread & Wine changed into Flesh & Blood./

5300 F°.53   Bread—Wine—not the Wheat-plant, and the
Vine!—Nature in the philosophy of the Gospel is not a Symbol of
the Divine (the Earth was cursed, Gen. II.). Moral Acts, without
Consequents, products, and signs of Moral Actions—οσα μεν εγε-
νετο δια ανθρωπων. To this, however, there are two exceptions—
Light and Life. But even here the Exception confirms the Rule—   *f24*
for the one is the eminently Subjective in Nature—her Ideal
Pole—viz. Light, and the other the *historical* in Nature itself,
Life, Birth, Generation; and neither of them a *Concrete*, as the
Sun, the Sea, Plants, Animals &c. The Idea of Christianity can
only be subjectively objectivized—for it denies the true Objectivity
of ~~the~~ Corporeal or rather of ~~the~~ Material Things—they all are
corrupt and will pass away—and ~~even~~ the *Law* of the Material
Universe, ο κοσμος εν τῷ κοσμῷ, is the *Cosmetor*—and therefore not
a Symbol—and besides this, *Xty* is a growth, a Becoming, a Progression, and on this account not symbolizable by Presences that
identify the Future with the Past, and consequently declare only
that which has already been.—HISTORY therefore, and History
under its highest form of Moral freedom, is that *alone* in which
the Idea of Christianity can be realized/the Synthesis not consisting
of the Infinite ✕ Finite; but of the simultaneous Infinite ✕ Successive Infinite. The Differential generates *the line* not in an Ellipse
but in a Parabola. Here therefore, as in all ~~practice of~~ other articles
of the Roman Church, against which Luther & his fellow-labour-
ers *protested*, we find a just IDEA metamorphosed and as it were by
the rennet of the Golden Calf coagulated into finite Superstitions/
morals cast in arbitrary moulds, Deeds frozen into *Things*/Priva-
tions and Automatic Performances substituted for the Mind, Life,
and Agency that were in Christ. Nevertheless ⟨as⟩ the ⟨Pseudo-⟩
Hagiography (Vitæ Sanctorum) of the Benedictine Annalists is the
appropriate objectivization of the Antichrist, so ~~would~~ must a true
Hagiography be of the Power of Christ. *The Idea* of the Christian
Religion can be realized only in the "Lives of Christians."—Even
the Miracles, the multitude & vulgarity of which render the Romish Hagiography a Goëtography (βιογραφία γοητων), are but the
substitutes for those true Wonder-works of Faith, which would
have indeed removed Mountains. What need of Romish Miracles
for Men who can refer to such credentials of their divine author-

ity, as the present State of Otaheite and its sister Islands compared
with their condition before the arrival of the Baptist Missionaries?

5301 F°.54   Where the Divine can be represented entire in
a Finite, Polytheism is the necessary Form of the Religion. For
the Divinity here is but the *Space*, and the Finite the Outline of
the Diagram—The Space exists absolutely in each of a hundred
Diagrams; but only in the Diagram *can* it *e*xist.—In Christianity,
on the contrary, the Logos existed previously to & independently
of its incarnation/it existed πρoς τoν Θεoν, being itself Θεoς.—But
even so, the Return of Christ (Χριστoυ, ηγoυν, τoῦ ὁρωμένoυ), the
Withdrawing of the visible Finite, was indispensable to the Descent of the *Spirit* of Truth, i.e. of the Christ as the *Mediator* &
therefore in union with the Father./My Father & I will come: &
we will dwell in you.—For I can not conceal the fact, that hitherto
I have not been able to discover any texts in the 4th Gospel, ex-
f24ᵛ   pressing the *distinct* personal Subsistence of the Holy Ghost, any
passage of which the existence of a third Person in the Godhead is
the direct import, and the proper *intendiment* of the Evangelist.
The Paraclete, the *Spirit* of Truth, is Christ himself; but the Spiritual Christ—Christ in the Spirit.—It does not follow, however,
that this article may not be clearly & convincingly inferred from
many or all the passages, which assert the divinity of our Lord
himself. I am fully persuaded, that the Church legitimately, and
of necessity, inferred it—the Idea of the Trinity being the only
possible form, under which the Divinity of the Redeemer could
be reconciled with the Unity of the Godhead; and the personality
(Eιμι, I-hood, Ichheit) of the Spirit proceeding a necessary term
in the Idea of the Trinity/—I mean only—that this article of Faith
is not the Proposition demonstrated; but a demonstrable Corollary
of the Proposition and Demonstration.—This, & if it be true,
would settle at once the controversy respecting the Verse in the first
Epistle of John. The divinity of Christ, and in what manner it
realized it and bore witness to, itself in the Regenerate, namely,
in and by, ⟨the⟩ Water (τo Φως), the Blood (ἡ ζωὴ), and the Spirit,
or joint Unity arising out of both, and their common Outbreath-
ing—and the conspiration of these three to the Birth and manifestation of the One Spiritual Christ.—A Trinity indeed is asserted

in this Chapter (1 John. IV.8.) but it is a Trinity of spiritual Powers in the ~~Soul~~ Person of the Believer, in which the One Christ/Χριστος Θεος εφανερωθη. The 7th Verse, therefore, is evidently an intrud~~ent~~er originating, I doubt not, in a mistaken Gloss of St Augustine, who supposed the form⟨ula⟩ of the Trinity which it took the Church three Centuries to bring to its final perfection, to have been as *explicit* and as familiar & *upper-most* in the Mind of the Apostle as in his own. But that this is confessedly the only Text in the whole New Testament—nay, that it is the only text in the Writings of an Apostle so fervently and constantly occupied in grounding the doctrine of regeneration on the divinity of Christ—this single fact would warrant a suspicion of its genuineness, even tho' no Manuscripts of equal antiquity with ~~those of~~ the Greek had been extant, and consequently none in which the Verse was missing. For where will ~~an~~ ⟨similar⟩ instance be found, after by occasion of the Arian Controversy, the ~~Id~~ compleated Idea of the Trinity had become an article of *explicit* Faith? So far is this from invalidating the doctrine of the Trinity, it is almost necessary for the maintenance of its Truth—against the learned Heretics—. For this affords the true & only satisfactory solution of the lax language of the Anti-nicene Fathers—

*f*25

5302 F°.55   With the Ancient Greeks, or the old civilized World, Civilization was the ultimate end. Ο πολιτης was the Aim, ο πολιτικος (the Statesman) the highest Character.—Ο φιλοσοφος was an anomaly—a prophetic Birth. In the new World, or Christendom (I speak of it as its proper Institutions characterize it—not of the woful declension from ⟨the⟩ ~~Ideas~~ into a lower than pagan Idolage) Civilization is but the Matrix—*Cultivation* being the Gem—. Again, in the old World the personality of the Gods was the ⟨open, exoteric,⟩ το φανερον και κοινον; their impersonality the esoteric, the Mystery. In the New World the ~~M~~ Impersonal (Nature, Natural Philosophy, Celeste Mechanique) is το φανερον και κοινον, the personality of the Godhead the Mystery.

5303 F°.56   What our Priestleian Metaphysickers call Necessity is but an empirical scheme of destroying one Contingency by the introduction of another, which is to be treated in the same manner—in short, a pushing back of Contingency ad infinitum, the unconquerable Foe retreating step by step, and still facing the Pursuer.—~~His contingent as~~ [?Taking] contingent a. the Necessitarian discovers a Cause in b. a becomes a necessary effect, and the Contingency is transferred to b.—But as a to b, so b to c, the Contingency playing at Leap-frog—as it ~~runs~~ vaults backwards—As if History could be thus explained; as if the Motives of Action were not a part of the Action—Here comes the Head ~~of the~~ and Neck of the Horse; but what was behind?—The Tail. Ergo, the Tail pushed the Head & Neck forward.

5304 F°.57   But tho' History of Christians, which cannot be rendered intelligible, without the History of Men or general History, be the proper real exponent of the Christian Idea still a focus is wanting, to collect the scattered rays of a Multitude of individual Subjects, and ~~to~~ above all to present their Unity, and as the Objective Form of the Idea, in which as permanent in all succession & entire in each & every Individual, this Unity is grounded.— Such is the CHURCH: and as the Hist. of Christians requires the light of general History, so neither can the Church be understood aright without reference to *the Christendom*, during each of its periods.—

f171   5305 29.144
         ☿ opposite to
         ☿ contrary to

5306 29.145
Οικονομια
Œconomy

5307 29.146

		F
		FΟΙΚΟΣ
Gothic + Ph.	Phoenician	Weicus
Greek − Latin		Vicus
Theotiscan		Civus
Anglo-saxon		Civis

English   Civitas
                                   Citta
                                   City

5308 F°.1   [An entry of 12 lines, heavily obliterated.]   *f1*ᵛ

5309 F°.6   [15 lines heavily scored out.]   *f2*

5310 F°.9   ∧ ∧ ∧ and bear in mind that the disjunction of MIND
from *life*, so as to permit the former to reveal its powers SEV-
ERALLY, must be *preceeded* by a state, in which the mind shews
itself IN *the Life*, on the *materiel* & immediate impulse of the facts,
occasions, and circumstances of his existing state ⟨moment of
Being⟩—I so to say in *the practical Concrete*.—In his verse-exer-
cises, his learning by heart, ⟨in Parsing,⟩ and (tho' in a less degree)
in his construing, there is an a *Sundering* of the mind from the
living present Base of his Self *en masses*/& hence he does better in
construing than in parsing, & worst of all in his Verses.

5311 F°.58   *"vrai* classicality" as Michael Kelly says of Na-   *f25*
varre's Ballet L'Iphagenia in Aulide—Vol. 2. p. 33. Reminis-
cences—

5312 F°.59   12 Janᵞ 1826. Assuredly, more than one advantage to the history of the Church would follow from the adoption
of Eichhorn's hypothesis respecting the Ep. to Titus & Timothy—
namely, that they were written by a disciple of the Apostle's, consisting in part of reminiscences of Sᵗ Paul's oral instructions, and
in part of inferences from these and from the general Principles
& positive Institutions found in the Epistles already published.—
Of Eichhorn's internal signs of their *unpaulinity* I do not think   *f25*ᵛ
much. They struck me as standing in the same predicament with
little potatoes, which, it is well known, are = no great things.
The difficulties of fixing on an occasion and period of the Apostle's
composing & send the three pastoral Charges or Circulars, that
can be reconciled with the recorded history of Sᵗ Paul's Mission &
life (tho' I think rather exaggerated by Eichhorn, and in more
than one instance chargeable with the sophistry of ~~advancing~~

grounding proofs of their spriouslyness on the assumption of the
same, since as long as their spuriousness is not *proved*, the Authority and uncontradicted Tradition of the Church bind us to
receive them as genuine; and if genuine, they form part of the
recorded History, or of the Materials for it)—these trad biographical and chronological difficulties & discrepancies are of more importance. And still weightier is the fact of their not forming a part
of Marcion's Apostolicon, for which no satisfactory reason can be
detected in the contents of the three Letters relatively to Marcion's
peculiar Tenets. On the contrary, while no part directly opposes
or precludes, Marcion's prominent dogma (namely, the independence of Christianity on Judaism, and the disjunction of the Gospel
from the Hebrew Scriptures) many passages would be construed
by him, as supporting and authorizing his it—.—On the other
side, I cannot with Eichhorn consider the assumption of this Apostle's Name as a harmless Disguise—a mere mono-dramatic form,
like Cicero's Dialogues—/The Greetings of individuals &c shock
my moral feelings, & render it very, very difficult for me to
believe that so good, and wise a man as the writer of these Pastoral
Charges must have been, could have condescended to so disingen-
uous an artifice. For whatever may be said of the principles and
institutions, as actually derived from Sᵗ Paul—⟨in⟩ these, the greetings, must the Writer must have been conscious that he was
lying.—Eichhorn talks of numerous analogous instances of Scripture pseudonymous Scriptures. Let him cite a single instance, that
can be fairly compared with the Epistle to Titus & Timothy.—

Nevertheless, I do not retract my first position—that the Hypothesis has its advantages. The imposing a Vow on the Deacon-
esses not to marry again—& making the breach of it a crime—is
very suspicious: and I should be more willing to would be able to
regard it as the dawn of the Anti-christ, the first Beginnings of the
Corruptions & Usurpations of the Church, than have to vindicate
it, as an act of the Great Apostle, whose ruling Maxim was, principiis Obsta—and likewise, it does not seem quite probable to me
that so early as the year 65 (the su most accredited Date of the 2ⁿᵈ
to Timothy, and during the short interval from the year 55 (the
supposed Date of the Ep. to Titus) the separation of the Deacons
Elders from the Deacons, and of *the* Bishop from the Elders,

should have already taken place/.Neither Titus nor Timothy could have needed this—as the Proxies & or Locum tenentes of the Apostolic Founder—*their* Churches, at least, would have felt no insufficiency in the πρεσβυτεροι, as collectively episcopal./And one excuse may be made for Eichhorn & Schleiermacher—that these letters have not the weight, την δεινοτητα the positiveness of purpose, that so eminently characterize the other Pauline Epistles.

5313 F°.60   13 Jany 1826. Thursday—Mr J. H. Frere   *f26* passed an hour or two with me in my Garret, & then took me with him in his Carriage to the Marquis of Hastings, at the Burlington Hotel—with whom I dined & stayed till past midnight—& was sent home in Mr Frere's Carriage—. Met besides the Marquis & Marchioness Hastings, Lady Flora (a young Lady of Genius) her Sister Lady Sara Hastings, her cousin Lady William Russel (a beauty) Lord W. Russel, Lord Rawdon—& in the evening Lady Westmoreland—&c &c. Was most pleased with the Marchioness.

5314 F°.61   A Man of Genius using a rich and expressive Language (the Greek, German, or English) is an excellent instance & illustration of the ever individualizing process & dynamic Being, of Ideas.—What a magnificent History of acts of individual minds sanctioned by the collective Mind of the Country a Language is—This Hint well deserves to be evolved and expanded in a *more auspicious* Moment.

Q.^y Whether words as the already organized Materials of the higher Organic Life (viz. as Vegetables which are the rude Material of Animal life) may not after a given period, become *effete*? How rightly shall we conceive this marvellous Result a Language?—A Chaos grinding itself into compatibility! But this would give only the negative attributes.

5315 F°.62   As I propose to give a sketch of two Schemes of Polit. Economy, in contrast with each other—the one beginning with Things, the other with Persons: so I would annex to my eight Letters on the right & superstitious use of the Scriptures a ninth Letter, comparing the Objective, or philogical, and (in the nar-

rower sense of the word, historical Handling of Scripture: and the
SUBJECTIVE, and historical in the large & most philosophic sense
of History—namely, that which they Scriptures have by divine
Providence become, as a mighty Agent, and into which they may
be realized ~~in~~ *Subjectively*—i.e. in the mind & spirit of the Readers & Hearers.—Each in its own place good & indispensable—
the former to prevent the texts of Scripture from being perverted
into authorities for fanciful Dogmata, or even of sounder Doctrines which, however, can be adequately and profitably vindicated
only by their own *trueness* and *consonancy* with the whole Spirit of
the Sacred Writings collectively.

5316 F°.63   It is of no rare occurrence, that we find ~~an as-
sertion~~ (text) in the Old Testament, the ~~con~~ ⟨direct opposite &⟩
apparent contrary of which the Christian may assert, not only without contradicting the former but in a Light which alone affords a
full insight into its truth.—Ex. gr. There is nothing new under
the Sun—The Christian, like the Poet, finds a perpetual novelty
in the Old/Why? The Christian contemplates Life in *growth*—im
Werden. Not the *thing* but the product of that thing on his own &
f26ᵛ   others' Souls. N.B. This is the relation in which the N.T. generally bears to the Old—it leaves the truth in its full worth & value,
even as it before stood, but it completes it, and then gives it a new
worth—viz. that of a necessary stage on the road./

5317 F°.64   Man, says Scripture, has many inventions—
Thus, he has invented for himself two duties of Sacrifice—
     1. to sacrifice the World to himself in all temporal interest
(Number *One*. Every man for himself & God for us all)—
     2. to sacrifice himself to the World in all ⟨his⟩ spiritual inter-
ests.—To sacrifice the world to himself in temporal; but himself
to the W. in Sp.—

5318 F°.65   If I were disposed to accept a pure and practical
code of Morals under the name of Religion, as Christianity, I
~~might~~ should adopt the Discourses of Dʳ Frederick Schleiermacher, as my Manual and Guide. But I want, I need, a Redeemer: and this is possible only under the two-fold Condition, which

I find asserted in the New Testament and in the Creeds of the Universal Church—that he is my fellow-*man*, yet not my fellow-*creature*. Dʳ Schleiermacher stands in the estimation of his Countrymen generally, at the head of those practical Divines who profess to separate Religion from Theology, and ⟨not to expose, but only⟩ to *imply*, the falsehood of the Dogmas of the Church by avoiding, or rather by seeming to avoid, all reference to them. They preach Christ and Christianity as far as the Person, Character, and Action of the One, and the Doctrines of the other, are *comprehensible*. (See Schleiermacher's Sermon on Good-Friday). But I waiving for the moment all consideration of the truth or falsehood of this Scheme and of its *comparative* worth, there are sundry Draw-backs, that attach to the Scheme itself—inconveniences of its own. Ex. gr. the difficulty of maintaining the language and conduct of Jesus, even as exemplary. ~~D~~ If he be presented merely as a ~~consumate~~ Moral Man, ~~it is questionable whether he would answer to this character~~/it is to be feared that his very morality would be questionable. He must be presumed to have a great deal more, not to be a great deal less/.—Secondly, the Objection so finely urged by Lessing in his *Nathan*—viz. the inju~~diciou~~stice & spirit-narrowing effect of confining our love, and admiration, to a single Character—and this impoverishing the field of Imitation and Sympathy. The late Mʳ Cumberland's slanderous attack on Socrates is but one instance among many of the hard uncharitable bigotry and jealousy, to which this monopoly has given occasion. Again, the comparatively few moral relations, in which Christ was placed, during the very short period, ~~of~~ to which our knowlege of him is confined.—And many other objections of no less weight might be added—all of which vanish, as soon as the secondary is restored to its rank as Secondary. We may apply to   *f*27
this what was said of Neroe—All thought him worthy of Empire till he became Emperor. Christ's humanity seems divine, in subordination to his Divinity.—but is shorn of half its rays, when substituted for it.

5319 Fᵒ.66   On the ~~misuse of~~ misconception of the term, Inspiration, as applied to the Scriptures—Motto for my 9 Letters on this subject.—

Quid enim, an semper silentio premenda erunt talia, in quibus ab aliis ⟨a plebe theologorum⟩ dissentimus? vel an non licebit dissentire ex iis quæ non sunt ad salutem necessaria vel requisita?

Dissentire bonos etiam de rebus iisdem

Incolumi licuit semper amicitia.

Præf. in Cocceii Opera—

Sunt autem quæ, inter αδιαφορα minime censenda sint, quamvis nec in primo ordine necessaria. Vera tamen cum sint et Verbo Dei consentanea, si quis ea ἑτερόδοξα dixerit, falsa et venenatæ lancis instar habenda, peccabit Doctor Ecclesiæ nisi ea, quamvis ~~taceat~~ non omnino necessaria, mordicus tueatur: quia omnis Veritas est Dei Veritas, cujus causam non deserit vir probus.

—Idem—

An potius putabit Vir obscurus, ~~et~~ Custos iste tenebrarum acerrimus, Deum mentitum fuisse, quando apud Danielem Cap. 12 indicavit fore ut "tempore finis scrutarentur multi, et augmentaretur Scientia"?—

5320 F⁰.67   In transcribing the Substance of my Marginal Notes on Schlʳˢ Essay on Luke—Mem. to urge the discourse of our Lord to his Disciples on their road to Emmaus—exorsus a Moses et per omnes Prophetos, quæ de ipso scripta erant, interpretatus est—

Luke 24. v. 25. A stronger support to my theory can scarcely be wished for./

5321 F⁰.68   Elohim = Robora, the Strengths, connected with the image & notion of the TRUNK of an Oak.—It is *vox collectiva*—Unitas Roborum. I neither agree with Eichhorn who would render it the Gods, Dii Immortales, and infers that the Author of this most ancient Cosmogony was a Polytheist; nor with the ~~theory of~~ more unorthodox Divines who would deduce the Trinity from the word. Qui ad probandam fidem utitur argumentis non cogentibus, cedit irrisioni infidelium: says Thomas Aquinas. But need we always address our arguments to Infidels, or argue with Christians, as if they were infidels.

f27ᵛ   For "vox collectiva" overleaf, read: Vox pluralis, plurium in singulo co-immanentiam exprimens.

5322 Fᵒ.69   Eichhorn, Vol. III. p. 11. Über die Paulinische
Briefe.

If this one incident of the Flash stood single, it certainly would
be rational to interpret the fact of Sᵗ Paul's Conversion, as Eichhorn has done. For in the period of only four years I had cut out
from the Newspapers three similar instances, where the persons
had been struck off their horse, heard voices, struck with blindness
& recovered their sight after two or three days.—But Ananias; but
Paul's own following Trance & Vision—in short, but all the con-
texture of the narrative—are these fables of Luke's? If so, what
trust can we have even in the truth of the passages, which Eichhorn
assumes as truth? And what must we suppose Luke's motives to
have been?/It seems as if Luke had composed his Work before the
death of Sᵗ Paul: and if he did, it is to the last degree improbable
that Sᵗ Paul should not have been made acquainted it with it. Is it
in Sᵗ Paul's Character?—and even a personal intimacy could
scarcely give a livelier impression of his character, or one that
more set at defiance all counterfeit & invention, than his Letters
give to every man of Taste, Tact, and sane Feeling—is it, I say,
in Sᵗ Paul's character to have consented to a novel founded on
facts—the facts being a brace or so of Minews and the Novel, alias,
garnish, some half dozen Cod Fish? I fulminate, No! Sᵗ Paul was
κατ' εμφασιν και κατ' εξοχην a GENTLEMAN.

On the other hand, I freely confess, that we do not find, and
probably ought not to expect, in Luke a scrutinizing philosophic
Historian, who previously to drawing up his Report had cross-
examined the Authorities as Dʳ Woolaston would do, supposing
him at the head of a Commission for reporting to the Government
the true state of the facts respecting Animal Magnetism. Not
doubting the great ultimate truths of the Gospel by Christ, in all
the detail, in all the putting together of the minor facts, Luke
thought more of spiritual *Edification*, than of historical precision.

The original sin of the German School is the comparing of this
or that extraordinary a narrative in the Gospel with some other
analogous fact in recent or profane History—instead of taking the
complexus of the New Testament Story & seeking for an analogy
to *this*, in any other series of events allowed not to be miraculous.
In imagination they snap each single Hair, with ease; but in reality,

the generous Steed would have kicked their Brains out at the first
ᵇ kick—as foul Play.—No!—You must try your strength on the
whole Tail.

f28   Luke not acquainted with Sᵗ Paul's Journey into Arabia: and
accordingly in the Speeches of Paul himself, in which he tracks
out the course of his Apostolical Travels no mention is made of
the same.—Ergo: these Speeches are *Livian?*—But why must this
ignorance on the part of Luke be supposed? He might & Sᵗ Paul
in two formal public Orations might well have passed over it,
because it was not connected with any memorable incidents or results—And yet in a Letter, when his Toils & Travels were to be
urged, the Apostle might very naturally introduce it.—But rash-
ness in conclusion—i.e. Luke's Silence *may* have arisen from his
ignorance of the Fact changed it—*must* have arisen—and then of
this journey into Arabia Luke *was* ignorant—this is characteristic
of the Neological School from Semler to Schleiermacher.

—δια δεκατεσσάρων ετῶν παλιν ανεβην εις Ιεροσολυμα—14
years from his Conversion, says Eichhorn who however admits
that this is not the sense of the *Greek*, but supposes Paul to have
mistaken the idiom.—But is it necessary to assert that when Paul
& Barnabas carried the contributions of the Christians of Antioch
to the distressed Brethren in Jerusalem & Judæa, the former proceeded to Jerusalem? Might not Barnabas have gone thither, and
Paul (knowing how much his presence would embitter the Jews &
perhaps not greatly please the Jerusalem Christians) might have
chosen the distribution of the Charity to Christian Communities in
the Country Towns?—

To be sure, what a Contrast does the noble upright Conduct &
Dominion of Paul present with the duplicity ⟨of Barnabas⟩ and
Bantam-Cock forwardness of ⟨⟨want of *Bottom* in⟩⟩ Peter!—These
instances are sufficient to gives us a hint, that Luke's phraseology
is often to be interpreted rhetoricaly & not without many qualifications as the satis et non plusquam satis of a matter of fact historian—but on the generally received notions of his Descent of the
H. G. on the Apostles, our Divines have improved on Luke, and
exaggerated the influence out of all compatibility with the recorded
facts.

5323 F°.70   8 Feb.ʸ 1826

It was by an effort of Self-denial that during my late severe indisposition I withdrew my especial study and meditation from the 4ᵗʰ Gospel and the Epistles of the Apostles John and Paul I. to a free examination of the three first Gospels, and a review of the Controversy respecting their authority & necessity begun by Lessing, and their authenticity and origin which commenced with Eichhorn's Theory of a Proto-euaggelion and continued to Schleiermacher's Counter-theory unfolded in his Essay on the Gospel of Luke which is the last work, that I at least have seen: and *f28ᵛ* II. to a careful continuous perusal of the Apocalypse in the original Greek and the Commentary of Coccëius (b. 1603, d. 1669), to whom long before Janus and Heumann the credit belongs of expunging the Nicolaitans from the list of Heresies, and evincing the little reliance that can be placed on the assertions of Irenæus and the Fathers generally, taken apart from their authorities— while even these are too often of a very suspicious character, from their want of all sound principles of Criticism in the discrimination of Spurious from genuine Works.—My motive for the former investigation was furnished by the translation and publication of Schleiermacher's Essay with a full account of the Controversy and all the controversial Works of any Note, that have appeared in Germany since Eichhorn's Introduction to the New Testament, and Bishop Marsh's Modification of Eichhorn's Theory in this Country. I had long foreseen, that this Disclosure must take place: and that no Cordon Sanitaire could exclude the infection; and from this conviction I wrote the 8 letters on the religious and superstitious veneration of the Scriptures—in the hope of preparing the minds of theological Students for the discussion by shewing that whatever the final result might be, the truth of Christianity stood on foundations of Adamant, and that this conviction emancipating the believer from the Spirit of fear would tend to render the result i[t]self different in no point of real and practical importance different from the common Belief in the Subject *actually* entertained by any man of Learning in the Church during the last half-century. Anxious however that the momentous Truths & Vindications of the Mysteries of our Faith from ~~other~~ unscriptural perversions & distortions set forth in the Aids to Reflection should have fair play, I suspended the publication of the Letters—/and do not on the whole regret it. The appeal to the Fact, as having taken place, will be a less questionable justification of my purpose, than the anticipations of it, as of probable occurrence.

To the second pursuit, viz. the study of the Apocalypse I was impelled solely by the rumours, that had reached me, of my friend, Edward Irving's, Aberrations (for such, I fear, they are) into the Cloud-land of Prophecies of The approaching fulfilment of certain Prophecies, his long Orations on the Millennium, the expulsion of the Gentiles from the Church analogous to that of the Jews, the collection of Gentile False-Believers in Armageddon— & what not of the Faber Insomnia—But these studies were against

f29 my inclinations & cravings. I needed Prayer for my Comfort: I needed unction and tenderness of heart for my Prayers: & this I could not hope to find from the thorns and brambles of critical disquisitions—Still I found the latter a duty of Love and Charity— and I earnestly asked for Light and a humble Spirit—and I trust, that my prayers were graciously heard—for the result has been an ~~extension of~~ enlargement of my views beyond a my hopes, and with it a calming of my mind on what had previously greatly perplexed me—I mean, the startling dissonance, heterogeneity of spirit, between the three Gospels, Matth. Mark, Luke—and the Gospel of Sᵗ John—& tho' in a somewhat less striking way between these Gospels κατα σαρκα & Sᵗ Paul's Epistles/—Equally or even more unexpected have been the enlightening & enlarging Insights obtained by the study of the Apocalypse—which now for the first time I perceive to be an important and even necessary Supplement of the Gospels according to the Flesh, the Gospel according to the Spirit, ~~and~~ with the Epistles—the Apocalypse uniting both & at the same time crowing the whole. In short, it is the Supplement to the New Testament and the Complement of the Christian Faith—.

1. The ~~three~~ Evangelic Triad I comprize under the common title of απομνημονευτα τα των Αποστολων, or Recollections of the Sermons and Discourses of the Eye-witnesses (See Luke I. v. 3.)— containing the acts and sayings of Jesus, as the *Founder* of the Christian Church.—

2. The Gospel of John, or the Acts and Discourses of the Incarnate Word, τοῦ Θεανθρώπου, as the *Object* of the Christian Faith.

3. The Epistles, as the Application of the latter to the establishment and confirmation of the former in its integral parts, i.e. for the ordering and edifying of particular Churches, whoseere while the larger portion of the reasonings and ordinances are common to all Churches & of permanent obligation & interest, in each epistle respect is had to the particular needs and dangers of the particular Church at the then time/—One especial & characteristic Purport of the Epistles is to clear up the true relation of the Gospel to the Dispensation under the Law & the Prophets—*Moses Evangelizatus.*

4. The Apocalypse—or Christ as the fulfilment of all the Prophecies respecting his Royalty—(even as the Gospels of all respecting his humiliation—Christ in his Spiritual Realm but yet not subjectively acting but *objectively*, as King, Conqueror, Avenger, Recompencer, Judge, to whom all Power is given in heaven & in earth—

5324 F°.71   Qʸ ~~That~~ Our present Matthew a translation of   *f29ᵛ* the Recollections of the Church at Pella, and other Churches in Judæa, for the Church at Rome & the Italian Churches generally?—The great number of the Jews, both free and captive, at Rome & throughout Italy immediately after the destruction of Jerusalem must have rendered this Gospel particularly desirable— why not into Latin rather than Greek?—First I answer—that the same question might be asked respecting Luke which is generally believed to have been intended for Christians of Italy—And secondly (which is the solution of both)—that t of the Jewish Captives & other Emigrants from Palestine, 99 understood Greek for one that understood Latin./Even in Palestine itself the number of Towns & Persons, that understood Greek and not Hebrew exceeded thate number of those that understood Hebrew and no Greek—as Hug has clearly proved—.And after all where is the impossibility that there may have been a Latin or Italic Version directly from the Syro-chaldaic—and that this may even have been earlier than our present

5325 F°.72   16 Feby 1826. B. Goldschmidt's Stoppage announced, whose House is said to have *netted* half a million sterling profit in the year, 1824—Vide Second Lay-Sermon, p. 95–104.—

5326 F°.73   Luther (Table-talk) deep, cordial, heroic on the Antithesis of the Law and the Gospel—/The free and dauntless use of the Catachresis makes the Chapter on this head less fit for the present race of religious Readers generally: and indeed at all times must have required a strong digestion. But nevertheless it is invaluable for those for whom it is safe/Like electric Wax, it attracts the doctrine of Antinomianism only to repel it/—In short, my Views is that ~~what~~ such as Religion ⚹ Science in ~~all which i~~ genere, such is the Law ⚹ the Gospel by relative opposition et in gradu.—In Science all appearance of Will is to be removed by being resolved into necessity of Reason: in Religion all the forms of Necessity are to be resolved into the determinations of Will. In Science Necessity appears as a Cause, precluding ~~freedom~~ Will— in Religion as an Effect, supposing it.—Now the Law is to the Gospel as Science to Religion: it is the *Science* of Religion, the Gospel the Religion of the Science. Without the Gospel the Law would not be Religion: without the Law the Gospel would have neither material on which, nor channel in which to manifest its power & ~~conquest~~ victory—it would want its *Rationale*.

5327 F°.74
Mem.

> When thou dost purport aught (within thy
>   power)
> Be sure to do it, tho' it be but small:
> Constancy knits the bones and makes us tower
> While wanton Pleasures beckon us to Thrall.
> Who breaks his own bond forfeiteth himself.
> What Nature makes a Ship, he makes a Shelf.
>   Herbert Church-porch

I would add—Therefore do not often make formal Resolves: but try to do the thing, & then say—Well! I have saved a *Resolve*. *f30* Use Resolves as young men should use Wine or Spirit—. When

I am weak, or ill, or in my decline I may want it: and then it will
have the force of fresh medicine/—Had I £10 to spare, I would
offer it as a Prize for the Eton Boy who should send in the best
Translation of Herbert's Church-porch, with about ¼th of the
Stanzas omitted, in Elegiac Latin Verse./

The Dialogue, p. 107.—supplies a thought of support and inward strength to me—

> Sweetest Saviour! if my Soul were but *worth* the Saving—It
>   were worth the Having!
> Quietly then should I control any thought of *waving*—i.e. of
>   giving it up ⌈. . .⌉—
> What, Child! is the Balance thine? Thine the Poize &
>   Measure?
> If I say, Thou shalt be mine—Finger not *my* treasure!
> What the gains in having thee Do amount to, only He
> Who bought thee ~~on~~ by the Cross can see.

It is a very difficult thing to return a sufficing answer, sufficing
I mean & satisfactory to the Answerer's own Judgement, to the
objection made as often as you complain of the irreligion of the
present age—/In what age have not the same complaints been made
in the same words?—But when I think of the great popularity with
the Readers of the Period from the year 1635 (the year of Herbert's Death) when he delivered the MSS to Mr Farrel ~~&~~ to the
1674, the date of the 10th Edition—& how large these ~~Editions~~
Impressions must have been appears from Isaak Walton, who not
long after the Death of Herbert states the number at 20,000 Copies—. When I read these poems, and compare my feelings &
judgements respecting them at different periods of my own life—
I cannot avoid drawing the Conclusion, that as the *Readers* did at
that time comprize the most thinking & competent Members of
the Community, there must have been more religious *experience*,
more serious interest in the Christian Faith as a business-like Concern of each Individual, than there is at present—when even
among serious people it is *Generals*, the broad total Truths only of
Religion, that are interesting or intelligible to them—When a man
begins to be interested *in detail, from hour to hour*, & ~~believes~~ feels
Christianity as a Life, a Growth, a Pilgrimage thro' a hostile

Country—then he will enjoy *The Temple*, for the same reason that men in general enjoy Franklin's Travels over the Frozen Zone or Parry's Voyages—

5328 F°.75   So as to Books of Education—those written 150 years ago were at all events excellently adapted to the plan & objects of the Educators—but now!—Scarcely half a dozen (out of myriads) Books of entertaining instruction, that can be confidently put into a Boy's or Girl's hands—and as to Books of SCHOOLING a blank—& yet an Alexandrine Library—

5329 F°.76   18 Feby 1826—.I hold it far more probable than I imagined, I should at the first Suggestion of the hypothesis, that the third Trumpet refers to the dreadful System of Robberies, & High-road, & Oppidan, and even in the Streets & Synagogues of Jerusalem itself the *commencement* of which was in Amarus (Marah, Bitterness: Exodus XV. 23.) and Eleazar.—Indeed, I do not see how a judicious Scholar can read the latter Chapters of Josephus's Jewish History; then his Life; & last, his Books of the Roman War, and hestitate to interpret the first four Trumpets of the Factions & the Anarchy that preceded the War—the 5th of the Zelotæ or Terrorists during the Siege; and the 6th of the Collection of the Roman Forces that executed the final Judgement on the murderous City and the P̶ rebellious People—And still observe (as an antidote or (better still) a Prophylactic against the literal chronological scheme of Interpretation) the constant reference to *Seven*— Six days shalt thou labor; on the Seventh &c—3½—either *half the week*, and more than half of the *working* time, the period of growth and process—or the same as the 42 months/—while the thousand Years, the Millennium seems to be the same (i.e. the whole time preparative & previous to the great Sabbath & Jubilee of the New Jerusalem, subtracting the 4th part as the period of Jewish and Imperial Persecution of the outward Church—/—

f30^v

5330 F°.77   Monday Night Feby 20th from the Times' Report Tuesday 21 Feby 1826—"Mr Canning did not suppose or set up that the Bank of England or any other Establishment would act for the public Interest to the exclusion of their own. He did not look for this—it was no part of their Charter a̶n̶—*their real tie to the Public was this (and it was always the safest one & the surest tie,* that the *Interest of the Public became collateral with their own.*"—Now this (less imprecisely worded) I propose to examine by the test of *facts*—*Does* Experience justify this superior Security of *un*moral Self-interest (I do not say, *im*moral)? I say, No! And more over I say, there is a gross fallacy in the Statement—for on a sufficiently large Scale the two (Interest and Duty) must be (not collateral as the Times' *Reporter* has blunderingly expressed it; but) confluent & coincident/therefore *not* on a sufficiently large Scale, nor with a sufficient *Fore*-cast—and therefore a false calculation/ and is it of false calculations, the offspring of blind & blinding Passions, that the surest and safest Ties are to be twisted?—

N.B. In th̶i̶s̶e Debate of this Night Mr Hume made a *surprizing* sensible Speech, as far the question respecting the Causes of the late & present Distress is concerned—and in his doubts respecting the compossibility of a currency exclusively metallic with a Commerce of the ⟨present⟩ vast extent and tendency to extend, I partake largely: tho' neither Mr Hume nor his Master, the late Dr Ricardo, have satisfied my judgement, that a paper currency adequate to the wants & (there is no practical distinguishing of the two) the cravings of such a Commerce & such a Commercial Spirit can co-exist with a metallic Currency without striking at one time against Scylla, and at another time drifting toward Charybdis—when all is smooth & fair, the latter will take place—the metallic currency will be only so much added to the whole mass of the circulating medium, & do its part in raising the prices of all articles of necessity, and luxury—at the first alarm, all will rush at once to procure the ultimate Security, the Subject of universal Confidence (for alas! Credo in Aurum et Argentum is a far more extensive Faith than Credo in Deum Patrem et Jesum Christum) and reduce the paper currency to *stationary* paper./   *f3*^1

5331 F°.78   Tuesday Night, 21 Feby 1826.—

That no reference to the testimony concerning Christ in Josephus is to be found in any of the elder Apologists of Christianity is decisive against the disputed §ph., if these Apologies supply any proof that the Writers were cognizant of Josephus's Works ⟨But this is certain of Justin Martyr at least) at all. The argument drawn from the evident connection between the preceding §ph. and the succeeding, and the utter ασυναρτητον of the intervening & suspected §ph. is strong of itself—and confirms the former. But in fact it is a bungling interpolation. The former half might have passed: for knowing how vehemently convinced a multitude of the first Jewish Christians, if not the majority of the Apostles themselves before their consultation with Paul, were of the Scheme & intention of our Lord to retain the Mosaic Law, reformed from the traditions of men, we cannot think it improbable that a man, like Josephus, (especially after sore experience had convinced him of the ruinous folly of that impatience of the Roman Yoke which Jesus lost his life for opposing) might judge very favorably of him, and be willing to receive him among the Prophets & Patriots whom his Countrymen had persecuted—But the latter Sentences, in which Josephus is made to repeat our Lord's own assertion concerning himself, as him of whom all the Prophets from Moses to Malachi had written—the imposture is too glaring.—Doubtless, therefore, the whole is an interpolation. Alas! h its worst feature is, that it shows us how little reliance we dare place on even the most learned of the Fathers, as Eusebius and Jerom, in any question of the authenticity of passages or books, that seemed to them to strengthen their cause!—And now comes the problem? How shall we most plausibly account for the silence, the utter silence of Josephus, respecting both our Lord and the so rapidly increasing Sect of Christians. A Statesman, Warrior, and Active Commander during the war, he could not but have had his attention forcibly drawn to the Christians by their unanimous refusal to join their Countrymen in the war, and by their abandoning Jerusalem, one & all, before the Siege.—And in this very circumstance I seem to find the solution of his Silence. When he commenced his History of the War, he had become a Flatterer of Vespasian & Titus, and a Partizan of the Roman Interests. To prove the sincerity of his Conversion by exposing the madness of the Rebellion, & at the same time to *palliate* the prominent part, he himself had taken in it, were the Objects, he had in view, in publishing the work. He could not therefore without gross & even dangerous & most suspicious inconsistency defame the Christians for their superior pru-

dence & loyalty to the Emperor & the Roman Government: and   *f31ᵛ*
yet enough of the old Leaven, the pharisaico-Jewish Hate &
Grudge toward a party, whom both as an ambitious ~~Statesman~~
Chieftain, and an active & enthusiastic Soldier, he had so long
despised as Cowards and detested as Traitors, to render it too bitter
a potion to speak of them in term of commendation. He therefore
contrived to consult his safety without doing violence to his feelings by not speaking of them at all.—It is possible, that his pretended belief & flattering attempt to persuade Vespasian to believe,
that *he*, Vespasian, was himself the Christ or Messiah, might have
had some share in the determination.—But after all, is utterly impossible that an active Politician of noble birth & high connections, engaged (according to his own account of himself) from
early youth in political intrigues & party-pursuits, might have
thought & cared very little about the Christians—or mistaken
them for one of the modifications of the *Essenes?*—His account of
these, & the existence of Fraternities & (as we should say) Congregations of Essenes ~~there~~ in the towns & cities of Judæa & its
vicinity is so inconsistent with what we have reason from other
authorities to suppose respecting the number & *Habitat* of the
Essenes, as very much to diminish the unlikelihood of this hypothesis. The whole passage concerning the Essenes, ~~and~~ its disproportionate length, disproportionate to the comparative importance of
the true Essenes, and ~~its~~ that it is manifestly made up of incorrect
~~hearsay~~ gossip, the circumstance of their eagerness in Martyrdom
& their steadfastness in persecution—all appear to me very like a
compost of confused quid pro quo Hearsay—/Add too their Baptism in consecrated water, their sacred social Meals—refractions
& distorted reports of the Christian Sacraments. Besides, if the
real Essenes had been as widely dispersed in knots throughout Palestine, is it probable that no mention of them should occur in the
four Gospels & the Acts of the Apostles—books in which the
Scribes, Sophists or Lawyers (οι νομικοι) the Pharisees and Sad-
ducees occur in almost every Chapter?—Whether this is a new
suggestion, or has been already advanced by Learned Men, I do
not know. It is so long since I have Lardner's Work in my hands,
that I have quite forgotten what he says of ~~the~~ Josephus & the
disputed passage except that he rejects it as spurious on grounds,

which at the time I read him—some 5 & 20 years ago—appear to me decisive.—

f32 5332 F°.79   De sputatione in ignem vividum vel carbonem ardentem—The black, the dusky stain, thin shadow, disappearance, former brightness—so minor our peccata, acts of infirmity, overtakings, in a soul in a state of Grace.—25 Feby 1826.

5333 F°.80   3 March. To trace & picture that sinkback of the Mind into an in *at animal* in which at length every thought not supported by *Things*, i.e. sensuous or sensual impressions, becomes dim & visionary—This state may begin with the mysteries of Religion; but it will end in the most admitted Historical Facts— the origin being the same—the dreadful mistake that the proper source & justification of *Belief* are in the *Senses*.—MEM. *important*

5334 F°.81   13 March, 1826. The passion of the Jews ~~after the state of the admitted association~~ from the time, when the Miracles & immediate manifestations of the Divine Influence, in the Temple or by Prophets especially called up, ⟨were admitted to have ceased—⟩ i.e. during the four Centuries before the Birth of Christ (Malachi is supposed to have finished his prophecies and the prophetic æra—436 B.C.)—the increasing Passion of the Jewish Church & Rabbis for the Miraculous, and with ~~it~~ this a Taste for the Symbolic & *Allo*graphical—(i.e. visual Allegory) for the purpose of giving a ~~miraculous and~~ supernatural air and semblance to doctrines and historical facts which they themselves did not ⟨actually⟩ regard as miraculous—a taste acquired during their sojourn on the Euphrates, ~~ass~~ fostered by their connection with the Medopersian Empire, and confirmed into habit and character by the scanty extent of their National Literature, the whole learning, genius ~~and industry~~ industry and inventiveness of the Nation being confined to the extrication, ⟨or exconjunction⟩ of meanings from the words of the Law & the Prophets—(the Psalms & Proverbs included)—and lastly, stimulated by the craving after a substitute for the wonders & glories of the Old Times, and the desire of appropriating the ~~con~~ more congenial portion of the Greek Philosophy, namely, the Pythagaræo-platonic, by a process of assimila-

tion without acknowleging the debt—/this Passion, I say, (blessings on the Man who invented that "*I say*", for the benefit of all
rambling polyparenthetical ⟨Sentence-⟩ jumblers!) ~~of~~ gave rise to
the early Cabbala—and to that katterfelto scheme of interpreting
the Scriptures, which spite of the ⟨tough⟩ Blow aimed at it by B.
Spinoza in his Tractatus Theologico-politicus remained in full possession of the Divinity Schools to the close of the 18th Century—
(i.e. till within the last 60 or 70 years) the epoch of Semler and
Eichhorn.—To this Spirit we owe the translation of Enoch—or
rather, the translation of the words recording his Death in the
prime of Life into the Miracle of his not dying at all—/An interpretation ⟨however,⟩ which, I doubt not, was earlier than the date
of the ⟨Completion of the⟩ historical Books, & suggested the poetic
drapery & symbolical Ornature of the death of Elijah; who possibly may have been interrupted by sudden death during the strenuous discharge of his prophetic functions, & perhaps have been
attacked ~~under the~~ in this very *æstus* and during the ~~conf~~ illapse of
the ~~prophetical~~ inspiring Power. N.B. I respect Eichhorn as much
as I despise Herder. Eichhorn honestly lets his Readers see what
he would be at. That Hume used, as a *Sneerer*, the admission of
our elder Orthodox Divines, that a Grace & Gift of Faith were
necessary in order to the full and unwavering Belief of the Facts
recorded in the Old and New Testament, is no proof that the same   *f32ᵛ*
declaration may not be made seriously and in good faith by better
men & even by ~~s~~ sincere and convinced Christians. In the second
Century of the Reformation (Counting from A.D. 1500) it became
the Subject of a Controversy among the Protestant Divines,
whether the external and properly historical Evidences of the
Christian Revelation were sufficient ~~to~~ of themselves, to ~~decide the
judgement of an inquirer~~ extort an assent to the truth of the facts
recorded ~~in~~ by the Sacred Historians from a competent inquirer,
so that the ~~position~~ unbelief or imperfect conviction may justly be
attributed wholly to some ~~similar warp or defect of defect of intel-
lect~~ hindrances and disturbing forces in the Inquirer's own ~~moral
state~~ State of Morals and Intellect?—In other words, whether abstracting from all influence of the Holy Spirit and from all subjective predispositions, whether predilection or prejudice, in the
Inquirer, and supposing a competency of Judgement and Infor-

mation, the outward proofs and evidences ~~of the (historical) Truth~~ of the ~~Gospels and~~ Sacred Records ~~sufficed~~ were adequate to the effecting a full and positive Conviction of their truth?—And the ~~larger Majority and~~ Divines, who decided in the Negative, exceeded the Affirmers of the question both in number and in weight of character. In the present day and in this Country the man, who should avow this opinion would be decried as a disguised Infidel, whatever protestations he might make to the contrary—and tho', as it might easily happen, he differed from his Defamers chiefly in the greater extent and orthodoxy of his religious Creed.—Now Eichhorn pretends to no *faith* in *spiritual* Christianity, and decides much as I should do, if I saw and had found in the Christian Religion nothing more or other than he sees and ~~foun~~inds. That is: he is an honest Philo-christian—loves and respects Christianity for its own merits and reverences it because he sees it to be & to have been under the protection and favor of the Divine Providence in a degree so superior and so much more evident, than he can discover in the history of any other Religion as to be equivalent to a difference in *kind*—in other words, sufficient to constitute it a *Religion*.—On the one hand, he does not ~~p~~ affect to disguise his opinion that a philosopher of the present day, educated under the present state of physical and psychological Research, would (could we suppose such a man to have existed) ~~in this age)~~ probably have seen the facts and incidents recorded in the Gospels or in the Old T. in a different light, and have given a somewhat different account of them, than the Sacred Penmen have done/who related what they saw or heard *as* they saw and heard it/.But on the other hand he declines with a smile all attempts to explain these extra ordinary incidents by physical & psychological *possibilities* & suppositions, first as forced & arbitrary, and secondly as scarcely less absurd than would be an attempt to explain the Fata Morgana, or the Vision of the Army on Saddleback, on the principles of ophthalmia—~~and~~ united with those of the Phantasmagoria & Magic Lanthorn./—

f33   In short, if I removed from Christianity the Eternal, and both the universal and my own individual *Subjective*, even as Eichhorn thinks and feels, so in the main should I.—But Herder is a paltry Juggler, a tricksy gaudy Sophist, a rain-bow in the Steam of a

Dunghill.—Christianity does not supersede or discourage the search after probable ~~grounds~~ reasons for the belief of a Future Life—in the depths of the Human Soul, in the course of Nature and the World (Von der Auferstehung, p. 92.) to *spier* after (nach zu spähen [nachzuspähen] Probability and Grounds. Nur das Christentum selbst ist nicht auf diese Wahrscheinlichkeiten, es ist auf den Glauben an eine Geschichte gebauet—Only Ch: itself is not built on these probabilities: it is built on *the Belief of a* HISTORY—i.e. ~~as fact recorded as historical~~ the Gospels."—~~Yet~~ Now observe the inconsistency of the Man! We are to found our trust in a future state on a fact of ~~History videlicet, the Resurrection of Jesus—Yet as and this by a Narrative (for the German Geschichte comprizes means either sometimes the same as our word, History, and answers to our Story, or and sometimes is equivalent to, and (elsewhere) [?organizes] the single narrative, the narration of an event or incident. Remove the depreciative sense (generally) connected on with it, and our "Story" answers best to the word in this place.)~~ Our hope of immortality is founded on a ⟨His-⟩Story—and yet according to Herder a ~~Story~~ History so disguised in Symbols, Jewish allusions, and short and long Allegories, that of the two main Facts which give their value to all the others, Herder believes in the literal sense neither the one nor the other, and does not favor us even with a hint, what we are to believe—i.e. *historically*—instead of them. If Herder's words have any determinate meaning, Christ neither really rose again from *Death*, nor really ascended to Heaven. But this latter, forsooth, is a mere trifle, unworthy of notice/a harmless inference of Luke's & the Apostles grounded on a popular prejudice.—The Deuce, it is?—What then became of Christ? If you reply, Mr Herder! that you neither know nor care—how can your faith be founded on your belief of a History?—A more offensive Conception I cannot imagine, than that the Apostles saw him die afterwards in consequence of his maltreatment before ~~& a~~ & during his Crucifixion, privately buried him & took no notice of the Circumstance—and never did my Soul recoil from a more blasphemous Supposition, than that Christ purposely withdrew from them, and like a second Empedocles, & hid himself in a Cave—or crept into some hole in the wilderness, to die like a sick animal in Solitude./And yet one or the other must have been the case—if there were nothing super-natural in his removal from this Earth!—

It is hard under any one name to designate Herder's Faith—if Faith it may be called which Faith is none—It is composed of contrary Elements in the attempt to balance each other; but by their cont heterogeneity incapable of any union by equilibrium of powers—this is not consolidated but in endless glowing and vibrating in endless fits alternations of attraction appulsion and repulsion. There is a sensibility, a certain refined Epicurism of Moral Sense, a desire to possess the sympathies of the Mass of Christians and an ambition to govern them by this hold on their Feelings—and yet an equal craving to be respected by the PHILOSOPHERS, the superior Intellects! He will linger in and about the Tenets of the Religious, as their fellow-soldier or ally. But then he will have, or he will forge for himself, a Ticket, a Permit, a Certificate from the Philosophic Board, authorizing him so to do!—Alas! but is not this very like a Spy?

f33ᵛ   The most amusing thing in all Herder's theological tracts *to me* is his cool, *vornehm*, i.e. *quality-like* Looking-down on the Founders of Christianity. Poor simple Creatures! excuse them, Gentlemen! They had very good hearts, take my word for it. And tho' they were somewhat silly, yet really put ourselves in their place, suppose that instead of *our* rank, education, and various immeasurable Superiorities, we had been poor vulgar superstitious ignorant Jew Blackguards; like Peter, John & the rest—really, Gentlemen!—do not be offended if I say, that we, even we ourselves, would have thought and acted much in the same way!— And this is a Defence of Christianity!!!—

The supposition that the greater part of Christ's declarations and promises respecting himself as the Son of Man, and his Kingdom, to made to his Disciples during the three years before his Crucifixion were Messianic Prejudices of his Education, Delusions which melted away after his re-animation—i.e. when the Disappointment, and anguish of mind and Body had cooled his imagination, and brought him to see matters in quite a different light (p. 43, 44. Wie anders sieht man die Welt von einem Sterbebette an, als man sie vorher sah! &c) is, I think, quite new—a morceau of the Herderian Sterne-Marivaux-Richardsonian psilanthropic Christianity!/

5335 f°.82   14 March. 1826. In our Lord's reply to Peter, the foundation-stone was evidently contained in the words, the Son of the Living God.—Many had long before supposed, and some fully satisfied themselves, that he was the Christ—i.e. the Messiah/ and this our Lord had repeatedly forbidden them to make public. For in the only sense, in which the Jewish People and the immense majority of the Rabbis attached to the m̶ title—viz. a Descendant of David, and the Restorer of the Throne of David, another and mightier David, as King, Conqueror and Prophet, who was to transfer the seat of Empire from Rome to Jerusalem, it was not only a groundless Tradition but a most immoral and dangerous Delusion, which—let Herder, and the Sect of Vice-christians say what they may—it was our Lord's objecti̶o̶n̶ from the beginning of his Mission to dissipate.—But the anointed, i.e. solemnly ordained and appointed to the redentorial and mediatorial office, who brought from Heaven "the words of *eternal* Life, instead of the ways and means of temporal Empire & Sovereignty, and of political emancipation, that Anointed One who was a̶n̶ properly and primarily *the* Son of the Living God, and only by assumption Son of Man, and by title of office Son of David, and according to Ezekiel David himself—i.e. that Substance of which David as the Type was named the Man after God's own Heart, i.e. the Word, the Expression, the Icon or Substantial Image of the Supreme Mind—the Infinite in the Finite even as the Father is the Finite in the Infinite/

This reply of Peter was indeed well worthy to be the Rock, a̶ on which ⟨and out of which⟩ the Church of Faith was to be built, and a truth which not Flesh & Blood—i.e. no conclusion which Peter's understanding could have drawn from aught he had seen or heard, but the result of an immediate a̶n̶ revelation by the Divine Spirit.

5336 f°.83   Herder—p. 98. I think, I might safely defy a   *f34* Polyhistor to produce a more amusingly impudent piece of Sophistry than in this antithesis of κηρυγμα Rule or Canon of Faith, and Δοξα = opinion of Divines, which Δοξαι when many consented became Dogmata = determined or settled Opinions, or Tenets— αρεσκοντα τοις θεολογοις. Αλλο γαρ δογμα, και αλλο κηρυγμα, says Basil.—Thus: Christ rose from the Dead. This is the Rule—this is

το κηρυγμα της πιστεως.—Well! and what is the Meaning of it—?
Did he rise from Death, having first bonâ fide given up the Ghost,
and been as truly dead as John the Baptist when his Head was on
the *Charger*?—O never mind which Or did he only awake out of
a trance, rose up from the Dead-clothes, and then rose from the
Grave—i.e. made his way out of the Sepulchre, in which he had
been layed?—O never mind! Which you like—this will be is only
a Δοξα, which, if you prefer the former, has been voted into a
Dogma.—II. Christ is the Son of God. This is το κηρυγμα! this is
the *Rule*—But what does it mean? That he was the co-eternal
Word, begotten by the Father from all eternity, and the even He
by whom all things were brought into existence?—Or only that he
was miraculously conceived ⟨by a Virgin Mother,⟩ the Spirit of
God being to him instead of as human Father? Or if this a legend
or an allegory; and do the words mean no more than that he was
an eminently pious, meritoriously, and especially favored Man?—
Never mind! Whichever of the three you like best—It is after all
only a Δοξα—and if you are desirous to have it a Dogma, you need
only look into the List of Sects—/ & you may say—Δογμα εστι·
αρεσκει γαρ ημετεροις θεολογοις, τοις σοφωτεροις, εαν μη τοις
πλειοσιν.

In whom we have remission of Sins.—This is κηρυγμα!—What
does this mean?—By teaching sound doctrine & setting a good
example? Or by any direct efficacious influence on the will & spirit
of the Believer? Or in consequence of a Contract with the Divine
Justice, by which God consented to receive the sufferings & death
pangs of his sinless Son as a satisfaction for the Sufferings, of
which Sinners were under bond of Judgement to have paid?—
Never mind!—How impertinently curious you are!—Which you
like. They are only opinions—take your Doxy here, as you would
on other occasions—according to your liking—. Marry her if you
will—or only take her on trial.—A lawfully wedded Doxy becomes a *Dogma*/Herder was a bit of a Papist in this respect—he
preferred Concubines—& a pretty Coterie he seems to have had—
with whom he semi-demi-quavered modo passerino most diacriti-
callydoxically!

5337   f°.84   18 March March 1826. Saturday—(19th Palm
Sunday. 26th Easter Sunday.)

It cannot be denied, that the foundation of Protestantism, the one intelligible First Position, common to all the Reformers, and separating the Faith of the Reformed Churches from the Tenets of the Romish Communion, is the Sufficiency of the Sacred Scriptures, as the ground and guide of Belief, Morals and Discipline *f34ᵛ* in all points necessary to Salvation. As little can it be denied, that the Reformers, one and all, grounded this *sufficiency* on the hypothesis of them plenary inspiration of the Sacred Writers, in some sense of the word, inspiration, in which, whether from diversity of *kind* or from difference of degree equivalent for all practical purposes to a difference of kind, it could not be legitimately applied to any other writers or writings, however eminent the one or excellent the other—in such a sense, that was in short, as justifies Christians in considering the various canonical Books, collectively and in detail, as the works of one and the same Author—namely, of the Holy and Infallible Spirit of Truth, to whom all the ostensible authors, Moses, David, Solomon, Isaiah, Matthew, Mark, Luke, John, Paul, Peter &c were but Amanuenses.—

But while no competently informed and tolerably candid Scholar will refuse his full assent to both these the truth of this statement, in both instances—the position of the Sufficiency of Scripture, and of their inspiration as the ground and reason of their Sufficiency; this does not forbid us to see and point out the difference between the *fact* that the Reformers *did* so ground the great Tenet, on which they divided from the Papal Church, and the necessity in Reason and Scripture of so doing. It may well happen, that the first Position, which is absolutely essential to Protestantism, may stand firm by its own weight and breadth of Basis: even tho' the Hypothesis, or Sub-basis, supplied by the second Position, should be rejected, if not as ⟨a⟩ false, yet as a doubtful, and unnecessary inference.

But least of all, ought it to be forgotten or overlooked, that this inference of the great Reformers was accompanied in by and inseparably connected with, another position, which, even tho' the former were an error, was proven must counter act the injurious disarm it of all its injurious qualities—namely, the necessity of the same Spirit in the Readers of the Scriptures—so that in those parts only, in which the Spirit in the Letter revealed itself to the Spirit *f35* in the Heart, were guiding *Scriptures* for each Individual—and nothing more was imposed on him than the duty, which both Humility and Charity dictated, of presuming that th all the other parts of Scriptures ⟨might have been⟩ for other Christians and ⟨might become⟩ for himself at some future time or and in other moods & states of spiritual insight, be the transparent Shrines of the same Spirit of Truth.—

Hence therefore it seems to me that the Church at present would be justified in expressing the true practical Rule of the Reformers, as resulting from the combined consideration of the second position and of third by which the second is qualified, in the following formula.—The Bible is the sole safe and sufficient Canon of Christian Faith and Practice: because whoever seeks therein within a right spirit that which is requisite for his spiritual welfare and final salvation, will infallibly find what he seeks. Or—

The Bibles contains all revealed truths necessary to Salvation, and for all men in all times: and every true believer has the promise of God that whatever he seeks in the spirit of Love and filial Trust the Spirit of Truth will enlighten him to find as far as it is profitable for him.—Or.

In all things profitable to our true Welfare the Bible is an infallible Guide for every true sincere Inquirer, who reads the Letter by the light of the Spirit for spiritual purposes & with spiritual desires.—

Observe, however, that this promise is not required and therefore not extended to those who take up the study of the Scriptures as a series of Books written by diverse Authors in diverse ages, for the purpose of understanding the whole historically and philologically. This is indeed a most worthy and honorable Object of Pursuit—commendable for all Christians who have leisure and the means of so doing, and a duty for the Doctors of the Church/—Here all the ordinary means and aidances of rightly interpreting ancient writings are requisite—the and such as the light of no single age can suffice to furnish—/Who indeed could even wish, that so elevating, so edifying a pursuit should ever cease to be an object of intellectual effort—which, were it absolutely completed, must be the case? One man & one age correct the mistakes and fill up the deficiencies of the preceding; leaving still as rich a Harvest for their successors.—Methinks this latter, in the study of which the Bible must be read as any other Book of similar antiquity in a dead language, is as distinct from the former, as the examination by a scientific Lapidary or Mineralogist of the 12 precious Stones in the Urim and Thummim of the High Priest from the contemplation of the revealing Light & Flashes from the same in the moment of the Holy Spirit's Presence in the whole/—

5338 F°.85   Αλλο μεν το ρημα, αλλο ο λογος. In which of our   *f34ᵛ* learned Divines shall I find more truth more nobly expressed than in the following §§ ph. of poor despised Jacob Behmen—Vol. II. p. 152—ad finem.

How dead is the Faith which stops at the knowlege, the notion! An historical faith is but the ~~belief~~ Hearing of a Story, ~~that is~~ where he, who hears it, has a notion that it is a true story. Is *this* the way to Eternal Life?

O no, all this avails nothing/—⟨It avails nothing⟩ that thou knowest and dost entertain thyself therewith! True Faith in Christ is quite another thing. It lies not barely in the History and in the Letter. The *Letter* is not the word/: it is but a leader and director to the Word. *The Word is living and hath the Spirit*: and the Right FAITH is the Right WILL, which enters into the living word.

5339 F°.86   Monday 20 March 1826.—To meditate on the   *f35ᵛ* personality of God, and on the personëity both of Good and of Evil. See J. Smith's Select Discourses, p. 463. If I cannot but feel, see and think that my intelligent Will gives origin to a new direction and determination of the physical as well as moral trains of causative acts, so that Things & Thoughts take other configurations and are productive of ~~other~~ events and phænomena that would ⟨not⟩ otherwise have taken place; ⟨& this⟩ without any disturbance of the order of the World, either ⟨the⟩ visible or the spiritual, and ~~without hindrance to any process leaving in~~ without preventing or jarring with the power & the means of rational Calculation or desirable Foresight—why may I not ~~far rather~~ attribute the same influence in ~~an infinitely~~ higher degree and more perfect form to the ~~Divine~~ Will ⟨of God⟩ without any subtraction from ~~the~~ *his* Wisdom and Providence? ~~of God?~~ And what more than this Belief is necessary for Prayer and in order to pray in

faith? Grant even—which however I discern no reason for granting but many and mighty grounds for denying—that Spinoza with
the necessitarian Predestinators were in the right, and that both the
Consciousness of free agency and the appearance of events and
products *originatinged* ⟨there-⟩by, ~~voluntary acts~~ were a delusion
imposed on us by the constitution of the Human Mind—Still it
remains a Law of Nature, which we must follow, and which we
cannot withstand without destroying the harmony of our own
Being, without a daily and hourly inconsistency between our
thoughts and feelings, our reflections and our actions, without, in
short, rending ourselves live asunder from the community of the
Human Race! If the Necessitarian boldly takes anchorage in Atheism, there is an end of the Question. Acknowlegement and
Thanksgiving are no less precluded than petitionary Prayer. But
if he stops short of this, if there be a God that sees and hears, a
Creator and Saviour, how can it be otherwise than ~~well pleasing to
him and~~ accordant with supreme Wisdom, that I should obey the
f36   Law, which ~~he has~~ itself implanted in my humanity?—How can I
suppose myself to walk humbly before the Lord my God, if I
strive to overfly *the* NATURE, in which he hath willed to create
me—and which constitutes me a Man? ⟨see p. 68⟩

What I *must* do, what I *do* do, in full confidence to my earthly
Friends and Superiors, asking and not doubting that I shall obtain
what I reasonably ask, and obtain it in consequence of my asking,
can I hesitate to do when I lift up my heart to my Almighty Friend
and Guardian?—If in the former instances I relied on the weakness, ignorance or corrupt passions of my Friends, then indeed I
might well dread to ~~ret~~ transfer my petitions to the Throne of
Eternal Strength, Wisdom and Holiness. But if I appeal to the
Goodness of my Benefactor, if I ground my hopes of Success on
~~the~~ his known or believed Judgement—if my motives for addressing my request to him rather than to any other of my Acquaint-
ances have been drawn from my conviction of his moral and intellectual excellence—then the measureless superiority of the
Divine Wisdom and Goodness can only tend to render the reason-
ableness of my preferring my petitions ~~to our Heavenly Father~~
thitherward, proportionally greater & more evident. If Reason
discountenances what Wisdom dictates, let me be irrationally wise
rather than foolishly rational! Let me pluck fruits from the Tree

of *Life*: the Apple from the Tree of ~~Knowlegeingness~~ I leave for the Devil to chew—/ ⟨The original Pip was of his Planting:—and let *him*⟩

"with spattering noise
And hatefullest disrelish writhe his jaws
With soot and cinder filled!

⟨l. 4. p. 67⟩ But am I not entitled to ask the Calvinist/—if ~~R~~   *f36ᵛ* my reason rejects the ~~ideas of~~ influence of petitions ~~to~~ on God, as incompatible with ~~absolute~~ his universal Prescience (and how could an omnipotent Power foresee & not predestine?) and with the divine Immutability; does it not equally reject the notion of a delusion generated & necessitated ~~by~~ in an intelligent creature by the Law of its Creation an incompatible with the Veracity of God, ~~making him~~ (in the bold language of the Beloved Apostle) making God a Lyar! And what if in the former case ~~not~~ it should not be Reason in its own sphere, ⟨that decides on the former,⟩ but the Light of Reason in the understanding equally certain indeed, ~~in the former, but~~ only not absolutely, but *conditionally?* Now one of these conditions is, that the terms are such as the Understanding is capable of adequately *presenting* to the Conclusive Power of the Reason?—And is this the Case with the connection of Will and Knowlege in an Eternal *I am?* Is not the very Prefix, Fore, ~~that~~is contraband from the Realms of Time & Place, this heterogene ~~weldeding in~~ out of Clay to Gold, a pretty good proof of the contrary?—And further, have we not ground to ~~believe~~ conclude (if the Belief in ⟨an⟩ all gracious & wise God be conceded as the Premise,) that our moral intuitions of ⟨God's⟩ Truth, Love, Holiness, are ⟨more to be relied on, are⟩ both clearer & ~~in~~ less inadequate, than our Conceptions of the intellectual Acts & Essences of ~~the~~ unique & (even on this account, were there no other cause) incomprehensible Being—with which ⟨act⟩ we have no concern except as they enter into the constitution of his *Wisdom?*—Absolute Will = Θεος; + Supreme Intelligence; = Divine Wisdom. Hence the Holy Spirit proceeding from the Father and from the Son was by the Fathers named Σοφια

Will	Int	Το Αγαθον	+	Ο Λογος	=	ἡ Σοφια
\ /		Father		Son		Holy Spirit
Wisd		Ο Αγαθος		Ο Αληθης		η Σοφια

f1ᵛ   5340 26.3   [Notes towards a Greek Grammar: in *SWF*]

f132ᵛ 5341 26.99   It is decided that different Nerves or Parts of
Nerves are instrumental to the Will, and to the notices from the
periphery—abducent & adducent. But these two are not the only
purposes of Nerves—ex. gr. those of the reproductive System, and
the imagination. Mechanic or chemical Stimulation of the Nerves
of the Heart do not quicken its beat, tho' they appear to increase
its excitability to Agents applied directly to it. The ~~Grape-cluster
skin~~ membrana botruoeides of the Eye is only not wholly insensate—& yet is amongst the most nerve-enriched Parts of the Body
in animals.—Generally, Sensibility stands in no calculable ratio to
the number or size of the nerves—the marrow-skin of the Bones
is nerveless yet exquisitely sensible—the voluntary muscles have
comparatively little feeling, and yet are rich in nerves.—The question then is: What is the formula, which expresses, distinguishes,
& comprehends all the functions & purposes of Nerves—Qʸ? Potential Insemination? Is the Nerve the proper *Male* of the Texture
& Structure, to which it belongs—? Is it the Transit-organ be-
f132 tween the Actual and the Potential? This might be heard (lässt sich
hören, as the Germans say) if the Nerves were all abducent or
adducent. But in those that originate elsewhere than in the Brain,
what & where is the Actual. Stahl would cut the knot at once; but
I ~~will~~ can not hold his doctrine † impossible, neither dare I assent
to it. My first and boldest Proposition is the best—ανδροπερμα
genericum in θηλυσπερμα specificum
f131ᵛ   It cannot be denied that there is a difficulty in the Hypothesis
of the Vis Vitæ organifica from its dependence on its product—
Castration stops for ever the seminal Secretion, Extirpation of the
Breasts the lacteal—a *difficulty* I say. ✳

f132 † Plausible grounds for the dependence of all on the Will in the
instances of those who could suspend their life by an act of their
will—& of many (Fontana asserts it of himself) who had subjected
the motions of the Heart & the Iris to their will. Of the former
facts a collection by Martin, 1777. Abhandlung der Schwedischen
Academie.—Where is the proof that every sense-nerve has its specific sensibility, whence Treviranus infers a distinct organization

in each? How is it known, that the nerves of Smell have no excitability by Light? May it not far more philosophically be explained
by the different *Tune* conveyed by each, by which whether Light
or Odor be the ab extra Cause the mind judges?—

Ganglia Trev. Biol. V. 358–361.—Precious Logic—G. necessary to intercept the effluences of the will; but (in answer to Hasse
[Haase], Prochaska &c the nerve may do this as well without
them.—Q:? A remnant of Insect life not yet worn out, the human
body still far from its ideal Type? The seat of insect Instincts
turned ad intra.

※ 22 March, 1826. Attempt to lessen this still by me admitted   *f131ᵛ*
difficulty. Consider an Artistan in his work-shop. Many of his
Tools may be made extempore, like Pens or Chalk-pencils—/Sev-
eral of them may be as it were regenerated at little cost & trouble—the edges & points, for instant, of his Cutting and piercing
instruments—others, when broken or spoilt may cost the Artist
hours, days, nay months to re-produce, and yet it may be worth
his while to do this, and it may be in his Power—. But there will
be some that had cost him years to make, and this during a period   *f131*
of his life when he was in possession of means & facilities that no
longer are at his disposal. It may be, he cannot afford the ~~necessary~~
requisite time & effort, having to maintain himself the while, &
he too living from hand to mouth/~~and~~ especially if the complex
and costly machine was for the finer works, ~~for the purposes of~~ to
gratify the luxury of the Eye & Taste, & that he could earn the
necessaries of life without it, or it may be, that this machine was
made by him at a time when he had assistants & by co-operation
(Vis vitæ uterinæ Matris). May not these ⟨as⟩ *analogies* suffice to
prove the possibility of the Organs being the workmanship of
Life, notwithstanding the dependence of the Latter on the former
in the instances above stated? The more so, that the processes destroyed are for temporary and extrinsic ends, and the organs such
as tho' not violently removed would yet undergo a *virtual* extirpation, many many years before the decay of those which had existed from the Birth?—

5342 26.100   Our Humian Psychology at the best is but   *f131ᵛ*
what chemistry would be, if it resolved every thing at once in the

first instance into Carbon, Nitrogen, Oxygen, Hydrogen & allowing no identity to the proximate units, *Camphor* &c—

5343 26.101

f130ᵛ
Tutor and Pupil

T.   Say, you had never seen our Neighbor, Mʳ Jones's, little Girl, (the Baby I mean) without either its Mama, or the Nursery Maid. But you can *imagine* it without either; and you can imagine Mʳˢ Jones without the Baby: and in like manner the Nursery Maid?

P.   To be sure. I can imagine either *separately*.

T.   Well said! That is the right word. And of course, you can *think* of them separately. Again—you have often seen Tom May *sitting still*, and you have, perhaps as often, seen him running: and you can imagine him either running or sitting still!

P.   ~~No doubt~~ What should hinder me? To be sure, I can.

T.   But can you imagine Running or Sitting still without Tom May, or any ~~else~~ one else! Can you imagine these, or either of these, *separately*. Think a moment before you answer! To *imagine* ~~a thing~~ is to ~~call up~~ have in your mind an *image* or ~~form~~ shape not actually in your sight. For if it is present, you say, I *see* it—not, I imagine it. We imagine things in our dreams, with our eyes
f130   shut. I have never *seen* the Pike of Teneriffe; but I can readily *imagine* it. Now my question is: Can you *imagine* Running by itself, without ~~an~~ the image of a man, woman, horse, dog, stone, river, or the like?—Try!—

P.   No. I cannot.

T.   Now suppose, that three men, of exactly the same size, drest exactly alike, and with masks on their faces, ran a race for a prize or a wager: and that you were the Judge, to award the prize. ~~And~~ Or suppose, that it was across a plain, and that first one ran—that a few minutes afterwards the second; and again, a little while after, the third—/that the Starting Post and the Goal were both out of Sight; and that you had layed a wager, that you would determine by your eye which of the three had reached the Goal in the shortest time—What would you confine your attention to?

P. To the Running.

f129ᵛ   T. Right. Then tho' ~~you~~ I cannot *imagine* Running *by* itself, ~~you~~ I can *think* of it *for* itself? I saw a Stone ~~running~~ rolling down a

Hill-side, and a man, a Horse, & a Grey-hound all abreast running beside it.

P. Why, yes! Or how could you say of ~~a~~ the Man, a Horse, a
Grey-hound, and a Stone ~~that set rolling down a Hill~~, that all four
were *running*, if ~~I could~~ you had not ~~think~~ought of *Running*, for
itself: before you saw either of the four?

T. I am glad to find, that you understand me. Now do you remember any word that expresses this way of thinking? You do not?
Well! I will tell you. It is called thinking *abstractly*. You cannot
imagine Running *separately*: but you can think of it abstractly.
What is abstraho in Latin?

P. To draw off, or withdraw.

T. Well! and your attention was withdrawn from the Man, the
Horse, and the Grey-hound, as to their *difference*, in order that you
may give your whole thought to the one point, which was common
to all three—namely, the *Running*. But you can go farther. Without thinking of or imagining any ⌈ . . . ⌉ particular person or
creature you can say—There is a great difference between Run- *f129*
ning, and Walking. Or—Running heats the Blood.—In such instances, you think and speak of Running in the *Abstract*.—You
understand this?

    P. Yes.

      T. Will you try to remember it?—Now
then, run off to your Play. To-morrow morning we will renew
our Question & Answer Lesson.

Dialogue II.

5344 F°.87 Good Friday. March 1826.—The moral purity *f36*
and worthiness of our Lord's Character in respect of his accomodation of the Truths of his kērugma to the popular Opinions of
the Jews not defensible without the admission of the truth of his
promise, My *Spirit* shall be always with you—or the doctrine of
the Holy Ghost & the Communion with the same, as an essential
& perpetual article of faith.

5345 F°.88 Easter Monday, 1826
 It is wonderful to me how so many acute men, who have adopted *f36ᵛ*
& defended the Calvinistic Doctrine of Predestination, and abso-

lute Reprobation should not have seen, that they stop short on the Road of Consequences—and in the very wantonest exercise of the Willkühr, free choice, which they reject & exclude, stop because they do not *like* to go further—when there is not even a Turn in the Road, or a Bar thrown across, to justify the Halt—The inevitable next step or two would & must have been a Universal-God—*all-God* ⟨an Oceanic God, Man, Beast and Plant being mere⟩ & ~~merely~~ wavelets & wrinkles on the ~~ocean~~ surface of the Depth—Wars and peaceful Æras, Creeds and Theories, the Smiles and Frowns on the "faces of the waters. Qy The dogma of predestined Reprobation, and of Creation of Multitudes for & with the immutable purpose of their everlasting Misery a *Verjuice Grin*?

5346 F°.89   1 April 1826.—

Mem. ~~for~~ to conclude the Essay or Dialogue on the Church with an ~~scheme of~~ earnest exhortation to, and Scheme of Union between our Est. and the really pious & orthod. Dissenters who have the interests of our common Christianity more at heart than the "Dissenting Interest."—A strange and ominous phrase! Vide p. 84, 85 of the Answer to the First Court Chaplain Dr Ammon—

f37 The Reformation commenced at the same time in very remote places & under very different circumstances/It must have been a miracle therefore or rather a ~~var~~ multitude of Miracles, if tho' they all rose out of the same spirit & were all built on the same foundation, they had been equally uniform in ceremonies, discipline and the details of doctrine/especially in parts where two opposite errors were to be avoided, two poles of one truth to be asserted & secured—viz. the predetermination of all things & events by the divine Providence for the salvation of men, and the responsible will of men without which man would be no subject of a moral Providence—the Power & Omniscience of God, on the one hand, ~~with~~ & his justice and goodness on the other. What wonder then, if one Community were under circumstances which made the one the predominating object in their mind and in their anxiety to secured had expressed the doctrine with too little reference to the other.—Calmer spirits will arise—& the sad consequences of division, past, mutual weakness & the exaltation of the common Adversary—and fanatical or semi-infidel Sects, the Cari-

catures of their differences—will, it may be hoped, prepared the
minds of the better members, the genuine Christians, of both Parties to co-operate with them—and the Spirit of Wisdom, which
~~results from~~ ascends at the moment in which the equbrium of the
~~equal & opposite but omnipowered~~ polar ~~half-truths~~ forces is re-
adjusted, and the half-truths interpenetrate, will give a blessing to
their labors. For Absolute ~~Power~~ Goodness & Supreme Intelligence become one in Infinite Wisdom—and Omnipotent ⟨Will⟩ is,
as it were, the ineffable Nature & Ground of All!

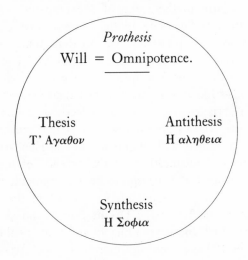

Prothesis
Will = Omnipotence.

Thesis   Antithesis
Τ' Αγαθον   Η αληθεια

Synthesis
Η Σοφια

5347 F°.90   "To hold the mystery of Faith in a pure Con-   *f37ᵛ*
science—τὸ μυστήριον τῆς πίστεως ἔχειν ἐν καθαρᾷ συνειδήσει—
instanced by Schleiermacher in his numerous list of unpauline &
απαξ λεγομενων words & phrases in the 1ˢᵗ ⟨to⟩ Timothy—.
I agree with Schl. in rejecting Theodoret's αντι του τοις εργοις
βεβαιοῦντας πίστιν, but cannot *reprobate* the phrase as unmeaning
but would illustrate it by the text in James C. I. v. 25. ο παρακύψαι
εἰς νόμον τέλειον τὸν τῆς ἐλευθερίας—Nay, I prize it as a noble
& simple enunciation of a most vital truth—that in the Conscience
is contained the Mystery of the Faith and should explain it as—
who in a pure conscience find the substance & true solution of the
Enigma of Faith—i.e. the fact & certainty of a more real reality
than that given by the sensuous or the sensitive ζωη ψυχικη—&

which must be *trusted in* above & in defiance of the inferences from the notices of the senses or the sensations.—

5348 f°.91   Εις Εδουαρδον.

First, what is a Sacrament? A Sacrament is a Symbol or Mystery consisting of ~~an outward~~ sensible Sign and a Spiritual Substantiative Act. An *Act*, observe: not a doctrine, ~~nor~~ nor even an event, however aweful, nor a duty: ~~for~~ else you would scarcely find one of the whole Rat-tangle of the Romish Ceremonies, which would not ~~b~~ have a claim to the name of a Sacrament.—[N.B. This definition, which is far more to the purpose that that which is implied in the Note to p. 55 of "Aids to Reflection," which so far partakes of this as to distinguish a Symbol or Mystery from a Ceremony, but does not determine the distinctive character of a Symbol that is ~~at~~ likewise a Sacrament. I therefore retract the position that "Marriage————————is perfectly a *sacramental* Ordinance": tho' the reasons annexed why it is not one of *the* Sacraments, or to be joined with Baptism and the Eucharist, are still valid, as additional justifications of the decision of the Reformed Churches. In order for Marriage to be a Sacrament, the substantiative Act must ~~have~~ be *spiritual*, i.e. an act of the ~~Heart~~ Soul corresponding to an Act of the Divine Spirit, and as it were the medium thro' which the ~~latter~~ gracious influence of the latter is ~~n~~ conveyed to the Believer, and not merely a *moral* Act—. Again— the ~~outward Act~~ sacerdotal Conjunction of the Parties as wholly declarative and benedictory, not essential to a true matrimonial union tho' in all ordinary circumstances indispensable because it is ⟨an⟩ indispensable duty to obey the Laws of the Land where they do not contravene the Laws of God, and because the Law in question is especially beneficent & expressly sanctioned both by the letter & the spirit of the Divine Law—the sacerdotal Form, I say, being wholly declarative & benedictory, is therefore properly entitled the Marriage *Ceremony*, ~~The Act~~ and by no means a Symbol. The Act indeed must be symbolic/or it is a mere Animal Concubitus & not a Christian Marriage,—symbolic of the *Moral* Union, in which ~~either~~ each of the two Persons morally perfects the other. Dimidia in ~~unum~~ totum concurrunt, like two opposite Mirrors, each containing the Image of the other; but in order for to be ⟨a⟩

sacramental Symbol, this moral Act should be not (as it *is*) a sign of a future Union of the Whole Church with Christ; but a Symbol, i.e. a sign co-existent & co-present with that which it signifies.— See p. 55.—Now then let us go back and restate my position—.

A Sacrament is a Symbol or Mystery consisting of a sensible   *f38* Sign and a *spiritual* Substantiative Act—the ~~first~~ predicate ⟨Spiritual⟩ distinguishing the Act ~~both~~ from a physical, and even from a *moral* act, unless in the latter case the act of the soul shall be correlative to an act of the Divine Spirit, and the medium thro' which the gracious influence of the Divine Spirit is conveyed to the Believer—while the *Act*, and the substantiative act, ~~a~~ is in distinction from a doctrine or Duty, ⟨or office⟩ or an event, however aweful & important: otherwise all the numerous Ceremonial rites of the Romish Church would be intitled to the name of Sacraments.—Thus definition thus explained excludes on the one hand ~~the ordin Romish~~ Penance, Ordination, Marriage &c from the list of Sacraments in opposit(ion) to the Romish Theologians; and the receiving of Bread and Wine, as exclusively a signum commemorans, in opposition to the *Zwinglian* Sacramentaries. (N.b. *not* the *Calvinistic*. Calvin's exposition is not so properly to be denounced as erroneous, as to be complained of, as *defective*: and as not containing any reason for the particular terms, Flesh and Blood.)

Well! ~~on~~ from this analysis of the term we learn, that every Sacrament is a Ceremony; but that every Ceremony is not necessarily a Sacrament. Now let us suppose a Sacrament, the ceremonial part of which had two or three several purposes, ~~the~~ one outward, another inward, ~~the~~ one general and public, another personal—and the former, again, divided into two—viz. an outward & public purpose in relation to a ~~larger~~ more distant, and a special and household purpose in relation to a ~~more~~ closer circle. ~~To~~ But in both divisions ~~of~~ the outward purpose ⟨was effected by⟩ the ceremonial part of the Sacrament alone. The Ceremony, I say, was the means to these ends: for the sensible Sign abstracted from the Spiritual act is, of course, a Ceremony: and in the present case the substantiative act is hidden & confined to the Soul of the individual Agent and Patient.—Further, let us suppose, that at the first institution of the Sacraments the circumstances were such that

all these several purposes, outward & inward, were a co-effectible
at one and the same time by one & the same ministration; but that
in the course of six or seven Generations the circumstances had
~~altered in so many~~ been so changed & almost reversed, that the
purposes could not but be separated in respect of time—that the
one was most wanted when the ~~other~~ attainment of the other was
wholly out of the question, and morally if not physically impossible.—~~What would Here, however, we must add supply~~. In this
dilemma what was to be done? But before we attempt to answer
this question, there is one fact to be mentioned that may perhaps
tend to lessen the difficulty—namely, that the Divine Institution
of the Sacrament had promised to the Church thro' all ages, as
long as it *remained his* Church, that he would be with them as a
guiding & suggesting Spirit always—and on the ground of this
perpetual & continued presence had communicated a power & authority to the Churches not indeed of altering or repealing his laws
& ordinances but of giving *effect* to them, and of preserving the
spirit & Substance of his Commands by the adoption of such
means, as the circumstances should dictate & require.—

f39   5349   F°.92

  Open a bounteous ear: for I'll be free,
     Ample as Heaven! Give my Speech more room;
  Let me unbrace my breasts, strip up my Sleeves;
     Stand like an Executioner to Vice
  To strike his head off with the keener edge
     Of my sharp Spirit!

                              Marston's *What you will.*

   I'll do that my dear Boy! which few of thy acquaintance do, love
thee; but I will not do that which they all do flatter thee, nor that
which many do, laugh at thee behind thy back/I'll tell thee the
truth—thou hast two humours, which I would have thee cashier—
the humour of Comparison, ⟨ex. gr. Jan. Steen & Wilkie—⟩ and
the pugnacious *viscous* humour, which causes thee to stick to an
argument, and draw out the threads thereof like boiled treacle/—
yea, would in mid dinner when thy neighbors are longing for a
change of viands—. Then thou leavest off reluctantly, with a restless look at thy mouth—Tut, man! drop it neatly—let ~~it~~⟨the shut-

tle-cock⟩ be ~~& take~~ tis a slug ⟨& weak-winged—⟩ & take up another shuttle-cock that will perhaps fly better & have lifesomer
feathers/—*Half* Marston's—

> ~~We~~ I too have been a Disputant & wrangled
> With much applause; but age & home-felt weakness
> Have drawn our eyes to search the heart of things
> And leave vain seemings—

The following from Marston's Parasitaster are fine—

By him, by whom we are! I think, a Prince Whose tender suf-
france never felt a gust of bolder Breathings; ~~that~~ but still liv'd
gently fann'd With the soft gales of his own flatterers' lips Shall
never ~~known~~ his own complexion.—Thou grateful Drug, sleek
Mischief, Flattery, Thou dreamful Slumber that dost fall on Kings
As soft and soon as their first holy oil, Be thou for ever damn'd! I
now repent Severe Indictĩons to some sharp styles. Freeness, so it
~~grown~~ not to licentiousness Is grateful to just States. Most spotless
Realm, And men oh happy! born beneath good Stars Where ⟨that
which honest men cannot but think, They may speak too, &⟩ what
is honest, ⟨honest men may think,⟩ ~~men may (freely think)~~ Speak
what they think, and write they do speak, ⟨publish what they
speak,⟩ Not bound to servile Soothings!—

In the first speech of Chapman's *Bussy D'Ambois* there is a most
beautiful thought spoilt by the lengthiness & tumid pastiness of
the language—The Ship that has put a girdle round the Earth
when near their haven *are fain* to call a poor fisherman or prattic
man who never passed sight of land to guide it in/

5350 F°.93   ~~Tuesd~~ Monday, April *10* for especial Meditation—"For who is God save the Lord? Who is our rock save our
God?"/

5351 F°.94   ~~Wed~~ Tuesday 11 April 1826.—I have just read
Clement's Ep. to the Corinthians, (Archbishop Wake's Translation) in Hone's Apocryphal N.T.—. (By the bye, it is much to be
wished both for poor Hone's Sake and for that the Book is really
a Desideratum in our cheap Literature supplied, that he could be
induced to make the Amende Honorable for the grievous faults

into which ⟨he had been hurried by his⟩ Illiterateness and the Self-conceit ~~as shewn in~~ which is the ~~ever~~ universal accompaniment of illiterate self-educat*ing* Men, who have good natural talents & warm feelings & aggravated in this ~~or~~ instance by ~~his ex~~ Zealotry for an imagined *New Light*—to ~~g~~ procure some sound thoroughly learned Man to prefix an accurate account ~~of~~ to each of the ~~C~~ Books, ~~distinguishing the existing Copies from~~ with the probable date of the Mock Gospels now extant, as well as the earliest authorities for the existence of the Works, ~~of~~ themselves spurious, & of ~~the~~ which these are vulgar falsifications—and all which/i.e. the first 8 in the collection, should have been divided, as a separate collection, from Clement, Barnabas, Polycarp, ⟨Ignatius⟩ & Hermas—of which latter the admitted interpolations & corruptions (τα νωθα) should be marked by a *—from the suspected but yet by many learned Critics vindicated passages, which might be pointed out by + − and the grounds and arguments advanced for either opinion/—and thus to give a new & unobjectionable Edition—to which I think the Book of Enoch in the Royal Library at Paris might be conveniently added.⟩—But before I come to Clement, let me note the amusement I have received from the perusal of the Manichaean Gospel of Nicodemus—Q:ʸ Had Milton read it? The Double person, the Death-King, ~~ae~~ which accords well with the name *Satan*, in its etymon, Circuitor, who walks over earth seeking whom to devour, as well as its derivative sense, Adversarius—the Last Enemy of Sᵗ Paul—, and the Hell-King, Beelzebub—is adopted by the Great Poet—and the whole Scene of our Lord's approach to the Gates of Hell is almost worthy of the Curse of Kehama.—But what particularly struck me, was the coincidence with the Arab. Nights Entert. in the Story of the Mule—. The Arab. Night have been long supposed to be of Persian Origin—from whence the Manichaeans are supposed to have come & the whole Tale of the Transformation has an oriental character/—But sat nugis—ducant in seria—& so to Clement.

f39ᵛ

I have not attended very closely to this Epistle: but the II Clem. ⟨C⟩ XVI. ⟨v⟩ 18. is the only one which struck me at first reading as a probable Gloss that had slipt into the text—for if Clement had really himself quoted from the Epistle to the Hebrews, I cannot help thinking that of so recent a work he would have marked the quotation by some introductory or inserted Sentence: and still more, that if the dogma concerning the person of Christ implied in the words "by *inheritance* obtained a more excellent name than they (the Angels) had been distinctly before the Good Bishop's mind, some traces of it would be found in other parts of ~~an~~ long Epistle in which the characteristic attributes of Christ form so frequent & so prominent a subject. And yet I cannot discover a line, ~~in~~ which a pious Socinian (n.b. *not* a Unitarian de scholâ Preistleio-Belshamensi, but a pious Socinian) addressing himself to those of his own flock homiletically & without any thought of controversy, might not have written.—This, however, tends to confirm my opinion that the doctrine of the Trinity, and the ⌈. . .⌉ union of the second person distinctly from the Father, and the Holy Spirit with the Human Nature in the person of Jesus, as the synthesis or tertium aliquid of both, may be legitimately deduced from very many passages of the New Testament—say rather, from the whole Canon, but is not expressed, nor, can I find satisfying reasons to suppose, that this great Truth was present to the minds of the Apostolic ~~F~~ Writers, as the immediate subject of their consciousness—in the same way, as the divinity of our Lord was. For had it been so, surely we should have found the same frequency and expressness in their declarations concerning it, and in their reference to it, as in the writings of the Fathers, after the doctrine had become an article of distinct Faith. But no! God & the Father are every where equivalent terms. It is not the God, the Father but the Father of all, God—who was fully in the Man, Jesus—the *Vehicle*, the conduit—It is one God, *from* whom—& the one ~~Man,~~ ~~by~~ one High-priest and Chosen one *by* and *through* whom.—See Chapt. XXIII. 1. 2. and 4 v.—

P.S. The obvious truth of the preceding remark relatively to Clement's first Epistle was probably the incentive to the fabrication of the Second, for the purpose of invalidating the argument, which the ~~Anti~~ Homoiousian & Samosatene Heretics might derive from the first—and ~~g~~ suggests a conditional presumption of ~~its~~ the spuriousness of the second/—The Trimestrian Critics may be as abusive as the Odium Theologicum could desire—they will not be able to do away the fact, that Christians of all sorts during the first 5 Centuries attached little or no criminality to to the sending forth

f40　　of Books under false Names—that where any good end (i.e. what
they thought such) was proposed, they made no conscience of forg-
ing Authorities to support it—and that between Catholic & Heretic, Orthodox & Heterodox, in *this* respect there was not *a pin* to
choose—"X is true & secundum regulam fidei—the Apostle
James, (or Peter, or Paul) was inspired and led into all truth—
ministring to faith—therefore into the truth X—therefore it can
be no harm to attribute to James doctrines, which he certainly
held, and thus to repair the breaches of Time & Accident—this
was the Logic of the Pious Fraudsmen of all denominations—&
the same principles produced the same effect in the Schools of the
Neoplatonists, as in the Churches of Christianity—Orphics, Py-
thagorics, ~~&c~~ Sibylline Prophecies, Hermetics, what not?—

By the bye, Archbp. Wake must have had an obtuseness of the
discerning faculty, more favorable to Credulity than conducive to
a right Faith—How otherwise could he have reconciled an epistle
which is little more than a *Cento* from the present Evangelic &
Epistolic Canon, with another so characteristically barren in all
⟨clear⟩ references to the writings of the N.T. that the ~~evidence of~~
single evident exception exposes itself to the suspicion of having
been a marginal Gloss—as Letters of the same Man to the same
Church./— The Trimestrian High-parson might have fished out
a pretty discovery, worth a snug piece of Preferment, by assuming
the genuiness of Clement's 2nd Epistle, as vindicated beyond all
modest objection by the profound Learning and Sagacity of that
bright Ornament of the Episcopacy, Archbishop Wake—& thence
concluding the solemn Settlement of the Canon of the New Testament in the interval between the writing of the 1st & 2nd Epistle,
as a *fact* demonstrated by the following axiom—

If a certain Truth = a could not be truth, if B be not ~~affirmed
as~~ true, B. is a certain truth.—or

That without which what is actual would not be possible is itself
real—or (better still) the necessary conditions of Realities are themselves real—or (best of all till another comes to my head—A
known Reality proves the reality of its necessary Condition./—

5352 F^{o}.95　　　Tuesday ⟨Night⟩, 11 April, 12 ? clock.—Have
read the first four Chapters of Barnabas, with Hone's blindly compiled preface. I am greatly interested in what I have read: & must

try to get some information respecting the grounds for and against its authenticity.—Even if Barnabas were an assumed name, ~~the~~ adopted to win a hearing from the Ebionites and Judaizing Churches, from Barnabas having quarreled with Paul, the great object of Nazarean & Ebionite Enmity, it bears every mark of an age not very distant from the Apostolic. I must get Cotolerius's Judicium de epist. St Barnabae— —in his Collection of the Apostolical Fathers—Its having been so great a favorite with the earliest Bishops ⟨& Teachers⟩ of the Alexandrine Church—natural enough if the tradition is to be relied on which makes Mark the founder & first Bishop of Alexandria—is no more an objection to this than to the Ep. to the Hebrews, which by the bye has been attributed to Barnabas—. I see at present no reason for asserting it spurious—Surely, ~~an~~ we are not so possessed by the *wide* word, inspiration, as to require that all the Apostles or Apostolic Elders should write equally well—or that Jude's Epistle is either equal in worth & value to St Paul's or not Jude's!—But if there be no reason against its genuineness, surely its testimony to the pre-existence of Christ as the Lord of the Old Testament, ought to give it a high value to an Orthodox Divine.—Even as an undoubted Work of the earlier part of the Second Century—scarcely more than a generation from the death of the Evangelist, John, gives importance to this testimony & makes it probable to have been the doctrine of the Apostles.—

f40^v

5353　F°.96　　　Wednesday Morning, 12 April 1826.—

5th and 6th Chapters of Barnabas—To be sure—somewhat too philo-judaic, alexandrine, edging on the fantastical—but more so, et magis et *alio* genere ac Epist. ad Hebræos? This I must freely and attentively examine into—especially, whether diverso genere.—The Scoffing Unbeliever, availing himself of the crass and superstitious notions concerning inspired Writings—namely, that the Writers were not penmen but pens man-shaped, or Automaton Scribes, might blaspheme in saying, that the Spirit was equally unfortunate in making and solving Riddles & Conundrums.

5354　F°.97　　　Wed. afternoon.—The 8th Chapter v. 10–14. decides the mainpoint, that of catholicity of Spirit—which gives the true force and ought to be the final test of Canonicity—and decides it in the negative. It may be an *authentic*; it *is* not a *Catholic* Epistle. It may have been written by Barnabas with a holy intention; it was not outbreathed from the Holy Ghost. The Particular, too often at no safe distance from the Peculiar & even the Whimsical, predominates characteristically over the Universal, the arbitrary and sectarian in the ways & means, the proofs, examples, and arguments overlays the ~~teaching~~ truth to be concluded. It is not that these ⟨innocent⟩ infirmities of humanity have a place in the Epistle, for it is a mistaken ~~view~~ Theory of Inspiration that would demand their exclusion from a canonical work; but that they occupy the prominent place—not that they occur, but that they are constantly recurring—and form the distinguishing character of the Whole.

In every man there is a Diagnostic, and a Differential. ~~and the one~~ The words sound the same; but the senses ~~is~~ are widely different, and cannot without grievous error be confounded, nor even safely overlooked. The differential evolved in its own energy unchecked and unmodified by disturbing forces ~~generates and~~ has ~~true~~ Individuality as its product and integration; and every true individual is a Radius, that never crosses or impinges on any other Individual, but is always harmonious and convergent. But the Diagnostic, that by which other men remember and recognize this man, as John, and not James, or Luke, or Joshua &c &c—this is the common product of the Differential and the disturbing & modifying forces, and is often most obtrusive where the *Differential* is ~~weakest~~ least energetic. The ratio is inverse ~~not~~ rather than direct—and Differential − 5 = Diagnostic + 5, even as in physiology the Sensible qualities of the secreted fluids increase as the vitality & health of the secretive glands diminish.—

There are numberless Vessels, but one Spirit—and it is Catholicity, attested by the respondence of the Spirit one & the same in all regenerate minds to the same Spirit in the Written Word, that can alone determine ~~it~~ the claims of any particular work to be received as a work of Inspiration. But how is this to be ascertained?

f41 Let me answer one question by another, litem lite resolvens? How is it ascertained, that Homer, Milton and Shakespear were gifted Poets, Men of Genius? Wherein consists the difference between *Fame* and *Reputation?*—We have the proof, you will reply, in the

co-incident admiration of the wise and great thro' a long succession
of Generations. Well! but how do you know, that these admirers
were the wise, the superior order of Minds?—Such men are the
smallest number in every age & country. You will answer & the
answer is most satisfactory—that Folly, and False Taste are ever
fickle, and ever take their direction from the fashion of their times;
which fashion again is always determined by accidental and transitory influences—that every Child of Fashion & Folly holds in
contempt the fashion of the Fools, his Predecessors—and that Wisdom only varies not. But further, the many, who are necessarily
the creatures of the fugitive associations of their own present period, cannot but dislike or ⟨at least⟩ be insensible to the products
of false Taste characterized by that had derived their charm from
by-gone circumstances & modes—t and are therefore well content
to have works of former distant ages under the name of Classical
set up against all other Mushrooms but those of their own growth.
And on the same principle they build Tombs to the Prophets whom
their Fathers had stoned to death & plunged into dungeons: and
as long as the wise & good of their own times go no farther than
the point last canonized Seer had gone, and are content to be re-
peaters of and commentators on past Prophets & Legislators without attempting to commence Prophets & Lawgivers themselves,
they will possess a certain portion of influence over their contemporaries which will be allowed to shew itself in the education of
the Young, and a classical education becoming a necessary advantage mark of distinction for the higher ranks, the Works of independent and enduring merit, the genuine products of Wisdom and
Genius will be preserved, handed down and multiplied from an
age to age, and if no unless some great revolution such as the
irruption of the Goths, and Vandals, or of the in the Latin, and of
the Saracens & Turks in the Greek Empire ⟨should violently over-
whelm, or suspend the process.—⟩ they will ⟨be⟩ more and more
dispersed and ready at hand to excite and kindle the few small
predisposed Few, scattered among the coarse Many, who by similarity of Genius Nature and thro' a portion of the same Genius
(for truly and adequately to love and admire the great Luminaries
of the intellectual World supposes a ray of the same Light, are
conformed to these works and thus enabled to recognize their dis-

tinctive character at first sight ⟨and instinctively.⟩ For an inward
pre-conformity revealing itself at the first presentation of its proper
corresponding Object is what we mean by Instinct, and is the only
true & intelligible definition of the word.—Now this accumulated
Suffrage of the ~~Few in every age~~ better & nobler Spirits in each
generation successively, the comparatively Few at any one moment
f41ᵛ but many and mighty by ~~a~~ perpetuation & survivorship of of aim,
~~objects~~ and Authority, forming the ⟨moral and intellectual⟩ Constancy of the Kind; ~~& therefore the legitimate Representative of
our proper Humanity~~ this common ~~tre~~ sentence and decree of the
only legitimate Representative of our proper Humanity, is *Fame*—
φημη, and by right of nature legislatorial, compelling tacit assent,
and unresisting Submission ⟨ab extra⟩, as ~~a the~~ *Law*, ~~even when~~
from those, who ~~from~~ not having ~~the~~ it within are therefore under
the Law—even as the Air crushes ~~& keeps down~~ with its weight
the ~~empty~~ Bladder that, ~~does not contain it~~ it does not fill—but
bringing confirmation, assurance, sympathy, and inciting Cheer to
the Elect, in whom Faith supersedes the Law by conformity and
Free Affection of Love. But for all alike the Decree hath been
pronounced—FATUM *est*—it is *Fate* ~~m~~—or FAME—κηρυγμα το των
σοφων πάλαι καὶ νῦν —and only by contrast therefore to be compared with Reputation, ταις, ηγουν, δοξαις των πολλων, which is
rightly named κενοδοξια—~~as~~ And so indeed does the word, Reputation, ~~does indeed define~~ define itself—Quod ~~hic~~ ille putat, hic
*r*eputat—what ~~this~~ one fool fancies, another fancies over again—
the oracles of Justice Shallow echoed by Master Slender, and his
two serving Men Simple and Davy!—

   But this ⟨sally against reputation⟩ is a digression—at least, let it
pass for such till we ~~have an~~ find occasion to apply it.

5355 F°.98   (Mem. (Thursday, 13 April) this is the answer
to the plausible Objection—the *Ep. of Barn.* (ex. gr.) was held
authentic & revered as inspired by ~~the~~ as great a majority of Christians of the first half of the 2ⁿᵈ Century, and for a century & more
afterwards, as several of the Canonical—for instance than the Ep.
to the Hebrews/—True! but with *me* this is no more than *reputation*—.

   Mem.—the folly of attempting to mete out the Spirit by measures, and determine it by weights—to ascertain, how *many* wise

men there must be to constitute the *fame* of a book, or in what parts of the Book the Spirit does or does not utter itself—

Mem. Q.ʸ in humility.—Whether the will of the Infinite to feel as the innocent Finite (referral) does not *constitute* the incarnation?—

5356 23.60 Spring Flowers, I have observed, look best in *f46ᵛ* the Day, and by Sunshine; but Summer or Autumnal Flower-pots by Lamp or Candlelight. 18 April, 1826—I have now before me a Flower-pot of Cherry-blossoms, Polyanthuses, double Violets, Periwinkle, Wall-flowers &c—but how dim & dusky they look!— The Scarlet Anemone is an exception & 3 or 4 of these with all the rest of the Flower-Glass Sprays of white Blossoms, and one or two Periwinkles for the sake of the dark-green Leaves, green stems, and flexible elegant forms—make a lovely Group, both by Sun & by Candlelight.—

5357 F°.99 ~~19ᵗʰ~~ 22 April 1826. according to Dʳ Ure & Mʳ *f41ᵛ* Faraday pure Caoutchouck is bi-elemented—~~and~~ by Ure, 90 Carb. 9.11. Hyd.—by Faraday 7 nearly (6.812) Carb.—1.000 Hyd. or 7 to 8 by weight—

Q.ʸ Does not this both confirm my Theory of Carb. = Fixity, Astringency, Appropriate Attraction, and Hydrogen = Dilation, or Continuous Expansion, forma primaria fluiditatis ⚹ Nitrogen = Volatility, self-separative Projection, and (per potentiam ad extra) Repulsion, and Oxygen = Contraction, Atomic or absolute Hardness, as opposed to Toughness & Hardness by Cohesion— and at the same time throw a gleam of Light on *Elasticity*?—Contrast Caoutchouc = Carbon + Hydrogen with the pure Cyanic Gas = Carb. + Nitrogen/the basis it appears of all *fulminating* compounds. In these, the most anti-elastic of Natures (N.b. I am well aware of the current opinion that Air is an *elastic Fluid*; but likewise persuaded of its falsity—Hydr. is fluidiform, Nitrogen aeriform) the Carbon is essential as a retarding fulcriform Attraction bringing the Explosion within sensible Time/

5358 F°.100 22 April, 1826—heard *the* Nightingales in *f42* Widow Cootes' Lane. The Gardner (n.b. so deaf that I was forced to *holler* in his ear) had heard them two days before./

5359 F°.101   25 April, Tuesday—How comes it (asked M^{rs}

G. Frere this morning, as we were speaking of the Eton Collegers) that well-educated *Men* are generally tender-hearted and Boys, as long as they remain at School, even to the age of 19 & 20, so *cruel?*—Now this question takes for granted, that the same Individuals are meant, that the tender-hearted Men had been cruel tyrannical Lads.—I am willing to believe that it may be so,—but it is not so with Men of Genius, of poetic Genius at least.—Man-like in Childhood, Child-like in Manhood I have ever found the characteristic of true Genius/But suppose the fact of ~~an~~ the generality—and our Public Schools seem to afford the proof—the solution must be found, in one or other or all of these—

1. That the lawless power & the opportunity & temptation of exacting it ceases with leaving School—/A Gentleman is disgraced by striking or ill-using a Servant, ~~or~~ would be rendered infamous at College by any act of wanton cruelty to an errand boy &c—& these in turn do not excite the same rage, as the impudence or resistance of a furious School-fellow, Consubstantial or ejusdem generis, tho' subordinate. For the same cause the Spanish Grandee treats his ~~Servants~~ Menials with more humanity, & allows of a greater familiarity than an English Gentleman ~~an~~ his hired Servants, and the West-India Planters allow their dogs ~~more~~ to take greater liberties with them than their Negroes, and ⟨treat⟩ their house-negroes with greater familiarity than their white Servants or even their inferior Clerks.—

2. Sense of Security, known subjection to & protection by established Law. Boys are under Privateer, & Piratical Constitutions./—

3. The amelioration & in better ~~men~~ natures the transformation of ~~Appet~~ Lust, in its own quality always akin to Rage (ex. gr. the Cats) by Love or the formation of individual Attachment. The coarsest ~~master~~ Fellow when he has *fallen in love*, begins to affect the *amiable*—He *sighs*! & gazes at the Moon! and says, POOR Fly! ~~I pity thee~~

4. Marriage—& children of their own./

But with all this, where Wealth & early Debauchery and a strong habit of Body & the Custom of Field-Sports & Studs combine in the same Individual, the cruel Boy & Lad passes into the cruel Man—& the Colonel Berkleys are by no means a Scanty Species—. These are the best materials for the solution of the Problem, that I can offer; but having no experience in my own past or present Nature, having from my childhood had not only a detestation of cruelty in others but a constitutional incapability of being cruel myself, I can readily believe that some simpler & more satisfactory reason exists—for I cannot get rid of the feeling, that even a cruel Lad or Boy must be of coarse & vulgar clay/—Accordingly to my recollections, cruel Lads were vulgar, lustful black-guard-souled Natures, sometimes clever but oftner stupid—

5360 F°.102   26 April 1826. Wednesday Night. This   *f42ᵛ* Morning a little before three suffered one of my most grievous and alarming ⟨Scream-⟩ Dreams—and on at length struggling ~~out of this~~ myself awake found just such a focus of Ferment just above the Navel as if the Dæmon of Aqua Fortis had just closed in with ~~some~~ the Genie Magnesia, or as if a Chocolate Mill were making a Water-spout dance a reel in dizzy-frisk.—It is strongly impressed on my mind, that I shall imitate my dear Father in this as faithfully as Nature imitates ~~&~~ or repeats him in me in so many other points—viz. that I shall die in sleep/—even as in the Epitaph I composed in my sleep under the notion that I had died, at an Inn at Edinburgh, during my Scotch Tower, the year Southey's Margaret died & he first came to Keswick—

Here lies poor Col. at length, and without Screaming,
Who died as he had always liv'd—a dreaming!
Shot thro' with pistol by the Gout within,
Alone and all unknown at Embro' in an Inn.

I remember, I awoke from the stimulus of pure vanity from the admiration of my own fortitude, coolness, and calmness in bearing my death so heroically—as to be able to compose my own Epitaph/.

Since I first read Swedenborg's De Cœlo et de Inferno ex Auditis et Visis, ~~p 119, § .299~~ every horrid Dream, that I have, my thoughts involuntarily turn to the passage in p. 119, § .299 (indeed to the whole Book I am indebted for imagining myself always in Hell, i.e. imagining all the wild Chambers, Ruins, Prisons, Bridewells, to be in Hell)—Sunt Spiritus, qui nondum in conjunctione cum Inferno sunt: illi amant indigesta et maligna, qualia sunt sordescentium Ciborum in Ventriculo—Swedenborg had often talked with them, and driven them away, & immediately the poor Sleeper's frightful Dreams were removed, they being the spiritual Linguifacture of these Toad-Imps' whispers.—Only that I ~~frame~~ modify this Miltonic Theory by supposing the Figures in my Dream to *be*, or to be assumed by, the Malignant Spirits themselves—for it is very curious, that they are more or less malicious.—One good effect, I trust, I ~~have~~ may attribute to these half and quarter earnest Melancholies—the deep sense of the exclusion from God's Presence to me (for this has for many years been my Conception of REASON, and I think it sanctioned by the first Chapt. of St John's Gospel)—But in serious whole Earnest, and however hypochondriacal the Spirit-theory may be, I dare avow, that no explanation of Dreams or attempt to explain them, that I have seen or heard, has in the least degree satisfied my judgement,

f43 or appeared to solve any part of the mysterious Problem / On the contrary, this is the very nakedness thro' the scant & ragged Breeches of the modern Hartleio-Lockean Metaphysics, with its Impressions, Ideas, and Sensations, and its Jack of all Trades, Association.—Now I purpose to note down the characteristics of Dreams, especially my infernal Dreams, as they occur to me—as so many parts of the Problem to be solved. For so far from any thing like a Solution having been given by Hartley, Condillac, Darwin ~~&~~ on one hand, or the Scotch Metapothecaries on the other, that the Problem itself has never been adequately, no nor even tolerably, stated—.

The first point of course is the Vision itself—that we see without eyes and hear without Ears.—

The second (& which I have never seen noticed) is—that we live without consciousness of Breathing. ~~No~~ You never suppose the Men & Women of the Dream to breathe—⟨you do not suppose them *not* to breathe⟩—the thought is wholly *suspended*—and absent from your consciousness.

The third concerns the qualities & relations of Somnial or Morphean Space—which I now must content myself by MEM-ming.

The fourth is the *spontaneity* of the Dream-personages—Each is its own center—herein so widely differing from the vivid thoughts & half-images of poetic Day-dreaming.—In sleep you are perfectly detached from the Dramatis Personæ—& they from you.

The 5th is the whimsical transfer of familiar Names and the sense of Identity and Individuality to the most unlike Forms & Faces. So the Dream, noted almost 30 years ago in one of my Pocket-books, of Dorothy Wordsworth/and last night of Mrs Gillman.—

Some others I could put down, but it is getting late—& I must defer them.—It is time to be saying my prayers, and to intreat protection "from the Spirits of Darkness"—a phrase in one of Jer. Taylor's fine Prayers, which I am always *inclined* to retain—tho' the fear of praying what I do not fully believe makes me alter it into—Afflictions of Sleep.

S. T. Coleridge—

P.S. 6th. Conversion of bodily Pain into some passion of the Mind—Heart-burn becomes intense Grief, with bitter Weeping; Pain in the Umbilical Region becomes Terror—& in like manner, I doubt not, that bodily pleasure becomes Hope, or intense Love nullo libidine mixtus/

7th. Imaginary Air-piercing, Air-shooting, skimming, soaring by successive Jerks of Volition or rather a nisus-analogue of ~~Ba~~ inward Volition./

8. & most interesting—the apparent representative character of particular Forms and Images, repr. I mean, each of some particular organ or structure—Ex. gr. I have never of late years awaked, desiderio mingendi, but the preceding Dream had presented some water-landskip, Lake, River, Pond, or Splashes, Water-pits. Mem. The frequent dreams, some years ago, of Snakes, and Serpents, green, yellow & black, all covering the roads & rocky path—& I skimming and shooting along about a yard high above them—I have not been afflicted of late in this way. But I suspect, the vermiform motion of the Bowels—& the predominance of the colors, & other things in dreams, I am disposed to refer *fæcibus* accumulatis—But these symptoms of clair-voyance & inward Light & sight in Dreams is a deep subject.

9. The *frustration* ~~of in~~ most common in Dreams.

10. Non-descript & yet not composite Animals—the magnificent Fassades of Architecture.

11. The occasional sui generis Elysean Sunshine—/

f43ᵛ 5362 Fᵒ.103   28 April 1826—Friday—Am I to go to town,
to dine at Sir G. Beaumont's & meet Mʳ J. H. Frere.—God's
grace attend me!—Last night even to this morning wrote marginal
notes on Jer. Taylor's Sufficiency of Scriptures in the 2ⁿᵈ Part of
his *Dissuasive* from Popery. And now for the ~~few~~ two hours before
I leave Highgate, I am reading Taylor's Sect. II. Book II. Of
Purgatory (P. 500 of "Polemical Tracts".)

Imprimis, I should say a priori that the Christians of the two
first Centuries thought too well of themselves and too ill of all
others, to feel any motive or occasion for a Purgatory. Their Prayers for the dead evidently referred to the Day of Judgement, and
the supposed fearful Accompaniments and immediate Precursors
of the same/or are to be ~~resolved~~ by the sound remark of Alphonso
de Castris—Sæpissime petuntur illa quæ certó sciuntur eventura
ut petuntur, et hujus rei plurima sunt testimonia—One will suffice—from the Masses *de defunctis*—Domine Jesu Christe, Rex
Gloriæ! Libera animas Fidelium defunctorum de Pœnis Inferni et
de Lacu profundo! Libera eos de ore Leonis, ne absorbeat eos
Tartarus, ne cadant in obscurum.—So Augustine praying for his
exemplary Mother, who had died in the Faith—Credo *jam* feceris
quod te rogo; sed voluntaria oris mei approba, Domine.—Lastly,
"the Father made prayers for the Patriarchs, Apostles, and the
blessed Virgin Mary."—

P. 505. Curious instance of the inconsistency of the Church with
the ~~Sacred Scriptures~~ Bible in Pope Innocent's attributing a sentence of Augustine's (Injuriam facit Martyri qui orat pro Martyre)
to the Holy Scriptures.

P. 507. Had the Papal Church contented itself with admitting
the notion of a remedial process in dormitione Redemptorum who
had not wholly emancipated themselves from the Consequences of
Sin, even as Diseases are sometimes removed in Sleep, as a per-
missible Opinion—it would not have laid~~n~~ open to any very
stronge Charge of *Innovation*—in the Fathers of the 2ⁿᵈ, 3ʳᵈ & 4ᵗʰ
Centuries—.But still it would need to be anxiously guarded in
order not to produce a portion of the immoral & Christ-dishon-
oring effects of the present Article of PURGATORY—i.e. as it is
actually taught & believed by only not all Catholics, and not as
Mʳ C. Butler may choose to represent it *in genere generalissimo*. I

believe (and I *trust* that ~~it~~ such is the doctrine of the New Testament) that the Death and redemptorial Act & Victory of Christ, together with the regeneration & birth of a new & heavenly Principle of Life ⟨in the penitent Believer⟩ thro' the Communion of the Flesh and Blood (Corpus *Noumenon*) of the incarnate Word, kill the root of Sin in the SOUL: so that the remaining imperfections and infirmities have their surface roots (as it were) in the fugitive unindividualizable Animal Life & its perishable Organism—and are therefore left in the Grave.—But with *his* almost Roman-Catholic Views of this Subject, and the very faint and obscure sort and quantum of efficacy attributed by him to the Cross of Christ—little in short, that Reason and Moral Sense would not expect from the Divine Goodness, without the Atonement ~~by~~ in the Cross, I cannot but think that Jer. Taylor must have been inwardly favorable to some modification of a Purgatory. Without some such Softner & Qualifier his System is too fearfully hopeless. Talk of Calvin! Calvin's austerest Decisions are Oil and Balsam compared with the Conclusions in Taylor's Unum Necessarium: or Doctrine & Practice of Repentance!—

5363 26.86   Lausdune, where the 365 children, Male &   *f159* Female, born at one birth by ~~Herman~~ Margarite Herman Comitissa &c were baptized, somewhere about 1460, Henry VI. Edward I. Qʸ—Where to find a good account of this—in some old book of Travels? It can scarcely be meant, that the Countess had procured the Baptism of this number of orphans—What is the date of the Inscription, in Dutch & Latin, that hangs over the large Table on the Wall on which stand (or stood) the Basins in which the Male & female Homunculi were baptized/

5364 26.85   Ὀινάιοι (or Ὀινοὴ) τὴν χαράδραν = ⟨ὁ⟩ Καρπάθιος τὸν λαγῶον two Gr. Proverbs of the same purport—viz. A boon of supposed advantage or pretence to benefit that cause the ruin or detriment of the receivers or planners—The Inhabitants of Œnoe, a Demus of Attica, diverted the course of a torrent to water their vinyards which in the next rain storm the Torrent swept away—
—so the ~~men~~ People of Carpathus introduced Hares into their

Island which multiplied so much as to destroy all their corn &
produce.—

f157ᵛ　5365 26.87　　　20 millions from (i.e. the Interest of the National Debt　　1. Malt. 2. Beer. 3. Hops. 4. Tea. 5. Sugar.
6. Spirits. 7. Wine. 8. Tobacco. 9. Coffee, Spices.—/

5366 26.88　　　5 May 1826. The repulsive effect of all attempts for party purposes to revise & *pare away* any of the Verdicts
& decided Points, the great moral Abstractions of History—as in
C. Butler's & Dʳ Milner's Apologies for the Sᵗ Dunstan Treachery
to Huss & Jerome of Prague, Massacre of Paris, Queen Mary the
Bloody &c/

5367 26.89
Observ.ⁿˢ on Croup
Infl. Stage every ⌈. . .⌉ exertion to cut it short by Bleeding from
the Arm or locally by *Leeches*—Emetic. blisters. emetic/Warm
bath. purgatives. the most useful apparently Leeches—& bleedᵍ
to[o] employ'd to great extent in the 1.ˢᵗ 48 hrs. in which period
the mischief the patient generally cut off either by spasm or coagu-
ble form'd ⟨so as⟩ to impede respiration—

5368 26.90
~~A. G.~~
f157　Was ne'er on earth Seen beauty like to this,
The concentrated satisfying Sight
~~That self sufficing~~ In its deep quiet ask no further bliss,
At once the form and Substance of Delight!

As in the driving Cloud the Shiny Bow,
That gracious Thing made up of ~~Smiles & Tears~~ Tears and
　Light
Looks forth ~~into the~~ upon the troubled air below
Unmoved, entire~~ly~~, inviolately bright.

f152ᵛ　5369 26.91　　$\divideontimes$ = opposite to　　　$\divideontimes$ contrary to
Sweet $\divideontimes$ Sour : Sweet $\divideontimes$ Bitter.—

5370 26.7   Armin.)(Calvinism.   *f2ᵛ*

Arm. is cruel to Individuals for fear of damaging the race by false hopes and improper confidences: while Cal. sounds horrible for the race but is full of Consolation to the Penitent Individual.

The oftner I read and meditate (& how few days are there in which I do not read and meditate) on J. Taylor's Writings, the more forcibly does the Justice of the preceding Note strike me. And it is so marvellous, such a hungry dry corrosive Scheme of Monacho-manichæan Ethics in so rich, so genial, so tender a Soul as Bishop Taylor's! That he should have strangled the philosophy of Love by the parasite network of rank weeds, the Logic of Casuistry. A̶n̶ moral ασκῆσις, or an ascetic Moral, that wears out the Spirit in an endless task-work of Self-examination, Self-accusation, Self-reproach, Self-torture, what can it do other than keep alive, with wind and fuel, the Hell of corruption within us by the con-   *f3* stant Blowing of the Imagination—the Imagination in its turn blackened & scorched and fetid by the constant neighborhood of impurity/—O what a treasure of moral thought on the idea of the Beatific Vision—or F̶r̶u̶i̶t̶i̶o̶n̶ ̶i̶n̶ fruitive Intuition! Is there a man who has d̶e̶e̶p̶l̶y̶ ̶a̶n̶d̶ truly and intensely loved a lovely and beautiful Woman, a Woman capable of gazing, in that *inwardmostest* communion of Silence, on Vale, Lake, and Mountain Forest, in the richness of a rising or setting Sun, h̶e̶r̶s̶e̶l̶f̶ she, as she stands by his side, smitten by the radiance & "herself a Glory to behold, the Angel of the Vision!"—t̶h̶a̶t̶ ⟨who has ever loved with such love & at such a moment, but must⟩ have n̶o̶t̶ felt, that it is the disquieting sense of e̶a̶r̶t̶h̶l̶y̶ Change ⟨the thought-flash, o̶f̶ "I shall lose her,   *f 2ᵛ* perhaps," that awakes DESIRE! The hollow w̶h̶i̶s̶p̶e̶r̶ Bodement of Inconstancy, the remembrance of⟩ o̶f̶ ̶t̶h̶e̶ ̶m̶u̶t̶a̶b̶l̶e̶,̶ ̶I̶n̶c̶o̶n̶s̶t̶a̶n̶t̶ the   *f3* transitory, the fugitive in all sublunary Loveliness, t̶h̶a̶t̶ ̶a̶w̶a̶k̶e̶s̶ D̶e̶s̶i̶r̶e̶ that disturbs the deep fruition of the simple uncompared Present, and w̶i̶t̶h̶ ̶a̶ ̶m̶i̶s̶t̶r̶u̶s̶t̶ that Fear the doubting infidel, untrusting of the Future, & yet dissatisfied with the Present ⟨it is that⟩ prompts ⟨him⟩ to press the Beloved Object closer to himself, as if to inclose it in his own Life, and to b̶l̶e̶n̶d̶ confound it with his Being, thus sacrificing in order to secure it!—But with this   *f3ᵛ* excitement of the Selfish L̶i̶f̶e̶ ̶N̶i̶s̶u̶s̶ Greed comes grasping with restlessness & turbid feelings/Lake, Vale, & Forest, Mountain &

the Glory of the Light are eclipsed.—And so it must be: for we are earthly—and the Earth claims its part in us—But happiest he, ~~or~~ for whom the ~~stain~~ Shadow passes soonest off, and the orb emerges from the brassy ⌈ . . . ⌉ Stain with brighter Light—Light—who ~~awakes refreshed from the Sleep starts up from the~~ awakes as from a brief Sleep/and ~~as refreshed~~ forgets the Dream in the reality!

f3ᵛ   5371 26.8   Mem. of Tell's Act—. Walter condemns it as unchristian—& will not take an Ivy Wreath from the Chapel—Hildegard, the lovely Catholic, divided between her feelings & her inability to ~~ans~~ deny Walter's assertions—Theodore admits that it was a vindictive act & that such revenge there is a disturbance of the Moral Order. He will not therefore extol the ~~Act~~ Death of Gessler as Heroic, still less a Christian, Act. Indignation at the Insolence of the oppressor, the Sting of Patriotic Wrath; Sense of his Country's wrongs, and the outraged Heart of a Father, with the glorious Thirst for Liberty, swelled confluent into one rush of
f4   Passion, that overflowed and burst thro' the dams & banks of Moral Law—Thus he became a blind Instrument; but yet an instrument of Justice & of God—It was the verdict of his Country, ~~of Human~~ which he executed on the Tyrant—and the Hearts of the Good & Great in all succeeding times have made it the verdict of the Human Race—and thus *the* Act, not as Tell's Act, but as a grand Incident of History, an Act of retributive Providence, obtains a sacred Character & deserves a Chapel—. Hildegard Whispered—You have expressed the whole feeling of my heart.—Ah well! but why *may* we, why *should* we, not suppose, that W. Tell himself viewed his Act in this light, considered himself, as the instrument & minister of righteous Vengeance! That he lost all thought of a particular Self—Generalized his own wrongs—felt them as the wrongs of ~~the~~ Fatherhood—To such a feeling in such
f4ᵛ   a moment I should (my soul convinces me) deliver myself up, the more absolutely, ~~if~~ had I been the hour before reading the Gospel of John, and the Narrative of the Meek Redeemer's Agony & ~~forgiving tears~~ Forgiving mercy with tears of passionate and adoring Love & Gratitude—& therefore I cannot, will not, pronounce the bold Deed of Tell an unchristian Act—. In this spirit I would compare Tell and Ehud & Deborah herself with Jael.—

5372 26.9   The Question to be solved is: Are we constrained
by our duty as Christians to receive the sub-texts, or sentences in
Scripture, which are merely illustrations, ~~of~~ or, for the purpose of
conciliating the minds of the Writers' Contemporaries to some
truth of Revelation, and the import of which sentences is not the
immediate end & purpose of the Sacred Writer, as proceeding
from the universal Spirit & therefore revealed truth, equally with
the texts that ~~do~~ are the proper & immediate purpose of the Sacred   *f5*
Writer?—And this too, when the Sub-texts are notoriously parts
of the popular Belief of the particular Age & Country (Zeitmein-
ungen)—& these opinions, that we know to have been of human,
nay (as in the instance of the Devil, of Spirits & Dæmons, of the
Destruction of the Planet by Fire, &c) Pagan & Heathenish Origin?—Were then no errors left for the influences & certain effects
of Christianity itself to remove? Were the Apostles made equal to
their Lord and Master in possessing all truth purified from all
error? Do they themselves pretend to any such prerogatives and
immunities? Does not Scripture assert the Contrary? Would it not
be a ~~mystery more obscure~~ miracle more astounding than all the
wonders recorded, that Matthew or Barnabas should have the
whole Light, and the Light of the Light, of the Sun of the Christian Faith through all ages concentered in his mind, as in a Focus?—In close connection with this is the other question—viz. re-   *f5ᵛ*
specting the formation of the existing N. T. Canon?—That it was
not formed or decided by authority of Revelation, that the Selectors
were not infallible or specially inspired for this purpose, all
learned Protestants admit. But it is with this subject, as with that
of our Liturgy & Homilies—the fallibility of the Compilers is
admitted but the least hint of any instance existing, even a single
sentence in which viri e confesso fallibiles ipso facto fallebantur,
is repelled with intolerant resentment.—Providence, it will be
said, watched over a proceeding so vitally important to a right faith
and the highest interests of Christianity. Granted! but how are we
to distinguish the result, as the work of an over-ruling Providence,
and not the consequence of the fallible human instruments, if there   *f6*
are not marks & proofs of both?—Of Providence, from the fact
of no ⟨known⟩ work, having any character of universality sufficient
~~to~~ even to ground a plausible question on, Was it not inspired?
having been excluded, of Providence—because the great majority,

the only not all, of the canonical Books are approved by the Conscience & Reason of all Christians, to be Words of the Spirit of
Truth—because no one has yet proposed a Truth that vitally concerns the Faith or Practice of a Christian, which may not be found
in, or undeniably deduced from, some passage of the Canonical
Scriptures".—In short, from the total effect—from that impression, which alone is received consciously by every simple heart,
like the total impression or Aspect of a fine Statue seen in the right
light at the due distance—On the other, of the fallible instruments,
in the existence of some, tho' few and unimportant, exceptions.

f6ᵛ That they possessed no unerring Judgement, these failures prove—
it is not to *this* therefore that we can attribute the fact ~~that their
judgement was in the main & practically~~ of the whole Canon answering to ⟨all⟩ the purposes intended by it, that for the Christian
seeking truth in order to salvation there is every thing to guide &
further, nothing to mislead or hinder—and that the few ~~failures~~
human errors exist—for those alone, whom they cannot harm, but
by their own evil spirit seeking harm?—Therefore this is the Hand
of Providence—It is the whole Chain, and its strength as a whole,
and the sustaining curve, ~~that~~ with inverted Arch forming the
Bridge, on which we pass with safety over the ~~torrent~~ rough &
turbid Stream of Life and the eddies & whirlpools of the Passions,

f7 that evidence the Mighty Artichitect, not the separate Links—and
what ⟨? tho'⟩ a collateral chain of inferior metal should have been
added where no stress falls? Or here and there a side link should
~~should~~ hang, that supports nothing and yet is~~of~~ too trifling ~~weight
and dimension~~ an addition to injure by its superfluous weight?
"May I not ~~speak of~~ truly characterize Paul's Epistle as a whole,
by its universality of Spirit (~~its~~ and Catholicity is the test of Inspiration—) because it contains a ~~sonton~~ request to bring him his
Cloak and Tablet, or a—give my love to this and that acquaintance—or a—my Fellow-prisoner, James, begs to be remembered
to Mʳ & Mʳˢ Trueheart? Or must I in defiance of common sense
introduce a miracleulous illumination of the Holy Spirit, and vi
et armis impregnate the words with a sense of universal concernment, or aerate them by means ⟨of⟩ a Swedenborgian Forcing-
Pump with a mystery? Or to put a case fully in point—does it
detract from, or in any way affect my judgement of Shakespear,

that I am persuaded that his ~~earnest~~ successive Editors ~~were~~ have ~~f7^v~~
been under an error in placing Titus Andronicus among his Plays?
While I give them credit & thanks for having rejected, what ~~at~~
yet ruder Judges in more credulous times had appropriated to our
mighty Bard, the Yorkshire Tragedy and London Apprentice?
Does it detract from or not rather increase, my reverence for his
Genius and Judgement, that ~~even~~ in some of his undoubtedly genuine plays some interpolations are to be found—and here and there
a passage of later date introduced by the Actors? If I could prove
this in the instance of the Porter's Speech in Macbeth, and make
its un-shakespearian ~~character~~ origin as evident to ~~other~~ the Public
as it is to myself, would not every true and enlightened Admirer
of Shakespear thank me?—I am sure, that I should deserve
thanks—and yet a higher meed would be my due, could I affix,
ecclesiâ consentiente, the asterisk of spuriousness to the last Ch.,
or the latter Half of the last Chapter of St Mark, and the ⟨two   *f8*
discrepant⟩ Evangelia Infantiæ in Matthew and Luke, & the Digit
of Suspicion to the first Epistle to Timothy—or perhaps to all three
of the Pastoral Letters—What one article of the Christian Creed
in its most comprehensive form would be touched!/Of the faith
preached by Luther at least not one, except the very point, I am
now agitating—viz. the inexplicable tenet of the inspiration or
rather the revelation of every sentence, word and syllable of the
Bible from Genesis to the Apocalypse.

5373 26.10   7 May, 1826.—Mem. to enforce and expound
the distinction between the Systematic Unity, which the Understanding made intelligential by the *Light* of Reason, ⟨strives after⟩
and the Identity in all Alterity or absolute Unity, peculiar to Reason in its own Sphere to Reason as opposed to Understanding and   *f8^v*
distinct from even the Light of Reason in the Understanding. Perhaps, *Union* or Totality would be more appropriate to the Syste-
matizing Tendency of the Understanding; while Unity might be
reserved for the higher Gift, Reason as the Source and Seat of
Ideas ~~&~~ or Spiritual Verities.—In short, this most important Principle of the essential difference of Reason and Understanding cannot be presented to the mind of the Pupil in too great a detail of
instances, examples and illustrations. As in the circle of Wicks in

an Argand's Lamp, if any one takes light, it kindles all the rest. So any one instance of the diversity of ~~the~~ R. and U. clearly ap-
f9 prehended and thoroughly mastered (and which of the number may be the successful one depends so much on the accidents of constitution and experience, in the individual Pupil's Mind that it cannot be known beforehand) all the other instances will become luminous on each side, till the whole blend in a circle of Light.

5374 26.11   7 May, 1826. Monday.—Mem.—The beneficial effect of Protestantism in counteracting and retarding the tend-
ency of Christianity generally to destroy Nationality, and ~~to~~ by attract⟨ing⟩ the different Masses of Men to each other & to repro-
duce a second Roman Empire, or Fifth Temporal Monarchy. The cause why it is *desirable*, that this ~~movement~~ tendency should be checked is—that this power of *this* tendency remains unaltered or ⟨is⟩ perhaps strengthened, by the corruptions of the Religion, and
f9ᵛ works onward while the purifying, enlarging and elevating influ-
ences and effects that would supply the place of Patriotism and national Individuality are torpid, or comparatively of feeble growth.—And this is the more considerable, because Christianity is in this ⟨amassing and assimilating⟩ operation in alliance with the ~~predom~~ ascendancy of Trade, Commerce, the Mechanic Arts and Sciences, & the predominance of whatever is scientific or belonging to the GENERIC, ⟨dem algemeine [allgemeine] *Verstande*⟩ (i.e. unmodified by the character of the particular country ~~or~~ and by the Genius of the Persons, from & for whom the knowlege exists)—
Astronomy, Geology, Physiology, Chemistry, Mechanics, over Literature, Poetry & other growths of individual minds, & har-
mony of ⟨particular⟩ circumstances—while the Sciences of Reason, die algemeine [allgemeine] Anschauungen der Vernunft, which would have afforded the requisite counterweight *den algemeinen* [*allgemeinen*] *Begriffen* des Verstandes, unfortunately lie under yet
f10 heavier discouragements than Poetry and Literature—. The strength of this tendency to the Non-national is evidenced in the growths of mind that are most intensely individual by the unde-
niable ~~ev~~ super-ordination of Music over Painting and ~~Music~~ Sculpture, and of these over Poetry—and in Music itself, of in-
strumental over vocal. It would be idle to compare the ~~protection~~

patronage afforded to Poetry with that so prodigally giving to ~~wha~~ the other Arts of Painting and Sculpture: & Music has had her Homers, Miltons & Pindars within our own Recollection.

The various ways, by which Protestantism in addition to its effect as Protestancy, & therefore divisive, ~~favors~~osters the national and patriotic Prejudices and Predilections, are worth mentioning tho' sufficiently obvious. It is not a flattering truth nor very creditable *f10ᵛ* to ~~the~~ Mankind, but a *truth* it is—that one of the strongest grounds and safeguards of Nationality, or *John-Bull*-ism, is the contempt for other Nations.—An habitual Conviction & Feeling of the ~~superiority~~ Excellence of our own, La grande Nation, is another strong ground; but not, in my opinion, at all equal in strength to the former, as a ground, and still less effective as a safe-guard. Nationality is most intense, tho' less ebullient and obtrusive, where the Contempt for other Nations is the positive Pole, the explicit ~~or~~ and conscious Passion of the mind, and the ⟨conviction of the⟩ superiority of our own (which may well exist without any over-weening Conceit of its excellence) is the negative Pole, the implicit vix conscita ~~passio~~ Affectio. Now there is no contempt so hearty and *thorough* as that which ⟨is engendered by⟩ the sense of the Folly and Absurdity of our neighbour's ~~Faith~~ Religious Creed, Cere-monies & Forms of ⟨Turn to p. 15⟩ ⟨*Remarks on the nationalizing* *f18* *effects of Protestantism continued from Seven Leaves back.*⟩ Worship, as far as and according to the proportion in which they differ from our own.—But this will acquire double & treble force, if it should be connected with resentment, ~~the ab~~ and moral indignation and abhorrence from historical recollections and popular traditions of outrageous Cruelty and Perfidy, and the et cetera of persecution, endured by ~~our Forefathers~~ the Professors of our own Belief and inflicted by the Church, ~~whose~~ the tenets and discipline of which we despised/and the ~~whole will be~~ crowning accession will be given, where the Sufferings, Courage and Perseverance of our Forefathers in braving and finally overcoming the power and rage of the persecuting Church form the most heroic, prominent and universally familiar parts of our National History—Ex. gr. How large a portion of the Scotch Nationality, as it exists in the most numerous class of the Scotch Nation, is built on fond recollections

& traditions of the Covenant Times, and the earlier heroic Con-
f18ᵛ flicts with Cardinal Beaton, and with Mary!—Now these Causes
are all confluent in Protestantism; and Mʳ Canning & the other
Tory Advocates of the Catholic Bill, who praise and prize national
Prejudices as the basis of National Virtues, should be made aware
of the inconsistency of their conduct with their general principles—

A second Aid to the conservation of Nationality, and of a less
equivocal character, is found *in der Verstandes-geist*, the predominance of the Understanding, or Discursive Intellect in Protestantism. There are Mystics and Followers of the Vie interieure in
Protestant Countries as well as in papal, to whom this remark will
not apply. But Mystics are exceptions in all established Religions
and are essentially the same in all times, and churches. As Tauler
was no Romanist, tho' a Romish Doctor: so Behmen ~~and George
Fox were~~ was no Lutheran, ~~no Protes~~ he went to an Evangelical
f62 Church. ⟨Turn to p. 101⟩ The ⟨*Remarks on the influence of Protestantism on the preservation of Nationality Continued from p. 16.*⟩
Logical, the Discursive is the presiding Element of Protestantism,
and alas! too exclusively—and this notwithstanding the fact, that
Luther, the Father of the Reformation, and the First *Protester*,
~~forms a glorious~~ set a different example. But Martin Luther was
a Hero and a Genius—Dionysus, ~~and~~ Apollo, ~~went halves in this
Swan in conjunction~~ and Venus Urania fix'd their Aspects in triplicity
on this consecrated Swan, and ~~shot converging rays~~ their several
influences ~~met~~ entered him with converging rays! ~~in the focus of
that~~—Hence—Who loves not Woman, Wine & Song Remains a
fool all his life long! But after him the ~~Restoration~~ Resuscitation
of the Evangelical Faith, the Restoration of the Christian Religion
degenerated into a Reformation of the Latin Church—and of the
f62ᵛ Reformed Churches, Lutheran or Calvinist, Episcopalian, Presbyterian, or Independent, the common Character is the subordination of the Intuitive to the Discursive, in both forms of Intuition, sensuous and supersensual—as a Balloon rises above Earth
yet is never the nearer to Heaven, so the Genius of Protestantism
leaves the images and idolatries of the Spiritual Babylon behind,
but never reaches the spiritual region, ~~of~~ where the Ideas live,
such as John uttered to the Reason and Paul interpreted ~~to the~~ and

accomodated to the Understanding. Paul—useds *Discourse*—i.e.
the logical faculty of the Soul—but it is ever "Discourse of Reason"—.But this is a digression—If Protestantism is defective by
negation of the ~~Highest~~ Spiritual it is most beneficent by exclusion
of the ~~mean~~ Sensual/Now ~~the~~ Reason and Sense are both universal
Poles—Reason of ~~the~~ our personal Being, Sense of our Animal—   *f63*
opposed to both is the Understanding, Λόγος ψύχικος) as the individual Pole. Every man has his own understanding, differing in
extent, and in its original constitution no less than in its degrees of
developement. Climate, Soil, Local Circumstance, modify it in
every several Man. Hence it strives after the Individual, the de-
finably *distinct*: for its proper function is to *comprehend*, and we
can only comprehend an object by separating it. But the Understanding, like the Reason, is two-fold, practical as well as theoretic
or intellective. But as practical, the Und.ⁿᵍ is the faculty of selecting
and adapting means to proximate ends; and if with this we connect
its former function, it will be seen as a faculty of adapting definite
means to definite individual ends, to results which become its end   *f63ᵛ*
and aim in great measure in consequence of the circumstantial
Agents, under the modifying influences of which it grew and
formed itself. Hence the generalizing Spirit of large Monarchies,
and a System of Laws as universal in their principle as a System
of pure Geometry, eked out in their application to an endless diversity of Cases by the alien agency of undefined discretional
power, is utterly adverse to the Spirit of Protestantism—which
craves and strives after CONSTITUTIONS, Customary and By-laws,
particular means for particular ends. It is ~~continually~~ instinctively
legislative— & ~~its~~ legislation is the continual Tense, a perpetuated
Present—but as the tendency to the individual must from the diversity of the Individuality in each different Mind lead to ⟨a⟩ collision and diffraction incompatible with the lowest degree of Unity   *f64*
of Will, with which a State can exist and perform its functions,
and which is only remediable by compromise, the ~~on~~ most effectual
mode and organ of which is a *representative* Body, each individual
member of which has liberty of speech and suffrage, to propose,
to support, to reject and to modify—hence Protestantism is essentially favorable to representative Governments, not only ~~that~~ national, but municipal, not only temporal but spiritual. Parlia-

ments, Common-councils, Presbyteries, provincial Synods, general Assembles, &c down to Vestry-meetings & Coroners' Inquests, together with Associations & Confederacies, ~~for all pur~~ and Committees of Delegates for all purposes, are the natural Growth of Protestantism, where its spirit is not cowed & contracted by

f64ᵛ opposing forces, ~~which its own~~ and congenial accidents—such as the number and smalle~~st~~ness of States, the neighborhood of mighty Despotisms and the necessity of a military system, in Germany—aided by the dis~~persive~~junctive and uncombining Character of Protestantism itself. (For remember that every deliberative & representative Body is a Conjunction disjunctive; and that confederacy is the consequence of the tendency to Individuality, as the specific Medicine is of the Disease)—But even in Germany the controlled but not subdued Passion for Constitutions & free federal states ~~under~~ is sufficiently manifest—.

Now by Collision and Concert prominent Character is formed—and peculiar Constitutions result, all bearing the marks of Compromise, and by the enduring action of check & Countercheck, Collision and Compromise anomalies in theory are ~~produced~~ harmonized in practice—or the remaining Discord is rendered bearable by Habit, nay, endeared, as a stimulus—But

f65 wherever there is most *Characters* ~~in~~ among the individuals, there will be most character in the People at large, most of marked and peculiar character in the ⟨manners,⟩ customs and institutions of that People—and where all these co-exist, there will be the strongest *Nationality*, and with it the ~~greatest security~~ strongest bulwark against foreign Conquest—while the very activity of innovation in the parts as the best security ~~against inne~~ for the retention of the Whole, in the Body Politic no less in the Body Natural. For who would change the power of changing?—

If I do not flatter myself, the preceding remarks throw a new or at least a stronger light on the difference between Protestant & Catholic States—and tend to prove, that the republican disposition charged on Puritanism and the Calvanistic Doctrines & Discipline

f65ᵛ are essential to Protestantism *in kind*: and that the excess has been the result of accidents, some of them unavoidable & not fairly chargeable on either party, and of gross errors & a papal spirit in the Cabinet and Hierarchy of the Stuarts—and that it did not cease with that dynasty, as the unhappy consequence of the Extrusion of the two or three thousand Ministers from the ~~Church~~ Establishment in the ~~St Bartholemews M~~ spiritual Massacre of the St Bartholemew's Day of the Church of England. It is notorious, that the so called Presbyterian, ⟨and anti-episcopal⟩ but more truly named the Anti-prelatic, Party sacrificed the Liberties of their Country to their predilection for a Monarchy—for their hereditary and legitimate King.—And a republic ⌈ . . . ⌉ compatible with an hereditary, and powerful tho' limited Monarchy, a loyal kingly republic—if this be meant, shame fall on the Briton, who is not a republican in Head and Heart, Body and ~~Soul~~pirit—If there be such a Slavish ~~Briten~~ Soul, let him keep his treachery sacred to the   *f66* ears of his ~~Shaveling~~ Father Confessor. He may be a very consistent Papist, and of a *Catholic* ~~Mind~~ Taste—he cannot be a true Protestant, or of a National Spirit!—Pat Riot you may be, my dear Honey! a Patriot you cannot be! and a native of *this* free Island, Scotch or English, I hope, you are not!—

S. T. Coleridge—Monday, 7 May 1926—

5375 26.12   Tuesday Morning, ~~6~~ 5 °clock, 8 May 1826— Sat up writing the preceding remarks, till ⟨it was⟩ past 1 °clock priusquam preces meos obtuli. Was more than commonly opened to the Love of Christ—but have awakened from a dreadful labyrinth of strangling, hell-pretending Dreams—Prayed fervently & with tears—that I might not be suffered ⌈ . . . ⌉ fall off from my faith & trust in God—but to take this merited chastisement meekly—.—Cf the moment of the Fall of Man. N.b.—how many   *f66^v* of the most important events & chains of Events in the History of Nations have depended on the decision of a moment! The momentum is indeed always of the moment. Tell's leaping out of the Boat, which he drives backward with the Vault—on this the Freedom of all Switzerland! But is not the Present always a moment—or rather is there no Present Moment, except when some decision & decisive act of the Will petrifies, like Gorgon's head, the dissolving Fluent—the evanishing Indifference of Past & Future! This latter is the true point of view.—This therefore is another Beauty in the wonderful Hebrew Philosophers!

5376 26.22   Milton and his great Compatriots were too   *f42* much Republicans because they were too little Democrats. The universal Habit of the Age, and of ages before them, among all educated men to exclude the Many, the Population, from all ~~share or~~ concern in political and national economy, as naturally and by a Law of God and Right Reason the Governed, and to confine all share and interest in Government and Legislature to the Gentry

f42ᵛ and the ~~Lett~~ Learned, i.e. the Offspring and the Authors of the Permanent—(Senatus Populusque were the Nobility, Gentry and Clergy—) and the confirming voice of the History of their Country, which ~~tau~~ gave them no other example but of Changes and beneficent Innovations effected by the FEW, the Mass of the people disregarded, and either passive or blindly following their Lords,—these go a great way to excuse ⟨them⟩ for the error, they committed in aiming at forms of Government and institutions beyond the moral and intellectual growth of the Nation at large, and (a yet more fatal error) without adverting to their progress in wealth and influence.—Even their aversion to the gauds of the Monarchy and Hierarchy, and to the rites and ceremonies which the first English Reformed Bishop had retained from the Papal Church in charitable & prudent condescention to the customs,

f43 prejudices and prepossession of the People at large, but which Charles's Prelates and Oxford Divines were busily increasing in Love and admiration for the things themselves—even this aversion had its main source in their Aristocratic Feeling and Principle. They despised and condemned them, as flatterers to the Populace—. Algernon Sidney's Essay on Government is one continued illustration of this remark.

5377 26.23   ⟨If the Soul be an immortal *essence*, it must either be a *Creation* in each individual, or its pre-existence must be asserted on the same ground, as its continuance after Death.—⟩

The question of an ante-natal as deduced from the assumption of a posthumous Life involves or rather perhaps provokes another—viz. how far the doctrine of immortality loses or returns its moral and religious worth and interest disjoined from the continuance of a Consciousness of the present state of our being? I have 30 years ago and more controverted Locke's assertion, that Consciousness (in the sense of Memory or the definite Consciousness of having been definitely Conscious) is the essence of Personal

Identity—observing that Locke might as rationally have asserted
Mile Stones to be the essence of the Road/. Now in the highest   *f43ᵛ*
sense of Consciousness, what the Germans call Urbewüsstseyn,
[*Urbewusstsein*], I cannot deny that a great deal may be said for
the deduction of pre-existence from the immortality of the Soul,
after this life. But no less undeniable does it appear to me, that
this (whether Idea in the divine Mind or a Soul) is not what we
mean by *us*. It is not my *I*—tho' it may be My eye or mihi—but
the source of it, not at all participating in its crimes or their consequences and infinite above its merits & attainment, even as God
is the source of Motion & animal Life without partaking ⟨of⟩
them—. But the main point on which I differ toto cœlo from the
newest Sect of religious Philosophy in German (the School of
Schleiermacher, and Solger) is their charging this tenet with an
unsafe sort of Pantheism or Christianity/& of extolling the faith
in immortality independent or even exclusive of individual Con-   *f44*
sciousness, as a Christian *Perfection*—a more exalted State of
Mind.—on the contrary, it seems to me to have been one grand
& continued purpose of our Lord and of the Christian Doctrine
of the Resurrection of the Body to draw the Believer's mind from
all speculative notions by asserting the resuscitation of *the* Man—
not of a Soul or Spirit but *of the Man*. The immortality of the
Soul may or may not be deducible from the New Testament. It is
not expressed or enforced as an Article of Faith.—But even as a
philosophical theme, I see in it no unusual difficulty to be grappled
with. If we assume, as all the facts ~~of~~ accumulated by the genius
and industry of the Constellation of Great Minds, who with John
Hunter as their Morning Star, have founded the Science of Comparative Anatomy & Physiology, authorize us to assume, a ~~scale~~
graduated Scale of ~~Consciousness~~ ascent from the minimum of   *f44ᵛ*
Consciousness, in ~~the facts of~~ *Habit* as a peculiar product or accompaniment of Life, and in the growth of *Sense* (of Sight for instance,
by the lingerings of past impresses manifested in the instinct anticipation & more and facile apprehension, of images ejusdem generis, up to the highest imaginable perfection of Consciousness,
that can exist in a *Creature*, there must be some first instance, in
which the Consciousness survives the metempsychosis of the Creature—even as there must be a first, in which the Consciousness

becomes *individual* (i.e. proper Self-consciousness)——. Now as this latter takes place *first* in Man, there is every reason ~~for~~ to suppose and none to deny, that ⟨Man will be the first instance of⟩ the former likewise—In the human Being *first* we assume a⟨n⟩ ~~successive~~ immortality of the Individual ⟨by succession of *states*⟩ instead of an immortality of the Race by a succession of Individuals: and it would be strange indeed, if the Self-consciousness which is *the Form* and indispensable *Mark* of the Individuality, should not partake in its destiny. Only ~~take care to~~ be aware of the full import of *"Form"* as here applied—Consciousness is not an impressed

f45　　Shape, as the Seal on the wax, or as the Pyriformity on a Marble Pear—nor can it be compared even to the characteristic Type, or distinctive ~~cons~~ Shape, resulting from the formative power of Life, in the natural fruit, or in each animal. No! It is Form, as the correlative of Essence—distinct but even in thought inseparable, and co-inherent.—In the ~~same~~ sense, that in discoursing on the Godhead, or (if that be forbidden or of doubtful right) in discoursing on the Attributes of Moral and responsible Creatures, we say that Intelligence is the *form* of the personal Will, and ~~this~~ Will the essential Ground of the Intelligence—since a Will not intelligent is no *Will*, but a tendency or blind Appetite—in this same sense must the term be understood, when I say that the Consciousness is the *form* of the personal *Individuality*.—N.B. The characteristic Formula of all *Spiritual* Verities or Ideas is an apparent *Circle*—i.e. a proposition which is predicated of Things or Conceptions, περι αισθητων, η περι λογων (εννοιων των λογικων) would produce~~d~~ a vicious Circle in Logic. And yet as the universal forms

f45ᵛ　　of Logic are for *us* the ~~sole and~~ necessary forms of all discourse, the indispensable conditions of all ratiocination, we ⟨are forced into a Compromise—i.e. we⟩ have no other means of reconciling the contradiction, than, first by shewing that an appearance of contradiction is the ⟨1.⟩ necessary consequence of ~~th~~ applying the Understanding to the immediate Truths of Reason, ~~and~~ in other words, of the attempt to *conceive* what being simple & unique, ~~may be~~ is essentially *inconceivable*—and 2. by shewing that by admitting this circle in the first instance, and only by admitting it we avoid all future circles, and obtain a staple of a ~~lo~~ chain logical in all its Links. Now the seeming self-contradiction, ~~that~~ in which

alone an Idea or Spiritual act, can be enunciated, is contained in
the following Formula A ⌈. . .⌉ ~~B~~ is the Cause of B, in as far as
B is the Cause of A. or B is the Effect of A, on condition that A
is the effect of B. or ⟨as⟩ A + B = A; so B + A = B. A and B   *f46*
mutually constitute, each the other; and yet remain distinct, A =
A, B = B.—Thus the essence of Self-Consciousness consists in
the distinction yet identity of the Subject and Object, Conscientis
et Consciti.—

We may therefore confidently assume, that if the Individuality
survive, the individual consciousness will likewise survive, the dissolution ⟨or Sloughing⟩ of its present Larva.—Yet another and
perhaps plainer proof may be drawn from the ~~articulated~~ Continuity necessarily supposed in all Consciousness—an articulated
continuity indeed, but yet continuous. We are self-conscious Creatures, and when we speak of our ~~being~~ consciousness after death
we mean that which we now *are*, and *have*. Yet we have no memory or consciousness of our first two, three, and with few and
doubtful exceptions, of our first 5 or 6 years: and Consciousness
would be a burthen not a Blessing or Perfection, were it otherwise.
It is sufficient that each ~~time or~~ Moment & hour is conscious of
the immediate antecedent/the more or the less of the past, farther
back, and ~~how~~ what length of ~~line~~ Time is contained between the   *f46ᵛ*
present, and the earliest recollection, together with the sort and
comparative value of the⟨se⟩ unerased fractions of the Line 5 ——
—————— 25, this depends on the laws of association modified and
determined by the character and circumstances of the Individual.
This, however, we know, that both the extent and the distinctness
of our Consciousness grows with the growth of the general intellect; ~~and~~ but it is not as commonly considered, tho' it is equally
true and a truth of yet higher interest, how close a connection there
subsists between the Consciousness and the Conscience, how
greatly both the quantity and quality of our Consciousness is affected by our moral character and the state of the Will. But especially, the *Quality*—The more advanced in the Life spiritual, the
more perfectly the Will of the Individual is self-subjected to the
Divine Light and Word (Ο Λογος ὁ φωσφορος, η το φως το λογικον—
John 1. v.1.4.9.) as the representative and exponent of the Absolute Will; the more habitually the understanding is ~~subordina-~~   *f47*

~~ted~~mitted to the Light of Reason shining therein, and this Light of Reason in the Understanding is itself subordinated to the Reason in the Conscience; the more does our individual consciousness partake of the stedfastness and identity of the personal Subsistence, which is the copula and Unity of all the ~~fac~~ acts and shapes of the mind, the less loose and detachable ~~are~~ is the ~~im~~ consciousness of the events and objects that make up the Man's Experience (τὸν ἑαυτοῦ βίον) from the Self-consciousness, which is the essential and inalienable Form of his Personal Identity. See the FRIEND Vol. I. p. 58.

Meantime, it must never be forgotten, that whatever the Soul, or Ground of each man's individual & personal Being, may be, it must ⟨can⟩ be no more than a potential entity, the dimidium sui, the half only of its *actual* Being: that (See Aids to Reflection, p. 262) "tho' Reason in finite Beings is not the Will—or how could the Will be ever opposed to the Reason?—yet it is *the condition*, the *sine quâ non* of a *free* —i.e. of *actual*) Will—Therefore, Reason

f47ᵛ and *the* Will are the *co.efficients* of *actual* personality. Now every Night brings home to us the aweful fact, that ~~Reason~~ the analogy between Reason and the *Common* Light, which gives to the former the name of the latter, holds throughout—and that it is not a mere metaphor or ornament of discourse that we avail us of, when we call Reason Light—"the Light that lighteth every man, that cometh into the World", or when we speak of the Light of Reason/ Like the Light of the Sun, it is but *dispensed* to us, but leant to ⌐. . .⌐ us for determinate periods, withdrawn & again restored, but at the moment of its withdrawal the Will too disappears as an actual & free will—& likewise the functions dependent on the Will, ex. gr. the comparing power. Alas! we not *have*, we *become*, a Dream. Well does the Hebraism express this truth, the Soul does not ~~merely~~ see Dreams; but the Soul dreameth dreams. Thus, without the Light of Reason (which is God's not our own) the soul either relapse into a merely potential Being (which not impossibly

f48   take place—at least, to which it probably approximates, in ⟨our⟩ *profoundest* Sleeps;) and remember, that the Evangelist, John, who is no where superfluous in his phrases, ~~speaks of the Logos~~, limits his position, "the Light that lighteth every man" by the additional sentence, "that cometh into the World"—i.e. that is taken up into

and as it were co-organized with, a system & community of Souls/
Now it is ~~to~~ this undeniable fact taken in connection with the arguments preceding, that I should ~~convert my attention~~ select as my
Guide and Compass, my ‡Way-weiser, as the Germans say, in
seeking my way thro' the questions of an intermediate state—
whichever side I might adopt.—For if I supported the Affirmative, I should rest the *possibility* on the Conscience and the relation
on which it stands to Consciousness, namely, as its antecedent &
source, and ~~its~~ the *probability* on the moral Affections and Com-
munions which are the offspring of Conscience in which the Conscience most immediately reflects itself, as partaking in equal proportions of intuition (~~of~~ forms outwardly perceived) and impulse
or action—in other words, as the synthesis of Mind and Will—　*f48ᵛ*
But if ⟨I took⟩ (as on the whole, and in the more frequent mood
of my thought,) I incline to take, the negative, I should draw my
arguments principally from the Scripture analogy of Death to
Sleep—from the fact that Growth chiefly is effectuated during
Sleep—that even in the imperfect Sleep, which is marked by
Dreams, *Pain* is transmuted into *mental* passions, Grief, Fear, Remorse, Hate, Revenge &c—that if the metempsychosis of Death
be of that infinite moment which the Scriptures attribute to it, viz.
as preparatory to the appearance of the perfected & thenceforward
unalterable I M A G O, it may very rationally be supposed that
the processes of growth may be such as would be intolerable to the
⟨awakened⟩ Sensibility of the Soul, consequent on its full consciousness—& in this manner. I should interpret the words, hidden in God—hidden in Christ—even as the Soul or persistent Life
of the impenia~~nt~~tent wicked may be hidden in the Evil Nature, ἐν
τῷ πονήρῳ. Such are my speculations—δοξαι, ηγουν μη δογματα up
to this Friday, 11 May 1826. P.S. It furnishes one slight pre-　*f49*
sumption, or material for argument, against the conscious intermediate state, that our ablest Divines, as Sherlock, Taylor &

‡ I have heard in some of our provinces, I am confident, tho' I　*f48*
do not distinctly recollect where—the country-folks ask—Can you
wise me the way ~~to~~ or the road to such or such a place—I do not
think it probable that this is a Corruption for advise, or (as the
Cockneys) ad*wise*!

others, have made such lame work of it in the attempt to answer
the so natural Objection—If the Soul exercise all its most glorious
functions not only without the body but in consequence of its deliverance from the Body, why should *it* desire or God effectuate,
its rejunction? Now tho' a portion of this difficulty is doubtless
derived from their strange preference of the Judaico-egyptian *Cat-
acomb* Superstition to the great Apostle's indignant Thou Fool! not
that which goeth into the Grave. &c—yet a large remainder will
be found, even with the right & Pauline Idea of the Resurrection/
For let it be that the Spiritual or celestial Body, in which the Man
arises, be the product of the Spirit—yet as no other Body is mentioned or supposed during the interval between Death & Resurrection—how is this compatible with an intermediate State of Consciousness? The conclusiveness of the preceding argumentation
depends of course on the justness of the conception respecting the
*f49*ᵛ   Body—(See p. 17.) I believe it to be the only philosophical view—
viz that it is (an to use a bold image) a fixed Tune or Harmony,
constantly arising from the reciprocal Action of the principium
individui (say, the Soul) and the system ab extra, with which it is
placed in intercommunion—or—the Body is the organ of that intercommunion of the Soul and the System of which she forms an
integral part, constantly pro- and e-duced by their conjoint action.
The position likewise, that the Body is the necessary condition of
Pain as distinct from mental passion & emotion I hold to be both
true and valuable.—How far, however, and in what particulars,
this conception is transferable to the Spiritual Body put forth by
the life-making Spirit, as distinguished by Sᵗ Paul from the living
Soul, is a question that requires thought before I venture to attempt an answer; yet the Analogy, and the Trumpet of the Arch-
angel, & several texts of Scripture, are all in favor of a spiritual
f50   Mundus circumstans—an action of the universal Spirit, of the
Spiritual Christ, on the individual spirit conformed thereto. Add
that this latter assumption supplies a ground, of which ⟨it⟩ is certainly in want, for the Zeit-meinung adopted by Sᵗ Paul of *a* day
of Judgement, and a total simultaneous Resurrection, the truth of
which is supposed in very terms of the origin question—Is it reasonable, and ~~acor~~ accordant with Scripture to expect an intermediate state of conscious existence?—

5378 26.6   14 May, 1826   tried to make a Crow-quill a   *f2*
Pen/a chance Rook-feather, and from the shorter wing-feathers.
Could I procure the largest and longest, I think I should success:
and the pens would be very useful for marginal notes.

S. T. Coleridge.

5379 26.32   Lord Bacon's Comment on the Slaying of Hera-   *f61ᵛ*
clitus—The Dry Light is the best Soul—viz. when the intellectual faculties are not drenched by the Affections, is no doubt a
pertinent Corollary from the adage/but the immediate Sense is incomparably deeper—Sᵗ John would have been a truer interpreter—
Vide Ch. I. v. 4.—

5380 26.33   15 May, 1826, Tuesday. Eton Montem—   *f66ᵛ*
James there/what a happy day to poor Hen Pen—& so fine a day
too—/I cannot help regarding it as a symptom of a coarse idealess   *f67*
Spirit, that lives most in the Understanding ⟨& the Senses,⟩ less
in *the Sense*, but least in the Reason when I see a Man of Letters,
a Polyhistor, dog- (or rather, magpie-) matizing contemptuously
on the characters of Jacob Behmen, Swedenborg, and other extraordinary men of this class.—Grant that there was ~~organic~~ structural
or functional derangement in the case of Swedenborg, in a wonderful manner blending the laws of Sleep with those of waking—.
still whether the language be words or images, the meaning is
the main point—Read Swedenborg's De Cœlo et Inferno as you
read the Vision of Mirza or the Tablet of Ceres—interpret his
~~facta~~ visa et audita into Symbols and Allegories/and if the result
be grand and rational—give the more honor & reverence to the
Man, who under such a visitation could retain and exercise so fine
and deep an intellect/.

5381 26.34   Mem.   *f67ᵛ*
The high-principled, idealizing, finely feeling Ildegard's conversion to Lutheranism, κατα πνευμα το Λυθήρου—or as Luther
would ~~have~~ preached were he now living, and had compared the
Protestantism of the present times with the ever the same Romish
Apostacy exemplified in the two instances of the Parthenolatry and
the Mass—and in each by convincing her, that the inward perfec-

tions, the affections and aspirations, which had endeared the Mass & the Image of the Virgin Mother, as the exciting causes, were in fact only narrowed by them & contracted into single & exclusive ~~mono~~ Particulars—their representative & symbolical character wholly lost—But especially by the comparison in detail between the contemplation of the Storgè, first in its ascent from ~~the~~ the Plant, του πανζωίκου in its indistinction and dawning minimum to the Insect (ex. gr. the Sister Ants) & from the Insect thro' th

f68   nobler animals (the Sea-Cows, &c) to its irradiation by the Reason & Conscience in the human Mother—2. ~~in its descent~~ beginning from the highest to touch the place & order of its genesis—so as to demonstrate that it loses all interest and meaning by the Romish Deification of it—i.e. by transferring to the Co-eternal Logos the necessary condition of the Logos in Man & in Time.—

f50   5382 26.24   19 May 1826.—I begin to question much, whether the Age can bear the whole truth respecting the essential Spirituality of the Christian Faith, and the necessity of keeping it constantly before our minds in the interpretation of the *historical* Form. Now interpretation κατα πνευμα requires that every historical Fact should be *symbolically* integrated/and the critical point to be determined is, how far the κηρυγματα των Μαρτυρων, οσοι ξυν Χριστω ησαν, were delivered as thus integrated—& wherein the supplement or completory consisted?—

f51ᵛ   5383 26.25   Prayer.—the focus of Religion.—Religion the
f52   relation of a Will to a Will, the Will in each instance being *deeper* than Reason ~~for~~ of a Person to a Person. The legitimate inference, that for Prayer as the realization, ~~and~~ the Act and Product, of the Will, only a negative Rationality can be demanded. ~~It must con~~ Reason must not contradict it.

2. As it is the end and aim of Religion to unite the *intuition* of this Truth—i.e. that God is a Person, with the *Life*, the most appropriate means of effecting this union must be a religious *Duty*. N.B. The union of our *Conceptions* with our Life is provided for by our *Senses*: but a union of Ideas with the Life, constituting a *lively* Faith, by Prayer alone—. Meditation being a form of Prayer—Our Father, who *art*—in Heaven. i.e. by a supersen-

suous Being—but even the world of the Senses will for the religious mind derive its intelligibility from the Divine Idea—Hallowed be thy NAME. Whatever thing manifests Order, Law, Beauty utters GOD—

Self-contempt, or a Sinking back into the potential, a willingness to evanescence of the Personal in us, is virtual Suicide—it is *f52ᵛ* truly a self-centering—we will not the will of God.—It is likewise presumption: for hereby we will to be lower than Reason.

5384 26.35   20 May 1826, Sunday.—   *f68*

After the Collect for the 25th Sunday after Trinity instead of the Epistle, a Section from Jer. 23.6—certainly, the clearest most unequivocal prediction of a ⅃ Messiah, such as the Jews during the interval between Malachi & our Lord imagined & expected; but (God enlighten me if to my blindness or eye-film it be owing!) how it can be appealed to as fulfilled in our blessed Redeemer I can not see! The name indeed (THE LORD OUR RIGHTEOUSNESS) is very striking; but is it more so than Melchisedec (King of Peace)? Can it be said *f68ᵛ* in any sense not utterly alien from Jeremiah's meaning, that Judah was saved in the days of Jesus Christ, and that Israel dwelt safely? Or that the seed of the House of Israel were led home from all countries whither God had driven them, to dwell in their own land?—If this be a prediction yet to be fulfilled in the person of our Lord, to which purposes did the Compilers of the Liturgy wish it to be applied?—. These bringings forward of Messianic Prophecies, and to confess the whole truth, the application of the term, Messiah, at all to the Redeemer of the World perplex me sadly./That the Word incarnate in the Son of Man, ~~and~~ Homo Universus, totius generis Humani Substantia, et unitas, and together with this personëity assuming personal individuality in Jesus, born of Woman, as what the Jews ought to have expected *instead of* expecting a Messiah—i.e. a Re-founder of the Th⟨r⟩one of David, and a Restorer of the Twelve Tribes under one Head, *f69* as the imperial Nation, to which the other States and Kingdoms of the World were to be subordinated—this I believe with my whole Heart!—and to this, it appears to me, all the Prophecies of the

Old Testament point, with exception of Daniel, Ch. IX—and two or three passages in Jeremiah and Ezekiel. But on the other hand, when I consider these exceptions, and can find in them no clue which could have guided the Jews to a purely spiritual & in fact allegorical interpretation of the promises contained therein, and yet am to believe that these prophecies were intended of our blessed Redeemer; I confess, that under my present light I find it difficult not to palliate, ~~the~~ the sin of blindness in the Jews in not recognizing our Lord, as the Messiah described in these Scriptures: tho' I fully admit, that even so their rejection ~~and pe~~ of him as a Prophet & more than a Prophet, in his own right & by his own evidence in word & work, remains inexcusable/and ~~their~~ conduct of the Priests & Rules fiendish & murderous. But if it be said,

f69ᵛ that these Prophecies would have been literally fulfilled if the Jews had received our Lord as their Messiah—how are we to reconcile this hypothesis with our Lord's express declaration, even from the beginning, that his Kingdom was not of this world? Or how make it compatible with the whole Scheme of Redemption by the Cross?—with the Lamb slain from the foundation of the World?— Dʳ Magee indeed and the very numerous school of his followers, who regard the Redemption, as an arbitrary act, as one way chosen out of many, by which the same result ~~would~~ might have been secured, may find the ~~difficulty~~ problem of no difficult Solution. But for as many as think with Paul and Luther, I see no other mode of solving it but by a second Advent of the Redeemer of the World as the Jewish Messiah—and this appears to have been the Belief of the Apostolic Age and of the Church even to this day. I see too the advantage of this scheme in retaining and carrying on the *historical* character of the Christian Faith—in supporting its

f70 objectivity, and giving a *body* to the Soul, an embodied Soul to the Spirit. Nevertheless, the difficulties, both philosophical & historical, that weigh upon the scheme, are such as would dispose me to welcome any plan of interpreting the more express Messianic prophecies, or any ~~Idea~~ Code of the Laws & Canons, by which the Hebrew Prophets generally are to be understood that would justify the transfer of temporal Images & Incidents to Spiritual Ideas & Epochs.

5385 26.36   The first Assault of Protestantism was on the Romish Doctrine of ritual merits; & the gifts to religious purposes (i.e. priestly uses); and to alms, given in the spirit of compensation & as equivalent for duties omitted or transgressed—in short, against the scheme of GOOD *works*, in the churchly acceptation of the Word—In opposition to this most pernicious Doctrine the Reformers preached FAITH as the only only principle or subjective Source of Salvation.—The second against the *Romish* Doctrine of Faith (i.e. implicit confidence) in the Pope & Bishops, instead of Faith in Christ & Belief of the Scriptures—in opposition to this, they preached Faith working obedience by Love. Then came the division between Protestants—and Arminianism obtained the victory over Calvinism in all the higher orders of Christians/and the consequence has been, a finer form of the old doctrine of meritorious words—the Protestants forgetting the living Faith in a lifeless Morality, the Romanists overlooking true morality in a lifeless Faith/   *f70ᵛ*

5386 26.37   —to *fill* our sphere, to develope in ~~even~~ due proportion the several faculties of our individual Being, and to live in harmony with himself & the World around him—. But what *is* the due proportion? What *is* the Harmony?—Nay, this is the Problem which every man is bound to solve in act & life—& you ask like an idle Schoolboy, who ~~can~~ not content with having the Rule & the question clearly explained to him, asks—but what is the Facit—Boy! that is your exercise—/go to work!

5387 26.38   Judge of the necessity of a divine Teaching = Revelation to the first Men by the Success of the Nations who have fallen away from it, and of their several experiments to solve the problem of Life for themselves—from the Boschman to the Chinese, from the Fetish-worship of Africa to the Human Sacrifices of Mexico—True!—but even Christendom/Yes! but shew a single instance in which the cause was not virtual Heathenism—.   *f71*

5388 26.39   Question which an honest man finds no difficulty in answering to his Conscience but ~~that~~ for the judgements of others—/39 Articles. Paleyanism ⨯ Rigorism—.the cause, the generalness of words—Hence the duty of precise terminology—.

f159   5389 26.81   Engaged to Mr T. Farrer's, Hampstead, Friday 9th June, 7° clock—1826. Friday 27—Friday 3.

f22   5390 26.102   Preconditions requisite for the reception and appreciation of Mr Green's Theory of Poesy/or Establishment of the Common Ground and the specific Differences of the Fine Arts./
First. An insight into the necessity of Ideas, as contra-distinguished from Conceptions & Images.
2. A knowlege of the negative characters of an Idea. 3. Of the positive Characters.

f22^v   4th Precond^n—Knowledge of the necessary relation of every Particular, having true Being, to a Universal ejusdem essentiæ.
5th Of the Faculties or attributes, of which the Human mind is the unity, and whence the possibility of both succesive & simultaneous Action.
6. The Law of Subj. & Obj./

n.b. the *mind* of Man may be conceived as *based* upon Life, as Sensatio existentiæ [?confusæ].

f159   5391 26.82   "Constancy lives in realms above"/
This exclusion of Constancy from the list of earthly virtues may be a poet's exaggeration, but certainly, it is of far rarer occurrence in *all* relations ⟨of Life⟩ than the Young and Warm-hearted are willing to believe/but ~~especially,~~ in cases of *exclusive* attachment (i.e. in Love, properly so called, and yet distinct from Friendship) and in the *highest* form of the Virtue, it is *so* rare, that I cannot help doubting, whether an instance of *mutual* Constancy in affection ever existed.—For there are two sorts of Constancy, the one negative—where there is no *transfer* of Affection, ~~and~~ where the ⟨Bond of⟩ attachment is not broken off, tho' it may be attenuated to a thread/this may be met with, not so seldom when there is
f158^v   goodness of Heart, it may be expected—but the other sort, or *positive* Constancy, where the Affection endures in the same inten-

s˙   with the same or increased tenderness & *nearness*—of this it is that I doubt whether once in an age an instance occurs, where ~~if~~ A feels it toward B & B feels it toward A, & vice versâ.—

5392 26.83   Unmuthigkeiten, tho' perhaps more strictly   *f158ᵛ* Disheartenings, Disgenialities, is the best German Substitute for our *Discomforts*. But for Comforts, Comfortable &c there is none, I fear.

5393 26.42   John X.—Wha 's the Door of the Sheep-   *f74* fold?—The practical Reason? The power of Reason in the Con- science? or Reason as the Entrance-way of Ideas?—In this sense of the term, Reason, the only sense in which ~~Reason~~ the term can be used to designate a *faculty of* the Human Mind, comprehended in its *propriety*, Reason is the capability of Ideas—and thus most truly the *Door of the Sheepfold*.—This verse 8ᵗʰ is an astounding Text. I want to possess the truth therein intended; and yet scarcely dare articulate the ~~n opinions~~ thoughts, that offer themselves as the pos- sible answer anticipated in the question, tho' the fang of affirmation is plucked out by the preceding *Is* it—! or Can it be—or the ⟨yet⟩ more timid form of asking, It cannᴜ be—/History mentions no ~~P~~pretende~~r~~d Christ, no ~~or~~ Usurper of the Messianic & office by anticipation! In a writing of Cerinthus, Marcion, or any of the anti-judaic Heretics the Sense would have been obvious. But in John we are in all reason to expect a spiritual Meaning.

May I venture to find an analogy in Luther's Table Talk, p. 189, 217, & elsewhere?

5394 26.43   10 June 1826. Saturday. May not the Flash and   *f74ᵛ* the Peal in Thunder be used to illustrate the possibility of proph- ecy—the prophetic Ειργασται? or even of the spiritual Act of the Will, the Will-flash, and the successive rolls of the *Deeds* conse- quᴀteent/. The Common because total Crash in Adam—the artic- ulated distinct yet never abscinded Sound-segments ~~of~~ thereof peal- ing on to this hour? The whiz-sparklet of a passing Fire-fly is a something won from utter darkness: and even the light of rotten wood cheers when it does not enlighten or guide!

5395 26.44   The Gospel Truths in ~~the~~ worldly Health, Wealth, and Lustihood = Lightning flashed across Sunshine. Even the Outward church, or the Ecclesia in Domino petrified by the Mammon of Apostacy into Ædes Kyriacas, "from whose arched roof Pendent by subtle Magic many a Row of Starry Lamps and blazing Cressets fed with Naphtha and Asphaltus, yielded Light As from a Sky", may need the Thunderbolt to reduce it to ruins & a wilderness of dark Caverns & Dungeons avenging the bedimmed Flashes from Heaven/that now glare on the amazed Consciences of the ~~con~~ prisoners enclosed & underwhelmed.

5396 26.45   Most truly does the profound Apostle speak of the Mystery of the Trinity, as wherein all treasures of Knowlege are hidden—That one κηρυγμα, that the Logos is no attribute or quality of ~~a~~ Being but itself ὁ ὤν, co-eternal indeed but yet second, ~~εκγονος~~ _υιος_ ὁ μονογενης, is the most pregnant & fundamental of all the prima principia philosophiæ.

f75

5397 26.46   To use the World *distinct* ⟨in division⟩ from our own Being (tho ⚬ to the Thesis, I) is Waking: to possess it by immediate communion is Sleep—and so interpret Sleep, in the New Testament—in which the Death of the Redeeming is Falling asleep in the Lord.—

5398 26.47   Can it alter the nature of a Community that it was formed & is continued for moral and religious purposes? Strange Logic to suppose, that the distinctive character of a Species could annul the essential character of ~~a~~ the Genus! That what is understood & taken for granted by all men in every other community, Society, Confederacy, Club and Band, in University, College, Senate, Bench &c should not hold of ~~the~~ a National *Church* Establishment—tho' a more plebeian and crass ~~fancy~~ Error can scarcely be conceived than the conceit that in the moral and spiritual sense of the word, religion, a Judge, Physician, Magistrate, Senator or ~~Member of~~ Cabinet Minister faithfully and zealously performing the Duties, he has severally undertaken to discharge, is less *religiously* employed than a Deacon, Rector or Bishop.—But here I find another instance in addition to a hundred

f75ᵛ

former ones, confirming my maxim, that there is no equivocal or multivocal Word in a language that is not the cause & occasion of more or less mischief. Short of opposition & contrariety, I do not see how two words can be more disparate than θρησκεῖα and ευσεβεια. Yet our anglicized Religion being used for both, the former and lower meaning (Cultus Sacerdotalis) is confounded with the latter (Godliness, Faith) and both ~~blend~~ pass into Superstition as the tertium aliquid of the Synthesis—Vide Definition of Superstition in the Aids to Reflection.—A number of honorable Men enter into an engagement with each other, express or tacit, to support a Ministry as long as these Ministers remain faithful to certain great _f76_ principles of the Constitution and to a Scheme of Policy which they deem indispensable or in the highest degree expedient under the existing needs & Circumstances of their Country, and because a ~~combina~~ union of this kind is the only or most effectual means of preventing the reins of Government from falling into the hands of a desperate Faction, Sect of Democrats or Rè-nettoists. Had it been possible or in any tolerable degree likely, that each & all of this party should on every ~~measure~~ point in the whole detail of executive and legislative measure think exactly alike, there could have no motive for the formation of Party. But because Lelius, disapproving of some particular measure or preferring some other, submits his judgement ~~in its influence on his~~ practically to that of the majority of his Friends—or had joined the party in the first instance because he agreed with them in all important matters, tho' there were one or two minor points of very subordinate interest— does it follow, or does any sober-minded person quote his example _f76ᵛ_ in justification of Clodius, who holding the whole scheme, all the most momentous Constituents of the Scheme, both in principle and practice, false or foolish or injurious to the best interests of his Country, nevertheless regularly votes for it, ~~and~~ harangues for it, actively circulates its manifestos & addresses, because he had, or expected to have a place or pension, & had chosen Government Politics as his way of Livelihood—or on the other hand having expressed with due scorn and reprobation of Clodius, exclaim— that Lelius was just such another?—No man of sober mind, guided by Reason & Conscience only, and not excited by Vanity, pharisaic Ostentation, or party-spirit, would ever dream of confounding the

two—. Now apply this to the Church, taking in the first instance
a young Clergyman holding the same opinions as myself—/—beginning with the reasons why he goes into the Church—the most
apostolic containing all that is necessary salvation, with more helps
f77   and and furtherances, and with fewer & less important drawbacks or
imperfections than in any other communion—on earth, I dare say
with little hesitation, tho' it were enough to have said, within the
Sphere in which Providence has placed me. I can pleno corde pray
its prayers, grieve its griefs, thank its thanksgivings, swell its
hymns & halelujahs—in the weekly performance of my duties to
others, I feed and feast my own Spirit.—But, as an individual, I
wish—the Pseudo-Ath. *& so on/*

    (*Momentous.*—Prayer, Praise, practical divinity, the Cultivation
of the religious Sense & sensibility cloath the Skeleton of dogmatic
Theology with the flesh & blood, the smooth & beautiful Skin, of
Humanity—/Nay, more!—the Church, & the Body Corporate of
regenerate Man, has the privilege of uniting the gifts & characters
of the lower & the high Class, the Testacea with the Vertebrates.
She has the supporting Bone-frame of the positive Statutes of
Faith, and the ⌈. . . .⌉ chain-armour of ~~negative &~~ defensive &
offensive Dogmata, to preclude & repel error in the persons of
her Warriors, her militant Forces—. But at home, around her
sacred Hearth, she lays aside her Coat of Mail—& even her inmost Framework is ~~implied~~ contained and understood. Hence,
*f77*ᵛ   from the very nature of the things, her Articles of Faith will have
a greater semblance of ~~Arminianism~~ what is falsely called Calvin-
ism/in fact the common Code of Theology formed by the first
Reformers in Unity of Spirit, as *Re*-formers—consequently, de-
nouncing the anti-scriptural additions & warpings of the Deforming ~~Interp Fana~~ Innovators, papal or fanatic, as well as establishing
the original form—and the Liturgy on the other hand will have a
greater semblance of Arminianism and even (~~of~~ because it is indeed
the substance & spirit of true Catholicity) to weak or inflamed eyes
of *Roman* Catholicism—.—My two neighbor Ministers, L. and
N. have not considered this—L. taking his tone from the Liturgy
professes himself an Arminian, and explains away certain of the
Articles & sundry passages of the Homilies as well as he can—N.
a man of deep yet stern mind, which has been formed & colored

by the study of the earliest Reformers & those Divines, who ~~under the name of Puritan~~ adhered to the Bishop of Edward VI & Elizabeth in opposition to the learned but less Anti-romish Prelates & Doctors who obtained the Rule of the Church during the Stuart Dynasty, in the latter half of the reign of James I & retained it, clings to the articles & Homilies—but feels scrupulous and uneasy at some parts of the Liturgical Offices/. Both are excellent men— but the fault of both is this, ~~that~~ in addition to the want of consid- *f78* ering the different nature & purposes of Liturgy and the Dogmatique, they neither had examined, what the Objects of a National Church were, and in what their Duties & Functions consisted as Fiduciaries and Ministers of that Church/Had they done this, they would, I am persuaded, have found that they had performed, both of them ~~equally~~ alike and with the same fidelity all the duties, they had engaged themselves to perform, in every sense in which the Church can without outraging common Sense— be supposed to have required this engagement at their hands— Now the Church desires & stipulates for two things—first, that her Ministers should be attached to her conscientiously on those grounds of fair & decided preference, which an Institution ~~framed and~~ established by human authority, and a scheme of Doctrine, ~~and~~ Worship, and Government framed by the imperfect tho eminent, wisdom and piety of men who not only layed no claim to any special ~~&~~ superhuman immunity from error for themselves, but demanded of all Fiduciaries of the Church ~~by their choice~~ the refusal of such immunity to any particular Church, National or *f78ᵛ* Provincial, their own included—men ~~wh~~ not without shades of difference in points of Theology among themselves, and in whose work indications of this difference & of the healing spirit of Christian Compromise which rendered it harmless, are not wanting— that is to say, passages & sentences which, by ~~a non violen~~ a moderated liberty of ⌐. . .⌐ interpretation ⟨they⟩ might be reconciled with each other, ~~but their~~ the ⟨more⟩ obvious sense of the words ~~are~~ appear at variance tho'—and consequently, a tacit ~~understanding~~ permission that the Successors of both opinions might unreproved so understand the words, as often as their ministerial functions required them to recite the same—the peace of the church ~~never~~ not disturbed, nor the ~~spiritual~~ spiritual edification of the

Flock not distracted, by disputes on subjects, in which as simple Christians they had no interest.

This is the first—the Second implied Stipulation is that every
f79 Fiduciary minister and officer of the Church should, in his place & functions make the known Aims of the ~~Founders of the Church his aim, and realize~~ Institutors and of those whom their authority has devolved & in whom they ~~are always~~ virtually survive his aim, and in all points fulfil the known Objects, and final causes of a National Church.—It were to suppose, that the Church should expect ~~of a succession Body of~~ in ten thousand Individuals in each generation more than conscientious devotion to her interests grounded on a sincere preference of her Forms and Doctrines, & adequate means to all her ends—or that having this she should wish ~~or intend~~ to exercise a further control over the ~~inward~~ freedom of their minds, as ~~Scholars~~ members of another Body, the republic of Letters I mean, or ~~to for~~ intend to force into an impossible identity all ~~their~~ differences of opinion that must necessarily exist in such ~~large a~~ a multitude of different men on points, ~~which or~~ some of which could never without ~~a~~ impertinence ~~come~~
f79ᵛ ~~before~~ be brought forward at all in ~~their~~ discharge of their ministerial functions; ⟨while in⟩ others, the practical result is the same whichever of two opinions the Minister may mentally prefer—and the one or two remaining are of such trifling importance whether we compare them with the Points in which all are supposed to be of one mind or with the peace of the Church and its effects on the moral and spiritual edification of the Flocks collected in her several Folds, that to deny the privilege of a modest ~~difference of~~ inward Dissent, or to declare it ~~unacceptable~~ irreconciliable in conscience with the public ~~form~~ performance of the Office, in which the words relating to this subject occur, is in fact to deny all opportunity and subject matter for the exercise of Charity and ~~the love of~~ brotherly Concord. Nay, I will go further, and referring to the essential difference between Truth (or a ~~determination of the Judgement~~ mental Conclusion which in each individual mind is whole and entire, and Action in order to the realization of the same which is an necessarily fractional—and in no one ~~pers~~ Agent more
f80 than a fraction utterly inadequate to ~~this~~ any other effect, ~~than~~

perhaps—than that of disturbance, I will venture to assert, that we cannot deny to the Minister of the Church in his separate charac- ter, as a ~~Man of Letters Learning addressing himself to a~~ Scholar, ~~and~~ addressing himself to Scholars, the right of ~~expressing un- blamed this dissent, with the grounds tha~~ a modest & respectful avowal & vindication of his opinion, and of ~~the~~ recommending the consideration of the point to the proper Authorities, without incurring the ~~dol~~ intolerable dilemma, either of transferring to an admitted Work of merely human Wisdom the perfection and con- sequent inalterability of Divine Revelation, or of deliberately pre- cluding all ~~progression &~~ improvement ~~however clearly generally the necessity or expedience therefrom of may be~~ —and advance- ment, ~~are~~ and all increase of knowlege that might lead to the desire of it, which for a Church calling itself protestant, and the first ~~Founders~~ Reformers and thereby Founders of which avowed the incompleteness of this Reform, and that the Ne plus ultra was fixed by the Circumstances of their Times, and not by ~~its~~ Commensu- rateness of the Work with their own Wishes & Judgements, is not   *f80ᵛ* even to be ~~thought~~ imagined. I am indeed persuaded, that even now a modest exercise of this right, ⟨limited & qualified as I have stated it,⟩ ~~by a Clergyman~~ will give offence to no ~~enlightened~~ sober or learned Divine; but should it be otherwise, I contend that this intolerance & narrowness of spirit arises out of the general inatten- tion, first to the true nature & purposes of a National Church, and the difference in kind between the Church, as the third great & venerable Estate of the Realm, and the Ecclesia, or ~~Com~~ Spiritual Community having Christ as its head, which is the mild opposite & at once Support and Antidote of ~~the~~ all States & Nations, ~~of~~ i.e. *the World*—and secondly, to the difference between Opinion, and Action.

5399 26.48   Herbert's Temple, p. 50-. II.-. The Spiritual Unity in the Bible = the *Idea* of the Organic World, as the pro- duct of one Spirit of Life but (N.B.) + 1, ~~not~~ a pregnant inclusive not a negative exclusive Oneness—such as is the Unity of Light, comprehending the Colors, and infinite shades or intensities of each   *f81* Color.

= 8. 1   The Culminant.   Red
    2   The Nadir—   Black
    3   The + Pole   Yellow
    4   The − Pole   Blue
    5   The Indifference of the + and − Pole.
                          Indecomponible Green.
    6   The Synthesis of the + and − Pole
                          Decomponible Green
    7   The Indifference between the Culminant &
        the + Pole.

                          Orange
    8   The Indifference between the Culminant
        and the − Pole.

                          Indigo.

5400 26.49   The more perfect the Liturgy, in the language
of Love & Holy Emotion, & therefore of accomodation, the more
necessary the Doctrinal Articles in the language of Science (&
therefore ~~languages~~ of propriety or declarative of the inadequacy
or inapplicability where proper terms are precluded by the unicity
or transcendence of the Subject) in order to prevent the accomodations from passing into the province of Doctrine, & speak expressing doctrines instead of emotions—

f81ᵛ 5401 26.50   Prayer = A sort of Tune which all things hear
and fear.—Herbert. ~~The more~~ Every time I read Herbert anew,
the more he grows in my liking. I admire him greatly—14 June
1826.

                          Antiphon. Men & Angels
Mem. − ⌣ − ⌣ − ⌣ − a   Chorus. Praisèd be the God of Love
        − ⌣ − b   M. Here below
        ⌣ − ⌣ − a   A. And here above.
        ⌣ − ⌣ − b   Ch. Who hath dealt his mercies so
    − ⌣ − ⌣ − ⌣ −
        − ⌣ − c   A. To his friend
        ⌣ − ⌣ − b   M. And to his foe

    − ⌣ − ⌣ − ⌣ − c   That both Grace & Glory tend

— ◡ — d	A. Us of old
◡ — ◡ — c	M. And us in th'end
— ◡ — ◡ — ◡ — d	✳The great Shepherd of the Fold
— ◡ — e	A. Us did make
◡ — ◡ — d	M. For us was sold

The ~~pe~~ last syllable of the penultimate line of each stanza rhyming
to the 1ˢᵗ & 3ʳᵈ lines of the following stanza.

✳ The licences are hidden by the *tune*/Such must be *read tuning*
He our foes in pieces brake. Him we touch—And him we take.   *f82*
Wherefore since that he is such   We adore   And we do crutch—
(crouch)
Who goes to bed and does not pray   Makesth two nights to every
day.—

5402 26.51   Curious & the completing 1000th of ~~my~~ the
instances of my favorite adage, Extremes meet!—is the coincidence
in ~~the~~ principle—i.e. the grounding Position assumed, between
my ἄρυμσχᾶρυμ νέφυ Ἔνρι, and Mʳ Irving—each drawing from
the same assumption ~~the~~ a contrary result. For I. asserts and ῾E.
implies ~~a~~ the direct politocratic power of the Gospel—the latter
proceeding on the puritan politics and Judaizing Eulen-spr~~ach~~ruch
(Dictum bubonium or Owl-oracle) of Sir Matthew Hale that the
Bible is the Law of England, and former asserting that it *ought* to
be so.—Hence Irving exclaims—This (say, Slavery) is abhorrent
from the Spirit of Christ's Commands—therefore extinguish it by
Act of Parliament.—῾E. on the other hand reasons—Sᵗ Paul did
not command his few wealthy converts to emancipate their
Slaves—therefore Slavery is not abhorrent from the Christian Re-   *f82ᵛ*
ligion.—evidently implying, that *if* Sᵗ Paul had in his apostolic
character admonished Philemon to emancipate Onesimus, *then* ~~the~~
our Parliament would have been bound to have set all consequences
at defiance and have abolished Slavery by ~~Statute~~ moral Law.—
The error common to both—viz. the confusion of ultimate ends
(which as long as a *World* in the N.T. sense of the word is in
being ~~are~~ is the sole Command of Xty) with the Mediate—i.e. the
ways and means dictated by existing circumstances to men exercis-

ing particular functions & consequently contained in the sphere of their Action as Functionaries of this particular name, of ~~appr for warding the~~ moving toward the realization of the ultimate end.— But then *Means* must be *Means*—i.e. they must be, first, practicable & secondly, adapted to & likely to effect, the intended purpose—not such as notoriously without a succession of Miracles would set the desired object at a greater distance than before—

f83

~~Form~~ Let the base line XX of the Isosceles Triangle represent ~~a~~ the Nation in its present condition, moral, intellectual, and political. Let the left-hand Leg, L. represent ~~Human~~ positive LAW, or Legislation, the right leg,

R. the influence of Religion/the two lines start from the opposite poles of the Base line, and ~~remaining par~~ separate tho' with everlessening distances to the moment of their meeting in the Apex, Θ—which represents *Theocracy*. Mr Irving ~~cannot force the Lines~~ would have a Triangle ◁▲ in which a perpendicular ~~wou~~ falls from the apex to the Base '◢ᴿ and then ~~force~~ change from an oblique to a perpendicular and then force it into contact & unition with the straight Line R. ◢ᴸ. But this is impossible without a succession of Miracles subversive of all moral freedom, & consequently of all responsibility, and consequently of Religion itself! But *some*thing he might do—Something the Puritans (~~in~~ during the Interregnum, commencing with the Civil War) in England & Scotland effected—and *some*thing the Romish Hierarchy has effected—viz. to ~~bring~~ turn the two lines L. and R. of the divinely described Isosceles Triangle into parallels that never

f83ᵛ

can meet at any distance/both necessarily ~~deal~~ missing the Θ. But a Religion which instead of moving forwards to Theocracy will ~~def~~ have thro' its whole Line without contra-distinguishing itself as Religion by acknowleging Law as its Antithesis, becomes Law itself—and a godless Law to boot.—My kingdom is not of *this world*—i.e. it is not a kingdom or realm of mediate purposes, dictated & the means determined by the understanding (φρονημα σαρκος) but of ultimate ends dictated by the Reason—& the means only as far as they are parts of the ultimate end—ex. gr. Purity & Charity as the means of Holiness, but likewise parts thereof—

Surely no two positions can well be more distant from each other
than Slavery is in accordance † with the Christian Religion—and
the refusal to ~~abolish~~ attempt an immediate abolition of ⟨Colonial⟩
Slavery by repeating the Acts of Parliament by which it has been
hitherto protected & passing penal laws for its prohibition in their
place, ~~is~~ argues no inconsistency in a Government, the members
of which ⟨are⟩ professed Christians—or may be an Act of Duty on   *f84*
the part of a Legislature, the members of which are individually
sincere Christians. A ~~Legis~~ Christian Legislator is no more bound
to consult the Gospel for the ~~rules of his Craft~~ making of Laws,
than a Christian Blacksmith for the making of Horse-shoes—to
both alike Christianity prescribes the *ultimate ends*; and in both
cases alike leaves the choice of the means and the question whether
the appropriate means ~~fall within~~ do not lie beyond the sphere of
his particular Craft, to ~~the~~ the man's Understanding and Common
Sense, ~~regulated (qualified) by Experience &/regulated~~ with the
times and opportunities of applying them in the application of past
experience with the time and manner of applying them to the
Man's own Common Sense, Knowlege of existing Circumstance &
Skill in his particular Craft or Calling—& in like manner too the
determination of the very important question, whether the appropriate means do not lie beyond the sphere of his particular Craft/
—However active and strenuous he may be in his individual capacity as a man & Christian, he may nevertheless see sufficient
grounds for abstaining from all interference as a Craftsman, in   *f84ᵛ*
obedience to the good old Precept, Ne Sutor ultra Crepidam, and
~~to the~~ because both Conscience & Common Sense teach us to take
the least of two Evils, and to do ~~to do nothing rather than~~ nothing
where we can only do mischief, or at best play the fool. Nihil
quam Nihili—nothing rather than Nothings.—. Surely, I repeat,
no two position can ~~be~~ well be more distinct than these—and yet
it is to the confusion of the two by Mʳ Canning & his Partizans
(my νεφυ for instance), or rather to their saying the first when in
fact they mean ⟨or rather began with meaning,⟩ the second, that
the main dispute is owing. For the Methodists, the African Soci-

† For "compatible" either means this: or the position is a truism,
equally valid of Whoredom or Profane Swearing as of Slavery.

ety, the Baptist Missionaries and my eloquent Friend Irving understand them to mean what their words mean—& ~~Mr Canning~~
~~the~~ οι αμφι Canning themselves by little and little, partly from the
~~confusing~~ heat & glare of Controversy and partly from the original
dimness of the conceptions & the want of ~~see~~ bringing both positions simultaneously & yet distinctly, ~~pass into the latter~~ and by
f85   defending the former to the degradation not to say defamation of
the moral Code of the Gospel. Saturday Midnight—17 June 1826.

5403 26.52   Mem. The same Licentia Spiritualis & seem-
ing-irreverent Boldnesses in Luther—& in Cotton Mather, or the
homely *Chalkhos*toms † of the Cameronian Tub—how different!
Pæne idem et nihilominus prorsus aliud.—i.e.—the ~~brilliant~~
spirit-starting Discords in a Beethoven or a Weber, and the teeth-
on-edge setting Discords of a Country Fidler.

                    Chrysostom
† χαλκοστομοι ⚹ χρυσοστομ

5404 26.53   Our knowleges are of three kinds, historical,
sciential, and the union of the two, ~~by the~~ and Psychology falls
into three Sections or Denominations, in correspondence with
    The Divisions or denominations of Psychology correspond with
those of the know
    Psychology falls under three denominations or divisions, in cor-
respondence with the three kinds of knowlege, which it is to arrange and systematize—viz. historical, sciential and ~~the union of~~
f85ᵛ   ~~the two~~ theoretical. The first, or historical (likewise entitled, empirical) acquires its material from the senses, the outward and the
inward sense by observation: the second or sciential Psychology ~~I~~
~~deter~~ sets forth the Laws or constitutive Forms of the intellectual
faculty itself, and ~~shows how~~ by shewing how the impressions on
the Senses are brought under ⟨and into coincidence with⟩ the inherent forms of the Understanding teaches the nature and conditions of EXPERIENCE: and it arrives at this knowlege by voluntary
reflection and meditation. In all experience, rightly so called, the
Senses supply the material, and the ~~Understanding~~ Mind the Rule:
and Experience is the union of the two.—Lastly, the third or the-

oretical Psychology, connects ⟨and reaffirms⟩ the data of Experience into scientific arrangement, in accordance with the formal functions or antecedent most general conceptions of the Understanding, ex. gr. Quantity, Quality, and Relation, the last comprizing the Relation of Substance and Accident, Cause and Effect, Action and reaction. And in this department we proceed by Contemplation the object of the process, being that of enabling the mind to comprehend all the several parts as a whole, and to see, as it were, the whole from one and the same point of View—And thus THEORY, from θεωρεῖν, contemplari—i.e. to see any given number of objects at the same time in consequence of their being so disposed as to appear connected Parts of the same Whole. And hence per metaphoram from the bodily eye to the eye of the Mind.

f86

To understand a thing is to know its conditions and relations: but so ⟨to⟩ place a thing as that the conditions of its existence and the relations, in which it exists, are rendered evident, is the meaning of Theory. The man therefore who cries out for Facts and no Theory, ~~or~~ for Practice in opposition to Theory, is very judiciously fitting his Soul at her next metempsychosis to enter into the form and functions of a Turn-spit Dog.

5405 26.54   The deficiency of the psilodynamic scheme is well exemplified in the Corresponding Opposites of Oersted's Juvenile Work—Oxygen Kindle-craft, Esqre and Lady Hydrogen Burn-craft, the incestuous Twins of Androgyn Oldcraft—more ~~rightly named~~ expressively englished, Sparkcraft and Tindercraft. But who does not feel that the term, kraft or power, must be taken in two different senses in order to constitute an intelligible difference in the two ~~Subjects~~ Factors, ⟨Zundkraft & Burnkraft⟩: that an active transitive *power* supposes a susceptibi~~lity~~le ~~over the~~ subject—a passio alīus which it seems strange to call *a Power*. The truth is, that neither the Atomic, nor the Dynamic System, singly, can answer the demand—the Matter is inactive without the Power—it is an accusative Case absolute—and on the other hand, the Power is objectless without the passive matter/It is a verb *transitive* without an accusative—i.e. without any thing, in quod *transeat*. Both are but nomina abstracta, the one = agere, the other = pati. Why not then go at once to a reality, that contains the agere

f86^v

f87

+ pati, and the agere = pati, + pati = agere, in its essential idea—i.e. to Life—first, as Unity and then under the condition of multëity (Lives)?

The point, in which all genuine Naturalists agree is: that all the phænomena and changes of Nature obey a Law—i.e. are reducible to some *form* coincident with Reason. But the misery of the matter is that not one in a Score of our Naturalists have ever asked themselves, what ~~they~~ he meant by a Law in Physics—content to know, that such or such is the Law in this or that, in consequence of which self-complaisant Carpenter's Ruler Sort of Science—Sight without Insight—nothing is more common than to hear a mere fact of frequent occurrence (ex. gr. a hard and thumping Pulse in a given state of Fever) called a Law. Facts, the constant recurrence of which under given conditions, as ascertained by legitimate Experiments carefully instituted & repeated by different philosophers, justify the presumption of their necessity, but ~~with all~~ where the source and nature of the necessity has not been seen into, should not be named LAWS, but Rules or Maxims of Experi~~ment~~ence.

But alas! it is a hopeless endeavour that of reforming the language of Thought in an unthinking Generation. The knowlege of Nature (as far as Facts without insight deserve the name of knowlege) will, I doubt not, continue to receive fresh and important accesssions from the present empirical Activity—the powers & conveniences of Society will be increased and enlarged.—but is it nothing that Man himself will not partake in the improvement—. That in point of moral dignity and intellective knowlege the very Inventors and Discoverers of these Utilities might as well have been employed as head Cooks in a French Nobleman's Kitchen, as head Chemists in a Royal Laboratory! . . The less depressive and perhaps most profitable way of setting forth this truth would, however, be by displaying the results and glorious consequences of a truly philosophic Science, in which the *ultimate* end and that which should evermore be *in aim*, tho' not always *in view*, and for which all lower knowleges should be contemplated as temporary Substitutes or approximations, is the ~~reduction~~ coincidence of Nature ~~to~~ with the necessities ⟨? necessary truths⟩ of Reason, or the Reduction of Facts to Ideas.

In such a System each ~~several~~ Philosopher in every discovery

f87ᵛ

f88

effected in his particular department would act on, and as it were
diffuse his growth into, the whole philosophic Senate—and thence
thro' the Statesman and the Theologian into the Society at large!
But first thy name must be hallowed, O Father which art in   *f88ᵛ*
heaven! before we can do more than wish and pray, that *thy Kingdom come*!

5406   26.55
Ideas

1. The Point.—2. The Point unfolding itself in all directions; yet
nevertheless remaining entire = Sphere. (P.S. An Idea is in its
purity necessarily inconceivable; for it is an Act and Form of a
Principle that transcends the human Understanding, ~~or~~ i.e. the
faculty of conceiving, *capiendi* hoc uná *cum* alio per notas ambobus
communes. Now what is inconceivable, is likewise inexpressible in
adequate terms or words. For Terms (termini, outlines, separative
boundaries) or Words, are the Products, and only *immediate* Objects, of the Understanding. Strictly speaking, we *understand*
words only. See Aids to Reflection p. 224. The result is, that there   *f89*
is no other way of expressing, rather say of conveying or designating an IDEA, but by two contradictory conceptions. "Before
Abraham *was*, I *am*." The Soul is *all* in every *part*. "The Divine
Power is a Sphere, whose *Center* is *every where* and its circumference *no where*—" &c.—Now in application to our present subject,
this seeming contradiction of a Point expanding or repeating itself
in all directions, yet abiding entire in itself designates the Idea,
and is realized in the Fact, of Generation. Hence the Ancient
Mathematicians, the Great Fathers of philosophic Arithmetic and
Geometry, employed the phrase, the Point generating the Sphere.
In the School of Pythagoras the Point produced the Line: ~~an~~ it was
reserved for a race of Pseudo-philosophers enslaved to the Outward Senses and Sensuous Imagination to degrade this into a Point
produced (i.e. elongated) into a Line. Now then *da capo*.) ⟨Turn
over⟩
1. The Point. 2. The Point repeating itself continuously, or ex-   *f89ᵛ*
panding in all directions = Sphere. 3. The radial Line, or the
generation of the Point contemplated in some one determinate direction ⟨from center to periphery.⟩ N.B. A Line produced inde-

terminately and causelessly from a point in ~~op~~ two opposite directions as W——————— . —————E, is a non-entity. Every
Line is essentially centro-peripherical; and must be assumed (*imagined* it cannot be) to move in one and the same act at once from
the center toward the periphery, and from the periphery to the
center. And this identity or union of Convergence and Divergence
constitutes the polarity, the $+ \ -$, of the Line. Every Line is bi-
polar—and essentially magnetic. The Centripetal is the universal
Pole = Gravity; the Peripheric or Centrifugal the Particular Pole,
f90   in which whatever is strives after individuality, distinction, the
Light Pole. The Source of Light is the Center of gravity—the
Sun. Light magnetic.—4. In every real periphery the extreme
points of the Radii contemplately continuously constitute the
Spherical Surface.—N.B. Plane Surfaces, by sections of the
Sphere, are necessarily fragmentary, and signify imperfection, and
death—In all such the apparent Surface is but the confused ~~collec-
tion~~ vision of the Lines, as in a horizontal Spider's Web, in which
the component threads are so close to each other as ⟨that⟩ at a small
distance the interspaces ~~one~~ become imperceptible. There is no true
difference between the lineal and the Superficial. Only the Spherical Surface constitutes a distinct essence, being always perpendicular to the Radius and never parallel with the Line. 5. As the
Radii are inseparable from the radiative Act and radial motion,
each Line must be ideally contemplated as continually produced by
the self-repeating motion. But what is true of every part must be
true of the whole. Every Sphere must revolve on itself, & have
f90^v   motion tho' not always an apparent or loco-motion. The Motion
~~or the Life from~~ abstracted loco-motion or change of Place is the
Life. 6. Whatever is not determinate is either = God as the Absolute Will, the αει προπρωτον, the sempiternal Ponent nunquam
positum; or = a universal Form, ex. gr. a ~~pl~~ Space; or an abortive
Effort of the Imagination, striving to present to itself the absolute
Will, or necessary *Antecedent* to all Being, in its own form—which
being impossible, the striving itself with the continually repeated
rejection and flux of phantom shapes, becomes the substitute for a
form—even as where bodies succeed each in too rapid motion for
any one to be seen distinctly, there results a visual *mist* (as the

golden mist seen in the Harp, in a rapid movement). Now this
⟨Phantom, or⟩ Substitute for a Phantom, is *Matter*.—All besides,
whatever *are* under whatever name of existence, Things or Acts or
(the identity of both) Persons, are determinate. Consequently all   *f91*
motion is determinate. Now Motion is the *Phænomenon* (Apparitio)
~~of~~ or *Space-form*, of Action—determinate Motion of determined
Action. But to every Phænomenon that is *Objective* (not merely
existing and for the *Subject*, as the Phænomena of Dreams) i.e.
that is an Appearance, not nakedly an Apparition, there belongs a
Noumenon, or Sufficient Cause (Causa *sub* faciens, quæ τό φαινό-
μενον *intelligibile* reddit). These Agents as the Causes of the Motions are of course in order of thought *antecedent* to the Motions,
as the Solar Orb to its rays, tho' without interval of Time—and a
fortiori antecedent to Fi*gur*e, which is generated by Motion. Now
then abstract from all Figure and Shape, and then meditate on
these determinate Energies, that express while they realize, each
its relation to the Indeterminable, determining all and containing   *f91*
eminenter all Determinates, and whose only visual Symbol is +o:
secondly, its comparative Value or Worth in reference to all other
determinate Energies: thirdly, its affections by Position with co-
existing Energies.

Furthermore (see 3) remember that every ~~Motive Energy~~ Line,
and consequently every lineal Motion, and consequently the motive
energy of which it is the Phænomenon, is centro-peripheric—that
~~its~~ the first act common ~~to it with all other~~ to all is the centripetal,
which in order of thought must be assumed as antecedent to the
act by which it is counteracted; but which therefore from this very
ideal anteriority & from its being common to all and therefore not
appropriated to any one peculiarly must appear as a with-holding,
retaining, or inhibitive act of the Center or Central Energy—and
after~~wards~~ its counteraction by the peripheric or centrifugal
Power, as an attractive Power—i.e. the center itself is the one pole   *f92*
of every radius.

Reflect again, that these motive energies are assumed as every
way determinate and characterized—⟨each⟩ expressing therefore
and realizing the determinate proportion of its Antagonism ~~or di-~~
~~vergent force~~ to the centripetal Force, or the comparative sum of

the energy by which it resists and to that extent overcomes or diminishes (practically) the withholding and attracting̶on of the Center.—

Now I say, thoughtfully master and bring together before your mind these several characters & attributes: and then I dare confidently ask you, what *more* appropriate, nay what other *proper* and significant *Name* can be assigned to these determinate Energies, that express themselves in determinate Motions, and at ~~once~~ first

f92ᵛ determining their relation to a common center then by motion generate determinate Figure and Dimension—if not substantial, ~~mo~~ living *Numbers*, Numeri numerantes! Try!—will you say Spirits? Souls? or the like?—But these are terms that express only a *Class*—and therefore necessitate the question—but what is a Spirit? What *are Souls?*—So if I should say, *Powers*—the Word is indeterminate, and signifies only a Principle of Action generally, without expressing the mode or ~~qualit~~ character of the action, and without rendering the Multëity asserted by the plural any way intelligible, and without affording any insight into the necessity or essentiality of this Multëity—much less of its relation to, & participation of, Unity—the Piú nel uno—or that in each of the Powers the many and the one exist determinately & ~~consequently different~~ and differentially.—For aught we could learn by the word,

f93 Powers, we might as significantly have substituted the Singular, Power. We have seen these determinate Energies determine, 1. ~~the each a determinate relation of proportion~~ a common relation to the central or inhibitive Power—and 2. each differentially exhibit a determinate relation of proportion to the same power—in other words, constitute 1. Gravity and 2. Specific Gravity—and then (in order of thought, ~~but coinstantaneous~~ tho' without interval of Time) generating the Sphere, the radial Line, and the ~~spherical~~ Surface— i.e. Figure, Dimension—Length, Breadth, and †Depth— And

†. Observe that Depth is Gravity in the *form* of relative Length— Length and Surface are proper and primary Expressions; but

f93ᵛ Depth is metaphorical, as applied to Vision and Space.—Hence we say *deep* Feelings, profound energy—a depth of Life &c—while a long or broad Thought would be ridiculous. Abstract from ponderable Body & Depth becomes a | on or from a————.

can we repeat without admiration the sacred Dictum—Numero,   *f94*
Pondere, et Mensurâ generantur omnia! How can determinate
Measures be induced on the indeterminate Space but by *numbering*
Time, and then *numbering* Space by ideal determinate Spaces? The   *f93ᵛ*
⟨philosophic⟩ Order of the Sciences is likewise on the preceding
grounds determined. First (if it be not rather a *Wisdom*, and the
Root of all knowleges) *Theology*. (Nay, why should the occurrence
⟨and abuse⟩ of the word in the writings of men, justly or unjustly
decried as Visionaries, and Enthusiasts, deter me from using it,
when I know that it is the more proper term of the two?—First,
and the A Ω of all knowlege—Theosophy. Second. Arithmetic.
Third, Static. Fourth, Geometry.—. Surely, if our venerable
Hooker had meditated more deeply or rather with less drawback
from prejudice on the subject he would neither have disturbed the
order of the words in this sublime declaration, by Number,   *f94*
Weight and Measure God made all things, nor have thought himself obliged to recur to a vehement Prepossession (how originated,
he does not tell us) as the ground of the Pythagorean Faith—Τ*α*ην
Αριθμῳ ουσιαν ἀϊδιον ειναι και δυναμιν—and that ~~the~~ Sages of the
Italian School, ~~and~~ such as Archytas and Archimedes, should re-
vive the profound Man of Samos and with him venerate τους
ζωοντας και οντως υπαρχοντας Αριθμους, ως αρχας προμαθεστατας
του παντος ουρανου και γης &c

P.S. The later Pseudo-pythagoreans, and Neo-platonists,˙ νοη-
ται μαλλον ἡ φιλοσοφοι, placed *Numbers* as the Transcendents of
IDEAS, which they placed in the second rank—thus seeking to   *f94ᵛ*
amalgamate the Platonic with the Samian Nomenclature, while
they ~~gar~~ intimated a mysterious Superiority ~~to~~ of Pythagoras over
Plato, in ~~order of~~ favor and furtherance of their scheme of setting
up ~~Pythagoras~~ the former as an inspired wonder—working
Prophet or Demigod, against Christ.—But there is no ground for
the distinction. The Pythagorean Numbers (Numeri numerantes,
Αριθμοι νοεροι και νοητοι) are the Ideas of Plato.—Αριθμοι, Ιδεαι,
Νομοι, Δυναμεῖς νομικοι, are Synonimes./

5407 Fᵒ.104   7 July 1826. Friday Noon.   *f44*
Curious instance of casual metre and rhyme in a prose narrative

(The Life of Jerome of Prague)—The metre is Amphibrach Dim-
eter Catalectic, i.e. ⌣ — ⌣ /⌣ : and the rhymes antistrophic—

Then Jerom did call   a
From his flame-pointed Fence   b
Which under he trod   c
As upward to mount   d
From the fiery flood   e

I summon you all   a
A hundred years hence   b
To appear before God   c
To give an account   d
Of my innocent blood!   e

5408 f°.105   When ~~in many~~ from several Points and in several directions simultaneously a ~~spirit of free~~ freedom of inquiry
shews itself, when in distant places men spring up ~~who~~ and as if
by some secret compact or guided by an invisible hand conduct the
apparently most dissimilar and unconnected studies to the same
End, we are assured, that the Spirit of History is awake, and ~~may
in~~ that a new epoch is near at hand.

5409 f°.106   You may see an *Idea* working in a man by
watching his tastes & enjoyments: tho' the man's understanding
may have been enslaved to the modern Metaphysics, or rather tho'
he may hitherto have no consciousness of any other reasoning but
that by conceptions & facts—On such a man you may hope to
produce an effect by referring him to his own experience & by
inducing him to institute an analysis of his own acts of mind and
states of being, that will prove the *negative* at last—viz. the not
only utterly *unsufficing* but the *alien* nature of all abstractions &
generalizations on the one hand, and of the negative units of the
outward Sight on the other, to the solution of his own intellectual
life.—But to talk of Ideas to men who neither have them or or
had by them, is profanation & folly to boot. Suppose your Hearer
a man of the most lucid logical talent, the utmost you can effect is
to make him understand that you imagine yourself to possess a
something which is *not* ~~any~~ either of the knowleges, or modes or
means of knowlege ~~of~~ with which he is acquainted.

5410 F°.107   The Papal Church split the Deity into a Pagan *Goddage*—the Protestants (after Luther) reformed it into a Judaic God, both equi-distant from the God of the Gospel, tho' the Protestant on the safer and more moral side.

5411 F°.108   Luther in his brave way often urges us to stir *f44ᵛ*
up ⟨God⟩ with prayer; and on the same ground vindicates language that seems to border on irreverence, outcries of Remonstrance and Inculpation not to say Objurgation. Nor can it be denied that the twofold precept of Prayer, viz. 1. perfect resignation to the Divine Will & ⟨not so truly prayer as⟩ grateful acknowlegement of the wisdom of the great Laws physical and spiritual, by which God governs the World, in the *guise* of Petition;—& 2ⁿᵈˡʸ ⟨Bonâ fide *Prayer*s,⟩ Prayers of importunity, *particular* requests persevered in with impassioned obstinacy and petitionary vehemence;—form a very remarkable and prominent Feature in our Lord's Discourses and seem to imply a twofold Ground of Prayer.—And whaterein can this be found if not in the Idea, of the του Θεου του υπερκοσμιου and of a αλλα και του Θεου πασχοντος, η του θειου πνευματος του Θ ἐγκοσμίου. ⟨We must hold⟩ Θεοτητα ὑποθετικην-many πνευμα δια πᾶσαν sc. κτισιν.—The necessityature of language Words forces us to speak metaphorically, ⟨and for the greater part⟩ in the language of the *eye*—and such metaphors of used of Spiritual things, above all of the Divine Spirit, must needs be *catachrestic*. Therefore if as in this instance the interests of faith and piety justify us in speaking at all, offence ne ought not to be taken at such phrases as *Deitas diffusa* and the like—as when Sᵗ Paul tells us, that the Spirit pleadeth to the Spirit with groans unutterable. An analogy might be drawn from Life in the organic realm; but more than an analogy would open out on this most profound but yet all-concerning point by the most methodical contemplation of *Life* in its lowest forms ⟨(a misgrowth ex. gr.)⟩ as distinct from and subordinate to Form, Type or the Principle of & the *Generic*—i.e. that which makes the Lion a Lion, the Eagle and Eagle.—2. of Organic Life, or the synthesis of the instrumental Life and the Form/then the relations of Life in both senses to Mind and Will—and lastly, the far higher than Life & typical generic Type, the principle of Individuality and Person—/Having thus ascended to

the Highest, viz. to the Prothesis, i.e. the Personëity of the Absolute Will—there rest ~~and~~ awhile, and then commence the descent—1. Thesis = I·M AM—the Supreme Mind in the form of
Will—/the Supreme Will in the form of Reason (Λογος) the union
of both in the SPIRIT, or celestial Life—The *chasm*—or apostasy,
or the self-position of the *Finite*—. From this point the ~~two~~ duplicity or two sides commences—/and in the condescension of the
Spirit and of the Word, in the work of Creation, as the first act of
the Redemption of the Finite, the Spirit & the Word—(the Principium a supra of Life and of Form) must be contemplated in a
two-fold relation, external and internal, lower & higher—to Life
and Form bodily, and to the ~~same~~ spiritual Life and Form—
whence the Former is of necessity the symbol of the Latter. Further, it is by Symbols alone that we can acquire *intellectual* knowlege of the Divine—. Every sincere & regenerate Believer possesses the truth in spiritual *Acts* and *States of Being*—and this is
enough for the Individual—but God will have his glory manifested in his *Church*, and therefore the *Church* requires a progressive evolution of intellectual Insight; & the instrumentality belongs
to those Individual (Doctors) to whom the Ability is given with
the Call, and the Call in the consciousness of the Ability & the
sense of the worthiness of the object:—But no other way exists but

f45   that of first obtaining intuitions of the action of Life on Life—the
stirring up of Life in many by Life in one—but yet efficiently &
for good only as far as it is *conditionally*—i.e. in accordance with
the higher Life and the commanding Form.—And then apply this
to *Prayer* in faith & in spirit—illustrated by the generation of
Heat and the elevation of the universal or thermo-metrical Heat—
For even these—viz. the absolutely continuous = Heat, and the
absolutely fractional = atoms, are but the lowest representations
of the condescended Spirit & Word (Deus Patiens, ὁ των κοσμιων
κοσμος)—But in order to this inquisition and to any part of it one
thing is previously necessary—viz. that the Inquisitor should believe that God IS—and *lives*—a faith in the *living* God.—The
depth of the Mystery is behind the Veil in the Vision of God
vouchsafed to Moses—Even he, could only be allowed to behold
the *back parts*, the skirts of Deity—i.e. ~~the~~ the Godhead as present
in and thro' all things, the ubiquity, not ~~the~~ God as to whom all

things are present, the supermundane Personal God—the only-
begotten before all worlds/—and the God, *in* whom all things are
present, even the Son himself and the Spirit, hath no one ever
seen—but the only-begotten sets if forth, is the Glory and the
Sound thereforeof from Eternity to Eternity!—Now we must begin with Moses, and learn to behold God in the Law, as the Skirts
et Infima Divina—and then ascend to Grace & Truth in Christ.

5412 F°.109   Of the causes of the delight which Men feel in
reading the History of great Warriors & Conquerors—& that this
is too broadly exprest—and with good mind is in great measure to
confined to Ancient History & especially that of Greece & Rome—

   Till States are in that self-standingness which admits of reciprocal Action, the epoch of mor international Morality is not yet
come—the Records do not yet as yet belong to the World of
Freedom/—& we read of these things as of the most interesting
parts of *Natural* History:—None but the vulgar (rich & poor)
felt Napoleon as they do Alexander the Great—Napoleon was an
Ape—. The difference of character in the conflicting nations was
wanting—not Greeks & Persians; but a wanton wicked Civil War
of ⟨a⟩ depraved knot of Co-europeans against men of the same
Arts, Sciences, habits &c. It was a civil war, not (I mean as far
as Napoleon was concerned) for any principle of Religion or Liberty but purely for an idle *Power*, merely nominal or and invested
in a few individuals. France as a state obtaining no additional
means of expanding perfecting herself—it was no expansion required in order to self-development, and therefore no *expansion* at
all; but a mere *notion*, that a man who resided ordinarily in Paris,
controlled & held in hate & terror the people in Amsterdam, Berlin & Naples—. WAR at present ought to be spoken of by all men
of genius as contemptible, vulgar, the dotage of second Childhood,
the letchery of Barrenness. The Holy Alliance in Idea was the
legitimate Product of just views respecting the constituent states of
Christendom; but usurped & debased by the substituting the fantastic interests of Individuals under the name of Governments, as
Proprietors of a power of doing mischief, or Wrong-lords, or of
a privileged order in each state versus the people—Had it been for
the securing the internal developement of each state by establishing

the law of equal action & reaction between all, it would have deserved the name—*Holy* Alliance.

f45ᵛ   5413 Fᵒ.110   July 18, 1826.—It is not enough to say that ~~I~~
we men by the nature and constitution of our limited Intellectual
are constrained to think of God in all these diverse relations—tho'
this both may and must be said: but we must believe that God
verily exists in these relations—i.e. they are not merely the Relations of our minds to the Idea of God, but the Relations in which
the Eternal I AM, who~~m~~ hath declared his own essence in the Hebrew words which literally translate (*as why should they not have
been?*) are—*I shall be that I will be* = my Will contains in itself
the ground of my own Being—on which account we without any
absurdity, on the contrary with the strongest reason, praise, thank
and glorify God for his own essential perfections.—But in believing the reality of these relations we must be most careful to declare
in our inmost spirit that he is One—one not by exclusion as in
~~finite an~~ the creatures where that which is A is therefore *not* B, but
one by the transcendent all-comprehendingness of his Will, which
excludeth imperfection ~~as~~ indeed but (observe! for it is most important!) because not being derived from any preclusive or inva-
sive Cause from without nor from any defect ~~or~~ deficiency, or
negation from within but ~~from~~ immediately from the Absolute and
infinite Perfection of his own Will it ceaseth to be imperfection.
The Patropassians erred grievously tho' I would not brand their
confused incorrespondent Conception with the name of Heresy;
but I cannot admit, that our Church Article is the right or adequate
Answer or Antidote to this error. The Article asserting the impas-
siveness of the Divine Being is true, but is not the whole truth—
Or rather the affirmation as thus worded is not all that belongs to
the full ~~comprehensive~~ expression of the Truth. To have sufficiently guarded the position, ab alio, or nisi per suum ipsius velle,
should have been added to *impassibilis*. Nevertheless the Will, the
ineffable Causa Sui, et Fons Unitatis in totâ infinitâ entis sui plen-
itudine, is evermore and eternally impassible—And since this is
personal in the Father, as το αυτοθετον Θελημα, Deus idem et
ipse—the Eternal Word υιος ο μονογενης being Deus alter et idem,
the Will eternally begotten (Will *of* Will, Very God *of* Very God)

in the form of Reason—therefore the Patropassian Hypothesis is a most grievous error, eclipsing the whole economy of the Trinity, & in its legitimate consequences leading to Pantheism, which is but a *live* Atheism in so far less repulsive but on that very account more dangerous than the lifeless Atheism of the Mechanic Materialists; such as Epicurus taught in old times and Le Land in our own times./Now we must not judge the Man by the consequences of his ~~Opinion~~ Doctrine of which he is not aware. But the doctrine itself we may & must. Say therefore that the Patripassian Doctrine is a condemnible Heresy tho' the Patripassians may not have been *f46* damnable Heretics.

P.S. The more I reflect, the more serious an evil does the retention of the Pseudo-athanasian ~~Church~~ Creed in our Church-liturgy appear. The Verses explicative of the Trinity may perhaps be dismissed as simply deficient—tho' I scarcely see how Bishop Bull or Dr Waterland could have refrained from marking ⟨as a positive error⟩ the confinement of the filial Subordination to the Humanity, and consequently denying its existence before the Birth of our Lord &!—That compared with the Nicene Creed, these Verses are wretched Verbiage—may be passed as a trifle—But the doctrine of the Nature & person in Christ I believe to be heterodox in theology; but the forcing this crude & arbitrary speculation unsanctioned by a single text of Scripture into a Creed or Compendium of Credenda essential to Salvation for all men—this is intolerable.

5414 F°.III   19 July 1826. The noblest feature in the character of Germany I find in the so general tendency of the young men in all but the lowest ranks (N.b. and highest) to select for themselves some favorite study or object of pursuit, beside their *Brodt*-wissenschaft—their Bread-earner—and where circumstances allowed, to choose the latter with reference to the former. But this, I am told, is becoming less and less the fashion even in Germany; but in England it is the misery of our all-sucking all-whirling Money-Eddy—that in our universities those, who are not idle or mistaking Verses for Poetry and Poetry for the substitute instead of (as it should be) the corolla & fragrance of the austere and many Sciences, appreciate all knowlege as means to some finite and tem-

poral end, the main value of which consists in its being itself a
means to a ~~some~~ another finite & common end—Knowlege—
Profession—Income—and consequently selecting their particular
Profession in exclusive reference to the probability of their acquir-
ing a good income & perhaps ultimate a Fortune thereby, then set
about getting in the easiest way exactly that sort and that quantity
of knowlege, which will pass them in their examinations for the
Profession, and which is requisite to or likely to forward their
~~professional~~ views of making money in ~~the~~ or by his Profession—
Now as the Many are most often the Judges & Awarders of the
Prize—or else, as in the Church, some Patron—Lord, Squire,
Bishop, or State-minister, we may readily determine, a priori,
what the qualifications will be that are most likely to be the means
to such an end—But this is the worst sort of Slavery: for herein
true Freedom consists, that the outward is determined by the inward, as the alone self-determinating Principle—what then must
be the result, when in the vast majority of that class in which we
are most entitled to expect the *conditions* of Freedom, and Freedom
itself as manifested in the *Liberal* Arts and Sciences, all Freedom
is stifled & overlaid from the very commencement of their career,
as men—namely, in our Universities, Schools of Medicine, Law
&c?

5415 F°.112   21 July 1826.—Those who in my life refuse
the kernel of my doctrine, said Luther, will after my death be glad
of the Shell if they could get it. ~~But~~ This was a great & prophetic
Truth—if we interpret, as in such Lightnings of Thought we are
entitled to do, *"those"* as meaning the same sort of people, the same
f46ᵛ *Minds* tho' in other bodies! For what were the controversies among
the Protestant Divines after Luther's Death, but a wrangling and
seeking for the identical Shell, in which Luther's Kernel chanced
to grow: that is, the exact *conceptions*, ~~and~~ the Logical Husks, in
which Luther swaddled the new-born Ideas, and sometimes mistook for them?—The words, however, suggest a still finer sense—
The man, who most vehemently rejected the whole doctrine when
first promulgated, would if he had born a century later, have been
the hottest zealot for the preservation of the Shell—but mark you,
of the hollow Shell. Offer him the kernel in another shell, much

more if you present it without a shell and shooting with its germinal Leafits, with marks of life and growth, the same enmity would break forth.

5416 F°.113   Custom more killing to Life & Truth than Sensuality. Hence the almost impossibility of Reformation but by Revolution = Luther: and then this again introduces the spirit of Negativity—Negamus: destruere oportet—Nihil restruendum, adstruendum, construendum—et postremo, hanc ipsam Negativitatem *estabilimus*—Extremes meet—Omnia credere et non credere = nihil credere.—

5417 F°.114   Tuesday 25 July 1826. Two classes in every profession—1. the almost all and 2. the scarcely any—The first point of diversity between them may be found in different sense of the word, Circumstances. With a man of the former class it means the sphere of his individual Practice, and whatever he hopes to include therein—his Town, Parish, Law-court, or Hospital. For the latter it means the whole sphere of his Art or Science. The second point of diversity is ~~the~~ to be found in the(ir) final Object. The one seeks to bring his Circumstances into harmony with his appetites, and ruling passions—i.e. with the inferior and animal portion of his Being—for the cravings for wealth, power, outward shew &c are as truly animal as Rage, Hunger, and Lust.—The other seeks to bring his Circumstances into harmony with his Intellect—and as to that narrower sense of Circumstances, he endeavors to bring his Wants and Wishes into harmony with them.—
    or I might express the thought thus:—
    There are two senses in which the word Circumstances may be understood—first, it may mean the sphere of a man's individual practice or what he hopes or wishes to include therein—and secondly, it may mean the whole sphere of the Art and the Science, which he professes.—In the first sense of the word, the man of the first class (viz. the almost all) seeks to bring his Circumstances into harmony with &c—while the man of the second class seeks to bring his wants and wishes into harmony with his circumstances.— In the other & wider sense of the word, the man of the first class

~~rather~~ cares nothing about them ~~or only as they are~~: the man of the second class strives to bring them into harmony with his Intellect—In short, the one ~~would fain~~ wishes to rise in his profession; the other to raise it.

5418 F°.115   Friday 28 July 1826. I will not ~~my~~ avail myself, tho' in all fairness I might do so, of the metaphors by which the N. Testament expresses the Punishment of ~~the~~ impenitent Sinners, and of the presumption, that as the texts cannot be interpreted *literally* of the particular Places (Tophet, Gehenna &c) neither *need* they be literally understood of *a Place* at all. Nor yet will I avail

f47 myself of the fact, tho' it be generally admitted, that throughout the Scriptures the positions must be understood in reference to Man's conceptions and ~~knowlege~~ Insight, not in reference to the divine knowlege: for whoever speaks, adapts his language to the known or supposed experience & capacity of the persons spoken to. For he speaks to be understood: and as soon as his words reach the ear of his Auditors, it is *their* mind that is to stand *under*, i.e. give the *substance* of thought to the sounds, not his own except as far as it can be identified with *theirs*. The mind of the Hearer may indeed be afterwards modified and enlarged ~~to~~ in consequence of the Words heard; but then they must have already been *words*, and not mere *Sounds*, in order to produce this Effect: and ~~they~~ Sounds become *Words* only by exciting in the mind of the Hearer images, thoughts or apprehensions already existing.

Thus: a process which does not contain in itself any necessity of its stopping at any time or point, in our conception of it—ex. gr. the division of any given Body—is said to be *endless*. We do not hesitate to say, that matter is divisible ad infinitum. But will this justify us in asserting, that any particular quantum has been or will be infinitely divided?—That which is beyond our power to define, ~~and is not~~ being *indefinite̶l̶y̶ably* great or long is for us infinitely such. The true interpretation therefore of all such phrases as expressed in the term, *incomparably*. There is no duration of which you have any experience, with which it can be compared.

But as I have said before, I will not avail myself of these Arguments. I admit, that the Soul is, without the intervention of a power equal to, and equally miraculous with, the power by which it was created, imperishable; that the nature, ~~and~~ or necessary tendency of sinful Habit, i.e. of Sin ripened into a habit, which is to destroy all the grounds and conditional causes of Well-being, and to substitute all the grounds and sources of Ill-being in all its forms of Pain, ~~in the~~ and misery, ~~are~~ is not ⟨itself⟩ affected ~~by the~~ or changed by the longer or shorter continuance of the Subject; but only the duration/.What matters it to the ever-flowing Brook whether the water-weeds that float on it & in it are annuals or perennials? As long as they are there, it bears & dashes them.— Now what do the Scriptures more than announce and affirm the great Law of the Spiritual World, that Sin generates misery and weakness, and that these instead of removing Sin, add to the strength of the Habit and diminish the Power of resistance; and this ~~descent~~ process of destruction has no other end or limit but that of the Subject, in which it is set up, and therefore if the one be imperishable, the other must be everlasting. Scripture has opened our eyes to the Abyss on ⟨the marge⟩ which every Sinner stands: but does it bid us push them in? or affirm of any one ~~soul~~ Individual Soul, that God has predestined *it* to fall—and that God never will control this fatal necessity, as he does so many others?— Is there no difference between the positions—God will put in force *f47ᵛ* the law of everlasting Death on such and such men—and—It has not been revealed to us, that God will *not?* Surely, this is our most striking instance of the propriety of a Negative Belief.—As sure as you have an immortal Soul, so certain is your everlasting damnation, if God does not interfere: and God has given you neither promise or assurance that he will! The impenitent Sinner that is proof against this, is ~~proof~~ a rock—which no force can make feel.

5419 F°.116   30 July 1826.—O my poor *Sara!*—I had hoped to have seen her once more before my decease! May God mercifully save my Understanding from being so weakened by bodily langor and low spirits, as to occasion my falling into Self-centering Superstitions—But this morning I awoke between 4 and 5—and having been thinking of the dispute concerning the effect of our Lord's Atonement on the state of the Resurgent Man, and whether ⟨the failure of⟩ an entire victory over Sin, by a cessation of all its consequences on the organic frame, be preclusive of the

Person's Salvation, or whether where the Sin is detested & bitterly confessed and lamented, and the consequences (ex. gr. where a poison destructive of life has become necessary to life) are felt as the merited punishment of past indiscretion and sinful weakness) the person anxiously laboring by all the means in his power to make compensation to his fellow-men and the Church of Christ, and ~~the~~ grounding his hopes wholly in God's infinite mercy in Christ Jesus, and strives with ~~whol~~ his whole soul and spirit to love God and his Saviour—we may not in this case hope that these remnants and sequels of Sin will by the power & efficacy of the Blood of Christ be *sloughed* and left with the Old Man in the Grave—

Musing on this, I say, I got out of bed, and took the Bible with an intention of reading the Epistle to the Romans and the Ep. to the Galatians—but I opened the Book on the 17ᵗʰ Chapter of Job, my eye falling on the first verse—My Spirit is spent, my days are extinct, the graves *are ready* for me—and then in the last line of Verse the 5ᵗʰ—"even the eyes of his children shall fail."—and it alarms & humiliates me to be forced to confess to myself, that this accident *troubled* me—Alas! to what depths of folly & imbecility do we not sink if for a moment God's grace be withdrawn—even to the Sortes Biblicæ.

f47ᵛ   5420 Fᵒ.117   30 July 1826. Sunday Night.—Wordsworth's & Southey's position that ~~God~~ pious prayers addressed to Idols, Saints, Virgin Mother &c find their way to the right Object and *f48ᵛ* are well-pleasing to God, is (thus—generally & unguardly worded, a very dangerous) error—Is not the *Love of Truth* a part of Christian Perfection? But this position necessarily tends to a spirit of indifference with regard to the false faith of our fellow-men of our own.

5421 Fᵒ.118   Tuesday, 1 August 1826.—Christianity ~~is~~ consists of *two* ingredients—the *first* is *History*—and my object is to restore it to religious *History*.—To those who pretend to know of no other ingredient; i.e. the persons commonly called the rational or liberal Divines of the Ch. of Engl—I would ask what the Doxology is—and for what purpose the Church introduces it so often in her public Service.—Glory to the F., the S. and the H.G. *as it was in the beginning, is now, and ever shall be.* That which is above Time, and indifferent to all times—that which has no appropriate exponent in any one particular thing, Act, Incident or Image—most certainly does not present itself to our minds, as historical. What then? Reflect a moment and ask yourself whether any other answer can be returned that it is an Idea or Eternal Truth. This, we say, is the only true *Idea* of God—or this is the Idea which the Christian Revelation teaches us to entertain of the God-head.—

This then is the other Element.—The facts of Religion in order to be religious facts or subjects of religious Belief must be grounded on Ideas and severally and collectively united with Ideas. As the Body with the Soul, in order to be a living Man—tho' not the converse/—But yet even those Ideas, which being antecedent to all as their common ground and presupposition cannot be embodied in a any fact of History, do yet acquire an historical character by the event or incident of their *revelation* to us.

Now this is my Aim—to bring back our faith & affections to the simplicity of the Gospel ~~History~~ Facts, by restoring the facts of the Gospel to their union with the Ideas or spiritual Truths therein embodied or thereby revealed.

Different from these spiritual facts, these incarnate Ideas are the historical events, by which their divine origin was attested (ex. gr. the destruction of the Temple & the Jewish State in fulfilment of our Lord's Prophecy) or their spread brought about. Yet the first Christians naturally expressed the idea or spiritual truth, of which this was one example, by figures and images abstracted from this example—and unfortunately the next generation forgot they were metaphors & made the figures of speech ~~the a~~ a component part of the truth itself.—N.b. remarkably verified in the various interpretations of the Apocalypse.

5422 F°.119   Two means of arriving at a sight of another *f48ᵛ* World that *now* is/and two preliminary conditions—
Condition I. That the person should feel the wish and want of *Common Sense.* For surely, the Sense of Sight, the representations of which ~~very with its p~~ are as different in different Individuals

as their relative positions, and n cannot be rightly called a Sense *common* to all. Example:—the 4 sided Pyramid which no one of nine persons saw ⟨with their bodily eyes:⟩ each of them might have seen with the eye of the mind—and this would be truly a common sense.

Condition II. That the person should feel an interest in knowing and understanding what he sees.—The Clown sees what he sees, and perhaps remembers the image impressed on his Senses & calls it by a name. But will it be said, that the Clown who ⟨Sirius pointed out to him⟩ being asked what Sirius it is, answers—why a *Star*—and in like manner, Jupiter—why, a *Star*—*knows* either? Did Kepler gain no advantage worth wishing for when feeling that the Ptolemaic System did not enable him to know or understand these Sights, discovered that the one was a Body like our Earth and moving round the same Sun, this Star Jupiter being 1000 times larger than our Earth, and the Sun a thousand times larger than Jupiter; and that Sirius was not such a body but a self-luminous one, like our Sun, and perhaps much larger.—

Way I. Distinguish the things themselves from their variable relations, of place, distance, subjective laws of vision &c—

Way II.—To understand a thing is to have an insight into the Power that *stands under* it—this is *substantial* knowlege—Now seek the intelligibility of every power from a higher power than itself— and this from a yet higher—till you arrive at a power, that ⟨in its own *definition*⟩ contains in its solution—or—the idea of which neither needs or permits an Antecedent.—

5423 F°.120   Tuesday Night, ⟨½ past 12.⟩ or rather Wednesday Morning—Of the large Moth with the immense proboscis that for half an hour had been with his back to the Candle trying every floret of 3 or four Scabiouses in my Flower-pot—and then turning round was struck with the Light & flew madly at the Candle—burnt scorch himself & fell—rose again, and dashed at it—I drove it off repeatedly—but in vain—again it dashed at the Light—till I succeeded in driving it about 3 yards off—& there the fascination seemed to cease.—Well worth thinking of—

f49 5424 F°.121   4 August 1826. This is a [? sore calamity/sorrowful] ⌜..........⌝!—God grant him the confirmation of his be-

lief, the fulfilment of his Hopes!—Likewise I had a Note from
M͏ʳ George Frère, in which, adverting to ⌜.......⌝ I have heard so
much good of my Son, John, that I was not happier on my Wed-
ding Day!—This *is* a Blessing!—Henry Gillman came home on
Tuesday Night. N.b.—*I have a fancy, that he will turn out an
eminent* ACTOR. He is *dramatic*—fond of dressing himself up, as
a young Lady, or an old Woman &c &c.—I was too ⌜..........⌝
to make it ⌜.........⌝ (Saturday, 30 July) the letter was delivered
to me which announced that She ⟨Sara⟩ had been taken so ill at
Kendal, that it was determined that M͏ʳ Gee should set off without
her.—O it was a bitter disappointment—for *her* sake even more
than for my own. For tho' I exceedingly regret that the attachment
between her & ✳ ✳ ✳ ✳ ✳ ✳ ✳ ✳ ✳ ✳ ✳ ✳ ✳ ⟨ever took
place⟩—for four momentous reasons; yet to know her to be unhappy, would be worse than *Regret*!

5425 F°.122   The Liver (the first perfected and first acting
Organ) I regard as the negative Pole of ~~the~~ negative Life; the
Lungs as the corresponding opposite (i.e. positive) Pole, and the
Heart, the Punctum indifferentiæ./But Life in the first Idea is
distinguished into positive and negative—the Nervous System
being the positive, and ⟨each of ⟩ the two other Systems negative
to *it*.—But when we contemplate all three vital Powers, then we
must say, that the Nervous System as the exponent of Sensibility
is the + Pole, the Glandulo-venous as the exponent of Reproductivity is the − Pole, and the Heart ~~or~~ & Musculo-arterial
⟨System⟩ as the exponent of Irritability, (better named, Instinctivity) is the Indifference.

The power & function which the seminal Contagium exercised on
the ovulum of the female, that same p. and f. the Brain exercises
on the lower organisms./

Cyanic Gas/Carbon + Nitrogene—explosive, forming rather
⟨than⟩ formed—this alternating with the predominance of Carbon
by aid of Hydrogen, and thus constituting a vital dynamic carbon-
ization of the Blood, I suspect to be the Function and character of
the Liver.

5426 F°.123   6 August, 1826.—If there be a Spiritual
World, if the linked Causes that in the same instant are Effects,
and Effects that are at the same moment Causes, when we contemplate the Material World in the form of Space and Co-existence,
and first Effect & then Cause (B, effect of a spiritual agent, that
forms no part of the Chain) B cause to C, C to D, D to E &c,
f49ᵛ   when we think of Nature in the form of Time & Succession—if I
say, this vast expanded and suspended Net-work, this complex
chain-armor of natural Necessity be but the reflected and refracted
Image of rather framed by the rays from the invisible Sun—the
world of Spirit, a system of Freedom, without generalization—
there is nothing prima facie improbable or extravagant in the supposition, that the same Incident might ⟨for the Bystanders of this
World and the Eyes and Ears of Flesh⟩ be a Thunder-storm and
a man on horseback struck down, blinded and thrown into a brief
Trance by the Lightning, and yet verily and really be the voice
and the spiritual presence of Jesus Christ to the awakened Spirit
of Sᵗ Paul. At all events, I would rather have recourse to this
Belief, than abuse Eichhorn for his explanation of the Miracle of
the Conversion without being able to disprove any one of his assertions, or to shew that his facts are false or not ejusdem generis—
It cannot be denied, that every part of the Incident, the prostra-
tion, the trance, the hearing of articulate sounds in the Trance
accompanied with the irres⟨is⟩tible conviction of a particular Person as the Utterer of the same, the temporary Blindness, and the
acceleration of the restitution to sight by the mighty excitant power
of faith, and the momentum communicated to the nerves by the
confidence of the Physician or Exorcist, has happened to other
Individuals, where there was neither reason nor pretence for any
miraculous interposition. Peculiar to the case of Paul are—first,
Cornelius's relation of interpretation belief of the coincidence of a
Dream with the arrival and purpose of the new Convert, or rather
the *Report* of this Circumstance, as heard and recorded by Luke,
Paul's Biographer—and this ⟨⟨Eichhorn would add⟩⟩ at a time and
in a country when & where men's minds were especially turned to
Dreams, Visions, and Omens—and second, the character and en-
suing Conduct & Success of Sᵗ Paul himself; to which I would
add, Sᵗ Paul's own assurances. For I cannot agree with Eichhorn

to interpret the texts in which the Apostle asserts his doctrines to have been learnt immediately from Christ by direct revelation, and on this fact rests his right of perfect equality with the other Apostles, as referring merely to the Vision on the road of Damascus, and the few words spoken to him at that time. These indeed were enough to ground his *Mission* on; but surely not the particular articles of Faith, so as to justify him in asserting & enforcing them against missionaries that were, or at least professed to be and were received by the Churches as having been, accredited from the Apostles themselves.—

Now on these last points of difference—viz. the object, the occasion, the *importance*, ~~of the share~~ the results, St Paul himself, the Apostle of the Gentiles, and the enduring Oracle of the pure Faith, I should rest my vindication of the *miraculous* character of the Incident, in any dispute with an Unbeliever—But even so I should begin by protesting against the fallacy & unfairness of detaching any single part from the Gospel History and reasoning on it as if it stood alone, and as if the magnetic energy in a complete~~ound~~ magnet, consisted of twenty or more ~~and~~ was not predicable of each during its station as a component part of the magnetic Engine—Even so is it with the credibility of the Gospel Facts—each *f5 1* must be appreciated by the credibility of the whole. Not—may an incident like that which occasioned the conversion of Paul of Tarsus not be explained by an accidental concurrence of natural causes, supposing it an insulated fact?—this is not the question!—Or if asked, the answer is—Yes! and in the insulated cases to which Eichhorn refers, and of which three occurred in the course of four years, as published in the Newspapers, no one ever thought of explaining them otherwise.—But the right question is—~~but~~ bearing in mind the time, the occasion, the results, the life and character of the Individual, and the close and *organic* connection of this Event with the whole History of Christianity, from the Baptism of John to the close of the Apostolic Age, and again the no less intimate connection of Christianity with the History, Laws and Prophecies of the Hebrew Nation, can we rationally refuse our assent to the Apostle's own inward Assurance and persistent Assertion of ~~the~~ its miraculous—i.e. supernatural, origin? If St Paul might have been deceived, yet Cornelius must have been a Liar, or Luke must have invented the story (i.e. been a Liar) or have suffered himself to be imposed on by Liars—Now the absence of all motive and object for a miraculous interposition must be very evident, before we could be justified in a making any one of these harsh conclusions—/*More* shocking still ~~would~~ will the wantonness and the uncharitableness of such an assertion ~~thu~~ appear when we advert to the very great probability that St Luke had t received his information from St Paul's own Mouth./

5427 F^o.124   If recorded facts are incompatible with our interpretation of one single text, must we not infer that we have given the words too wide a meaning, or have mistaken or over-looked their intended application? Ex. gr. the text in which our Lord promises the Apostles that the Holy Spirit will bring back to their minds all that he had said to them. If we take into view the poverty, laxity and simplicity of the Hebrew or Aramaic Lan-guage, in which our Lord conversed, we shall, I think, be inclined to understand these words of the general tenor of our Lord's In-structions, and as far as was requisite for each Apostle's Mission. At least, it would remove several difficulties, that perplex a thoughtful and reflecting Reader on the present generally received notion of plenary inspiration, enjoyed by all alike, and not bounded by any reference to the part, allotted ⟨by Providence⟩ to the Apostles collectively and to each specially, in the first planting of ⟨the⟩ Christian Church—it would lessen if not remove, I say, not a few difficulties in the 3 first Gospels, if we might venture to suppose that in some instances the Evangelists (for I ~~do~~ can not forget that the explaining the words according to St Matthew as equivalent to written by Matthew, is a purely arbitrary interpre-tation, and highly improbable to boot) had misconceived the Apos-tle/—or the Apostle whose preachings, κηρύγματα, he had collected (*taken notes of*, as we now say) have not comprehended their divine Master.—This remark was occasioned by the celebrated texts re-specting the Sin against the Holy Ghost—the most probable solu-tion of which is ὡς ἔμοίγε δοκεῖ, by the supposition that our Lord referred to the Sin of the Apostate Spirits, who had perverted the spiritual ground of their Life to the position of a false center, ~~for~~

*f*5 1^v

to the dishonor of the Universal Spirit, whose effluence constituted the power so rebelliously evoked.

5428 f°.125   7 August, 1826, ½ past 7—beautiful Sunset, as indeed for the last six months of this wonderful tho' to me overwhelming *Season* what evening has not been such—as I was pacing alongside the ivied wall that divides our Garden from Mr Nixon's Kitchen Garden, a dell or bottom to which ours is a Terrace, and musing on the ordinary exclusive attribution of Reality to the phænomena of the passive Sense (*See*, the *reverse* of a Verb Deponent: for as this is a Verb Active in the form of a Verb-passive, the other is a Verb Passive in the form of a Verb Active), and on the impossibility that a Mind in this sensual trance should attaching any practical lively meaning to the Gospel Designation of a Christian as living *a life of Grace by Faith*, in the present state, and to pass to a life of Glory; as opposed to those, who *live* without God in the World; and (to comprize all in one) of the unmeaningness or dark superstition of the Eucharist to such men, and the consequent necessity of knowing and communing with an *other* world that now is, in order to an actual and lively Belief of another world *to come*—the Question started up in my mind—but must this knowlege be explicit, and be conveyed in distinct conceptions. If so, what shall I think of a *such* a Woman *as Mrs Gillman*? Can I deny that she lives with God?—At this moment my eyes were dwelling on the lovely Lace-work of those fair fair Elm-trees, so richly so softly black between me and the deep red Clouds & Light of the Horizon, with their interstices of twilight *Air* made visible—and I received the solution of my difficulty, flashlike, in the   *f*52 word, BEAUTY! in the intuition of the *Beautiful*!—This ⟨too⟩ is *spiritual*—and a the Goodness of God this is the short-hand, Hieroglyphic of Truth—the mediator between Truth and Feeling, the Head & the Heart—⟨The Sense⟩ Beauty is *implicit* knowlege—a silent communion of the Spirit with the Spirit in Nature not without consciousness, tho' with the consciousness not successively unfolded!—The Beauty of Holiness! the Beauty of Innocence! the Beauty of Love! the Beauty of Piety! Far other is the pleasure which the refined Sensualist, the pure Toutos-kosmos Man, received from a fine Landscape—for him it is what a fine specimen of Calligraphy would be to ~~a R~~ an unalphabeted Rustic—To a spiritual Woman it is Music—the intelligible Language of Memory, Hope, Desiderium/the *rhythm* of the Soul's movements

To whatever we attribute reality, with that we claim kindred: for reality is a transfer of our own sense of Being.

5429 f°.126   Friday, 12 August 1826.—Difference of Reason & Understanding.—

Reason = ⟨the⟩ all ⟨~~and the All~~⟩: Understanding = *a* Whole.—Reason = Identity or Cöinherence of Means and End. Understanding = Separation of Means and Ends. Hence in the present state both of Man and of Nature, the materials being heterogeneous and imperfect, the highest possible State is a *State* of Understanding, το αμεινον. The greater number of the components parts of the resulting Whole must be MEANS where they are not Ends.—(Illustrate by the Optic Cylinder—all the scratches and fragments are indeed so arranged as to conspire in the Image of a HERO or of a Palace—But for an eye out of the Circle.)—To αγαθον (& το αριστον is either the same, or means less) is only conceivable in a State of REASON; but this supposes perfect and homogeneous Materials.—Real Bridges cannot possess the properties of Mathematical Arches: and why? ~~Because Bodies are not homogeneous, Spaces.~~

5430 f°.127   Rome took the *ideas* of Greece not into her Being but into her *Service*: She *made use of them.*—Rome was the proper Type of the PATRON. Pericles to Phidias & his Compeers was one Man of Genius befriending another; but Mecænas and Augustus Cæsar were PATRONS of the Fine Arts

5431 f°.128   By the substitution of Powers (Kräfte) for Things (Erscheinungen, Phænomena) *ungeheuer* viel ist gewonnen, *f52ᵛ* says Heinroth in his Anthropology—to which I affixed the marginal note—"This for the life of me I cannot see—inasmuch as every power is measured by its product." I did not mean that nothing was won; but I could not assent at once to the *enormity* of the advantage—.Now I must try to state the question fairly—and then to make out *what* the gain is, and under what use and conceptions of the term, Powers. For at first sight it seems a mere logical change in the formula—by repeating the effect under the notion of Cause—as for instance in the substitution of radii colorifici for r. colorati, or in calling Heat Calorific instead of Caloric. A Power of Vegetation will not explain to me any one Vegetable in particular. It must be a Moss-rose Power that produces a Moss-rose.—Nota bene—I do not intend this as an argument of settled validity; but merely as a clearing up of the question—which well deserves, and God permitting shall receive an orderly enucleation.

5432   F°.129   14 Aug. 1826—i.e. Tomorrow. And what if I died during the two remaining Hours of To Night!—

Feeling and Sensation seem to be comprized in Empfindung, by the German Psychologists. Are they really equivalent terms, Tautonimes?

I think not; and that even the Germans would do well if they confined Empfindung to those cases, in which we feel something mentally as well as bodily. I feel (Ich empfinde) an indescribable Calm on my Spirit. I have a smarting sensation in the part, where the wound was; but an *empfindung* of Delight at the thought of meeting my so long absent Daughter.—

But probably I am over-refining.—

Be this, however, as it may, Heinroth (Lehrbuch der Anthropologie (Leipzig, 1822) p. 414 et seq. seems to me to have given but a confused account of Sensation & Feeling, in contra-distinction from Will and Thought: and his conception of *Bewüss*tseyn is shadowy as latest Twilight to me.—I should say—that Sensation and Feeling belong to *Life*; but that there is a twofold Life, a spiritual and a natural, a celestial and a terrestrial, even as there Bodies Celestial & Bodies terrestrial—and can not therefore consider this inward Finding as of always and of necessity contrary to Freedom.

But let us confine our inquiry to Sensation, including Pain and Pleasure bodily, as likewise of Heat and Cold. Is there any necessity for separating it toto genere from *Perception*? Is it other than   *f53* simple Perception, ~~the~~ while Perception (so called) is comparative or the perception of two or more objects in relation to each other?—

But I must think on this subject.

5433 F°.130   Sunday Night—14 Aug. 1826. Past a comfortable day, from 10 °clock——The Psalms for the Day, my favorite Prayer the 71st (as in the Prayer-book) and that sublime Rapture of Prophecy the 72nd—Surely, if the Version be in any degree faithful, the Promises can have no other application but to the Shiloh, the Delight of Nations—whom the Jews after the Captivity nationalized & degraded into their Messiah. Applied to David and Solomon, or to Solomon & Rehoboam the Language is too extravagantly disproportionate even for Oriental Hyperbole— even supposing, what I deem altogether false, that the Hebrew Poetry is characterized by Hyperbole—a fond~~est~~ness for which is the Sign and offspring of Imbecility, (Children hyperbolize) whereas Energy is the distinctive of the Hebraic Muse.—Prayed (the Confession, the Te Deum, the Litany, Lord's Prayer & General Thanksgiving) with depth & sensible comfort—returned from my Bower-Oratory in the Paradise of Fitzroy Farm by ½ past 12—and found my dear friend, J. H. Green—and passed something more than four Hours with him in discourse and disquisition not unworthy of the Day, and to our mutual satisfaction—⟨I was sad but not sorrowful; subdued but not dejected.—⟩

—Of the very many fine Sunsets ⟨we have had of late—⟩ that of this evening most glorious—and now what a lovely Moonlight ~~Nature~~ Night with these soft flakes of white clouds, ⟨the cloudlets & bands immediately over the Moon /⟩ died in tenderest Blue and on my table the two flower-glasses and one flower-pot, in an oblique line :/. raised each over the other, so that the 2nd had the cylinder-*glass* of the first, and the Flower-pot, almost concealed by the Jasmines & Honeysuckles, hides that of the Second—.I was looking out of my window, saying to myself—What a beautiful Scene! when the ~~Ser~~ Maid came in to my room & said—What beautiful Flowers!—and it immediately occurred to me to ask myself—how many portions of a barley-corn T. Phillips's (R.A.)

Musical Scale of Proportions would go to explain the sense &
sensation of *Beauty* excited by either!

5434 23.26   N.B. *No elements* in the Bible; nor even one of   *f23*
the words which are equivalent or nearest at least to our elements.
Fire is not mentioned. MR HURWITZ, August 23, 1826.

Tohu = the το θαμβουν of Plato—*Bohu*—*in it was*—

5435 23.27   It is an old complaint, that a man of Genius no
sooner appears but the Host of Dunces are up in arms to repel the
invading Alien: and this observation would be more convincing,
were it conveyed more dispassionately and with a less contemptuous
Antithesis. For Dunces substitute the ὁι πολλοι, the "τουτος κοσμος" of the Apostolic writers, and then by a thoughtful examination
into the nature and natural effects first of *difference*; 2.nd of *diversity*
(not overlooking the frequency & facility with which the perception of the former passes into a sensation of the latter, in conse-   *f23^v*
quence of) 3.rd the not understanding what ~~is~~ they yet offer~~ed~~ and
expect~~ed~~ to ~~be~~ understo~~od~~and ⟨as if they had a *right* to do *so*.⟩ (For
an original Mathematical work, or any other requiring appropriate
symbols, will excite no uneasy feelings or scarcely: such feelings,
being commonly preclud~~ing~~ed with Mathematicians by the immediate determinability of the truth or falsehood of the proposed
accession to the science; & with all others, because they neither
expect~~ed~~ or are expected to understand it.) 4.th The misunderstanding certain to follow in cases, where the unfit person finding no
outward marks (arbitrary symbols, diagrams, or technical phrases)
informing him that the Subject is one which he does not pretend
to know, or wish to appear to do so) will attach some meaning—
& as he is out of humour with the author, such a meaning as he
can censure or ridicule.
    But above all, the whole world almost of minds is divided into
the two classes of the busy-indolent, and the lazy-Indolent: & to   *f24*
both alike all Thinking is painful, and all attempts to rouse them
to think, whether in re-examining the grounds of their former
convictions, or rather, takings-for-granted, or in the reception of

new Light, are irritating.—"He may be very clever—but Lord
me keep me from him—He would crunch my brain in a fortnight!—I like a little comfortable chit-chat, a little easy cheerful
conversation in which every man can take his share. One does like
to have one's brain on a stretch—Indeed, I cannot endure to see a
man so on the stretch himself.—One wants relaxation & amusement in one's social hours!—Well! but in their *studious* hours?
when their Bow is bent—and they are apud Musas, in the company
of the Muses? If not the *man*—yet the Books?—O it is just the
same—ipsas etiam apud Musas the same call for amusement, relaxation—entertainment—or at least, somewhat that returns them
their own thoughts in the tricksy style which they would like to
f24ᵛ   express them in themselves./ The attention must not be fastened
down—and this the man of Genius cannot help doing—and this
every work must do which is a work of Genius.—

A popular work meant in former times one that adapted the
results of studi~~aso~~ous meditation & scientific Research to the capacity
of the People by presenting in the concrete & by instances &
examples what had been ascertained in the Law & abstractly from
particulars. But now that is a popular work which ~~gives back to~~
flatters the People ~~thus~~ by giving them back their own errors &
prejudices & secures them the comfortable prospect that their children, who are to form their minds out of these books, will not be
tempted into the presumption of being better or wiser than their
parents!—

5436 23.28   The best plan, I think, for a man who would
wish his mind to continue growing, is to find, in the first place,
some means of ascertaining for himself whether it does or no.—
f25   And I can think of no better than early in life, say after 3 & 20,
to procure gradually the works of some two or three great writers—say, for instance, Bacon, Jeremy Taylor, and Kant, with the
De republicâ, de legibus, the Sophistes, and Politicus of Plato,
and the Poetics, Rhetoric and περι πολιτειας of Aristotle—and
amidst all other reading, to make a point of reperusing some one,
or some weighty part of some one, of these every four or five
years—having for the beginning a ⟨separate⟩ note-book for each of
these Writers, in which your impressions, suggestions, Conjec-

tures, Doubts, and Judgements are to be recorded, with the date
of each, & so worded as to represent most sincerely the exact state
of your convictions at the time, ~~abstracted~~ such as they would be
if you did not (which this plan will assuredly make you do, sooner
or later) anticipate a change in them from increase of knowlege.
"It is probable that I am in the wrong—but so it now appears to
me, after my best attempts—& I must therefore put it down, in
order that I may find myself so, if so I am.—It would make a
little volume, to give in detail all the various moral as well as
intellectual advantageous, that would would result from the sys-   *f25ᵛ*
tematic observation of this plan. Diffidence and Hope would reciprocally balance and excite each other. A continuity would be
given to your Being, and its progressiveness ensured. All your
knowlege otherwise obtained whether from Books, or Conversation, or Experience, would find centers round which ~~they~~ it would
organize itself. And lastly, the habit of confuting your past self,
and detecting the causes & occasions of your having mistaken or
overlooked the Truth, will give you both a quickness and a winning kindness resulting from sympathy in exposing the errors of
others, as if you were persuading an alter ego of his mistake. And
~~souch~~ indeed will ~~the~~ your antagonists appear to you, another =
your past Self—in all points on which the falsity is not too plainly
a derivative from a corrupt heart & the predominance of bad passions or worldly interests over-laying the love of Truth *as* Truth.
And even in this case the liveliness ~~of~~ with which you will so often
have expressed yourself in your private Note-books, in which the   *f26*
words unsought-for and untrimmed because intended for your own
eye exclusively were the first-born of your first impressions, when
you were either enkindled by admiration of your writer, or excited
by a humble disputing with *him*, re-impersonated in his Book,—
will be of no mean rhetorical advantage to you, especially in public
& extemporary Debates, or animated conversation.

5437 F°.131   6 Septʳ 1826. Thursday Night—.Reading   *f53*
Hooker's Preface. See p. 56. 57—The Spirit of Wisdom and of
Meekness equally translucent.—Mem.—No sophistry more piti-
ful yet alas! few more common than that of reasoning by possible—
or more truly, by imaginable—consequences, without attention to

f53ᵛ

the difference—Ex. gr. If one Clergyman may omit the Athena-
sian Creed because he disapproves of the damnatory preface, another may omit the Litany—&c &c—. No! it is not simply that
he disapproves—but that it is an undesirable fact that it is a source
of scandal to congregations generally—because &c &c &c and if
all these *becauses* applied equally to another part—why, then omit
that too—and but if there were many such, the Clergyman would
not have been a Clergyman—his Conscience would have forbid his
taking orders in such a Church.—

f139ᵛ   5438 3½.119 P.S.   P.S. 12 Septʳ 1826.—Hitherto the quantitative properties of the Metals have been too exclusively attended
to/but Metal = m *Quality.*

f53ᵛ   5439 Fᵒ.132   Pythagoras at Babylon—Daniel, as the Archi-
mage. Pythagoras demands the solution of two Riddles—Man and
the World's—Daniel refers ⟨him⟩ to the Book of the Law—Pythagoras returns after a time—restores the Volume—and relates his
Dream, as the reason—(The stream direct from a Fountain to the
a Fountain/another from the feet of Pythagoras to the latter. The
apparent drying up of the first Stream on its arrival at the Second
Fountain &c)—Daniel refers him to Meditation on the Eternal I
Am—III.—Pythagoras complains, that he cannot preserve his intellect Spirit in that *quiet motion*, which is requisite for freedom of
intellect—Now the Beauty—now the Holiness—now the Goodness, of the Supreme—either with emotions of Joy, or Awe, or
Love & Gratitude—or a deep motionless Concentration of Spirit
in the last meditation on the Superessential—Then Daniel unfolds
his doctrine of Symbols—commencing with an current abstraction,
consequently the minimum of objective reality—and progressively
potenziating the Sym same by *Symbols*—Here turn to the *Clasp
book (G's receipt-book* originally) p. 154.—

f94ᵛ   5440 26.56   14 Septʳ 1826. Thursday.—On Tuesday the
12, ΦʹΡΗ ρά Ο καλοκαγαθος μετα νεον μηνα τῳ Ἡπατοκολυμβήθρῳ.—
For this I bless and thank but not the more for this do I love,
honor and revere το καρα φιλτατον· Πλεον γαρ ερωτος η το κεαρ
f95   εμου—επει παντοιων καλων και αγαθων φρεαρ εστι βαθυ φρεαρ.

5441 26.58 ⟨Mementos in the handwriting of the Right *f95ᵛ*
Honorable John Hookham Frere, τον καλοκαγαθου.⟩
Oracles of Themis refer to the Patriarchial Laws, or prophecies—
Omnia duplicia unum contra unum—

5442 26.57 It is a sad thing that men in general are so *f95*
prone and prompt to think contemptuously of the Understandings
of other men—even of the most celebrated if only they flourished
in remote periods and under a form of Science or philosophy, long
superannuated according to the Register of Fashion. If an opinion
attributed to an ancient philosopher, or even to a Contemporary of
another Country is not at the first hearing understood and admitted
by them—out flies at once the scorn—What Nonsense! how absurd! &c—Surely, the palpable absurdity, the glaring Nonsense of
the words interpreted as they had interpreted them, ought to have
supplied a strong presumption that such was *not* the Sense in which
the Asserter of the Position meant them to be understood. For the
minds of men have no predilection for evident nonsense, as a gen- *f95ᵛ*
eral Rule: and it would be odd, if the intellectual Giants of the
Race, whose fame is of a thousand or perhaps two thousand years
standing, should form the exception. Pythagoras's Name has survived him 2400 years, I believe. Now really it is somewhat too
much to believe, that a man whose intellect had exerted so deep
and lasting an influence on his countrymen, could have meant the
numeral characters, which School-boys make on their slates or copy
out on their Cyphering Books, when he spoke of divine and eternal
Agents, the αρχαι προμαθεσταται του Ουρανου και γης και της *f96*
μεταξυ φυσεως· ετι δε και θειων και θεων και δαιμονων διαμονῆς
ριζαι—
After all, it is a question of proper names—x y z an are essential
Powers intelligent and intelligible, determinate themselves and the
determining and constitutive Causes of all other Forms—αγγελοι
Θεου δημιουργικοι—Having defined these sufficient Causes (Sub-
facients) as truly by an enumeration of their common and differential characters or attributes, and demonstrated the necessity of
assuming them actual existence—the question comes—By what
name or title shall we designate them? And of several more or less
significant names which shall we prefer as most significant, most

appropriate and adequate?—By these canons must the fitness and convenience of the Pythagorean *Name* (Αριθμοι αιδιοι, Numeri numerantes, be tried.—

f96ᵛ Q.ʸ have those ⟨Christians,⟩ who laugh or stare at this name, forgotten that the Divine Agent, by whom ~~the~~ all things were made according to the Will of Him, *from* whom all things were and are, is named. The *Word*—the living and substantial *Word*—the incarnate *Word*!—or that the ~~Source~~ Author and Giver of Life, & Love, ~~and~~ the Sanctifier and the Comforter is ~~no~~ named by less than a Word. viz. a Breathing or *Breath*?—Would it have been an improvement in dignity if for Αριθμοι, ⟨Numbers,⟩ Pythagoras had substituted πνευματα or ͟ψ͟υ͟χ͟α͟ι—i.e. *Puffs* and *Butterflies?*

For the ⌜. . .⌝ introduction to this—& continuance, refer to Thin Folio with red leather back, p. 100.

5443 26.59   *The hitting jump* that indivisible Point
Or centre wherein Goodness doth consist a chance Pentam. Iambic from Hooker, p. 82.

f97 It is rare to meet an idiom of this sort in Hooker—tho' his diction is native English throughout—the language of a thoughtful learned Englishman indeed, but still English, if not our Mother ~~tongue~~, yet our genuine *Father*-tongue. As Wine consists of Hydrogen, Carbon and Oxygen, or of Alcohol and sugared Water & malic Acid—yet it must *compose itself* to be the Unit, WINE— sound old Port or Sherry, so does the English consist of Saxon, Norman French, and Latin direct—but ~~the~~ it is a combination ~~of vital~~ in a living process—not a mixture, or mechanical juxta-position.—Water is as homogeneous in itself, as either of its two constituent Gases—and 5 (my hand, for instance) as true ~~the a ri~~ a Unit as 1 (a one fingered hand, for instance) tho' a richer more powerful one—But Language (I should have said) is an Organic Growth—and each several Tongue together with the type of the Class has a type of its own, a specific Type—and in this species there are (as in the noblest animal) individual types, yet in perfect
f97ᵛ harmony with & inclusion of the Type of the Species (English, Italian, Greek or whatever it may be)—And the nobler the Species, the more numerous and more characteristic the individual

types yet the more concordant with the National, or Specific—
Where it is otherwise, it is proof and symptom of DISEASE.—and
a specimen that no has no long life or principle of continuance,—
unless in the Glass-cases of a critical Philologist's pathological Museum.

   P.S. Hooker (p. 81) distinguishes Spirit from Soul; and as far
as I understand him, forms the same conception of Spirit as I have
done in the Aids to Reflection—namely, as a focal energy from the
union of the Will and the Reason—i.e. the *practical* Reason, the
source of Ideas as ultimate Ends.—Ah! if Hooker had initiated &
as it were matriculated his philosophy with the *prodocimastic*
Logic—or previous examination of the *Weights* & *Measures* in use!
S.T.C.
Thursday night   14 Septr 1826
p. 89. Eccles. Pol.—An exquisite passage on the instinctive *Hu-*   *f98*
manity of Men.
"A manifest token that we wish after a sort of universal fellow-
ship with all men appeareth in the wonderful delight, men have,
some to visit foreign Countries, some to discover Nations not
heard of in former Ages; we all (*all of us*) to know the Affairs and
Dealings of other People, yea, to be in league of Amity with them.
And this not only for Traffic's sake, or to be more strong by confederacy; but for such cause also, as moved the Queen of Sheba to
visit Solomon, *and in a word, because Nature doth presume, that how
many Men there are in the World, so many Gods*, as it were, there
are: or at leastwise such they should be towards Men.
   P. 92. All creatures below man seek that reality which is best
for them; the perfection of Man alone consisteth in that which is
simply best./Love supposes Likeness—in the very act of loving
Men Dogs acquire a mysterious affinity to Man.—The S.S. entitle   *f98^v*
the Gentiles, or Heathen nations in relation to the chosen people
DOGS. *These* Dogs have become Men: and what if He, who of
Stones could raise Children to Abraham, should fulfil the poor
Indian's F charitable faith?—David Hartley (Vol. II, ad finem)
has some interesting remarks on this subject. But altogether that
2nd Volume is quite independent of the first: and how could reconcile the truths of the One with the theory of the other, I cannot
understand.

f1   **5444** 26.2   16 Septr 1826, Sunday Afternoon, 3 ?clock, Sara Coleridge arrived, on the Northampton Coach, at the Wellington Arms—& thence in ~~a~~ *the Fly* to our House, Grove, Highgate.

f53^v   **5445** F°.133   Sunday, 16 Septr 1826.—Sara Coleridge arrived. Afternoon. 3 °clock—

5446 F°.134   18 Sept^r—I have (p. *27 of this Book*) noted my conjecture respecting White—namely, that it is the Indifferent Point in the minimum affection of Light by Body—and thus an antithetic to Green, as the Punct. Indiff. in the maximum affection of Light by Body.—Now on this principle how am I to explain— the progress of incandescence, beginning with RED (Color emphaticè et κατ᾽ εξοχην) proceeding to yellow and completed in full white Light, by increments of Heat. ?The Heat. Is the action of the ⌈. . .⌉ Body more and more pre-occupied and detained by its conversion into Warmth? Action increased yet detained is Vibration. Is the increasing Vibration of the Body the cause of ~~the~~ its diminishing Action ~~of~~ on the portion of Ether converted from the Indifference of 3 and 4 (i.e. του αλλου και του μεταλλου—vid. *p. 29*) i.e. Warmth into the 3—in other words, on the portion of warmth polarized?

So far is, I think, plain: that the fact of incandescence proceeds as according to my hypothesis it ought to do—from Red, as the Balance of του Αλλου και του Μεταλλου, the dynamic Light and Substantial Darkness—removing further from the latter (to the positive Pole of Red) in Yellow—and at its furthest in White.—?

What I doubt is, the propriety of the term, Indifferent, as applied to White—But this is only a part of a much more comprehensive Query—viz. whether the logical or rather logo-noëtic Pentad must not in its application to Powers phænomenally manifested under the Form of Multëity, admit of subdivisions in some
f54   or all of the five Positions of the Power contemplated in the Idea or universally?

Thus the Idea, Life, in the form of *Unity*—i.e. universally contemplated—

I

Identity

2	4	3
Thesis	Indifference	Antithesis

5

Synthesis

1. Life. 2. Excitability. 3. Resistance. 4. Sensibility, or Self-finding. 5. Self-seeking.—

But when I we resume the Idea in the form of Multëity, viz. Life as existing in a gradation of different intensities from a minimum to a maximum; the 5th or Synthesis of 2 and 3, subdivides into a lower and higher value or dignity—viz. $5^{(1}$ = Productivity and $5^{(2}$ = Irritability, or the Zoè phytoeidès and the Zoè entomöeidès.—

Thus too, in Language, we have the modification of 2 by 3 and of the 3 by the 2, = Adnoun and Adverb—. And again in Chemistry the subspeciation of the 5—Synthesis into ⟨1⟩ the − neutral, ⟨2⟩ + neutral and ⟨3.⟩ predominant—ex. gr.—1 Water. 2. Salt. 3. Oil or Alcohol—

Now the Problem is—to find some one ⟨Ideal⟩ Subject, whenich contemplated under the predicament of Multëity shall supply a Model or Canon, and therewith a nomenclature or scheme of Terms for the functions and affections of all other Subjects. And the most promising Subject for an experiment of this kind seems to me to be Light, as Light and as Color.—Preparatory to this, however, the several phænomena of Radiation, or rectilineal; of Scattering or hemispherical; of Reflection; Refraction; Absorption; Modification (the so called *Interference* of the Ray of Light); and of polarization; must be reduced to *Ideas*.

5447 F°.135   Saturday 29 Sept. 1826.—

My present notion respecting *White* is—that it is the *transitional* state between Light and Color, the immediate Antecedent to Color—and the Indifference is not an expedient term in a System in which it has already an appropriate sense, as the 4th Position of the Polar Pentad. It is not the Indifferent of Color; but indifferent to Colors. Hence it must be studied by itself: and it is easy to see that there must be two forms of White, viz. 1 that which marks the minimum affection of Light by Body 1. from the defect in the action of the latter; and 2. from the energic action of the former (the Light) in its own absence, and as resisting modification.— And so we say—a *dead* White, a vivid White—But above all—we must bear in mind the distinction between the Allon or Power of Light, and the Lumen or Sensible Light. With respect to the former, the Metallon must be conceived as so potenziated by the Lumen as evermore to contain in itself *potentially* the Allon, in greater or less energy: or in other words to be in the same state in which we must suppose it at the moment, before its polarization, is the ideal Chaos. It is the Substantial Darkness with a disposition to become Light-power—i.e. to act at the same moment in two opposite directions. (Vide, my other Mem. Book on Ideal Numbers—and my etymological Letter—Unless the Inquirer has learnt to understand the phrase, directions and opposite, as metaphors of vision for subjects essentially invisible, as terms of art in philosophic Logic—unless, in short, he has been initiated into the mystery of the 8 , and of the primary chrystal, the Hexaeder resulting from the double Teträeder—this and indeed the whole polar Logic as applied to the generative Powers, must be mere Jargon. ~~This alone~~ I expect to be intelligible to such only as know that the ~~Identity~~ very Thing, το οντως ον, is the Identity which is at once Thesis, Antithesis, and Indifference—. This which the Hebrew Legislator names Darkness, or the Container, I call *Nature*. And Nature, I say, must be assumed as existing simultaneously as the *Powers* of Weight, Warmth and Light.)

f54ᵛ

There must exist then a moment in which the self-counteracting Power of the Darkness (= the energy of Light) begins to be phænomenal—and this Phænomenon is—White (as in the Roots and Pith of Plants, in the White of Regeneracy and ? of Cold— Altogether distinct from this is the Lumen or Sensible Light, the product of the Allon—and this, the Lumen, exists in two forms or states, the radial and the Surface—and in the latter it *begins* to undergo the action of the Metallon, but yet with such resistance or energy statum proprium servandi as renders it a synthesis of *Pre-*

dominance—and this which stands in the same relation to the radial Light as the Shadow to the corpuscular Body, is + White; and if I am not mistaken, is the superstratum of Color even as Shadow is the Substratum. If this be so, White ⚹ Shadow, not to Black. (Mem. The white Linen interposed by Titian between his Crimson Drapery or *Sopha* and the Skin or naked Limbs of his Venuses and Nymphs.

5448 26.4   Matter = the phantom of the Absolute Will—   *f1*
Mr Green called it most happily the *Body* of a Ghost.

5449 26.62   *f99*
   John Coleridge's Children
John Duke Coleridge—   5 last 3rd of December.
Henry James   D^o 4 27 Septr 1826
Mary Frances Keble Coleridge 2 (*will be*) 27th Novr 1826
Aletheia Buchanan Coleridge born 4 July, 1826

5450 26.60   Motto for my Letters on the right & the su-   *f98^v*
perstitious veneration of the SS. "Whatsoever is spoken of God or of things appertaining to God, otherwise than as the truth is, tho' it seem an honor is an injury. And as incredible praises given unto men do often abate and impair the credit of their deserved com-mendation: so we must likewise take great heed, lest in attributing unto Scripture more than it can have, the incredibility of that do *f99* cause even those things which it hath most abundantly, to be less reverendly esteemed."
        Hooker's Eccles. Polity: B. III. ad finem.—*p. 124.*

5451 26.61   The Logic—2. Prayer—3. κολλ.—4. Pas-sions—5. Human Psychology—

5452 26.1   P. 174. The motto for my Letters on the Scrip-   *f1*
tures—

5453 F^o.136   16 Octr 1826. Monday Morning.—   *f55*
   War, Man's highest Honor or the basest Trade—. Tom Paine's celebrated Aphorism—"Society in ~~it's imp~~ its least perfect forms a

Blessing, and Government in its best a necessary Evil" was the significant Echo of the Times/implying the separation, nay, hostile adversion of Elements, the perfect Unity of which constitues a *free* STATE. Compare the public Moralé of Russia with that of England—in which latter see instanced the influence of the IDEA, that the Act of the Parliament is every free Man's own personal Act, even tho' he should have resisted the measure during its deliberation & voted against it—. Hence Atwood's Plan ~~was~~ made no way with the public mind—& Cobbett's, tho' supported by Curwen & other agricultural Short-sights, was abhorred—/—Every Man felt—tho' not perhaps in the form of a distinct *conception*—that both parties understood that the Lenders were to be repaid if payed off, in the same *nominal* Sum, let its relative & intrinsic Value be more or less, provided nothing were done with the intention of decreasing or increasing it—And hence lies the Q.ʸ respecting the honesty of Atwood's proposal—He says, that M.ʳ Peele's Bill *did* alter the value, to the wrong and damage of the whole Community considered as the Borrowers—But the Problem is singularly complex—The Lenders being at the same time a component part of the Borrowers and Payers—.

N.B. Left Highgate Wednesday Morning, 11 Oct.ʳ—and the Custom House Steps 5ᵐ· after 8—which from 5 stoppages, two ~~on~~ to prevent running down Barges in the crowded Reaches of the River, & 3 to take in & let out Passengers was increased to 20ᵐ·—and yet we arrived at the Pier Stone Steps precisely at 4—i.e. 13 miles an hour the whole way—or 100 miles in 7ʰ 40ᵐ!—At our old House, 8 Waterloo Plains—Sunday, 15ᵗʰ—a *delightful* drive in the *tiny* Vis a vis with one Donkey, M.ʳ G. & I to Kingsgate.— Susan *Steele* left at Walmer, whither we went & spent the day on Friday, 13ᵗʰ—/

5454 F°.137   Friday, 20 October 1826.—My Birthday.— Went in the Gemini Geminæ Vis a Vis, drawn by FANNY and his asinine Highness, LOFTY, Dominus, alias Don Cú, et Domina, alias, Donna Cú, to Margate. Instead of that scummy Pool Baths are now building on the Cliff. But a winding Tunnel leads down to the edge of the Sea—and all sorts of Baths, Shower & Plunge,

f55ᵛ

Hot and Cold, Cameral and Sub dio Oceanic, are building or preparing for, at the bottom and in breast-works excavated at different heights in the chalk Precipice/—But Margate will be Margate, do what they will—Jewrausalem and Hounsditch, and where the Israelitest Bucks and Does are all agog, then will be *Si*nagog!— It is essential to Margate, with its Stone *Pierlet painted green*, that in no one part, however fine in some respects, are you out of the Neighborhood of Vulgarity—low ~~or~~ hovels, tawdry new houses, check shirts, flannel petticoats, and Linen Tag Rags fluttering in the Sea-breeze!—This day last week Mr Gillman thrown out of his Gig, while driving down Highgate Hill, the Horse stumbling, and the Shafts broken. God be praised! a bruised Elbow seems to have been the extent of the Damage. But what it might have been!!—

P.S.—Superstitition is its own punishment. I had pre-determined that this day would be the specimen of the Year/~~I~~ Midnight. The day is at an end— —/————. . . . .*Ou—oou.*

5455 F°.138   Saturday, 21 Octr 1826.—. ⟨Papyrus erepta— Mem.—⟩

The fewer persons attached to a Government in contra-distinction from the People, the greater will be the ⟨popular⟩ attachment to the State—i.e. to the Government as the Representant of the Nation—.—

5456 F°.139   Thursday 26 th—Letter from E. C.—Alas! a fatality seems to follow our Ramsgate journey!.—

5457 F°.140   Saturday 28.—And the manifest improvement in M^{rs} G's Looks, Feelings, Strength, Spirits nipped and blighted—for the time at least—by this Shock. ~~I am persuaded that it is all for the best and that they cannot understand it as~~ ⌈. . .⌉ ~~it would~~ ⌈. . . . .⌉

5458 F°.141   28 Octr 1826.   *f*56

Music—Mozart's Quintette's for instance—prophecies of Thought—*words* (λογοι) hunted after thro' the labyrinth of life, and Sensation beginning to chrystallize, imitating in its fluidity by imperfect momentary *hinted* figure the forms and stabile organisms of *Mind*—a continual particularizing of the Universal (viz. proportion, in-number, and quality of tone) and of the Abstracts of Emotion and Passion, yet so as to remain Universals & Abstracts—augmenting in import, but never resting in any one expression long enough to render it possible to determine it as this or that—a *fluxion/*

5459 F°.142   9 November—. No! I cannot approve of a man, with sense, and sensibility like yours, marrying under the circumstances stated—supposing you, after an acquaintance of years with Aphanasia, not to have deceived yourself in the statement. ~~She~~ You feel an honorable but ardent Love for her. She regrets, that she cannot return it *in kind*; but professes, and I doubt not, feels, the highest esteem and regard for you—all that a Sister could have for an elder Brother/and her heart is not engaged by love for any other. If you marry her, you may rely on her for all the duties of a Wife, and for all the solicitudes of a faithful Friend, whose interests are identified with yours— —.

No! my friend! I cannot approve of the scheme—. If you have yourself given up all hope of ~~qualifying~~ vivifying her friendship into Love, you must (however severe the struggle may be) deaden your Love into Friendship. I could give you convincing reasons—. Who shall secure you against causeless jealousy with all its dreams & torments?—Besides, that which is pure and elevating/ —let L express its character—when it is L in correspondence to L, cannot but lose a portion of its finer Spirit, when it is L in correspondence to F − L. Alas! it may too soon be transmuted into Desire ⚹ Disgust.—⟨In short, Love and Love reciprocally

inclose and circum*vest* each the other like cycloeidal plates.

But Love ~~&~~ in the man + Friendship in the Woman may too soon degenerate into Desire met by Disgust. F − L i.e. Friendship without Love. ~~is born and~~)
(− minus or without—
⚹ in antithesis to)

Had the difference been in *degree* only, and tho' you had loved Aphanasia four times more intensely than she loved you, I should not doubt of your happiness. But where there is diversity in the *kind* of the Affection only, the Risk is far far too great.—

5460 F°.143   As the sensorial power in cases of Blindness *f56ᵛ*
appears to retire into the nerves of Touch, so the Loss of Poetic
Genius in a Nation produces a transfer of poetry to the Prose. This
is discernible even in Tacitus and both the Plinies; but in Apuleius
and the Latin writers after him it is manifest.—There is no longer
any Prose in their Literature—but a sort of hybrid Poetry—Like
the rough Copies of Hints taken down by a Poet—

5461 F°.144   The Ramsgate Muffin-man's Song—or Mu-
sical Cry—far superior to any other Cry, I ever heard—& the
Fellow's Voice is strong and mellow—I should like to get the
Notes.

5462 F°.145   (Love and Love mutually inclose and invest (or
*circum*vest) each other. But Love however refined met only by
Friendship however tender & feminine will too probably degenerate into Desire answered by Disgust.)

5463 F°.146   Love is always the same in *essence*; tho' it will
receive a different shade according to its object.—The Mother
loves her infant, the Sister *loves* ~~an~~ her amiable Brother—the
Brother *loves* his kind and lovely Sister: and *even so*, in marriages
really and verily of mutual Love, the Husband *loves* the Wife and
the Wife the Husband.—The ground of (or rather the pretext for)
the too common mistake on this point, is this: that in the latter
relation, from the nature of the *Object*, ~~beloved, the Love~~ in consequence of which—one and the same Person is the Object likewise
of another passion—in other words, ~~the one~~ Love, is found in co-
existence and occasionally in combination with, sexual Desire.—
So does Sugar co-existence with Lemon-juice, and Water with
Spirit, in Punch/but ~~does~~ this does not make Sweet Sour, nor Alcohol Water—.Much less when as in the case in question, the
combination is only occasional and momentary—and where, even
when the two passions are as cause and effect, the nobler & continual Passion is the Antecedent & the occasion of the temporary

Desire/Surely, the dank Vapor of the Earth and the Heavenly
Light are different in kind. Yet the Light excites and calls forth
the Vapor—but what it excites, it raises, and rarefies, and trans-
pierces in all its parts, and in the same instant ~~as~~ covers it with
its own brightness as with a veil or garment of Glory, concealing
the Vapor by glorifying it.—Now for the earthly Humor read
f57   Sexual Desire, and for Light read LOVE: and you have my exact
meaning.—But, you will say, if Love be essentially different from
Desire ⟨Λυστ⟩, and yet distinguishable from the tenderest Friendship—what *is* Love? I answer—Ask the Mother! Contemplate her
as she gazes on her infant with its little hands spread on her
Bosom—or while she is tending her Child in its various infirmities.—She, she can tell you the sense of the simple Scripture
Words, in which God himself speaking of conjugal Love says—
And they shall be *one Flesh.* Would it not be ridiculous to say, that
one Limb had a Desire for the other—the left Thigh for the
right?—Yet they touch each the other, as itself. They are *one
flesh.*—Even Desire as under the fitting circumstance so far included in Love, that as Friendship supposes Sympathy, so Love
aims at total Union—as far as the nature of things permits, and it
is not precluded by some other and positive Law—So in the Love
of a Brother for a favorite Sister. Here the total Union is forbidden by a positive Law, grounded, I doubt not, ~~in~~ on some ~~sure
protection~~ necessity of Nature, according to which Marriages in
the same stock would tend to the degeneracy of the Race—Still, I
say, that the Love of a Husband sitting by the sick bed of a beloved Wife, and that of a Brother by the sick bed of a dear Sister
would differ only in *degree*—and perhaps in appearances, occasioned by the habits of acting and feeling consequent on the universality, and universal knowledge and admission, of the positive
Law which forbids the Love to be that of the Total Being.—I
would sacrifice my Life for my FRIEND—I delight in his Society,
but yet I should shrink from the touch of his Body as from an
Alien Somewhat, without the most distant imagination of Sex, even
as a thousand times I might approach to the Wife of my Love
without the slightest emotion or purpose of Desire—And why?—
They shall be *one Flesh.* Love is Sense of Union: and all its acts
are tendencies to union, and ways of making ourselves conscious
of the Same. Finally, *Love is Love*—essentially the same, whether

the Object be a helpless Infant, our Wife or Husband, or God
himself—Hence I say, that Love does not fly from us; but we   *f57ᵛ*
from Love—and that Love is lost not by age or infirmity or Satiety
(all these are fatal only to Desire) but by Selfishness, or Vice, or
worldly Anxiety. Whatever forces us to contemplate or to feel an
Object as *essentially* different from ourselves, and therefore incapable of Union, it with us or we with it, is proportionally detractive
from Love.

5464 ꜰ°.147   The true object of Natural Philosophy is to discover a central Phænomenon in Nature; and a central Phæn. in
Nature requires & supposes a Central Thought in the Mind.

Again—the *notional* Boundaries or Ne plus ultras of Nature are
a part that ɨ relatively to no ~~others~~ minor particles is a Whole, i.e.
an Atom: and a Whole, which in no relation is a Part: i.e. a
Universe.

The System of Epicurus, that a finite Universe composed of
Atoms, is *notionally* true. But it is expresses the limits and necessities of the human imagination and understanding, not the truth
of Nature. An atom and a finite Universe are both alike Fictions
of Mind, entia logica.

~~But what can be found no where absolutely~~ Nevertheless not the
Imagination alone, but the Reason, requires a Center. It is a necessary Postulate of Science. That therefore which can be found no
where absolutely and exclusively, must be ~~found~~ imagined every
where relatively & partially. Hence the law of Bi-centrality—i.e.
that every Whole, whether without parts, ~~and wh~~ or composed of
parts, and in the former whether without parts by defect or lowness
of Nature, = a material atom, or without parts by the excellence
of its nature = a Monad, a Spirit, must be conceived as a possible
center in itself, and at the same time as having a Center out of
itself, and common to it with all others parts of the same System.

Now the first and fundamental Postulate of universal Physiology, comprizing both organic & inorganic Nature—or the fundamental Position of the *Philosophy* of Physics & Physiology—is:
that there is in Nature a tendency to realize this possibility, where
ever the conditions exist: and the first problem of this Branch of
Science is—What are the Conditions, under which a Unit having
a Center in the distance can ~~itself~~ manifest its own centrality—i.e.

be the center of a system, and as in dynamics the power of the Center acts in every point of the area contained in the circumference, be the center and the *copula* (principium unitatis in unoquoque Toto) of a System. Such a Unit would have three charac-

f58   ters—1. It would be a composite part of a System having a Center not of itself or to use a geometrical metaphor it would be a point in some one of the concentrical Lines, composing a common circle. 2. It would be itself the center and copula, the attractive and cohesive force, of a system of its own. 3rdly *For itself* (as far as it exists *for* itself) it would be the Center of the Universe, in a perpetual tendency to include whatever else exists relatively to *it* in itself and what it could not include, to repel. Whatever is not contained in the System, of which it is the Center and Copula, either does not exist at all *for* it—or exists as an Alien, which it resists—and in resisting either appropriates (digestion, assimilation) or repels—or ceases to be, i.e. dies. These three characters concur in every living Body—and hence there necessarily arise two directions of the contemplative act. The Philosopher may either regard any body or number of bodies in reference to a Common Center, the action of which is Center constitutes the general Laws of the System—and in *this* view all Bodies are contemplated as inanimate—and of those, the in which he can discover none of the *conditions* indispensable to the Body's being contemplated in any other view, he considers as positively inanimate/and the aggregate of these we call inorganic Nature. Or he may contemplate a Body as containing its center or principle of Unity in itself: and as soon as he ascertains the existence of the conditions requisite to the manifestation of such a principle, he supposes Life: and these bodies collectively are named Organic Nature.

In Nature there is a tendency to repeat the Whole herself so as to attempt in each part what she had produced in the Whole/but with a limited power and under certain *conditions*.

N.B. In this view, the only scientific, one View Nature itself is assumed as the Universal Principle of Life, and like all other *Powers* as contemplated under the two primary Ideas of Identity and Multëity—i.e. alternately as one and as Many. In other words, exclusively of *degree*, or as subsisting in a series of different intensities.

5465 F°.148   9 Decr 1826—Alas! a spirit-withering Interval
of Erysipelas *threating* Ulcer or perhaps *Spacelus* in the left Leg—
of the intolerable Sleep-subsectizing Humour cum immani *pruritu*
Scroti—of a whitloe more painful & enfevering than either in the
midfinger of my Right hand—⌐. . . . .⌐ Nec amet   *f58ᵛ*
quemquam, *nec ametur ab ullo*—But still I have gained something.
With more entireness of Will and even of Emotion I can say, Thy
Will, not mine be done!—

5466 F°.149   Prayer is the great object of my thoughts at
present—and I make this note to remember the marks thro these
of a divided sway between General Laws and the Volitions & modifying, & counteracting these general Laws, of individual Animals, of all classes: but the individual movement of mere power
as the Class is higher—ergo, highest in man—. What corresponds
to this in the Divinity?—
2.   The maze & exquisite subtlety, and yet the ⌐. . .⌐ probable
dependence on Moral *individual* causes, of the disparity of male &
female Births in different families—Suppose Bruce's Statements,
Vol II. p. 178–185, to be relied on, yet is it more likely that they
are the results of Polygamy, and not (as B. would have us believe)
its natural occasion & justifying cause?—The Personality, the I
AM, of the Abysmal Will & Absolute Reason. What a deathy
Preteritum Perfectum would the N Denial of Prayer petrify the
Universe into!—and this not in Heaven, not for the Future, not
in the identity of Necessity & Freedom, but in a world of imperfection—of rebellion—And ere yet the Son has subdued all enemies under his feet—Is not this *one* of the sundry sublime Meanings of this wonderful Text of the philosophic Apostle—that till
the Victory and the Sabbath when God shall be all in all, the Word
(the Absolute Reason itself) must be personal—and cloathe itself
in the form & assume the functions of the Understanding, or
finally of *selecting* present means to immediate purposes not pre-
determined by necessity (as in Science) but according to variable
Circumstances—and hence we must in all petitionary prayers, as
distinguished from acknowlegements of Eternal *Wisdom*, and
Thanksgivings, pray to the Eternal *thro'* the Son coeternal indeed

but not to him only as coeternal but specially as incarnate *in time*—
We pray to the Word, but not simply as THE WORD but to &
thro' Jesus Christ?—

f59   5467 Fº.150   Wordsworth's and Southey's assertions that the
mistake in [?the] object addressed (Sᵗ Catharine or the Virgin
Mary) will not prevent the efficacy of the Prayer where there are
pious feelings—.O not to speak of the fearful cruel consequences
of this as a general principle, what right have we to take away all
free grace from God's mercy, ~~to~~ in individual cases, by preaching
it as the general Rule—. Let us declare God's *strict Law*—& leave
God to make the exceptions. We are certain that Idolatry is forbidden, certain that in all cases it is dangerous & can only hope that
in particular instances it may be forgiven—What would a Father
think of a Servant, who was constantly anticipating the free mercy
of his affection to an erring Child by telling him, when he had
disobeyed, O don't be afraid!—Your Father can't help forgiving
you/—
        O the cruelty of modern Liberality!

5468 Fº.151   What a frightful callus of heart and hand, what
a conscience-proof Reprobacy, in the Italian Clergy, especially of
the Court of Rome, does not the placing of the Riforma d'Italia
instantly on its appearance in the Index Lib. prohib.—present to
my mind! How alienated from all sense & feeling of Truth must
the Soul of a Romish Priest of the least Learning & Intelligence
be to peruse such notorious truths so free from all heretical dogmata even in their own code of Heresy, and feel only a lust to
suppress the work & murder the Writer!—O it *is* antichrist: if
there be meaning in words!

        There is nothing †opposed to the Creed of Paul IV, not even
to any one of his 15 additions to the Nicene, in this work: & yet
what true Christian of the Church of England would hesitate to
give his hand & heart to such a Catholic—So easily might be the
Churches be if not united in forms, yet in love & christian Brotherhood—were only the *abuses* of the Roman Errors removed—i.e.
alas! the WICKEDNESS of their Clergy!

† except perhaps the denial that the Pope has any legitimate coercive power over other Bishops—tho' great deference is due to his authority as the first in Rank, by usage of Ages—tho' that this arose not from the few odd Texts of Scripture but from Rome being the Metropolis of the Empire is evident from the Bishop of Constantinople assuming an equal Rank when the Emp. was divided into E. and W.—

5469 F°.152   12 Dec' 1826.—Practical Domestic Economy   f59ᵛ
with Estimates published by Colborn, 1824—/A very mischievous
Book that ought to have been & might have been, a very useful
one—by the absurdity miscalculations. For almost every article,
you must add 25 per cent. for the cheapest parts of England; but
in all places near London or in London at least 40 per cent.—Still
the Plan is excellent: and a book ought to be written, with cautious
adherence to the true average of expences with careful Housekeepers, who are yet not to be supposed to employ their whole thought
in *contrivances*—but with a the necessary advertence to the moral
& in the majority of House-keepers obliged to be careful in making both ends meet, the politic & prudential Rule of Live & let
live. A medical Man must, a Clergyman ought to buy of his
Neighbors—. We have meteorological journals kept in almost
every great town thro' the Island—Now I will try to remember
(& for this purpose I have written this note) to ask Alaric Watts,
the Editor of the Amulet, &c to recommend Economic Journals
for each of our Counties—constructed on the principle above mentioned—viz. Do not set enough with the notion of showing, for
how little such & such an establishment might be kept, under a
confluence of wholesale purchases, inexorable System &c &c—but
what in fact and on the average the several & total expences really
are—

5470 26.5   M. 29ᵗʰ—the day before my dinner at Mʳ An-   f2
stey's—
      [. . . . .]

5471 3½.37   Revᵈ Mʳ La fitte   f42ᵛ
    8 Park Place
      Corner of Upper Baker St.

A CHRONOLOGICAL TABLE

Dates in square brackets are not supplied in Coleridge's text. Dates in pointed brackets are later insertions in the entry in question.

Series	N Entry	Date	Series	N Entry	Date
			4532	27.68	[Apr–June 1819]
			4533	27.69	[Apr–June 1819]
	1819		4534	18.322	[May 1819]
4505	27.25	[Apr 1819]	4535	18.323	[May 1819]
4506	27.26	[Apr 1819]	4536	18.324	[May 1819]
4507	27.27	[Apr 1819]	4537	18.325	6 May 1819
4508	27.28	[Apr 1819]	4538	18.326	[May 1819]
4509	27.29	[Apr 1819]	4539	27.90	[c 6 June 1819]
4510	27.30	[Apr 1819]	4540	27.31	[June 1819]
4511	29.14	⟨16 Apr 1819⟩	4541	27.32	[June 1819]
4512	29.15	16 Apr 1819	4542	27.33	[June 1819]
4513	29.16	[Apr 1819]	4543	27.34	8 June 1819
4514	29.17	[16 Apr 1819]	4544	27.35	[9–14 June 1819]
4515	29.21	[? Apr 1819]	4545	27.36	[c 10 June 1819]
4516	29.22	[? Apr 1819]	4546	27.84	[c 10 June 1819]
4517	27.70	[Apr 1819]	4547	27.86	10 June 1819
4518	27.71	[Apr 1819]	4548	27.87	[c 10 June 1819]
4519	27.72	[Apr 1819]	4549	27.85	[c 10 June 1819]
4520	27.73	[Apr 1819]	4550	27.89	[c 10 June 1819]
4521	27.74	[Apr 1819]	4551	27.88	[c 10 June 1819]
4522	27.75	[Apr 1819]	4552	27.37	14 June 1819
4523	27.76	[Apr 1819]	4553	27.38	[June 1819]
4524	27.77	[Apr 1819]	4554	27.39	[June 1819]
4525	27.78	[Apr 1819]	4555	27.40	[June 1819]
4526	27.79	[Apr 1819]	4556	27.41	[June 1819]
4527	27.80	[Apr 1819]	4557	27.42	[June 1819]
4528	27.81	23 Apr 1819	4558	27.43	[June 1819]
4529	27.82	[Apr–June 1819]	4559	27.44	[June 1819]
4530	27.83	[Apr–June 1819]	4560	27.45	[June 1819]
4531	27.66	[Apr–June 1819]	4561	27.46	[June 1819]

Series	N Entry	Date	Series	N Entry	Date
4562	27.47	[June 1819]	4606	21½.84	20 Oct 1819
4563	27.48	[June 1819]	4607	21½.85	21 Oct 1819
4564	27.49	[June 1819]	4608	21½.86	[Oct 1819]
4565	27.50	[June 1819]	4609	21½.87	[Oct 1819]
4566	27.51	[June 1819]	4610	21½.88	[Oct 1819]
4567	27.52	[June 1819]	4611	21½.89	[Oct 1819]
4568	27.53	[June 1819]	4612	21½.90	[Oct 1819]
4569	27.54	[June 1819]	4613	21½.91	[Oct 1819]
4570	27.55	[June 1819]	4614	21½.92	[Oct 1819]
4571	27.56	[June 1819]	4615	21½.93	[Oct 1819]
4572	27.57	[June 1819]	4616	29.26	[Oct 1819]
4573	27.58	[June 1819]	4617	29.27	[Oct 1819]
4574	27.59	[June 1819]	4618	29.28	[Oct 1819]
4575	27.60	[June 1819]	4619	29.29	[Oct 1819]
4576	27.61	[June 1819]	4620	29.30	[Oct 1819]
4577	27.62	[June 1819]	4621	29.31	[Oct 1819]
4578	27.63	[June 1819]	4622	29.32	[Oct 1819]
4579	27.64	[June 1819]	4623	29.33	[Oct 1819]
4580	27.65	[June 1819]	4624	29.34	[Oct 1819]
4581	27.67	[June 1819]	4625	29.35	[Oct–Dec 1819]
4582	28.1	[July 1819]	4626	29.36	[Oct–Dec 1819]
4583	28.2	[July 1819]	4627	29.37	26 Dec 1819
4584	28.3	16 July 1819	4628	29.38	[1819–20]
4585	28.86	[16 July 1819]	4629	21½.94	[1819–20]
4586	28.100	[July 1819]	4630	21½.95	[1819–20]
4587	28.99	[July 1819]	4631	21½.96	[1819–20]
4588	28.101	[July 1819]	4632	21½.98	[1819–20]
4589	28.37	[Aug 1819]	4633	21½.97	[1819–20]
4590	24.8	2 Sept 1819	4634	17.209	[1819–25]
4591	24.69	5 Sept 1819	4635	17.220	[1819–25]
4592	24.3	[c Sept 1819]	4636	17.221	[1819–25]
4593	29.13	[c 28 Sept 1819]	4637	29.184	[1819–25]
4594	21½.72	[Oct 1819]			
4595	21½.73	[Oct 1819]			
4596	21½.74	[Oct 1819]			
4597	21½.75	[Oct 1819]		**1820**	
4598	21½.76	[Oct 1819]	4638	29.3	[Jan 1820]
4599	21½.77	[Oct 1819]	4639	29.39	[30 Jan–5 Feb 1820]
4600	21½.78	[Oct 1819]	4640	29.40	[30 Jan–5 Feb 1820]
4601	21½.79	[Oct 1819]	4641	29.41	[30 Jan–5 Feb 1820]
4602	21½.80	[Oct 1819]	4642	29.42	[Feb–Mar 1820]
4603	21½.81	[Oct 1819]	4643	29.43	[Mar 1820]
4604	21½.82	[Oct 1819]	4644	29.44	[Mar 1820]
4605	21½.83	[Oct 1819]	4645	28.4	[early 1820]

Series	N Entry	Date	Series	N Entry	Date
4646	28.5	[early 1820]	4690	23.21	[1820]
4647	28.6	[early 1820]	4691	23.22	[1820]
4648	28.7	[early 1820]	4692	23.23	[1820]
4649	28.8	[early 1820]	4693	23.24	[1820]
4650	28.9	[early 1820]	4694	23.25	[1820]
4651	28.10	[early 1820]	4695	23.31	[c June 1820]
4652	28.11	[early 1820]	4696	23.32	[c June 1820]
4653	28.12	[early 1820]	4697	29.45	[May–July 1820]
4654	28.13	[early 1820]	4698	29.46	[May–July 1820]
4655	28.14	[early 1820]	4699	29.47	[May–July 1820]
4656	28.15	[early 1820]	4700	29.48	9 July 1820
4657	28.16	[early 1820]	4701	29.49	[c July 1820]
4658	28.17	[early 1820]	4702	29.50	[c July 1820]
4659	28.18	[early 1820]	4703	29.51	[c July 1820]
4660	28.19	[early 1820]	4704	29.52	[c July 1820]
4661	28.20	[early 1820]	4705	29.53	[c July 1820]
4662	28.21	[early 1820]	4706	29.56	[July–Nov 1820]
4663	28.22	[early 1820]	4707	29.57	[July–Nov 1820]
4664	28.23	[early 1820]	4708	29.58	[July–Nov 1820]
4665	28.24	[early 1820]	4709	29.195	[early Sept 1820]
4666	28.25	[early 1820]	4710	29.196	[early Sept 1820]
4667	28.26	[early 1820]	4711	29.194	[Sept 1820]
4668	28.27	[early 1820]	4712	29.193	[Sept 1820]
4669	28.28	[early 1820]	4713	29.197	[15/21 Sept 1820]
4670	28.29	[early 1820]	4714	29.198	[15/21 Sept 1820]
4671	28.30	[early 1820]	4715	29.199	[15/21 Sept 1820]
4672	28.31	[early 1820]	4716	29.200	21 Sept 1820
4673	28.32	[early 1820]	4717	29.201	[c 21 Sept 1820]
4674	28.33	[early 1820]	4718	29.202	[c 21 Sept 1820]
4675	28.34	[early 1820]	4719	28.48	9 Oct 1820
4676	28.35	[early 1820]	4720	28.49	[Oct 1820]
4677	28.36	[early 1820]	4721	28.50	[Oct 1820]
4678	28.38	[10/16] Apr 1820	4722	28.51	[Oct 1820]
4679	28.39	[Apr–May 1820]	4723	28.52	[Oct 1820]
4680	28.41	[Apr–May 1820]	4724	28.53	[Oct 1820]
4681	28.42	[Apr–May 1820]	4725	28.54	[Oct 1820]
4682	28.43	5 May 1820	4726	28.55	[Oct 1820]
4683	28.44	[5 May 1820]	4727	28.56	[Oct 1820]
4684	28.45	[May–June 1820]	4728	60.1	[c Oct 1820]
4685	28.46	[May–June 1820]	4729	60.2	[Oct 1820]
4686	28.47	[May–June 1820]	4730	60.3	[Oct 1820]
4687	23.18	[1820]	4731	60.4	[Oct 1820]
4688	23.19	[1820]	4732	60.5	18 Oct 1820
4689	23.20	30 June 1820]	4733	60.6	[c Oct 1820]

Series	N Entry	Date	Series	N Entry	Date
4734	60.7	[c Oct 1820]	4770	29.69	[22 Nov 1820–
4735	60.8	[c Oct 1820]			3 Jan 1821]
4736	60.9	[c Oct 1820]	4771	29.70	[22 Nov 1820–
4737	60.10	[c Oct 1820]			3 Jan 1821]
4738	60.11	[c Oct 1820]	4772	28.87	[1820–21]
4739	22.79	[c Nov 1820]	4773	28.88	[1820–21]
4740	22.81	Nov 1820	4774	28.89	[1820–21]
4741	22.80	[Nov 1820]	4775	28.90	[1820–21]
4742	22.82	[c Nov 1820]	4776	28.91	[1820–21]
4743	28.40	[Nov 1820]	4777	28.92	[1820–21]
4744	29.59	22 Nov 1820	4778	28.93	[1820–21]
4745	29.60	[Nov 1820]	4779	28.94	[1820–21]
4746	29.61	[Nov 1820]	4780	28.95	[1820–21]
4747	24.104	[Nov 1820]	4781	28.96	[1820–21]
4748	24.103	[Nov 1820]	4782	28.97	[1820–21]
4749	24.105	[Nov 1820]	4783	28.98	[1820–21]
4750	24.101	[Nov 1820]	4784	29.203	[1820–21]
4751	24.106	[Nov 1820]	4785	29.209	[1820–21]
4752	24.107	[Nov 1820]	4786	29.210	[1820–21]
4753	24.108	[Nov 1820]	4787	29.204	[1820–21]
4754	24.109	[Nov 1820]	4788	29.205	[1820–21]
4755	61.39	[1820]	4789	29.206	[1820–21]
4756	61.40	[1820]	4790	29.207	[1820–21]
4757	61.41	[1820]	4791	29.208	[1820–21]
4758	61.42	[1820]	4792	29.211	[1820–21]
4759	61.43	[1820]	4793	29.212	[1820–21]
4760	61.44	[1820–21]	4794	29.54	[1820–23]
4761	61.45	[1820–21]	4795	29.55	[1820–23]
4762	61.46	[1820–21]			
4763	29.62	[22 Nov 1820–			
		3 Jan 1821]		**1821**	
4764	29.63	[22 Nov 1820–			
		3 Jan 1821]	4796	29.71	[c 8 Jan 1821]
4765	29.64	[22 Nov 1820–	4797	29.72	[c 8 Jan 1821]
		3 Jan 1821]	4798	29.73	[c 8 Jan 1821]
4766	29.65	[22 Nov 1820–	4799	29.74	[c 8 Jan 1821]
		3 Jan 1821]	4800	28.57	[13 Feb 1821]
4767	29.66	[22 Nov 1820–	4801	28.58	[17 Feb 1821]
		3 Jan 1821]	4802	28.59	[17 Feb 1821]
4768	29.67	[22 Nov 1820–	4803	28.60	[17 Feb 1821]
		3 Jan 1821]	4804	28.61	[17 Feb 1821]
4769	29.68	[22 Nov 1820–	4805	28.62	[17 Feb 1821]
		3 Jan 1821]	4806	28.63	[17 Feb 1821]
			4807	28.64	[17 Feb 1821]

Series	N Entry	Date	Series	N Entry	Date
4808	28.65	[17 Feb 1821]	4849	20.1	[1821–5]
4809	28.66	[17 Feb 1821]	4850	20.4	[1821–5]
4810	28.67	[17 Feb 1821]	4851	28.84	[1821–5]
4811	29.75	[Jan–Sept 1821]	4852	28.85	[1821–5]
4812	29.76	[Jan–Sept 1821]			
4813	29.77	[Jan–Sept 1821]			
4814	29.78	[Jan–Sept 1821]		**1822**	
4815	29.79	[Jan–Sept 1821]	4853	21½.99	[c Jan 1822]
4816	29.80	[Jan–Sept 1821]	4854	21½.100	[c Jan 1822]
4817	29.81	[Jan–Sept 1821]	4855	21½.101	[c Jan 1822]
4818	29.82	[Jan–Sept 1821]	4856	21½.102	[c Jan 1822]
4819	29.83	[Jan–Sept 1821]	4857	21½.103	[c Jan 1822]
4820	29.94	[Jan–Sept 1821]	4858	21½.104	[c Jan 1822]
4821	20.21	[17/18 Apr 1821]	4859	21½.105	[c Jan 1822]
4822	20.22	[April 1821]	4860	21½.106	[c Jan 1822]
4823	20.23	[Apr 1821–	4861	21½.107	[c Jan 1822]
		May 1825]	4862	21½.108	[c Jan 1822]
4824	20.24	[Apr 1821–	4863	21½.110	[c Jan 1822]
		May 1825]	4864	21½.109	[c Jan 1822]
4825	29.183	11 July 1821	4865	21½.111	[c Jan 1822]
4826	30.59	[c Sept 1821]	4866	21½.112	[c Jan 1822]
4827	M.28	[c Sept 1821]	4867	21½.113	[c 18 Jan 1822]
4828	M.29	[c Sept 1821]	4868	21½.114	[Jan 1822]
4829	29.85	[1821]	4869	21½.115	[Jan 1822]
4830	29.86	[1821]	4870	21½.116	[Jan 1822]
4831	29.87	[1821]	4871	21½.117	[Jan 1822]
4832	29.88	[1821]	4872	21½.118	[Jan 1822]
4833	29.89	[1821]	4873	21½.119	[Jan 1822]
4834	29.90	[1821]	4874	29.93	3 Mar 1822
4835	29.91	[1821]	4875	29.94	[Mar 1822]
4836	29.92	Sept 1821	4876	29.95	[Mar 1822]
4837	22.160	[1821–2]	4877	29.96	[Mar 1822]
4838	29.213	[1821–2]	4878	29.250	23 Mar 1822
4839	29.214	[1821–2]	4879	23.35	[c Apr 1822]
4840	29.216	[1821–2]	4880	23.36	[c Apr 1822]
4841	29.215	[1821–2]	4881	23.37	[c Apr 1822]
4842	29.217	[1821–2]	4882	23.38	[c Apr 1822]
4843	29.218	[1821–2]	4883	23.39	[c Apr 1822]
4844	29.219	[1821–2]	4884	23.40	[c Apr 1822]
4845	18.327	[1821–2]	4885	23.41	[c Apr 1822]
4846	20.50	[1821–3]	4886	23.42	2 Apr 1822
4847	20.55	[1821–3]	4887	23.43	[2–9 Apr 1822]
4848	20.56	[1821–3]	4888	23.44	[2–9 Apr 1822]

Series	N Entry	Date	Series	N Entry	Date
4889	23.45	[2–9 Apr 1822]	4933	60.12	[1822–3]
4890	23.46	[2–9 Apr 1822]	4934	60.13	[1822–3]
4891	23.47	[2–9 Apr 1822]	4935	21½.120	[1822–5]
4892	23.48	[2–9 Apr 1822]	4936	23.59	[1822–6]
4893	23.49	[2–9 Apr 1822]			
4894	23.50	[2–9 Apr 1822]		**1823**	
4895	23.51	[2-9 Apr 1822]	4937	29.226	14 May 1823
4896	23.52	[2-9 Apr 1822]	4938	29.227	[16] May 1823
4897	23.53	9 Apr 1822	4939	29.228	[May 1823]
4898	23.54	[9 Apr 1822]	4940	3½.77	[May–July 1823]
4899	23.55	[c Apr 1822]	4941	3½.78	[May–July 1823]
4900	23.56	[c Apr 1822]	4942	3½.79	[May–July 1823]
4901	23.57	[c Apr 1822]	4943	60.14	[May–July 1823]
4902	23.58	[c Apr 1822]	4944	60.15	[May–July 1823]
4903	29.97	6 July 1822	4945	3½.112	[June 1823]
4904	29.98	[6 July 1822]	4946	3½.113	21 June 1823
4905	29.99	[15] July 1822	4947	2½.114	[21 June 1823]
4906	29.100	[July 1822]	4948	3½.115	22 June 1823
4907	29.101	[July 1822]	4949	3½.116	[June–July 1823]
4908	29.102	[July 1822]	4950	3½.1	[2 July + 1823]
4909	29.103	29 July 1822	4951	3½.11	[July 1823]
4910	29.104	[July 1822]	4952	3½.86	[c 2 July 1823]
4911	29.105	[July 1822]	4953	3½.85	[c 2 July 1823]
4912	29.106	[July 1822]	4954	3½.80	[c July 1823]
4913	29.107	[July 1822]	4955	3½.15	[c July 1823]
4914	29.108	[July 1822]	4956	3½.16	[c July 1823]
4915	29.109	[July 1822]	4957	3½.17	13 July 1823
4916	29.110	[July 1822]	4958	3½.87	[July 1823]
4917	29.111	[July 1822]	4959	3½.88	[July 1823]
4918	25.98	[Aug–Sept 1822]	4960	3½.89	[July 1823]
4919	25.99	[Aug–Sept 1822]	4961	3½.90	[July 1823]
4920	25.100	[2 Sept 1822]	4962	3½.91	[July 1823]
4921	25.101	[1822]	4963	3½.92	[July 1823]
4922	25.102	[1822]	4964	3½.93	[July 1823]
4923	29.220	[1822]	4965	3½.101	[July 1823]
4924	29.221	[1822]	4966	16.389	[July–Sept 1823]
4925	29.222	[1822]	4967	3½.95	[July–Sept 1823]
4926	29.223	[1822]	4968	3½.96	[July–Sept 1823]
4927	29.224	16 Nov 1822	4969	3½.97	[July–Sept 1823]
4928	29.225	[16 Nov 1822]	4970	3½.98	[July–Sept 1823]
4929	23.34	[?1822/1827]	4971	3½.99	[July–Sept 1823]
4930	25.68	[1822–3]	4972	3½.100	[July–Sept 1823]
4931	25.103	[1822–3]	4973	25.4	[c July–Sept 1823]
4932	25.104	[1822–3]	4974	25.54	[c July–Sept 1823]

Series	N Entry	Date	Series	N Entry	Date
4975	25.55	[c July–Sept 1823]	5019	30.75	14 Oct 1823
4976	25.56	[c July–Sept 1823]	5020	30.76	[14 Oct 1823]
4977	25.57	[c July–Sept 1823]	5021	30.77	[14 Oct 1823]
4978	25.58	[c July–Sept 1823]	5022	30.78	[14 Oct 1823]
4979	25.59	[c July–Sept 1823]	5023	30.79	[14 Oct 1823]
4980	25.60	[c July–Sept 1823]	5024	30.80	[14 Oct 1823]
4981	25.61	[c July–Sept 1823]	5025	30.81	15 [Oct 1823]
4982	25.62	[c July–Sept 1823]	5026	30.82	[15 Oct 1823]
4983	25.63	[c July–Sept 1823]	5027	30.83	15 Oct [1823]
4984	25.64	[c July–Sept 1823]	5028	30.84	17 Oct [1823]
4985	25.65	[c July–Sept 1823]	5029	30.85	[17 Oct 1823]
4986	25.66	[c July–Sept 1823]	5030	30.86	[17 Oct 1823]
4987	25.67	[c July–Sept 1823]	5031	30.87	[20–21 Oct 1823]
4988	20.57	27 Aug 1823	5032	30.88	[20–21 Oct 1823]
4989	20.58	[27 Aug 1823]	5033	30.89	[20–21 Oct 1823]
4990	20.60	[c Aug 1823]	5034	30.90	[20–21 Oct 1823]
4991	30.62	[c 1–9 Sept 1823]	5035	30.6	[Oct–Nov 1823]
4992	3½.94	[c 10 Sept 1823]	5036	30.7	[Oct–Nov 1823]
4993	3½.102	10 Sept 1823	5037	30.8	[Oct–Nov 1823]
4994	3½.103	[Sept 1823]	5038	30.9	[Oct–Nov 1823]
4995	3½.110	[Sept 1823]	5039	30.10	[Oct–Nov 1823]
4996	3½.117	[Sept 1823]	5040	30.11	[Oct–Nov 1823]
4997	26.13	[Sept 1823]	5041	30.12	[Oct–Nov 1823]
4998	26.14	[Sept 1823]	5042	30.13	[Oct–Nov 1823]
4999	26.15	[Sept 1823]	5043	30.14	[Oct–Nov 1823]
5000	26.16	[Sept 1823]	5044	30.15	[Oct–Nov 1823]
5001	16.392	[Sept–Oct 1823]	5045	30.16	[Oct–Nov 1823]
5002	16.393	[Sept–Oct 1823]	5046	30.17	[Oct–Nov 1823]
5003	16.394	[Sept–Oct 1823]	5047	30.18	[Oct–Nov 1823]
5004	30.3	[Sept–Oct 1823]	5048	30.19	[Oct–Nov 1823]
5005	30.60	Autumn 1823	5049	30.20	[Oct–Nov 1823]
5006	30.61	[Oct 1823]	5050	30.21	[Oct–Nov 1823]
5007	30.63	[Oct 1823]	5051	30.22	[Oct–Nov 1823]
5008	30.64	12 Oct 1823	5052	30.23	[Oct–Nov 1823]
5009	30.65	[12 Oct 1823]	5053	30.24	[Oct–Nov 1823]
5010	30.66	[12 Oct 1823]	5054	30.25	[Oct–Nov 1823]
5011	30.67	13 Oct 1823	5055	30.26	[Oct–Nov 1823]
5012	30.68	[13 Oct 1823]	5056	30.27	[Oct–Nov 1823]
5013	30.69	[13 Oct 1823]	5057	30.28	[Oct–Nov 1823]
5014	30.70	[13 Oct 1823]	5058	30.29	[Oct–Nov 1823]
5015	30.71	[13 Oct 1823]	5059	30.91	[Nov 1823– Jan 1824]
5016	30.72	[13 Oct 1823]			
5017	30.73	[13 Oct 1823]	5060	30.92	[Nov 1823– Jan 1824]
5018	30.74	[13 Oct 1823]			

Series	N Entry	Date	Series	N Entry	Date
5061	30.93	[Nov 1823–Jan 1824]		1824	
5062	30.94	[Nov 1823–Jan 1824]	5098	30.1	[Jan 1824]
			5099	30.97	19 Jan 1824
5063	30.95	[Nov 1823–Jan 1824]	5100	30.98	[20 Jan 1824]
			5101	30.99	[22 Jan 1824]
5064	30.96	[Nov 1823–Jan 1824]	5102	30.100	[22–26 Jan 1824]
			5103	30.101	[22–26 Jan 1824]
5065	30.30	[Dec 1823]	5104	30.102	[Jan 1824]
5066	30.31	[Dec 1823]	5105	30.2	[26 Jan 1824]
5067	30.32	[Dec 1823]	5106	30.56	26 Jan 1824
5068	30.33	[Dec 1823]	5107	30.57	[26 Jan 1824]
5069	30.34	[Dec 1823]	5108	30.55	[27 Jan 1824]
5070	30.35	[Dec 1823]	5109	30.58	[27 Jan 1824]
5071	30.36	[Dec 1823]	5110	29.229	27 Jan 1824
5072	30.37	[Dec 1823]	5111	29.230	[Jan–Feb 1824]
5073	30.39	[12 Dec 1823]	5112	29.231	[Jan–Feb 1824]
5074	30.38	12 Dec 1823	5113	29.232	[Jan–Feb 1824]
5075	30.40	[Dec 1823]	5114	29.233	[Jan–Feb 1824]
5076	30.41	[Dec 1823]	5115	29.234	[Jan–Feb 1824]
5077	30.42	[Dec 1823]	5116	29.235	[Jan–Feb 1824]
5078	30.43	[Dec 1823]	5117	29.236	[Jan–Feb 1824]
5079	30.44	[Dec 1823]	5118	29.237	[Jan–Feb 1824]
5080	30.45	[Dec 1823]	5119	29.238	[Jan–Feb 1824]
5081	30.46	[Dec 1823]	5120	29.239	[Jan–Feb 1824]
5082	30.47	[Dec 1823]	5121	29.240	[Jan–Feb 1824]
5083	30.48	[Dec 1823]	5122	29.241	[Jan–Feb 1824]
5084	30.49	[Dec 1823]	5123	29.242	11 Feb 1824
5085	30.50	[Dec 1823]	5124	29.243	[Feb 1824]
5086	30.51	[Dec 1823]	5125	29.244	[Feb 1824]
5087	30.52	[Dec 1823]	5126	29.245	[Feb 1824]
5088	30.53	[Dec 1823]	5127	29.246	[Feb 1824]
5089	30.54	[Dec 1823]	5128	29.247	[Feb 1824]
5090	3½.69	[c 1823]	5129	29.248	[Feb 1824]
5091	3½.68	[c 1823]	5130	29.249	⟨20 Feb 1824⟩
5092	3½.23	[c 1823]	5131	29.251	[20–28 Feb 1824]
5093	25.95	[c 1823]	5132	29.252	[20–28 Feb 1824]
5094	25.97	[c 1823]	5133	29.253	[20–28 Feb 1824]
5095	25.96	[c 1823]	5134	29.254	28 Feb 1824
5096	30.4	[Dec 1823–Jan 1824]	5135	26.97	23 Mar 1824
			5136	26.98	[Mar 1824]
5097	30.5	[Dec 1823–Jan 1824]	5137	29.255	[Mar–May 1824]
			5138	29.256	[Mar–May 1824]

Series	N Entry	Date	Series	N Entry	Date
5139	29.257	[Mar–May 1824]	5175	28.73	[1824]
5140	29.258	[Mar–May 1824]	5176	28.74	[1824]
5141	29.259	[Mar–May 1824]	5177	28.75	[1824]
5142	29.260	[Mar–May 1824]	5178	28.76	[1824]
5143	26.17	8 April 1824	5179	28.77	[1824]
5144	26.18	[April 1824]	5180	28.78	[1824]
5145	26.19	[April 1824]	5181	28.79	[1824]
5146	28.68	24 April 1824	5182	28.80	[1824]
5147	28.69	26 April 1824	5183	28.81	[1824]
5148	28.70	[26 April 1824]			
5149	26.84	[18–25 May 1824]		**1825**	
5150	29.261	20 May 1824	5184	29.262	3 Jan 1825
5151	29.112	[4 June 1824]	5185	29.122	⌜6 Jan 1825⌝
5152	29.113	[4 June 1824]	5186	28.82	[c 25 Jan 1825]
5153	29.114	4 June 1824	5187	29.263	[Jan–Aug 1825]
5154	3½.118	[after July 1824]	5188	29.264	[Jan–Aug 1825]
5155	3½.119	[after July 1824]	5189	29.265	[Jan–Aug 1825]
5156	3½.120	[after July 1824]	5190	20.2	9 Feb 1825
5157	3½.122	[July–Aug 1824– Sept 1826]	5191	20.3	[9 Feb 1825]
			5192	29.126	21 Feb 1825
5158	3½.123	[July–Aug 1824– Sept 1826]	5193	29.127	[Feb–May 1825]
			5194	29.128	[Feb–May 1825]
5159	3½.124	[July–Aug 1824– Sept 1826]	5195	29.129	[Feb–May 1825]
			5196	20.29	[Apr–May 1825]
5160	3½.125	[July–Aug 1824– Sept 1826]	5197	20.30	[Apr–May 1825]
			5198	20.31	[Apr–May 1825]
5161	3½.126	[July–Aug 1824– Sept 1826]	5199	20.32	[Apr–May 1825]
			5200	20.26	[May 1825]
5162	3½.127	[July–Aug 1824– Sept 1826]	5201	20.27	[May 1825]
			5202	20.28	[May 1825]
5163	3½.128	[July–Aug 1824– Sept 1826]	5203	20.25	[May 1825]
			5204	20.33	2 May 1825
5164	16.395	29, 30 Sept 1824	5205	20.34	[May 1825]
5165	16.396	[Sept 1824]	5206	20.35	[May 1825]
5166	29.115	20 Oct 1824	5207	20.36	[May 1825]
5167	29.116	[Oct–Nov 1824]	5208	20.37	[May 1825]
5168	29.117	[Oct–Nov 1824]	5209	20.38	[May 1825]
5169	29.118	27 Nov 1824	5210	20.39	[May 1825]
5170	29.119	[Nov 1824]	5211	20.40	[May 1825]
5171	29.120	[Dec 1824]	5212	20.41	[May 1825]
5172	29.121	[Dec 1824]	5213	20.42	[May 1825]
5173	28.71	[1824]	5214	20.44	[May 1825]
5174	28.72	[1824]	5215	20.43	[May 1825]

Series	N Entry	Date	Series	N Entry	Date
5216	29.123	[May 1825]	5260	F°.12	[Nov 1825]
5217	29.124	[May 1825]	5261	F°.13	[Nov 1825]
5218	29.125	[May 1825]	5262	F°.14	[Nov 1825]
5219	29.130	7 May 1825	5263	F°.15	[Nov 1825]
5220	29.131	23 May 1825	5264	F°.16	[Nov 1825]
5221	29.132	23 [May 1825]	5265	F°.17	[Nov 1825]
5222	29.133	[May 1825]	5266	F°.18	[Nov 1825]
5223	29.134	[May 1825]	5267	F°.19	[Nov 1825]
5224	29.135	[May 1825]	5268	F°.20	[Nov 1825]
5225	29.136	[May 1825]	5269	F°.21	[Nov 1825]
5226	29.137	[May 1825]	5270	F°.22	[Nov 1825]
5227	29.138	[May 1825]	5271	F°.23	[Nov 1825]
5228	29.139	[May 1825]	5272	F°.24	[Nov 1825]
5229	29.266	[May 1825]	5273	F°.25	[Nov 1825]
5230	29.267	[May–Aug 1825]	5274	F°.26	[Nov 1825]
5231	20.62	[May–Sept 1825]	5275	F°.27	[Nov 1825]
5232	20.63	[May–Sept 1825]	5276	F°.28	[Nov 1825]
5233	20.64	[May–Sept 1825]	5277	F°.29	[Nov 1825]
5234	29.268	3 Aug 1825	5278	F°.30	[Nov 1825]
5235	20.71	19 Aug 1825	5279	F°.32	[Nov 1825]
5236	29.140	6 Sept 1825	5280	F°.33	[Nov 1825]
5237	29.1	[c 6 Sept 1825]	5281	F°.34	[Nov 1825]
5238	29.2	2 Aug 1825	5282		[Nov 1825]
5239	29.5	[c 6 Sept 1825]	5283	F°.35	[Nov 1825]
5240	20.45	[Sept 1825]	5284	F°.36	[Nov 1825]
5241	20.46	[Sept 1825]	5285	F°.37	29 Nov 1825
5242	20.47	[c Sept 1825]	5286	F°.38	[29 Nov 1825]
5243	20.48	[c Sept 1825]	5287	F°.39	[Nov–Dec 1825]
5244	20.49	[c Sept 1825]	5288	F°.40	[Dec 1825]
5245	20.59	[c Sept 1825]	5289	F°.42	[Dec 1825–
5246	20.61	[c Sept 1825]			Jan 1826]
5247	20.65	[c Sept 1825]	5290	F°.43	[Dec 1825–
5248	20.67	[c Sept 1825]			Jan 1826]
5249	20.66	[c Sept 1825]	5291	F°.44	[Dec 1825–
5250	20.68	[c Sept 1825]			Jan 1826]
5251	20.69	[c Sept 1825]	5292	F°.45	[Dec 1825–
5252	20.70	[c Sept 1825]			Jan 1826]
5253	29.181	[c Sept 1825]	5293	F°.46	[Dec 1825–
5254	29.182	[c Sept 1825]			Jan 1826]
5255	29.143	[c Sept 1825]	5294	F°.47	[Dec 1825–
5256	21½.121	[c Sept 1825]			Jan 1826]
5257	F°.7	1 Nov 1825	5295	F°.48	[Dec 1825–
5258	F°.10	[Nov 1825]			Jan 1826]
5259	F°.11	[Nov 1825]			

Series	N Entry	Date	Series	N Entry	Date
5296	Fº.49	[Dec 1825–Jan 1826]	5328	Fº.75	[16–18 Feb 1826]
5297	Fº.50	[Dec 1825–Jan 1826]	5329	Fº.76	18 Feb 1826
5298	Fº.51	[Dec 1825–Jan 1826]	5330	Fº.77	20 Feb 1826
5299	Fº.52	[Dec 1825–Jan 1826]	5331	Fº.78	21 Feb 1826
5300	Fº.53	[Dec 1825–Jan 1826]	5332	Fº.79	25 Feb 1826
5301	Fº.54	[Dec 1825–Jan 1826]	5333	Fº.80	3 Mar 1826
5302	Fº.55	[Dec 1825–Jan 1826]	5334	Fº.81	13 Mar 1826
5303	Fº.56	[Dec 1825–Jan 1826]	5335	Fº.82	14 Mar 1826
5304	Fº.57	[Dec 1825–Jan 1826]	5336	Fº.83	[14–18 Mar 1826]
5305	29.144	[1825]	5337	Fº.84	18 Mar 1826
5306	29.145	[1825]	5338	Fº.85	[18–20 Mar 1826]
5307	29.146	[1825–26]	5339	Fº.86	20 Mar 1826
5308	Fº.1	[1825–26]	5340	26.3	[Mar 1826]
5309	Fº.6	[1825–26]	5341	26.99	⟨22 Mar 1826⟩
5310	Fº.9	[1825–26]	5342	26.100	[Mar 1826]
			5343	26.101	[Mar 1826]
			5344	Fº.87	24 Mar 1826
		1826	5345	Fº.88	27 Mar 1826
			5346	Fº.89	1 Apr 1826
5311	Fº.58	[Jan 1826]	5347	Fº.90	[1–10 Apr 1826]
5312	Fº.59	12 Jan 1826	5348	Fº.91	[1–10 Apr 1826]
5313	Fº.60	13 Jan 1826	5349	Fº.92	[1–11 Apr 1826]
5314	Fº.61	[Jan–Feb 1826]	5350	Fº.93	10 Apr 1826
5315	Fº.62	[Jan–Feb 1826]	5351	Fº.94	11 Apr 1826
5316	Fº.63	[Jan–Feb 1826]	5352	Fº.95	11 Apr 1826
5317	Fº.64	[Jan–Feb 1826]	5353	Fº.96	12 Apr 1826
5318	Fº.65	[Jan–Feb 1826]	5354	Fº.97	12 Apr 1826
5319	Fº.66	[Jan–Feb 1826]	5355	Fº.98	13 Apr 1826
5320	Fº.67	[Jan–Feb 1826]	5356	23.60	18 Apr 1826
5321	Fº.68	[Jan–Feb 1826]	5357	Fº.99	22 Apr 1826
5322	Fº.69	[Jan–Feb 1826]	5358	Fº.100	22 Apr 1826
5323	Fº.70	8 Feb 1826	5359	Fº.101	25 Apr 1826
5324	Fº.71	[8–16 Feb 1826]	5360	Fº.102	26 Apr 1826
5325	Fº.72	16 Feb 1826	5361	Fº.2	[26–28 Apr 1826]
5326	Fº.73	[16–18 Feb 1826]	5362	Fº.103	28 Apr 1826
5327	Fº.74	[16–18 Feb 1826]	5363	26.86	[May 1826]
			5364	26.85	[May 1826]
			5365	26.87	[May 1826]
			5366	26.88	5 May 1826
			5367	26.89	[May 1826]
			5368	26.90	[May 1826]
			5369	26.91	[1826]
			5370	26.7	[c 7 May 1826]
			5371	26.8	[c 7 May 1826]

Series	N Entry	Date	Series	N Entry	Date
5372	26.9	[c 7 May 1826]	5416	Fº.113	[21-25 July 1826]
5373	26.10	7 May 1826	5417	Fº.114	25 July 1826
5374	26.11	7 May 1826	5418	Fº.115	28 July 1826
5375	26.12	8 May 1826	5419	Fº.116	30 July 1826
5376	26.22	[c 11 May 1826]	5420	Fº.117	30 July 1826
5377	26.23	11 May 1826	5421	Fº.118	1 Aug 1826
5378	26.6	14 May 1826	5422	Fº.119	[1 Aug 1826]
5379	26.32	[14–15 May 1826]	5423	Fº.120	[2] Aug 1826
5380	26.33	15 May 1826	5424	Fº.121	[2 Aug 1826]
5381	26.34	[15–20 May 1826]	5425	Fº.122	[2–6 Aug 1826]
5382	26.24	19 May 1826	5426	Fº.123	6 Aug 1826
5383	26.25	[20 May 1826]	5427	Fº.124	[6–7 Aug 1826]
5384	26.35	20 May 1826	5428	Fº.125	7 Aug 1826
5385	26.36	[20 May 1826]	5429	Fº.126	12 Aug 1826
5386	26.37	[May 1826]	5430	Fº.127	[12–13 Aug 1826]
5387	26.38	[May 1826]	5431	Fº.128	[13 Aug 1826]
5388	26.39	[May 1826]	5432	Fº.129	14 Aug 1826
5389	26.81	25 May 1826	5433	Fº.130	14 Aug 1826
5390	26.102	[May 1826]	5434	23.26	23 Aug 1826
5391	26.82	[9 June 1826]	5435	23.27	[Aug 1826]
5392	26.83	[9 June 1826]	5436	23.28	[Aug 1826]
5393	26.42	[June 1826]	5437	Fº.131	6 Sept 1826
5394	26.43	10 June 1826	5438	3½.119 P.S.	12 Sept 1826
5395	26.44	[10–12 June 1826]	5439	Fº.132	[12–13 Sept 1826]
5396	26.45	[12 June 1826]	5440	26.56	14 Sept 1826
5397	26.46	[12 June 1826]	5441	26.58	[14 Sept 1826]
5398	26.47	[10-14 June 1826]	5442	26.57	[14 Sept 1826]
5399	26.48	[10-14 June 1826]	5443	26.59	14 Sept 1826
5400	26.49	[10-14 June 1826]	5444	26.2	16 Sept 1826
5401	26.50	14 June 1826	5445	Fº.133	16 Sept 1826
5402	26.51	17 June 1826	5446	Fº.134	18 Sept 1826
5403	26.52	[June 1826]	5447	Fº.135	29 Sept 1826
5404	26.53	[June 1826]	5448	26.4	[Sept 1826]
5405	26.54	[June 1826]	5449	26.62	[Sept–Nov 1826]
5406	26.55	[June 1826]	5450	26.60	[Sept–Nov 1826]
5407	Fº.104	7 July 1826	5451	26.61	[Sept–Nov 1826]
5408	Fº.105	[7–18 July 1826]	5452	26.1	[Sept–Nov 1826]
5409	Fº.106	[7–18 July 1826]	5453	Fº.136	16 Oct 1826
5410	Fº.107	[7–18 July 1826]	5454	Fº.137	20 Oct 1826
5411	Fº.108	[7–18 July 1826]	5455	Fº.138	21 Oct 1826
5412	Fº.109	[7–18 July 1826]	5456	Fº.139	26 [Oct 1826]
5413	Fº.110	18 July 1826	5457	Fº.140	28 [Oct 1826]
5414	Fº.111	19 July 1826	5458	Fº.141	28 Oct 1826
5415	Fº.112	21 July 1826	5459	Fº.142	9 Nov 1826

Series	N Entry	Date	Series	N Entry	Date
5460	Fº.143	[Nov 1826]	5466	Fº.149	[9–12 Dec 1826]
5461	Fº.144	[Nov 1826]	5467	Fº.150	[9–12 Dec 1826]
5462	Fº.145	[Nov 1826]	5468	Fº.151	[9–12 Dec 1826]
			5469	Fº.152	12 Dec 1826
5463	Fº.146	[Nov 1826]	5470	26.5	1826
5464	Fº.147	[Nov 1826]	5471	3½.37	[1826–30]
5465	Fº.148	9 Dec 1826			

DATE DUE
